Lecture Notes in Computer Science 4749

Commenced Publication in 1973
Founding and Former Series Editors:
Gerhard Goos, Juris Hartmanis, and Jan van Leeuwen

Bernd J. Krämer Kwei-Jay Lin
Priya Narasimhan (Eds.)

Service-Oriented Computing – ICSOC 2007

Fifth International Conference
Vienna, Austria, September 17-20, 2007
Proceedings

Springer

Volume Editors

Bernd J. Krämer
FernUniversität Hagen
D-58084 Hagen, Germany
E-mail: Bernd.Kraemer@FernUni-Hagen.de

Kwei-Jay Lin
University of California
Irvine, California 92697-2625, USA
E-mail: klin@ece.uci.edu

Priya Narasimhan
Carnegie Mellon University
Pittsburgh PA 15213, USA
E-mail: priya@cs.cmu.edu

Library of Congress Control Number: 2007934544

CR Subject Classification (1998): C.2, D.2, D.4, H.4, H.3, K.4.4

LNCS Sublibrary: SL 2 – Programming and Software Engineering

ISSN 0302-9743
ISBN-10 3-540-74973-X Springer Berlin Heidelberg New York
ISBN-13 978-3-540-74973-8 Springer Berlin Heidelberg New York

Springer is a part of Springer Science+Business Media

springer.com

Printed in Germany

Typesetting: Camera-ready by author, data conversion by Scientific Publishing Services, Chennai, India
Printed on acid-free paper SPIN: 12124367 06/3180 5 4 3 2 1 0

Preface

This volume contains all of the Research-Track, Industry-Track and Demo-Track papers that were selected for presentation at the Fifth International Conference on Service-Oriented Computing (ICSOC 2007), which was held in Vienna, Austria, September 17–20, 2007.

ICSOC 2007 followed the footsteps of four previous successful editions of the International Conference on Service-Oriented Computing that were held in Chicago, USA (2006), Amsterdam, The Netherlands (2005), New York City, USA (2004) and Trento, Italy (2003). ICSOC is recognized as the flagship conference for service-oriented computing research and best practices. ICSOC covers the entire spectrum from theoretical and foundational results to empirical evaluation, as well as practical and industrial experiences. ICSOC 2007 continued this tradition while introducing several new themes to further these goals.

Service-oriented computing brings together ideas and technologies from many diverse fields in an evolutionary manner in order to address research challenges including service-based application modeling, service composition, discovery, integration, monitoring and management of services, service quality and security, methodologies for supporting service development, grid services, and novel topics including information as a service and service-oriented architecture (SOA) governance.

To provide a balanced coverage and an equal emphasis across all aspects of service-oriented computing, ICSOC 2007's topics were divided into seven major areas: Business Service Modeling, Service Assembly, and Service Management, addressing research issues and best practices in the primary life-cycle phases of a service, modeling, assembly, deployment, and management; SOA Runtime and Quality of Service, covering issues spanning all stages of the life-cycle; Grid Services and Service Architectures, combining grid infrastructure concepts with service-oriented computing; and Business and Economical Aspects of Services.

Our solicitation of Industrial- and Research-Track submissions was extremely aggressive, particularly given the short time span between ICSOC 2006 (in December 2006) and ICSOC 2007 (in September 2007). The Research Track's paper-selection process was stringent, given the large number of excellent submissions that we had to select from in a very short time. In addition, matching the diversity of paper topics and reviewer expertise was a challenge, considering the multi-discplinary and emergent nature of service-oriented computing research. We worked closely with and consulted the designated Area Coordinators, with two experts leading the review process for each of the areas, for reviewer selection and also for resolution in the case of papers with conflicting reviews. In the paper-selection process, the quality of the submission was the ultimate deciding factor. We also strived to achieve a balance across all of the areas that encompass service-oriented computing. Of the 139 submissions to the ICSOC 2007 Research Track, only 30 full papers and 14 short papers were accepted for the program.

Our Industrial Track focused on three topic areas: Information as a Service, SOA Governance, and SOA Runtime and Registries. Each of these topic areas was covered on separate days. Each conference day started with a review of the state of the art, followed by a panel discussion reviewing key issues, both technical and practical, that were relevant to that area. The panel discussion was followed by a presentation of the accepted Industrial-Track papers in the form of multiple sessions throughout the day. The Industrial Track specifically solicited submissions covering the state of practice and real-world experience in service-oriented computing, especially in the three focused topic areas. Of particular interest were papers that described innovative service-based implementations, novel applications of service-oriented technology, and insights and improvements to the state of practice along with case studies and lessons learned from practitioners that emphasized applications, service technology, system deployment, organizational ramifications, or business impact. Of the 28 submissions to the ICSOC 2007 Industrial Track, only 13 full papers were accepted for the program.

In addition to the Research and Industry Tracks, ICSOC 2007 featured top-notch keynotes, presented by influential and recognized leaders in the industrial and academic community. The program included five tutorials and hands-on sessions on SOA, BPEL, Monitoring and Testing, Non-functional Properties, and Web APIs on Rails that were developed and presented by renowned researchers and practitioners. Also featured in the program were three panels addressing innovative issues like Information as a Service, SOA Governance, and Registries and SOA Runtime. Five pre-conference workshops on Engineering Service-Oriented Applications, Business-Oriented Aspects concerning Semantics and Methodologies in Service-oriented Computing, Non-functional Properties and Service-Level Agreements in Service-Oriented Computing, Web APIs and Services Mashups, and Telecom Service-Oriented Architectures completed the attractive conference program.

This outstanding conference program was a testament to the efforts of many dedicated individuals who were committed to the success of ICSOC 2007.

We start by acknowledging the Area Coordinators, the Program Committee members, and the reviewers for their painstaking efforts and integrity in the review and paper-selection process, especially given the pressures of time. We also acknowledge the significant contributions of Eva Nedoma and Uwe Zdun in the local organization; Karl Goeschka for handling finances; Soila Pertet and Alexander Stuckenholz for handling publicity-related activities. We also thank the Workshop Chairs, Elisabetta Di Nitto and Matei Ripeanu; the Demo Chairs, Martin Bichler and Ming-Chien Shan; Tutorial Chair, Marco Aiello; the Panel Chairs, Klaus Pohl and Robert D. Johnson; the Ph D ssSymposium Chairs, Tudor Dumitras, Andreas Hanemann and Benedikt Kratz. We would also like to single out individuals for their special help and contributions: Renate Zielinski and Volker Winkler for assisting the Program Chairs in compiling the proceedings, Harald Weinreich, who set up and adapted Conftool for our use and who was extremely responsive throughout.

We would like to express our deep gratitude to the Steering Committee members: Fabio Casati, Paco Curbera, Mike Papazoglou and Paolo Traverso for their constant guidance. Finally, we would like to acknowledge the cooperation of Springer, the ACM Special Interest Group on Hypertext, Hypermedia and the Web (SIGWeb), the ACM Special Interest Group on Software Engineering (SIGSoft) and the Networked European Software and Services Initiative (NESSI).

Finally, we thank the authors of our accepted papers for submitting their work to ICSOC 2007. Without the high-quality work of these researchers and practitioners, and their efforts in the area of service-oriented computing, such an excellent conference program would not have been possible.

It was our privilege and pleasure to compile this outstanding ICSOC 2007 conference proceedings. We sincerely hope that you find the papers in this volume as interesting and stimulating as we did.

July 2007

Asit Dan
Schahram Dustdar
Bernd Krämer
Kwei-Jay Lin
Priya Narasimhan
Stefano De Panfilis
Bobbi Young

Organization

ICSOC 2007 Conference Chairs

General Chairs	Asit Dan, IBM Software Group, USA Schahram Dustdar, Vienna University of Technology, Austria
Program Chairs	Bernd Krämer, FernUniversität in Hagen, Germany Kwei-Jay Lin, University of California, Irvine, USA Priya Narasimhan, Carnegie Mellon University, USA
Workshop Chair	Elisabetta Di Nitto, Politecnico di Milano, Italy Matei Ripeanu, University of British Columbia, Canada
Demo Chairs	Ming-Chien Shan, SAP Martin Bichler, Technische Universität München, Germany
Tutorial Chair	Marco Aiello, University of Groningen, Netherlands
Panel Chairs	Klaus Pohl, LERO, Ireland and University of Essen, Germany Robert D. Johnson, IBM Software Group, USA
Industrial Chairs	Stefano De Panfilis, NESSI and Engineering, Italy Bobbi Young, Unisys, USA
Industrial-Academic Coordination Chair	Robert D. Johnson, IBM Software Group, USA
Ph D Symposium Chairs	Tudor Dumitras, Carnegie Mellon University, USA Andreas Hanemann, Leibniz-Rechenzentrum, Germany Benedikt Kratz, Tilburg University, The Netherlands
Publicity Chairs	Soila M. Pertet, Carnegie Mellon University, USA Alexander Stuckenholz, FernUniversität in Hagen, Germany

Local Organization Chair	Uwe Zdun, Vienna University of Technology, Austria
Financial Chair	Karl M. Goeschka, Vienna University of Technology, Austria

Area Coordinators

Service Modeling	Boualem Benatallah, University of New South Wales, Australia
	Ingolf Krüger, University of California, San Diego, USA
Service Assembly	Tiziana Margaria, University of Potsdam, Germany
	Vincenzo D'Andrea, University of Trento, Italy
Service Management	Fabio Casati, University of Trento, Italy
	Heiko Ludwig, IBM Research, USA
SOA Runtime	Karsten Schwan, Georgia Tech, USA
	Frank Leymann, University of Stuttgart, Germany
Quality of Service	Doug Schmidt, Vanderbilt University, USA
	Elisa Bertino, Purdue University, USA
Grid Services	Jörn Altmann, International University, Germany, and Seoul National University, Korea
Business and Economical Aspects of Services	Christos Nikolaou, University of Crete, Greece
	Michael Huhns, University of South Carolina, USA

Program Committee

Research Track

Mikio Aoyama	NISE, Japan
Luciano Baresi	Politecnico di Milano, Italy
Elisa Bertino	Purdue University, USA
Bishwaranjan Bhattacharjee	IBM Research Hawthorne, USA
Walter Binder	EPFL, Switzerland
Marina Bitsaki	University of Crete, Greece
M. Brian Blake	Georgetown University, USA
Athman Bouguettaya	Virginia Tech, USA
Tevfik Bultan	UC Santa Barbara, USA
Nathan Caswell	IBM T.J. Watson Research, USA
Kuo-Ming Chao	Coventry University, UK
Shing-Chi Cheung	Hong Kong University of Science and Technology, China

Paco Curbera	IBM T. J. Watson Research, USA
Flavio De Paoli	University of Milan, Italy
Tommaso Di Noia	University of Bari, Italy
Wolfgang Emmerich	UC London, UK
Gianluigi Ferrari	University of Pisa, Italy
George Feuerlicht	University of Technology Sydney, Australia
Dennis Gannon	Indiana University, USA
Dimitrios Georgakopoulos	Telcordia, USA
Claude Godart	University of Nancy, France
Andy Gordon	Microsoft, UK
Paul Grefen	Eindhoven University of Technology, Netherlands
John Grundy	University of Auckland, New Zealand
Mohand-Said Hacid	University of Leon, France
Bernhard Holtkamp	Fraunhofer ISST, Germany
Bettina Kemme	McGill University, Canada
Alfons Kemper	Technische Universität München, Germany
Rania Khalaf	IBM T.J. Watson Research, USA
Roger Kilian-Kehr	SAP, Germany
Patricia Lago	Free University of Amsterdam, Netherlands
Neil Maiden	City University of Hong Kong, China
E. Michael Maximilien	IBM Almaden, USA
Massimo Macella	University of Rome, Italy
Brahim Medjahed	University of Michigan, USA
David O'Hallaron	CMU, USA
Anna Perini	University of Trento, Italy
Marco Pistore	University of Trento, Italy
Axel Polleres	Universidad Rey Juan Carlos, Spain
Wolfgang Reisig	Humboldt-Universität zu Berlin, Germany
Thomas Risse	Universität Hannover, Germany
Norbert Ritter	Universität Hamburg, Germany
Colette Rolland	University of Paris, France
Akhil Sahai	HP, USA
Jakka Sairamesh	IBM T. J. Watson Research, USA
Volker Sander	Fachhochschule Aachen, Germany
Jun Shen	University of Wollongong, Australia
Jianwen Su	UC Santa Barbara, USA
Angelo Susi	ITC, Italy
Stefan Tai	IBM T.J. Watson Research, USA
Kian-Lee Tan	NU Singapore, Singapore
Djamshid Tavangarian	Universität Rostock, Germany
Farouk Toumani	ISIMA, France
Karthikeyan Umapathy	Penn State, USA

Julien Vayssiere	SAP, USA
Yan Wang	Macquarie University, Australia
Mathias Weske	Universität Potsdam, Germany
Martin Wirsing	Universität München, Germany
Jian Yang	Macquarie University, Australia
Jih-Shyr Yih	IBM T.J. Watson Research, USA
Gianluigi Zavattaro	University of Bologna, Italy
Wenbing Zhao	Cleveland State University, USA
Wolfgang Ziegler	Fraunhofer SCAI, Germany
Christian Zirpins	Universität Hamburg, Germany

Industrial Track

John Falkl	IBM, USA
Paul Freemantle	WSO2, UK
Steve Graham	IBM, USA
Mansour Kavianpour	Unisys, USA
Robert Maksimchuk	Unisys, USA
Roger Milton	USA
Jeff Mischinsky	Oracle, USA
Andy Mulholland	CapGemini, UK
Srinivas Narayannan	Tavant, USA
Greg Pavlik	Oracle, USA
Alberto Sardini	IBM, Italy
Gunter Sauter	IBM, USA
Karl Schulmeisters	Unisys, USA
Harini Srinivasan	IBM, USA
Lynne Thompson	Twin Pearls Consulting Services, USA
Mahesh Viswanathan	IBM, USA
Sanjeeva Weerawarana	WSO2, Sri Lanka
Hemesh Yadav	Unisys, USA

Table of Contents

Part I: Research Track Full Papers

Service Deployment

Business Process Design

Service Discovery

Workflow

Quality of Service Support

Testing and Validation

Service Assembly

Service Properties

Service Modeling

SOA Composition

SOA Experience

SOA Runtime

Part II: Research Track Short Papers

SOA Adoption

Service Modeling

QoS and Composite Service Support

Part III: Industrial Track Full Papers

Information as a Service

Service Properties

SOA Governance

SOA Runtime

Part IV: Demo Track Short Papers

Pattern Based SOA Deployment

William Arnold, Tamar Eilam, Michael Kalantar, Alexander V. Konstantinou, and Alexander A. Totok

IBM T.J. Watson Research Center, Hawthorne, NY, USA
{barnold, eilamt, kalantar, avk, aatotok}@us.ibm.com

Abstract. A key function of a Service Oriented Architecture is the separation between business logic and the platform of its implementation and deployment. Much of the focus in SOA research has been on service design, implementation, composition, and placement. In this paper we address the challenge of configuring the hosting infrastructure for SOA service deployment. The functional and non-functional requirements of services impose constraints on the configuration of their containers at different levels. Presently, such requirements are captured in informal documents, making service deployment a slow, expensive, and error-prone process. In this paper, we introduce a novel approach to formally capturing service deployment best-practices as model-based patterns. Deployment patterns capture the structure of a solution, without bindings to specific resource instances. They can be defined at different levels of abstraction supporting reuse, and role-based iterative refinement and composition. We show how we extended an existing model driven deployment platform to support pattern based deployment. We formally define pattern semantics, validation, and refinement. We also present an algorithm for automatically instantiating such patterns on multiple distributed service environments. Our approach has been verified in a large prototype that has been used to capture a variety of functional and non-functional deployment constraints, and demonstrate their end-to-end maintenance and realization.

1 Introduction

Much of the focus in SOA research has been on service design, implementation, composition, and placement [1]. In order to fully realize the promise of SOA, similar attention must also be paid to the deployment, configuration, and runtime management phases of the service life cycle. While SOA allows designers and programmers to access business logic independent of implementation platform, from the operator's view the situation is the extreme opposite. SOA services are typically implemented using standard distributed application platforms such as J2EE, CORBA, and .NET, and are hosted on large middleware stacks with complex configuration interdependencies. Deployment of SOA services, and the composite applications that implement them, often involves creation of operational resources such as databases, messaging queues, and topics. The runtime container of the service must then be configured to access these resources. Establishing access may require installation and configuration of client software,

B. Krämer, K.-J. Lin, and P. Narasimhan (Eds.): ICSOC 2007, LNCS 4749, pp. 1–12, 2007.

security credentials, as well as network-level configuration. Deployers must assure that all service resources have been correctly instantiated and configured, satisfying all functional and non-functional requirements. Cross cutting interdependencies and constraints make this a very challenging and error-prone task [2]. In addition to the communication and hosting configuration challenge, SOA poses additional challenges in transforming non-functional requirements and goals to deployment solutions including configuration for security, availability, and performance.

One approach to reducing the complexity of designing the deployment of services is to capture common deployment patterns. Such patterns describe proven solutions that exhibit certain non-functional properties. For example, experts in WebSphere Process Server (WPS) have identified 12 best practices patterns for WPS deployment [3]. Each pattern offers a different set of capabilities (high availability, scalability, security) and supports classes of applications with different characteristics. Today, these SOA deployment patterns are still captured informally in lengthy unstructured documents. Information about what combinations of products and versions are known to work must be looked up in manuals and documents libraries. Tradeoffs between cost, availability, security, scalability, and performance are investigated in an ad hoc fashion. There are no models, methodology and tools to define, reuse, assemble, customize, validate, and instantiate SOA deployment patterns.

In this paper we present a novel approach to capturing SOA deployment patterns through formal methods, models, and tools. We use and extend a model-driven deployment platform that we have previously presented in the context of middleware[4] and network[5] configuration design, validation and deployment. We present how we extend the platform with the ability to express model-based patterns representing abstract deployment topologies. These models are used by experts to capture the essential outline and requirements of a deployment solution without specific resource bindings. We formally define the semantics and validation of the realization of such abstract patterns. Using our deployment platform, we enable non-expert users to safely compose and iteratively refine such patterns to design a fully specified topology with bindings to specific resources. The resulting desired state topology can be validated as satisfying the functional service requirements, while maintaining the non-functional properties of the pattern. We also show how automatic resource binding can be introduced to reduce the steps required to reach a valid and complete deployment topology. The desired state of the complete deployment topology can then be provisioned automatically by generating a one-time workflow as we presented in [6].

The paper is structured as follows. In Section 2, we describe our deploy platform resource model, architecture and concepts. In Section 3, we present our novel pattern modeling constructs, their semantics and validation. We also present an algorithm to automate the instantiation of patterns over an existing infrastructure. Section 4 covers related work. Finally, we conclude with a brief discussion of our prototype implementation and on-going work.

2 Deployment Platform

Our model-driven SOA deployment platform supports the construction of desired deployment state models that are complete, correct, and actionable. These models include detailed software stacks and configuration [4,5]. They are consumed by provisioning automation technologies [7] to drive automated provisioning [6]. The deployment platform is built on a core configuration meta-model, and exposes a number of services for model extension, validation, problem resolution, resource discovery, query, and provisioning.

2.1 Core Configuration Meta-model

The core model captures common aspects of deployment configuration syntax, structure and semantics. Core types are extended to capture domain-specific information. Domain objects and links are instantiated in a *Topology* which is used to design the *desired* state of the infrastructure after deployment. The *Unit* core type represents a unit of deployment. A *Topology* contains *Unit* instances that may represent resources that are already installed, or ones that are to be installed. The install *state* of a unit is a tuple $(init, desired)$ representing the install state of the unit when it was provided to the topology, and its state after publishing. The values of $init$ and $desired$ can be one of $\{uninstalled, installed\}$. Installable *Units*, may be associated with one or more *Artifacts*. A *Unit* may also represent a configuration node, such as J2EE data source, in a hierarchical structure (current or desired). A *Unit* can contain any number of *Capability* instances. Subtypes of *Capability* group domain-specific configuration attributes by function. The relationships of a *Unit* with other *Units* are expressed through containment of *Requirement* objects. The core model defines three types of relationships: *hosting*, *dependency*, and *membership*. Each *Requirement* is associated with one of these types. Relationships are represented using a *Link* association class. All these types extend a common *DeployObject* super-type. All *DeployObject* can be associated with any number of *Constraint* instances. The semantics and validation of a *Constraint* are defined by the subtypes extending it. The context of *Constraint* evaluation is the object on which it is defined. In the case of a *Constraint* contained in a *Requirement*, the constraint context is the target of the requirement link. This allows users to define constraints that must be satisfied by the resource at the other end of a relationship. Figure 1 outlines a deployment *Topology* instance model example. The topology captures the deployment of a new J2EE Enterprise Application (EAR) on an existing IBM WebSphere Application Server (WAS), using a pre-configured J2EE data-source. We have similarly defined extension schemas and instance models for a variety of other product domains and vendors.

2.2 Deploy Platform Architecture

The overall architecture of our model-based SOA deployment platform is depicted in Figure 2. At its base lies the core configuration model, on top of which

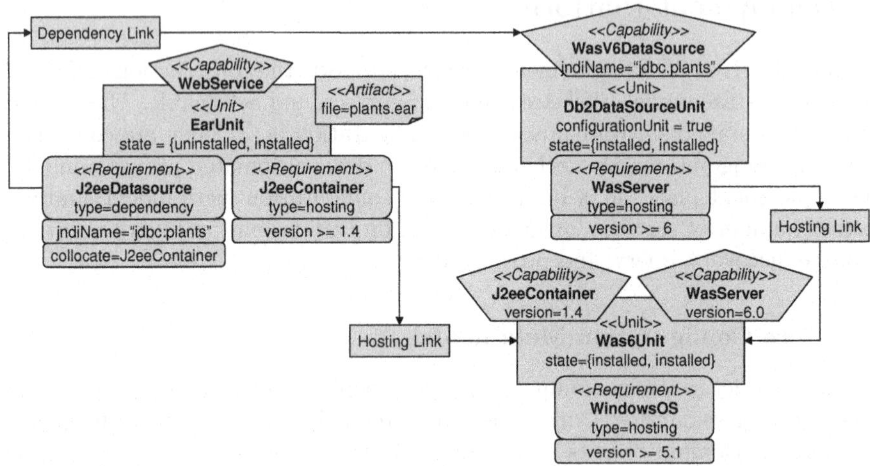

Fig. 1. Topology instance example modeling the deployment of a J2EE Application

a number of extensible services are supported. The platform defines the deployment service interfaces and provides the managers for registering extensions. The *Domain Service* is used to extend the core model types in domain-specific schemas. The *Validation Service* is used by domain authors to inject semantic validation logic. An example validation rule may express that the database name attribute of a J2EE datasource must match the actual name of the database on which it depends. The validation service invokes the validation rules when types from the domains with which they are associated are instantiated or changed. Validation rules generate semantically rich status errors markers. These error markers identify the areas in the model that violate a registered validation rule. The *Resolution Service* is used to declare logic for fixing the errors underlying the markers generated by validators. For example, in the earlier datasource database name validation example, a resolution may be declared to propagate the name of the database to all of the datasources that have a *dependency* relationship to it. For a given error status, the resolution service can be queried to provide the list of possible resolution actions. These resolutions can be invoked, either manually or programmatically, to modify the model. The core platform is packaged together with a core set of *Constraints*, *Requirements*, and an accompanying set of core validation and resolution rules. The *Provider Service* is used to discover and query configuration repositories (e.g. CMDBs), so that units that represent existing resources can be discovered and incorporated in deployment topologies. The *Publisher Service* is used to register provisioning agents whose role is to configure the infrastructure to match the desired state expressed in the topology. Finally, the platform supports a *Core Editor* which is a standard graphical interface for creating and editing topologies. The editor interfaces with the existing platform services for resource discovery, topology validation, error resolution, and publishing.

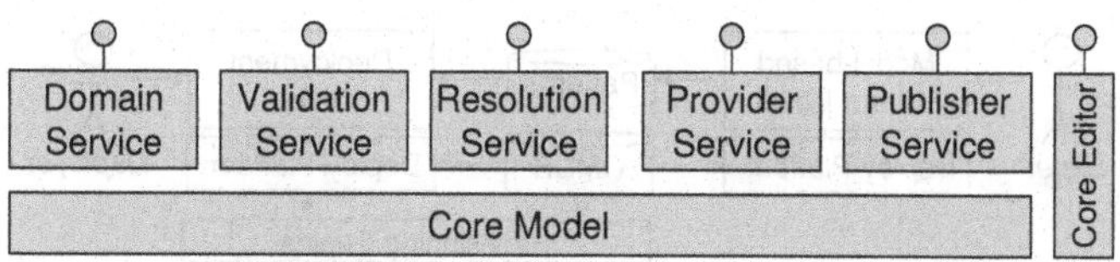

Fig. 2. Deployment Platform Extension Architecture

2.3 Valid Deployment Models

Users construct deployment models by adding or modifying units, and by executing resolution rules. The goal is to reach complete and valid deployment topologies that do not contain any error markers. A topology is validated against a set of core validation rules, a set of domain-specific type-level rules, and the constraints associated at the object instance level. The core validation rules check the cardinality of the topology links, as well as the type and configuration of their endpoints. Domain-specific validation rules can be expressed at the type level, to apply to all instances, or at the instance level as constraints. Formally, we say that a topology T is *valid w.r.t. a given set of validation rules* V iff (1) all core link validation rules are satisfied, (2) all type-level validation rules $v \in V$ evaluate to *true* on any object $u \in T$, and (3) all constraints on topology objects evaluate to *true* in the context of their evaluation. Recall that for a constraint defined in a capability the evaluation context is the capability's attribute set, while for a constraint defined in a requirement the context is the target of the relationship (and its contained capabilities). The logic for evaluating constraints is itself extensible.

3 Pattern Platform

A common requirement across different SOA deployments is the ability to describe a deployment topology at various levels of abstraction. At a base level of abstraction, the topology may represent a fully defined deployment structure that is only missing the relationships to the specific resources on to which it will be deployed. At higher levels of abstraction, the topology may partially specify the configuration of resources, focusing on key parameters and structures, while leaving others to be determined at deployment time. The deployment platform described in the previous section is well suited for modeling the *concrete* desired state of services, components, and their relationships that are directly mappable to native configuration models. In this section, we describe how we extend the deployment platform to support abstract models, termed *patterns*. As depicted in Figure 3, pattern models are defined by experts using a rich design tool and instantiated by deployers, potentially using a simple installation wizard for resource and parameter selection. First, we describe the modeling extensions, including structural constraints, virtual units, and realization links. Then we describe how we use views to execute the original set of validation rules

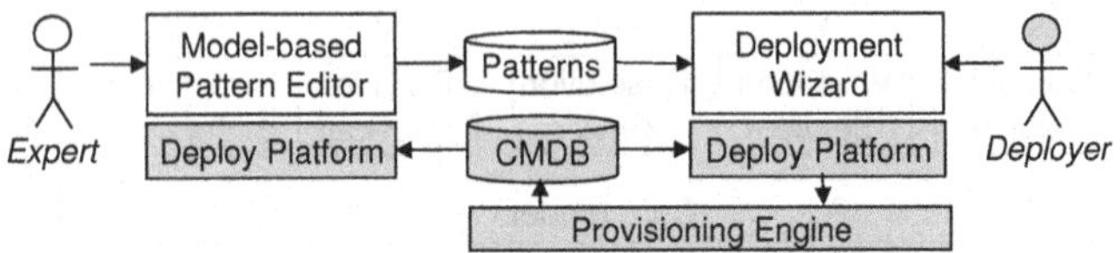

Fig. 3. Pattern use-case

on the extended class of models. Last we describe an approach for automatically realizing pattern topologies on multiple distributed environments.

3.1 Pattern Modeling Extensions

Structural Constraints. When defining patterns, it is often necessary to express structural constraints. For example, a fail over high-availability service pattern may include a structural constraint to anti-collocate the primary and standby services at the operating system level. To support structural constraints, we introduce a new *constraint* link type, and we extended it for two common types of structural constraints: collocation and deferred host.

A *collocation* constraint restricts the valid hosting of two units. It is associated with a *type* property which determines the type of the host on which the two units' hosting stacks must converge (anti-collocation can be defined similarly). *Deferred hosting* is a constraint that the source unit be eventually hosted on the target. For example, a deployer may wish to constrain the deployment of a service on a particular system without having to model the entire software stack. A valid topology, realizing a pattern with a deferred host constraint, must include a direct or indirect hosting link path from the source to the identified target.

Virtual Units and Realization Links. Many patterns can be expressed in the form of a model with partially specified units of abstract or non-abstract types. Our approach to presenting such patterns is through the concept of a *virtual unit.* A virtual unit is one which does not directly represent an existing or installable service, but instead must be *realized* by another unit. The *Virtual* property of a unit is a Boolean attribute on the base *Unit* type. Typically, virtual units will include capabilities with unspecified values and associated constraints. Every unit type can be instantiated as a virtual unit. A new *realizedBy* relationship can be defined between any two objects, where the source is virtual. The semantics of the relationship is that the source acts as a constraint over its target. Often, a *realizedBy* link will be defined from a virtual unit to a concrete (non-virtual) unit, although it may also target a more specific virtual unit. For simplicity, in this paper we restrict ourselves to the case where virtual units are realized only by concrete units. In cases where Unit-level realization is ambiguous in terms of the mapping of contained objects such as capabilities and requirements, additional realization links may be required between these objects. In the rest of

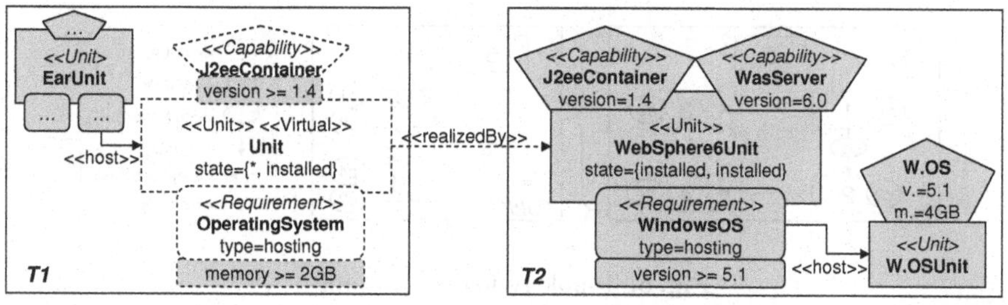

Fig. 4. Example of a virtual unit realized by a concrete unit

the paper, in order to simplify the formal definition, we assume all capabilities and requirements of realized units are also *explicitly* realized.

Figure 4 is a valid realization example which shows a virtual unit in a topology T_1 that is realized by a unit in a topology T_2 representing an installed WebSphere Application Server. Note that all constraints are satisfied by the realizing unit, and the type hierarchy is respected. The rules for locally validating a realization relationship between two units are formally defined in two stages as follows.

For any two model objects o_1, o_2, $matchR(o_1, o_2)$ iff (1) $supertype(type(o_1), type(o_2))$, (2) For every attribute $a \in attributes(type(o_1))$, $isSet(o_1, a) \rightarrow value(o_1, a) = value(o_2, a)$, and (3) For every constraint $c \in constraints(o_1), c(o_2)$.

For any two unit objects u_1, u_2, $validR(u_1, u_2)$ iff (1) $virtual(u_1)$, (2) $matchR(u_1, u_2)$, (3) For every capability $c_1 \in cap(u_1)$, there exists a unique capability $c_2 \in cap(u_2)$ s.t. $realizedBy(c_1, c_2) \wedge matchR(c_1, c_2)$, and (4) For every requirement $r_1 \in req(u_1)$, there exists a unique requirement $r_2 \in req(u_2)$ s.t. $realizedBy(r_1, r_2) \wedge matchR(r_1, (r_2))$.

3.2 Pattern Validation

By design, patterns are incomplete topologies. To meaningfully validate patterns, we have to distinguish between two sources of errors: model violations and model incompleteness. To formalize this concept we define three different validation states on attributes, relationships, or constraints, associated with virtual units in the model: $undefined$, $satisfied$, and $violated$. An element O is in an $undefined$ state in a model M if objects can be added to M, and undefined attributes set, such that O transitions to a $satisfied$ state.

The deferred host structural constraint between a source A and a target B is $undefined$ as long as the hosting stack for A is incomplete and there is no hosting link path from A to B' where $type(B') = type(B) \wedge B \neq B'$. The collocation relationship, with target type t, between units A and B is $undefined$ as long as there are no hosting link paths from A to C and from B to C' where $type(C) = type(C') = t$. A topology T is *weakly valid* iff all constraints, requirements and links associated with virtual units are in either $satisfied$ or $undefined$ states. For example, consider a pattern containing a virtual unit u with an associated hosting requirement r. If r is not linked, then the model will still be weakly valid, however if its linked to two different units it will be invalid.

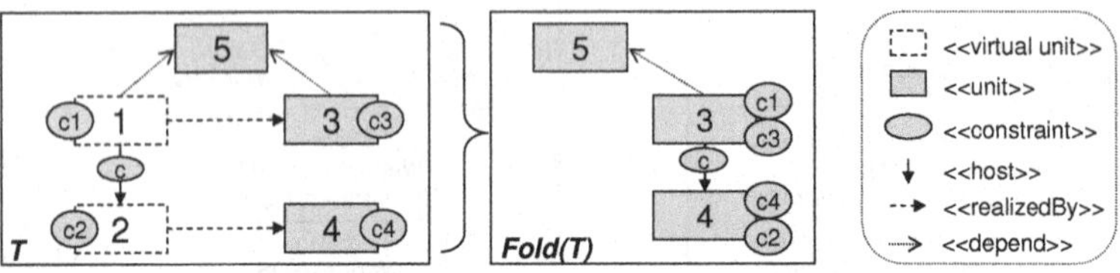

Fig. 5. Topology folding example

Topology Folding. Given a topology (or a set of topologies) with virtual units and realization links, it is not enough to locally check the validity of individual realization links using the rules defined in the previous section. For example, in Figure 4, the realization would be locally valid even if the WebSphere Application Server is hosted on an operating system with less than $2GB$ of memory. As another example, consider a virtual unit u hosted on a non virtual unit v. A valid local realization of u can map it to a non virtual unit u' hosted on a non virtual unit v' where $v' \neq v$. In this section we complete the semantic definition of patterns by defining the full set of validation and realization rules.

For this purpose, it is helpful to define the *folded topology* $foldR(T)$ of a given topology T, where, intuitively, we collapse all realized virtual units, relationships and constraints. An example of a folded topology is illustrated in Figure 5. The folded topology $foldR(T)$ satisfies the following rules: (1) For every $o \in T$, $o \in foldR(T)$ iff o is not the source of any *realizedBy* relationship, (2) For every $o \in T$, *constraints*(o) is the union of constraints defined on all $o' \in T$ such that *realizedBy*(o', o), (3) For every $o_1, o_2 \in foldR(T) : \exists r$ of type t from o_1 to o_2 iff there exists a relationship $r' \in T$ s.t. *type*$(r') = t$, and for $o_1' =$ *source*(r') : $((o_1 = o_1') \vee realizedBy(o_1', o_1))$ (resp. *target*(r') and o_2), and (4) For every $r \in foldR(T)$, *constraints*(r) includes the union of constraints defined on the set of relationships $r' \in T$ as defined in item (3).

A *strict folded topology* $foldR^S(T)$ of a topology T, is $foldR(T)$ where all virtual units and their associated relationships are removed. Note that the class of strict folded topologies is identical to the class of concrete topologies defined in Section 2. Thus, for a given pattern T all of the core deploy platform validation rules can run on $foldR^S(T)$ without requiring any changes.

Topology Realization Semantics. Given our definition of a locally valid realization, and the folded view of a topology, we can now define the validity of a topology containing multiple realization links. Given a topology T, T forms a *valid topology realization* iff the following properties are satisfied: (1) Every virtual unit is realized by at most one unit, (2) Each realization link in T is locally valid, and (3) $FoldR(T)$ is weakly valid (defined earlier in this section). Note that Item (3) guarantees that links between virtual units "agree" with links between their realizing concrete units (if they don't we will get a link multiplicity constraint violation in the folded topology). A topology realization is *complete* when it is valid and all its virtual units are realized. Note that if T forms a complete topology realization then $foldR(T) = foldR^S(T)$. Now that we extended the set of topologies defined in Section 2 to include patterns, the definition of a valid topology must be generalized, as follows. A topology T is *valid** iff (1) T forms a valid and complete realization, and (2) $foldR(T)$ is valid (according to the definition in Section 2). Note that for the provisioning phase of a *valid** topology T, only $foldR(T)$ is needed.

3.3 Automatic Pattern Realization

In the beginning of this section, we introduced the idea of automatically instantiating patterns in multiple environments. To do that, we have to have a way to automatically generate a *valid** topology T', given an input pattern T_1 and a target topology T_2 representing the target environment. To simplify the discussion, lets assume that the inputs T_1 and T_2 are merged into one topology T. Now, T must be automatically modified by adding realization links between virtual units originating in T_1 and concrete units originating in T_2. When the modified topology T' forms a valid and complete realization, it may still be necessary to automatically execute some resolution rules to reach a *valid** state. For example, values of attributes, originating in objects in T_2 may need to be propagated to units originating in T_1. An approach for automatic resolution execution was proposed in [4]. Hereafter, we limit the discussion to the automatic realization function.

Following is the formal definition of the automatic realization problem. Given a source topology T_1 and a target topology T_2, let R be a set of realization links from T_1 to T_2, and let $T' = T_1 \cup T_2 \cup R$ be the merged topology. The tuple (T_1, T_2, R) is a *maximum valid realization* iff (1) T' forms a valid realization, and (2) $|R|$ is maximum. The goal of the automatic realization problem is to find a maximum realization for given source and target topologies.

Note that a maximum valid realization may be incomplete: unrealized virtual units may exist. An incomplete topology may still be automatically completed to a *valid** topology in some cases. We defer the discussion of automatic completion to future publications.

Our approach to address the automatic realization problem is based on the observation that the problem is reducible (with some variations) to the error correcting subgraph isomorphism problem [8], where realization links play the role of the isomorphism mapping. Given T_1, T_2, R, and T', as defined above, let r be the mapping function. Then we define the following changes to the original definition of the error correcting subgraph isomorphism problem. For every two units $a \in T_1$ and $b \in T_2$, $r(a) = b$ is permissible only if the following conditions are satisfied. (1) $validR(a, b)$, (2) every constraint $c \in constraints(a)$ is not in a *violated* state in $foldR(T')$, and (3) for every link $l \in T_1$ with $source(l) = a$, the corresponding link l' in $foldR(T')$ is not in a *violated* state.

Consider the example in Figure 6, where colored nodes represent concrete units. The mapping r in all of the of the topologies in the figure is a valid error correcting subgraph isomorphism mapping. However, only topologies (a) and (c) show valid mapping according to our modified definition of the problem, and according to the definition of a valid realization in the previous section. Topologies (b) and (d) violate Item (3) in the the definition above.

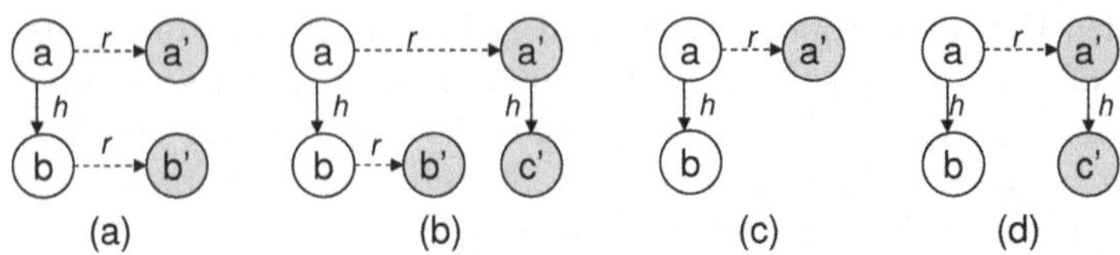

Fig. 6. Valid and invalid mappings according to our modified definition of error correcting subgraph isomorphism

Clearly, existing algorithms for error correcting subgraph isomorphism can be modified to handle the modified version defined above. The formal definition of such an algorithm is beyond the scope of the paper. We implemented and studied the performance of a simpler variant of the problem, where all virtual units must be matched. Preliminary performance results are on the practical side, although maximum subgraph isomorphism is NP-Complete. We speculate that this is because our graphs are heavily labeled, and sparse.

4 Related Work

Service deployment often refers to service selection [9] and service composition to satisfy functional and QoS requirements, for example, [10,11]. In contrast to this, our work focuses on the deployment, configuration and management of complex services including their supporting middleware. Work that addresses this depth of deployment and configuration often assumes a simplified model such as common middleware already deployed [10] or knowledge of the specific target environment so that provisioning steps are known in advance [12]. In [13] models are used to realize a conceptual service interface with one or more interfaces of its concrete implementation. The focus is on interface realization, not middleware configuration and deployment. Models are also used to capture non-functional aspects in [14] at the service design level. Such constraints can be used as input to our deployment refinement process.

The use of object-relationship models for the design and configuration of systems[15] and networks[16] has been widely adopted in industry[17,18] and their use is being standardized for service deployment models as SML[18]. [19] used a spreadsheet-style system to propagate configuration attributes over an object-relationship structure. Design tools for application deployment[5,20] have adopted Model Driven Architecture (MDA)[21] approaches.

Patterns have been used for the deployment of network services[22]. In this case, a pattern represented a detailed description of the conditions needed for the deployment of a service. While our patterns can be used as a key to find necessary conditions, they can also be used to create the necessary conditions. Patterns were used as a mechanism for service deployment in [12]. In this latter case, patterns are pre-defined and associated with concrete provisioning steps or workflows. Pattern selection is identified by mapping from a service level agreement. In our work, we divorce the pattern from the provisioning actions.

Instead, the pattern can be used to drive resource selection and to complete configuration planning, creating a detailed configuration plan. Such a plan can then be consumed by other tools such as [23,6] for provisioning.

5 Future Work

The model extensions for patterns that we have presented in this paper have been implemented in our model-driven deployment platform prototype. We are currently using this prototype to capture deployment patterns for complex domains such as WPS [3], as well as complex high-availability patterns for databases, messaging, and application servers. We have also implemented same basic structural constraints, such as collocation and deferred hosting, as well as more complex ones, such as communication. A rich visual interface supports simple model-based pattern creation and refinement. An initial implementation of the automatic realization algorithm allows users to automatically realize complex patterns over existing infrastructure resources. We plan on extending our implementation to also support installation of resources that may be missing. In future research we plan on investigating automated pattern composition, reverse pattern discovery, and pattern maintenance.

Acknowledgements

The authors would like to thank Daniel Berg, Andrew Trossman, Michael Elder, Edward Snible, and John Pershing for helping to shape our vision, contributing ideas, and assisting in implementation.

References

1. Curbera, F., Ferguson, D., Nally, M., Stockton, M.L.: Towards a programming model for service oriented computing. In: Benatallah, B., Casati, F., Traverso, P. (eds.) ICSOC 2005. LNCS, vol. 3826, pp. 33–47. Springer, Heidelberg (2005)
2. Brown, A.B., Keller, A., Hellerstein, J.: A model of configuration complexity and its applications to a change management system. In: Integrated Management (2005)
3. Redlin, C., Carlson-Neumann, K.: Websphere process server and websphere enterprise service bus deployment patterns. Technical report, IBM (2006)
4. Eilam, T., Kalantar, M., Konstantinou, A., Pacifici, G.: Reducing the complexity of application deployment in large data centers. In: Integrated Management (2005)
5. Eilam, T., Kalantar, M., Konstantinou, A., Pacifici, G., Pershing, J., Agrawal, A.: Managing the configuration complexity of distributed applications in internet data centers. IEEE Communication Magazine 44(3), 166–177 (2006)
6. El Maghraoui, K., Meghranjani, A., Eilam, T., Kalantar, M., Konstantinou, A.: Model driven provisioning: Bridging the gap between declarative object models and procedural provisioning tools. In: van Steen, M., Henning, M. (eds.) Middleware 2006. LNCS, vol. 4290, pp. 404–423. Springer, Heidelberg (2006)
7. IBM: Tivoli Provisioning Manager (TPM) (2006)

8. Tsai, W., Fu, K.: Error-correcting isomorphisms of attributed relational graphs for pattern recognition. IEEE Trans. on Sys., Man, and Cybernetics 9, 757–768 (1979)
9. Su, X., Rao, J.: A survey of automated web service composition methods. In: SWSWPC (2004)
10. Kichkaylo, T., Karamcheti, V.: Optimal resource-aware deployment planning for component-based distributed applications. In: HPDC, Washington, DC, USA, pp. 150–159. IEEE Computer Society Press, Los Alamitos (2004)
11. Canfora, G., Penta, M.D., Esposito, R., Perfetto, F., Villani, M.L.: Service composition (re)binding driven by application-specific QoS. In: Dan, A., Lamersdorf, W. (eds.) ICSOC 2006. LNCS, vol. 4294, pp. 141–152. Springer, Heidelberg (2006)
12. Ludwig, H., Gimpel, H., Dan, A., Kearney, B.: Template based automated service provisioning supporting the agreement driven service life-cycle. In: Benatallah, B., Casati, F., Traverso, P. (eds.) ICSOC 2005. LNCS, vol. 3826, pp. 283–295. Springer, Heidelberg (2005)
13. Emig, C., Krutz, K., Link, S., Momm, C., Abeck, S.: Model-driven development of SOA services. Technical report, Forschungsbericht (2007)
14. Wada, H., Suzuki, J., Oba, K.: Modeling non-functional aspects in service oriented architecture. In: IEEE Int. Conf. on Service Computing, IEEE Computer Society Press, Los Alamitos (2006)
15. Sloman, M.: Management for open distributed processing. DCS 1(9), 25–39 (1990)
16. Sengupta, S., Dupuy, A., Schwartz, J., Yemini, Y.: An Object-Oriented Model for Network Management. In: OO Databases with Applic. to CASE, Networks and VLSI CAD. Series in Data and Knowledge base systems, Prentice-Hall, Englewood Cliffs (1991)
17. DMTF: Common Information Model (CIM). Technical report, DMTF (2006)
18. W3C: Service Modeling Language, version 1.0. Technical report (2007)
19. Yemini, Y., Konstantinou, A., Florissi, D.: NESTOR: An architecture for self-management and organization. In: JSAC, vol. 18(5) (2000)
20. Microsoft: DSI: Applications of model-based management (Technical report)
21. Soley, R.: Model driven architecture. Technical report, OMG (2000)
22. Bossardt, M., Mühlemann, A., Zürcher, R., Plattner, B.: Pattern based service deployment for active networks. In: ANTA (2003)
23. Keller, A., Hellerstein, J., Wolf, J., Wu, K.L., Krishnan, V.: The CHAMPS system: change management with planning, and scheduling. In: NOMS, IEEE Press, Los Alamitos (2004)

A Domain-Specific Language for Web APIs and Services Mashups

E. Michael Maximilien[1], Hernan Wilkinson[2], Nirmit Desai[3], and Stefan Tai[1]

[1] IBM Research
{maxim, stai}@us.ibm.com
[2] Universidad de Buenos Aires
hernan.wilkinson@gmail.com
[3] N.C. State University
nvdesai@ncsu.edu

Abstract. Distributed programming has shifted from private networks to the public Internet and from using private and controlled services to increasingly using publicly available heterogeneous Web services (e.g., REST, SOAP, RSS, and Atom). This move enables the creation of innovative end-user-oriented composed services with user interfaces. These services *mashups* are typically point solutions to specific (specialized) problems; however, what is missing is a programming model that facilitates and accelerates creation and deployment of mashups of *diverse* services. In this paper we describe a domain-specific language that unifies the most common service models and facilitates service composition and integration into end-user-oriented Web applications. We demonstrate our approach with an implementation that leverages the Ruby on Rails framework.

1 Introduction

There are two paradigm shifts occurring on the Web that are changing the way software is developed. The first is the increasing availability of Web APIs (or Web services) in the form of Representational State Transfer (REST) [2] and SOAP services, as well as RSS and Atom data services. These Web APIs enable external partners (or software agents) to incorporate business data and processes of the service providers into their own Web application or Web client. Indeed, the proliferation of these Web APIs have resulted in various composed services with UIs, or *mashups*, which provide solutions to very specific and narrow problems. An example is Podbop.org, which combines the API and data retrieved from Eventful.com with MySpace.com, as well as other MP3 databases, to create a site for music lovers who want to sample music of new (unknown) artists performing in local bars and clubs.

The second paradigm shift is a movement to increasingly program Web applications using dynamic programming languages and frameworks, e.g., JavaScript with AJAX, Ruby with Ruby on Rails (RoR), Python with Zope, Smalltalk with Seaside, as well as PHP. These languages allow for rapid application development and testing; and not only afford programmers expressive and powerful

B. Krämer, K.-J. Lin, and P. Narasimhan (Eds.): ICSOC 2007, LNCS 4749, pp. 13–26, 2007.

frameworks, but they also lead to the use of high-level abstractions which are more representative of the domain in question.

In many ways these two paradigm shifts are complementary since they essentially help realize the vision of a *programmable Web*. However, frameworks focused directly on facilitating the creation and deployment of mashups of diverse Web APIs and services are missing. For instance, each type of service (REST, SOAP, RSS, and Atom) has heterogeneous means of exposing the service interface or none at all. Additionally, there is a need to help address common distributed systems issues that arise [3].

In this paper we present a domain specific language (DSL) for services mashups that alleviates some of these issues. In particular, our DSL (1) allows for a common interface representation among diverse service types, (2) facilitates exposing asynchronous and synchronous method invocations, (3) gives a uniform model for service data and service operations' interactions, and (4) enables basic service data caching. We demonstrate an implementation of our language using Ruby and the RoR framework.

1.1 Organization

The rest of this paper is organized as follows. Section 2 gives an overview of our platform architecture. We also provide a more thorough definition of services mashups. Section 3 gives a more precise definition of our language and some brief examples of the language in action. Section 4 describes our implementation. Finally, Section 5 follows with a discussion of our approach which includes related works and limitations.

2 Background and Architecture

In order to demonstrate our approach to mashups and how a DSL can facilitate mashup creation, it's useful to first have a more precise definition of mashups along with possible implementation approaches. We then illustrate our architecture with a brief overview of the base platform that we use.

2.1 What Are Mashups?

At its core, a mashup is a Web application that aggregates multiple services to achieve a new purpose. Conceptually, mashups are new Web applications used for repurposing existing Web resources and services. They include all three aspects of a typical Web application (model-view-controller) with additional functionality. For us, a mashup includes three primary components:

1. *Data mediation* involves converting, transforming, and combining the data elements from one or multiple services to meet the needs of the operations of another. For instance, mediating between data models of tags represented in both the Flickr [1] and the Eventful's APIs.

[1] http://api.flickr.com

2. *Process (or protocol) mediation* is essentially choreographing between the different services to create a new process. For instance, process mediation includes invoking the various service methods, waiting for asynchronous messages, and sending any necessary confirmation messages.
3. *User interface customization* is used to elicit user information as well as to display intermittent and final process information to the user. Depending on the domain, the user interface customization can be as simple as an HTML page, a more complex series of input forms, or an interactive AJAX UI.

2.2 Mashup Implementation Approaches

Two example technologies used to build mashups are the Google Web Toolkit (GWT) [2] and plain RoR. As an example, consider implementing a mashup that updates personal calendars from Atom feeds, and allows adding rating information for events. Assume, without loss of generality, that each user's calendar can be accessed via a REST API using a key parameter to authenticate users. The Atom feeds generate heterogeneous event entries for each up-coming talks. And finally, each user has an account in Eventful, which exposes a common data model for events and REST APIs to add, search, rate, and retrieve events.

Using GWT, two main components of the mashups are to represent the various talk feeds entries and converting them to the uniform *Event* data model of Eventful. This involves data mediation between the model for a *Talk* entry from the Atom feed to an the *Event* model in Eventful. For instance, the former may have a location data as a string which needs to be parsed into the different fields for location represented by the latter.

GWT does not have built-in libraries for accessing REST or Atom services. This means that for each service type, there is a need to find an appropriate Java ™library or creating one manually and binding and testing to the services in question.

Next, we need to mediate the protocols of the three services to achieve the goals of our mashup. For instance, assume that the first page of our mashup simply displays all up-coming events in the next two-weeks that are not already added to the user's calendar. One possible choreography between the three services to achieve this goal is:

1. Retrieve entries from all feeds for up-coming talks. Additional consideration for this step are: caching public entries for subsequent access or for other users and enabling asynchronous updates of the cache.
2. Query the user's calendar to get all talk entries for the next two weeks.
3. Mediate between the user's calendar entries and the feed entries. Decide on comparison criteria, e.g., time, date, location, and so on.
4. For each talk not present in the user's calendar, create a common representation of these talks as events in Eventful and add to the Eventful database via REST API. Eventful events include a model for speakers which also needs to

[2] http://code.google.com/webtoolkit

be mediated from the data feeds. If the talk is already present, then retrieve it and mediate between the reconciled event in previous step and this one.
5. Present a formatted page to the user with each new event with checkboxes and a button to enable the user to add events to her calendar.
6. Allow user to view events in her calendar. For each event: (1) display event data; (2) allow user to delete the event; and (3) allow user to indicate attendance.

It's worth noting that using GWT to implement the choreography above results in adding custom code for the data mediation steps, for resolving the choreography, as well as for any data caching. Additionally, there is no reuse of the various steps across mashups of the same services.

Using RoR is effectively similar to using GWT, though simpler for some aspects. For instance, RoR's built-in support for databases via *ActiveRecord* would facilitate caching the feed entries into a relational database. However, this would need to be manually done for each type of *Talk* feed added to the system.

2.3 Ruby on Rails

The Ruby on Rails (RoR) framework enables agile development of Web applications. The framework contains primitives to help efficiently implement all aspects of an Model-View-Controller (MVC) Web application. Each MVC Web application contains: (1) *Model* classes representing the data elements of the application's domain. Model objects can persist their state in a database using a series of conventions; (2) *View*s are the dynamic pages displayed to the user of the Web application. Each view file contains HTML and embedded Ruby code which is translated into JavaScript, HTML, and CSS on the server before being sent to the client (i.e., browser); and (3) *Controller*s constitute the middle layer between models and views. Controllers are classes whose names and methods map to the application URL path. Controller methods contain business logic by operating on model objects and accessing remote services.

Additionally, RoR also includes basic facilities to allow controllers to invoke external SOAP Web services and to access remote Web resources. However, the RoR Web API support lacks some key features needed to streamline and create mashups, e.g., lack of consistent and uniform representation for all different types of services, lack of support for asynchronous invocation of services' operations that can work across all service types, and lack of provisions for easily manipulating complex XML data (beyond parsing).

2.4 Architecture Overview

To address the above deficiencies (and others) as well as to provide a uniform model for building and sharing services mashup we created the *Swashup* platform. Our architecture extends the RoR architecture with a new DSL, supporting libraries, as well as associated platform models and services. Figure 1 illustrates the high-level components of our architecture.

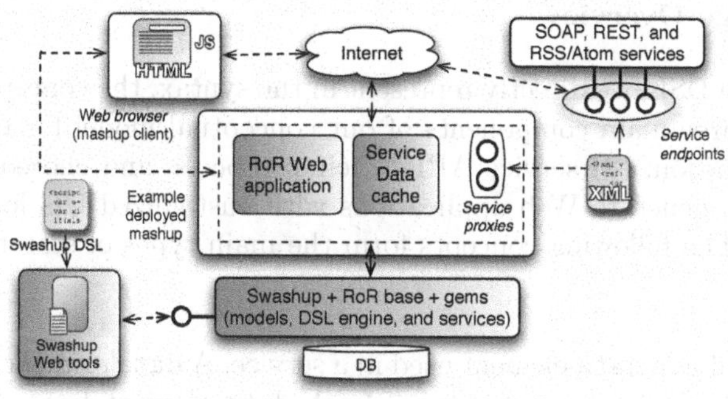

Fig. 1. Swashup high-level architecture

Using the Swashup Web UI tools, an end user creates, edits, and deploys a Swashup project which contains the necessary information for describing the services to be mashed up as well as the mashup information. Using the Swashup platform services, the Swashup project is deployed as a complete RoR Web application with all necessary service proxies, models, and initial views for each mashup.

3 Swashup DSL

We now introduce our language and discuss the main requirements for any DSL as well as some criteria for judging their value.

3.1 What Are DSLs?

A domain-specific language (DSL) is a 'mini' language built on top of a hosting language that provides a common syntax and semantics to represent concepts and behaviors in a particular domain. In general, using or designing a DSL helps achieve the following goals: (1) **Abstraction** by enabling programming at a level higher than what is available with the host programming language constructs or its libraries. A DSL allows the domain concepts, actions, and behaviors to be represented directly in the new syntax; (2) **Terse Code** as a side effect of programming in a higher-level of abstraction; (3) **Simple and Natural Syntax**, which leads to easy to write and read code; (4) **Ease of Programming**, which is desirable of any programming language and also somewhat difficult to judge. However, since a DSL enables the expression of constructs that map directly to a domain, it generally makes programming easier (for applications in the domain) than using the underlying language directly; and (5) **Code Generation** is how a DSL primarily functions. Essentially, the DSL statements are translated at runtime into code that uses the underlying language and its libraries. This can be either using metaprogramming techniques or by code generation of program files.

3.2 Language Overview

In the Swashup DSL, we directly represent in the syntax, the concepts necessary to cover the three main components of our conceptual model for mashups: (1) data and mediation; (2) service APIs, their protocols, and choreography; and (3) a means to generate Web applications with customized UIs for the resulting mashups. The following concepts form the main types of statements in our language.

- **data** describes a `data` element used in a service. A `data` element corresponds to an XML schema complex type. Each `data` element has a name and a series of `member` attributes. These attributes' types can be either regular XSD simple types or other data elements. Section 4 gives more details on our XML mapping approach including conventions and rules.
- **api** gives a complete description of a service's interface. This includes descriptions for the service's API, including operation names, parameters, and data types. An operation data type is either a simple type (e.g., string or integer) or refers to a `data` element. Section 4.1 discusses the conventions for creating `api` definitions for SOAP and REST services, as well as Atom and RSS services.
- **mediation** describes the transformation of one or multiple data elements to create a new one. Essentially, a `mediation` is a mapping between `data` elements with some possible transformations.
- **service** binds a service `api` with a concrete service. Part of the binding is to indicate the service's type (e.g., SOAP, REST, RSS, or Atom), the service's endpoint, as well as give an alias for the service instance.
- **recipe** constitutes a collection of `services` and `mashups`. A recipe also includes views for each of the mashup `wiring`. Some views are automatically generated and others are customized by the user.
  - **mashup** is a composition of one or multiple services. It comprises a collection of `wiring` declarations. Each `mashup` translates into a composed service which may be exposed externally and used for further mashups.
  - **mediate** invokes a `mediation` declaration with instances of the data elements to mediate. The result of a `mediate` call is a primitive type instance or another data element instance.
  - **wiring** which comprises two levels of granularities of connecting the services that are part of a `mashup`: (1) **:protocol** is a top-level structure of a mashup. It represents one or multiple operation `wirings` and `steps` invocations. It also associates with views as specified in Section 3.3 and (2) **:operation** is the wiring of one or multiple services' operations. Operation wiring includes the ability to invoke services' operations in an asynchronous fashion by automatically setting up callbacks.
  - **step** constitutes one atomic step in a protocol mediation. A step can be invoked multiple times as part of a protocol wiring. A `step` is invoked by the `step`'s name as a method call.

- **tag** and **tags** allows users to annotate terms to the various components of a Swashup `recipe` as well as `data` and `api` definitions. These types of tagging allows for some level of comments and idiosyncratic semantics to the various components.

For brevity, a complete formalization of our language in BNF (Backus-Naur form) is not described in this paper.

3.3 Conventions

Following one of RoR's main philosophy, namely, *using conventions over configurations* [3] our Swashup DSL includes a series of conventions. The use of conventions is meant to simplify the language's usage and to make the resulting code more compact.

- *Naming* are added to most statements as the first parameter and as a Ruby symbol or string. Names use either a camel-case (e.g., :SomeDataElement) format or lower-case (e.g., :some_mashup) using underscore to separate words. The `data` and `api` require camel-case. Other language constructs accept either camel-case or lower-case with underscore, e.g., `wiring` constructs.
- *Variables* are always lower-case with underscore separating the words in the variable's name.
- *Recipes* when deployed are complete RoR Web applications with controllers matching each of the `mashup`.
- *Mashups* are converted to a RoR Web application controller and every protocol `wiring` translates into an action for the Web application. This allows the application to be exposed as a service as well as adding views.
- *Views* by RoR convention associate with a controller's action and therefore with a protocol `wiring`. Using an `async` parameter to operation `wiring` allows the views to be created with AJAX JavaScript that can check back with the controller for updated data and refresh the view's content.

3.4 Examples

To illustrate the power of our DSL we now give a complete example. Briefly, our example mashes the data and protocol of two available services: (1) Google's SOAP search Web service and (2) Yahoo! Flickr's photo REST API. The main purpose of our mashup is to allow users to search for a phrase or word using the Google search service and display the top results. Additionally, we display the top thumb nail photos associated with the searched words from Flickr by matching the tags that the Flickr community has used for the shared photos.

Our mashup's `recipe` is divided into four listings (Listings 1.1 to 1.4), each illustrating one aspect of the solution. Listing 1.1 shows how we use the DSL's `data` construct to represent the data coming from Flickr (starting line 1). The API definition starts at line 5.

[3] http://www.rubyonrails.org/

Listing 1.1. Example Swashup `data` and `api` definitions.

```
data :Photo do
    member :url, :xml_text
    member :tags, [:string], :xml_text
end
api :FlickrApi do
  api_method :find_photos,
             :expects => [{:tags => [:string]}],
             :returns => [[:Photo]]
end
```

Listing 1.2 shows the start of our Google search SOAP API and Flickr REST API mashup `recipe`. We start by tagging the `recipe` in lines 11. Next we use the `service` construct to create a binding to the Flickr REST service, giving it an alias name of `f` and we would include similarly for all other services used.

The `service` construct unifies the different types of services supported in our DSL. It includes type specific parameters, e.g., `:wsdl` for a SOAP service, and type independent parameters, for instance, the `:endpoint` which is used for SOAP and REST services and used to indicate the RSS or Atom feed URL. The `service`'s `:api` parameter points to the defined API (Listing 1.1) for SOAP or REST services and is implicit for RSS and Atom feeds (see Section 4.1). However, RSS and Atom feeds require a `:entry` parameter to indicate the `data` definition for the expected entries of of the data feed.

Listing 1.2. Example Swashup `recipe` showing `tag`(s) and `service`(s) definitions.

```
9  recipe :GoogleFlikcrRecipe do
     tag 'recipe',
11       :synonyms => ['example', 'exemplar', 'pattern']
     service :flickr_service, :alias => :f
13           :type => :rest,
             :api => :FlickrApi,
15           :endpoint => 'http://rest.flickr.com/api'
       # service for Google search service
17     # constants declarations, other service definitions, $\ldots$
   end
```

Next, we illustrate how to define `mediators`, `wirings`, and `steps`. These are shown in Listing 1.3. Our `extract_tags` mediator starts in Line 20 and takes a string input and divides it into a set of keywords by first filtering them.

Each `wiring` is converted into a method that can be called in the context of the `recipe`, e.g., *search 'flickr mashups'*, however, the value added for the creating wiring (besides the design values and potential for reuse) is the ability to automatically make the wiring invoke operations in an asynchronous fashion.

This is achieved by either passing a Ruby block that is called back with the result of the `wiring` when the operation completes or by passing a block or Ruby method taking one parameter using the automatically generated setter method named `search_callback=`. The result of last invocation of a `wiring` is also automatically added to an instance variable by the wiring name.

Listing 1.3. Example Swashup `recipe` and `mashup`.

```
recipe :GoogleFlikcrRecipe do
    # tag(s), tags, service(s), and CONSTANT(s)
    mediator(:extract_tags, :data) do |string|
        keywords = []
    string.split.each do |s|
        keywords << s unless NON_KEYWORDS.include?(s)
        end
        return keywords
    end
    wiring(:find_images, :operation, :async) do |words|
        @urls = []
        words.each do |w|
            url = f.find_photo(w).url
            @urls << url unless urls.include?(url)
        end
        return @urls
    end
  step :search_and_images do |string|
        @results = search(string)
        @keywords = extract_tags(string)
        @urls = find_images(keywords)
  end
    # other mashup(s)
end
end
```

Listing 1.4 completes our example `recipe`. It illustrates how different `mashups` are added to a `recipe` by adding different protocol `wirings`. Each protocol `wiring` can accept parameters as a Ruby block parameters and can make calls to `steps`, `mediators`, and operation `wirings`. Importantly, each `mashup` can have it's protocol `wirings` exposed as SOAP, REST, RSS, or Atom services. This is achieved using the `expose_operation` construct. For RSS and Atom services the protocol `expose_operation` uses an `:entry` parameter which binds to a `data` indicating the format of the RSS or Atom entry and instance variable that will contain the updated entry data.

Listing 1.4. Example Swashup `recipe` and `mashup`.

```
recipe :GoogleFlikcrRecipe do
    # tag, tags, service, and any CONSTANT(s)
    # mediator(s), wiring(s), and step(s)
  mashup :spell_search_images_mashup do |g, f|
    tags ['mashup', 'spell']
        wiring(:images_for_keywords, :protocol) do |words|
            expose_operation :soap,
                         :expects => [{:keywords => :string}]
                         :returns => [[:Photo]]
            find_images(words)
        end
    wiring(:search_and_images, :protocol) do |string|
            expose_operation :atom,
                         :entry_data => :GoogleSeearchResult,
                         :entries => @results,
                         :atom_metadata => [{:author => 'Jane Doe'}]
            spelled = spell_search(string)
        search_and_images(spelled)
        end
  end # mashup
end # recipe
end
```

3.5 Value of DSL

As mentioned in Section 3.1 our DSL enables mashup programming at a higher-level of abstraction than frameworks supporting Web application programming. This is primarily achieved by defining high-level constructs that facilitate mashup creations. Specifically:

1. *Uniform treatment of diverse services (REST, SOAP, RSS, and Atom).* This is especially useful for REST, RSS, and Atom services which do not have standard machine readable definitions (such as WSDL for SOAP services).
2. *Facilitate asynchronous operation calls.* For each wiring operation you can specify `:async` as an option which will add (via metaprogramming) all necessary code to call methods asynchronously and deal with callbacks and so on.
3. *Uniform treatment of service data elements.* This includes having a definition of the data elements passed and returned to the `service` constructs. Additionally, our `data` construct help: (1) *facilitate data mediation and reuse* and (2) *facilitate service data caching*

4. *Uniform design for mashups.* Using our language we give some structure to the design of service mashups while also enabling the full support of a modern language and framework for Web application development.
5. *Integrate into RoR.* First by using Ruby as the implementation language (which makes RoR integration seamless) but also in how to expose a `recipe` as a RoR Web application.

4 Implementation

Our Swashup platform is implemented completely in Ruby and RoR. We leverage the RoR framework by using and extending various aspects. Using Ruby's metaprogramming support and the rich view capabilities of the RoR platform every recipe is converted into a Web application that can be customized to create rich AJAX Web applications. In addition, every recipe's `mashup` can be exposed as a Web service (SOAP, REST, RSS, or Atom). This is achieved using the DSL constructs and a series of conventions.

Our metaprogramming approach is enabled using a series of class and object templates for the different constructs of our DSL. For instance, each `data` construct is translated into three classes: (1) a ROXML [4] class to enable parsing and generation of XML; (2) an *ActiveRecord* class to allow the data element to be cached in a relational database; and (3) a Ruby class that seamlessly aggregates the other two classes' functionalities.

For each `recipe` we generate a full RoR Web application with a controller class for each `mashup`. Each `api` construct translates into a RoR *ActionWebService* API classes that make use of the `data` classes. We extend the RoR classes to deal with REST and other types of services. Each `service` construct translates into an object that proxies the service it binds. The proxy exposes the `api` interface and is adjusted for each type of service supported.

The `mediator` and operation `wiring` translate into Ruby methods that are added to a `module` created for each `recipe`. This module includes the Swashup platform modules and is included itself into the generated controller classes for each of the `mashup` constructs. Finally for each `mashup` we also generate an API class with `api_method` for each protocol `wiring` that includes an `expose_operation` construct call. This is how a mashup is exposed as a service.

For each protocol `wiring` we generate the following view related artifacts:

1. A partial view that includes an HTML form for the parameters of the protocol `wiring`. If the protocol `wiring` does not have parameters then no partial view is generated. Using Ruby and *ActiveRecord* conventions we use text fields for strings, numbers, and `data` fields marked `xml_attribute`; and we use an HTML form for fields that point to other `data` element using `xml_object`.
2. An RHTML template view with the name of the protocol `wiring` that includes the partial views and with some default text to indicate that this view associates with the action and needs to be customized.

[4] http://roxml.rubyforge.org

3. An action method in the generated `mashup` controller class that uses the data from the partial view (if any is present) to call the protocol `wiring` method and displays the view page.

4.1 Details

We achieve uniform `data` and `service` and `api` descriptions by extending the RoR platform and using a series of conventions when describing services. First, the service `data` are described by using the XML schema. For SOAP services this schema is part of the WSDL and for REST, RSS, and Atom it can be inferred, by the human designer, from service's documentation, or from example input and output messages. The representation of the `api` for a service depends on the service's type.

- SOAP services are expected to have an associated WSDL which makes the API definition somewhat automatic. Each SOAP `portType` maps to an `api` definition. Each `operation` in a `portType` maps to an `api_method` in the associated `api` and uses the input messages as `expects` parameters and output messages for the `returns` hash [5]. The input and output message's XSD types translate one-to-one to a `data` definition. The `service`'s `endpoint` parameter maps to the SOAP endpoint in the WSDL's `service` section.
- REST services require additional conventions, especially since REST services do not have associated standard description languages. Each REST service specifies its endpoint as the root URI that is common across all of its operations. For instance, we use `http://api.evdb.com` for the Eventful's API since all REST operations have this root URI in common. The `api_method` for a REST `api` definition can also take a third `:http_method` parameter to specify either if this operation should be an HTTP `:get` (default), `:post`, `:put`, or `:delete`.
  REST operations use a simple convention to convert the path into a Ruby method. For path names that do not contain the underscore character (i.e., '_') in the operation's path elements translate into a Ruby method that uses underscore to separate its sections (if any). For instance, the path 'search/-customer' translates into the operation named 'search_customer'. If the path contains the underscore character then it is assumed that the path section translates into two underscores when converting to a Ruby method. For instance, the path 'search_all/customers' translates into the Ruby method 'search__all_customers'.
- RSS and Atom services follow the same `api` so it never needs to be specified. Figure 2 shows the UML class diagram for Atom services showing the operations available for any Atom service.
  Since RSS and Atom services are feeds that contains recurring elements, the type of the element must be specified in the `service` construct. That type is specified as a `data` construct which uses its *ActiveRecord* part to enable caching of the feed's data entries.

[5] A Ruby hash is equivalent to maps or dictionaries in other languages.

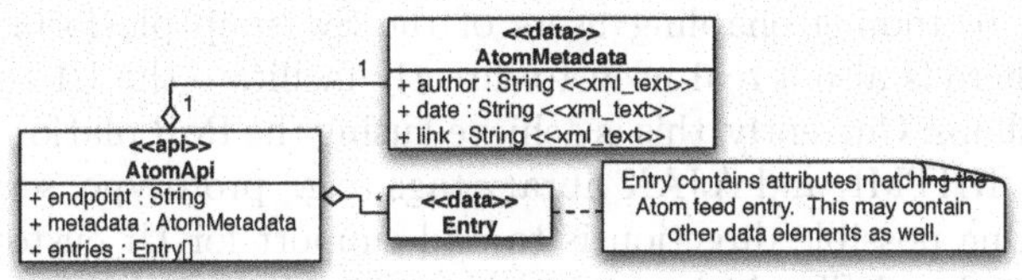

Fig. 2. Atom service API UML class diagram

5 Discussion

The Swashup DSL gives a high-level abstraction and language to create service mashups. Our initial implementation leverages and extends the RoR framework to create a set of tools that facilitate mashup creation as well as management.

5.1 Related Works

We divide related works into two main categories: mashup tools and frameworks and service compositions and service workflows.

Yahoo! Pipes [6] is an example of a mashup tool available on the Web. In Yahoo! Pipes, services (primarily RSS and Atom data services) can be 'piped' together (à la UNIX pipes) to create more complex data composition mashups. IBM's QEDWiki [7] is another example of a mashup tool. However, unlike Yahoo! Pipes, QEDWiki allows users to create widgets that access different services and data sources. Using the wiki metaphor, QEDWiki aims to make the composition process iterative and collaborative. While similar in objectives, both Pipes and QEDWiki differ from the Swashup platform, which focuses instead on giving common structures to mashups and creating a language to facilitate their creation and sharing.

Since Swashup, at some level, is essentially a platform for services composition, related works in services composition and workflows are important to note. BPEL is a workflow language adapted for services—instead of orchestrating a flow of activities, it orchestrates a flow of services [1]. Although BPEL has gained currency as a services composition solution, it is not geared toward UI-ready situational applications and mashups.

5.2 Directions

While with the current Swashup DSL we are able to create `recipes` which encompass different types of services and somewhat complex data and protocol mediation, there is a need to test our language and platform with even more complex services and mediations. For instance, the types of mediations necessary for back-end enterprise integration. For examples, services such as the ones available in the SalesForce.com's AppExchange [8] platform.

[6] http://pipes.yahoo.com

[7] http://services.alphaworks.ibm.com/qedwiki

[8] http://www.salesforce.com/appexchange

In addition to tooling enabling users of the Swashup platform to program in our DSL, there is also a real need to directly facilitate the UI customization aspects of mashups. Currently, this is achieved using the RoR platform's UI primitives by using RHTML and AJAX library tags (e.g., prototype, script.aculo.us, and others). One possible direction is to add support for UI customization directly in our mashup DSL which could make `recipes` more complete at the point of their creation.

Another direction is enabling the system and platform for collaboration [4]. We started in that direction by enabling the various components of a `recipe` to be tagged with information. In addition we would like to explore adding directly the ability to share, reuse, copy, restrict, and measure the effectiveness of recipes in our tools. This may result in some changes to the DSL, especially in the area of restricting access to recipes for instance. Additionally, with enough usage the tags in the recipes may form a folksonomy, [9] which might help users discover recipes and reuse them.

References

1. Curbera, F., Goland, Y., Klein, J., Leymann, F., Roller, D., Thatte, S., Weerawarana, S.: Business Process Execution Language for Web Services, Version 1.0 (2002), `http://www-128.ibm.com/developerworks/library/specification/ws-bpel/`
2. Fielding, R.T.: Software Architectural Styles for Network-based Applications. Ph.D. thesis, University of California, Irvine, CA (January 2000)
3. Goff, M.K.: Network Distributed Computing: Fitscapes and Fallacies. Prentice Hall, Upper Saddle River, NJ (2003)
4. Tai, S., Desai, N., Mazzoleni, P.: Service communities: applications and middleware. In: SEM-06. Proceedings of the 6th International Workshop on Software Engineering and Middleware, Portland, OR, pp. 17–22 (2006)

[9] http://en.wikipedia.org/wiki/Folksonomy

BPEL4Job: A Fault-Handling Design for Job Flow Management

Wei Tan[1,*], Liana Fong[2], and Norman Bobroff[2]

[1] Department of Automation, Tsinghua University, Beijing 100084, China
[2] IBM T. J. Watson Research Center, Hawthorne, NY 10532, USA
tanwei@mails.tsinghua.edu.cn, llfong@us.ibm.com,
bobroff@us.ibm.com

Abstract. Workflow technology is an emerging paradigm for systematic modeling and orchestration of job flow for enterprise and scientific applications. This paper introduces BPEL4Job, a BPEL-based design for fault handling of job flow in a distributed computing environment. The features of the proposed design include: a two-stage approach for job flow modeling that separates base flow structure from fault-handling policy, a generic job proxy that isolates the interaction complexity between the flow engine and the job scheduler, and a method for migrating flow instances between different flow engines for fault handling in a distributed system. An implementation of the design based on a set of industrial products from IBM is presented and validated using a Montage application.

1 Introduction

Originating from the people-oriented business process area, the applicability of workflow technology today is increasingly broad, extending to inter and intra organizational business-to-business interactions, automatic transactional flow, etc [1]. With the advent of web services as a new application-building paradigm in a loosely-coupled, platform-independent and standardized manner, the use of workflow to orchestrate the invocation of web services is gaining importance. The Web Service Business Process Execution Language [2] (WS-BPEL or BPEL for short), proposed by OASIS as a standard for workflow orchestration, will enhance the inter-operability of workflow in distributed and heterogeneous systems. Although many custom workflow systems have been developed by the scientific application community [3-5], the inter-operability of BPEL workflow systems has attracted many researchers [1, 6-10] to experiment with BPEL for applications in distributed environments such as grid.

BPEL-based workflow is particularly relevant in orchestrating batch jobs for enterprise applications, as job flow is an integral part of the business operation. There are obvious advantages in standardizing on a common flow language, such as BPEL, for both business process and batch jobs. Although some workflow systems are used for enterprise applications [11, 12], these workflow systems use proprietary flow languages.

* The work was done while the author was on an internship at IBM T.J. Watson Research Center, NY, USA.

B. Krämer, K.-J. Lin, and P. Narasimhan (Eds.): ICSOC 2007, LNCS 4749, pp. 27–42, 2007.

The use of BPEL for job flow is not without technical challenges, as BPEL was not designed with job flow requirements. These challenges include defining a job[1] entity within BPEL, expressing data dependency (usually implicitly expressed in the job definition), and passing of large data between jobs. Another key challenge is to manage the predominately asynchronous interaction between the BPEL engine and the job scheduling partners. Finally, support for fault tolerance and recovery strategy is important due to the long-running nature of jobs, as well as the interaction of grid services with dynamic resources [13]. This paper addresses the latter issues of asynchronous interactions and fault handling in job flow by proposing a design called BPEL4Job.

BPEL4Job includes three unique features. First, a two-stage approach for job flow modeling is presented. In stage one the flow structure and fault-handling policies are modeled separately. Stage two combines and transforms the flow model and policy into an expanded flow that is then orchestrated by a BPEL-compliant engine. The advantage of this approach is that it separates the concerns of application flow modeling from fault handling. Second, a generic job proxy is inserted between the BPEL engine and the job scheduler to facilitate job submission and isolate the flow engine from the asynchronous nature of status notification, including fault events. Finally, we propose several schemes for flow-level fault handling, including a novel method for instance migration between flow engines. Instance migration is important for scalable failure recovery in a distributed environment. For example, a flow that fails due to resource unavailability may be migrated to another resource domain.

The design and implementation work in this paper is based on the IBM BPEL-compliant workflow modeler and execution engine, as well as the service oriented job scheduler.

The following section introduces BPEL4Job, the overall design approach to incorporating fault handing features into the BPEL design and execution process. Section 3 discusses integrating fault policies at the flow's design stage. Section 4 presents the fault handling scheme and especially, the technique for flow instance migration and flow re-submission. Section 5 introduces our prototype system, and demonstrates our fault handling method using the Montage application [14]. Section 6 surveys related work and Section 7 concludes the paper and suggests future directions.

2 BPEL4Job: A Fault-Handling Design for Job Flow Management

In this section, we introduce our overall design, BPEL4Job, which facilitates the advanced fault handing in BPEL both the flow modeling tools and execution environments. More specifically, BPEL4Job has the following unique features:

- Adding a flexible fault handling approach based on policies. These policies can express a range of actions from simple job retry, to how and at what point in the flow to restart for a particular type of execution failure. The policies allow options to clean or retain the state of the jobs flow in the flow engine database.

[1] The terms "job" and "job step", and "job flow" and "flow" are used interchangeably in this paper. A job flow consists of one or more jobs.

- Introducing a functional element called a 'job proxy' that connects and integrates the high level BPEL engine with the lower level job scheduler that accepts and executes jobs. The proxy captures the job status notifications from the scheduler and relays them to the BPEL engine. The proxy serves as an arbiter and filter of asynchronous events between the BPEL engine and the job scheduler.
- Supporting migration of the persisted state of a BPEL job flow to another engine. This capability provides fault tolerance by allowing a flow that has failed, for example, because of resource exhaustion in one environment to continue execution in another environment.

The design of BPEL4Job consists of three layers: the *flow modeling* layer, the *flow execution* layer and the *job scheduling* layer, as shown in Fig. 1. First, we describe the *flow modeling* layer. The flow modeling in BPEL4Job takes a two-stage approach in modeling job flow. In the first stage, the *base flow,* the *job definitions,* and the *fault-handling policies* are defined. The base flow is a BPEL expression of the control flow of jobs for a process or an application. Each job definition describes a unit of work (e.g. an executable file together with parameters and resource requirements) to be submitted to scheduler and is expressed by a markup language such as Job Submission Description Language (JSDL) [15]. The fault-handling policies define the actions to be taken in case of job failures and can be described using the web service policy language WS-Policy [16]. In the second stage, the base flow, job definitions, and fault-handling policies are transformed into an expanded flow that is an executable BPEL process. This two-stage modeling approach has many advantages. First, the flow designer defines the job flow structure and fault-handling

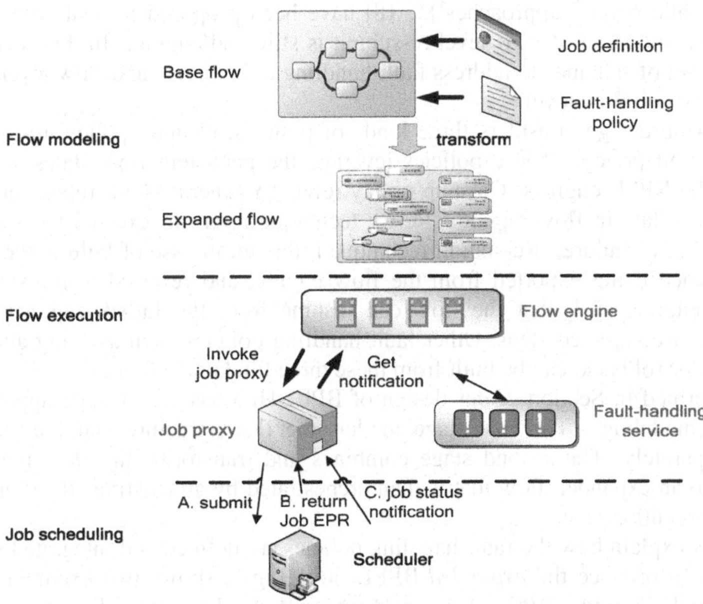

Fig. 1. BPEL4Job: fault-handling design for job flow management

policies separately, and needs not be concerned on how to implement these policies in BPEL. Second, the base flow and policies can be reused and combined if necessary. More details and examples are provided in Section 3.

The flow execution layer consists of three major components: the flow engine, the job proxy, and the fault-handling service. The flow engine executes the expanded BPEL originating in the flow modeling layer. For each job step in the expanded flow, the job proxy is invoked by the flow engine. The job proxy submits the job definition to the scheduler, listens for job status notification, and reports job success or failure to the flow engine. In the case of job failure, the flow engine invokes the fault-handling service if necessary. Otherwise, if successful, the flow engine proceeds to the next job step. The fault-handling service is discussed in Section 4.

The job-scheduling layer accepts jobs, returns a unique end-point reference (EPR) for each job, and sends notification on job status changes. We assume that the schedulers are responsible for resources matching and job execution management. Some schedulers also implement failure recovery techniques such as re-try. In BPEL4Job, we supplement this capability with a set of fault-handling techniques at the flow execution layer including re-try from another job step, as well as flow instance migration to other engines.

3 Integrating Fault-Handling Policies with Job Flow Modeling

Yu et al. [5] and Hwang et al. [17] classified the fault-handling methods of grid workflow into two levels: task level and flow level. From their work, we observe that, re-try and re-submit are the most elementary methods in these two levels respectively. Second, while several approaches [5, 18] have been proposed to deal with the task level re-try, the issue of flow level re-submit is still challenging. In this section, we provide a set of schemes to address fault-handling at both task and flow levels and to put emphasis on flow level.

BPEL4Job design considers three kinds of policies: cleanup policy, re-try policy and re-submit policy. These policies leverage the persistent flow states storage in most of the BPEL engines. Cleanup policy refers to generate fault report and delete the instance data in flow engine. Re-try technique refers to execute the same task again in case of failure. Re-submit technique refers to, in case of failure, the state of flow instance being exported from the flow engine, and restored to the same or a different engine, such that the flow can resume from the failed step without re-execution of completed steps. Other fault-handling policies such as using alternative resources, or rollback, can be built from these three fundamental ones.

As described in Section 2, our design of BPEL4Job has a two-stage approach for job flow modeling. The first stage models the flow structure and fault-handling policy separately. The second stage combines and transforms the flow model and policy into an expanded flow that is then orchestrated by an existing BPEL engine in the flow execution layer.

We now explain how the fault-handling policies are defined and integrated with the *base* flow to produce the *expanded* BPEL flow. Fig. 2 shows two exemplary fault-handling policies and a BPEL skeleton of a base flow. The first policy, named *retry-policy*, specifies that when job failure occurs, the flow will re-try from the current job step (by setting the value of element *RetryEntry* to *itself*), and after an interval of 300 seconds (by setting the value of element *RetryTimes* to *Unlimited*, and *RetryInterval* to *300s*). The second policy, named *resubmit-policy*, specifies that when job failure occurs, the flow will resume at another flow engine if desired. When it resumes, it restarts from the previous step of the failed job (by setting the value of element *RescueEntry* to *previous-step*. The base flow consists of two sequential job steps, *SubmitJob1* and *SubmitJob2*. In the base flow, the *retry-policy* is linked to *SubmitJob1* (<bpws:invoke name="SubmitJob1" faultHandling:policy="retry-policy" />), and *resubmit-policy* linked to *SubmitJob2* (<bpws:invoke name="SubmitJob2" faultHandling:policy= "resubmit-policy" />).

The re-try policy of *SubmitJob1* is realized by transforming the base flow to the expanded flow as shown in Fig. 3, and described as follows:

- Add a variable *RETRY* to indicate whether the job should be retried and set its value to *TRUE* before the job.
- Add an assign activity after the job to set variable *RETRY* to *FALSE*.
- Add a scope enclosing the job and succeeding assign activity.
- Add a While loop on top of the newly-added scope, and set the condition for the While loop to (*RETRY* == *TRUE*).
- Add a fault handler for the newly added scope to catch the fault. Advanced re-try schemes, including re-try for a given times, re-try after a given time of period, and re-try from a previous job, could all be implemented in this fault-handler block.

In case of job failure, the control flow goes to the fault handler (the *Catch All* block in Fig. 3), and when the fault-handling block completes, the control flow proceeds to the beginning of the While loop. Because the newly added scope does not complete when failure occurs, the value of variable *RETRY* is still *TRUE*, so the flow will continue at the beginning of the While loop (*Submit Job1* in Fig. 2), by this means the re-try policy is realized. It is important to note that expanded flow contains all the necessary fault-handling blocks, unlike other approaches in supporting runtime fault-handling selection [18].

```
<?xml version="1.0" encoding="UTF-8" ?>
<wsp:Policy xmlns:wsp="..." xmlns:jobFlow="..."
        name="retry-policy">
 <jobFlow:Retry wsp:Usage="wsp:Required">
  <jobFlow:RetryEntry>self</jobFlow:RetryEntry>
  <jobFlow:RetryTimes>Unlimited</jobFlow:RetryTimes>
  <jobFlow:RetryInterval>300s</jobFlow:RetryInterval>
 </jobFlow:Retry>
</wsp:Policy>
```

```
<?xml version="1.0" encoding="UTF-8" ?>
<wsp:Policy xmlns:wsp="..." xmlns:jobFlow="..."
        name="resubmit-policy">
<jobFlow:Rescue wsp:Usage="wsp:Required">
<jobFlow:RescueEntry>previous-step?
 </jobFlow:RescueEntry>
</jobFlow:Rescue>
</wsp:Policy>
```

```
<?xml version="1.0" encoding="UTF-8" ?>
 <bpws:process xmlns:bpws="..." xmlns:faultHandling="...">
  <bpws:partnerLinks>...</bpws:partnerLinks>
  <bpws:variables>...</bpws:variables>
   <bpws:sequence name="HiddenSequence">
    <bpws:receive createInstance="yes" name="ReceiveJobRequest" />
    <bpws:invoke name="SubmitJob1" faultHandling:policy="retry-policy" />
    <bpws:invoke name="SubmitJob2" faultHandling:policy="resubmit-policy" />
    <bpws:reply name="Reply" />
   </bpws:sequence>
</bpws:process>
```

Fig. 2. The re-try and re-submit policy, and the base flow embedded with these policies

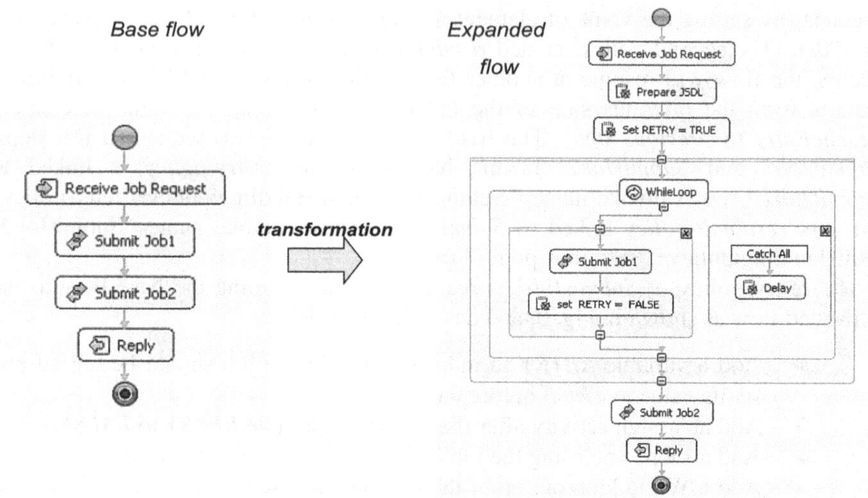

Fig. 3. The transformation to implement the re-try policy of *Job1*

4 Fault-Handling at the Flow Execution Layer in BPEL4Job

Job execution may fail due to a variety of reasons, such as resource and data unavailability, application failure, scheduler or human input error, etc. The fault handling at flow execution layer needs two mechanisms: the capability to recognize various job failures and the capability to handle the failures according to the policies defined at flow modeling layer.

In BPEL, faults can be raised by an invoked service and be caught by the invoking service. BPEL also provides a Java-style support for fault handling, using constructs like *Catch*, *Catch All*, *Throw*, *Rethrow*, etc. A BPEL fault handler catches faults and can handle them by, for example, calling a suitable fault-handling service. In addition, most of BPEL engines store persistent states of the flow and the use of states can support resumption of flow execution from a failed task. The design of fault handling in BPEL4Job would leverage the BPEL basic fault-handling features and enhance specific capabilities to recognize job failures and to handle faults according to defined policies. The following section addresses both aspects by introducing: i) the generic job proxy for job submission and job status notification (especially for fault recognition), and ii) the fault-handling schemes for various policies at the task level and flow level.

4.1 The Generic Job Proxy

The generic job proxy connects and integrates the higher-level BPEL workflow engine with the lower-level job scheduler. For each job submission invocation, the proxy submits jobs, captures the job status notifications from the scheduler, and returns the job failure/success result in a synchronous manner. It serves as an arbiter and filter of asynchronous notification events of jobs. When a job fails, the job proxy raises a fault to the workflow engine. Then, the workflow engine would invoke fault-handling service after catching the fault.

Fig. 4 shows the control flow of a generic job proxy. The explanation is as follows:

1. Receive a job submission request.
2. Forward the job request to a scheduler, and start to listen for the job state notification from it. The state notifications from different schedulers may vary, but usually they include *Submitted, Waiting_For_Resources, Resource_Allocation_Received, Resource_Allocation_Failed, Executing, Failed_Execution, Succeeded_Execution*, etc.
3. When state notifications come, filter the states. For states indicating the success/failure of job comes, forward this information to flow engine and returns, otherwise continue listening for the notification.

The job proxy provides a compact job-submission interface to the flow engine, so that for each job the flow engine does not need to use two separate activities to submit job and query job status respectively. The function of job proxy is not limit to fault handling, and it is actually a single entrance for job schedulers and can handle the complexity stemmed from the heterogeneity of different schedulers.

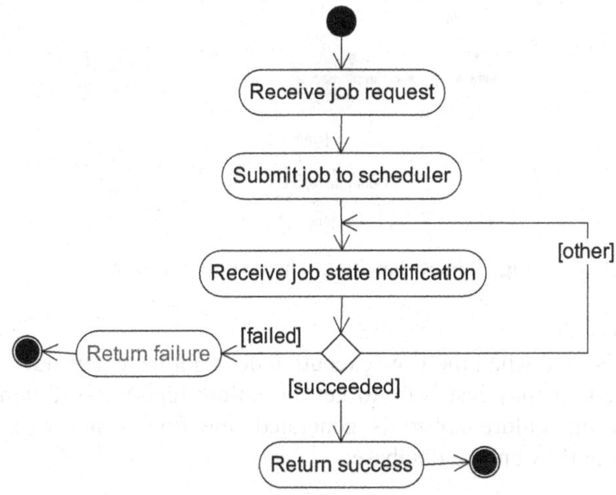

Fig. 4. Control flow of the generic job proxy

4.2 Fault-Handling Schemes in BPEL4Job

The fault-handling logical schemes of BPEL4Job are illustrated in Fig. 5, though the design is not limit to these policy schemes. When a job step is in state *Ready*, the flow engine submits it (*Submit Job*) and listens for the notification from the job proxy (*submitted*). If the job *succeeds*, flow engine *navigates to next job* and the flow proceeds. If the job *fails*, flow engine reacts according to the fault-handling policy for that job. If the policy is *cleanup*, the fault report is generated and flow instance is deleted in flow engine database. If the policy is *re-try*, the engine find the *re-try entry* (the re-try entry is the point to re-try a single job step, it can be at current failed job step, or at some previous step which has already completed) and submit the job to the scheduler. If the policy is *re-submit*, flow engine suspends the current flow instance, export the instance data to a permanent storage (for example, to a XML or other portable formats), and delete the instance data in current flow engine database. The exported flow instance can be re-submitted to the original engine when the source of the fault has been fixed, or be re-submitted to another flow engine to resume. After the flow instance is imported to the flow engine (either the original one or a new one), the flow instance is resumed at the *re-submit entry* (similar to the re-try entry, the re-submit entry is the point to re-start a job flow, it can be at the failed job step, or at some previous step which has already completed).

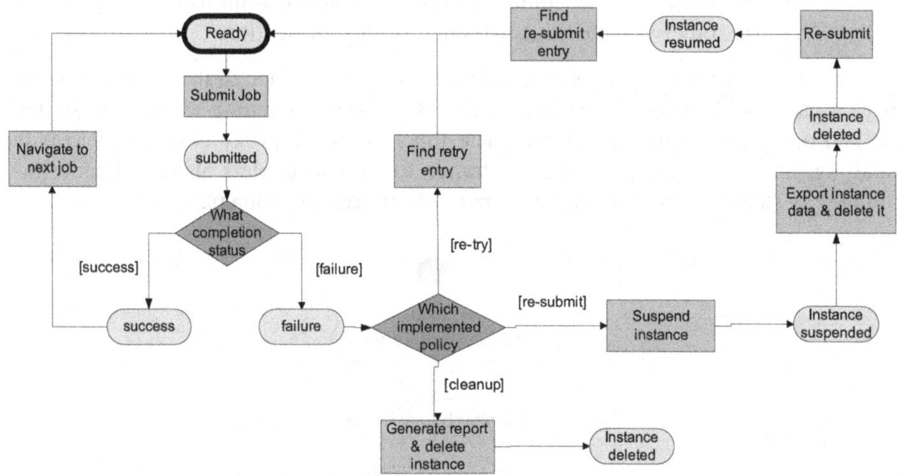

Fig. 5. Fault-handling scheme in BPEL4Job

4.2.1 Cleanup

Cleanup policy is used when the flow execution does not have any side effect resulted from failure, the user may just want to get the failure report and terminate the flow. Therefore, after the failure report is generated, the flow instance can be deleted (cleanup) from the flow engine database.

4.2.2 Task Level Re-try

We have shown the realization of a re-try policy as an example in section 3 where we explain how to integrate policy with job flow. The re-try policy is accomplished by adding a scope, a While loop and other additional constructs. Re-try policy can be extended to more advanced schemes, for example, to alter input parameters for the re-try job such as instructing the job proxy to use alternative schedulers or resources.

4.2.3 Flow Re-submission and Instance Migration

Now we investigate BPEL's capability to continue un-executed job steps without re-execution of successful job steps of a flow in the event of a fault. Many other job flow systems support restarting a flow regardless whether or not they persist job state during execution. Here are two of the exemplary systems:

1. DAGMan [3] is the flow manager of Condor [19] jobs. While executing, DAGMan keeps in memory a list of job steps of the flow, their parent-child relationships, and their current states. When a flow fails, it produces a Rescue DAG file for re-submission with a list of the job steps along their states and reasons of failures. The Rescue DAG can then be submitted later to continue execution.
2. Platform LSF [20] supports job dependency and flow restarting with the "requeue" feature. In LSF, job steps are executed sequentially unless they have a conditional statement on the success of failure or preceding steps. If "requeue" is specified for a job flow, for example "REQUEUE_EXIT_VALUES = 99 100", the flow will be requeued if the return code of a step matches the *requeue_exit* criteria and the requeued job flow will restart from this particular step.

BPEL4Job supports re-submit and facilitates instance migration if desire. The motivation to do job flow re-submission and instance migration is two-fold. The first reason is the performance issue. For long-running job flows, flow instance data is stored in the flow engine's database. This instance data include instance state information, the navigated activities, the value of messages/variables, etc. Depending on the flow definition and the run-time data used in the instance, a relatively large amount of data can be created with each instance. Unlike business processes, scientists may submit job flows in very large numbers and may not return to handle the flows immediately. A strategy for removing the failed flow instance out of the database is desirable to lessen the burden on the data storage or database.

The second reason is for job flow re-submission to a different engine. When a job flow instance *f* fails during the execution, the flow user or administrator may find that resource needed for *f* to proceed is unavailable in current resource domain. Thus, an alternative is to export and delete *f* in current flow engine, choose another resource domain in grid environments, re-submit *f* to the flow engine in that domain and resume it. (See Fig. 6 for an example.)

In order to realize flow re-submission, we introduce the concept of *instance migration*. Instance migration refers to the technique to export job flow instance data in one flow engine, and import it into anther one so that the flow instance can resume in it. When we do instance migration, the challenge is to collect sufficient data from the source flow engine, so that the target engine could re-build the status of the on-going job flow. The job flow instance database schemas vary with the different implementation, and in Fig. 7 we give a conceptual and high-level flow instance data model. Next section presents our implementation based on IBM Webshpere Process Server [21].

In Fig. 7, a process instance (or flow instance) has an attribute named *ProcessInstanceID*, and an attribute *ProcessTemplateID* to refer to the process template it belongs. A process instance can consist of multiple activity instances, task instances, correlation set instances, scope instances, partnerlink instances, variable instances, etc. Each of these instances has an attribute *ProcessInstanceID* to refer to the process instance it belongs.

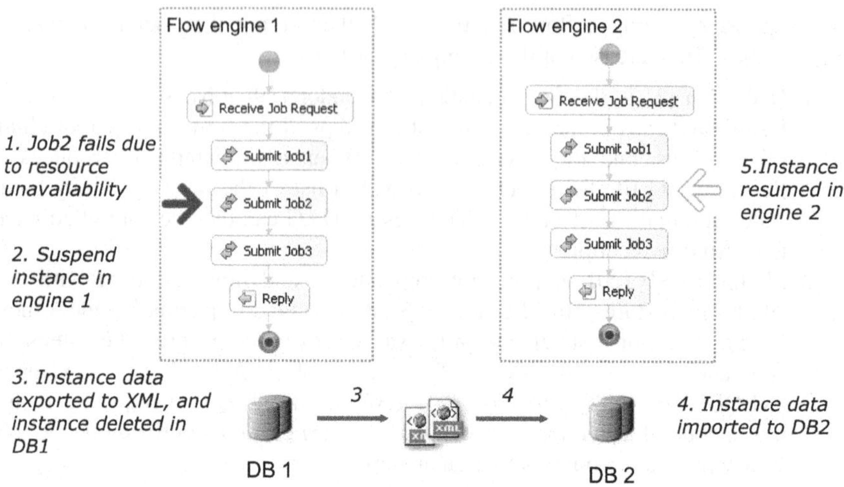

Fig. 6. An illustration of instance migration and flow re-submission

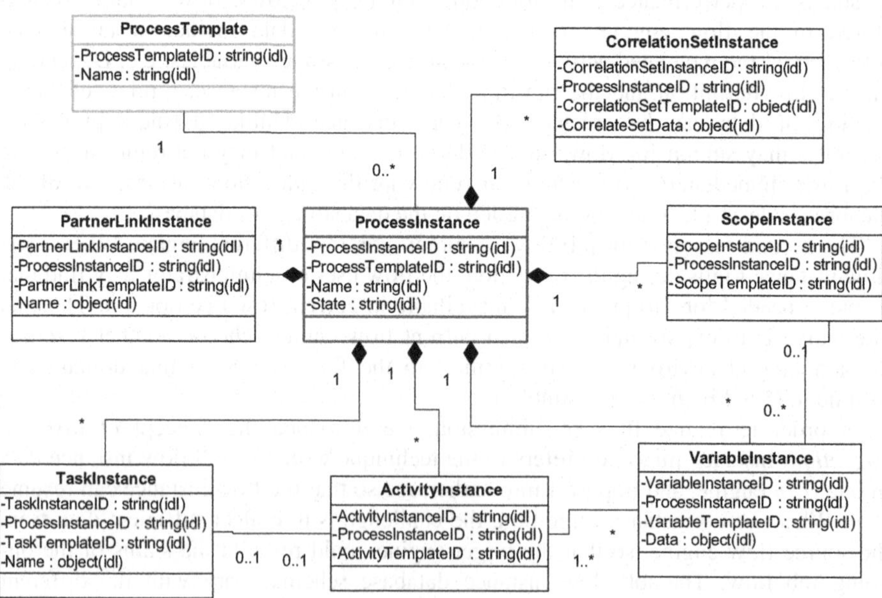

Fig. 7. Class diagram of flow instance data model

5 System Implementation and Case Study

A system is developed to validate the design of BPEL4Job. In our implementation, IBM Websphere Integration Developer (WID) [22] is used as BPEL modeling tool, IBM Websphere Process Server (WPS) [21] as BPEL engine, and IBM Tivoli Dynamic Workload Broker (ITDWB) [23] as job scheduler. In flow modeling layer, a

WID plug-in is developed to facilitate the use of JSDL for job step definition and the use of WS-Policy for policy definition. In flow execution layer, a generic job proxy is devised, and a fault-handling service is developed to implement the fault-handling schemes proposed in Section 4. For the job scheduling layer, we use ITDWB which provide job management web service API including job submission and job status notification.

We take an example from Montage astronomy mosaic generation application [14], named *m101 Mosaic*, to demonstrate the implementation of BPEL4Job. This example application takes several raw images (we use four images in our exemplary job flow), reprojects them and then combines them into a mosaic. We model the procedure of this application into a BPEL-based job flow (Fig. 8(a)). The first job, *mImgtbl*, generates an image metadata table describing the content of all the four raw images. Followed are four parallel jobs (*mProject1*, *mProject2*, *mProject3*, and *mProject4*), each of which reprojects one image. After all the images have been reprojected, a new metadata table is generated by job *mImgtbl1*, then job *mAdd1* generates a mosaic from the reprojected images, and finally job *mJPEG* transforms the mosaic into jpeg format.

Then we define fault-handling policies for job *mProject2* and *mAdd1*, respectively. The policy for job *mProject2* is to re-try after 10 seconds in case of failure; for job *mAdd1*, the policy is to re-submit the flow to another engine and re-start from its preceding job *mImgtbl1*. It is more logical to apply the re-submit policy on the flow scope such that re-submit will be triggered in any failed job step. But, we believe these two scenarios here are illustrative enough to demonstrate our different fault handling policies.

In Fig, 8, we show that the base flow plus the two policies are transformed into an expanded flow with JSDL and fault handling capability (Fig. 8 (b)). For space limit consideration, here we only give the JSDL definition of job *mAdd1* (Fig. 8(c)).

We will demonstrate the effects in migrating instance between two WPS servers, i.e., from server *saba10* to server *weitan*. The Montage job flow is instantiated at *saba10*, and when *mAdd1* fails, the flow instance is migrated to *weitan*. We use Business Process Choreographer (BPC) explorer [24] to monitor the orchestration of the Montage flow. The Montage flow is initiated with the name *Montage_saga10*. When job *mProject2* fails, the flow will automatically re-try it after 10 seconds (as discussed in Section 3). When job *mAdd1* fails, the fault-handling service suspends the flow instance at *saba10* (Fig. 9 (a)), and the flow instance data is exported into a XML file named *rescue.xml* (the size is about 560KB). When the user decides that *Montage_saga10* should be re-submit to server *weitan*, the fault-handling service imports *rescue.xml* to *weitan* (see Fig. 9 (b) for the BPC explorer at *weitan*, please be noted that the flow instance is restored from *saba10* to *weitan*). Then *Montage_saga10* will resume in *weitan* following the policy, that is, to restart from job *mImgtbl1* (Fig. 9 (c)). If we compare Fig. 9 (a) and (c), we could find jobs *mImgtbl1* and *mAdd1* are activated (submitted) at different time on two servers (for example, job *mImgtbl1* is activated on *saba10* at 5/8/07 4:26:28 PM and on *weitan* at 5/8/07 10:36:40 PM), this shows that when *Montage_saga10* is resumed at *weitan*, jobs *mAdd1* and *mImgtbl1* are executed for a second time (and the BPC explorer only show the latest execution time of them). That is to say, when *Montage_saga10* is resumed on *weitan*, the flow is re-started from the preceding job of *mAdd1*, i.e., *mImgtbl1*.

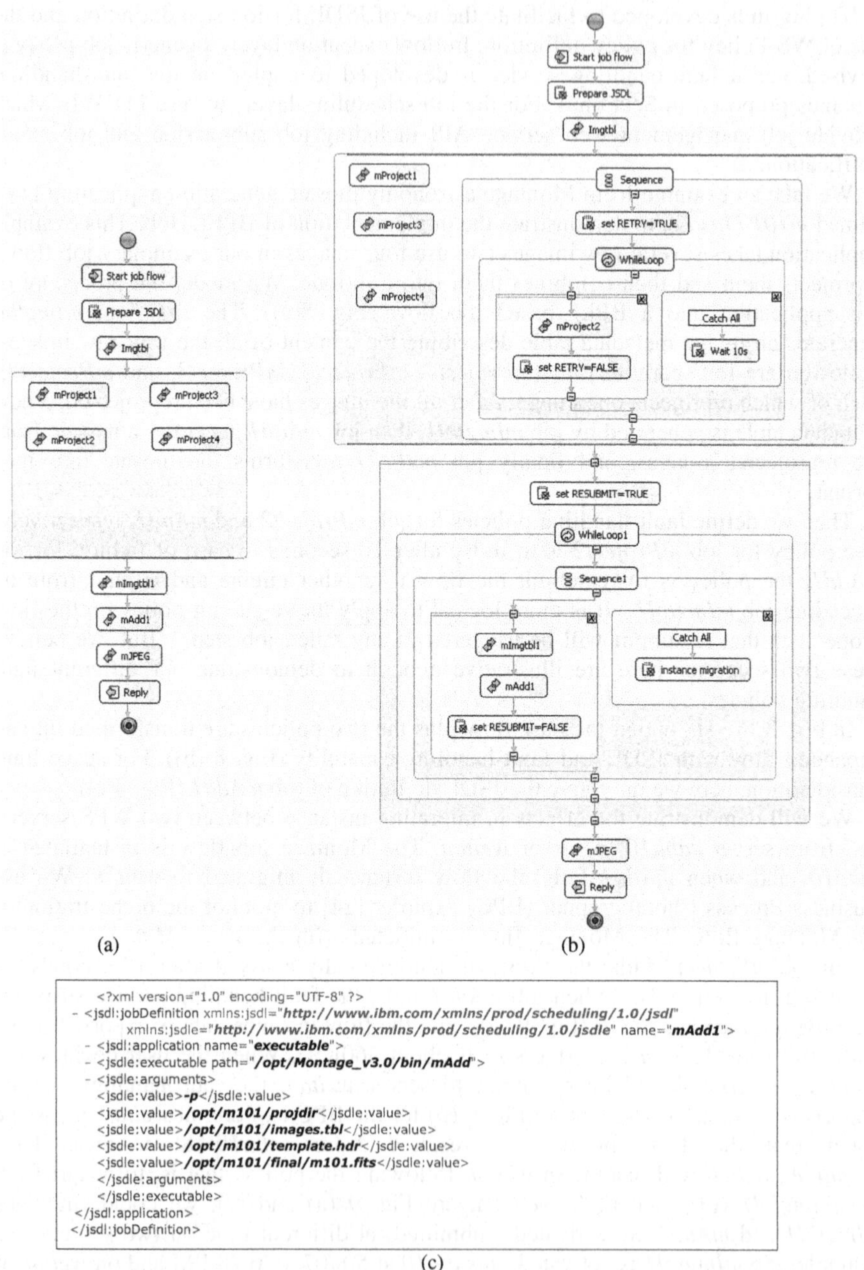

Fig. 8. Sample Montage application: (a) base flow (b) expanded flow (c) JSDL description of job *mAdd1*

Details | Process Input Message | Activities | Events | Related Processes | Tasks | Custom Properties

Activity Name	State	Kind	Owner	Activated
MAdd1	Failed	Invoke		5/8/07 4:26:44 PM
MImgtbl1	Finished	Invoke		5/8/07 4:26:28 PM
MProject2	Finished	Invoke		5/8/07 4:25:21 PM
MProject4	Finished	Invoke		5/8/07 4:25:18 PM
MProject3	Finished	Invoke		5/8/07 4:25:18 PM
MProject1	Finished	Invoke		5/8/07 4:25:18 PM
Imgtbl	Finished	Invoke		5/8/07 4:23:51 PM
Startjobflow	Finished	Receive		5/8/07 4:23:50 PM

(a) *Montage_saba10* initiated at *saba10*

Details | Process Input Message | Activities | Events | Related Processes | Tasks | Custom Properties

Activity Name	State	Kind	Owner	Activated
MAdd1	Failed	Invoke		5/8/07 4:26:44 PM
MImgtbl1	Finished	Invoke		5/8/07 4:26:28 PM
MProject2	Finished	Invoke		5/8/07 4:25:21 PM
MProject4	Finished	Invoke		5/8/07 4:25:18 PM
MProject3	Finished	Invoke		5/8/07 4:25:18 PM
MProject1	Finished	Invoke		5/8/07 4:25:18 PM
Imgtbl	Finished	Invoke		5/8/07 4:23:51 PM
Startjobflow	Finished	Receive		5/8/07 4:23:50 PM

(b) *Montage_saba10* re-submitted to *weitan*

Details | Process Input Message | Process Output Message | Activities | Events | Related Processes | Tasks | Custom

Activity Name	State	Kind	Owner	Activated
Reply	Finished	Reply		5/8/07 10:37:31 PM
MJPEG1	Finished	Invoke		5/8/07 10:37:16 PM
MAdd1	Finished	Invoke		5/8/07 10:37:01 PM
MImgtbl1	Finished	Invoke		5/8/07 10:36:40 PM
MProject2	Finished	Invoke		5/8/07 4:25:21 PM
MProject4	Finished	Invoke		5/8/07 4:25:18 PM
MProject3	Finished	Invoke		5/8/07 4:25:18 PM
MProject1	Finished	Invoke		5/8/07 4:25:18 PM
Imgtbl	Finished	Invoke		5/8/07 4:23:51 PM
Startjobflow	Finished	Receive		5/8/07 4:23:50 PM

(c) *Montage_saba10* re-started and completed at *weitan*

Fig. 9. The BPC explorer to illustrate flow instance migration between *saba10* and *weitan*

6 Related Works

Most works on using BPEL for job flow can be classified into two categories. The first approach [8] extends BPEL model elements, which make the flow model intuitive and simple. However, the workflow engine needs to be modified to deal with the model extension for jobs. The second approach [7, 25, 26] uses standard BPEL activity, so that the models are less intuitive and sometimes verbose to meet the needs of job flow. However, these models adhere to the standard BPEL and thus portable among BPEL-compliant flow engines. Our work falls into the second category of approach. However, the two-stage modeling approach gracefully hides the complexity to deal with jobs submission and fault-handling, while keep the advantage of using existing BPEL engine.

Sedna [10] is a BPEL-based environment for visual scientific workflow modeling. Domain specific abstraction layers are added in Sedna to increase the expressiveness of BPEL for scientific workflows. This method is similar to our two-stage approach. However, fault-handling issue is not addressed in that work.

TRAP/BPEL [18] is a framework that supports runtime selection of equivalent services for monitored services. An exemplary usage of this framework is for selection of recovery services when monitored services fail. By introducing a proxy as the generic fault handler, the logic in the proxy can dynamically select various recovery services according to some configurable recovery polices during runtime. Unlike the runtime dynamic support in TRAP/BPEL, the fault-handling services and policies for job flow are specified during modeling time in BPEL4Job. We require process and application flow modelers to provide directives on the scope (e.g. task or flow level) and types (e.g. re-try, re-submit) of fault recovery.

GridSam [27] provided a set of generic web services for job submission and monitoring. Our generic job proxy takes inspiration from this work. However, in our job proxy, job submission and job status query are combined into a single synchronous scheduling service invocation, with which the job failure/success status is returned. This approach provides a more compact job-submission interface to the flow engine, so that for each job submission the flow engine does not need to use two separate activities to submit job and query job status respectively.

DAGMan used in Condor is popular in many grid job management systems to manage job flow. The fault handling mechanism in DAGMan is re-try and rescue workflow (a kind of re-submit). Our idea of flow re-submission is similar to rescue DAG. Unlike DAGMan, our approach is policy-based and needs to consider the persistent states of job flows in BPEL-compliant engines.

7 Conclusion and Future Work

In this paper, we address two challenging issues in using WS-BPEL for job flow orchestration: the predominantly asynchronous interactions with job execution on dynamic resources, and the fault handling in job flow. We propose a design, called BPEL4Job, to illustrate our approach. BPEL4Job has three unique features: a two-stage approach for job flow modeling with integration with fault-handling policies, a generic job proxy to facilitate the asynchronous nature of job submission and job status notification, and a rich set of fault handling schemes including a novel method for instance migration between different flow engines in distributed system environment.

One direction of future work includes support for the definition and enforcement of more complicated fault-handling policies other than the proposed clean-up, re-try and re-submit. Our solution to instance migration can be extended to other related scenarios such as load balance between flow engines and versioning support for long-running processes. For the versioning support for long-running BPEL processes, if a template of a long-running BPEL process changes during the execution of many instances, the process instances that conform to the old template may need to be migrated to conform to the new one.

References

1. Leymann, F.: Choreography for the Grid: towards fitting BPEL to the resource framework. Concurrency and Computation-Practice & Experience 18(10), 1201–1217 (2006)
2. Jordan, D., et al.: Web Services Business Process Execution Language Version 2.0 (2007), Available from: http://docs.oasis-open.org/wsbpel/2.0/CS01/wsbpel-v2.0-CS01.pdf

3. Couvares, P., et al.: Workflow Management in Condor. In: Taylor, I.J., et al. (eds.) Workflows for e-Science, Springer, Heidelberg (2007)
4. Oinn, T., et al.: Taverna/myGrid: Aligning a Workflow System with the Life Sciences Community. In: Taylor, I.J., et al. (eds.) Workflows for e-Science, pp. 300–319. Springer, Heidelberg (2007)
5. Yu, J., Buyya, R.: A taxonomy of scientific workflow systems for grid computing. Journal of Grid Computing 34(3), 44–49 (2006)
6. Slominski, A.: Adapting BPEL to Scientific Workflows. In: Taylor, I.J., et al. (eds.) Workflows for e-Science, pp. 212–230. Springer, Heidelberg (2007)
7. Amnuaykanjanasin, P., Nupairoj, N.: The BPEL orchestrating framework for secured grid services. In: ITCC 2005. International Conference on Information Technology: Coding and Computing (2005)
8. Dörnemann, T., et al.: Grid Workflow Modelling Using Grid-Specific BPEL Extensions. In: German e-Science Conference 2007, Baden-Baden (2007)
9. Emmerich, W., et al.: Grid Service Orchestration using the Business Process Execution Language (BPEL). In: UCL-CS Research Note RN/05/07, University College London, UK (2005)
10. Wassermann, B., et al.: Sedna: A BPEL-Based Environment for Visual Scientific Workflow Modeling. In: Taylor, I.J., et al. (eds.) Workflows for e-Science, pp. 428–449. Springer, Heidelberg (2007)
11. Gucer, V., Lowry, M.A., Knudsen, F.B.: End-to-End Scheduling with IBM Tivoli Workload Scheduler Version 8.2., pp. 33–34. IBM Press (2004)
12. BMCSoftware: Meet Your Business Needs Successfully With CONTROL-M For z/OS. Available from: www.bmc.com/USA/Promotions/attachments/controlm_for_os390_and_zOS.pdf
13. Slomiski, A.: On using BPEL extensibility to implement OGSI and WSRF Grid workflows. Concurrency and Computation: Practice & Experience 18(10), 1229–1241 (2006)
14. Montage Tutorial: m101 Mosaic (2007), Available from: http://montage.ipac.caltech.edu/ docs/ m101tutorial.html
15. Anjomshoaa, A., et al.: Job Submission Description Language (JSDL) Specification v1.0. Proposed Recommendation from the JSDL Working Group (2005), Available from http://www.gridforum.org/documents/GFD.56.pdf
16. W3C: Web Services Policy 1.2 - Framework (WS-Policy) (2006), Available from http://www.w3.org/Submission/2006/SUBM-WS-Policy-20060425/
17. Soonwook, H., Kesselman, C.: Grid workflow: a flexible failure handling framework for the grid. In: HPDC'03. 12th IEEE International Symposium on High Performance Distributed Computing, Seattle, WA USA (2003)
18. Ezenwoye, O., Sadjadi, S.M.: TRAP/BPEL: A Framework for Dynamic Adaptation of Composite Services. In: WEBIST-2007. International Conference on Web Information Systems and Technologies, Barcelona, Spain (2007)
19. Condor. Available from: http://www.cs.wisc.edu/condor/
20. Platform LSF. Available from: http://www-cecpv.u-strasbg.fr/Documentations/lsf/html/ lsf6.1_admin/E_jobrequeue.html
21. IBM Websphere Process Server. Available from: http://www-306.ibm.com/software/ integration/wps/
22. IBM Websphere Integration Developer. Available from: http://www-306.ibm.com/ software/ integration/ wid/

23. IBM Tivoli Dynamic Workload Broker. Available from: http://www-306.ibm.com/software/tivoli/products/dynamic-workload-broker/index.html
24. Starting to use the Business Process Choreographer Explorer (2007), Available from: http://publib.boulder.ibm.com/infocenter/dmndhelp/v6rxmx/index.jsp?topic=/com.ibm.wsps.ins.doc/doc/bpc/t7stwcl.html
25. Kuo-Ming, C., et al.: Analysis of grid service composition with BPEL4WS. In: 18th International Conference on Advanced Information Networking and Applications (2004)
26. Tan, K.L.L., Turner, K.J.: Orchestrating Grid Services using BPEL and Globus Toolkit 4. In: 7th PGNet Symposium (2006)
27. GridSAM - Grid Job Submission and Monitoring Web Service (2007), Available from: http://gridsam.sourceforge.net/2.0.1/index.html

Faster and More Focused Control-Flow Analysis for Business Process Models Through SESE Decomposition

Jussi Vanhatalo[1,2], Hagen Völzer[1], and Frank Leymann[2]

[1] IBM Zurich Research Laboratory, Säumerstrasse 4, CH-8803 Rüschlikon, Switzerland
{juv,hvo}@zurich.ibm.com
[2] Institute of Architecture of Application Systems, University of Stuttgart
Universitätsstrasse 38, D-70569 Stuttgart, Germany
frank.leymann@iaas.uni-stuttgart.de

Abstract. We present a technique to enhance control-flow analysis of business process models. The technique considerably speeds up the analysis and improves the diagnostic information that is given to the user to fix control-flow errors. The technique consists of two parts: Firstly, the process model is decomposed into single-entry-single-exit (SESE) fragments, which are usually substantially smaller than the original process. This decomposition is done in linear time. Secondly, each fragment is analyzed in isolation using a fast heuristic that can analyze many of the fragments occurring in practice. Any remaining fragments that are not covered by the heuristic can then be analyzed using any known complete analysis technique.

We used our technique in a case study with more than 340 real business processes modeled with the IBM WebSphere Business Modeler. The results suggest that control-flow analysis of many real process models is feasible without significant delay (less than a second). Therefore, control-flow analysis could be used frequently during editing time, which allows errors to be caught at earliest possible time.

1 Introduction

The quality of a business process model becomes crucial when it is executed directly on a workflow engine or when it is used for generating code that is to be executed. A correct model is also important when one tries to obtain realistic business measures from a process model through simulation. Detecting and fixing errors as early as possible can therefore substantially reduce costs.

The control flow of a business process can be modeled as a *workflow graph* [11,14]. A workflow graph that has no structural errors such as *deadlocks* or *lack of synchronization* [11] is said to be *sound* [14]. Soundness can and should be checked automatically during the modeling phase. To achieve a high acceptance among the users, the soundness check should

- be as fast as possible and not delay the process of constructing the model — note that a fast soundness check that can be done after each small change of the model allows the user to identify the change that introduced an error — and
- produce useful diagnostic information that helps to locate and fix errors.

B. Krämer, K.-J. Lin, and P. Narasimhan (Eds.): ICSOC 2007, LNCS 4749, pp. 43–55, 2007.

When reviewing the techniques currently available for deciding soundness, there seems to be a trade-off between the two requirements. The fastest technique known (cf. [14,6]) translates the workflow graph into a *free choice Petri net* (cf. [2]) and then decides soundness of that Petri net using the *rank theorem* (cf. [2]). This technique uses time that is cubic in the size of the workflow graph, but does not provide useful diagnostic information. The best diagnostic information is currently provided by a search of the state space of the workflow graph. This can return an execution sequence that leads to the error but it can use time that is exponential in the size of the workflow graph. Esparza [3] (cf. also [2]) provides a technique that can be used to decide soundness in polynomial time (more than cubic) which could potentially provide some diagnostic information, but the latter has not yet been worked out. The analysis tool Woflan [17] can decide soundness and provide diagnostic information, but because the tool ultimately resorts to state space search, it can also take exponential time.

Some authors provide algorithms for deciding soundness for the special case of acyclic workflow graphs. Perumal and Mahanti [10] gave an algorithm that takes quadratic time, which improves on previous approaches for that special case, which were either slower [7] or incomplete [11].

Given any complete technique for deciding soundness from above, we propose two enhancements in this paper. Firstly, we propose to decompose the workflow graph into a tree of *single-entry-single-exit (SESE) fragments*. This technique is known from compiler theory and can be done in linear time [5]. To check soundness of the workflow graph, one can now check soundness of each fragment in isolation. The overall time used now depends mainly on the size of the largest fragment. We show by experimental evidence on a large number of industrial workflow models that the largest fragment of a workflow graph is usually considerably smaller than the workflow graph itself.

Zerguini [18] and Hauser et al. [4] have proposed similar techniques of deciding soundness through decomposition into fragments. However, they decompose into multiple-entry-multiple-exit (MEME) fragments. These fragments are more general, and include SESE fragments as a special case. This however implies that a fragment can be less intuitive in general. Moreover, their decomposition into fragments is no longer unique and their decomposition algorithms are slower; while Zerguini's algorithm [18] uses quadratic time, the time complexity of the approach of Hauser et al. [4] is unknown, but we conjecture it to be at least quadratic. Both techniques could be used after our fast SESE decomposition.

A nice feature of the decomposition (SESE or MEME) approach is that each error is contained in a fragment. Thus, the error can be shown in a small local context, which in turn should help fixing the error. Errors that are located in disjoint fragments are likely to be independent. Hence, the decomposition also allows multiple independent errors to be detected in one pass.

The second enhancement we propose are two heuristics that can prove soundness or unsoundness of some fragments in linear time. The heuristics are meant to be used before any of the complete techniques from the literature are used, because the latter are likely to be more expensive. The heuristics are based on the observation that many of the fragments found in real process models have a simple structure that can be recognized quickly. The first heuristic uses ideas from Hauser et al. [4].

Note that simple *reduction rules* (e.g. [2,11,15]) can also be used to speed up the verification. Usually applied with low cost, they reduce the process model while preserving soundness.

We have implemented our technique and tried it on two libraries of altogether more than 340 industrial process models. 81% of the process models can be completely analyzed with the SESE decomposition and the heuristics alone. For the remaining cases, the analysis task becomes considerably smaller through SESE decomposition.

Mendling et al. [9,8] have analyzed more than 2000 EPC process models using the Woflan tool [17] for a relaxed version of soundness. We are not aware of any other published case study with large industrial data.

This paper is structured as follows. In Sect. 2, we recall the definition of workflow graphs and their soundness. Section 3 describes our approach in detail. Section 4 presents the results of the case study. Missing proofs can be found in a technical report [16].

2 Sound Workflow Graphs

In this section, we recall the definition of sound workflow graphs [11,14]. We also give an equivalent characterization of soundness, which will be used later in this paper.

2.1 Workflow Graphs

A *workflow graph* is a directed graph $G = (N, E)$, where a node $n \in N$ is exactly one of the following: a *start node*, a *stop node*, an *activity*, a *fork*, a *join*, a *decision*, or a *merge* such that

1. there is exactly one start node and exactly one stop node; the start node has no incoming edges and exactly one outgoing edge, whereas the stop node has exactly one incoming edge but no outgoing edges;
2. each fork and each decision has exactly one incoming edge and two or more outgoing edges, whereas each join and each merge has exactly one outgoing edge and two or more incoming edges; each activity has exactly one incoming and exactly one outgoing edge;
3. each node $n \in N$ is on a path from the start node to the stop node.

It follows from the definition that no node is directly connected to itself. Figure 1 shows an example of a workflow graph. An activity is depicted as a square, a fork and a join as a thin rectangle, a decision as a diamond, and a merge as a triangle. Start and stop nodes are depicted as (decorated) circles. The unique outgoing edge of the start node is called the *entry edge*, and the unique incoming edge of the stop node is called the *exit edge* of the workflow graph.

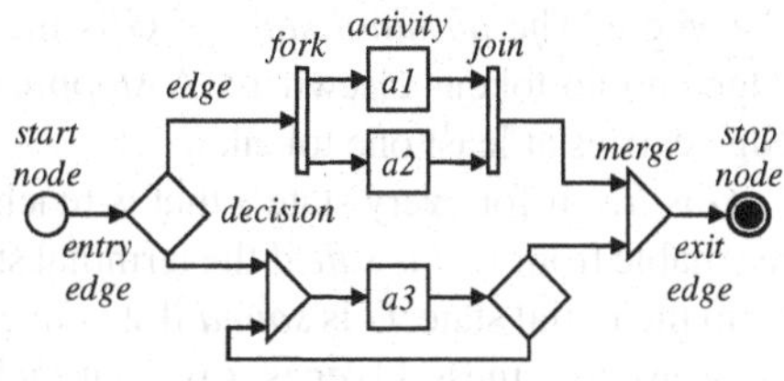

Fig. 1. A workflow graph

The semantics of a workflow graph is, similarly to Petri nets, defined as a token game. A state of a workflow graph is represented by tokens on the edges of the graph. Let $G = (N, E)$ be a workflow graph. A *state* of G is a mapping $s : E \to \mathbb{N}$, which assigns a natural number to each edge. When $s(e) = k$, we say that edge e carries k *tokens* in state s. The semantics of the various nodes is defined as usual. An activity, a fork, and a join remove one token from each of its ingoing edges and add one token to each of its outgoing edges. A decision node removes a token from its incoming edge, nondeterministically chooses one of its outgoing edges, and adds one token to that outgoing edge. A merge node nondeterministically chooses one of its incoming edges on which there is at least one token, removes one token from that edge, and adds a token to its outgoing edge.

To be more precise, let s and s' be two states and n a node that is neither a start nor a stop node. We write $s \xrightarrow{n} s'$ when s changes to s' by executing n. We have $s \xrightarrow{n} s'$ if

1. n is an activity, fork or join and
$$s'(e) = \begin{cases} s(e) - 1 & e \text{ is an incoming edge of } n, \\ s(e) + 1 & e \text{ is an outgoing edge of } n, \\ s(e) & \text{otherwise.} \end{cases}$$
2. n is a decision and there exists an outgoing edge e' of n such that
$$s'(e) = \begin{cases} s(e) - 1 & e \text{ is an incoming edge of } n, \\ s(e) + 1 & e = e', \\ s(e) & \text{otherwise.} \end{cases}$$
3. n is a merge and there exists an incoming edge e' of n such that
$$s'(e) = \begin{cases} s(e) - 1 & e = e', \\ s(e) + 1 & e \text{ is an outgoing edge of } n, \\ s(e) & \text{otherwise.} \end{cases}$$

Node n is said to be *activated* in a state s if there exists a state s' such that $s \xrightarrow{n} s'$. A state s' is *reachable from* a state s, denoted $s \xrightarrow{*} s'$, if there exists a (possibly empty) finite sequence $s_0 \xrightarrow{n_1} s_1 \ldots s_{k-1} \xrightarrow{n_k} s_k$ such that $s_0 = s$ and $s_k = s'$.

2.2 Soundness

To define *soundness* [14] of a workflow graph G, we use the following notions. The *initial state* of G is the state that has exactly one token on the entry edge and no tokens elsewhere. The *terminal state* of G is the state that has exactly one token on the exit edge and no tokens elsewhere. A *stopping state* of G is a state of G in which the exit edge carries at least one token.

G is *live* if for every state s that is reachable from the initial state, a stopping state is reachable from s. G is *safe* if the terminal state is the only stopping state that is reachable from the initial state. G is *sound* if it is live and safe. The soundness criterion is a global view on correctness. Liveness says that each run can be completed, and safeness says that each completion of a run is a proper termination, i.e., there are no tokens inside the graph upon completion. The workflow graph in Fig. 1 is sound. Figure 2 shows simple examples of unsound graphs. The graph in part (a) is not live, the graph in part (b) is not safe.

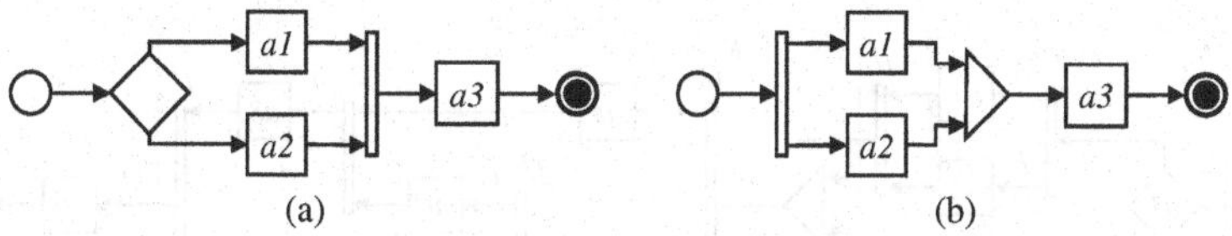

Fig. 2. Structural conflicts: (a) a local deadlock (b) a lack of synchronization

The two examples of unsound workflow graphs in Fig. 2 are examples of a *structural conflict*, viz. a *local deadlock* (part a) and a *lack of synchronization* (part b) [11]. A *local deadlock* is a state s such that there exists a join n where (i) at least one incoming edge of n carries a token in s and (ii) there is an incoming edge e of n such that e does not carry a token in any state s' that is reachable from s. That is, that join will never get 'enough' tokens. A state s of G has *lack of synchronization* if there is a merge n such that more than one incoming edge of n carries a token, i.e., that merge gets 'too many' tokens. Note that a lack of synchronization can lead to a state where there is more than one token on a single edge. Van der Aalst et al. [14] have shown that for acyclic workflow graphs, soundness is equivalent with the condition that neither a local deadlock nor a state with lack of synchronization is reachable from the initial state. We generalize this here for arbitrary workflow graphs, therefore providing a local view of correctness for arbitrary workflow graphs.

Definition 1. *Let G be a workflow graph. G is* locally live *if there is no local deadlock that is reachable from the initial state. G is* locally safe *if no state is reachable from the initial state that has more than one token on a single edge.*

Theorem 1. *A workflow graph is sound if and only if it is locally safe and locally live.*

3 Enhanced Control-Flow Analysis

In this section, we explain the decomposition of a workflow graph into SESE fragments and show how some fragments can be quickly recognized as sound or unsound.

3.1 Decomposition into Fragments

Figure 3 shows a workflow graph and its decomposition into *SESE fragments* (cf. e.g. [5]). A SESE fragment is depicted as a dotted box. Let $G = (N, E)$ be a workflow graph. A *SESE fragment* (*fragment* for short) $F = (N', E')$ is a nonempty *subgraph* of G, i.e., $N' \subseteq N$ and $E' = E \cap (N' \times N')$ such that there exist edges $e, e' \in E$ with $E \cap ((N \setminus N') \times N') = \{e\}$ and $E \cap (N' \times (N \setminus N')) = \{e'\}$; e and e' are called the *entry* and the *exit* edge of F, respectively.

The workflow graph shown in Fig. 3 has more fragments than those that are shown explicitly. For example, the union of fragments J and K, denoted $J \cup K$, as well as $K \cup L$ are fragments. Those however are not of interest here and they are subsumed in fragment X. Interesting fragments will be called *canonical*, which are defined in the following. We say that two fragments F and F' are *in sequence* if the exit edge of F is

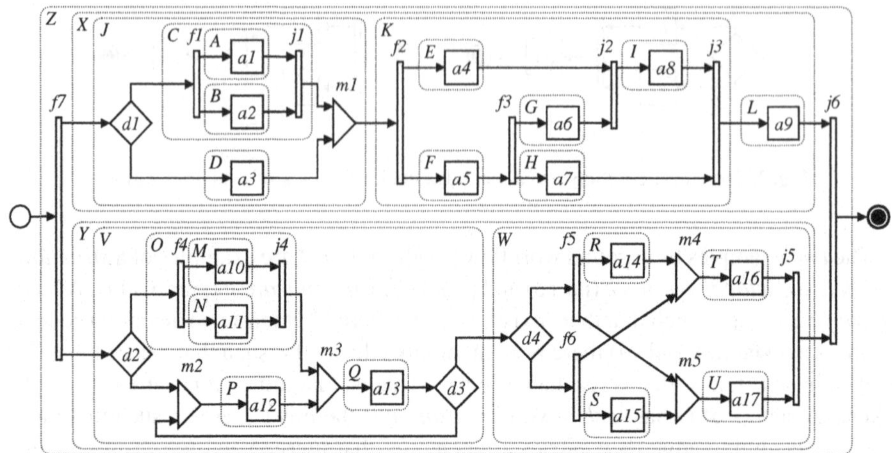

Fig. 3. Decomposition of a workflow graph into canonical fragments

the entry edge of F' or vice versa. The union $F \cup F'$ of two fragments F and F' that are in sequence is a fragment again. A fragment F is *non-canonical* if there are fragments X, Y, Z such that X and Y are in sequence, $F = X \cup Y$, and F and Z are in sequence; otherwise F is said to be *canonical*.

The fragments shown in Fig. 3 are exactly the canonical fragments of that workflow graph. Canonical fragments do not overlap. Two canonical fragments are either nested or disjoint [5]. Therefore, it is possible to organize the canonical fragments in a unique tree, similarly to the Program Structure Tree shown in [5]. We call this tree the *process structure tree* of a workflow graph. It can be computed in time linear in the size of the workflow graph [5][1]. As we are only interested in canonical fragments, we mean 'canonical fragment' whenever we say 'fragment' in the following.

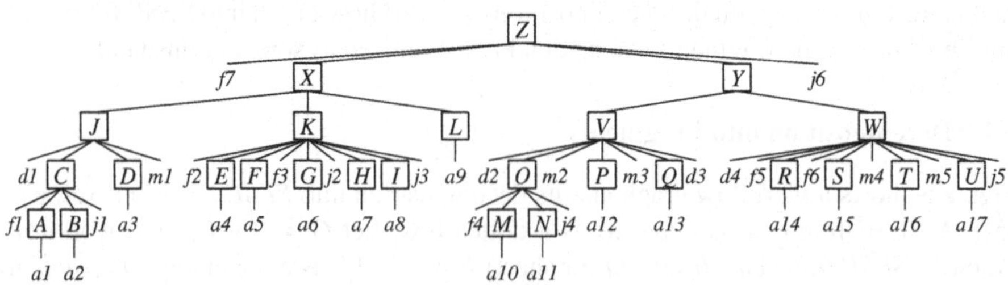

Fig. 4. The process structure tree of the workflow graph in Fig. 3

Figure 4 shows the process structure tree of the workflow graph from Fig. 3. A fragment is represented as a boxed tree node. In addition, we represent the nodes of the workflow graph as leaves in the tree. The *parent* of a fragment F (a workflow graph

[1] Note: Ananian [1] gives a slightly modified linear time algorithm that includes corrections.

node n) is the smallest fragment F' that contains F (n). Then, we also say that F is a *child fragment* of F' (n is a *child node* of F').

To check the soundness of a workflow graph, it is sufficient to analyze the soundness of its fragments in isolation. Note that a fragment can be viewed as a workflow graph by adding entry and exit edges as well as a start and a stop node. Hence we can apply the notion of soundness also to fragments. The following theorem follows from classical Petri net theory (e.g. [12], cf. also [13,14,18]).

Theorem 2. *A workflow graph is sound if and only if all its child fragments are sound and the workflow graph that is obtained by replacing each child fragment with an activity is sound.*

Checking soundness of fragments can therefore be done along the structure of the process structure tree, starting from the leaves upwards. If a fragment F was checked for soundness, checking soundness of the parent fragment (in the tree) can abstract from the internal structure of F, i.e., F can be treated as an activity in the parent fragment. Figure 5 shows fragments J and V from Figs. 3 and 4, where fragment J abstracts from the structure of the child fragments C and D and fragment V abstracts from the structure of fragment O.

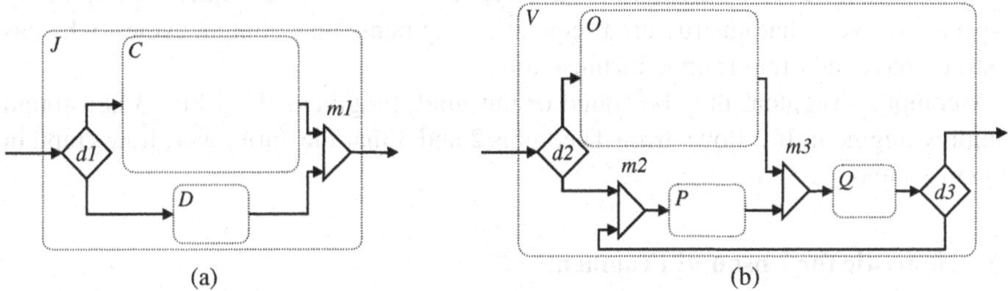

Fig. 5. Fragments J and V ignoring the structure of their child fragments

3.2 Heuristic for Sound Fragments

Many fragments that occur in practice have a simple structure that can easily be recognized, which identifies those fragments as being sound. To this end, we define the following categories, based on definitions given by Hauser et al. [4].

Definition 2. *Let F be a fragment of a workflow graph. F is*

1. well-structured *if it satisfies one of the following conditions:*
   - *F has no decisions, merges, forks or joins as children in the process structure tree (*sequence*),*
   - *F has exactly one decision and exactly one merge, but no forks and no joins as children. The entry edge of F is the incoming edge of the decision, and the exit edge of F is the outgoing edge of the merge (*sequential branching*),*
   - *F has exactly one decision and exactly one merge, but no forks and no joins as children. The entry edge of F is an incoming edge of the merge, and the exit edge of F is an outgoing edge of the decision (*cycle*),*

- *F has exactly one fork, exactly one join, no decisions and no merges as children. The entry edge is the incoming edge of the fork. The exit edge is the outgoing edge of the join. (*concurrent branching*).*

2. *an* unstructured concurrent *fragment if F is not well-structured, contains no cycles, and has no decisions and no merges as children.*
3. *an* unstructured sequential *fragment if F is not well-structured and has no forks and no joins as children.*
4. *a* complex *fragment if it is none of the above.*

It is easy to see that it can be decided in linear time to which of the four categories listed above a fragment belongs.

Theorem 3. *If a fragment F is well-structured, an unstructured concurrent, or an unstructured sequential fragment, then F is sound if and only if all its child fragments are sound.*

This theorem was already observed by Hauser et al. [4]. Note that all fragment categories ignore the structure of child fragments, taking only the top-level structure into account. In Fig. 3, fragments *X* and *Y* are well-structured (sequence) and so are also fragments *C*, *O*, *Z* (concurrent branching) and *J* (sequential branching). Fragments *K* and *V* are examples of unstructured concurrent and unstructured sequential fragments, respectively. Note that unstructured sequential fragments may contain cycles, whereas unstructured concurrent fragments must not.

A complex fragment may be sound or unsound. Fragment *W* in Fig. 3 is a sound complex fragment. It follows from Theorems 2 and 3 that the entire workflow graph in Fig. 3 is sound.

3.3 Heuristic for Unsound Fragments

Some complex fragments can be efficiently determined as not being sound:

Theorem 4. *A complex fragment F is not sound if it satisfies one of the following conditions:*

1. *F has one or more decisions (merges), but no merges (decisions) as children in the process structure tree,*
2. *F has one or more forks (joins), but no joins (forks) as children,*
3. *F contains a cycle, but has no decisions or no merges as children.*

It is again easy to see that this heuristic can be applied in linear time. We actually found numerous errors in real process models using this heuristic (see Sect. 4.2). The relative strength of this heuristic is due to the fact that, similar to the heuristic in Sect. 3.2, the structure of child fragments is ignored.

4 Case Study

In this section, we describe the results of an application of our proposed technique in a case study with industrial data.

4.1 The Data

We have analyzed the soundness of more than 340 workflow graphs that were extracted from two libraries of industrial business processes modeled in the IBM WebSphere Business Modeler. Although the modeling language used there is more expressive than workflow graphs, it was possible to translate the process models into workflow graphs because strict guidelines were used for the construction of these process models. The description of the translation is beyond the scope of this paper.

Library 1 consists of more than 140 processes. The extracted workflow graphs have, on average, 67 edges, with the maximum being 215. Library 2 is an experimental extension of Library 1. It contains similar processes, but many features were added to the processes and also some processes were added. It contains more than 200 processes, the extracted workflow graphs have 99 edges on average, with the maximum being 342.

4.2 The Results

We analyzed the libraries using an IBM ThinkPad T43p laptop that has a 2.13 GHz Intel Pentium M processor and 2 GB of main memory. The entire Library 1 is analyzed in 9 seconds, and Library 2 in 15 seconds. Thus, the average analysis time per workflow graph is less than 0.1 seconds.

SESE Decomposition. As described in Sect. 1, the worst-case time a complete technique needs for checking the soundness of a workflow graph can be polynomial or exponential in the size g of the workflow graph, which is defined to be its number of edges. Similarly, the size of a fragment is defined as its number of edges plus 2 (for the entry edge and the exit edge). If we use a complete technique after the SESE decomposition according to the procedure in Sect. 3.1, the time used is linear in the number of fragments. Note also that the number of fragments in a workflow graph is at most twice the number of nodes. The overall time used therefore mainly depends on the size $f_{\max}$ of the largest fragment to which we have to apply the complete technique. If the complete technique uses polynomial time g^c for some constant c, then the reduction that SESE decomposition could achieve is $g^c/f_{\max}^c = (g/f_{\max})^c$. If the complete technique uses exponential time c^g, then the possible reduction is $c^g/c^{f_{\max}} = c^{g-f_{\max}}$. Table 1 shows the values for $g/f_{\max}$ and $g - f_{\max}$ for Library 1 as an indication of the reduction achieved due to SESE decomposition.

Figure 6 shows the largest fragment size in relation to the graph size for each workflow graph in Library 1. It shows that the graph size has only a minor impact on the

Table 1. Graph size (i.e., number of edges) compared to the size of the largest fragment in the graph and size reductions for the workflow graphs in Library 1

	Graph size g	Largest fragment size $f_{\max}$	Reduction $g - f_{\max}$	Reduction $g/f_{\max}$
Maximum	215	51	191	9.0
Average	67	24	44	2.8
Minimum	11	11	0	1.0

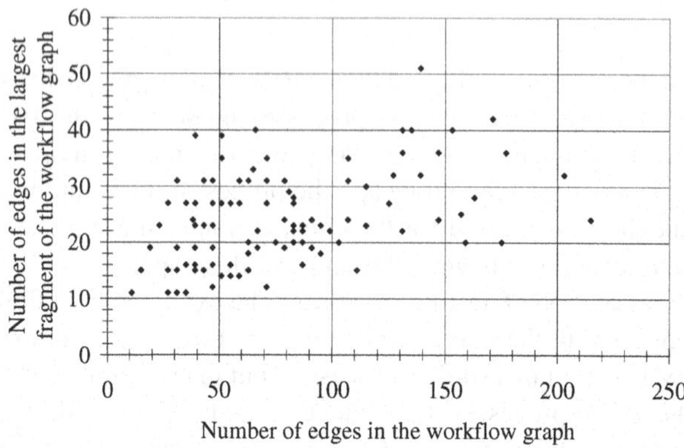

Fig. 6. Size of largest fragment in relation to graph size for all workflow graphs in Library 1

largest fragment size. Therefore, the reduction increases as the graph size increases. Thus, the technique is most useful when the complete techniques would be most time consuming. Even a small reduction can be significant, as the complete techniques for checking soundness can take a time that is cubic or exponential in the graph size.

Table 2 shows the reduction statistics for the workflow graphs in Library 2. The graphs are larger, and also the reduction is higher.

Table 2. Graph size compared to the size of the largest fragment in the graph, and size reductions for Library 2

	Graph size g	Largest fragment size $f_{\max}$	Reduction $g - f_{\max}$	Reduction $g/f_{\max}$
Maximum	342	82	328	24.4
Average	99	21	78	5.6
Minimum	12	6	5	1.5

Using both heuristics from Sect. 3, we can decide soundness for 68.5% of the workflow graphs in Library 2. For the remaining graphs, our prototype tool highlights the complex fragments that may be unsound. A complete analysis method is needed to decide their soundness, or they can be reviewed manually. The reduction statistics for these remaining workflow graphs are shown in Table 3.

Fragment Categories. Even though our heuristics from Sect. 3 are incomplete, we were able to decide soundness for all the workflow graphs from Library 1. They are all sound.

The first column in Table 4 illustrates the distribution of fragments according to the categories defined in Sects. 3.2-3.3 for Library 1. We excluded here any fragments that are well-structured sequences from these statistics, because most fragments are sequences and those are trivially sound and thus not interesting.

Table 3. Library 2: Graph size, largest fragment size, and reduction for the remaining 31.5% of workflow graphs for which soundness is unknown after applying our heuristics

	Graph size g	Largest fragment size $f_{\max}$	Reduction $g - f_{\max}$	Reduction $g/f_{\max}$
Maximum	334	82	284	10.4
Average	126	32	94	4.3
Minimum	40	12	25	1.6

We can also put entire workflow graphs into the various categories. For example, a workflow graph is *complex* if it has at least one complex fragment. Complex graphs are further divided into those known to be not sound by applying the heuristic in Sect. 3.3 and those for which soundness is unknown. A workflow graph is *unstructured* if it has at least one unstructured fragment and no complex fragments. Otherwise, a graph has only *well-structured* fragments and it is therefore called *well-structured.* Column 3 of Table 4 shows the distribution of workflow graphs in Library 1 in the various categories. The last two columns present the same statistics for Library 2.

Most fragments are well-structured, which makes it attractive to analyze fragments separately. However, only a third of the workflow graphs are well-structured and there is a considerable number of sound unstructured workflow graphs. Therefore, although well-structuredness is also an appealing correctness requirement, it seems to be overly restrictive. As unstructured fragments occur often, it makes sense to detect those with fast heuristics before using a complete analysis technique. Our heuristics can decide soundness not only for many fragments, but also for a significant proportion of the workflow graphs.

In Library 2, 43.5% of the workflow graphs contain at least one complex fragment. Only one workflow graph has more than one complex fragment. 19.7% of the fragments in Library 2 are complex fragments. Our heuristic recognized 27.3% of these fragments as being unsound. We have not yet checked the soundness of the remaining complex graphs by integrating our tool with a complete analysis method. The high error rate in Library 2 is due to its experimental nature.

Table 4. Categories of fragments and workflow graphs in the libraries

Fragment category / Workflow graph category	Library 1 Percentage of fragments	Percentage of graphs	Library 2 Percentage of fragments	Percentage of graphs
Well-structured (sound)	54.8%	37.5%	65.4%	33.3%
Unstructured (sound)	45.2%	62.5%	14.9%	23.1%
- Unstructured concurrent	1.4%	-	6.0%	-
- Unstructured sequential (acyclic)	29.2%	-	4.4%	-
- Unstructured sequential (cyclic)	14.6%	-	4.6%	-
Complex	0.0%	0.0%	19.7%	43.5%
- Complex (not sound)	0.0%	0.0%	5.4%	12.0%
- Complex (soundness unknown)	0.0%	0.0%	14.3%	31.5%

5 Conclusion

We proposed a technique to focus and speed up control-flow analysis of business process models that is based on decomposition into SESE fragments. The SESE decomposition could also be used for other purposes such as browsing and constructing large processes, discovery of reusable subprocesses, code generation, and others.

We also proposed a partition of the fragments into various categories, which can be computed fast. We think that tagging a fragment with its category may help to better understand the process model and may help to establish modeling patterns. It also helps to speed up the control-flow analysis as many of the correct fragments that occur in practice have a simple structure.

We plan to integrate our prototype with existing complete verification techniques and measure the impact of SESE decomposition on the analysis time. In addition, we plan to investigate the errors that occur in Library 2, together with approaches to fix them.

Acknowledgments. We thank Michael Friess for suggesting to apply SESE decomposition to workflow graphs. We thank Wil van der Aalst, Rainer Hauser, Rania Khalaf, Jana Koehler, Oliver Kopp, Jochen Küster and Ksenia Ryndina for helpful discussions and comments.

The work published in this article was partially supported by the SUPER project (http://www.ip-super.org/) under the EU 6th Framework Programme Information Society Technologies Objective (contract no. FP6-026850).

References

1. Scott Ananian, C.: The static single information form. Master's thesis, Massachusetts Institute of Technology (September 1999)
2. Desel, J., Esparza, J.: Free Choice Petri Nets. Cambridge University Press, Cambridge (1995)
3. Esparza, J.: Reduction and synthesis of live and bounded free choice Petri nets. Inf. Comput. 114(1), 50–87 (1994)
4. Hauser, R., Friess, M., Küster, J.M., Vanhatalo, J.: An incremental approach to the analysis and transformation of workflows using region trees. IEEE Transactions on Systems, Man, and Cybernetics - Part C (June 2007) (to appear, also available as IBM Research Report RZ 3693)
5. Johnson, R., Pearson, D., Pingali, K.: The program structure tree: Computing control regions in linear time. In: PLDI. Proceedings of the ACM SIGPLAN'94 Conference on Programming Language Design and Implementation, pp. 171–185. ACM Press, New York (1994)
6. Kemper, P.: Linear time algorithm to find a minimal deadlock in a strongly connected free-choice net. In: Ajmone Marsan, M. (ed.) Application and Theory of Petri Nets 1993. LNCS, vol. 691, pp. 319–338. Springer, Heidelberg (1993)
7. Lin, H., Zhao, Z., Li, H., Chen, Z.: A novel graph reduction algorithm to identify structural conflicts. In: HICSS-35 2002. Proceedings of the 35th Hawaii International Conference on System Sciences, p. 289 (2002)
8. Mendling, J.: Detection and Prediction of Errors in EPC Business Process Models. PhD thesis, Vienna University of Economics and Business Administration (WU Wien), Austria (May 2007)

9. Mendling, J., Moser, M., Neumann, G., Verbeek, H.M.W., van Dongen, B.F., van der Aalst, W.M.P.: Faulty EPCs in the SAP reference model. In: Dustdar, S., Fiadeiro, J.L., Sheth, A. (eds.) BPM 2006. LNCS, vol. 4102, pp. 451–457. Springer, Heidelberg (2006)
10. Perumal, S., Mahanti, A.: A graph-search based algorithm for verifying workflow graphs. In: DEXA 2005. Proceedings of the 16th International Workshop on Database and Expert Systems Applications, pp. 992–996. IEEE Computer Society, Los Alamitos (2005)
11. Sadiq, W., Orlowska, M.E.: Analyzing process models using graph reduction techniques. Inf. Syst. 25(2), 117–134 (2000)
12. Valette, R.: Analysis of Petri nets by stepwise refinements. Journal of Computer and System Sciences 18(1), 35–46 (1979)
13. van der Aalst, W.M.P.: Workflow verification: Finding control-flow errors using Petri-net-based techniques. In: van der Aalst, W.M.P., Desel, J., Oberweis, A. (eds.) Business Process Management. LNCS, vol. 1806, pp. 161–183. Springer, Heidelberg (2000)
14. van der Aalst, W.M.P., Hirnschall, A. (Eric) Verbeek, H.M.W.: An alternative way to analyze workflow graphs. In: Pidduck, A.B., Mylopoulos, J., Woo, C.C., Ozsu, M.T. (eds.) CAiSE 2002. LNCS, vol. 2348, pp. 535–552. Springer, Heidelberg (2002)
15. van Dongen, B.F., van der Aalst, W.M.P., Verbeek, H.M.W.: Verification of EPCs: Using reduction rules and Petri nets. In: Pastor, Ó., Falcão e Cunha, J. (eds.) CAiSE 2005. LNCS, vol. 3520, pp. 372–386. Springer, Heidelberg (2005)
16. Vanhatalo, J., Völzer, H., Leymann, F.: Faster and more focused control-flow analysis for business process models though SESE decomposition. IBM Research Report RZ 3694 (July 2007)
17. (Eric) Verbeek, H.M.W., Basten, T., van der Aalst, W.M.P.: Diagnosing workflow processes using Woflan. Comput. J. 44(4), 246–279 (2001)
18. Zerguini, L.: A novel hierarchical method for decomposition and design of workflow models. Journal of Integrated Design and Process Science 8(2), 65–74 (2004)

Discovering Service Compositions That Feature a Desired Behaviour*

Fabrizio Benigni, Antonio Brogi, and Sara Corfini

Department of Computer Science, University of Pisa, Italy
{benigni,brogi,corfini}@di.unipi.it

Abstract. Web service discovery is one of the key issues in the emerging area of Service-oriented Computing. In this paper, we present a complete composition-oriented, ontology-based methodology for discovering semantic Web services, which exploits functional and behavioural properties contained in OWL-S service advertisements to satisfy *functional* and *behavioural* client queries. To this aim, we build on top of the results contained in two recent articles, where we presented (1) a suitable data structure (viz., a dependency hypergraph) to collect functional information of services, and (2) a suitable notion of behavioural equivalence for Web services. We also discuss the architecture and the main implementation choices of the matchmaking system applying such a methodology.

1 Introduction

Service-oriented Computing (SoC) [1] is emerging as a new promising computing paradigm that centers on the notion of service as the fundamental element for developing distributed software applications. In this setting, Web service discovery is a major issue of SoC, as it allows developers to find and re-use existing services to rapidly build complex applications.

The standard service description language (WSDL) provides services with purely syntactic descriptions, not including neither behavioural information on the possible interaction among services, nor semantics information to describe the functionality of services. Yet, both behavioural and semantic information may be necessary, for example, to satisfy complex queries that require to compose the functionalities offered by different services, as well as to automatise the processes of service discovery and composition.

During the last years, various proposals have been put forward to feature more expressive service descriptions that include both semantics (viz., ontology-based) and behaviour information about services. One of the major efforts in this direction is OWL-S [2], a high-level ontology-based language for describing services. In particular, OWL-S service descriptions include a list of semantically annotated functional attributes of services (the *service profile*), and a declaration of the interaction behaviour of services (the so-called *process model*).

* Research partially supported by EU FP6-IST STREP 0333563 SMEPP and MIUR FIRB TOCAI.IT.

B. Krämer, K.-J. Lin, and P. Narasimhan (Eds.): ICSOC 2007, LNCS 4749, pp. 56–68, 2007.

In this paper, we present a composition-oriented, ontology-based methodology for discovering OWL-S described services. In particular, we employ semantic information to select available services that can be exploited to satisfy a given query, and we employ behaviour information to suitably compose such services to achieve the desired result.

The methodology integrates the results recently presented in [3,4]. In [3] a suitable data structure (viz., a dependency hypergraph) to collect relationships among ontology-annotated inputs and outputs of services (i.e., semantic information) was introduced. It is important to stress that the construction of such a hypergraph does not affect the query answering time, as it is built off-line and updated whenever a new service is added to the local service repository. In [4] we defined a suitable notion of behavioural equivalence for Web services. Such a notion allows to establish whether two services, described by means of a simple variant of standard Petri nets, are behaviourally equivalent, i.e., such that an external observer can not tell them apart. An interesting feature of this methodology is the ability of addressing both *functional* and *behavioural* queries, i.e., respectively, queries specifying the functional attributes of the desired service, and queries also requiring a specific behaviour of the service to be found. In particular, in case of a behavioural query, the methodology – besides satisfying the query functional requirements – guarantees that the returned service features the desired behaviour.

In this paper we also present a system – called SAM, for Service Aggregation Matchmaking – implementing the discovery methodology here introduced. The main features of the new version of SAM can be summarised as follows:

- *Composition-oriented matching* – that is, the capability of discovering service compositions. When no single service can satisfy the client query, SAM checks whether the query can be fulfilled by a suitable composition of services.
- *Ontology-based matching* – that is, the ability of "crossing" different ontologies and performing flexible matching automatically. Given that different services are typically described in terms of different ontologies, SAM determines relationships between concepts defined in separate ontologies, so to establish functional dependencies among services.
- *Behaviour-aware matching* – that is, the ability of guaranteeing behavioural properties. Given a query synthetising the behaviour of a service, SAM searches for (compositions of) services which are behaviourally equivalent to the query. Each matched service (composition) can be used interchangeably with the service described by the query.

It is also worth observing that, with respect to its first version described in [5], SAM is now capable of properly coping with the problem of "crossing" different ontologies (thanks to the introduction of the hypergraph), as well as of suitably addressing behavioural queries.

The rest of the paper is organized as follows. Section 2 describes the composition-oriented, ontology-based methodology for discovering services. Section 3 is devoted to discuss the architecture, the main implementation choices, and possible future extensions of the system applying such a methodology. Finally, some concluding remarks are drawn in Section 4.

2 A Methodology for a Composition-Oriented Discovery

In this Section, we present a methodology for discovering compositions of semantic Web services which takes into account both *semantic* and *behavioural* information advertised in the OWL-S service descriptions. In particular, we employ "semantics", namely all those ontological information regarding the functional attributes (i.e., inputs and outputs) of services, to select services with respect to "what they really do", and we employ "behaviour", namely, information concerning the order with which messages can be received or sent by each service, to guarantee some useful properties of selected services. Before presenting the discovery methodology, we describe hereafter the data structures and formalisms we employ to summarise service descriptions.

2.1 The Internal Representation of Services

As briefly mentioned in the Introduction, the complete behaviour of a service is described by the OWL-S process model, which may include conditional and iterative constructs. Hence, a service may behave in different ways and feature different functionalities. We say that a service may have different *profiles*, each of them requiring/providing different inputs/outputs. Hence, as one may expect, we represent each service with two distinct items: a *set of profiles*, to summarise the different sets of functional attributes employed by each profile of the service, and a *Petri net*, to model the whole service behaviour.

More precisely, a profile S_n represents a dependency between the set of the inputs and the set of the outputs employed by the specific behaviour n of a service S. Service profiles are collected into a hypergraph, whose nodes correspond to the functional attributes of the service profiles, and whose hyperedges represent relationships among such attributes. It is worth observing that each node v of the hypergraph, that is, each functional attribute, is associated with a concept, which is defined in one of the ontologies referred by the service employing v. The hypergraph also includes equivalent and sub-concept relationships among nodes, viz., among ontology concepts. (A formal definition of the hypergraph and the algorithms for its construction can be found in [3,6].)

Example. Let us consider the simple service T, defined as a choice of two atomic operations. The former inputs a *zipCode* (Z) and returns the corresponding *geographicCoordinates* (GC), and the latter inputs a *location* (L) and a *date* (D), and returns the computed *wheatherInformation* (W). The service T has hence two profiles, T_1 and T_2, represented by the hyperedges $\{Z\} \xrightarrow{T_1} \{GC\}$ and $\{L, D\} \xrightarrow{T_2} \{W\}$, respectively. Consider next the service S, which inputs a *city* (C) and a *nation* (N), and returns the corresponding *zipCode* (Z). Service S exposes a single profile S_1 represented by the hyperedge $\{C, N\} \xrightarrow{S_1} \{Z\}$. The

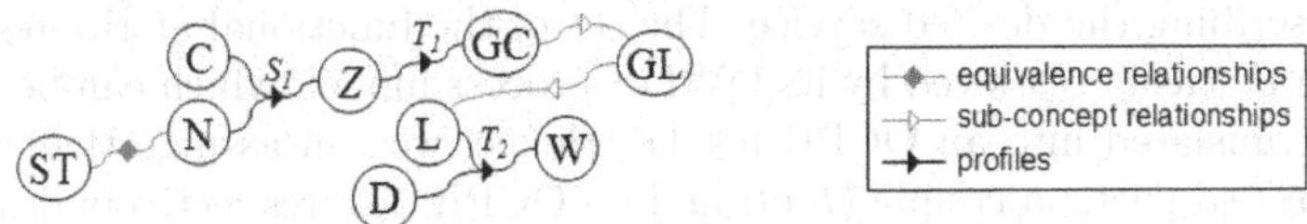

Fig. 1. A simple hypergraph

hypergraph including profiles S_1, T_1, T_2 is illustrated in Figure 1. Note the equivalent relationship linking together *state* (ST) and *nation* (viz., ST and N are synonyms), as well as, the sub-concept relationship linking *geographicCoordinates* and *geographicLocation* (GL) (viz., GC is a sub-concept of GL).

While a profile describes a particular behaviour of a service from a functional point of view, the complete interaction behaviour of a service is represented by an OCPR net. OCPR nets (for Open Consume-Produce-Read nets) [4] are a simple variant of the standard Condition/Event Petri nets, designed to naturally model the behaviour of services, and in particular the persistency of data (i.e., once a data has been produced by some service operation, it remains available for all the service operations that input it). Briefly, an OCPR net is equipped with two disjoint sets of places, namely, control and data places, to properly model the control flow and the data flow of a Web service, and with an interface, which establishes those data places that can be observed externally. Hence, whilst control places can be produced and consumed, data places can be read, produced but not consumed. We formally defined OCPR nets in [4], where a mapping from OWL-S process models to OCPR nets is also presented. Intuitively speaking (see [4] for details), transitions map (OWL-S) atomic operations, while data and control places respectively model the availability of data and the executability of atomic operations. It is worth observing that when a service is translated into an OCPR net, all the data places of the net are externally observable by default.

Example. Figure 2 (which will be explained in more detail later) illustrates four simple OCPR nets, where rectangles, circles and diamonds respectively represent transitions, data places and control places. The initial control place i as well as the final control place f of each net are emphasised in light gray. Furthermore, each net is delimited by a box which represents the net interface, namely, the set of places which can interact with the environment. Hence, those data places that lie on the box are the ones that can be observed externally.

2.2 Discovering Compositions of Services

So far, we have introduced the internal representation of services that we use to store them in a local repository. We can now propose a complete composition-oriented methodology for discovering services. The methodology takes as input the so-called *behavioural queries*, that is, queries specifying both the inputs and outputs, as well as the expected behaviour of the service to be found. A behavioural query, for example, can be expressed in terms of the OWL-S process model describing the desired service. The set of the functional attributes of the query can be easily retrieved by its OWL-S process model, which can be in turn suitably translated into an OCPR net [4]. Hence, we can assume that a query consists of two parts: a couple (I, O) and an OCPR net, respectively describing the set of the inputs and outputs, and the behaviour of the service to be found.

The discovery methodology we are going to propose consists of two main phases: a *functional analysis* and a *behavioural analysis*, that we describe below.

Functional Analysis

This first phase consists in a sort of *functional filter*, indeed, services are selected according to their functional attributes only. More precisely, the functional analysis focuses on the first functional part of the query (viz., the couple (I, O) of inputs and outputs), and returns those set of services which satisfy the functional requirements of the query. Hence, for each set of services S passing the functional filter: (1) all the query outputs are provided by the services in S, (2) all the inputs of the services in S are provided by the query (or they can be produced by some service in S).

As described in the previous subsection, we summarise functional information of the services stored in the repository in an hypergraph. The functional analysis hence consists of a visit of the hypergraph. It is worth noting that by exploring *profiles*, we address the discovery of sets of services, as well as by exploring *sub-concept* and *equivalent* relationships we properly reason with (different) ontologies. In particular, the functional analysis explores the hypergraph starting from those nodes corresponding to the query outputs, and it continues by visiting backwards the hyperedges until reaching, if possible, the query inputs. The profile-labelled hyperedges which take part in an hyperpath from the query outputs to the query inputs determine a set of service profiles satisfying the query. A detailed discussion of the algorithm for visiting the hypergraph can be found in [6]. Furthermore, it is also worth noting that we have enriched the functional analysis with a *minimality check* [5], in order to avoid constructing non-minimal sets of service, that is, sets containing (at least) a service not strictly necessary to satisfy the query.

Example. Consider the simple hypergraph illustrated in Figure 1, and the query taking as input a *city* (C) and a *state* (ST) and providing as output the corresponding *geographicLocation* (GL). The functional analysis visits the hypergraph starting from the query output GL. Then, by exploring the sub-concept relationship $\{GC\} \rightarrow \{GL\}$ and the profile T_1, it reaches the node Z. Next, by visiting the profile S_1 and by crossing the equivalence relationship $\{ST\} \rightarrow \{N\}$, it reaches both the query inputs $\{C, ST\}$. Hence, the set of profiles $\{S_1, T_1\}$ satisfies (the functional requirements of) the query.

Behavioural Analysis

As previously described, every set of profiles determined by the functional analysis satisfies the query from a functional perspective. Consider now a specific set P of profiles. The behavioural analysis checks whether the services included in the

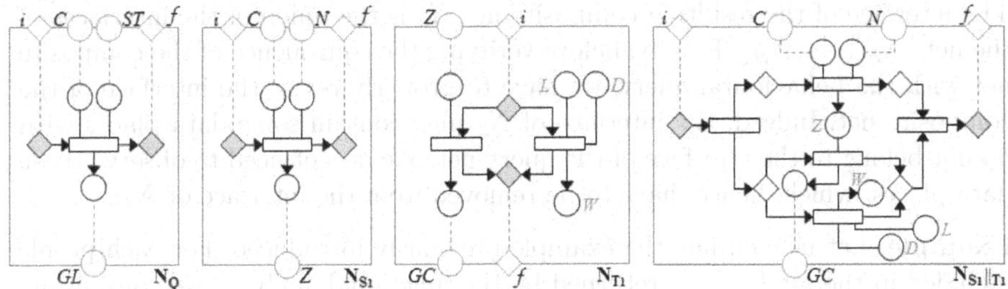

Fig. 2. OCPR nets

set, and suitably composed together, are *behaviourally* equivalent to the client query. The behavioural analysis consists of the following two main steps.

(1) Constructing the composite service. The objective of this step is to construct the OCPR net modelling the parallel composition of the service profiles included in P. Firstly, for each service profile S_n in the set, we retrieve from the local repository the OCPR net modelling the complete behaviour of the corresponding service S. As described in subsection 2.1, all the data places of an OCPR net are externally observable by default (viz., all the data places of the net belong to the net interface). Yet, a profile identifies a specific portion (i.e., behaviour) of the service, which may partially employ the inputs and outputs of the whole service. Hence, let S_n be a profile of a service S, and let N_S be the OCPR net modelling S. Then, we remove from the interface of N_S those data places which do not belong to the inputs and outputs of the profile S_n.

We can now construct the composite OCPR net $N_{\|}$ modelling the parallel composition of the OCPR nets $N_{S_1}, \ldots, N_{S_n}$ associated to the profiles $S_1, \ldots, S_n$ belonging to the set P. Note that, if the set of profiles returned by the functional analysis contains n profiles of the same service S, we insert into the composite net n copies of the OCPR net modelling S, each of them typically providing a different interface. In other words, we are considering multiple executions of the same service.

As stated before, the data places which belong to the net interface are the only ones that can interact with the external environment. Consequently, in order to compose OCPR nets, we have to operate on their interfaces. To build $N_{\|}$ we first perform the disjoint union of the transitions, data places and control places of the nets $N_{S_1}, \ldots, N_{S_n}$. Next, we collapse those data places which are equivalent and which occur in the interfaces of $N_{S_1}, \ldots, N_{S_n}$. It is worth noting that we qualify as equivalent data places, those data places which are syntactically and/or semantically equivalent. For example, we collapse two data places corresponding to two syntactically different, yet synonyms concepts. Moreover, in order to perform the parallel composition of $N_{S_1}, \ldots, N_{S_n}$, we add to $N_{\|}$ the necessary additional transitions and control places, according to the OCPR mapping of the parallel composition (viz., the OWL-S `split+join` construct) given in [4]. It is important to observe that the initial control places as well as the final control place of an OCPR net are externally observable by default.

The interface of the resulting composite net $N_{\|}$ is the union of the interfaces of the nets $N_{S_1}, \ldots, N_{S_n}$. Finally, before verifying the equivalence of the composite net with the behavioural query, we have to properly revise the interface of the composite net. Indeed, the interface of $N_{\|}$ may contain some data places with do not belong to the interface of the query net. We do not need to observe those data places, which, hence, have to be removed from the interface of $N_{\|}$.

Example. Let us continue the example previously introduced. For each profile included in the set $\{S_1, T_1\}$ returned by the functional analysis, we consider its OCPR net representation. The OCPR nets N_{S_1}, N_{T_1}, respectively representing the profiles S_1, T_1, are illustrated in Figure 2. While all the data places of N_{S_1} belong to the net interface (as they belong to the single profile S_1 of S), the interface of N_{T_1} contains only the data places employed by the profile T_1. We perform next the parallel composition of the two nets N_{S_1} and N_{T_1}. The resulting net $N_{S_1\|T_1}$ is depicted in the right part of Figure 2. Finally, note that we removed Z from the interface of $N_{S_1\|T_1}$, since it does not belong to the query.

(2) Analysing the service behaviour. The second step of the behavioural analysis checks whether the composition of those services previously selected during the functional analysis is capable of satisfying the query from a behavioural perspective. Let N_Q denote the net representing the behavioural query. Namely, this step checks whether N_Q and $N_{\|}$ are equivalent, that is, whether they are externally indistinguishable.

To this end, we defined in [4] a suitable notion of behavioural equivalence for Web services, which features *weakness*, as it equates structurally different yet externally indistinguishable services; *compositionality*, as it is also a congruence; and *decidability*, as the set of states that an OCPR net can reach is finite. More precisely, a state of an OCPR net is the marking of its observable places. In the initial state only the initial control place contains a token, while all the other places belonging to the net interface are empty. Then, in each state, an OCPR net can execute two types of actions, namely, it can put a token in one of the data places of its interface, or it can perform τ-transitions (i.e., it can fire transitions not requiring any additional token). Hence, intuitively speaking, in order to verify whether N_Q and $N_{\|}$ are equivalent, the second step of the behavioural analysis checks whether for each state s of N_Q: (1) there exists a state t of $N_{\|}$ which can perform all the actions executable by s; (2) for each state s' reachable from s by executing the action a, t can reach a state t' by executing the same action a, such that s' and t' are equivalent. It is important to observe that if s reaches s' by performing a single τ-transition, t can reach a state t' equivalent to s' with one or more τ-transitions. Dually, this step checks whether similar conditions hold for each state of $N_{\|}$. If so, the query and the composite net are equivalent, that is, the found service composition fully satisfies the query.

Example. Consider the nets N_Q and $N_{S_1\|T_1}$, illustrated in Figure 2, and respectively representing the client query and the previously built composite service. According to [4], the nets N_Q and $N_{S_1\|T_1}$ are equivalent. In particular, note that if we add a token in C and ST (namely, N, since ST and N are equivalent), N_Q

reaches the final state in a single τ-transition, while $N_{S_1 \| T_1}$ needs of performing four τ-transitions.

3 Implementation of the Methodology

We discuss below the architecture and the main implementation choices of the system (viz., SAM) applying the discovery methodology described in Section 2.

Architecture
Figure 3 illustrates the overall architecture of the matchmaking system implementing the proposed discovery methodology. The system – available as Web service – is designed to cope with two classes of users, *clients* and *providers*, which, mainly, can query the system, and add a new service to the system, as reflected by the WSDL interface depicted in Figure 3.

The client queries are handled by the *search engine* core component, which consists of two building blocks, namely, the *functional analyser* and the *behavioural analyser*, respectively implementing the functional analysis and the behavioural analysis of the discovery methodology described in subsection 2.2. In particular, functional queries can be satisfied by the functional analyser only, while behavioural queries need of the joint work of both functional and behavioural analysers. It is worth noting that the implementation of the *behavioural analyser* makes use of the algorithm presented by Fernandez and Mounier in [7] for verifying the bisimilarity of two systems. Clients can also list available services and ontologies: the *service browser* component satisfies these requests.

When a provider adds a new service to the system, the *hypergraph builder* and the *OWL-S2PNML* components translate the service into the internal representation described in subsection 2.1. The hypergraph builder determines the profiles of the service. Moreover, it exploits SemFiT [8], a tool for "crossing" different ontologies, to establish the semantic (viz., equivalence and sub-concept) relationships among ontology concepts. In particular, the hypergraph builder determines the relationships concerning those concepts defined in the new ontologies employed by the service to be added, and those concepts which belong to the ontologies previously registered to the system. A more detailed description of the behaviour of the hypergraph builder component is available in [6].

OWL-S2PNML translates the OWL-S process model of the service into an OCPR net, which is described by a corresponding PNML file. The Petri Net Markup Language[1] (PNML) is a XML-based and customizable interchange format for Petri nets. We employ PNML in order to enhance the modularity and portability of the system. Providers can also add single ontologies: in such a case, the hypergraph builder component suffices to update the hypergraph.

It is also worth noting that, before adding a new service as well as a new ontology, a provider has to login the system. The authentication service is managed by the *account manager* component.

[1] `http://www2.informatik.hu-berlin.de/top/pnml/about.html`

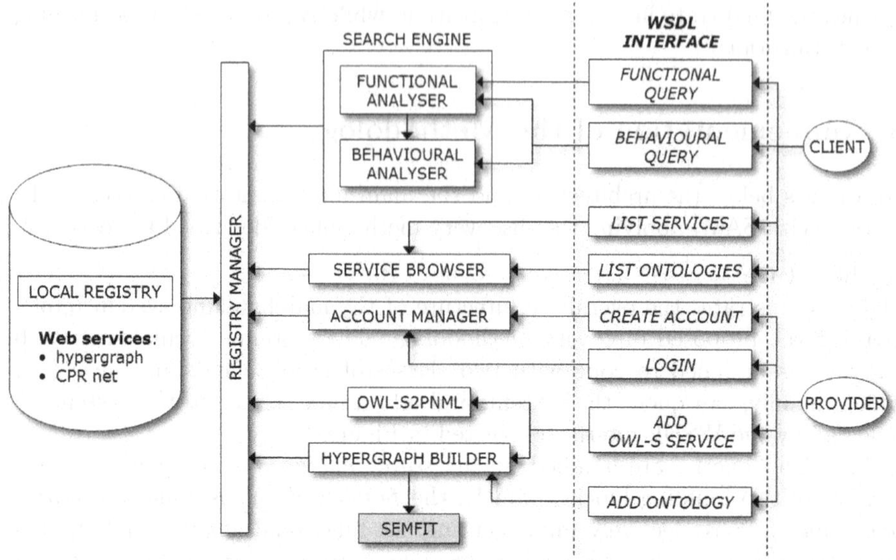

Fig. 3. System architecture

Service internal descriptions (i.e., profiles and semantic relationships, and PNML files), ontologies and account information are stored in the *local registry*. All system components can access the local registry by means of a suitable *registry manager*.

Implementation

We discuss hereafter the main implementation aspects of SAM, the matchmaking system previously described in Section 2. In particular, the implementation of SAM has been conditioned by the following requisites.

- *Portability* – the system consists of Java packages, each of them wrapped in a standard Java EE 5 component. SAM is accessible as a Web service, described by a standard WSDL interface as well as by an OWL-S advertisement.
- *Extensibility* – SAM is deployed as a multitiered Java enterprise application, which allows for high levels of modularization and ease of substitute/add logic components (e.g., the integration with SemFiT, remotely accessed by its WSDL interface). Furthermore, the use of Java language allows us to employ many existing Java libraries and tools (e.g., OWL-S parsers).
- *Scalability* – Java EE platform natively guarantees suitable performance and scalability to component-based and multitiered applications.
- *Use of standards* – Besides the use of Java EE platform, the system implementation relies on other standard languages and well-known technologies:
  - PNML, to describe OCPR nets by means of standard XML files,
  - javaDB, to deploy the database (which is accessible via JDBC API directly by the Java EE component containers),

- Mindswap OWL-S API, to validate, marshal/unmarshal OWL-S descriptions,
- PNML framework API, to marshal/unmarshal PNML descriptions.

The domain logic of SAM is implemented by three Java libraries: SamFeedLogics, which implements the *OWL-S2PNML* and *hypergraph builder* components of Figure 3, SamFunctionalLogics, that implements the *functional analyser* component, and SamBehaviouralLogics, which implements the *behavioural analyser* component. It is worth noting that each library is connected to the rest of the architecture by facade EJB (Enterprise Java Beans) components, that automatically retrieve other components' references by Java EE server injection. Hence, each functional component is totally independent from the overall architecture, and it can be tested in a Java SE 5 environment by employing suitable stubs and drivers. Furthermore, facade components declaratively instruct the application server (by means of Java 5 annotations included in the class files) to expose relevant methods as (WSDL described) Web services.
The implementation of SAM is completed by the following Java EE components.

- SamPersistence – which, by abstracting from the actual data representation, provides two interfaces to respectively view and modify (only upon authorization) the data contained in the local registry of SAM.
- SamDBBrowser – which implements a simple database browsing tool (viz., the *service browser* component).
- SamAccountMgmt – which grants (or denies) access to SamFeedLogics component. In particular, the current security management allows only registered users to submit new OWL-S descriptions and new ontologies. Moreover, it keeps trace of every submission to discourage any abuse. Future improvements of security management may be implemented in order to prevent possible leaks in quality of service.
- SamGWTServlet – which provides SAM with a friendly Web interface, developed with the Google Web Toolkit.

Extending the Implementation
For testing the system concisely presented in this section, we manually produced several OWL-S service descriptions. Although the behaviour of each single part of the system has been properly checked, currently, we are not able to provide a serious experimental assessment of the system. Please, note that no standard test collection for OWL-S service retrieval does exist, yet. To be more exact, by accurately scanning the Web, we found two OWL-S repositories[2], both generated with semi-automatic WSDL annotators. However, as one may expect, WSDL annotators generate very simple OWL-S process models, typically a list of atomic operations, as no behavioural information is available in WSDL descriptions. Obviously, such process models are not useful for testing the system.

To overcome this problem, a brute force (time-consuming and error-prone) solution could be to manually create a test collection of OWL-S services. Yet, given

[2] http://moguntia.ucd.ie/repository/owl-ds.html
http://www-ags.dfki.uni-sb.de/ klusch/owls-mx/index.html

that WS-BPEL [9] has been recently approved as an OASIS standard, we plan to extend our system in order to cope with WS-BPEL services. For instance, a possible solution is to translate BPEL processes into OWL-S services, by plugging into the system the BPEL2OWL-S [3] translator developed by Aslam et al. in [10]. Yet, there is still a prominent problem, namely, the lack of ontological information in WS-BPEL descriptions. Hence, when a provider adds a WS-BPEL process into the system, firstly, the WS-BPEL process is translated into a "rough" OWL-S service, and secondly, the provider is asked to complete the OWL-S description, by annotating the service parameters with ontology concepts (e.g., by employing some friendly ontology editor, such as Protégé (`http://protege.stanford.edu`). The new OWL-S service can be then registered into the system as described in the previous subsections.

Finally, given the high computational (viz., exponential) complexity of the functional and behavioural analysers, another important line for future work is to develop indexing and/or ranking techniques (as search engines do for Web pages) in order to sensibly improve the efficiency of the discovery methodology.

4 Concluding Remarks

In this paper, we have introduced an automated composition-oriented, ontology-based methodology for discovering (semantic) Web services. We have also presented a matchmaking system, called SAM, which prototypically implements such a methodology. SAM is the first matchmaker – at the best of our knowledge – that takes properly into account functional, semantic and behaviour information provided by service descriptions. More precisely, given as input a query specifying inputs, outputs and expected behaviour of the service to be found (viz., a *behavioural* query), SAM returns an ordered list of (compositions of) services, each of them (1) requiring as input a subset of the query inputs, (2) providing as output all the query outputs (or more), (3) featuring a behaviour equivalent to the query. In particular, it is important to observe that feature (3) makes our system suitable to be employed to address emerging issues of the Service-oriented Computing area, such as service replaceability.

Recently, automatic matchmaking of Web services has gained prominent importance and new approaches are frequently introduced. For the lack of space, we briefly discuss hereafter only some of the widely known approaches.

The first effort towards the automation of Web service discovery has been put forward by some of the authors of OWL-S in [11]. Their algorithm performs a functionality matching between service requests and service advertisements described as DAML-S (the predecessor of OWL-S) service profiles. This approach was the first at introducing the notion of an automatic and flexible matching by suitably considering subsumes and plug-in relationships among the ontology-annotated attributes of services and service requests. Yet, the algorithm proposed in [11] does not deal with the ontology crossing problem, that is, it is not able to determine relationships between attributes annotated with concepts of separate

[3] `http://bpel4ws2owls.sourceforge.net`

ontologies. To this aim, it is worth mentioning the service matchmaking approach presented by Klusch et al. in [12], which employs both logic based reasoning and IR techniques to properly relate concepts of different ontologies.

A common drawback of [11,12] is that they search for a *single* service capable of satisfying a client query by itself. However, as previously described, composing functionalities of different services may be necessary to satisfy a query. An approach to a composition-oriented discovery is presented by Benatallah et al. in [13], where the matchmaking problem is reduced to a best covering problem in the domain of hypergraph theory.

With respect to the approach presented in this paper, it is important to stress that none of the mentioned proposals takes into account behavioural aspects of services. Indeed, our matchmaker – differently from [11,13,12] – is capable of solving behavioural queries, guaranteeing, as well, some behavioural properties of the returned (compositions of) services.

Behavioural aspects of services are partially taken into account by the approach of Agarwad and Studer, that proposed in [14] a new specification of Web services, based on description login and π-calculus. Their algorithm consider semantic and temporal properties of services, yet, their matchmaking approach is limited to a single service discovery.

References

1. Papazoglou, M.P., Georgakopoulos, D.: Service-Oriented Computing. Communications of the ACM 46(10), 24–28 (2003)
2. OWL-S Coalition: OWL-S: Semantic Markup for Web Service (2004), http://www.ai.sri.com/daml/services/owl-s/1.2/overview/
3. Brogi, A., Corfini, S., Aldana, J., Navas, I.: Automated Discovery of Compositions of Services Described with Separate Ontologies. In: Dan, A., Lamersdorf, W. (eds.) ICSOC 2006. LNCS, vol. 4294, pp. 509–514. Springer, Heidelberg (2006)
4. Bonchi, F., Brogi, A., Corfini, S., Gadducci, F.: A behavioural congruence for Web services. In: Arbab, F., Sarjani, M. (eds.) Fundamentals of Software Engineering. LNCS, Springer, Heidelberg (2007) (to appear)
5. Brogi, A., Corfini, S.: Behaviour-aware discovery of Web service compositions. International Journal of Web Services Research 4(3) (2007) (to appear)
6. Brogi, A., Corfini, S., Aldana, J., Navas, I.: A Prototype fot Discovering Compositions of Semantic Web Services. In: Tumarello, G., Bouquet, P., Signore, O. (eds.) Proc. of the 3rd Italian Semantic Web Workshop (2006)
7. Fernandez, J.C., Mounier, L.: "On the Fly" verification of behavioural equivalences and preorders. In: Larsen, K.G., Skou, A. (eds.) CAV 1991. LNCS, vol. 575, pp. 181–191. Springer, Heidelberg (1992)
8. Navas, I., Sanz, I., Aldana, J., Berlanga, R.: Automatic Generation of Semantic Fields for Resource Discovery in the Semantic Web. In: Andersen, K.V., Debenham, J., Wagner, R. (eds.) DEXA 2005. LNCS, vol. 3588, pp. 706–715. Springer, Heidelberg (2005)
9. BPEL Coalition: WS-BPEL 2.0 (2006), http://docs.oasis-open.org/wsbpel/2.0/wsbpel-v2.0.pdf

10. Aslam, M.A., Auer, S., Shen, J., Herrmann, M.: Expressing Business Process Models as OWL-S Ontologies. In: Eder, J., Dustdar, S. (eds.) Business Process Management Workshops. LNCS, vol. 4103, pp. 400–415. Springer, Heidelberg (2006)
11. Paolucci, M., Kawamura, T., Payne, T., Sycara, K.: Semantic Matchmaking of Web Services Capabilities. In: Horrocks, I., Hendler, J. (eds.) ISWC 2002. LNCS, vol. 2342, pp. 333–347. Springer, Heidelberg (2002)
12. Klusch, M., Fries, B., Sycara, K.: Automated semantic web service discovery with OWLS-MX. In: AAMAS'06, pp. 915–922. ACM Press, New York (2006)
13. Benatallah, B., Hacid, M.S., Léger, A., Rey, C., Toumani, F.: On automating Web services discovery. VLDB J. 14(1), 84–96 (2005)
14. Agarwal, S., Studer, R.: Automatic Matchmaking of Web Services. In: IEEE Int. Conference on Web Services, pp. 45–54. IEEE Computer Society Press, Los Alamitos (2006)

An Hybrid, QoS-Aware Discovery of Semantic Web Services Using Constraint Programming*

José María García, David Ruiz, Antonio Ruiz-Cortés, Octavio Martín-Díaz, and Manuel Resinas

Universidad de Sevilla
Escuela Técnica Superior de Ingeniería Informática
Av. Reina Mercedes s/n, 41012 Sevilla, España
josemgarcia@us.es

Abstract. Most Semantic Web Services discovery approaches are not well suited when using complex relational, arithmetic and logical expressions, because they are usually based on Description Logics. Moreover, these kind of expressions usually appear when discovery is performed including Quality-of-Service conditions. In this work, we present an hybrid discovery process for Semantic Web Services that takes care of QoS conditions. Our approach splits discovery into stages, using different engines in each one, depending on its search nature. This architecture is extensible and loosely coupled, allowing the addition of discovery engines at will. In order to perform QoS-aware discovery, we propose a stage that uses Constraint Programming, that allows to use complex QoS conditions within discovery queries. Furthermore, it is possible to obtain the optimal offer that fulfills a given demand using this approach.

Keywords: Discovery Mechanisms, Quality-of-Service, Semantic Matching, Constraint Programming.

1 Introduction

Most approaches on automatic discovery of Semantic Web Services (SWS) use Description Logics (DLs) reasoners to perform the matching [7,13,15,18,26,27]. These approaches have limitations regarding with the expressiveness of searches, especially when there are Quality-of-Service (QoS) conditions integrated within queries. For instance, a condition like "find a service which *availability* ≥ 0.9, where $availability = MTTF/(MTTF + MTTR)$"[1] can not be expressed in DLs. Although there are proposals that extend traditional DLs with concrete domains in many ways [9], they still have limitations on expressing complex conditions [1,14], as in the previous example. These complex conditions usually

* This work has been partially supported by the European Commission (FEDER) and Spanish Government under CICYT project Web-Factories (TIN2006-00472).

[1] $MTTF$ stands for "Mean Time To Failure", while $MTTR$ stands for "Mean Time To Repair". Both of them are QoS parameters often used to define service availability.

B. Krämer, K.-J. Lin, and P. Narasimhan (Eds.): ICSOC 2007, LNCS 4749, pp. 69–80, 2007.

appear when performing a QoS-aware discovery, so in this case DLs reasoning is not the most suitable choice.

QoS conditions are contemplated in several SWS discovery proposals. For instance, Wang *et al.* extend WSMO framework to include QoS parameters that allow to discover the best offer that fulfills the demanded conditions [30]. Benbernou and Hacid propose the use of constraints, including QoS-related ones, to discover SWS [3]. Moreover, Ruiz-Cortés *et al.* model the QoS conditions as Constraint Satisfaction Problems (CSPs) [23], but in the context of non-semantic Web Services.

Our proposal is an hybrid architecture to discover SWS. Discovery may be split into different stages, each of them using the best suited engine depending on the features of the corresponding stage. We identify at least two stages in this process: QoS-based discovery and functional (non-QoS) discovery. The former may be done using Constraint Programming (CP), as proposed in the case of non-semantic Web Services in [23], while the latter is usually performed by DLs reasoners, although it is not restricted to use other techniques.

Our approach allows to filter offers, stage by stage, using a proper search engine until the optimal offer that fulfills a demand is found. This optimization is accomplished due to the proposed use of CP in the QoS-aware discovery stage, also enabling the definition of more complex conditions than defined ones using DLs. Furthermore, our proposed architecture is loosely coupled and extensible, allowing the addition of extra discovery engines if necessary.

The rest of the paper is structured as follows. In Sec. 2 we introduce related works on discovering SWS, discussing their suitability to perform a QoS-aware discovery. Next, in Sec. 3 we present our hybrid discovery proposal, explaining the proposed architecture and how CP can be used in a QoS-aware semantic discovery context. Finally, in Sec. 4 we sum up our contributions, and discuss our conclusions and future work.

2 Discovering Semantic Web Services

In this Section, we discuss related work on discovering SWS, describing the different approaches and analyzing their suitability to handle QoS parameters and conditions, in order to perform a QoS-aware discovery.

2.1 Preliminaries

Each proposal uses its own terminology to refer to the entities involved in the discovery process, especially its descriptions of the requested and provided services. For the sake of simplicity, we use one single notation along this paper.

We refer to a demand (denoted by the Greek letter delta, i.e. $\delta emand$) as a set of objectives that clients want to accomplish by using a service that fulfills them. It may be composed of functionality requirements and QoS conditions that the requested service must fulfill, such as "find a service which $availability \geq 0.9$, where $availability = MTTF/(MTTF + MTTR)$". The different proposals refer to demands as goals [22], queries [2,3,13], service request [7,19,27] or user requirements [30].

An offer (denoted by the Greek letter omega, i.e. *ωffer*) of a service is the definition of a SWS that is publicly available from a service provider. An offer may be composed of functionality descriptions, orchestration, choreography, and QoS conditions of the given service. For instance, an offer can consist in a QoS condition like "$MTTF$ is from 100 to 120 inclusive and $MTTR$ is from 3 to 10 also inclusive". Different approaches refer to offers as advertisements [2,13,30], service capabilities [19,22,27], or service profiles [7,15,16].

Most proposals on discovering SWS are built upon one of the following description frameworks. Firstly, OWL-S [16] is a DARPA Agent Markup Language program initiative that defines a SWS in terms of an upper ontology that contains concepts to model each service profile, its operations and its process model. It is based on OWL standard to define ontologies, so it benefits from the wide range of tools available. Secondly, the Web Service Modeling Ontology (WSMO) [22] is an European initiative whose goal, as OWL-S, is to develop a standard description of SWS. Its starting point is the Web Service Modeling Framework [6], which has been refined and extended, developing a formal ontology to describe SWS in terms of four core concepts: ontologies, services, goals and mediators. Finally, the METEOR-S project from the University of Georgia takes a completely different, but aligned approach than the others. Its main target is to extend current standards in Web Services adding semantic concepts [25], among others contributions discussed here. These extensions make use of third party frameworks, including the previous two, to semantically annotate Web Service descriptions. These proposals have extensions to take care of QoS parameters.

2.2 Related Work

In the context of DAML-S (the OWL-S precursor), Sycara *et al.* show how semantic information allows automatic discovery, invocation and composition of Web Services [27]. They provide an early integration of semantic information in a UDDI registry, and propose a matchmaking architecture. It is based on a previous work by Paolucci *et al.*, where they define the matching engine used [19]. This engine matches a demand and an offer when this offer describes a service which is "sufficiently similar" to the demanded service, i.e. the offered service provides the functionality demanded in some degree. The problem is how to define that degree of similarity, and the concrete algorithm to match both service descriptions. They update their work to OWL-S in [28].

Furthermore, there are proposals that perform the matchmaking of SWS using DLs [7,13,15]. Particularly, González-Castillo *et al.* provide an actual matchmaking algorithm using the subsumption operator between DLs concepts describing demands and offers [7]. They use existing DLs reasoners, as RACER [8] and FaCT [11], to perform the matchmaking. On the other hand, Lutz and Sattler [15] do not provide an algorithm, but give the foundations to implement it using subsumption, like Li and Horrocks [13], who also give hints to implement a prototype using RACER.

These three works define different matching degrees as in [27], from exactly equivalents to disjoint. All of them perform this matching by comparing inputs and outputs. Apart from that, neither of them can obtain the optimal offer using QoS parameters. However, Benatallah *et al.* propose to use the degree of matching to select the best offer in [2], but it results to be a NP-hard problem, as in any optimization problem [4].

On the other hand, Benbernou and Hacid realise that some kinds of constraints are necessary to discover SWS, including QoS related ones, so they formally discuss the convenience of incorporating constraints in SWS discovery [3]. However, instead of using any existing SWS description framework, their proposal uses an *ad-hoc Services Description Language*, in order to be able to define complex constraints. In addition, the resolution algorithm uses constraint propagation and rewriting, but performed by a subsumption algorithm, instead of a CSP solver.

Concerning WSMO discovery, Wang *et al.* propose an extension of the ontology to allow QoS-aware discovery [30]. The matchmaking is done by an *ad-hoc* algorithm to add QoS conditions to offers and demands. Their implementation has some limitations, as the algorithm can only be applied to real domain attributes, and is restricted to three types of relational operators.

Ruiz-Cortés *et al.* provide in [23] a framework to perform QoS-aware discovery by means of CP, in the context of non-semantic Web Services. They show the soundness of using CP to improve the automation of matchmaking from both theoretical and experimental points of view. Although CP solving is a NP-hard problem, the results of their experimental study allow to conclude that CP-based matchmakers are practically viable despite of its, theoretical, combinatorial nature. This work is the starting point of our approach on using CP to perform QoS-related stages of our hybrid SWS discovery proposal.

2.3 Frameworks

As an application of their previous work, Srinivasan *et al.* present an implementation to development, deployment and consumption of SWS [26]. It performs the discovery process using the proposals introduced in [19,27]. They show performance results and detail the implementation of OWL-S and UDDI integration, so it can be used as a reference implementation to OWL-S based discovery, but without QoS conditions.

IRS-II [18] is an implemented framework similar to WSMF [6], that is able to support service discovery from a set of demands. It uses descriptions of the reasoning processes called Problem Solving Methods (PSM), similar to OWL. Moreover, IRS-III [5] updates this previous implementation, using WSMO ontology to model SWS, and providing an architecture to discovery, composition and execution SWS. All of them can not handle with QoS conditions, although they are extensible so they may support them.

Another interesting proposal is done in [24], where Schlosser *et al.* propose a graph topology of SWS providers and clients, connected between them as in a peer-to-peer (P2P) network. In this scenario, searching, and specially publishing, are done very efficiently, without the need of a central server acting as a register of offers and demands. In addition, the network are always updated, due to an efficient topology maintenance algorithm. This structure of decentralized registries is proposed in METEOR-S for semantic publication and discovery of Web Services [29]. The semantic matching algorithm uses templates to search inputs and outputs of services described with ontological concepts, without the use of a specific reasoner, or the possibility to express QoS conditions. Although the matchmaking is too simple, the idea of a P2P network can be adopted in our proposal without troubles.

Our proposal is open to be implemented in the context of any of the presented frameworks in this section. The proposed architecture that we present in the following section does not impose any restriction on the SWS framework used (i.e. OWL-S, WSMO or METEOR-S), and can be composed of any number of the discovery engines discussed in Sec. 2.2, due to its hybrid nature. Furthermore, it can be materialized as the discovery component of implementations like IRS-III [5] or OWL-S IDE [26].

3 Our Proposal

The addition of constraints, specially QoS-related ones, to SWS descriptions, turns most approaches on discovering SWS insufficient, because they mainly use DLs, which are usually limited to logical and relational expressions when describing QoS conditions. CP becomes necessary to manage more complex QoS conditions, so a demand can be matched with the best available offer. Instead of using solely CP to perform the discovery, we present an hybrid solution that splits the discovery into different stages.

3.1 Hybrid Semantic Discovery Architecture

An abstract architecture of our proposal is sketched in Fig. 1, where we show how the different components are connected between them. Here, the dashed line defines the boundaries of our hybrid discovery engine.

Q document corresponds to the query that a client wants to use to discover services, i.e. the demand. This query may be expressed in any desired language that the scheduler can handle, such as a SPARQL query [21], a WSMO goal, a faceted search [20], or even it may be defined visually using a GUI.

R is the result set of offers that fulfill the query Q. It is the output of the discovery process, possibly being an empty set, the best offer, or an ordered list of offers by an optimality criterion. The format of this output should conform the specification of a concrete SWS framework in order to successfully invoke the discovered service(s).

The different stages of the hybrid discovery are performed by the best suited discovery engine. In Fig. 1, $E_1 ... E_n$ represent the engines to be used in each corresponding stage. The core component of our proposed architecture is responsible to send the input data to each engine, by decomposing the query Q

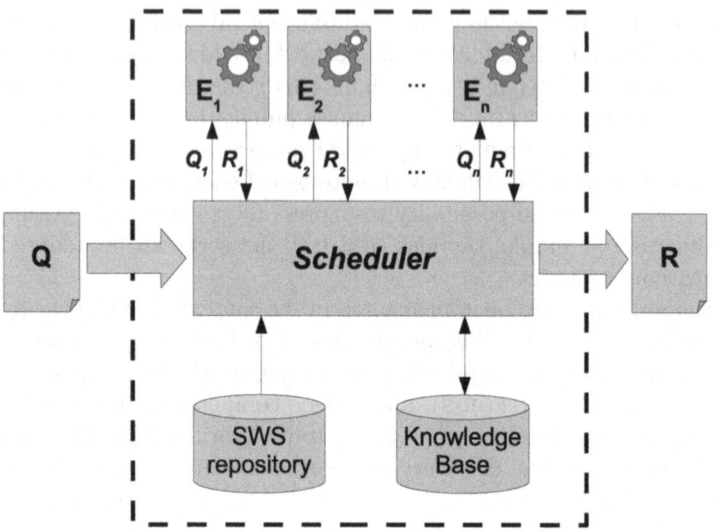

Fig. 1. Architecture of our hybrid discovery proposal

in subqueries (Q_i), and to recover its corresponding output (R_i), joining all of them to output the final result R. These input and output formats depend on the concrete engine of each stage. Thus, if we are performing a QoS-aware stage, the input must be modeled as a CSP, so CP can be applied to perform this kind of stage. Additionally, it is possible to use a DLs engine to perform non-QoS discovery, or a template matchmaker [29], for instance.

Offers have to be published in some kind of repository so they can be matched with demands by means of the different discovery engines used in our approach. This SWS repository may be implemented in different ways: as a semantically-extended UDDI registry [26], as a decentralized P2P registry [29], or as a WSMO repository [5], for instance.

In addition, our architecture takes care of the NP-hard nature of optimization [4], so we propose to include a knowledge-base (KB) that cache already performed discoverings, so the execution of the discovery process becomes faster. Thus, we store executed queries related with their result set of SWS from the repository component, into the KB. IRS-II implementation uses a similar idea to accelerate discovery [18].

Finally, the core component of our proposal is the scheduler. It has to analyze the query Q, split the discovery task into stages, and communicate with discovery engines, in order, providing them with a correct input, and obtaining a corresponding output. These different outputs are processed stage by stage, so the set of matching offers from the SWS repository are gradually made smaller. Each discovery stage may be concurrently or sequentially launched in order, depending on the query nature. Moreover, the scheduler update the KB using the results of discovery process, which is output as R.

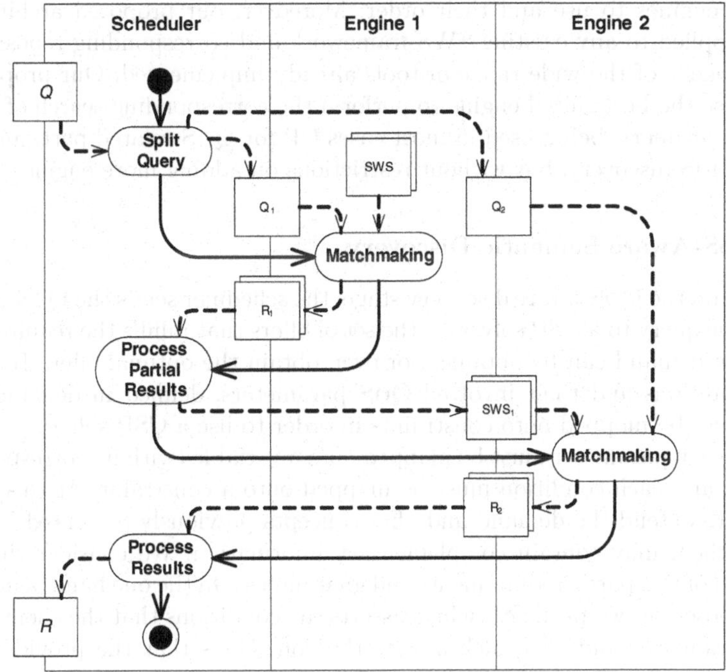

Fig. 2. Activity diagram of our discovery process

Fig. 2 shows the activity diagram of an hybrid discovery process performed in two stages using two different engines. This diagram can be easily extended if we need more stages. For instance, using a similar format from [13], a query $Q = (ServiceProfile \cap A \geq 0.9)$, where A corresponds to availability, is split by the scheduler into two subqueries: $Q_{DL} = (ServiceProfile)$ being the part expressed in DLs, and $Q_{CP} = (\{A\}, \{[0..1]\}, \{A \geq 0.9, A = MTTF/(MTTF + MTTR)\})$ the part modeled by a CSP.[2] $ServiceProfile$ corresponds to the definition of a demand in terms of the OWL-S profile of a service. In this scenario, the scheduler perform a matchmaking firstly using a DLs engine with Q_{DL}, obtaining the offers that satisfy this subquery. Then, with this resulting subset of SWS from the registry, the scheduler performs a matchmaking using a CP engine and Q_{CP}, so the final result is the optimal offer that satisfies the whole query Q. For the sake of simplicity we do not contemplate the KB role in Fig. 2, because it only provides a way to speed up the process.

This hybrid discovery architecture has many advantages. It is loosely coupled, due to the possibility to use any discovery engine. Also, the input query format is not restricted, as the scheduler can analyze a given query, so it can infer the

[2] A CSP consists in a three-tuple of the form (V, D, C) where V is a finite, non-empty set of variables, D is a finite, non-empty set of domains (one for each variable) and C is a set of constraints defined on V. The solution space of a CSP is a set composed of all its possible solutions, and if this set is not empty, the CSP is said to be satisfiable.

concrete engines to use and their order. Moreover, our proposed architecture can be applied to any existing SWS framework and corresponding repositories, taking benefit of the wide range of tools already implemented. Our proposal is able to use the best suited engine to perform the corresponding search of a part of the input query, being used in most cases CP for QoS-related part, and DLs for non-QoS discovery, but without restrictions on adding more engines.

3.2 QoS-Aware Semantic Discovery

Focusing on the QoS-aware discovery stage, the scheduler sends the QoS-related part of the query to a CSP solver, so the set of offers that fulfills the requirements of a given demand can be obtained, or even obtain the optimal offer. To do so, QoS conditions and their involved QoS parameters, defined in demands and offers, must be mapped onto constraints in order to use a CSP solver.

Thus, each parameter must be mapped onto a variable (with its corresponding domain), and each condition must be mapped onto a constraint. At this point, we have to extend the demand and offer concepts previously presented because both of them may contain complementary information. We consider they are composed of two parts: requirements and guarantees. On the one hand, a demand δ is composed of two parts: δ^γ, which asserts the conditions that the client meets (i.e. γuarantees), and δ^ρ, which asserts the conditions that the provider shall meet (i.e. ρequirements). Similarly, an offer ω can also be considered composed of ω^γ (what it guarantees) and ω^ρ (what is required from its clients).

For example, consider the demand "The availability shall be less than 0.9, where $A = MTTF/(MTTF + MTTR)$" (δ^ρ); and the offer "The mean time to failure is from 100 to 120 minutes inclusive, while the mean time to repair is from 3 to 10 minutes inclusive" (ω^γ). Assuming that $MTTF$, $MTTR$ and A range over real numbers, their corresponding CSPs are defined as follows:

$$\begin{aligned}\delta^\rho &= (\{A, MTTF, MTTR\}, \{[-\infty, +\infty], [0, +\infty], [0, +\infty]\},\\ &\quad \{A \geq 0.9, A = MTTF/(MTTF + MTTR)\})\\ \omega^\gamma &= (\{MTTF, MTTR\}, \{[0, +\infty], [0, +\infty]\},\\ &\quad \{100 \leq MTTF \leq 120, 3 \leq MTTR \leq 10\})\end{aligned}$$

Additionally, the demand may also contain the condition "My host is in Spain" (δ^γ); and the offer "For American and British clients only" (ω^ρ), so the offer provider requires from its clients some guarantees. Consequently, assuming that $COUNTRY$ variable ranges over the powerset of $\Lambda = \{ES, US, UK, FR\}$, i.e. $\mathcal{P}(\Lambda)$, their corresponding CSPs are defined as follows:[3]

$$\begin{aligned}\delta^\gamma &= (\{COUNTRY\}, \{\mathcal{P}(\Lambda)\}, \{COUNTRY = \{ES\}\})\\ \omega^\rho &= (\{COUNTRY\}, \{\mathcal{P}(\Lambda)\}, \{COUNTRY \subseteq \{UK, US\}\})\end{aligned}$$

[3] Note QoS parameters can be linked together in order to express more complex conditions, such as $\{COUNTRY = \{ES, UK, FR\} \Rightarrow 5 \leq MTTR \leq 10, COUNTRY = \{US\} \Rightarrow 5 \leq MTTR \leq 15\}$. These conditions can be interpreted as "the $MTTR$ is guaranteed to be between 5 and 10 if client is Spanish, British, or French, else between 5 and 15 if client is American".

The conditions previously expressed in natural language should be expressed in a semantic way, using QoS ontologies such as the one proposed by Maximilien *et al.* in [17]. Thus, semantically defining QoS parameters that take part in such conditions, and integrating these descriptions in any SWS framework, they can be interpreted later as a CSP so a solver can process them in the corresponding discovery stage.

These CSPs allow to check for consistency and conformance of offers and demands. A demand or an offer is said to be consistent if the conjunction of its corresponding CSPs (of requirements and guarantees) are satisfiable. On the other hand, an offer ω and a demand δ are said to be conformant if the solution space of the CSP of the guarantees of the offer (denoted by ψ_ω^γ) is a subset of the solution space of the CSP of the requirements of the demand (ψ_δ^ρ), and vice versa ($\psi_\delta^\gamma \subseteq \psi_\omega^\rho$) [23]. In the previous example, ω and δ are consistent, but they are not conformant, because $COUNTRY$ is guaranteed to be ES, but the offer requires it to be UK or US.

Finally, the ultimate goal of the matchmaking of offers and demands is to find a conformant offer that is optimal from the client's point of view. To do so, it becomes necessary to model the optimization task as a CSP, as with consistency and conformance checks. More specifically, finding the optimal can be interpreted as a Constraint Satisfaction Optimization Problem (CSOP), which requires to explicitly establish a preference order on the offer set. This order can be defined using a weighted composition of utility functions, which can be taken as a global utility function for the client.

Thus, each QoS parameter can have a utility function defined, and an associated weight to successfully describe how important the values that can take are for the client. Fig. 3 shows an example of how to discover optimal offers. In this case, we are assuming that the demand only specifies its requirements (Fig. 3a) and the offer only specifies what it guarantees (Fig. 3b), so the offer is conformant with the demand. The corresponding utility functions of the QoS parameters involved, i.e. $MTTF$ and $MTTR$, ranging over $[0,1]$, are shown in Fig. 3c and 3d, respectively.

The utility function for $MTTF$ (Fig. 3c) is a piecewise linear function that defines a minimum utility if $MTTF$ is below 60 minutes; the utility grows linearly if $MTTF$ is between 60 and 120 minutes, and the utility reaches its maximum value if $MTTF$ is above 120. On the other hand, the utility function for $MTTR$ showed in Fig. 3d is a decreasing piecewise linear function. In order to obtain a global utility function of the offer, we consider that $MTTF$ has a weight of 70% and $MTTR$ 30%.

The offer from Fig. 3b must be checked for conformance with the demand from Fig. 3a, supposing that both descriptions have been previously checked for consistency, and that both are based on same QoS parameters, or they are defined using a compatible ontology. In this case, there is only one offer conformant, but there could be more than one, being necessary to obtain the optimal offer. To do so, utility functions for each offer have to be computed in order to compare them and get the maximum utility value, which corresponds with the optimal offer. In Fig. 3e we show the OPL [10] model for the computing of the utility function of the showed offer.

$$\delta^\rho \equiv A \geq 0.9 \wedge$$
$$A = \frac{MTTF}{MTTF + MTTR}$$

(a) Demand requirements.

$$\omega^\gamma \equiv 100 \leq MTTF \leq 120 \wedge$$
$$3 \leq MTTR \leq 10$$

(b) Offer guarantees.

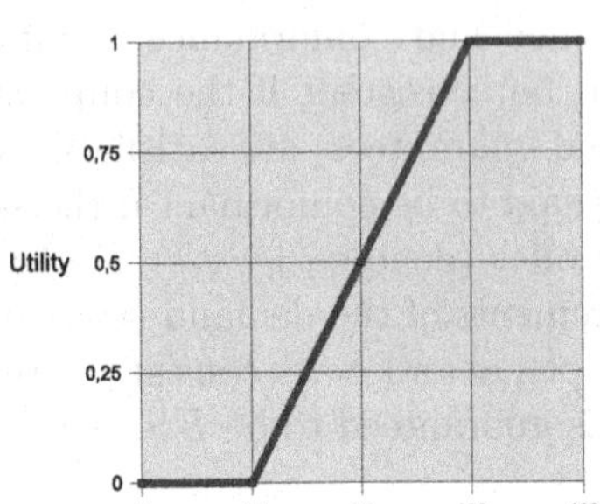

(c) $MTTF$ utility function.

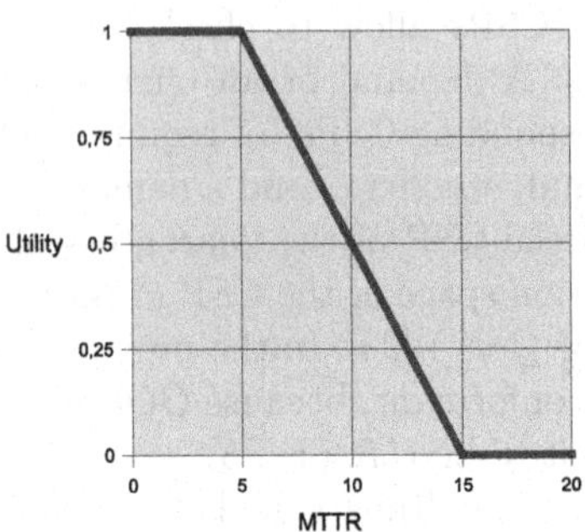

(d) $MTTR$ utility function.

```
//variables
range TYPE_MTTF 0..255;
var TYPE_MTTF MTTF;
range TYPE_MTTR 0..255;
var TYPE_MTTR MTTR;
range TYPE_UTILITY 0..100;
var TYPE_UTILITY U_MTTF;
var TYPE_UTILITY U_MTTR;
var TYPE_UTILITY UTILITY;
minimize
 UTILITY
subject to {
 // Offer guarantees
100<=MTTF<=120;
3<=MTTR<=10;
// Utility function of MTTF
MTTF<=60 => U_MTTF=0;
60<MTTF<=120 =>60*U_MTTF=MTTF-60;
MTTF>120=> U_MTTF=1;
// Utility function of MTTR
MTTR<=5 => U_MTTR=1;
5<MTTR<=15 => 10*U_MTTR=15-MTTR;
MTTR>15 => U_MTTR=0;
// Utility aggregate of matching
UTILITY = 70*U_MTTF + 30*U_MTTR;
};
```

(e) OPL model for computing utility.

Fig. 3. An example on obtaining optimal offers

Note that we compute the minimum value of the utility function, taking the worst-case scenario. This way, we say that an offer ω is optimal with regard to a utility function U if the minimum value of this function is the maximum among minimum values of all conformant offers. It is also possible to take other approaches when computing the utility function, like using the maximum value, a mean value, or the more general case of a weighted composition of the maximum and minimum value [12].

4 Conclusions and Future Work

In this work, we show that using a unique engine to discover SWS is not appropriate, due to each engine is usually designed for a concrete kind of search. For instance, DLs reasoners are well suited when discovering SWS in terms of concepts and relations, but they can not handle complex numerical QoS conditions. Although there are extensions to allow concrete domains in DLs, reasoners have to implement them, and they may bring undecidability results.

We present an hybrid solution that consists in a n-stages discovery process, where each stage is performed using the most appropriate technique. Furthermore, we propose to use CP to perform QoS-aware discovery stages, so the optimal service(s) offered that fulfills a given demand can be found. In addition, our proposed architecture is extensible and loosely coupled, allowing to define complex QoS conditions, and to use utility functions based on QoS parameters to obtain the optimal offer. This architecture does not impose any restriction on the SWS framework and repository to use, allowing its materialization as a discovery component for current SWS implementations.

For future work, we are considering to define more precisely the scheduler and its interaction with the rest of the components. The query split mechanism has to be characterized, so do the results merging for each engine. Thus, a catalog of stages would be defined, including their order of execution. Moreover, we are considering to extend current SWS frameworks using a QoS ontology to define QoS parameters and conditions, allowing to express complex arithmetic, relational, and logical expressions in demands and offers.

Acknowledgments. The authors would like to thank the reviewers of the 5th *International Conference on Service Oriented Computing*, whose comments and suggestions improved the presentation substantially.

References

1. Baader, F., Sattler, U.: Description logics with aggregates and concrete domains. Information Systems 28(8), 979–1004 (2003)
2. Benatallah, B., Hacid, M., Rey, C., Toumani, F.: Semantic reasoning for web services discovery. In: WWW Workshop on E-Services and the Semantic Web (2003)
3. Benbernou, S., Hacid, M.: Resolution and constraint propagation for semantic web services discovery. Distributed and Parallel Databases 18(1), 65–81 (2005)
4. Bonatti, P., Festa, P.: On optimal service selection. In: 14th international conference on World Wide Web, pp. 530–538 (2005)
5. Cabral, L., Domingue, J., Galizia, S., Gugliotta, A., Tanasescu, V., Pedrinaci, C., Norton, B.: IRS-III: A broker for semantic web services based applications. In: International Semantic Web Conference, pp. 201–214 (2006)
6. Fensel, D., Bussler, C.: The web service modeling framework WSMF. Electronic Commerce Research and Applications 1(2), 113–137 (2002)
7. González-Castillo, J., Trastour, D., Bartolini, C.: Description logics for matchmaking of services. Technical Report HPL-2001-265, Hewlett Packard Labs (2001)
8. Haarslev, V., Möller, R.: RACER system description. In: Goré, R.P., Leitsch, A., Nipkow, T. (eds.) IJCAR 2001. LNCS (LNAI), vol. 2083, pp. 701–706. Springer, Heidelberg (2001)
9. Haarslev, V., Möller, R.: Practical Reasoning in RACER with a Concrete Domain for Linear Inequations. In: Int. Workshop on Description Logics (2002)

10. Van Hentenryck, P.: Constraint and integer programming in OPL. INFORMS Journal on Computing 14(4), 345–372 (2002)
11. Horrocks, I.: FaCT and iFaCT. In: Int. Workshop on Description Logics (1999)
12. Kritikos, K., Plexousakis, D.: Semantic QoS metric matching. In: ECOWS 2006, pp. 265–274. IEEE Computer Society Press, Los Alamitos (2006)
13. Li, L., Horrocks, I.: A software framework for matchmaking based on semantic web technology. In: Int. World Wide Web Conference, pp. 331–339 (2003)
14. Lutz, C.: Description logics with concrete domains – a survey. In: Advances in Modal Logic, pp. 265–296 (2002)
15. Lutz, C., Sattler, U.: A proposal for describing services with DLs. In: Int. Workshop on Description Logics (2002)
16. Martin, D., Burstein, M., Hobbs, J., Lassila, O., McDermott, D., et al.: OWL-S: Semantic Markup for Web Services. Technical Report 1.1, DAML (November 2004)
17. Maximilien, E.M., Singh, M.P.: A framework and ontology for dynamic web services selection. IEEE Internet Computing 8(5), 84–93 (2004)
18. Motta, E., Domingue, J., Cabral, L., Gaspari, M.: IRS-II: A framework and infrastructure for semantic web services. In: Fensel, D., Sycara, K.P., Mylopoulos, J. (eds.) ISWC 2003. LNCS, vol. 2870, pp. 306–318. Springer, Heidelberg (2003)
19. Paolucci, M., Kawamura, T., Payne, T., Sycara, K.: Semantic matching of web services capabilities. In: Horrocks, I., Hendler, J. (eds.) ISWC 2002. LNCS, vol. 2342, pp. 333–347. Springer, Heidelberg (2002)
20. Prieto-Díaz, R.: Implementing faceted classification for software reuse. Commun. ACM 34(5), 88–97 (1991)
21. Prud'hommeaux, E., Seaborne, A.: SPARQL Query Language for RDF. Technical Report Working Draft, W3C (March 2007)
22. Roman, D., Lausen, H., Keller, U.: Web Service Modeling Ontology (WSMO). Technical Report D2 v1.3 Final Draft, WSMO (October 2006)
23. Ruiz-Cortés, A., Martín-Díaz, O., Durán Toro, A., Toro, M.: Improving the automatic procurement of web services using constraint programming. Int. J. Cooperative Inf. Syst. 14(4), 439–468 (2005)
24. Schlosser, M., Sintek, M., Decker, S., Nejdl, W.: A scalable and ontology-based P2P infrastructure for semantic web services. In: Peer-to-Peer Computing, pp. 104–111 (2002)
25. Sivashanmugam, K., Verma, K., Sheth, A., Miller, J.: Adding semantics to web services standards. In: Intl. Conference on Web Services, pp. 395–401 (2003)
26. Srinivasan, N., Paolucci, M., Sycara, K.: Semantic web service discovery in the OWL-S IDE. In: Hawaii International Conference on Systems Science (2006)
27. Sycara, K., Paolucci, M., Ankolekar, A., Srinivasan, N.: Automated discovery, interaction and composition of semantic web services. J. Web Sem. 1(1), 27–46 (2003)
28. Sycara, K., Paolucci, M., Soudry, J., Srinivasan, N.: Dynamic discovery and coordination of agent-based semantic web services. IEEE Internet Computing 8(3), 66–73 (2004)
29. Verma, K., Sivashanmugam, K., Sheth, A., Patil, A., et al.: METEOR-S WSDI: A scalable P2P infrastructure of registries for semantic publication and discovery of web services. Inf. Tech. Management 6(1), 17–39 (2005)
30. Wang, X., Vitvar, T., Kerrigan, M., Toma, I.: A QoS-aware selection model for semantic web services. In: Dan, A., Lamersdorf, W. (eds.) ICSOC 2006. LNCS, vol. 4294, pp. 390–401. Springer, Heidelberg (2006)

Architectural Decisions and Patterns for Transactional Workflows in SOA

Olaf Zimmermann[1], Jonas Grundler[2], Stefan Tai[3], and Frank Leymann[4]

[1] IBM Zurich Research Laboratory, Säumerstrasse 4, 8803 Rüschlikon, Switzerland
olz@zurich.ibm.com

[2] IBM Software Group, Schönaicher Strasse 220, 71032 Böblingen, Germany
jonas.grundler@de.ibm.com

[3] IBM T.J. Watson Research Center, 19 Skyline Drive, Hawthorne, NY 10532, USA
stai@us.ibm.com

[4] Universität Stuttgart, IAAS, Universitätsstraße 38, 70569 Stuttgart, Germany
frank.leymann@iaas.uni-stuttgart.de

Abstract. An important architectural style for constructing enterprise applications is to use transactional workflows in SOA. In this setting, workflow activities invoke distributed services in a coordinated manner, using transaction context-propagating messages, coordination protocols, and compensation logic. Designing such transactional workflows is a time-consuming and error-prone task requiring deep subject matter expertise. Aiming to alleviate this problem, we introduce a new analysis and design method that (a) identifies recurring architectural decisions in analysis-level process models, (b) models alternatives for these decisions as reusable, platform-independent patterns and primitives, and (c) maps the patterns and primitives into technology- and platform-specific settings in BPEL and SCA. Our method accelerates the identification of decisions, empowers process modelers to make informed decisions, and automates the enforcement of the decisions in deployment artifacts; tool support is available. We demonstrate value and feasibility of our method in an industry case study.

Keywords: BPEL, BPM, patterns, transactions, MDA, SCA, SOA, workflow.

1 Introduction

Service-Oriented Architecture (SOA) with transactional workflow support is a state-of-the-art architectural style for constructing enterprise applications. In this context, enterprise resources such as databases and message queues are exposed as distributed services, which are invoked concurrently by diverse service consumers including end user applications and executable workflows. The *integrity* of the enterprise resources must be preserved at all times [4]. System-level transaction techniques such as Atomicity, Consistency, Isolation, and Durability (ACID) transactions and business-level solutions such as compensation-based recovery are two ways of addressing this requirement [8]. However, defining transaction boundaries and implementing compensation logic are complex, time-consuming, and error-prone tasks requiring deep subject matter expertise. Neither reusable architectural patterns nor methodological

B. Krämer, K.-J. Lin, and P. Narasimhan (Eds.): ICSOC 2007, LNCS 4749, pp. 81–93, 2007.

support exist today; development tools do not guide process modelers sufficiently. This lack of support is diametrically opposed to SOA design goals such as increased agility, flexibility, and reusability – in our opinion, a key inhibitor for real-world adoption of transactional workflows in SOA.

In this paper, we introduce a new analysis and design method that aims to eliminate this inhibitor by combining architectural decision modeling techniques, reusable patterns composed of primitives, and mappings of the primitives to concrete technologies such as the Business Process Execution Language (BPEL) and the Service Component Architecture (SCA). Our method covers the entire lifecycle from analysis to conceptual design to technology selection and runtime engine configuration. This end-to-end coverage speeds up the identification of design alternatives for transactional workflows in SOA and helps to make the decision making process repeatable; architectural knowledge can be shared across project and technology boundaries. Pattern-aware design tools can map the primitives to platform-specific technology specifications and deployment artifacts, e.g., in BPEL/SCA engines and other middleware.

The remainder of this paper is organized in the following way. Section 2 defines the context for our work. Section 3 scopes the problem to be solved by identifying recurring architectural decisions in a real-world case study. Section 4 defines three conceptual transaction management patterns and three underlying primitives, along with an exemplary technology- and asset-level transformation. Section 5 discusses related work, and Section 6 concludes with a summary and an outlook to future work.

2 Background

The objective of our work is to support the design and development of *enterprise applications* that require transactional semantics. An example is a Customer Relationship Management (CRM) system that serves many concurrent users via multiple access channels and processes, including an Internet self-service and a call center. In this CRM, business-relevant customer profile information is persisted in databases and accessed via Web-accessible services; external systems also have to be integrated.

SOA and Web services. SOA reinforces general software architecture principles such as separation of concerns and logical layering. A defining element of SOA as an architectural style is the possibility to introduce a *Service Composition Layer (SCL)* [18], which promises to increase flexibility and agility and to provide better responsiveness to constantly changing business environments. (Re-)assembling workflows in the SCL does not cause changes on the underlying service and resource layers; computational logic and enterprise resource management are separated from the service composition. We refer to a SOA with such a SCL as a *process-enabled SOA*.

XML-based Web services are a state-of-the-art implementation option for process-enabled SOAs [19]. The Web Services Description Language (WSDL) [15] describes service interfaces, SOAP [12] service invocation messages. BPEL [14] is a workflow language with operational semantics that can be used to realize the SCL. Component models for the implementation of services are emerging; SCA is such a model [9]. Service components in SCA are defined from several perspectives: an *interface* describing the input and output parameters of the operations of a component, *references* to other components, and component *implementations*. Via *imports*, a component implementation can reference external services.

In the CRM example, let us assume that process-enabled SOA has been chosen as the architectural style. The business processes to be implemented are modeled explicitly during requirements analysis; their execution as SCL workflows is later automated using a *BPEL engine*. The tasks in the processes are realized as atomic and composed Web services, which have a WSDL interface and can be invoked at runtime through transport protocol bindings, e.g., SOAP/HTTP. We further assume that these services are implemented as SCA components or integrated via SCA imports.

Transactional workflows. In the CRM system, relational database tables and message queues provided by integration middleware [5] serve as *enterprise resources* persisting and exchanging customer profiles. Concurrent and distributed access to transactional enterprise resources can be coordinated by *transaction managers*, which are in charge of ensuring the ACID properties; Relational Database Management Systems (RDBMS) and queue managers then take a local *resource manager* role subordinate to a transaction manager [8].

The SCL in a process-enabled SOA can be seen as a workflow application. If a BPEL engine in the SCL serves as a transaction manager, its process flows become *transactional workflows* [8]. Transactional workflows coordinate the outcome of the local and remote service invocations that access and manipulate the enterprise resources. Transactional workflows in process-enabled SOA are particularly challenging to design due to the potentially long-lived nature of processes, the loose coupling and autonomy of services, the existence of non-transactional resources, and the diversity in coordination and communication protocols (synchronous and asynchronous message exchange patterns). Traditional system transactions alone are not directly applicable in a SOA setting; a more decentralized *coordination* model and application-level *compensation* strategies have to be added. To address these needs, WS-Coordination, WS-AtomicTransaction (WSAT), and WS-Business Activity Framework (WBAF) complement the Web services specifications introduced above [17].

3 Recurring Architectural Decisions in Process-Enabled SOA

Today's SOA tools use default transaction management settings when translating analysis-level process models into BPEL workflows, Web services and SCA components [20]. Often, these settings are inappropriate and have to be changed during the later development steps. This is error-prone, platform-specific work; software quality issues arise and technical project risk increases. This problem can be overcome by:

A method for the systematic design of transaction management settings in process-enabled SOA, which (a) identifies the required architectural decisions in analysis-level process models, (b) captures proven design options as patterns which facilitate the decision making, and (c) transforms the patterns to platform-specific settings.

Sample process. Refining our CRM example, we now discuss the SOA enablement of an existing system of a telecommunication service provider that is organized into several Lines of Business (LOB), including wireline and wireless telephony. The business event triggering the sample process is a customer requesting an upgrade from prepaid to regular wireless service, e.g., by calling a call center agent.

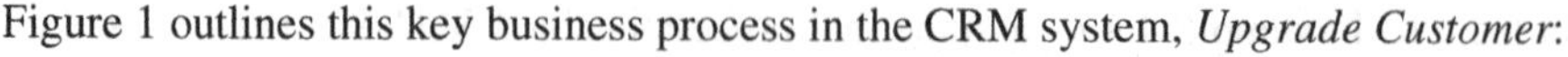

Figure 1 outlines this key business process in the CRM system, *Upgrade Customer*:

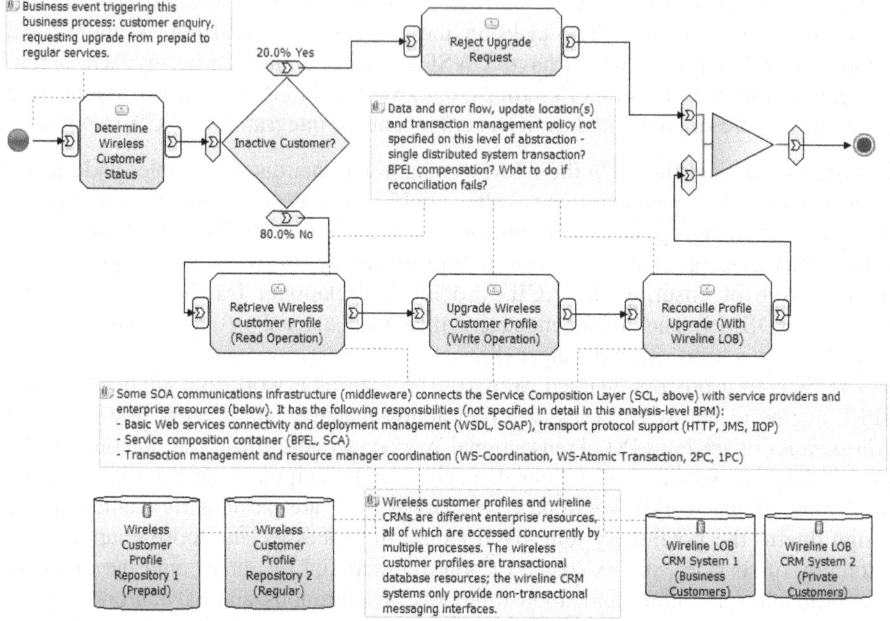

Fig. 1. Sample CRM process: analysis-level BPM including enterprise resources

The analysis-level Business Process Model (BPM) specifies that first the customer status has to be determined (*Determine Wireless Customer Status*), so that the customer profile, an enterprise resource spread over several repositories, can be retrieved (*Retrieve Wireless Customer Profile*). Next, a tentative *Upgrade Wireless Customer Profile* task is executed; however, the status change can only be finalized if a subsequent *Reconcile Profile Upgrade* task completes successfully. This task sends approval request messages to the two CRM systems of the wireline LOB. If any of these CRM systems declines the upgrade or does not respond within a working day, the upgrade process has failed, and the wireless customer profile must remain unchanged. Other business processes work with the customer profile while this process is running.

An analysis-level BPM such as Figure 1 is typically created by a business domain expert, not a software architect or workflow technology specialist. Such a BPM is not directly executable in a workflow engine; typically it does not cover design concerns such as data flow, resource protection, and error handling sufficiently. In the CRM example, the customer profiles are the enterprise resources to be protected with system and/or business transactions.[1] Another transactional enterprise resource might be the process instance state maintained by the engine; a BPEL engine in transaction manager role may have to roll back process parts when handling errors, even if

[1] Not all resources have to be protected by transactions, e.g. immutable resources meet the ACID characteristics trivially. On the other hand, not all resources worth protecting can actually be protected by transaction managers, e.g., due to legacy system constraints.

activities that do not participate in the same transaction (the one in which the BPEL process runs) have been committed on the system level already.

Recurring architectural decisions. It is technically feasible to transform the analysis-level BPM from Figure 1 into a design-level process model, e.g., via basic BPEL/SCA export utilities provided by commercial SOA tools [7]. However, such predefined transformations do not obey any *architectural decisions* that are made in response to project-specific requirements [20]. Many of these architectural decisions must be made for any process-enabled SOA, not just our CRM example: Which *composition paradigm* and *resource protection* approach should be selected? Who *coordinates* the transactions? Which *invocation protocols* are best suited to invoke services from the process activities in the SCL? Should the process activities and the service invocations run in separate *transaction islands* or form a *transaction bridge*? Which *compensation technology* should be used, and where should it be *placed*?

As step (a) of our method, Figure 2 organizes these recurring decisions by their *abstraction level* and *scope*. The abstraction level refines from conceptual issues such as selection of a composition paradigm (here: workflow) to technology and asset selection (here: BPEL language and BPEL engine). The scope of a decision assigns it to design model elements; in the CRM example, the activity *transactionality* has to be decided for Reconcile Profile Upgrade and the other four tasks shown in Figure 1.

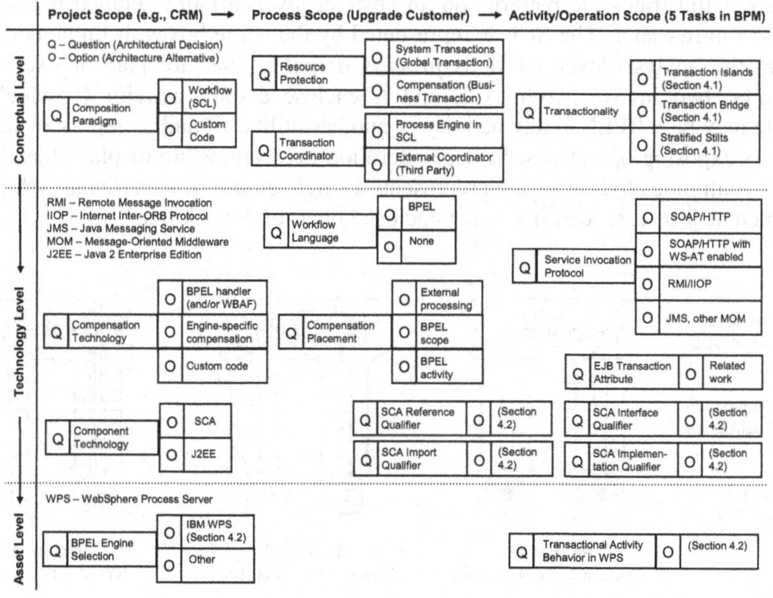

Fig. 2. Architectural decisions and alternatives for transactional workflows in SOA

4 Architectural Patterns as Decision Alternatives

As step (b) of our method, we now introduce three conceptual patterns as solution options (architecture alternatives) for the activity *transactionality* decision from

Figure 2. These conceptual patterns comprise of platform-independent primitives that we map to BPEL and SCA technology and engine deployment artifacts in step (c). The primitives are designed in such a way that other mappings can also be provided.

4.1 Conceptual Patterns and Primitives

The tasks from Figure 1 require different transactional treatment: Determine Wireless Customer Status does not change any enterprise resource; transactional execution is not required. The retrieval should execute as fast as possible. Upgrade Wireless Customer Profile updates wireless customer profiles; the service operation is co-located with that realizing the Retrieve Wireless Customer Profile task. Changes must be executed with all-or-nothing semantics. The CRM systems contacted in Reconcile Profile Upgrade offer messaging interfaces and may take days to respond. Still, all-or-nothing semantics is required; if any of the reconciliation request messages returns an error or times out, the updates to the wireless customer profile made by Upgrade Wireless Customer Profile must be undone.

TRANSACTION ISLANDS, TRANSACTION BRIDGE, and STRATIFIED STILTS are three patterns commonly used to address resource protection requirements such as those in the CRM. In theory, more design options exist; however, faithful to established pattern capturing principles, we only present patterns observed and proven in practice.

Figure 3 illustrates the patterns on an abstract level; a more detailed pattern description follows later. The SCL is represented by the white boxes. It implements the tasks in the analysis-level BPM as *process activities* that are part of executable workflows; two invoke activities I_1 and I_2 enclose a third activity U, which for example may be a BPEL assign activity or another utility. S_1 and S_2 represent *service providers* exposing operations. Service operation invocations are displayed as dotted lines. A contiguous light grey area represents a single *global transaction* as defined in [8], which may be extended if it is not enclosed by a solid black line.

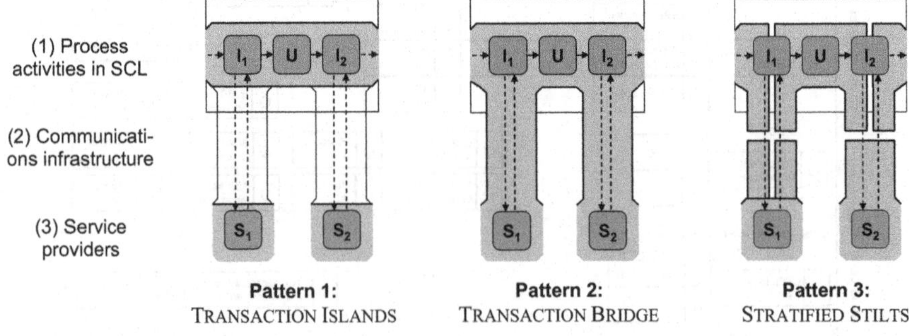

Fig. 3. Transaction context sharing options between process activities and service operations

These patterns comprise of three types of *primitives* that correspond to the architectural layers from Figure 3: (1) Process Activity Transactionality (PAT) primitives for the *process activities* in the SCL. (2) Communications Transactionality (CT) primitives modeling the capabilities of the *communications infrastructure* (invocation protocol, component technology). (3) Service provider Transactionality (ST) primitives stating the capability and willingness of *service providers* to join a transaction.

These primitive types are conceptual, platform-independent abstractions of concepts for example found in today's BPEL/SCA technology, and can be viewed as design time statements of architectural intent. Figure 4 illustrates the primitives:

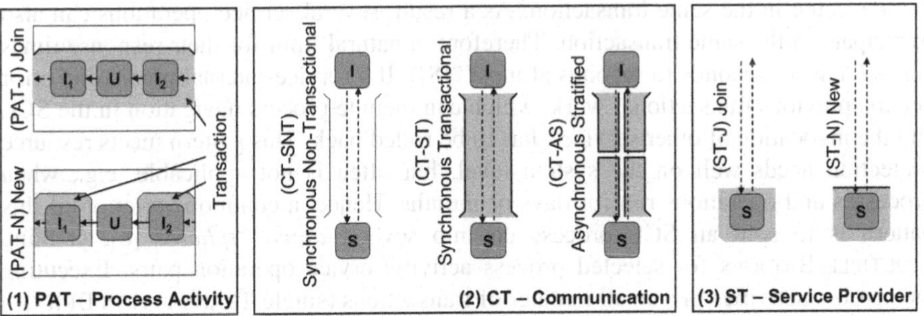

Fig. 4. Conceptual primitives as pattern building blocks (notation same as in Figure 3)

To elaborate upon the defining characteristics of the patterns and the primitives, we now present them in a format commonly used in the design patterns literature.

Intent. All patterns and primitives share the objectives motivated in Sections 2 and 3: To protect enterprise resources against integrity and correctness threats that may occur during concurrent process execution, e.g., when multiple processes and activities in the SCL invoke distributed services via a SOA communication infrastructure.

Pattern 1. Decoupled TRANSACTION ISLANDS (PAT-J+CT-SNT+ST-N in Figure 3)

Problem. How to isolate SCL process activities from service operation execution?

Solution. Do not propagate the transaction context from the SCL to the service.

Example. In the CRM case study, this pattern is applicable for Determine Wireless Customer Status. This analysis-level task is realized as a process activity that invokes a read-only operation which in this example should execute non-transactionally.

Forces and consequences. If a service operation fails, the process navigation in the SCL is not affected, and vice versa. If a service works with shared enterprise resources, its operations must be idempotent, as they may be executed more than once due to the transactional process navigation in the SCL. In many cases, the service provider must offer compensation operations, and higher-level coordination of the compensation activities is required (e.g., via business transactions; various models have been proposed). In practice, this pattern is often selected as a default choice.

Pattern 2. Tightly coupled TRANSACTION BRIDGE (PAT-J+CT-ST+ST-J shown in Figure 3); MULTIPLE BRIDGES variant (PAT-N+CT-ST+ST-J).

Problem. How to couple process activity execution in the SCL and service operation execution from a system transaction management perspective?

Solution. Configure process activities, communications infrastructure, and service providers in such a way that the SCL transaction context is propagated to the service.

Example. In the CRM case study, this pattern addresses the all-or-nothing requirements stated for Retrieve/Upgrade Wireless Customer Profile (co-located services).

Forces and consequences. Process activities and the service operations invoked by them execute in the same transaction. As a result, several service operations can also participate in the same transaction. Therefore, a natural limit for their response times exists ("tens of seconds to seconds at most" [8]). If a service-internal processing error occurs, previous transactional work, which can include process navigation in the SCL and the invocation of other services, has to be rolled back. This pattern meets resource protection needs well on the system level, but often is not applicable, e.g., when processes and operations run for days or months. Hence, a common variation of this pattern is to split an SCL process up into several *atomic spheres* [8], creating MULTIPLE BRIDGES for selected process activity/service operation pairs. Executing the process activities in a small number of transactions (single TRANSACTION BRIDGE) reduces the computational overhead for process navigation; splitting the process up into several atomic spheres (MULTIPLE BRIDGES) increases data currency.

Pattern 3. Loosely coupled STRATIFIED STILTS (PAT-J+CT-AS+ST-J in Figure 3)

Problem. How to realize asynchronous, queued transaction processing in SOA?

Solution. Use message queuing as SOA communication infrastructure.

Example. In the CRM case study, this pattern must be applied for Reconcile Profile Upgrade, as the wireline CRM systems only provide messaging interfaces (e.g., JMS); additional compensation logic is required. In Figure 3, I_1 and S_1 use *stratified transactions* (as defined in [8]) during service invocation; on the contrary, service S_2 reads the request message and sends the response message within a single transaction.

Forces and consequences. Services do not have to respond immediately; the delivery of the messages is guaranteed by the communications infrastructure. If the execution of the service operation fails, the process may not get an immediate response; additional error handling is required, often involving compensation logic. This pattern often is the only choice in process-enabled SOA, e.g., when integrating legacy systems.

PAT primitives. As Figure 4 shows, Process Activity Transactionality (PAT) defines two primitives for the SCL, transaction context sharing or *Join (J),* and transaction context separation or *New (N).* If set to PAT-J, a process activity executes in the same transaction context as the adjacent activities in the same process; it *joins* an existing context. As a consequence, the process activity's work might be rolled back if any other process activity or service operation that participates in the same transaction fails. With *PAT-N*, a process activity is executed in a *new* transaction context. Both PAT-J and PAT-N are valid choices in all three composite patterns; PAT-J is shown in Figure 3 and commonly used in practice. In TRANSACTION BRIDGE, PAT-N models the MULTIPLE BRIDGES variant. Deciding for PAT-N is justified if two process activities should be independent from each other from a business requirement point of view. Furthermore, some process models contain loops that are too complex to fit into a single, short-lived system transaction (e.g., due to retries, refinement/completion cycles, and service provider limitations).

CT primitives. We model three Communication Transactionality (CT) primitives, *Synchronous Non-Transactional* (CT-SNT), *Synchronous Transactional* (CT-ST), and *Asynchronous Stratified* (CT-AS). CT-SNT is used in the TRANSACTION ISLANDS pattern. It represents a synchronous service invocation from the process activity without propagation of the transaction context. As a consequence, the activity waits until the call to the service returns. Once the service has been called, there is no possibility to influence the work the service conducts. For example, the CT-SNT service invocation may cause the transaction to exceed the maximum duration configured in the SCL, which may result in a transaction timeout and a subsequent rollback. With CT-SNT, undoing the work of the service can not be included in this rollback.

CT-ST is required to build a TRANSACTION BRIDGE. It models a synchronous service invocation with transactional context propagation. As a consequence, the process activity waits until the call to the service returns; a rollback may occur after the service execution has completed (the service participates in the SCL coordination).

CT-AS is part of the STRATIFIED STILTS pattern. It represents an asynchronous service invocation without transaction context propagation. In CT-AS, long-running services can be invoked without loosing transactional behavior, as the process navigation is part of a *stratified transaction* [8]. At least three transactions are involved in the invocation of a long-running service: the request message is sent in a first transaction; in a second transaction, the message is received by the service provider and the response message is sent; in a third transaction, the process activity receives the response from the service. As shown in Figure 3, depending on the service implementation, the second transaction (provider side) may be split up into two transactions: receive the message and commit, and later on, send the response in a new transaction. Such stratification details are described further in [8].

ST primitives. Two choices and corresponding primitives exist for the Service Provider Transactionality (ST): *join* an incoming transaction (ST-J) or create a *new* one (ST-N). ST-J is used in TRANSACTION BRIDGE, ST-N in TRANSACTION ISLANDS. In ST-J, the service provider participates in the transaction of the caller (if a transaction exists). As a consequence, process activity execution in the SCL and the invoked service operation influence each other, e.g., when causing a rollback. In ST-N, the service provider does not participate in the incoming transaction. As a consequence, if the transaction in which the process activity runs is rolled back and the activity is retried later (e.g., due to process engine-specific error handling procedures), the service may operate on enterprise resources that have been modified in the meantime.

4.2 Sample Mapping of Primitives to BPEL/SCA Technology and Engine

As step (c) of our method, we now map the three PAT, CT, and ST primitives to BPEL and SCA and other technology platforms. We expect that BPEL engines provide settings that allow configuring the transactional behavior at least for *invoke activities*. Services are invoked via protocols such as SOAP/HTTP, IIOP and JMS, which differ in their support for transaction context propagation and (a)synchrony. The transactional behavior of SCA components is defined by SCA *qualifiers*.

Qualifiers specify the behavior desired from the point of view of the service consumer (SCA reference and SCA import) and the service provider (SCA interface, SCA implementation).

(1) The PAT primitive from Figure 4 does not have a direct BPEL realization; typically, BPEL engine vendors add proprietary support for it. Furthermore, additional standardization work is underway; for example, the BPEL for Java (BPEL4J) specification introduces *ACID scopes* [2]. The exact semantics are BPEL engine-specific. For example, during a rollback an engine may let the entire process fail, request resolution by a human operator, or retry one or more activities at a later point in time (potentially with a different transactional scope). While this is engine-specific behavior outside of the scope of the BPEL specification, the process modeler must be aware of it when selecting between PAT-J and PAT-N. (2) CT-SNT as a synchronous invocation not propagating the transactional context maps to SOAP/HTTP or IIOP as transport protocol. CT-ST maps to SOAP/HTTP with WS-AtomicTransaction support or to IIOP. CT-AS can be implemented with JMS; however, no standardized WSDL bindings exist at present. CT also determines the SCA qualifiers on reference, import, and interface level, e.g., `SuspendTx` and `JoinTx`. (3) ST can be mapped to the SCA qualifier `Transaction` on component implementation level.

Table 1 maps the three conceptual patterns from Section 4.1 to CT and ST primitives and corresponding SCA qualifiers. At the time of writing, these qualifiers resided in a non-standard namespace [7], not yet in one of the emerging SCA standards [9]. The full mapping reference can be provided.

Table 1. Mapping of conceptual patterns to primitives and SCA qualifiers

Primitive / Qualifiers / Patterns	**CT** **SCA reference** (BPEL process as component invoking others)	**CT** **SCA import** (reference to external service)	**CT** **SCA interface** (service provider component)	**ST** **SCA implementation** (service provider component)

TRANSACTION ISLANDS	CT-SNT
	`DeliverAsyncAt=n/a`
	`SuspendTx=true`
		CT-SNT
		`JoinTx`
		`=false`
			CT-SNT
			`JoinTx`
			`=false`
				ST-N (or ST-J)
				`Transaction`
				`=local|global|any`

TRANSACTION BRIDGE	CT-ST
	`DeliverAsyncAt=n/a`
	`SuspendTx=false`
		CT-ST
		`JoinTx`
		`=true`
			CT-ST
			`JoinTx`
			`=true`
				ST-J
				`Transaction`
				`=global`

STRATIFIED STILTS	CT-AS
	`DeliverAsyncAt`
	`=commit`
	`SuspendTx=false`
		CT-AS
		`JoinTx`
		`=n/a`
			CT-AS
			`JoinTx`
			`=n/a`
				ST-J
				`Transaction`
				`=global`

Mapping to IBM WebSphere Process Server (WPS). WPS [7] provides a BPEL engine, which exposes processes and services as SCA components; in WPS, a BPEL-based SCL connects to the underlying architectural layers via SCA. The SCA qualifiers from Table 1 govern the transactional context propagation and behavior. Furthermore, PAT translates into a proprietary invoke activity configuration attribute called `transactionalBehavior` which can be set to `requiresOwn` (PAT-N) and `participates` (PAT-J). Two additional vendor-specific values exist, which we did not model as primitives, `commitBefore` and `commitAfter` [7]. We implemented this PAT mapping in a decision injection tool prototype. The tool reads the conceptual pattern selection decision in and configures the WPS process model accordingly.

5 Related Work

Transactional workflows and business-level compensation have been studied extensively. However, existing work primarily focuses on advancing transaction middleware, runtime protocol, and programming model design. Methodological and modeling aspects for engineering transactional workflows from business requirements to conceptual design to low-level implementation details, however, are covered only insufficiently. SOA-specific challenges such as logical layering (e.g., SCL) and loose coupling are not addressed in detail. Reusable decision models or pattern catalogs do not exist.

Papazoglou and Kratz [10] propose a design approach for business transactions based on standard business functions such as payment and delivery in supply chains. Our approaches are complementary as they focus on different design decision points.

Witthawaskul and Johnson [16] use unit-of-work modeling to express transactional primitives in a Model-Driven Architecture (MDA) context; they provide sample transformers to Hibernate and J2EE (but not SOA). Our PAT and ST primitives are inspired by their platform-independent transactionAttribute (UnitOfWork stereotype).

The WS-BPEL specification [14] defines operational semantics for executable business processes, touching upon well-known transactional behavior without going into details. For instance, it provides the concept of isolated scopes in order to support exclusive access to particular resources. However, the BPEL specification does not define which coordination protocols and service component models should be used in order to comply with the specification; this is left to BPEL engine implementations.

SOA patterns have begun to emerge over recent years. For example, Zdun and Dustar define a pattern language for process-driven SOA [18]. In enterprise application architecture literature, we find a service layer pattern and general coverage of transaction management issues, but no coverage of workflow applications [3]. Hohpe and Woolf introduce a PROCESS MANAGER mainly concerned with message routing; their TRANSACTIONAL CLIENT allows sharing a transaction context over a message queue, but does not cover forces and consequences in process-enabled SOA [5]. The Patterns for e-business initiative [6] provides top-down design guidance, but does not cover transaction management details of the EXPOSED PROCESS MANAGER. There are workflow patterns [13], transactional workflow patterns [1], and service integration patterns [11], which focus on control flow and interaction structure, but do not address system transaction or business compensation design. These patterns also do not cover SOA implementation technology details such as WSDL transport bindings or BPEL and SCA deployment settings. Even if the existing patterns do not cover transaction management design aspects in detail, our decision and pattern-centric method leverages the pattern vocabulary and given design advice as background information.

6 Summary and Outlook

In this paper, we introduced a new analysis and design method leveraging architectural decision models and patterns in support of the full lifecycle of designing transactional workflows, a particularly challenging problem in the construction of process-enabled SOA. We motivated the need for such an approach by (a) identifying recurring, reusable architectural decisions. We then (b) defined three conceptual patterns, TRANSACTION ISLANDS, TRANSACTION BRIDGE, and STRATIFIED STILTS, consisting of platform-independent primitives modeling system transactionality on (1) process activity, (2) communications infrastructure, and (3) service provider level. We (c) defined and implemented a mapping from the conceptual primitives to known technical uses in BPEL and SCA and one particular BPEL/SCA engine. Such a full-lifecycle analysis and design method allows sharing conceptual architectural knowledge across technology and platform boundaries, but also takes platform-specific aspects into account. This is required because legacy systems limitations constrain the decision making in practice, for example the transaction boundaries of existing software assets and commercial packages implementing parts of the business process.

Future work includes documenting more variations and pattern selection guidance for our three patterns. The three primitives can be mapped to more runtime platforms such as the Spring framework. To extend the method, architectural patterns for other recurring decisions, for example business-level compensation, should be documented. Finally, we plan to investigate whether our design-time patterns can be represented as runtime policies in emerging SOA runtimes, for example future versions of SCA.

References

[1] Bhiri, S., Gaaloul, K., Perrin, O., Godart, C.: Overview of Transactional Patterns: Combining Workflow Flexibility and Transactional Reliability for Composite Web Services. In: van der Aalst, W.M.P., Benatallah, B., Casati, F., Curbera, F. (eds.) BPM 2005. LNCS, vol. 3649, Springer, Heidelberg (2005)
[2] BPELJ: BPEL for Java, ftp://www.software.ibm.com/software/developer/library/ws-bpelj.pdf
[3] Fowler, M.: Patterns of Enterprise Application Architecture. Addison Wesley, Reading (2003)
[4] Gray, J., Reuter, A.: Transaction Processing: Concepts and Techniques. Morgan Kaufman Publishers, San Francisco (1993)
[5] Hohpe, G., Woolf, B.: Enterprise Integration Patterns. Addison Wesley, Reading (2004)
[6] IBM Patterns for e-business: Exposed Serial Process application pattern, http://www.ibm.com/developerworks/patterns/b2bi/at8-runtime.html#soa
[7] IBM WebSphere Business Modeler: Integration Developer, Process Server, http://www.ibm.com/developerworks/websphere/zones/businessintegration
[8] Leymann, F., Roller, D.: Production Workflow. Prentice Hall, Upper Saddle River (2000)
[9] Open Service Oriented Architecture, http://www.osoa.org/display/Main/Home
[10] Papazoglou, M., Kratz, B.: A Business-aware Web Services Transaction Model. In: Dan, A., Lamersdorf, W. (eds.) ICSOC 2006. LNCS, vol. 4294, Springer, Heidelberg (2006)
[11] Service Integration Patterns, http://sky.fit.qut.edu.au/~dumas/ServiceInteractionPatterns

[12] SOAP 1.1, http://www.w3.org/TR/2000/NOTE-SOAP-20000508

[13] v.d. Aalst, W.M.P., ter Hofstede, A.: Workflow Patterns, www.workflowpatterns.com

[14] Web Services Business Process Execution Language (BPEL), http://www.oasis-open.org/committees/tc_home.php?wg_abbrev=wsbpel

[15] Web Services Description Language (WSDL) 1.1, http://www.w3.org/TR/2001/NOTE-wsdl-20010315

[16] Witthawaskul, W., Johnson, R.: Transaction Support Using Unit of Work Modeling in the Context of MDA. In: Proc. of EDOC 2005, IEEE Press, Los Alamitos (2005)

[17] WS-AtomicTransaction: WS-Business Activity Framework, WS-Coordination, http://www.ibm.com/developerworks/library/specification/ws-tx

[18] Zdun, U., Dustdar, S.: Model-Driven and Pattern-Based Integration of Process-Driven SOA Models, http://drops.dagstuhl.de/opus/volltexte/2006/820

[19] Zimmermann, O., Doubrovski, V., Grundler, J., Hogg, K.: Service-Oriented Architecture and Business Process Choreography in an Order Management Scenario. In: OOPSLA 2005 Conference Companion, ACM Press, New York (2005)

[20] Zimmermann, O., Gschwind, T., Küster, J., Leymann, F., Schuster, N.: Reusable Architectural Decision Models for Enterprise Application Development. In: Overhage, S., Szyperski, C. (eds.) Proc. of QoSA 2007. LNCS, Springer, Heidelberg (2007)

Bite: Workflow Composition for the Web

Francisco Curbera, Matthew Duftler, Rania Khalaf, and Douglas Lovell

IBM T.J. Watson Research Center, Hawthorne, NY 10532, USA
{curbera, duftler, rkhalaf, dclo}@us.ibm.com

Abstract. Service composition is core to service oriented architectures. In the Web, mainstream composition is practiced in client-side or server-side mashups, such as providing visual widgets on top of Google Maps results. This paper presents an explicit, workflow based composition model for Web applications called Bite. In contrast with prior attempts to bring workflow capabilities to the Web environment, Bite can deal with data integration as well as interactive, asynchronous workflows with multi-party interactions, and is architected to support protocols currently in use by Web applications. The Bite development model is designed for simplicity and short development cycle by taking a scripting approach to workflow development.

1 Introduction

It is probably fair to say that service oriented architectures [1] deliver two main values: extended interoperability (runtime as well as tools) and service composition. It is hard to argue at this point with the success of the SOC approach, as its wide adoption by enterprises and public organizations demonstrates.

In the last few years, however, questions have been raised from Web-centric developers about the complexity and overhead of the SOA and Web services models [2]. Interoperability, it is argued, was delivered by the Web years ago and at a much lower overhead to both runtime systems and developers. While failing to address the need for end-to-end quality of service and tools in enterprise settings, this argument is certainly appropriate in the context in which it is made: Web application development. This paper is not concerned with this debate, but with the related question of how to bring composition capabilities like those at the heart of SOA to a Web-centric environment.

Composition is of course not new to the Web. The resource oriented architecture of the Web has favored data-centric composition models such as those underlying most "mashups." Mashups [3] can be supported at both the client and the server sides, but in either case the focus is consistently on data aggregation. In contrast, SOA composition focuses on behavioral aggregation of services. This paper presents an approach to deliver composition capabilities in a resource-centric environment, such that data and behavioral compositions are seamlessly supported by a common workflow oriented model.

The approach taken is to adapt well known workflow techniques to the resource-centric model, and to extend it beyond simple resource interactions

B. Krämer, K.-J. Lin, and P. Narasimhan (Eds.): ICSOC 2007, LNCS 4749, pp. 94–106, 2007.

to cover fully asynchronous, interactive processes. However, since our goal is to deliver native Web workflow composition, matching the interaction and modeling principles of the Web is not enough. This research also paid special attention to lowering the development overhead of existing workflow models in order to address the short-cycle, highly iterative development model prevalent in the Web.

The result of this work is "Bite," a minimalist choreography language and runtime built to support the Web. Bite offers a workflow based development model for server-side scripting of all kinds of applications that interact with browser clients, e-mail clients, REST resources, remote functions available through URL encoded RPC, JSON-RPC, and local functions available through Java or JavaScript method invocations. Bite supports low overhead development by enabling a script oriented approach in which developers can choose what advanced capabilities to use according to the problem requirements. Variable and interface typing are not required, but are supported. Likewise, simple data flows can be created with the use of just a few constructs of the language, which is also able to support powerful long-running asynchronous processes including conditional and parallel processing.

A significant base of internet applications accessible through HTTP interfaces is currently available from Web sites such as Google, Yahoo, EBay, PayPal Amazon and many others, demonstrating a significant body of practice and commerce built around straightforward Web protocols. Bite provides a simple to use, solid composition model to leverage this growing trend.

The rest of this paper is organized as follows. Section 2 reviews prior work in the area. Section 3 presents an overview of the Bite language and its design principles. Section 4 explains how the Bite model addresses two major forms of Web composition, data and interactive flows. In Section 5 a sample Bite process is discussed in detail, and in Section 6 we discuss the implementation of the Bite runtime. Finally we present the conclusions of this work and new research directions in Section 7.

2 Related Work

The most relevant source of related work refers to Web-based workflows. We use the BPEL language [4] as our reference for service oriented process models. For a full survey of other approaches in Web services composition, see [5]. In this section, we focus on workflows that operate using the Web in a first class manner. Prior research can be summarized in the five categories below.

- **State machine based workflow.** A finite state machine is used in [6] to provide REST-centric, workflows that interact with a browser. The goal is to support single browser applications in which clicking on a link or posting a form results in the state machine transitioning to a new state.
- **Continuations.** A continuation [7] is a low-level programming primitive that stores execution context at a pre-determined location in the code, allowing different mechanisms to restore it later. A continuation point is associated with a wait state in the "flow" and with an event (such as an

incoming HTTP request) that will trigger restoration of context and allow execution to continue. Continuations are available in several languages such as Ruby[8] and Scheme, and externally supported for others such as Cocoon's FlowScript API [9] or JavaFlow[10]. Continuations support "flow-like" programming in traditional Web programming languages. One can send a user a form that contains a unique identifier of the continuation while maintaining a "continuations repository" [11,12]. Once the user fills out the form, the application knows exactly which continuation to go to. Anton van Straaten [13] advocates making the continuation itself a REST resource, giving each a URI.

- **Web Services Derivations.** In [14], the authors introduce a BPEL-like workflow for browser interaction in a REST-centric manner. Factories and process entry points are associated with externally visible URIs, and specialized semantics are provided for certain HTTP operations. It provides a single client model. Other proposed workflow models that use Web-centric interactions, but extend the HTTP verbs with additional commands, include SWAP, ASAP and Wf-XML.
- **Meta-data driven.** Another approach is to overlay meta-data on top of a service's implementation, such that the metadata describes the workflow semantics and directs the interaction with a browser. The Web Calculus [15] defines a directed graph where the nodes are document nodes and the edges may have closures. A client interacts with the service described by such a graph using a combination of graph-traversal and closure invocations.
- **Data Flows.** Examples of pure data flow approaches include Yahoo Pipes [16] and XProc [17]. However, they focus on manipulating data in response to a single incoming request. They are not geared to aggregating user interactions.

Bite shares certain aspects of its interaction model with [14], but extends an array of capabilities that make it particularly well adapted to the Web interaction model (including multi-protocol support) and different types of workflows (multi-party asynchronous flows and also data flows). The next Section describes the Bite approach in detail.

3 The Design of a Web-Centric Flow Language

Designing a process language for a REST oriented environment like the Web requires adapting the two-level programming model underlying workflow development to the resource-centric view. In addition, any programming model for Web applications needs to support the short-cycle, highly iterative development practice enabled by such systems as PHP and Ruby. In this paper we investigate the adaptation of BPEL's composition model to satisfy these two requirements. The goal is to leverage the accumulated experience of process-centric composition in SOA environments to deliver process composition in a Web environment.

We consequently need to address two major concerns: how a process executes within a REST environment, and how to support the Web's fast paced, lightweight development model. Before explaining how this is done, we present a brief overview of the Bite language.

3.1 Bite Language Summary

As with most workflow languages, Bite contains two main constructs: activities and links. Activities define units of work and links define dependencies between activities. As in BPEL, activities have a "joinCondition" based on the status of the incoming links and links have a "transitionCondition." The execution semantics of links and activities is the same as <flow> in BPEL with "suppressJoinFailure" set to "yes," which itself is derived from FDL [18].

The language comes with a predefined set of basic constructs, shown in Table 1. The small set of built–in activities was chosen to embody basic actions in Web workflow, as described in the Notes column. However, additional activity types can easily be added by the user/developer community: the activity set is extensible as explained in section 3.2. The rest of this paper will elaborate on the different aspects of these constructs, with examples in Section 5.

Table 1. Overview of Bite Constructs

Activities	Notes
<receive>, <reply>,<receive-reply>	Receiving and replying to messages. Optional relative url attribute may be used to match incoming message. <receive-reply> shorthand for the two activities linked together, for the common pattern of callers just retrieving data
<invoke>	Call to an external party. Mandatory "invocationTarget" attribute, whose value is an expression, inlines service location and must resolve to a URI. Optional content-type and httpMethod attributes.
<local>	Call local code, such a static Java method or a script.
<wait>, <empty>, <terminate>	Utility activities: wait for fixed time, no–op, terminate the process instance.
<assign>	Basic data manipulation.
<pick>	External choice: contains an ordered list of external request and/or timer "choice" elements.
<while>	Loop as long as a condition is true.
Other Constructs	**Notes**
<source>	Control link. Also behaves as a data link if the "input" attribute is set to "yes."
<variable>	Optional variable declaration. May contain a "content-type" attribute, among others.

3.2 Deep Integration with the Web

Processes as active resources. In a SOA-centric model, a deployed business process interacts with its environment by invoking external services and by offering itself to requesters as a service over one or more service endpoints [4]. Likewise, in a REST oriented environment a process should interact with other entities as resources, and be itself exposed as a resource.

There is a deep similarity between the BPEL implicit factory model (in which a startable receive generates a new process instance for an incoming message), and the ATOM protocol by which a POST request creates items in an ATOM collection [19]. We thus model a deployed process as a logical collection whose members are process instances. The process itself is exposed as a collection resource whose URL address corresponds to the startable receive of the process (see [4]). An HTTP POST against the process URL results in the creation of a new logical "item"– a process instance in the process collection. Following [19], a new URL is assigned to the newly created instance (resource), and returned in the HTTP Location header.

REST interactions on the new process instance URL have a specific meaning, providing process management calls not available to regular clients. GET and DELETE verbs respectively retrieve a representation of the process's state and terminate the running instance. A PUT request is not defined in Bite. Bite process instances are "active" resources with lifecycle and termination controlled by the internal logic of the process execution.

To support interaction between external requesters, a process instance exposes one or more URLs as logical addresses of the instance's nested resources. POST requests directed to these URLs are dispatched to the individual <receive> activities in the process model using the relative URLs defined in the activities' url attribute.

In BPEL, the partner link construct represents external partners (applications or people, see [20]). Bite represents external partners using their resource identifiers. Requests initiated by the process create HTTP requests (usually but not strictly GET or POST) directed at one of these external resources.

One note of caution is in order. The operation of the Web relies on more than REST interactions. Other protocols, in particular e-mail exchanges, are fundamental components of most complex Web interactions. For that reason, any workflow language directed at Web applications must be able to support alternative interaction protocols, and e-mail in particular. Bite's <invoke> activity, described in Section 3.1, enables processes to send generic invocations in different protocols identified by the scheme of the invocation target URI: "mailto:" sends an e-mail over SMTP and "http:" sends an HTTP request.

Dynamic data types. One characteristic of web interactions is the runtime discovery of request metadata, of which content-type [21] is particularly important. HTTP requests and responses carry content-type information used by the requestor's application to interpret the response. Bite supports dynamic content-type for incoming messages as well as optional statically defined content-type for outgoing requests (<invoke>).

Bite variables are associated with a content-type. The content-type of a variable used to save an incoming request is automatically set to the content type of the incoming message. As the variable gets used by the process, the content type is carried with the data. It is set in the corresponding HTTP header when the data is sent out. The result is that a flow may be designed to operate with different incoming content-types (such as XML and JSON), as long as no dependency on the specific data format is built into the code.

Content type can be statically set in the process definition for both variables (if the variable is declared) and <invoke> activities. An error is generated when a content-type mismatch is detected between data copied into a variable and a static content-type declaration.

Extensible activity set. Bite's activity set is extensible, enabling communities of users to define domain specific activities in addition to Bite's built–in ones. Such new activities may capture well known actions such as data sort, append, etc. Bite provides for extensions by a tag library model similar to that of Java Server Pages ([22]). To define a new activity, developers register an XML parsing class and associate it with an execution class in the tag library registry. The parsing class will read the information provided in the activity definition within a process model and make it available to the execution class. At runtime, the Bite engine invokes the execution class providing access to the activity definition. The execution class gets its input from the process and writes its output back to the process; it is not given read or write access to any other part of the process state.

3.3 Lightweight Process Model

The workflow development model provides significant advantages over traditional procedural and object oriented implementation languages. Foremost is its ability to capture the end-to-end business logic of an application in a single definition. With long-running, asynchronous flows, traditional development models (such as servlets) necessarily fracture the application logic into multiple separate code artifacts. The result is the obfuscation of the coordination mechanisms by programming constructs such as hash tables, state machines, etc.

In order to deliver this value to Web developers it is crucial to offer a radically simplified workflow model and development process. In this section we examine how these two aspects are addressed by the Bite language.

Flat graph model. Much of the barrier to entry for BPEL is in its combination of flat and structured programming models. Bite's process model is a graph model with no nesting (except for loops), but with rich execution semantics similar to BPEL activities within a BPEL flow activity. Because of the lack of scope nesting, exception handling in Bite is fundamentally different from BPEL's [23]. Exceptions may be handled at the activity level through exception-labeled outgoing links as in [18]. Otherwise, they may be handled at the process level with an exception handler block.

Two of BPEL's structured activities find their way into Bite: <while> and <pick>. Structured iteration loops (<while>) significantly simplify the definition of correct iterative flows (as opposed to unstructured loops built using backward links). An example is shown in section 5.

The <pick> activity allows the flow to react to an exclusive choice from a set of different possible external inputs. External choice is a required feature [24] of interactive processes. Bite adapts the pick construct to the "flat graph" model by turning it into a flat activity whose output variable contains: which choice was taken (using an index or the choice's name if provided), and the received message data. The process may use the variable like any other, especially in link transition conditions to go down a different branch based on the selected choice.

Workflow scripting. Most of today's workflow languages are strongly typed with respect to both data and behavior (interfaces). There is a clear rationale for strongly typed languages in general (ability to detect errors, overall consistency, etc.) and workflows in particular. From the practice of Web application development, however, we have learned that the overhead imposed by typing and other forms of required artifacts external to the workflow logic itself creates a barrier of entry that excludes most Web developers. (See [2] for a good discussion on the topic.)

With this consideration in mind, Bite takes a "scripting" approach to workflow definition. By this we specifically mean:

1. The principle of "use implies definition:" Variables can be directly used without requiring prior declaration or explicit typing. This is similar to the use of variable in languages like JavaScript. However, a developer may choose to explicitly define and type a variable using the optional <variable> element.
2. The principle of "convention over configuration." Bite conventions dictate that the output of an activity is contained within an implicitly defined variable with the same name as the activity. Additionally, a control link may also specify that the output data of its source activity be used as part of the input of its target activity.
3. Radical reduction of extraneous constructs while eliminating levels of indirection. Invocation targets on invoke activities are encoded as literal URLs or as data variables (see section 5) No typing of the resource being accessed is required (i.e.: message types). Contrast this with the BPEL model, where an invocation must reference a partner link construct that is in turn typed by a predefined partner link type, which in turn depends on WSDL port types and XML Schema definitions, and which is finally bound to physical service endpoint by an implementation dependent mechanism that is out of the scope of the BPEL language.

Flexible configurability. Bite processes provide configurability by enabling values of variables to be set outside of the workflow definition. This is similar to "properties" in Java. This capability may be used for actions such as: late binding of partner URLs, or turning paths of a process on or off by setting values of variables used on transition conditions or the condition of a while loop.

4 Web Workflow Scenarios

We focus on two scenarios for which Web workflow provides significant value added— data-centric flows and interactive flows.

4.1 Web Data Flows

The resource-centric nature of many Web applications makes data integration common for simple Web integration scenarios. The approach is well illustrated by the Yahoo Pipes tool [16], and its model is also captured by the XProc language [17]. The common pattern is a set of processing steps connected by explicitly stated data dependencies. Execution of a step takes place as soon as all required inputs are available.

This model is natively supported in Bite, taking advantage of the fact that a data dependency always implies a (direct or indirect) control dependency. The execution semantics of Bite imply that an activity targeted by a link, defined using <source> in Bite, waits for completion of the link's source before proceeding. An activity may contain <input value="..."> subelements that explicitly provide it with data. The value is an expression that of course may refer to any of the process's variables. The <source> element provides an "input" attribute that enables one to treat it as a combined control link and <input>. The source's "name" attribute refers to the link's source activity. If "input" is set to "yes," it indicates that the output of the source activity (contained in an implicit variable with the same name, see Section 3.3) is treated as one of the inputs of the target activity. Therefore, an activity's input data set consists of the ordered list of <source input="yes"> and <input> elements. The following code snippet shows a data flow connection between two activities, as do lines 2-9 of the example in section 5.

```
<invoke name="getBBCTopStories"
   invocationTarget="'http://rss.news.yahoo.com/rss/topstories'"/>
<local name="sort" invocationTarget="'java:util.Sort'" operation="sort">
   <source name="getBBCTopStories" input="yes"/>
</local>
```

Data flow composition is thus a particularly simple application of Bite's general workflow model. Data flows are typically executed synchronously in response to a single external request for data retrieval (such as through a GET request), and they have very limited error handling capabilities (see [17]).

The main value of encoding a data flow as a workflow lies in explicitly exposing data dependencies. Bite's support for more complete workflow execution semantics (including error handling and asynchronous execution) allows seamless extension of data flow logic into more functional workflows.

4.2 Interactive Flows

Most Web applications are highly interactive. Beyond delivering information to end users, they often receive customer data through HTML forms and contact customers back via e-mail. They often involve several parties and potentially back–end applications. Many typical Web transactions are potentially long running (resolved in the course of days or weeks) and asynchronous, involving a combination of synchronous HTTP interactions and asynchronous e-mail messages.

Bite's model is particularly well suited to support these types of applications. Remaining fundamentally Web centered, both in protocols and interactions models, it has significant advantages over other development approaches:(1) the application logic is defined in a single file where the interaction with all the parties and their relationships are explicitly encoded; (2) the workflow model natively supports asynchronous execution, as opposed to object or procedural models; (3) multi-protocol capabilities support seamless integration of traditional Web interaction models, e-mail, and back-end interactions. In addition, Bite supports multi-party interactions natively since it supports a Web-centric version of BPEL's partner link model.

5 Example Bite Workflow: Special Order

The following example illustrates Bite's salient features. It demonstrates a mix of automatic and human interaction in a scenario involving multiple parties and agents. A customer requests a special order item at a high–end store as shown in Figure 1. The employee submits the order to the process (order) and gets back a URL of where to go to confirm receipt once the order arrives in the store. The process sends the order to an automated authorization service (autoApprove). If it is not approved, it goes to a manager via e-mail (rqstApproval) for a deeper evaluation. The manager gets a link in the e–mail notifying her of the order and approves or rejects the order (authorize). If the manager does not approve, the process ends. If either the service or the manager had approved the order, the process sends an e-mail to the designer to create the item (makeItem). Then, a loop is entered that waits until the employee confirms receipt of the item. In the pick (pick1), the employee has 7 days (reminder) to confirm (confirmation) after which he gets an e–mail reminder (remind) to find out why the item is delayed. If he confirms, he gets a reply acknowledging that (confirm). Once the process is notified that the item is in store, the customer is notified via e-mail (itemArrived).

We now look at the complete Bite process, shown below, and containing nearly all the language elements. Activity names match the labels in the figure, so we focus on highlighting interesting aspects of the script. Consider the receive-reply (lines 2–6). It receives the order from the client, at which time a process instance is created and the value of ProcessId is set, and replies with the value inlined in "input." ProcessId is a reserved variable available to every Bite process instance containing the id of that instance. The full URL is also available in the reserved Location variable. The reply contains a URL that is routable back exactly to this process instance: notice the "ProcessId."

The activity "autoApprove" (line 7–9) shows an example of a service invocation as well as a control link that transmits data. The "source" element has "input" set to yes, meaning that the message sent to the service is the message received from "order." The next invoke, "rqstApproval" (line 10–16) shows an e–mail style invoke. Notice the "mailto" scheme in the URL. The "invocationTarget" attribute takes an expression so one can build the value directly from the received message in "order." Recall that the default output variable of an activity has the same name as the activity. Therefore, the order, containing the manager's e–mail, is in the variable "order." Notice the URL used for the manager to send back a response: it will be received by "authorize" (line 17–20).

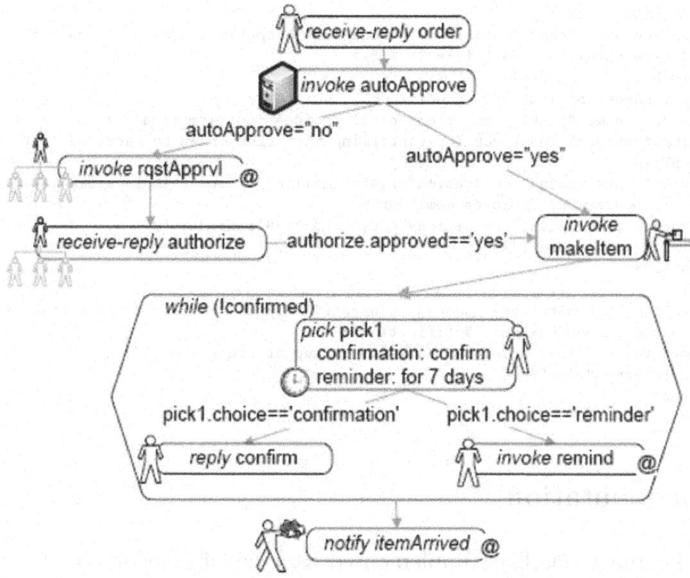

Fig. 1. Sample Bite process for a special order. Icons by activities represent the person or service the activity interacts with.

From here, an interesting part is the pick activity (line 29–32). It has a message–based choice (line 30) that waits for the employee to confirm an alarm (line 31). Notice how one uses the selected choice in the transition condition of the links entering "confirm" (line 34) and "remind" (line 39).

```
1.  <process name="orderItemPlus">
2.    <receive-reply name="order" url="/initiateCase">
3.      <input value=
4.       "'When the item arrives, confirm here: http://localhost:8080/demo/order/'
5.        + ProcessId + '/confirm'"/>
6.    </receive-reply>
7.    <invoke name="autoApprove" invocationTarget="'http://example.com/orderAuthorization">
8.      <source name="order" input="yes"/>
9.    </invoke>
10.   <invoke name="rqstApproval" invocationTarget=
11.          "'mailto:'+ order.managerEmail[0]" operation="Manager Approval">
12.      <source name="autoApprove" condition="autoApprove=='no'"/>
13.      <input value=
14.      "'Please go here to approve an order: http://localhost:8080/demo/approvalform/'
15.        + ProcessId"/>
16.   </invoke>
17.   <receive-reply name="authorize" url="/approvalResponse">
18.     <input value="'Thank you for responding.'"/>
19.     <source name="rqstApproval"/>
20.    </receive-reply>
21.   <invoke name="makeItem"  invocationTarget="'mailto:' + order.designerEmail[0]"
22.                            operation="Manufacturer Request">
23.     <source name="authorize" condition="authorize.approved[0]=='yes'"/>
24.     <source name="autoApprove" condition="autoApprove=='yes'"/>
25.     <input value="order"/>
26.   </invoke>
27.   <while name="loop" condition="!confirmed">
28.     <source name="makeItem"/>
```

```
   <pick name="pick1">
     <choice name="confirmation" url="/confirm" outputVariable="confirmed"/>
     <choice name="reminder" for="'P7D'"/>
   </pick>
   <reply name="confirm" url="/confirm">
     <source name="pick1" condition="pick1.choice=='confirmation'"/>
     <input value="'Thank you for confirming that this order has arrived.'"/>
   </reply>
   <invoke name="remind" invocationTarget="'mailto:' + order.employeeEmail[0]"
           operation="Employee Reminder">
     <source name="pick1" condition="pick1.choice=='reminder'"/>
     <input value="order"/>
   </invoke>
 </while>
 <invoke name="itemArrived" invocationTarget="'mailto:' + order.customerEmail[0]"
         operation="Customer Notification">
   <input value="'Your order is ready for pickup at the store.'"/>
   <source name="loop"/>
 </invoke>
</process>
```

6 Implementation

The Bite language has been implemented as a set of embeddable Java components. A "BiteManager" (referred to simply as manager) implements the language's core execution semantics. A servlet is used to service incoming HTTP requests, forwarding them to the manager. This servlet has been tested through deployment into Jetty installations.

We now briefly describe the runtime operation of the Bite engine. Incoming requests to URLs matching the <receive> activities in the process model are mapped to execution events. The target process instance is identified from the request's URL, and its instance data is retrieved from a map of process context data. The manager uses a thread pool to serve requests to multiple concurrent process instances. The hand-over of events between worker threads in the thread pool and the servlet thread associated to the incoming request is supported using event queues stored as part of the instance data. In addition to <receive>, wait, pick, and invoke also wait for events coming from the manager notifying them, respectively, of when the alarm has gone off, a message or alarm matching a 'choice' has occured, or the response to the invocation has arrived. A worker thread navigates a process instance until all paths block, or the process completes. A path blocks when a receive, invoke, pick, or wait activity is encountered and there is no suitable event queued that can matches the activity. Such an activity is then added to a list of waiting activities for new events.

7 Conclusion and Future Work

This paper has presented the Bite Web–centric flow composition model through a discussion of its main design points and an overview of the language and implementation. Devlivering an composition mechanism for the development of Web applications and leveraging their workflow model, Bite supports explicit encoding of compositional logic in a single programming artifact.

The Bite model is aligned with the resource-centric view of the Web, but is not limited to REST interactions alone, in line with current practice in the Web. Bite supports sophisticated asynchronous, multi-part workflows as well as simple data composition ones. In Bite, workflows are developed with minimal up-front overhead, aligning the development model with fast paced development practices of Web scripting languages. The runtime has been developed in Java and tested on the Jetty servlet engine, but is designed as an embeddable component that can be used in other runtimes.

To fully exploit the potential of Web–centric compositions, we are starting new work in several areas. We are exploring a dedicated scripting syntax, as an alternative to Bite's current use of XML. While XML ensures wide familiarity among developers, a scripting alternative can improve readability and usability. We are also planning to identify and support well known interaction patterns, such as the e-mail and form interaction shown in Section 5, using Bite's tag library mechanism. We are considering a <choice-reply> under <pick> to mirror the <receive-reply> shortcut, and investigating whether a simplified form of BPEL correlation would be a useful addition. The difficulty there is in simplifying the definition of a correlation set especially for the case of untyped messages. Finally we are extending our effort to provide increased transparency and control with respect to the use of interaction protocols by exposing HTTP and e-mail artifacts such as protocol headers directly in the flow language.

Since the submission for publication, a later version of the Bite language and runtime, under the title "the Project Zero assembly flow language," has become publicly available [25].

Acknowledgement. The authors would like to thank Marc-Thomas Schmidt for his comments and advice regarding the general design of the Bite language and Xin Sheng Mao for his input on the use of Bite for data flows.

References

1. Weerawarana, S., Curbera, F., Leymann, F., Storey, T., Ferguson, D.: Web Services Platform Architecture: SOAP, WSDL, WS-Policy, WS-Addressing, WS-BPEL, WS-Reliable Messaging, and More. Prentice-Hall, Englewood Cliffs (2005)
2. Bosworth, A.: ICSOC 2004 keynote talk. Adam Bosworth's Weblog (2004), http://www.adambosworth.net/archives/000031.html
3. Anonymous: ProgrammableWeb.com (2007), http://www.programmableweb.com/
4. OASIS: Web Services Business Process Execution Language Version 2.0. (2007), http://docs.oasis-open.org/wsbpel/2.0/wsbpel-v2.0.html
5. Dustdar, S., Schreiner, W.: A survey on web services composition. Int. J. Web and Grid Services 1(1) (2005)
6. Kuhlman, D.: Workflow and REST how-to. Personal Web site (2003), http://www.rexx.com/~dkuhlman/workflow_howto.html
7. Ruby, S.: Continuations-for-curmudgeons. Blog post (2005), http://www.intertwingly.net/blog/2005/04/13/Continuations-for-Curmudgeons

8. Thomas, D., Fowler, C., Hunt, A.: Programming Ruby: The Pragmatic Guide, 2nd edn. Addison-Wesley, Reading (2004)
9. Apache: Apache Cocoon, Control Flow. (2006), http://cocoon.apache.org/2.1/userdocs/flow/index.html
10. Apache Jakarta: Javaflow (2006), http://jakarta.apache.org/commons/sandbox/javaflow
11. Tate, B.: Crossing borders: Continuations, web development, and java programming (2006), http://www-128.ibm.com/developerworks/java/library/j-cb03216/?ca=dgr-jw22StatelessWeb
12. Belapurkar, A.: Use continuations to develop complex web applications. IBM developerWorks (2004), http://www-128.ibm.com/developerworks/library/j-contin.html
13. Straaten, A.V.: Continuations continued: the REST of the computation (2006), http://114.csail.mit.edu/slides/rest-slides.pdf
14. zur Muehlen, M., Nickerson, J.V., Swenson, K.D.: Developing web services choreography standards - the case of REST vs. SOAP. Decision Support Systems 37 (2004)
15. Waterken Inc.: Web-Calculus. (2005), http://www.waterken.com/dev/Web/Calculus/
16. Yahoo Inc.: Yahoo pipes (2007), http://pipes.yahoo.com
17. Walsh, N., Milowski, A.: XProc: An XML pipeline language. Working draft, W3C (2007), http://www.w3.org/TR/xproc/
18. Leymann, F., Roller, D.: Production Workflow. Prentice Hall, New York (2000)
19. Gregorio, J., de hOra, B.: The atom publishing protocol. Internet draft, IETF Network Working Group (2007), http://bitworking.org/projects/atom/draft-ietf-atompub-protocol-15.html
20. Active Endpoints, Adobe, BEA, IBM, Oracle, SAP AG: WS-BPEL extension for people (BPEL4People). IBM developerWorks (2007), http://www.ibm.com/developerworks/webservices/library/specification/ws-bpel4people/
21. Fielding, R., Gettys, J., Mogul, J., Frystyk, H., Mastinter, L., Leach, P., Berners-Lee, T.: Hypertext transfer protocol – http/1.1. Request for Comments 2616, IETF Network Working Group (1999), http://www.ietf.org/rfc/rfc2616.txt
22. Sun Microsystems: JSR-000245 JavaServer Pages^{TM} 2.1. (2004), http://jcp.org/aboutJava/ communityprocess/final/jsr245/index.html
23. Curbera, F., Khalaf, R., Leymann, F., Weerawarana, S.: Exception handling in the BPEL4WS language. In: van der Aalst, W.M.P., ter Hofstede, A.H.M., Weske, M. (eds.) BPM 2003. LNCS, vol. 2678, Springer, Heidelberg (2003)
24. Milner, R.: Communicating and Mobile Systems: the Pi-Calculus. Cambridge University Press, Cambridge (1999)
25. IBM: Project zero (2007), http://www.projectzero.org/

Stochastic Modeling of Composite Web Services for Closed-Form Analysis of Their Performance and Reliability Bottlenecks

N. Sato[1] and K.S. Trivedi[2]

[1] IBM Research
[2] Duke University

Abstract. Web services providers often commit service-level agreements (SLAs) with their customers for guaranteeing the quality of the services. These SLAs are related not just to functional attributes of the services but to performance and reliability attributes as well. When combining several services into a composite service, it is non-trivial to determine, prior to service deployment, performance and reliability values of the composite service appropriately. Moreover, once the service is deployed, it is often the case that during operation it fails to meet its SLA and needs to detect what has gone wrong (i.e., performance/reliabilty bottlenecks).

To resolve these, we develop a continuous-time Markov chain (CTMC) formulation of composite services with failures. By explicitly including failure states into the CTMC representation of a service, we can compute accurately both its performance and reliability using the single CTMC. We can also detect its performance and reliability bottlenecks by applying the formal sensitivity analysis technique. We demonstrate our approach by choosing a representative example of composite Web services and providing a set of closed-form formulas for its bottleneck detection.

1 Introduction

Composition of multiple Web services is growing in popularity as a convenient way of defining new services within a business process. By combining existing services using a high-level language such as BPEL [13], service providers can quickly develop new services. When deploying these services, service providers often commit service-level agreements (SLAs) with their customers, which include performance and dependability-related metrics. For example, the mean response time and the service reliability for each incoming request are guaranteed. Since a composite Web service may have complex application logic, it is non-trivial to check whether or not the composed service will meet its SLA. In this paper, we develop an analytical approach to determining the overall performance and reliability of composed Web services.

As an example of such a Web service, we consider a business process, called TravelAgent (Figure 1). Figure 2 shows a concrete implementation of this process in BPEL. An interesting part of this process is that it tries to make the airline reservation in a unique manner: First, it looks up two different airlines for vacancy in parallel. When they respond, it chooses one of the airlines based on some criterion such as fare, schedule, etc.

B. Krämer, K.-J. Lin, and P. Narasimhan (Eds.): ICSOC 2007, LNCS 4749, pp. 107–118, 2007.

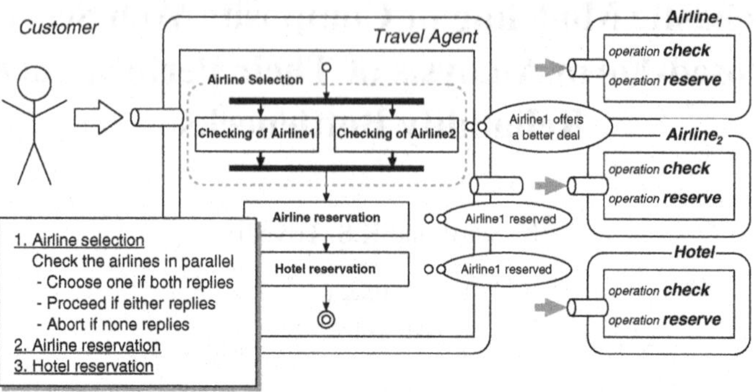

Fig. 1. TravelAgent process

Otherwise, when either of the two airlines fails to respond, it chooses the other airline. In case *both* fail to respond, then it gives up and aborts. Any other Web service may fail to respond, from which we attempt to recover by means of a restart.

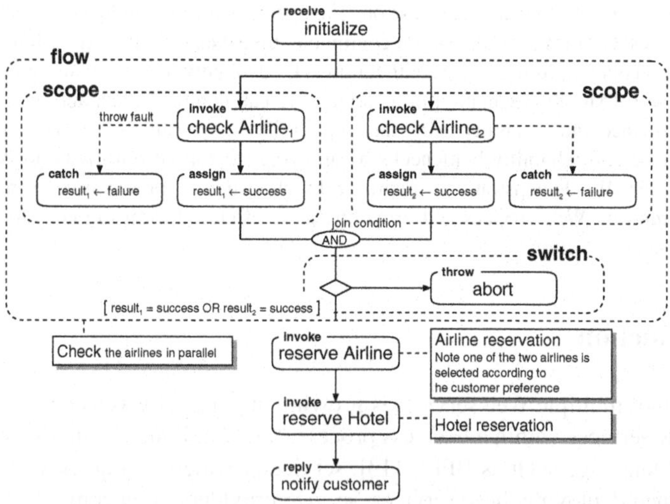

Fig. 2. TravelAgent process (BPEL)

Issues we observe here are summarized as follows: (1) Before starting the service, the provider needs to estimate what can be guaranteed to its customers. (2) During operation, it needs to keep its SLA, and in case something goes wrong and the system suffers from degradation, it needs to detect the bottleneck and resolve the problem.

To resolve these issues, we develop a set of Markov models, for *computing the performance and the reliability* of Web services and *detecting bottlenecks*. In so doing, we address the following specific challenges: (1) Web services are defined using a rich set of control constructs. These include switch, while, flow, and scope. Our model will include all the control constructs allowed in BPEL. (2) Restarts in failed activity is allowed in BPEL via fault handlers. We will include restarts in our model. (3) We will discuss parameterization based on experiments and monitoring. (4) We will primarily be concerned with bottleneck detection, based on sensitivity functions and optimization.

Our contributions are four fold: First, we provide a *continuous-time Markov chain* (CTMC) formulation of composite Web services *with failures*. Then, closed form expressions of the mean response time and the reliability of TravelAgent are derived. Thirdly, bottleneck detection using the formal sensitivity analysis is carried out. Lastly, outline of a solution in the general case is also given.

There are several research efforts related to ours. The IBM BPM engine [4] supports performance *simulation* of BPEL processes. In contrast, we take an analytic approach and we introduce failures and recoveries from failures. In addition, we also consider sensitivity analysis. Our reliability model is related to a paper by Laprie [7]. But ours is cast in the BPEL context and sensitivity analysis that we carry out is new. The paper by Sharma and Trivedi [14] is the closest to current effort. But we find closed form results and carry out formal sensitivity analysis. The computation method for the mean response and reliability we use is described in the paper by Wang [21] and in the book by Trivedi [18]. The computation of sensitivity functions is discussed in [1,8].

2 CTMC Formulation of Composite WS

We assume throughout that times to complete all individual Web services are exponentially distributed. Similarly we assume that the the overhead time to conduct a restart is also exponentially distributed. If desired, these restrictions can be removed, as presented in [19].

2.1 CTMC for a Process with Concurrency

We start with a simple case where we never encounter failures. In such a case, the BPEL process in Figure 1 can be encoded to the CTMC in Figure 3(a). The parallel invocation in Figure 1 gets translated into 3 states [9]. In the state labeled Airline selection (1,2), both activities are ongoing. After one of them finishes, only the other one is active. Finally, when both finish, we proceed to make the reservation.

We note here that the model here assumes no contention for hardware or software resources. In future, we will introduce contention for resources using a product-form queueing network [18] or a non-product-form network [2,22].

2.2 CTMC with Failures

Each execution of a BPEL process may *fail*. Thus, for example, we suppose that the invocations of the airlines may result in failures. To take account of these possibilities, we add a single failure state to the CTMC. When failure states are added to a CTMC, we need to modify the transition rates of the CTMC in the following manner. Suppose an operation q_1 takes λ^{-1} on average and it has a probability of R for successful completion (i.e., $(1 - R)$ for failure). Then, the successful transition now has a rate $\lambda \cdot R$, while the

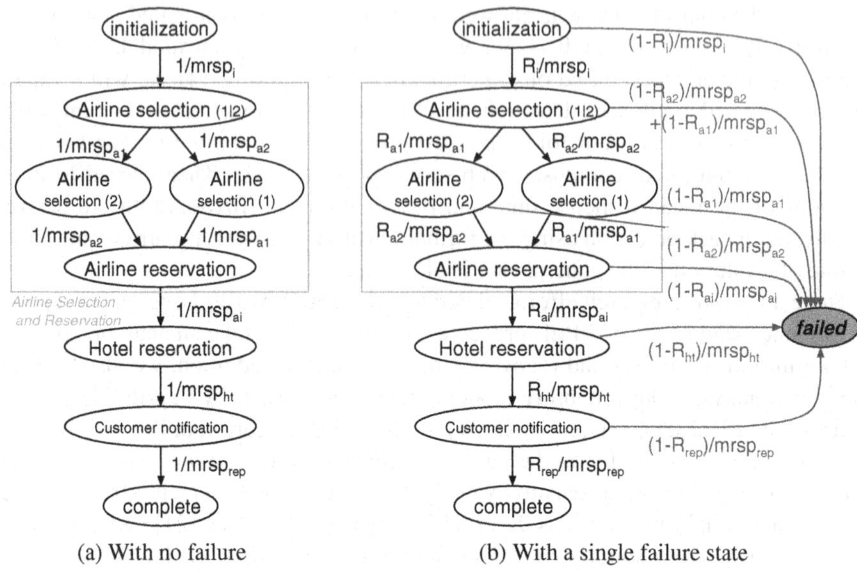

(a) With no failure (b) With a single failure state

Fig. 3. CTMCs for the TravelAgent process

other transition (to the failure state) has a rate $\lambda \cdot (1 - R)$. Figure 3(b) is the revised CTMC with failures introduced in the CTMC of Figure 3(a). Note that only if both airline invocations return successfully then we continue, otherwise we abort.

2.3 CTMC with Restarts

For high reliability, BPEL processes often specify recovery procedures, called *fault-handlers*, which are invoked for restarting failed invocations [13]. Figure 4 shows the CTMC with failures and restarts. We have assumed that restart may be successful with probability C while it fails with probability $1 - C$. We also allow for an overhead time for restart. Thus, for instance, upon the failure of the hotel invocation, a restart attempt is made with the mean overhead time of $mrsp_{ht}$ and probability of success as C_{ht}. We assume that there is no restart for the airline invocation. Further that if either one or both airlines invocation is successful, we proceed further in the flow. Upon the failure of both invocations, we abort.

2.4 Response Time and Service Reliability

Now, we are ready to compute the mean response time and the service reliability based on the CTMCs we have developed in the preceding sections. We derive closed form expressions for the mean response time and service reliability based on the CTMCs we have developed in Figure 3(a), 3(b), and 4.

Response Time. We start with the simple CTMC in Figure 3(a). In this case, the mean response time can easily be computed as follows.

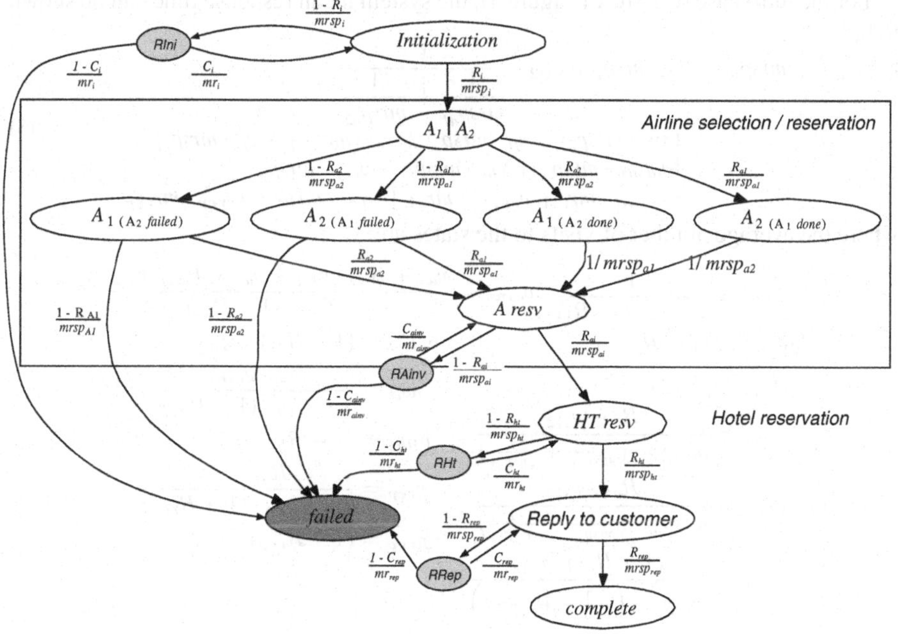

Fig. 4. CTMC with restarts

$$mrsp_{sys} = mrsp_i + \left(mrsp_{al} + mrsp_{a2} - \frac{1}{\frac{1}{mrsp_{al}} + \frac{1}{mrsp_{a2}}} \right) + mrsp_{ai} + mrsp_{ht} + mrsp_{rep} \tag{1}$$

The expression in the parentheses above is a well-known one for the parallel construct [16].

For the second case (CTMC of Figure 3(b)), the system mean response time can be shown to be:

$$\begin{aligned} mrsp_{sys} &= mrsp_i \\ &+R_i \cdot \left(\frac{1}{\left(\frac{1}{mrsp_{a1}} + \frac{1}{mrsp_{a2}} \right)} \cdot \left(1 + R_{a2} \cdot \frac{mrsp_{a1}}{mrsp_{a2}} + R_{al} \cdot \frac{mrsp_{a2}}{mrsp_{a1}} \right) \right. \\ &\left. + R_{al} \cdot R_{a2} \cdot \left(mrsp_{ai} + Rai \cdot \left(mrsp_{ht} + R_{ht} \cdot mrsp_{rep} \right) \right) \right) \end{aligned} \tag{2}$$

Note that the mean response time will reduce due to failures since some fraction of requests will not traverse the graph to completion. Also, notice that the above expression (2) reduces to the expression (1) when all reliability values are set to 1.

For the third case (CTMC of Figure 4), the system mean response time can be shown to be:

$$\begin{aligned} mrsp_{sys} = {} & v_i \cdot mrsp_i + v_{1|2} \cdot \frac{1}{\frac{1}{mrsp_{a1}} + \frac{1}{mrsp_{a2}}} \\ & + v_{a2} \cdot mrsp_{a2} + v_{f1} \cdot mrsp_{a2} + v_{a1} \cdot mrsp_{a1} + v_{f2} \cdot mrsp_{a1} \\ & + v_{ainv} \cdot mrsp_{ai} + v_{ht} \cdot mrsp_{ht} + v_{rep} \cdot mrsp_{rep} \\ & + v_{rinit} \cdot mr_i + v_{rainv} \cdot mr_{ai} + v_{rht} \cdot mr_{ht} + v_{rrep} \cdot mr_{rep} \end{aligned} \tag{3}$$

where the average number of visits to the states are:

$$v_i = \frac{1}{1 - C_i(1 - R_i)} \qquad v_{ainv} = \frac{v_{a1} + R_{a2} \cdot v_{F1} + v_{a2} + R_{a1} \cdot v_{F2}}{1 - C_{ai} \cdot (1 - R_{ai})}$$

$$v_{Rinit} = (1 - R_i) \cdot v_i \qquad v_{Rainv} = (1 - R_{ai}) \cdot v_{ainv}$$

$$v_{1|2} = R_i \cdot v_i \qquad v_{ht} = \frac{R_{ai} \cdot v_{ainv}}{1 - C_{ht} \cdot (1 - R_{ht})}$$

$$v_{a1} = \frac{R_{a2} \cdot v_{1|2}}{mrsp_{a2} \cdot (\frac{1}{mrsp_{a1}} + \frac{1}{mrsp_{a2}})} \qquad v_{Rht} = (1 - R_{ht}) \cdot v_{ht}$$

$$v_{a2} = \frac{R_{a1} \cdot v_{1|2}}{mrsp_{a1} \cdot (\frac{1}{mrsp_{a1}} + \frac{1}{mrsp_{a2}})} \qquad v_{rep} = \frac{R_{ht} \cdot v_{ht}}{1 - C_{rep} \cdot (1 - R_{rep})}$$

$$v_{Rrep} = (1 - R_{rep}) \cdot v_{rep}$$

$$v_{F1} = \frac{(1 - R_{a1}) \cdot v_{1|2}}{mrsp_{a1} \cdot \left(\frac{1}{mrsp_{a1}} + \frac{1}{mrsp_{a2}}\right)}$$

$$v_{F2} = \frac{(1 - R_{a2}) \cdot v_{1|2}}{mrsp_{a2} \cdot \left(\frac{1}{mrsp_{a1}} + \frac{1}{mrsp_{a2}}\right)}$$

Check again that when all R_k's are set equal to 1, the above expression reduces to Expression 1. Note also that the mean response time in this case will tend to be larger due to: (1) multiple executions of the same activity and (2) overheads of restarts.

For the general case, it will be impossible to find closed-form answers. After first generating CTMC, we can numerically solve for the overall mean response time using a package such as SHARPE [10]. Alternatively, we can first construct a stochastic Petri net from the BPEL description and then automatically generate and solve the underlying CTMC using a software package such as SPNP [17] or SHARPE. Equations to compute the mean time to absorption in a CTMC can be found in [18,21].

Service Reliability. The service reliability is computed in closed form using the equations provided in [21,18]. Refer also to [11] for the reliability computation. In the case without failures (CTMC of Figure 3(a)), overall service reliability is 1.

In the case with failures (CTMC of Figure 3), the overall service reliability can be easily written down as:

$$R_{sys} = R_i \cdot R_{a1} \cdot R_{a2} \cdot R_{ai} \cdot R_{ht} \cdot R_{rep} \tag{4}$$

Finally, in the case with failures and restarts (CTMC of Figure 4), the overall service reliability in closed-form can be shown to be:

$$\begin{aligned} R_{sys} = {} & \frac{R_i}{(1 - C_i \cdot (1 - R_i))} \cdot \frac{(R_{a1} + R_{a2} - R_{a1} \cdot R_{a2}) \cdot R_{ai}}{(1 - C_{ai} \cdot (1 - R_{ai}))} \\ & \cdot \frac{R_{ht}}{(1 - C_{ht} \cdot (1 - R_{ht}))} \cdot \frac{R_{rep}}{(1 - C_{rep} \cdot (1 - R_{rep}))} \end{aligned} \tag{5}$$

We note that Expression (5) above does not reduce to Expression (4) if we set each of the coverage probability to 0. In fact, in that case we obtain the lower bound of R_{sys} as follows:

$$R_{sys} = (R_{a1} + R_{a2} - R_{a1} \cdot R_{a2}) \cdot R_{ai} \cdot R_{ht} \cdot R_{rep} \quad (C_k = 0 \text{ for all } k) \tag{6}$$

The reason is that our fault handling procedure says that if either airline succeeds we proceed. Also note that if all C_j are set equal to 1, the upper bound turns out as follows:

$$R_{sys} = R_{a1} + R_{a2} - R_{a1} \cdot R_{a2} \quad (C_k = 1 \text{ for all } k) \tag{7}$$

This is the best case reliability we can obtain.

2.5 Parameterization

To compute performance/reliability metrics of TravelAgent, we need to specify the rate parameters of the CTMC for TravelAgent. Specifically, these rate parameters are computed from the following types of primitive values:

1. Execution time of each activity (i.e., mean response time of each activity)
2. Reliability (i.e., success probability) of each activity
3. Overhead time for restart of each activity
4. Success probabilities for each restart
5. Branching probabilities in the original BPEL graph (if any)

Note that in our particular example, there are no branches in the original BPEL graph.

Execution time of an activity. From a collected sample of n values, the sample mean and sample variance can be computed. We can then use the *Student t* distribution to compute the interval estimate of the mean response time of each activity. We can either use the expression for this together with critical values of the t-distribution from a text such as [12,15,18], or use a statistical analysis package such as R [5].

Reliability. Since we are concerned only with software failures, the service reliability can also be measured through execution. Actual measurements give us counts of the number of successful tries n_s out of a total of given number of trials n. The ratio n_s/n is the sample mean. We can also determine confidence intervals, using formulas based on the Bernoulli sampling [18] or using a statistical analysis package.

Overhead time for restarts. The same method as in execution time of each activity.

Success probabilities for restarts. Same method as in the reliability above.

Branching Probabilities. Since BPEL process definitions often include conditional branches (switch) and loops (while), it turns out that we need to transform these parts of the definitions into probabilistic forms. Same method as in the execution time above.

3 Bottleneck Detection

In order to detect bottlenecks to pinpoint the particular activity or parameter that is the cause of bad behavior, we carry out a formal sensitivity analysis. This can be used at design time to point out the activity/parameter that needs to be improved. We can also use this in a realtime setting during the operational phase.

The basic idea is to compute the derivatives of the measure of interest with respect to all the input parameters. These derivatives can then be used to pinpoint the bottleneck [1].

For the Overall Response Time $mrsp_{sys}$. We can argue that scaled sensitivities are the relevant quantities in this case so that bottleneck device I is obtained, using the sensitivity S_k (k ranges over the activities), as follows.

$$\textit{Bottleneck } I = \text{argmax}_k \, |S_k| \quad (i.e.\ |S_I| = \max_k\{|S_k|\})$$

$$\textit{Sensitivity } S_k = \frac{mrsp_k}{mrsp_{sys}} \cdot \frac{\partial mrsp_{sys}}{\partial mrsp_k}$$

For the first case (CTMC of Figure 3(a)), the scaled sensitivity values are derived as follows:

$$S_{a1} = \frac{mrsp_{\mathrm{a1}}}{mrsp_{\mathrm{sys}}} \cdot \frac{\partial mrsp_{\mathrm{sys}}}{\partial mrsp_{\mathrm{a1}}} = \frac{mrsp_{\mathrm{a1}}}{mrsp_{\mathrm{sys}}} \cdot \left(1 - \left(\frac{mrsp_{a2}}{mrsp_{a1} + mrsp_{a2}}\right)^2\right)$$

$$S_{ht} = \frac{mrsp_{\mathrm{ht}}}{mrsp_{\mathrm{sys}}}$$

For the second case (CTMC of Figure 3(b)), the scaled sensitivity values are derived as follows:

$$\begin{aligned} S_{a1} = \frac{mrsp_{\mathrm{a1}}}{mrsp_{\mathrm{sys}}} \cdot R_i \cdot \Bigg(& \frac{{mrsp_{a2}}^2}{(mrsp_{al} + mrsp_{a2})^2} \\ & + R_{a2} \cdot \frac{{mrsp_{al}}^2 \cdot mrsp_{a2} + 2 \cdot mrsp_{al} \cdot {mrsp_{a2}}^2}{(mrsp_{al} + mrsp_{a2})^2} - R_{a1} \cdot \frac{mrsp_{a2}}{(mrsp_{al} + mrsp_{a2})^2} \Bigg) \end{aligned}$$

$$S_{ht} = \frac{mrsp_{\mathrm{ht}}}{mrsp_{\mathrm{sys}}} \cdot (R_i \cdot R_{a1} \cdot R_{a2} \cdot R_{ai})$$

For the third case (CTMC of Figure 4), the scaled sensitivity values are derived as follows:

$$\begin{aligned} S_{a1} = \frac{mrsp_{\mathrm{a1}}}{mrsp_{\mathrm{sys}}} \cdot \Bigg(& v_{1|2} \cdot \left(\frac{mrsp_{a2}}{mrsp_{al} + mrsp_{a2}}\right)^2 + \left(\frac{\partial v_{a2}}{\partial mrsp_{al}} + \frac{\partial v_{f1}}{\partial mrsp_{al}}\right) \cdot mrsp_{a2} \\ & + \left(\frac{\partial v_{a1}}{\partial mrsp_{al}} \cdot mrsp_{al} + v_{a1}\right) + \left(\frac{\partial v_{f2}}{\partial mrsp_{al}} \cdot mrsp_{al} + v_{f2}\right) \\ & + \frac{\partial v_{ainv}}{\partial mrsp_{al}} \cdot mrsp_{ai} + \frac{\partial v_{ht}}{\partial mrsp_{al}} \cdot mrsp_{ht} + \frac{\partial v_{rep}}{\partial mrsp_{al}} \cdot mrsp_{rep} \\ & + \frac{\partial v_{Rainv}}{\partial mrsp_{al}} \cdot mr_{ai} + \frac{\partial v_{Rht}}{\partial mrsp_{al}} \cdot mr_{ht} + \frac{\partial v_{Rrep}}{\partial mrsp_{al}} \cdot mr_{rep} \Bigg) \end{aligned}$$

$$S_{ht} = \frac{mrsp_{\mathrm{ht}}}{mrsp_{\mathrm{sys}}} \cdot v_{ht}$$

where

$$\frac{\partial v_{a1}}{\partial mrsp_{al}} = R_{a2} \cdot v_{1|2} \cdot \frac{mrsp_{a2}}{(mrsp_{al} + mrsp_{a2})^2} \qquad \frac{\partial v_{a2}}{\partial mrsp_{al}} = R_{a1} \cdot v_{1|2} \cdot \frac{-mrsp_{a2}}{(mrsp_{al} + mrsp_{a2})^2}$$

$$\frac{\partial v_{f1}}{\partial mrsp_{al}} = (1 - R_{a1}) \cdot v_{1|2} \cdot \frac{-mrsp_{a2}}{(mrsp_{al} + mrsp_{a2})^2} \qquad \frac{\partial v_{f2}}{\partial mrsp_{al}} = (1 - R_{a2}) \cdot v_{1|2} \cdot \frac{mrsp_{a2}}{(mrsp_{al} + mrsp_{a2})^2}$$

$$\frac{\partial v_{ainv}}{\partial mrsp_{al}} = \frac{1}{1 - C_{ai} \cdot (1 - R_{ai})} \cdot \left(\frac{\partial v_{al}}{\partial mrsp_{al}} + R_{a1} \cdot \frac{\partial v_{f1}}{\partial mrsp_{al}} + \frac{\partial v_{a2}}{\partial mrsp_{al}} + R_{a2} \cdot \frac{\partial v_{f2}}{\partial mrsp_{al}} \right)$$

$$\frac{\partial v_{rainv}}{\partial mrsp_{al}} = (1 - R_{ai}) \cdot \frac{\partial v_{ainv}}{\partial mrsp_{al}} \qquad \frac{\partial v_{ht}}{\partial mrsp_{al}} = \frac{R_{ai}}{1 - C_{ht} \cdot (1 - R_{ht})} \cdot \frac{\partial v_{ainv}}{\partial mrsp_{al}}$$

$$\frac{\partial v_{Rht}}{\partial mrsp_{al}} = (1 - R_{ht}) \cdot \frac{\partial v_{ht}}{\partial mrsp_{al}} \qquad \frac{\partial v_{rep}}{\partial mrsp_{al}} = \frac{R_{ht}}{1 - C_{rep} \cdot (1 - R_{rep})} \cdot \frac{\partial v_{ht}}{\partial mrsp_{al}}$$

$$\frac{\partial v_{Rrep}}{\partial mrsp_{al}} = (1 - R_{rep}) \cdot \frac{\partial v_{rep}}{\partial mrsp_{al}}$$

For the Overall Reliability R_{sys}. For this case, we can argue that unscaled derivatives can be used to pinpoint the bottleneck: The bottleneck J should be determined as follows.

$$\textit{Bottleneck } J = \text{argmax}_k |S_k|$$

$$\textit{Sensitivity } S_k = \frac{\partial R_{\text{sys}}}{\partial R_k}$$

Applying this to the second case (CTMC of Figure 3), we obtain the following formula:

$$\frac{\partial R_{\text{sys}}}{\partial R_k} = \frac{R_{\text{sys}}}{R_k}$$

For the third case (CTMC of Figure 4), we show some of its sensitivity values as follows.

$$\frac{\partial R_{\text{sys}}}{\partial R_{\text{al}}} = \alpha \cdot \frac{(1 - R_{a2}) \cdot R_{ai}}{(1 - C_{ai} \cdot (1 - R_{ai}))}$$

$$\frac{\partial R_{\text{sys}}}{\partial R_{\text{ht}}} = \beta \cdot \frac{1 - C_{ht}}{(C_{ht} \cdot R_{ht} + (1 - C_{ht}))^2}$$

where

$$\alpha = \frac{R_i}{(1 - C_i \cdot (1 - R_i))} \cdot \frac{R_{ht}}{(1 - C_{ht} \cdot (1 - R_{ht}))} \cdot \frac{R_{rep}}{(1 - C_{rep} \cdot (1 - R_{rep}))}$$

$$\beta = \frac{R_i}{(1 - C_i \cdot (1 - R_i))} \cdot \frac{(R_{a1} + R_{a2} - R_{a1} \cdot R_{a2}) \cdot R_{ai}}{(1 - C_{ai} \cdot (1 - R_{ai}))} \cdot \frac{R_{rep}}{(1 - C_{rep} \cdot (1 - R_{rep}))}$$

By definition, the sensitivity metric for an activity tells us about the potential contribution of *its* improvement to the *overall* improvement. Thus, it is natural to identify the activity with the highest sensitivity as the bottleneck.

4 Evaluation

We have evaluated the effectiveness of our approach, using the example in Figure 1: We have defined a BPEL process for the example and run it on IBM WebSphere Process

Table 1. MRSP Results

	$1a$	$1b$	$1c$	$2a$	$2b$	$2c$	$3a$	$3b$	$3c$
Computed, using the closed-form expressions ($mrsp_i = mrsp_{rep} = 1$, $R_i = R_{rep} = 1$, $C_{ai} = 1$, $C_{ht} = 0$, $mr_{ai} = 0.15$)									
MRSP									
$mrsp_{a1}$	2.000	1.000	2.000	2.000	1.000	2.000	2.000	1.000	2.000
$mrsp_{a2}$	2.000	2.000	2.000	2.000	2.000	2.000	2.000	2.000	2.000
$mrsp_{ai}$	1.000	1.000	1.000	1.000	1.000	1.000	1.000	1.000	1.000
$mrsp_{ht}$	2.000	2.000	1.000	2.000	2.000	1.000	2.000	2.000	1.000
Reliability									
$R_{a1/a2/ai/ht}$	0.9/0.9/0.9/0.9			0.1/0.9/0.9/0.9			0.1/0.1/0.9/0.9		
$mrsp_{sys}$	8.002	7.336	7.012	7.679	7.012	6.769	4.768	4.101	4.578
S_{a1}	0.187	–	–	0.196	–	–	0.315	–	–
S_{ht}	0.247	–	–	0.237	–	–	0.080	–	–
Measured on WPS									
MRSP									
$mrsp_i$	1.000	1.066	0.976	0.975	0.938	0.932	0.930	1.075	1.054
$mrsp_{a1}$	1.855	0.954	1.886	2.061	1.159	1.936	1.866	0.959	1.826
$mrsp_{a2}$	2.072	1.964	2.177	1.947	1.857	1.999	2.028	1.890	1.960
$mrsp_{ai}$	1.028	1.029	1.032	1.031	1.029	1.028	1.029	1.030	1.028
$mrsp_{ht}$	2.045	2.044	1.053	2.043	2.042	1.043	2.047	2.046	1.044
$mrsp_{rep}$	1.029	1.028	1.032	1.029	1.027	1.026	1.035	1.033	1.030
$mrsp_{sys}$	8.081	7.425	7.171	7.751	6.991	6.825	4.670	4.083	4.530

† *Between (a) and (b) / (c), only the colored parameters have intentionally been changed*

Table 2. Reliability Results

	$1a$	$1b$	$1c$	$2a$	$2b$	$2c$	$3a$	$3b$	$3c$
Computed, using the closed-form expressions ($R_i = R_{rep} = 1$, $C_{ai} = C_{ht} = 1$)									
R_{a1}	0.800	0.900	0.800	0.100	0.200	0.100	0.100	0.200	0.100
R_{a2}	0.800	0.800	0.800	0.800	0.800	0.800	0.100	0.100	0.100
R_{ai}	0.900	0.900	0.900	0.900	0.900	0.900	0.900	0.900	0.900
R_{ht}	0.800	0.800	0.900	0.800	0.800	0.900	0.800	0.800	0.900
R_{sys}	0.768	0.784	0.864	0.656	0.672	0.738	0.152	0.224	0.171
S_{a1}	0.160	–	–	0.160	–	–	0.720	–	–
S_{ht}	0.960	–	–	0.820	–	–	0.190	–	–
Measured on WPS									
R_{a1}	0.804	0.903	0.807	0.103	0.199	0.102	0.099	0.200	0.101
R_{a2}	0.803	0.801	0.797	0.804	0.801	0.797	0.099	0.101	0.101
R_{ai}	0.805	0.800	0.804	0.800	0.805	0.809	0.809	0.803	0.812
R_{ht}	0.800	0.802	0.905	0.800	0.806	0.901	0.796	0.799	0.895
R_{sys}	0.768	0.786	0.868	0.660	0.679	0.736	0.150	0.224	0.171

Server (v6.0). As for the reliability parameters, we have artificially caused failures in the 4 service invocations, namely $\mathsf{Airline}_{1/2}$ (for selection), Airline (for reservation), and Hotel. We have assumed perfect reliability for the other activities ($R_i = R_{rep} = 1$), and chosen $C_{ai} = C_{ht} = 1$ for the coverage parameters. Our evaluation is divided into two parts, and the results are summarized in Table 1 and 2.

First, we focused on performance bottlenecks / improvement in 3 different cases, in each of which we changed either $mrsp_{a1}$ or $mrsp_{ht}$ and evaluated its effect on $mrsp_{sys}$ (Table 1). For example, in Case 1a, *mrsps* are set to $mrsp_{a1} = mrsp_{a2} = mrsp_{ht} = 2.0, mrsp_{ai} = 1.0$, and R_i, R_{a1}, R_{ht} are all set to 0.9. Then, in Case 1b (1c), $mrsp_{a1}$ ($mrsp_{ht}$) are improved to 1.0. As its result, $mrsp_{sys}$ is improved from 8.002 to 7.336 (7.012). Notice that the higher contribution of the improvement of $mrsp_{ht}$ parallels the fact that S_{ht} is larger than S_{a1} ($0.247 > 0.187$). This applies to the other two cases as well.

Subsequently, we evaluated effects of improvements of reliability values. Since the service reliability does not depend of the *mrsp* values, we do not mention their values. Again, as shown in Table 2, the sensitivity values S_{a1} and S_{ht} successfully suggest which service should be chosen for improving the overall service reliability.

5 Conclusion

We have developed an approach to computing the overall mean response time and the overall reliability of composite Web services. We find closed-form expressions in a typical example. We show how sensitivity functions can be used to detect bottlenecks. Experimental results are used to validate our theoretical expressions. We have also developed an availability model (not shown in this paper) of the system under consideration. We plan to extend our work by providing a tool to carry out such an analysis in the general case. We plan to remove several assumptions made here such as: no contention for resources. We could also remove several distributional assumptions. We plan to use the sensitivity function in a formal optimization setting. We will consider our scheme in a realtime control theoretic setting. We propose to also extend the availability model to include hardware redundancy and software replication as in [6] and consider interactions between the availability model and performance model as in [14],[20], or [3].

References

1. Blake, J., Reibman, A., Trivedi, K.: Sensitivity analysis of reliability and performability measures for multiprocessor systems. In: ACM SIGMETRICS, pp. 177–186. ACM Press, New York (1988)
2. Bolch, G., Greiner, S., de Meer, H., Trivedi, K.: Queueing networks and Markov chains: modeling and performance evaluation with computer science applications, 2nd edn. Wiley-Interscience, New York, NY, USA (2006)
3. Chimento, P., Trivedi, K.: The completion time of programs on processors subject to failure and repair. IEEE Trans. Comput. 42(10), 1184–1194 (1993)
4. Chowdhary, P., Bhaskaran, K., Caswell, N.S., Chang, H., Chao, T., Chen, S., Dikun, M., Lei, H., Jeng, J., Kapoor, S., Lang, C.A., Mihaila, G., Stanoi, I., Zeng, L.: Model driven development for business performance management. IBM Systems Journal 45(3) (2006)
5. Fox, J.: An R and S-Plus Companion to Applied Regression. Sage Publications, Thousand Oaks (2002)

6. Garg, S., Kintala, C., Yajnik, S., Huang, Y., Trivedi, K.: Performance and reliability evaluation of passive replication schemes in application level fault tolerance. In: the 29th Annual International Symposium on Fault-Tolerant Computing, p. 322 (1999)
7. Goseva-Popstojanova, K., Trivedi, K.: Architecture-based Approach to Reliability Assessment of Software Systems. Performance Evaluation 45(2/3), 179–204 (2001)
8. Goyal, A., Lavenberg, S., Trivedi, K.: Probabilistic Modeling of Computer System Availability. Annals of Operations Research 8, 285–306 (1987)
9. Heidelberger, P., Trivedi, K.: Analytic Queueing Models for Programs with Internal Concurrency. IEEE Transactions on Computers 32(1), 73–82 (1983)
10. Hirel, C., Sahner, R., Zang, X., Trivedi, K.: Reliability and Performability Modeling using SHARPE 2000. In: Haverkort, B., Bohnenkamp, H.C., Smith, C.U. (eds.) TOOLS 2000. LNCS, vol. 1786, Springer, Heidelberg (2000)
11. Littlewood, B.: A reliability model for systems with markov structure. Applied Statistics 24(2), 172–177 (1975)
12. Meeker, W., Escobar, L.: Statistical Methods for Reliability Data. John Wiley & Sons, West Sussex, England (1998)
13. OASIS: Specification: Business Process Execution Language for Web Services (1.1) (2004)
14. Sharma, V., Trivedi, K.: Reliability and performance of component based software systems with restarts, retries, reboots and repairs. In: International Symposium on Software Reliability Engineering (2006)
15. Tobias, P., Trindade, D.: Applied Reliability, 2nd edn. Kluwer, Dordrecht (1995)
16. Towsley, D., Browne, J., Chandy, K.: Models for Parallel Processing within Programs: Application to CPU:I/O and I/O:I/O Overlap. CACM 21(10), 821–831 (1978)
17. Trivedi, K.: SPNP User's Manual Version 6.0. Duke University (September 1999)
18. Trivedi, K.: Probability and Statistics with Reliability, Queuing, and Computer Science Applications. John Wiley & Sons, West Sussex, England (2001)
19. Wang, D., Fricks, R., Trivedi, K.: Dealing with Non-Exponential Distributions in Dependability Models. In: Performance Evaluation and Perspectives, pp. 273–302 (2003)
20. Wang, D., Trivedi, K.: Modeling User-Perceived Service Availability. In: Malek, M., Nett, E., Suri, N. (eds.) ISAS 2005. LNCS, vol. 3694, pp. 107–122. Springer, Heidelberg (2005)
21. Wang, W., Choi, H., Trivedi, K.: Analysis of Conditional MTTF of Fault-Tolerant Systems. Microelectronics and Reliability 38(3), 393–401 (1998)
22. Whitt, W.: The queueing network analyzer. Bell System Technical Journal 62(9), 2779–2815 (1983)

SLA-Based Advance Reservations with Flexible and Adaptive Time QoS Parameters

Marco A.S. Netto[1], Kris Bubendorfer[2], and Rajkumar Buyya[1]

[1] Grid Computing and Distributed Systems (GRIDS) Laboratory
Department of Computer Science and Software Engineering
The University of Melbourne, Australia
ICT Building, 111 Barry Street, Carlton, VIC 3053
{netto, raj}@csse.unimelb.edu.au

[2] School of Mathematics Statistics and Computer Science
Victoria University of Wellington
Wellington 6140, New Zealand
kris@mcs.vuw.ac.nz

Abstract. Utility computing enables the use of computational resources and services by consumers with service obligations and expectations defined in Service Level Agreements (SLAs). Parallel applications and workflows can be executed across multiple sites to benefit from access to a wide range of resources and to respond to dynamic runtime requirements. A utility computing provider has the difficult role of ensuring that all current SLAs are provisioned, while concurrently forming new SLAs and providing multiple services to numerous consumers. Scheduling to satisfy SLAs can result in a low return from a provider's resources due to trading off Quality of Service (QoS) guarantees against utilisation. One technique is to employ advance reservations so that an SLA aware scheduler can properly manage and schedule its resources. To improve system utilisation we exploit the principle that some consumers will be more flexible than others in relation to the starting or completion time, and that we can juggle the execution schedule right up until each execution starts. In this paper we present a QoS scheduler that uses SLAs to efficiently schedule advance reservations for computation services based on their flexibility. In our SLA model users can reduce or increase the flexibility of their QoS requirements over time according to their needs and resource provider policies. We introduce our scheduling algorithms, and show experimentally that it is possible to use flexible advance reservations to meet specified QoS while improving resource utilisation.

1 Introduction

Service Level Agreements (SLAs) are an important element of the service oriented computing paradigm and define a mutually agreed upon set of consumer expectations and provider obligations. Typically SLAs encode Quality of Service (QoS) parameters such as resource availability, response time and completion deadlines. The role of the consumer is usually limited to specifying their QoS parameters and perhaps revising those parameters if an SLA cannot be agreed.

B. Krämer, K.-J. Lin, and P. Narasimhan (Eds.): ICSOC 2007, LNCS 4749, pp. 119–131, 2007.

We assume a scenario where access to a utility computing provider's computational resources is acquired through agreed SLAs [1]. The SLAs define the time and quantity of computation along with other QoS parameters, in return for a certain price. Access to computational resources may require consideration of *external* constraints, such as the need for access to simultaneous multiple resources (co-allocation for parallel computation) or to reflect timing dependencies when computing a workflow. In order to meet such external constraints, a QoS scheduler must allow consumers to reserve resources in advance.

When a provider accepts an advance reservation, the consumer expects to be able to access the agreed resources at the specified time. However, changes may occur in the scheduling queue between the time the consumer submits the reservation to the time the consumer receives the resources. There are a number of reasons for such changes including: consumers cancelling requests, consumers modifying requests, resource failures, and errors in estimating usage time in the consumer requests. Therefore, from the resource provider's perspective, a good time-slot for the consumer at the time the SLA was agreed may be a bad time-slot in the future due to increased fragmentation. This fragmentation reduces the potential scheduling opportunities and results in lower utilisation. Indeed, even finding a free time-slot can be a challenging task since fixed advance reservations fragment the resource's availability, and limit the positions in which other jobs can be scheduled. In order to minimise low system utilisation due to advance reservations, researchers on this area have introduced and investigated the impact of flexible time intervals for advance reservations [2,3,4,5,6].

We extend the existing solutions and contribute to the research field in the following ways: (i) we introduce the concept of adaptive time QoS parameters, in which the flexibility of these parameters are not static but adaptive according to the user needs and resource provider policies (Sect. 2); (ii) we present heuristics for scheduling the advance reservations (Sect. 3); and (iii) we perform experiments through extensive simulations to evaluate the advance reservations with flexible and adaptive time QoS parameters (Sect. 4). We show the results on the impact of system utilisation using different scheduling heuristics, workloads, time intervals, inaccurate estimation of execution times, and other input parameters. Moreover we investigate cases when users accept an alternative offer from the resource provider on failure to schedule the initial request.

2 SLA Specification from Execution Time QoS Scenarios

This section defines the set of parameters that we need in addition to any normal SLA parameters such as incentives and penalties, security or trust requirements, etc. Following are the three different time requirement scenarios:

1. **Strict start and completion time:** Consumers require the resource at exactly this time, and for the duration specified. There is no flexibility permitted to the scheduler. This scenario maps well to the availability of a physical resource that may need to be booked for a specific period.

2. **Relaxed start time, strict completion time:** Consumers require that the execution completes prior to a deadline. This scenario typically applies when there are subsequent dependencies on the results of this computation.
3. **Flexible interval:** There is a strict start time and a defined finish time, but the time between these two points exceeds the length of the computation. This scenario fits well with forward and backward timing dependencies, such those encountered in a workflow computation.

2.1 Scheduling Issues and Incentives

These cases as given above are simplistic; however scheduling them is complicated. Consider both cases 2 and 3, as the actual deadline approaches, the apparent priority of scheduling must increase to ensure that the execution completes prior to the deadline. Also early acceptance of SLA requests of rigid advance reservations fragments the availability of the resource, which may result in wasted computation time, increased rejections, reduced utilisation and consequently reduced revenue.

The idea of having flexible intervals for advance reservations is to make it possible to modify or reallocate existing advance reservations when new jobs are submitted to the scheduler. Once an SLA has been agreed upon, the scheduler may schedule the workload within those flexible constraints. We would expect that any pricing model would reward more flexible consumers with a lower price and in turn penalise consumers with less flexibility by charging a higher price. In addition, the SLA itself could be renegotiated (adaptive) if the resource provider needs to solve a scheduling impasse or consumer needs to react to a change in circumstance. In this case a consumer who accepts a resource providers SLA adaptation request for more flexibility would expect some form of incentive payment, whereas a consumer who requests a less flexible SLA adaptation should expect some penalty.

2.2 SLA Parameters

The advance reservations are defined in the SLA by a set of timing constraints, budget and computational resources. Following is the notation and parameter definitions for a job j, which can be either rigid or moldable (parallelism versus execution time trade off):

- R_j^{min} and R_j^{max}, where $1 \leq R_j \leq m$: minimum and maximum number of resources (e.g. cluster nodes or bandwidth) required to execute the job;
- f_j^{mol}: $R_j \rightarrow T_j^e$: moldability function which specifies the relation between number of resources and execution time T_j^e;
- T_j^s: job starting time—time determined by the scheduler;
- T_j^r: job ready time—minimum starting time determined by the user;
- T_j^c: job completion time—defined as $T_j^s + T_j^e$;
- D_j: job deadline;
- B_j: job budget—maximum amount of money that the user is willing to spend to execute the job with the required QoS;

- C_j: job cost—the cost determined by the resource provider in order to execute the job j with the above specifications.

3 Job Scheduling

The scheduling of a job consists on finding a free time-slot that meets the job requirements. Rather than providing the user with the resource provider's scheduling queue, we assume that the user asks for a time-slot and the resource provider verifies its availability. This is sensible in competitive environments where resource providers do not want to show their workloads, as consumers and other resource providers may exploit this commercially sensitive information. We also consider the scheduling to be on-line, where users submit jobs to the resource provider's scheduler over time and the scheduler makes its decisions based only on the currently accepted jobs.

Scheduling takes place in two stages. Firstly all jobs that are currently awaiting execution on the machine (and therefore have accepted SLAs) are sorted based on some criteria. Then this list is scheduled in order, and if the new job can be scheduled, the SLA is accepted. If the job cannot be scheduled, then the scheduler can return a set of scheduleable alternative times.

3.1 Sorting

Firstly we separate the jobs currently allocated into two queues: running queue $Q^r = \{o_1, ..., o_u\} \mid u \in \mathbb{N}$ and waiting queue $Q^w = \{j_1, ..., j_n\} \mid n \in \mathbb{N}$. The first queue contains jobs already in execution and cannot be rescheduled. The second queue contains jobs that can be rescheduled. The approach we adopt here is to try to reschedule the jobs in the waiting queue by sorting them first and then attempting to create a new schedule. We use five different sorting techniques in this paper: Shuffle, First In First Out (FIFO), Biggest Job First (BJF), Least Flexible First (LFF), and Earliest Deadline First (EDF). The only sorting criteria that needs explanation is LFF, which sorts the jobs according to the flexibility terms of starting time and deadline. This approach is based on the work of Wu et al [7], but considers only the time intervals. We define the time flexibility of a job j as follows:

$$\Delta_j = \begin{cases} D_j - max(T_j^r, CT) - T_j^e\text{: } \textit{for advance reservation jobs} \\ D_j - CT - T_j^e\text{: } \textit{for jobs with deadline} \end{cases}$$

Obviously other potential criteria can be used to perform this sort, one that we will be exploring in the future is sorting based on expected revenue. In the evaluation Sect. 4 we present results comparing these sorting techniques.

3.2 Scheduling

Algorithm 1 gives the pseudo-code for scheduling a new job j_k at the current time CT, returning true if it is possible to scheduled it, or false and a list of optional possible schedulings. Before the scheduling of a new job, the state of the system is consistent, which means that the current scheduling of all jobs meets the users QoS requirements. Therefore, during the scheduling process, if a job j_i is rejected there are two options: (i) $j_i = j_k$, the new job could not be scheduled; or (ii) $j_i \neq j_k$, the new job was scheduled but generated a scheduling problem for another job $j_i \in Q^w$. In the second case we change the positions of j_k with j_i and all jobs between j_k and j_i go back to the original scheduling—function that we call *fixqueue*. In our current implementation, each job is scheduled by using first fit approach—the first available time-slot is assigned to the job. For jobs with deadline the scheduler looks for a time-slot between the interval $[CT, D_j - T_j^e]$ and for advance reservations the scheduler looks for a time-slot within the interval $[T_j^r, D_j - T_j^e]$.

Algorithm 1. Pseudo-code for scheduling a new job j_k.

```
Q^w ← Q^w ∪ {j_k}
sort Q^w according to some criteria (e.g. EDF or LFF)
k ← new index of j_k
jobscheduled ← true
for ∀j_i ∈ Q^w | i ≥ k and jobscheduled = true do
  if schedulejob (j, Q^w, Q^r) = false then
    jobscheduled ← false
  end if
end for
if jobscheduled = false then
  if i ≠ k then
    fixqueue(Q^w, i, k) { update index of j_k (k ← i)}
  end if
  return reschedule ∀j_i ∈ Q^w | i ≥ k
end if
return true
```

When job j_k is rejected, all the jobs in Q^w after j_k, including j_k itself, must be rescheduled (Algorithm 2). However, in this rescheduling phase, other options are used to reschedule j_k. The list of options Ψ is generated based on the intersection of the new job j_k, the jobs in the running queue and the jobs in the waiting queue that are before j_k. For each job j_i that intersects j_k, job j_k is tested before T_i^r and after D_i. Once the list of options Ψ is generated, it is possible to sort it according to the percentage difference ϕ between the original T_j^r and D_j values and the alternative scheduler suggested options $OPTT_j^r$ and $OPTD_j$:

$$\phi_{opt} = \begin{cases} \frac{OPTD_j - D_j}{T_j^e} : \textit{option generated by placing } j_k \textit{ after } j_i \\ \frac{OPTT_j^r - T_j^r}{T_j^e} : \textit{option generated by placing } j_k \textit{ before } j_i \end{cases}$$

Once defined the possible positions of the new job j_k, all jobs in Q^w after j_k (including it) are rescheduled. If a job j_i is rejected, we have again two options: (i) $j_i = j_k$, the new job could not be scheduled; or (ii) $j_i \neq j_k$, the new job was scheduled but generated a scheduling problem for a another job $j_i \in Q^w$.

Algorithm 2. Pseudo-code for rescheduling rejected part of Q^w using the list of options Ψ for the rejected new job j_k.

```
OT_k^r ← T_k^r, OD_k ← D_k {keep original values}
while ∀OPT ∈ Ψ do
  jobscheduled ← true
  for ∀j_i ∈ Q^w | i ≥ k and jobscheduled = true do
    if j_i = j_k then
      set T_k^r and D_k with option OPT
    end if
    jobscheduled ←schedule(j_i)
  end for
  if jobscheduled = false then
    if i ≠ k then
      fixqueue(Q^w, i, k)
      T_k^r ← OT_k^r, D_k ← OD_k {restore original values}
      return reschedule ∀j_i ∈ Q^w | i ≥ k
    else
      return false {already tested new options for j_k}
    end if
  else
    {valid option OPT in Ψ—inform user about this possibility}
  end if
end while
if ∃ OPT ∈ Ψ | OPT generates a possible scheduling then
  return true
end if
return false
```

In constrast to Algorithm 1, in Algorithm 2, when $j_i = j_k$, it means that the scheduler has already tried all the possibilities to fit j_k in the queue, and hence, j_k will not be rescheduled again. However, if $j_k \neq j_i$, then the queue Q^w is fixed, the index of j_k is updated, T_k^r and D_k are set to the original values, and the rest of Q^w is again rescheduled. This process finishes when there are no more scheduling options to test. For a consumer who does not require an advance reservation, the first successful option should be enough.

4 Evaluation

The basis for the design of the scheduling algorithms and the improvement in utilisation, is predicated on the idea that scheduling advance reservations with some specified flexibility will allow better scheduling decisions to be made. The experimental results in this section demonstrate that the principle is sound.

4.1 Experimental Configuration

We evaluated the use of flexible QoS parameters for advance reservation on an extended version of the PaJFit (Parallel Job Fit) simulator [8]. We used the workload trace from the IBM SP2 system, composed of 128 homogeneous processors, located at the San Diego Supercomputer Center (SDSC)[1] as a realistic workload to drive the simulator. This workload contains requests performed over a period of two years. However, for reasons of tractability we conducted our experiments using 15 day intervals. We also removed any requests with a duration of less than one minute.

As the workload has no deadline specifications, and there are no traces with this information available, we modelled them as a function of the execution time. We observe that many workload distributions exhibit Poisson lifetimes and assume that this would also be true for deadlines. Therefore, for each job j, $D_j = T_j^{sub} + T_j^e * p$, where p is a random number defined by a Poisson distribution with λ=5, and T_j^{sub} is the request submission time defined in the workload traces. As we are working with advance reservations, we defined the release time of jobs as $T_j^r = D_j - T_j^e$. To model higher loads and the subsequent performance of the scheduler, we increased the frequency of request submissions from the trace by 25% and 50%.

We also analysed four different flexible interval sizes, which we again define as a Poisson distribution: fixed interval, short interval ($\lambda \leftarrow \phi = 25\%$), medium interval ($\lambda \leftarrow \phi = 50\%$), long intervals ($\lambda \leftarrow \phi = 100\%$). For all experiments using flexible intervals, we modified only half of each workload, the other half continues to have fixed intervals. We believe a portion of users would continue to specify strict deadlines even though the resource provider would probably reduce the price for more flexible and therefore *easier* consumers.

4.2 Results and Analysis

For the first experiment we evaluated the importance of sorting the jobs in the waiting queue according to specific criteria. Figure 1 shows the results, comparing LFF, BJF (sorted by the job's size = $T^e * R$), EDF, and FIFO, against a random shuffle; all of them with backfilling strategy. The results are presented as the difference in utilisation from the random baseline. In all cases, EDF with flexible intervals produced a schedule with the highest utilisation. It is worth noting that the results are not load sensitive, shown as the load increases — from normal (top graph) to high (bottom graph) in Fig. 1. As in our experiments we show comparative results, it is important to mention the system utilisation values to have an idea of the magnitude of these results. The values for the original workload and the two modifications on the frequency of request submissions, using FIFO approach, are: 46.8 ± 3.3 %, 50.9 ± 3.5 %, and 54.7 ± 3.7 %.

Using the EDF heuristic, we next evaluated the impact of the flexible time interval *duration* on resource utilisation. We observe in Fig. 2 that the longer the interval size, the higher the utilisation. This is because longer interval sizes provide the scheduler with more options for fitting (juggling) advance reservations and thereby minimising the resource fragmentation.

[1] We used the version 3.1 of the IBM SP2 - SDSC workload, available at the Parallel Workloads Archive: http://www.cs.huji.ac.il/labs/parallel/workload/logs.html.

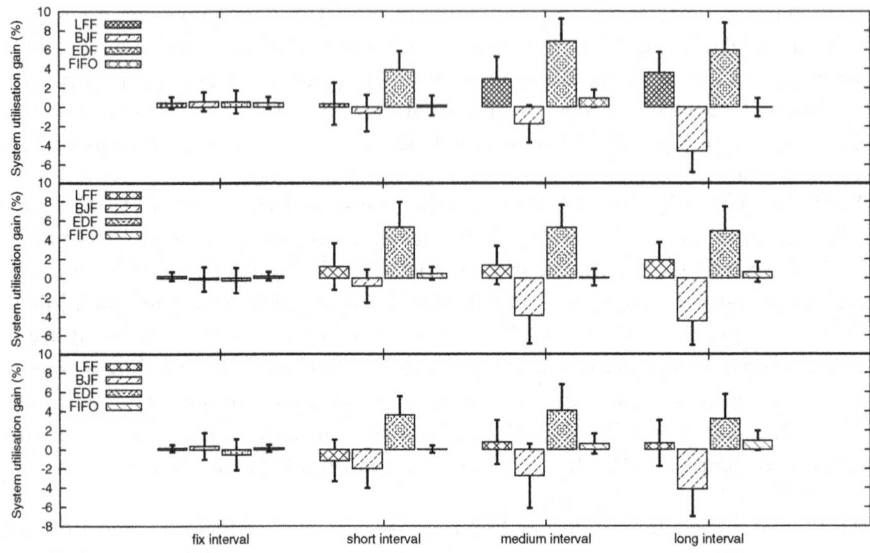

Fig. 1. Impact of sorting criteria on system utilisation

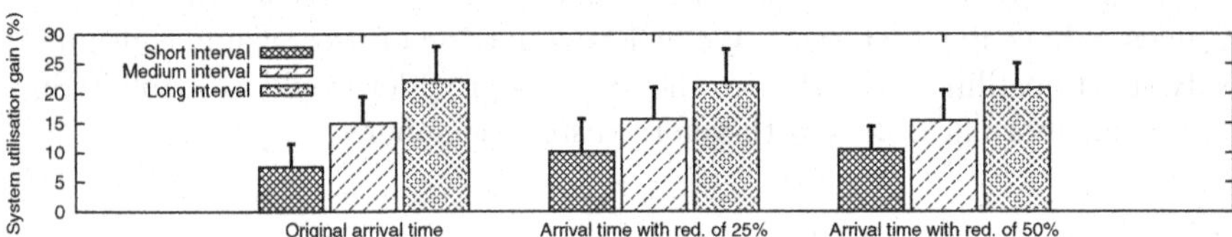

Fig. 2. Impact of time interval size on resource utilisation

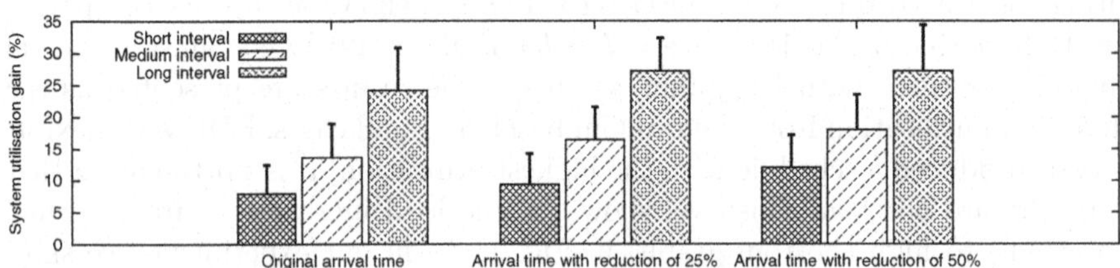

Fig. 3. Impact of time interval size on resource utilisation with inaccurate estimation time

In a real scenario, users may not estimate their execution time accurately. To understand the impact of incorrect execution time estimates we performed the following experiment. We modified the actual execution time in the workload trace by a factor determined from a Poisson distribution with λ=80—we assume the users in general overestimate the execution time [9,10].

Compared to the results in Fig. 2, we can observe in Fig. 3 that the flexible intervals have more impact when users overestimate their execution time, since otherwise the requests create small fragments that cannot be used by rigid time QoS requirements.

Consumers may want to know with some assurance when their jobs will execute. They can ask the resource provider to fix their jobs when the time to receive the resources gets closer, i.e. remove the time interval flexibility by renegotiating the SLA. We evaluated the system utilisation by fixing the T_j^r and D_j of each job j when 25%, 50%, and 75% of the waiting time has passed. We compared these results with an approach that fixes the schedule immediately the job is accepted.

As in the first set of experiments (Fig. 1) we performed runs for different workloads. However in this case the results for all workloads were similar, therefore we only present the graph for the medium workload in Fig. 4. We observe that the longer a user waits to fix their job, the better is the system utilisation. This is a pleasing result as this is indeed what we would expect because the scheduler has more opportunities to reschedule the workload.

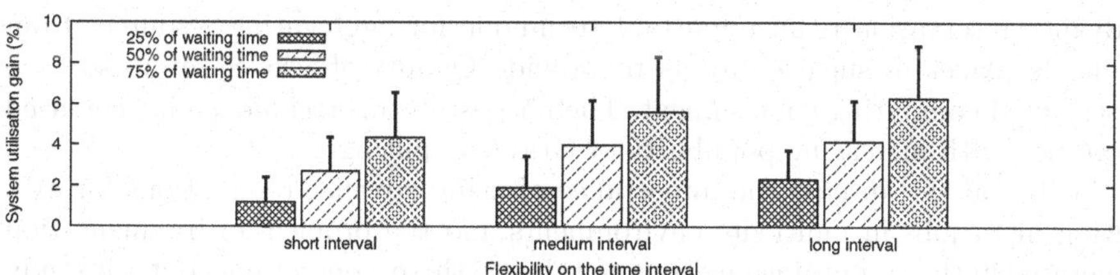

Fig. 4. The longer a job remains flexible, the better the utilisation—premature fixing of a job's place in the schedule consistently has an adverse effect on resource utilisation

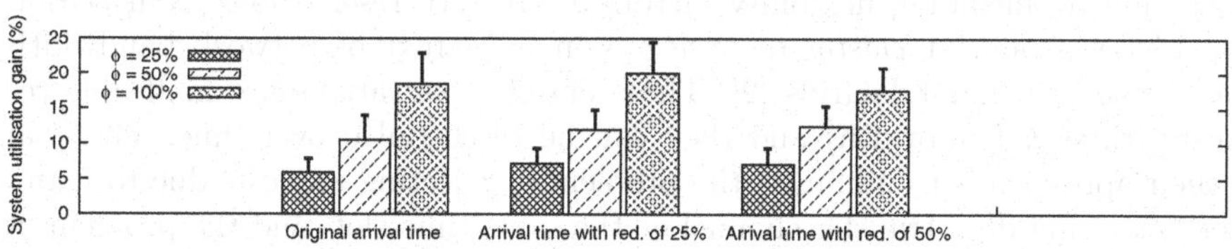

Fig. 5. System utilisation using suggested option from resource provider

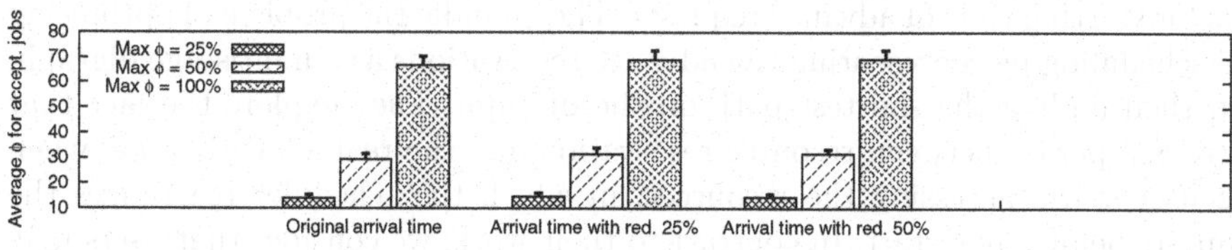

Fig. 6. Average actual ϕ of jobs accepted through suggestion by resource provider

Instead of using flexible intervals to meet time QoS requirements of users, we wanted to see what would happen when the resource provider offered an alternative slot to the consumer. When the resource provider cannot schedule a job j with the required starting time, it provides the user with other options (if possible) before and after the interval $[T_j^r, D_j]$. We selected the lowest difference ϕ of the options for each job j, given a threshold of 25%, 50% and 100%. Figure 5 shows that while this approach does increase the system utilisation, it does not perform as well as the flexible interval technique. Nevertheless, the approach of returning to the consumer with an alternative option is a useful technique for users who cannot accept flexible intervals.

We also measured the difference between the actual and the thresholds ϕ for the jobs accepted through the option suggested by the resource provider. From Fig. 6 we observe that in average case, the value of ϕ is not significantly less than the maximum ϕ defined by the resource provider.

5 Related Work

Advance reservation is an important technique for aggregating resources from multiple places in such a way as to provide Quality-of-Service for users in a distributed computing environment. The interest in this technique has increased alongside with increasing popularity of Grid Computing.

Snell et al [11] discuss the importance of using advance reservations for executing meta jobs in multi-site environments and the problem of fragmentation generated in the computing environment due to these reservations. In their study they assume that advance reservations are strictly rigid in terms of time QoS requirements.

More recently researchers have become interested on how to improve system utilisation by including flexibility factors in advance reservations. Naikasatam and Figueira defined *elastic reservations* in a context of network bandwidth management in LambdaGrids [2]. These elastic reservations are malleable requests (time X bandwidth) and they can be rescheduled over time. The goal of their approach is to minimise the problem of rejecting requests due to many users requiring data transfer channel at the same time-slot, and the problem of bandwidth fragmentation. In contrast to their work, we focus on the flexibility on the requests time intervals and not on the request malleability.

Chen and Lee [3] propose a flexible reservation model based on flexible intervals for starting time of advance requests. They handle the problem of optimising the scheduling by representing the advance reservations as a multistage digraph, and then finding the shortest path on the digraph. They explore the fact that there is a period between resource reservation and the real allocation, i.e. when the user starts accessing the resources, in which the scheduler rearranges the requests before they start. In contrast to their work, we consider that users may decide to fix their time schedule. That is, the flexibility is allowed until a certain period of time, since users may need to know the exact starting time to be reported some time in advance. Furthermore they do not consider requests for multiple resources.

Kaushik et al [4] study the use of flexible time intervals, which they call flexible time-windows, for advance reservations. They investigate the relation between the time-window size and the request waiting time, assuming that the request inter-arrival time follows the Pareto distribution. In our experiments we relied on inter-arrival requests from real workload from a supercomputing centre, and the Poisson distribution for defining the minimum starting time. We also consider that requests can come out of order. Furthermore they do not consider requests for multiple resources.

Castillo et al [12] use concepts of computational geometry to handle resource fragmentation caused by advance reservations. In their study they consider only jobs with strict time intervals, and as in the other related work, only jobs requiring a single resource.

Röblitz et al [5] present an algorithm for reserving computing resources that allows users to define an optimisation criteria (e.g. cost and completion time) when multiple candidates match the minimum users' requirements. They use a flexible advance reservation model where start and end time, duration and number of requested CPUs are flexible. Unlike our work they do not explore the rescheduling of existing flexible advance reservations.

Farooq et al [6] evaluate a set of algorithms for mapping advance reservations. They allow advance reservations to be flexible in terms of starting time and deadline. They also introduce an algorithm called Minimum Laxity Impact, in which rescheduling can be performed each time a new job arrives, but the scheduler minimises the extent to which existing jobs are pushed closer to their deadlines. The principle is to create more space for incoming jobs with more difficult scheduling options.

None of the related projects evaluate returning other scheduling options on failure to schedule the initial request. Moreover, the existing studies on flexible advance reservations assume that the parameters for flexibility are static, and in our case are adaptive according to the user needs and resource provider policies.

6 Conclusions and Further Work

In this paper we outlined consumer scenarios for advance reservations with flexible and adaptive time QoS parameters and presented the benefits for resource providers in terms of system utilisation. We evaluated these flexible advance reservations by using different scheduling algorithms, and different flexibility and adaptability QoS parameters. We investigated cases where users do not or can not specify the execution time of their jobs accurately. We also examined resource providers that do not utilise flexible time QoS parameters, but rather return alternative scheduling options to the consumer when it is not possible to meet the original QoS requirements.

In our experiments we observed that system utilisation increases with the flexibility of request time intervals and with the time the users allow this flexibility while they wait in the scheduling queue. This benefit is mainly due the ability of the scheduler to rearrange the jobs in the scheduling queue, which reduces the fragmentation generated by advance reservations. This is particularly true when users overestimate the execution time of their jobs.

For future work we can draw useful conclusions from these results. In particular the results can be used as a solid foundation for a utility computing pricing model as we have quantified the effects of varying degrees of flexibility on the utilisation of the provider's resources. Our work will include a pricing system for charging consumers for resources and give incentives or discounts for those users who are willing to provide flexibility within their QoS requirements and therefore include time flexible SLA parameters. We believe that this approach will allow resource providers to satisfy the full range of QoS timing requirements and in particular add a new option for some difficult scheduling domains such as workflow applications and resource co-allocation.

Acknowledgments

We would like to thank Marcos Dias de Assunção and the anonymous reviewers for their valuable comments. This work is partially supported by research grants from the Australian Research Council (ARC) and Australian Department of Education, Science and Training (DEST).

References

1. Auyoung, A., Grit, L., Wiener, J., Wilkes, J.: Service contracts and aggregate utility functions. In: HPDC. Proceedings of the 15th IEEE International Symposium on High Performance Distributed Computing, Paris, France, June 19–23 2006, pp. 119–131. IEEE Computer Society Press, Los Alamitos (2006)
2. Naiksatam, S., Figueira, S.: Elastic reservations for efficient bandwidth utilization in lambdagrids. Future Generation Computer Systems 23(1), 1–22 (2007)
3. Chen, Y.T., Lee, K.H.: A flexible service model for advance reservation. Computer Networks 37(3/4), 251–262 (2001)
4. Kaushik, N.R., Figueira, S.M., Chiappari, S.A.: Flexible time-windows for advance reservation scheduling. In: MASCOTS. Proceedings of the 14th International Symposium on Modeling, Analysis, and Simulation of Computer and Telecommunication Systems, Monterey, USA, September 11–14 2006, pp. 218–225 (2006)
5. Röblitz, T., Schintke, F., Reinefeld, A.: Resource reservations with fuzzy requests. Concurrency and Computation: Practice and Experience 18(13), 1681–1703 (2006)
6. Farooq, U., Majumdar, S., Parsons, E.W.: A framework to achieve guaranteed QoS for applications and high system performance in multi-institutional grid computing. In: ICPP. Proceedings of the 35th International Conference on Parallel Processing, Columbus, USA, August 14–18 2006, pp. 373–380. IEEE Computer Society Press, Los Alamitos (2006)
7. Wu, Y.L., Huang, W., Lau, S.C., Wong, C.K., Young, G.H.: An effective quasi-human based heuristic for solving the rectangle packing problem. European Journal of Operational Research 141(2), 341–358 (2002)
8. Netto, M.A.S., Buyya, R.: Impact of adaptive resource allocation requests in utility cluster computing environments. In: CCGRID. Proceedings of the 7th IEEE International Symposium on Cluster Computing and the Grid, Rio de Janeiro, Brazil, 14-17 May 2007, IEEE Computer Society Press, Los Alamitos (2007)

9. Chiang, S.H., Arpaci-Dusseau, A.C., Vernon, M.K.: The impact of more accurate requested runtimes on production job scheduling performance. In: Feitelson, D.G., Rudolph, L., Schwiegelshohn, U. (eds.) JSSPP 2002. LNCS, vol. 2537, pp. 103–127. Springer, Heidelberg (2002)
10. Lee, C.B., Snavely, A.: On the user-scheduler dialogue: Studies of user-provided runtime estimates and utility functions. International Journal of High Performance Computing Applications 20(4), 495–506 (2006)
11. Snell, Q., Clement, M.J., Jackson, D.B., Gregory, C.: The performance impact of advance reservation meta-scheduling. In: Feitelson, D.G., Rudolph, L. (eds.) IPDPS-WS 2000 and JSSPP 2000. LNCS, vol. 1911, pp. 137–153. Springer, Heidelberg (2000)
12. Castillo, C., Rouskas, G., Harfoush, K.: On the design of online scheduling algorithms for advance reservations and QoS in grids. In: IPDPS. Proceedings of the 21st IEEE International Parallel & Distributed Processing Symposium, Long Beach, USA, March 26–30 2007, IEEE Computer Society Press, Los Alamitos (2007)

Monitoring the QoS for Web Services

Liangzhao Zeng, Hui Lei, and Henry Chang

IBM T.J. Watson Research Center Yorktown Heights, NY 10598
lzeng,hlei,hychang@us.ibm.com

Abstract. Quality of Service (QoS) information for Web services is essential to QoS-aware service management and composition. Currently, most QoS-aware solutions assume that the QoS for component services is readily available, and that the QoS for composite services can be computed from the QoS for component services. The issue of how to obtain the QoS for component services has largely been overlooked. In this paper, we tackle this fundamental issue. We argue that most of QoS metrics can be observed/computed based on service operations. We present the design and implementation of a high-performance QoS monitoring system. The system is driven by a QoS observation model that defines IT- and business-level metrics and associated evaluation formulas. Integrated into the SOA infrastructure at large, the monitoring system can detect and route service operational events systemically. Further, a model-driven, hybrid compilation/interpretation approach is used in metric computation to process service operational events and maintain metrics efficiently. Experiments suggest that our system can support high event processing throughput and scales to the number of CPUs.

1 Introduction

Web services are autonomous software systems identified by URIs which can be advertised, located, and accessed through messages encoded according to XML-based standards such as SOAP, WSDL and UDDI. Web services encapsulate application functions and information resources, and make them available through programmatic interfaces, as opposed to the human-computer interfaces provided by traditional Web applications. Since they are intended to be discovered and used by other applications across the Web, Web services need to be described and understood in terms of both functional capabilities and non-functional, i.e., Quality of Service (QoS) metrics.

Given the rapidly increasing number of functionally similar Web services available on the Internet, there is a need to be able to distinguish them using a set of well-defined QoS metrics. Further, in situations where a number of component services are aggregated to form a composite service, it is necessary to manage the QoS for the composite service based on the QoS for individual component services. Most systems for QoS-aware service selection [2][4][5][6] and management [22][23] assume that the QoS information for component services is pre-existing. How to obtain this QoS information is largely overlooked. In this paper, we try to address this fundamental issue.

B. Krämer, K.-J. Lin, and P. Narasimhan (Eds.): ICSOC 2007, LNCS 4749, pp. 132–144, 2007.

In general, QoS metrics can be classified into three categories, based on the approaches to obtaining them:

- Provider-advertised metrics. This type of metrics is usually provided by service providers, which is subjective to service providers. One example is the execution prices advertised by service providers.
- Consumer-rated metrics. This type of metrics can be computed based on service consumer's evaluations and feedback, which is therefore subjective to service consumers. For example, the service reputation is considered average according to service consumers' evaluations.
- Observable metrics. This type of metrics can be observed, i.e., computed, based on monitored service operational events, which is objective to both service providers and consumers. Majority of QoS metrics in fact can be observed, including those of IT level and of business level. IT-level metrics include service execution duration, reliability, and etc. At business level, metrics are usually domain-specific and require some modeling efforts to define the formulas [5]. For example, the metric "forecast accuracy" for forecast services in supply chain management is usually defined as:

$$\sum_{i=0}^{n} \frac{|\, actualDemand_i - forecastDemand_i \,|}{actualDemand_i}$$

  In order to compute such a metric value, both actual demand and forecasted demand need to be monitored. It should be noted that the metric value needs to be recomputed whenever the execution of a service instance is completed.

In this paper, we focus on these observable metrics. We adopt a model-driven approach to the definition and monitoring of Web service QoS metrics. We introduce an observation metamodel that specifies a set of standard building blocks for constructing various QoS observation models. An observation model defines the specific QoS metric types that are of interest, as well as rules on when and how the metric values are computed.

An observation model has to be executed by a QoS monitoring system. There are two main issues in designing and implementing such a monitoring system:

- Service monitoring architecture. To detect service operational events, service monitoring needs to be integrated into the SOA infrastructure at large. It is important to leverage existing components in the SOA infrastructure, and to enable detection and routing of the service operational events systematically.
- QoS metric computation. There are three main challenges in designing an efficient computation runtime:
  - *High volume of service operational events.* In large-scale SOA solutions, there can be thousands of business process instances concurrently running. Even if each process instance generates only one operational event per second, there may be thousands of events that need to be processed per second. It is thus important for the runtime to support high event-processing throughput.
  - *Complexity of metric computation.* The ECA rules for metric computation actually create a workflow representable as statecharts. The complexity of metric computation stems from two aspects: the topology of the statecharts and

the formulas for computing the metric values. For example, hundreds of expressions may be triggered directly or indirectly to update a series of metric values due to the occurrence of a single service operational event. Unlike most complex event processing systems that focus on event filtering and composite event detection, metric computation is concerned with the expression evaluation triggered by events. The potentially large number of expressions that need to be evaluated significantly increases the overall complexity of the system.

- *Metric value persistence*. QoS metric values need to be saved in persistent storage after they are computed/updated, in order to make them available for other components (e.g., service selectors). Given the high volume of service operational events and the complexity of metric networks, an appropriate persistence mechanism is required, in order to support both efficient metric value persistence and queries.

Given QoS metrics are time-critical and time-sensitive information, it is important to develop a high performance metric computation engine that can compute/update metric values in real time.

In order to tackle the above challenges, we design and implement a service *Q*oS monitoring system. It provides a user-friendly programming model that allows users to define the QoS metrics and associated ECA rules. It enables declarative service QoS monitoring in the SOA infrastructure. It employs a collection of model-analysis techniques to improve the performance of metric computation. In a nutshell, the main contributions of this paper are:

- *Monitoring-enabled SOA Infrastructure*. Building upon our previous work on semantic service mediation [21] and semantic pub/sub [18] that enables flexible interoperation among Web services, we further enrich the SOA infrastructure to enable declarative event detection and routing in dynamic and heterogeneous environments. Such an extension allows the QoS for Web services to be monitored with small programming efforts.
- *Efficient QoS computation*. We present a novel hybrid compilation-interpretation approach to QoS metric computation. A series of model-analysis techniques is applied to improve event processing throughput. At build time, custom executable code is generated for each ECA rule. The custom code is more efficient to execute than generic code driven by ECA rules. At runtime, model-driven mediators interpret a transformed observation model to invoke generated code at appropriate points. Also, model-driven planning is adopted to enable wait-free concurrent threads for metric computation, which eliminates the overhead of concurrency control. Our experiments suggest that the system not only can support high event throughput but also can scale to the number of CPUs.

The rest of this paper is organized as follows. Section 2 presents the QoS observation metamodel. Section 3 illustrates the SOA infrastructure that enables service QoS monitoring. Section 4 discusses the design of a high performance metric computation engine. Section 5 briefly describes the implementation and experimentation. Following discussion on related work in Section 6, Section 7 provides concluding remarks.

2 QoS Observation Model

In the presence of multiple Web services with overlapping or identical functionality, service requesters need some QoS metrics to distinguish one service from another. We argue that it is not practical or sufficient to come up with a standard QoS model that can be used for all Web services in all domains. This is because QoS is a broad concept that encompasses a large number of context-dependent and domain-specific nonfunctional properties. Therefore, instead of trying to enumerate all possible metrics, we develop a QoS observation metamodel which can be used to construct various QoS observation models. The observation models in turn define the generic or domain-specific QoS metrics.

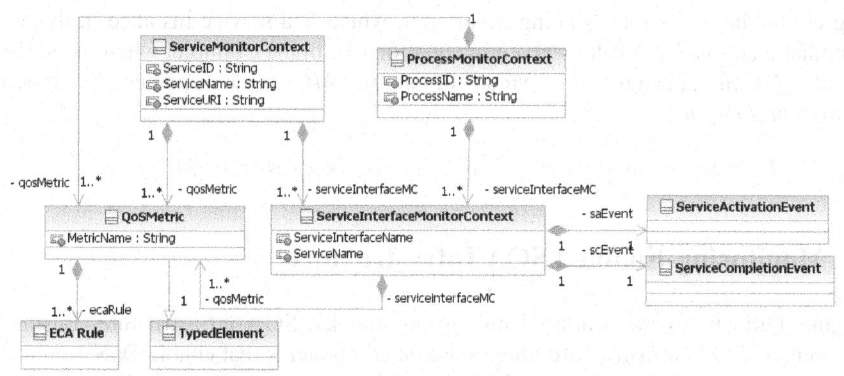

Fig. 1. Simplified Class Diagram of the Observation Metamodel

As indicated by the metamodel in Figure 1, an observation model can include three types of monitor contexts. Each type of monitor context corresponds to a type of entity to be monitored. A *ProcessMonitorContext* corresponds to a business process and specifies how a composite service should be observed. A *ServiceMonitorContext* (resp. *ServiceInterfaceMonitorContext*) corresponds to a service (resp. service interface). These two kinds of monitor contexts specify how component services should be observed. Users can define a collection of QoS metrics in a monitor context. A QoS metric can be of either a primitive type or a structure type, and can assume a single value or multiple values. For the computation logic, we adopt Event–Condition-Action (ECA) rules (c.f. Expression 1) to describe when and how the metric values are computed. Such a rule-based programming model frees users from the low-level details of procedural logic.

$$\text{Event(eventPattern)[condition]|expression} \quad (1)$$

In an ECA rule, the event pattern component indicates either a service operational event or the value change of a metric value. For example, when a service instance starts execution, a service activation event can be detected. The condition component in a rule is a Boolean expression specifying the circumstance to fire the computation action described in the expression component. The expression consists of an association predicate and a value assignment expression. The association predicate identifies which monitor context instance should receive the event. The operators allowed in the predicate expressions include relational operators, event operators, vector operators, set operators, scalar operators, Boolean operators and mathematical operators, etc. An example ECA rule for metric computation is given in equation (2).

$$Event(E_1 :: e)[e.a_2 > 12] \mid (MC_1.serviceID == e.serviceID)\ MC_1.m_2 := f_1(e) \quad (2)$$

In the above example, when an instance of event E_1, denoted as e, occurs, if $e.a_2 > 12$, then the event is delivery to the instance of MC_1 whose serviceID metric matches the serviceID field of event instance e, and the metric value of m_2 is computed by function $f_1(e)$. When there is no matching context instance, a new monitor context instance is created. It should be noted that the monitor context represents the entity that is being monitored, which is a service instance in this case. Another example ECA rule is given in equation (3). In the example, when the value of metric $MC_1.m_2$ changes, the value of metric $MC_1.m_3$ is updated by function $f_2(MC_1.m_1, MC_1.m_2)$.

$$Event(changeValue(MC_1.m_2)[] \mid MC_1.m_3 := f_2(MC_1.m_1, MC_1.m_2) \quad (3)$$

3 Monitoring-Enabled SOA Infrastructure

Figure 1 illustrates the proposed monitoring-enabled SOA infrastructure. Basing on the generic SOA infrastructure, three specific components that enable QoS monitoring are introduced. The *Web Service Observation Manager* provides interfaces that allow users to create observation models. The *Metric Computation Engine* generates executable code, detects service operational events and computes and saves metric values. The *QoS Data Service* provides an interface that allows other SOA components to access QoS information via a *Service Bus*. In this section, we mainly focus on the creation of observation models and the detection of service operational events. The details of metric computing and saving are presented in next section.

3.1 Observation Model Creation

We start with the observation model creation. When importing a process schema, the Web Service Observation Manager generates a ProcessMonitorContext first. For each service request in the process, it creates a ServiceInterfaceMonitorContext definition, in which two types of event definitions are also created, namely *execution activation event* and *execution completion event*. For example, if a service request is defined as R (*TaskName*, C_{in}, C_{out}), where C_{in} (C_{in}=<C_1, C_2,..., C_n >) indicates input types and C_{out} (C_{out}=<C_1, C_2,..., C_m >) indicates excepted output types, then the execution activation event can be defined as E_s(*PID, SID, TimeStamp, TaskName, ServiceName, ServiceInterfaceName*, <C_1, C_2,..., C_n>), where the *PID* is the process instance ID and the *SID* is the service ID. The execution completion event is defined as E_c(*PID, SID, TimeStamp, TaskName, ServiceName, ServiceInterfaceName*, <C_1,C_2,...,C_m>). Based on these service operational event definitions, the designers can further define the QoS metrics and their computation logic by creating ECA rules.

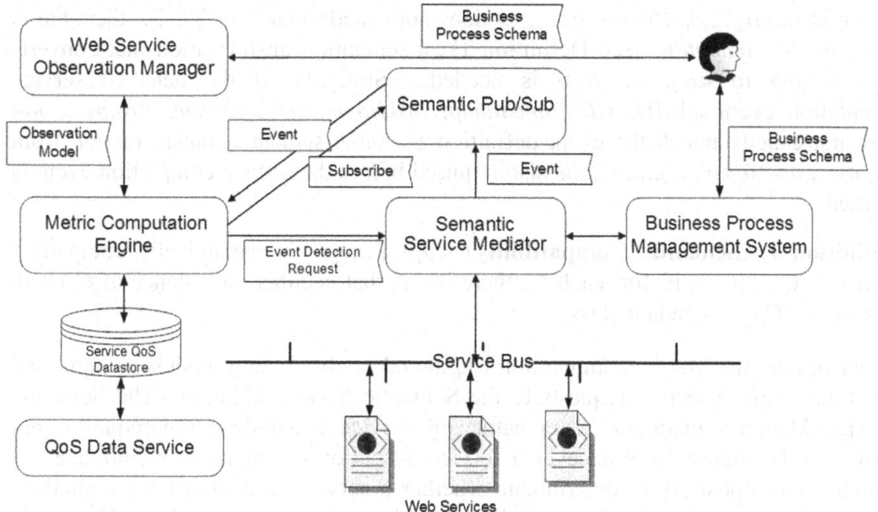

Fig. 2. Simplified QoS Monitoring-enabled SOA infrastructure

3.2 Detection and Routing of Service Operational Events

Given that the observation model is an event-driven programming model, there are two main steps before processing the events to compute the QoS metric values: event detection and event routing. If we assume that the data types are standardized across different process schemas and service interfaces, these two steps can be performed based on the syntactic information on service interfaces and service operational events.

However, such an assumption is impractical. Since services are operated in heterogeneous and dynamic environments, it is inappropriate to assume that all the service providers adopt the same vocabulary to define service interfaces. To improve the flexibility of SOA solutions, we have introduced semantics in service mediation [3], wherein service interfaces can be semantically matched with service requests. Therefore, when there are not any syntactically matched service interfaces for a service request, semantic match is applied to identify service interfaces. In cases of semantic matches, the data format transformations are required when invoking the matched service and returning the execution results to service consumers. In such cases, semantic matching is also required between the event definitions in observation models and the actual operational events detected. Fortunately we can leverage the same semantic-mapping capability provided by semantic service mediation to transforms operational events into formats that conform to the event definitions in the observation model.

If we assume that a service request is defined as $R(TaskName,\ C^r_{in},\ C^r_{out})$ and C^r_{out}=$<C_1,C_2,\ldots,C_m>$, the generated service activation event definition in the observation model is then $E_c(PID,\ SID,\ TimeStamp,\ TaskName,\ ServiceName,$ $ServiceInterfaceName, <C_1,C_2,\ldots,C_m>)$. We also assume that the matched service interface is defined as $i\ (serviceInterfaceName,\ C^i_{in},\ C^i_{out})$, and that the execution output is $<o_1,o_2,\ldots,o_l>$. If $<o_1,o_2,\ldots,o_l>$ does not exactly match $<C_1,C_2,\ldots,C_m>$, but is *semantically compatible* (see Definition 1),, a semantic transformation that converts $<o_1,o_2,\ldots,o_l>$ to $<o'_1,o'_2,\ldots,o'_m>$ is needed. Similarly, if the detected service completion event e_c(*pID, sID, timeStamp, taskName, serviceName,* $<o_1,o_2,\ldots,o_l>$) dose not exactly match the event definition E_c, same semantic transformation from $<o_1,o_2,\ldots,o_l>$ to $<o'_1,o'_2,\ldots,o'_m>$ is also required before the service completion event is emitted.

Definition 1. (Semantic Compatibility) $<o_1,o_2,\ldots,o_l>$ is semantically compatible with $<C_1,C_2,\ldots,C_m>$, if for each C_i, there is a o_j that is either an instance of C_i or an instance of C_i's descendant class.

In our design, the Metric Computation Engine takes observation models as input and generates event detection requests to the Semantic Service Mediator. The Semantic Service Mediator maintains a repository of service event detection requests (not shown in the Figure 1). Whenever a service execution is activated or completed, it searches the repository to determinate whether a service activation (or completion) event needs to be emitted. The search is done by semantically matching the service input and output with entries in the event detection request repository.

Similarly, it is impractical to assume that different process schemas use standardized data types and service interfaces. Therefore, when the event definitions in observation models are derived from service requests, it is necessary to consolidate those semantically matched monitored events. For example, consider two service requests R^1(*TaskName*^{1}, C^1_{in}, C^1_{out}) and R^2(*TaskName*^{2}, C^2_{in}, C^2_{out}) in two process schemas PS^1 and PS^2. Two execution activation event definitions can be generated as E_s^1 (*PID, SID, TimeStamp, TaskName, ServiceName ServiceInterfaceName,* $<C_1, C_2,\ldots,C_n>$) and E_s^2 (*PID, SID, TimeStamp, TaskName, ServiceName, ServiceInterfaceName,* $<C_1, C_2,\ldots,C_m>$) in two observation models OM^1 and OM^2 respectively. If $<C_1, C_2,\ldots,C_n>$ is semantically matched with $<C_1, C_2,\ldots,C_m>$, then the service operational events detected when executing PS^1 (resp. PS^2) should also be transformed and delivered to context instances in OM^2 (resp. OM^1). These transformations are performed by a semantic pub/sub engine [4]. Specifically, the Metric Computation Engine takes observation models as input and generates event subscriptions for the semantic pub/sub engine, relying on the latter to perform event transformation and event routing. For example, given OM^1, the Metric Computation Engine subscribes to event E_s^1 (*PID, SID, TimeStamp, TaskName, ServiceName, ServiceInterfaceName,* $<C_1, C_2,\ldots,C_n>$). When an event e_s^2 (*pID, sID, timeStamp, taskName, serviceName, serviceInterfaceName,*$<o_1,o_2,\ldots,o_m>$) (an instance of E_s^2) is published from the service mediator, the event is transformed to e_s^1(*pID, sID, timeStamp, taskName, serviceName, serviceInterfaceName,* $<o'_1,o'_2,\ldots,o'_n>$) by semantic pub/sub and delivered to the appropriate context instances of OM^1.

4 High Performance Metric Computation Engine

Given a monitoring-enabled infrastructure to detect and route service operational events, it is imperative that these events be processed efficiently, and that the QoS metric values be computed and saved efficiently as well. The main challenges of the system design are tri-fold: high volume of service operational events, complexity of expressions involved in metric computation and persistence of metric values. Although most complex event processing systems [12][13][14][15] support high throughput of events, they primarily focus on event filtering and compound event detection. They do not address metric computation, where event data triggers and contributes to a complex flow of computation. Further, they don't consider the issue of state persistence. In this paper, we advocate a series of model analysis techniques to improve event throughput in a monitoring environment. In this paper, we only sketch out the high-level design but omit more detailed descriptions, due to the limitation of space. More complete descriptions of these techniques can be found in [11].

4.1 Model Transformation and Execution Framework

As we discussed earlier, event-driven rule-based programming is user friendly, particularly for business integration developers. However, because of the overhead in locating rules to be executed at runtime, the event-driven model does not lend itself to efficient execution, especially when the number of rules is very large, such as in the case of service QoS monitoring. In our design, the rule-based model is transformed to a state-based model, wherein statecharts are adopted to reorganize the rules. The rationale for such a model transformation is that statecharts organize the rules by states, which can greatly reduce the overhead in locating rules at runtime.

The construction of statecharts is based on user-defined ECA rules: a state represents either an event or a metric, while a transition between two states represents the triggering relationship (see Table 1). For example, if the event pattern is a service operational event in an ECA rule (see expression 2 for an example), then there is a transition from the event state to the metric state. In another case, the event pattern is the value change of a metric (see expression 3 as an example), and the corresponding transition is from one metric state to another metric state.

Table 1. Transforming the ECA rules to Statecharts

ECA rule type	Control-flow Transitions in Statechart
Event pattern is a service operational event	Event → Metric
Event pattern is value change of a metric	Metric1 → Metric2

With the above transformation, each service operational event initiates a statechart. Thus, the execution of the ECA rules is converted to the execution of statecharts. An example of transformation is shown in Figure 3. In the example, three statecharts are generated from twelve ECA rules. The advantage of executing statecharts is that the overhead of a full rule set scan is eliminated when identifying the rules to be executed at runtime, as the next rules that need to be executed can be located via the outgoing transitions of the current state.

There are two approaches to executing statecharts, compilation and interpretation. Both approaches have their own advantages and drawbacks. We discuss the interpreting approach first. In order to execute the statecharts, the interpreter not only interprets the state transition logic, but also interprets the expressions in the rules. Given that the operators that appear in expressions can be relational, set, vector, scalar, and etc., interpretation is less efficient than compilation [9]. With a compilation approach, executable code is generated from a statechart. As custom code is generated at buildtime for the execution of statecharts, this reduces CPU cycles at runtime. However, the compilation approach entails another potential performance issue. When using multi-threads to process events, thread scheduling relies on the lock-based scheduling mechanism provided by either the operating system or language runtime (e.g., JVM). Such lock-based scheduling usually results in high system overhead [10], especially in multiple CPUs systems.

We take advantages of both approaches and propose a hybrid approach. In the hybrid approach, state transition logic is interpreted, while the expression in a rule is compiled into standalone executable code. The advantages of such a hybrid approach are twofold. On the one hand, by interpreting the state transition logic, the computation engine can plan the execution of rules in finer granularity, i.e., at the transition level instead of the statechart level. For example, information about the dataflow among the rules can be used to plan the wait-free execution of the expressions (details can be found in next subsection). On the other hand, the execution of an individual expression is done by executing pre-complied code, which enjoys the efficiency of the compilation approach.

Adopting the hybrid approach, we further develop a queuing network to execute the statecharts, in order to enable dynamic CPU allocation at runtime. At deployment time, the ECA rules in different statecharts are distributed to a collection of mediators.

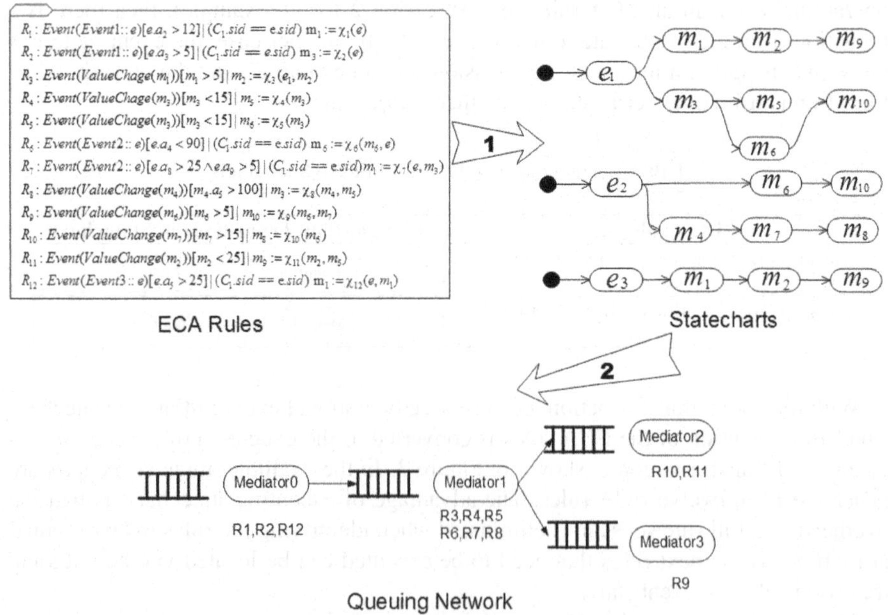

Fig. 3. Execution Model Transformation

Each mediator in the network possesses a work item queue, an interpreter and a thread pool. The queue buffers available work items. The interpreter executes the complied code of expressions in the rules. The thread pool enables multi-thread concurrent processing on work items, wherein the number of thread can be configured dynamically. The threads in different thread pools have the same level of priority. The CPU resource allocation for a mediator is determined by the size of its thread pool. By configuring the size of the thread pool dynamically, CPU resource can be dynamically allocated.

The collection of mediators forms a queuing network, wherein the number of mediators and the topology of the network are determined by the topologies of statecharts. The strategies for constructing the queuing network are: (i) The order of rule execution is preserved by the network topology. This is achieved by first sorting the rules based on the execution sequence in each statechart and then distributing the rules to an ordered collection of mediators based on the rules' execution order. (ii) The communication cost among mediators is minimized by eliminating data access contention among the threads in different mediators. This can be done by distributing rules that access the same data into the same mediator. An example of queuing network is shown in Figure 3.

4.2 Execution Planning

One of the key techniques for improve event processing throughput is multi-threaded concurrent processing. However, event throughput normally is not proportionate with the number of concurrent threads deployed, because of the runtime overhead incurred by the concurrency control mechanism. QoS monitoring requires that QoS metric values be persistent and we use a relation database for this purpose. In order to reduce the amount of I/O between the Metric Computation Engine and the datastore, a cache is also instituted. Therefore, either the datastore or the cache needs to provide concurrency control. Although modern RDBMs support row-level locking, such an option substantially deteriorates database performance. On the other hand, if concurrency control is implemented in the cache, a rollback segment needs to be maintained for each transaction. Given the large volume of events and that each event occurrence initiates a transaction, a large number of rollback segments need be managed by the cache. These rollback segments occupy significant memory and eventually impair performance. Therefore, an approach of supporting concurrent threads without locking, such as a lock-free approach, is more appealing [16][17]. However, these lock-free approaches rely on either the hardware or programming language support on for compare-and-swap [3]. Aiming at a solution that is independent of hardware or programming languages, we plan the execution ahead of time using information in the observation model The basic idea is that we plan the rule execution in each mediator: if the execution of two rules update the same metric or one rule produces operands for another rule, then these two rules need to be executed sequentially; otherwise these two rules can be executed concurrently. It should be noted that the execution order relationships between the rules are derived before the runtime. Therefore, there is not much runtime overhead involved when planning the executions.

5 Implementation and Experimentation

Our implementation leverages the Websphere Process Server (WPS) [24]. WPS is a SOA solution platform that contains a BPEL engine and provides a service bus for Web services. The proposed Metric Computation Engine uses a message driven bean to receive service operational events routed from the semantic pub/sub engine. *We have also developed a dashboard to display the metric values from the QoS Data Service.* We have conducted a series of experiments to demonstrate the functionality of Web service QoS monitoring. We first created a business process called *"patient visit" (see Figure 4) and deployed it on WPS. From the service request definitions in the process, a skeleton observation model was generated by the Web Service Observation Manager that consisted of one process monitor context, six service interface monitor contexts and twelve service operational event definitions. Given the skeleton model, we then created about forty metric definitions and ECA rules. We deployed the complete model into the Metric Computation Engine, wherein the model information was transformed and executable Java classes were generated. These generated Java classes were distributed to five mediators. When the process "patient visit" is executed, the related service operational events are detected and published to the Semantic Pub/Sub engine. When these events are routing to the Metric Computation Engine, the metric values are computed and saved. Eventually, the computed metric values are displayed on the dashboard in realtime fashion.*

To test the system throughput, we designed an event emitter that sends simulated service operational events to the Metric Computation Engine with a given sending rate (i.e., number of events per second). On an Intel CPU Linux server, the Metric Computation Engine can process 660 events/sec. In order to test its salability, we deployed the Metric Computation Engine on multiple CPU hardware platforms (2 and 4 CPUs). The experiment results (1210 events/sec and 2012 events/sec respectively) demonstrate that our system is scaled to the number of CPUs.

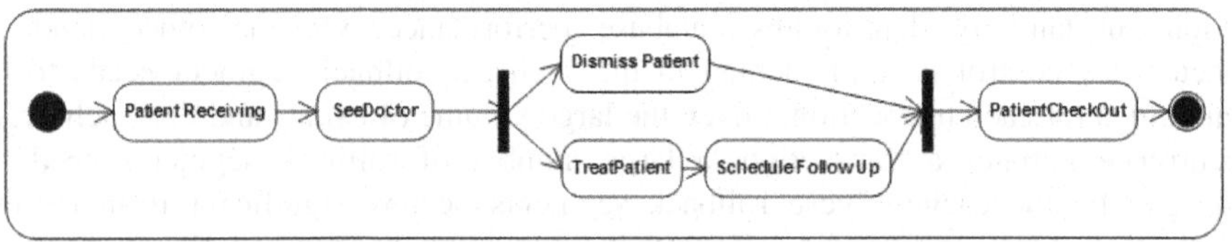

Fig. 4. An Example of Business Process

6 Related Work

In this section, we review work in the areas of QoS management and event processing systems. QoS management has been widely studiesd in the context of middleware systems [18][19][20]. These efforts have addressed the following issues: QoS specification to allow description of application behavior and QoS parameters, QoS translation and compilation to translate specified application behavior into candidate application configurations for different resource conditions, QoS setup to appropriately select and instantiate a particular configuration, and QoS adaptation to runtime resource fluctuations. Most efforts in QoS-aware middleware, however, are focused on the network transport and system level. Little work has been done at the application and business process levels.

QoS-Aware service composition [1][2][4][5][6][7][8][19][20] aims for selecting component services to optimize the overall QoS of a business process. In [2][7], the system assumes that the QoS information of components is pre-existing, and therefore, the overall QoS of composite service can be computed based on formulas. In [8], the formulas that compute the QoS of a workflow based on both the QoS of component services and the workflow schemas are discussed. However, it only focuses on the QoS at IT level. In [5], a QoS-aggregation system is presented. It provides an editor for the QoS aggregation function that allows users to specify QoS attributes and their aggregation formulas. It also provides an interpreter that evaluates a workflow's global QoS. Again, it assumes that the QoS information of component services is pre-existing. Further, it does not provide the details on how to compute the aggregation formulas efficiently. Different from above works, this paper tries to tackle the fundamental issue: monitor and compute the QoS of component/composite services, both at IT and business level. Further, it discusses the design and implementation of a high performance metric computation engine.

Complex event processing systems [12][13][14] focus on event filtering and compound event detections However, in service QoS monitoring, event filtering logic is relatively simple. Complicated computation happens after the events are filtered, i.e., when the event data is used to compute/update a collection of metrics. rFurther, most of the complex event processing systems do not support state persistence, even though it is a critical requirement for a service QoS monitoring system to save metric values.

7 Conclusion

In this paper, we advocate computing the QoS metrics of services by monitoring the executions. An observation model is proposed, which allows users to define the metric types and formulas. We design a monitoring-enabled SOA infrastructure to enable the systematic detection and routing of service operational events. Further, we implement a high performance metric computation engine that can support high event throughput. Our further work includes supporting the metric network (i.e., probabilistic, system dynamics and extensible user-defined dependency) and a careful study of the system.

References

1. Menasce, D.A.: QoS Issues in Web Services. IEEE Internet Computing 6(6) (2002)
2. Zeng, L., Benatallah, B., Dumas, M., Kalagnanam, J., Sheng, Q.Z.: Quality Driven Web Services Composition. In: WWW 2003 (2003)
3. Prakash, S., Lee, Y.H., Johnson, T.: A Nonblocking Algorithm for Shared Queues Using Compare-and-Swap. IEEE Transactions on Computers 43(5) (1994)

4. Canfora, G., Di Penta, M., Esposito, R., Villani, M.L.: An Approach for QoS-aware Service Composition based on Genetic Algorithms. In: GECCO 2005, ACM Press, New York (2005)
5. Canfora, G., Di Penta, M., Esposito, R., Perfetto, F., Villani, M.L.: Service Composition (re)Binding Driven by Application-Specific QoS. In: Dan, A., Lamersdorf, W. (eds.) ICSOC 2006. LNCS, vol. 4294, Springer, Heidelberg (2006)
6. Nguyen, X.T., Kowalczyk, R., Han, J.: Using Dynamic asynchronous aggregate search for quality guarantees of multiple Web services compositions. In: Dan, A., Lamersdorf, W. (eds.) ICSOC 2006. LNCS, vol. 4294, Springer, Heidelberg (2006)
7. Zeng, L., Benatallah, B., Ngu, A.H.H., Dumas, M., Kalagnanam, J., Chang, H.: QoS-Aware Middleware for Web Services Composition. IEEE Transactions on Software Engineering 30(5) (2004)
8. Cardoso, J., Sheth, A.P., Miller, J.A., Arnold, J., Kochut, K.J.: Modeling quality of service for workflows and web service processes. Web Semantics Journal: Science, Services and Agents on the World Wide Web Journal 1(3), 281–308 (2004)
9. Rao, J., Pirahesh, H., Mohan, C., Lohman, G.M.: Compiled query execution engine using jvm. In: ICDE 2006 (2006)
10. Goetz, B., Peierls, T., Bloch, J., Bowbeer, J., Holmes, D., Lea, D.: Java Concurrency in Practice. Addison-Wesley Professional, Reading (2006)
11. Zeng, L., Lei, H., Chang, H.: Model-analysis for Business Event Processing. IBM Systems journal (2007) (to appear)
12. Wu, E., Diao, Y., Rizvi, S.: High-performance complex event processing over streams. In: SIGMOD 2006 (2006)
13. Wang, F., Liu, P.: Temporal management of RFID data. In: VLDB 2005 (2005)
14. Complex Event Processing, http://en.wikipedia.org/wiki/Complex_event_processing
15. Luckham, D.: Power of Events: An Introduction to Complex Event Processing in Distributed Enterprise Systems, 1st edn. Addison-Wesley Professional, Reading (2002)
16. Ennals, R.: Efficient Software Transactional Memory, Intel Research Cambridge Technical Report: IRC-TR-05-051 (2005)
17. Herlihy, M.P., Luchangco, V., Moir, M.: Obstruction-free Synchronization: Double-ended Queues as an Example. In: ICDCS (2003)
18. Zeng, L., Lei, H.: A Semantic Publish/Subscribe System. In: IEEE CEC (East) (2004)
19. Gillmann, M., Weikum, G., Wonner, W.: Workflow Management with Service Quality Guarantees. In: SIGMOD 2002 (2002)
20. Nahrstedt, K., Xu, D., Wichadakul, D., Li, B.: QoS-Aware Middleware for Ubiquitous and Heterogeneous Environments. IEEE Comm. Magazine 39(11) (2001)
21. Zeng, L., Benatallah, B., Xie, G.T., Lei, H.: Semantic Service Mediation. In: Dan, A., Lamersdorf, W. (eds.) ICSOC 2006. LNCS, vol. 4294, Springer, Heidelberg (2006)
22. Zeng, L., Lei, H., Jeng, J.-J., Chung, J.-Y., Benatallah, B.: Policy-Driven Exception-Management for Composite Web Services. In: IEEE CEC 2005 (2005)
23. Zeng, L., Jeng, J.-J., Kumaran, S., Kalagnanam, J.: Reliable Execution Planning and Exception Handling for Business Process. In: Benatallah, B., Shan, M.-C. (eds.) TES 2003. LNCS, vol. 2819, Springer, Heidelberg (2003)
24. Websphere Process Server, http://www-306.ibm.com/software/integration/wps/

Q-Peer: A Decentralized QoS Registry Architecture for Web Services*

Fei Li, Fangchun Yang, Kai Shuang, and Sen Su

State Key Lab. of Networking and Switching, Beijing University of Posts and Telecommunications
187#,10 Xi Tu Cheng Rd., Beijing,100876, P.R. China
pathos.lf@gmail.com, {fcyang, shuangk, susen}@bupt.edu.cn

Abstract. QoS (Quality of Service) is the key factor to differentiate web services with same functionality. Users can evaluate and select services based on their quality information. Traditionally, run-time QoS of web services is collected and stored in centralized QoS registry, which may have scalability and performance problem. More importantly, centralized registry can not operate across business boundaries to support global scale application of web services. In this paper, we propose a P2P (Peer-to-Peer) QoS registry architecture for web services, named Q-Peer. The architecture is a Napster-like P2P system, where query of QoS is naturally achieved by getting QoS storage address from service registry. Q-Peer employs object replication mechanism to keep load-balance of the whole system. We present two types of replication schemes and conduct comparison study. A prototype of Q-Peer has been implemented and tested on Planet-lab. Experimental results show that Q-Peer can automatically balance load among peers in different circumstances, so the system has good performance and scalability.

1 Introduction

Using web service to integrate business applications is one of the major trends in distributed computing. Web service, which specified by a set of XML (eXtensible Markup Language) based standards[1], is a standard way to improve interoperability between software running on different platforms over internet[2]. Web services can be published by providers and discovered by requesters based on their description. Services[1] can further be composed to a more powerful service to improve reusability. When using a certain web service, user experience is largely depends on quality of the service, so QoS information is essential in web service framework and should be properly processed.

* This work is supported by the National Basic Research and Development Program (973 program) of China under Grant No.2003CB314806; the Program for New Century Excellent Talents in University (No:NCET-05-0114); the Program for Changjiang Scholars and Innovative Research Team in University (PCSIRT); the Hi-Tech Research and Development Program (863 Program) of China under Grant No.2006AA01Z164; Collaboration Project with Beijing Education Committee.

[1] In this paper, we use *web service* and *service* interchangeably.

B. Krämer, K.-J. Lin, and P. Narasimhan (Eds.): ICSOC 2007, LNCS 4749, pp. 145–156, 2007.

Quality of service is non-functional properties of service, such as response time, availability, and price. It is a commonly accepted procedure that service requesters discover services by functional description and select services by QoS. Generally, service function is relatively stable throughout service lifetime, while QoS can change frequently with system status, load, network condition, etc. Maintaining the two types of information has different system requirements and design considerations. Thus service discovery and service selection are often accomplished on two entities respectively, called *service registry* and *QoS registry*. Currently, service registry in P2P manner is a hot research topic, but most of the published QoS registry works are still in centralized manner. They are sharing common shortcomings of centralized systems, like scalability, performance and single point failure. More importantly, because of business boundaries between different regions or management domains, a centralized system may not be able to support global scale web service interoperations.

In this paper, we propose a P2P QoS registry system for web services, named Q-Peer. The basic idea and a preliminary load-balance approach has been published as a work-in-progress paper in[3]. This work expanded our previous study by improving the load-balance approach and analyzing system performance in a series of experiments. Q-Peer is a P2P system which provides large-scale QoS storage, monitoring, collecting and query services. It can work with either centralized or decentralized service registries like UDDI (Universal Description, Discovery and Integration)[4] and other P2P service discovery system[5]. Every peer has its own policy to decide whether to accept a QoS registration request or a load-balance request. Q-Peer solves QoS object query problem by adding peer address into service registration information. User gets a peer address which storing the requested QoS object and accesses the peer directly, so that it does not need a query routing mechanism internally. QoS data of similar or identical services is clustered together, which makes query and comparison of QoS very efficient. Peers find other light-loaded peers to be neighbors by an autonomous load information dissemination scheme. Neighbors are expected to share load when needed. Data replication mechanism is applied on all peers to adjust load and improve availability. We propose two replication mechanisms and compare their effect by experiments. We have implemented the Q-Peer prototype and tested it on Planet-lab[6]. Experimental results show that Q-Peer has very good scalability and performance.

The rest part of this paper is organized as follows: Section 2 reviews some related works. Section 3 introduces the general model and design consideration of Q-Peer. Section 4 presents how to disseminate QoS and load information in Q-Peer. Section 5 proposes the load balancing approaches in Q-Peer. Section 6 presents the detail of experiments and analyzes the results. The paper is concluded in Section 7.

2 Related Works

QoS information processing is an important issue in web service framework. Most of the previous works are focused on how to evaluate and select web services, although they all mentioned certain kinds of QoS registries. Centralized QoS registry architecture has been proposed before. Maximilien et al. [7] proposed an agent based architecture for processing QoS information. An ontology framework is builded to represent QoS knowledge. Serhani et al. [8] presented a QoS broker architecture and clarified its relationship with other entities in web service. Liu et al. [9] designed a QoS registry for a hypothetical phone service market place. The registry collect QoS information from two sources: one is active monitoring on service provider, another is user feedback. The registry can execute their QoS computation algorithm to rank services. Yu et al. [10] presented a broker based framework for QoS-aware web service composition. It maintains QoS information and integrates services on user's behalf. As far as we know, the only work mentioned a distributed QoS registry architecture is by Gibelin et al. [11]. They use hash-table based QoS indexing which is not efficient for QoS query problem. No detailed design information could be found in the paper.

In past several years, peer-to-peer paradigm has gained considerable momentum as a new model of distributed computing. P2P systems are created for file sharing at first, as Napster[12], Gnutella[13] and Kazaa[14]. P2P systems can be roughly divided to two categories by content distribution approach: structured and unstructured[15]. They have different query mechanisms, which should be chosen for different application scenarios. For scalability, autonomy and robustness of P2P systems, the P2P model has been introduced into distributed storage and information retrieving[16]. Some applications of P2P have already contributed to web service research, as distributed service discovery[17]. Replication is an important approach to improve P2P system performance. Cohen et al.[18] analyzed search efficiency by different replication strategies in unstructured P2P systems. Otherwise, we adopt replication mechanism to balance-load in Q-Peer.

3 System Model

Q-Peer is a peer-to-peer database system for register, storage and query of web service QoS. QoS data is recorded in XML documents. QoS query in Q-Peer is not conducted by query routing among peers, but by the support of service registry. For each service, service registry stores its functional description and at least one peer address containing its QoS. Users get QoS by directly access the address. This query mechanism can work with either centralized or decentralized service registry. The mechanism is suitable for QoS query, although different to common P2P database system. To query QoS without service description is meaningless, because no service user cares about service quality without known its function. The query mechanism in Q-Peer is similar to the most original P2P system-Napster[12], by a centralized index server cluster.

Services can be classified by their functionality, so corresponding QoS is naturally classified to QoS classes. QoS in a same class have same QoS metrics[7]. In Q-Peer, a QoS class is stored at one peer at first, but QoS data could be replicated when needed. Organizing storage by QoS class can improve efficiency because users often retrieve QoS of functional-identical services to compare and select from them. Different service selection algorithm can be deployed on peers to assist users[9][19]. If a service stored its QoS at a certain peer, the peer acts as its run-time monitor.

All peers are equal in Q-Peer. We do not use super-peer[20] because super-peer often intends to improve query efficiency, which is not a problem in our system. Peers employ a replication based load-sharing policy which utilizing spare resource on light loaded peers. Every QoS record may have several replicas on different peers. Service registry has a list of candidate peers for every service and chooses a random one when user query QoS. Peers have an autonomic mechanism to exchange run-time load information. Every peer keeps several other light-loaded peers as its neighbors for load sharing. The detailed mechanism will be presented in following sections.

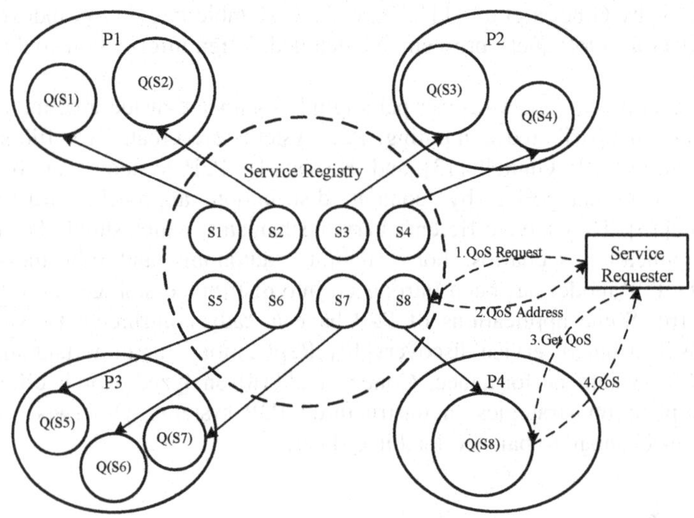

Fig. 1. General model of Q-Peer

Figure.1 illustrates a sample Q-Peer system containing 4 peers and 8 classes of services. Replicas are hided for illustrating our model clearly. Service registry in the figure can be either centralized or decentralized architectures. S_i is a service class which contains a number of same or similar service description. The QoS data set of a service class S_i is $Q(S_i)$. Each peer stores several QoS classes. Every service description contains the address of its QoS, as a pointer. When a service user needs to query QoS of a certain service, it sends a QoS request to service registry, then the registry will reply with a peer address. Service user can get QoS by direct accessing the peer.

4 Information Dissemination

In Q-Peer, two types of information change frequently which should be constantly updated and properly disseminated in the system. The first is service QoS. The second is load status of peers.

4.1 QoS Update

For a service *s* to be registered, which belongs to service class *S*, the service has functional and non-functional properties—service description *D(s)* and quality of the service *Q(s)*. *D(s)* is registered at service registry. If no service of *S* has been registered before, service registry will choose a random peer to store its QoS information. The selected peer is the *main peer* of *Q(S)* and the QoS data stored in this peer is the *main replica* of *Q(S)*. If *S* has been registered, *Q(s)* is added to its main peer. As soon as a peer decided to accept *Q(s)* of a new service, the peer contacts with the service and get current QoS for the first time.

For sharing load and improving availability, any *Q(s)* may have several replicas at different peers (The replication mechanism is presented in next section). These peers are called *replica peers* of *Q(s)*. Every time a service update its QoS, it only updates to the main peer. Then the other replicas are passively updated by the main peer.

4.2 Load Update

In Q-Peer, peer's load and capacity are characterized by the QoS access frequency on a peer. We assume every peer always has enough storage space for the cost of increasing storage is much lower than which of increasing CPU power or network bandwidth. QoS access comes from two major operations: one is update of QoS; another is query of QoS. For a peer *P* storing *n* services' quality information: $\{Q(s_1),Q(s_2),...,Q(s_n)\}$, each service has an updating frequency $f^u(s_i)$ and a query frequency $f^q(s_i)$, the load of the peer is:

$$L(P)=\sum_{i=1}^{n}\left(f^u(s_i)+f^q(s_i)\right) \tag{1}$$

The estimated maxim allowed access frequency of *P* is the *maxim capacity* $C^M(P)$. The *available capacity* $C^A(P)$ is: $C^A(P)=C^M(P)-L(P)$.

Every peer has a list of several other peers' address, called Neighbor List (NL). The peers in NL are candidate peers to accept replication request of the NL owner. A neighbor item in NL is $N_i=\langle P_i,C^A(P_i)\rangle,(i=1...m,a\le m\le b,0<a<b)$, where *m* is the total neighbor number, *a* and *b* are the lower and upper limit of *m*. Neighbor list is sorted by C^A in descent order. Items in NL can be dynamically added and deleted according to load change. When a new peer *P* adds to Q-Peer system, it will get a random list of peers as neighbors. *P* periodically sends its own $C^A(P)$ to neighbors and update NL by getting neighbors' C^A back from reply messages. If any peer received an unknown peer's C^A which was better than the last item in its NL or the NL was not full, the new peer is inserted as a neighbor. If NL exceeded the maxim number limit *b*, the last item is removed. A peer has a lowest capacity limitation *l* to take another peer as its neighbor. For any P_i in NL which $C^A(P_i)<l$, it is deleted. If item number in NL were lower than *a*, peer initiates a random walk process to find new neighbors. The random walk begins from a random peer in its NL. Random walk message contains the initiator's C^A for other peers to update NL if satisfied. For any

peer walked through, it sends a random item in its NL back to the initiating peer and forwards message to the item. The random walk stops for TTL limitation.

By this load information exchange approach, peers tend to take light-loaded peers as neighbors which are more likely to be able to accept replication requests. For peers with less available capacity which have not been taken as neighbor of any other peers, they still have chance to use other peers' resource. When they have more available capacity, they are added to its neighbor's NL.

5 Replication and Load Sharing

If a peer found itself under load pressure, it can request other peers to replicate some of its data for load-sharing. We present two replication schemes in this section: *Replicating QoS Class(RQC)* and *Replicating QoS Object(RQO)*.

5.1 Replicating QoS Class

Replicating QoS class considers load status of a whole QoS class and takes QoS classes as operation unit. This replication scheme makes service selection can be done at any peer containing a replica, because every replica is a whole class of QoS.

Every QoS class has $r(1 \le r \le K)$ replicas including the original one, where K is the maxim allowed replica number for a QoS class. If a peer's load were approaching threshold, it tries to replicate the most popular QoS class to the neighbor with most available capacity, which is the first neighbor in NL. A peer accepts replication request when all of the three conditions hold: the QoS class has less than K replicas, the spared capacity of the neighbor can satisfy load requirement, the neighbor has not stored this QoS class. Assume P_1 is the replication target peer, and $Q(S_i)$ is the class to replicate, the load satisfaction condition is:

$$C^A(P_1) > f^u(Q(S_i)) + \frac{r \times f^q(Q(S_i))}{r+1} \text{ and } r < K \tag{2}$$

In (2), we can find that by replicating a QoS class, replication peer can share $1/r+1$ of the class' query load, but update load can not be leveraged because all replicas should keep consistency. With the growing of replica number, load sharing by replication can have less and less effect because $r/r+1$ is approaching 1. Furthermore, keeping more replicas consistent adds more load on the system. Thus, K should be a small number to make the approach effective.

If the available capacity of first neighbor $C^A(P_1)$ could not satisfy the replication requirement, the random walk process will be initiated to refresh the neighbor list. As soon as a replication peer is found, a replication request of $Q(S_i)$ is sent to new peer. Service registry is informed that a new replica can be selected to query QoS after replication is successfully performed.

If all QoS class in a peer had K replicas but it was still under load pressure, a random replica is chosen to delete. Service registry is informed before deletion, so that it would not get the class of QoS from this peer. Main peer of the QoS class is also informed so that it would not update QoS to this peer. If the deleted replica was the main replica of the service class, another replica would be chosen as main replica and related service providers would be informed to update QoS to the new main peer.

5.2 Replicating QoS Object

The scheme of replicating QoS object replicates only one service's quality data every time. This replication scheme would not affect service selection function because a complete replica of a QoS class is still exists at the main peer which is responsible for updating QoS to all replicas.

When a peer finds itself under load pressure, it tries to replicate the most loaded QoS object. If the peer were still heavy loaded after a replication (This is highly possible if only one QoS object is replicated), it replicates the most loaded QoS object again. The new most loaded QoS object may or may not be the previous replicated one. This replication process would repeat until the peer's load is under predefined threshold. Every replication request is sent to the neighbor with most available capacity. We do not limit the replica number of a QoS object in this scheme, because for a single heavy loaded QoS object, its access frequency is always much higher than its update frequency.

In replication process, neighbor list may run out of neighbors because neighbor's available capacity is consumed. Random walk will be initiated when neighbor number is lower than limitation.

If neighbor list had been updated and run out again, and the peer were still under load pressure, peer begins to delete QoS object by descent order of object access frequency. Another deletion scheme is always taken periodically at all peers: if the query frequency of a QoS object was lower than its update frequency, it is deleted no matter what the peer status is. Only objects which are not main replica can be deleted.

6 Experiments

The Q-Peer prototype is developed in JAVA. We deploy our prototype on Planet-lab platform to test the performance and effectiveness of the system. "Planet-lab is a global research network that supports the development of new network services."[6] The platform can provide us nearly realistic distributed network environment.

6.1 Experiment Environment

The experiment environment is illustrated in Fig.2. Service registry is only a simulation program for testing the Q-Peer prototype, providing service classification and QoS address query function. Test agent simulates QoS access operations of service providers and requesters, which generates load to Q-Peer. We allocate a number of hosts in Planet-lab and deploy Q-Peer prototype on every host.

6.2 Evaluation Methodology

We expect that by replication, we can balance load among peers in Q-Peer which will result in better system performance. We characterize the Q-Peer performance by *system utility*, *balance degree*, and *request loss ratio*.

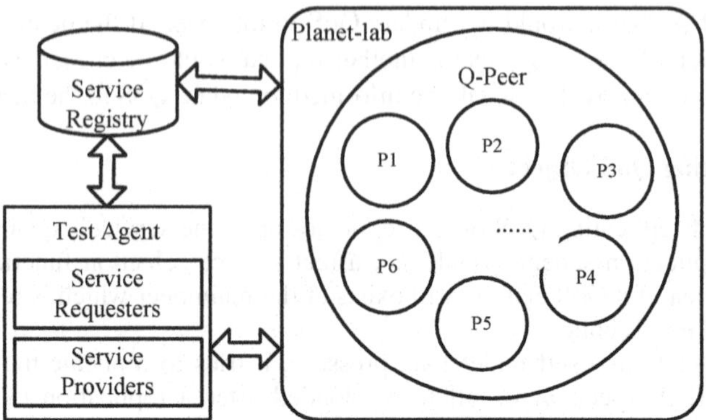

Fig. 2. Experiment environment

- System utility: the percentage of total successful query frequency to the total allowed capacity of all peers.
- Balance degree: the standard deviation of utility at all peers.
- Request loss ratio(RLR): the percentage of refused requests to total requests. A peer will refuse QoS access request when the load achieves allowed capacity.

The performance have been evaluated in three replication schemes: without replication, QoS class replication and QoS object replication. We allocated 50 hosts as 50 peers. Each host had a maxim allowed capacity randomly set from 500 to 10,000 (access/minutes). QoS data was added by the service provider simulator from test agent. Every provider updated its QoS once a minute. QoS query requests was simulated following Zipf distribution[21]. That is, a small portion of the QoS objects is queried much frequently.

Different scenarios was tested to find out the effect of replication schemes in different system status: 1, fixed QoS object number with growing request; 2, different QoS object number and class number with growing request; 3, different parameter configuration and their effect on load-balance. In the first scenario, 200 classes of QoS was generated and randomly distributed in peers. There were randomly 100-500 QoS objects in each class. Average request frequency was set at 50,000 requests/minutes., and grew 1000 every minute. The maxim replica number in RQC was set at 5. In the second scenario, two cases were tested. One was that we tested the performance when total QoS object number increased with a step of 1,000, but keeping the total class number at 200. The other was that we increased total class number by adding new classes to the system, but average QoS object number in each class did not change. In both cases, we grew requests frequency until RLR achieves 10%. The third scenario tested the effect of different system configuration. The maxim neighbor list length was set from 6 to 20 with a step of 2. Random walk TTL was set at 10. For the sake of peers' policy, not every peer is so generous to accept replication request. We tested the system utility when 10%-70% of peers would refuse other peers' replication request. In each configuration, we still tested system utility with growing request frequency until RLR achieves 10%.

6.3 Results and Analysis

In Fig.3, we illustrate the Q-Peer performance in different replication schemes. Figure 3(a) shows request loss ratio when request frequency grows. The no replication case has a linear growth of RLR because some of the peers are unable to response all the request at the beginning. With the request frequency growing, more and more peers are reaching capacity limits and more requests will be dropped. Obviously, replication cases can make the system scale up easily. The RQO case has better scalability because it balance load more accurately. Only the QoS object which needs replication will be replicated in RQO while the RQC replicates some light-loaded QoS object with the whole class. Figure 3(b) also shows that RQO has better balance degree. The balance degree keeps high at the beginning because requests are not evenly distributed in all peers and most of the peer has no need to replicate. When request frequency increases to system limit, the balance degree is decreased under 0.1 by RQO.

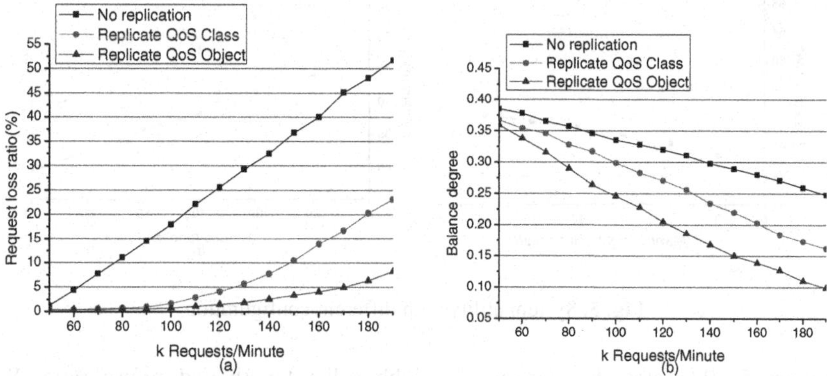

Fig. 3. (a) Request loss ratio with request frequency growing. (b) Balance degree with request frequency growing.

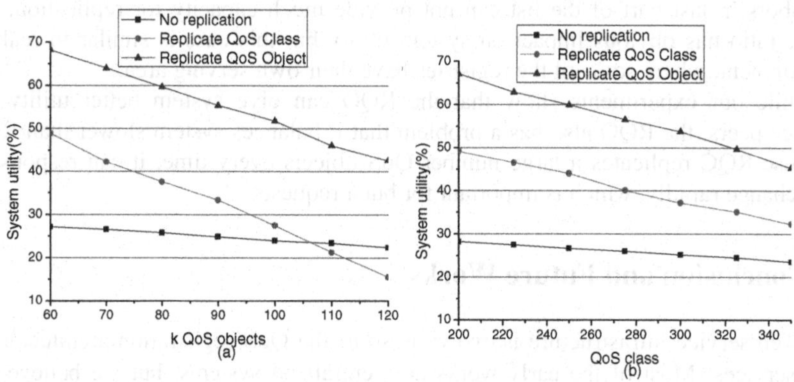

Fig. 4. (a)System utility with different QoS object number. (b) System utility with different QoS class number.

The total QoS number and its classification also has significant impact on Q-Peer performance because when QoS number growing, the QoS update operation will consume a significant part of total system capacity. Replications will increase update operations because we have to keep consistency of all replicas. In Fig 4, we can find that no replication case keeps a very low system utility at 20%-30%. The RQO case's system utility decreases with QoS number growth and drops to about 40% when QoS object number achieves 120,000. Considering our total system capacity is about 250,000, the system utility is still very good. A problem of ROC is illustrated in Fig 4(a). The system utility drops rapidly with total QoS number growing by expanding every class. The reason is that RQC has to replicate more QoS object when QoS number in each class growing. Surprisingly, system utility of RQC is worse than no replication case when total QoS number is approaching 110,000.

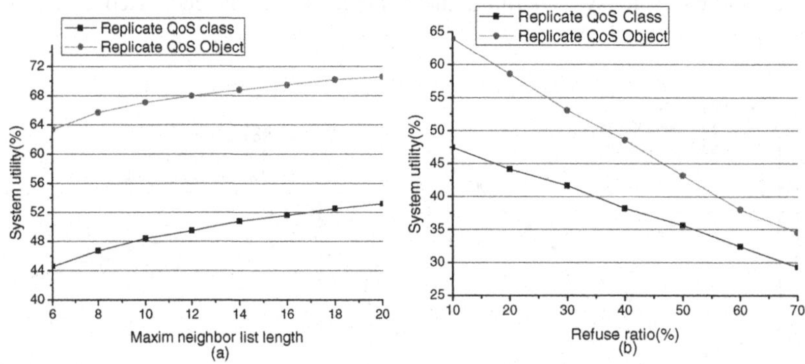

Fig. 5. System utility with different configuration

Figure 5 illustrates the impact of neighbor list length and refuse ratio. With neighbor list length growing, system utility can be improved. But long neighbor list can generate more network overhead for neighbor load update. And system performance improves slowly when neighbor list is long enough, because the neighbors in last part of the list can not provide much capacity for replication. The refuse ratio has obvious impact on system utility but this case is similar to realistic environment, where some of the registries have their own serving area.

While our experiments show that the RQO can give system better utility and balance peers, the RQO also has a problem that it balances system slower than RQC. Because RQC replicates a large number QoS objects every time, it can response to load change rapidly, which is important for burst requests.

7 Conclusion and Future Works

The web service infrastructure is evolving, so as the QoS registration architecture of web services. Most of the early works are centralized systems, but we believe that decentralized system is more suitable for global service oriented environment. In this paper, we presented a distributed web service QoS registry—the Q-Peer architecture.

The architecture is based on Napster-like unstructured peer-to-peer model. Every QoS object address is stored in service registry with its service description. Same or similar services' QoS is clustered together to conveniently expand other QoS operation like service selection. We designed simple but effective mechanisms to exchange load information between peers. Every QoS has several replicas to share load on different peers. Replication is based on load status exchange mechanism among peers. We presented two replication schemes—replicating QoS class and replicating QoS object, which have different granularity of replication. We tested the system performance with two replication schemes. RQO showed good load-balance effect in various system statuses.

We are still improving Q-Peer on the replication scheme. A more accurate and rapid load sharing approaching is needed. We are conducting theoretical analysis on replication behavior and effect of different configurations, which will make the system more adaptive on different scale and network status.

References

1. Tsalgatidou, A., Pilioura, T.: An Overview of Standards and Related Technology in Web Services. Distributed and Parallel Databases 12(2), 135–162 (2002)
2. Web Services Architecture, W3C (February 2004)
3. Li, F., Yang, F.C., Shuang, K., et al.: Peer-to-Peer based QoS Registry Architecture for Web Services. In: DAIS 07. The Proceedings of the 7th IFIP International Conference on Distributed Applications and Interoperable Systems. LNCS, vol. 4531, Springer, Heidelberg (2007)
4. UDDI version 3.0, OASIS
5. Verma, K., Sivashanmugam, K., Sheth, A., et al.: METEOR-S WSDI: A Scalable P2P Infrastructure of Registries for Semantic Publication and Discovery of Web Services. Information Technology and Management 6(1), 17–39 (2005)
6. Planet-Lab Homepage, http://www.planet-lab.org/
7. Maximilien, E.M., Singh, M.P.: A Framework and Ontology for Dynamic Web Services Selection. IEEE Internet Computing 8(5), 84–93 (2004)
8. Serhani, M.A., Dssouli, R., Hafid, A., et al.: A QoS broker based architecture for efficient Web services selection. In: ICWS'05. Proceedings of IEEE International Conference on Web Services, pp. 113–120. IEEE Computer Society Press, Los Alamitos (2005)
9. Liu, Y., Ngu, A.H., Zeng, L.Z.: QoS computation and policing in dynamic web service selection. In: Proceedings of the 13th International Conference on World Wide Web, pp. 66–73. ACM Press, New York (2004)
10. Yu, T., Lin, K.J.: A Broker-based Framework for QoS-Aware Web Service Composition. In: EEE-05. Proceeding of IEEE International Conference on e-Technology, e- Commerce and e-Service, Hong Kong, China, IEEE Computer Society Press, Los Alamitos (2005)
11. Gibelin, N., Makpangou, M.: Efficient and Transparent Web-Services Selection. In: Benatallah, B., Casati, F., Traverso, P. (eds.) ICSOC 2005. LNCS, vol. 3826, pp. 527–532. Springer, Heidelberg (2005)
12. Napster Homepage, http://www.napster.com
13. Gnutella Homepage, http://www.gnutella.com
14. KaZaA Homepage, http://www.kazaa.com

15. Lua, E.K., Crowcroft, J., Pias, M., et al.: A Survey and Comparison of Peer-to-Peer Overlay Network Schemes, IEEE Communications Survey and Tutorial (March 2004)
16. Koloniari, G., Pitoura, E.: Peer-to-peer management of XML data: issues and research challenges. In: ACM SIGMOD Record, vol. 34(2), ACM Press, New York (2005)
17. Schmidt, C., Parashar, M.: A peer-to-peer approach to Web service discovery. In: Proceedings of the 13th International Conference on World Wide Web, pp. 211–229 (2004)
18. Cohen, E., Shenker, S.: Replication Strategies in Unstructured Peer-to-Peer Networks. In: Proceedings of the 2002 conference on Applications, technologies, architectures, and protocols for computer communications, pp. 177–190. ACM Press, New York (2002)
19. Li, F., Su, S., Yang, F.C.: On Distributed Service Selection for QoS Driven Service Composition. In: Bauknecht, K., Pröll, B., Werthner, H. (eds.) EC-Web 2006. LNCS, vol. 4082, Springer, Heidelberg (2006)
20. Nejdl, W., Wolpers, M., Siberski, W., et al.: Super-peer-based routing and clustering strategies for RDF-based peer-to-peer networks. In: Proceedings of the 12th international conference on World Wide Web, pp. 536–543. ACM Press, New York (2003)
21. Adamic, L.A., Huberman, B.A.: Zipf's Law and the Internet. Glottometrics 3, 143–150 (2002)

Business Process Regression Testing

Hehui Liu, Zhongjie Li, Jun Zhu, and Huafang Tan

IBM China Research Laboratory, Beijing 100094, China
{hehuiliu, lizhongj, zhujun, tanhuaf}@cn.ibm.com

Abstract. Business Process Execution Language(BPEL) has been recognized as a standard for the service orchestration in Service Oriented Architecture(SOA). Due to the pivotal role played by BPEL in service composition, the reliability of a business process becomes critical for a SOA system, especially during its evolution.

Regression testing is well known as an effective technology to ensure the quality of modified programs. To reduce the cost of regression testing, a subset of test cases is selected to (re)run, known as regression test selection. Previous work addressing this problem will fail in the presence of concurrent control flow, which is an important and widely used feature of BPEL in describing service orchestration. In this paper, a regression testing approach for BPEL business processes is presented. In this approach, an impact analysis rule is proposed to identify the test paths affected by the change of BPEL concurrent control structures. Based on the impact analysis result and process changes identification, the impacted test paths are classified into reusable, modified, obsolete and new-structural paths. Experiments show that our approach is feasible.

1 Introduction

Service Oriented Architecture (SOA) is continually gaining more application in software industry for the automation of business processes and the integration of IT systems. In SOA, the service orchestration that combines several web services into a more complex one is a crucial building block [2]. Business Process Execution Language(BPEL) is a standard for describing such service orchestration. For the pivotal role played by BPEL in service composition, the reliability of business processes becomes especially critical for a SOA system. More importantly, the dynamic and adaptive nature of SOA also requires the business processes evolve more quickly and meanwhile puts forward more rigorous demand on the quality of the processes during the maintenance of a SOA system.

Regression testing is well known as an effective technology for verifying the behavior of modified programs [5]. After a program has been changed, obviously, the simplest way is to rerun all test cases, which is called as retest-all strategy [5] in regression testing. However, this strategy is expensive for executing unnecessary tests. Another strategy called as selective strategy [5] is applied to select only a subset of test cases to (re)run. Two problems have to be addressed in this

B. Krämer, K.-J. Lin, and P. Narasimhan (Eds.): ICSOC 2007, LNCS 4749, pp. 157–168, 2007.

strategy: (1) the problem of selecting impacted tests from the test suite of original program and (2) the problem of determining where additional test cases may be required and generating them. A lot of work has been done around the first problem [7, 1, 4, 9, 3], which is known as regression test selection problem. An earlier work proposed a test path comparison approach to select the impacted test cases [1]. In this approach, the test paths of the original and the new programs are compared one by one, test paths not included in the new paths are selected out as impacted paths, and all test cases attached with the impacted paths should be rerun. This path comparison approach could only be used when white box test paths exist. Whereas, in real projects, test cases may be black box and are no associated white box test paths, and the test paths are not always generated. So more generally and widely used approaches are based on the comparison of control flow graphs or source codes [7, 4, 9]. These approaches are based on the assumption that when a node/edge on the control flow or a statement of the source code is changed, only the test cases that could cover this node/edge or statement will be impacted. This assumption is true for programs without concurrent control flow. However, in the presence of concurrent control flow, even a minor change to the synchronization condition may affect many concurrent execution paths that don't contain the changed condition. Furthermore, the impact is not only related with the changed synchronization condition, but also with other synchronization conditions. So, in the presence of concurrent control flow, the traditional work [7, 4, 9] will fail and cannot be applied directly. While in BPEL, the concurrent control flow is used as an important feature and is widely used in business processes.

In previous work [6, 8], the authors have implemented a test path generation tool for a BPEL business process under the path coverage criteria. This tool can generate test paths automatically, and the generated test paths need to be further refined manually into runnable test cases by adding complete test data and so on. The application of this tool in real cases leads to the requirement on the regression testing of a business process under the path coverage criteria. To meet such requirement, in this paper we propose a regression testing approach to select the (re)run test cases for a modified business process. Suppose that we have two sets of test paths, one for the old process, one for the new process, and an old test case set. Our goal is to work out a new test case set and select a test case subset to (re)run. All test paths can be classified into four categories with regression test selection technique:

- **reusable paths:** not impacted by the process changes, representing common test paths of the old and new processes;
- **modified paths:** impacted, in the sense that conditional branches on the test paths are the same but activity attributes or non-conditional activities are somehow changed, representing old and new test paths that have minor differences;
- **obsolete paths:** only valid for the old process, representing old test paths that will not exist for the new process;
- **new-structural paths:** only valid for the new process, representing new test paths having no correspondence in the old process.

Once we have this classification performed on the old and the new test paths, we can take actions to get the new test cases. Old test cases of the reusable paths are added to the new test case set; old test cases of the modified paths are updated into new test cases; and new-structural test cases are derived from the new-structural paths. Then all modified and new-structural test cases are selected to (re)run. In order to do the test path classification, in this paper, the differences between the old and the new processes are firstly identified. An impact analysis rule is proposed to analyze the affected test paths by the changes of concurrent control structures. Based on the process change information and impact analysis result, a test path selection algorithm is used to select the test paths, (re)run test cases. Different with previous work [1], we select the impacted test paths based on the business processes comparison instead of path comparison. Therefore, even if the test paths of the business processes are not generated, our approach could still be applied to select the impacted test cases via the linkage of source codes with test cases. The rest of this paper is organized as follows: section 2 gives some background of BPEL. Section 3 introduces our regression testing approach for business processes. Section 4 presents related work and section 5 closes this paper with conclusion and future work prediction.

2 Business Process Execution Language

A BPEL process is composed of BPEL activities, which can be either atomic or structured. Atomic activities define constructs for web service interactions and data handling, such as receive (wait to receive an event), reply (return an response to its caller), assign (assign a value to a variable). Like other programming languages, BPEL has typical control structures including sequence, switch, while, etc. In addition, BPEL uses the flow construct to provide concurrency and synchronization. These are called structured activities, which will be the container for atomic activities. A BPEL activity could have some attributes like name, invoked service and variable name.

Inside a flow construct, synchronization between concurrent activities is provided by means of links. Each link has a source activity and a target activity. Furthermore, a transition condition (a boolean expression) is associated with each link and is evaluated when the source activity terminates. Only after the source activity has terminated, the transition condition is evaluated. And only if the transition condition is true, the target activity could be executed. In this paper, activities that allow control logic divergence (e.g. switch, link with a transition condition) are called decision points. As the link activity has special meaning for regression analysis, we'll take it as a special kind of activity, and call all the other activities "general activities".

Figure 1 gives an example loan process. This process begins by receiving a loan request. The *InvokeAssessor* and *InvokeApprover* are two invoke activities to invoke risk assessment and loan approval services respectively. All the activities of this process are contained within a flow, and their (potentially concurrent) behavior is staged according to the dependencies expressed by links. The

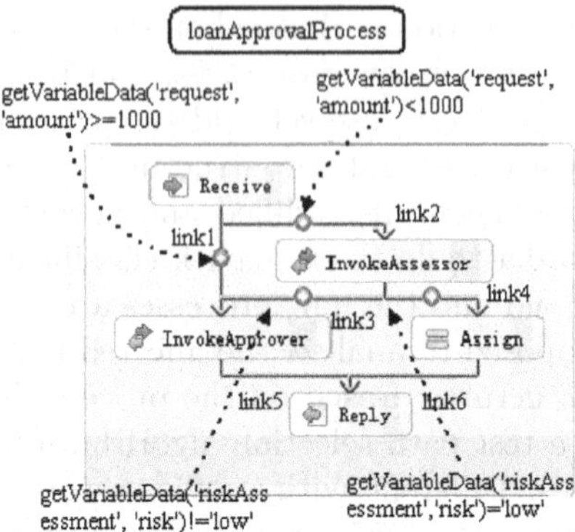

Fig. 1. The Loan Process

transition conditions on the links determine which links get activated. Finally the process responds with either a "loan approved" or a "loan rejected" message.

3 BPEL Regression Testing

The objective of regression test selection of a business process is to identify the impact of business process changes to test cases, and then take proper test case update actions accordingly and determine the subset of test cases to (re)run.

In this paper, we classify the test paths for the original process and the new process into four categories: reusable, obsolete, modified and new-structural, as is shown in figure 2. The exact meaning of this classification has been explained in the introduction section. Take the processes in figure 2 as an example, for the three test paths in the old process, path 1 is reusable as it is not impacted by the process changes, path 2 is obsolete, path 3 is modified into a new test path by adding a new activity 10 and modifying the activity 6. The new process introduces two new test paths: path 4 and path 5.

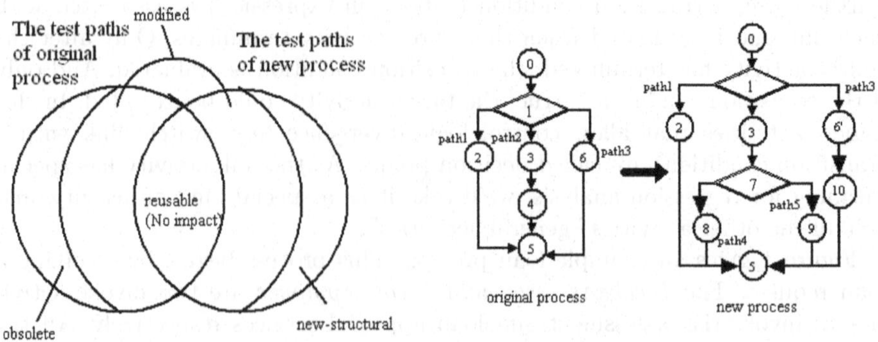

Fig. 2. The test paths classification and process change scenario

3.1 Regression Test Selection Problems Introduced by Concurrent Control Flow

Based on the path classification, the mission of path selection is to identify the reusable, obsolete, new-structural and modified test paths after a business process has been changed. For different types of activities, the change impact to test paths is different. For a general activity change, only test paths containing this activity will be impacted. According to the activity type and change information, the category(modified, obsolete, and new-structural) of impacted test paths could be determined. For example, if a while activity is deleted, all test paths containing this activity in the original path set will become obsolete. However, for a link activity, the problem becomes complex and this simple rule is not true any more. Once a link activity is changed, the impacted test paths will not be limited to those containing the changed link. For example, if the transition condition of link2 in the process of figure 1 is modified to the condition showed in the process of figure 3(1), the path with request.amount >= 1000 not containing link2 in figure 1 will be modified(the condition of this path becomes request.amount >= 2000). At the same time, two new-structural test paths are introduced into the new process(the path with 1000 <= request.amount < 2000 and riskAssessment.risk != 'low' and the path with 1000 <= request.amount < 2000 and riskAssessment.risk = 'low'). Whereas, if the transition condition of link2 is changed to request.amount >= 1000, as showed in the process in figure 3(2), all the test paths in the original process will become obsolete, and two new-structural paths will be generated in the new process.

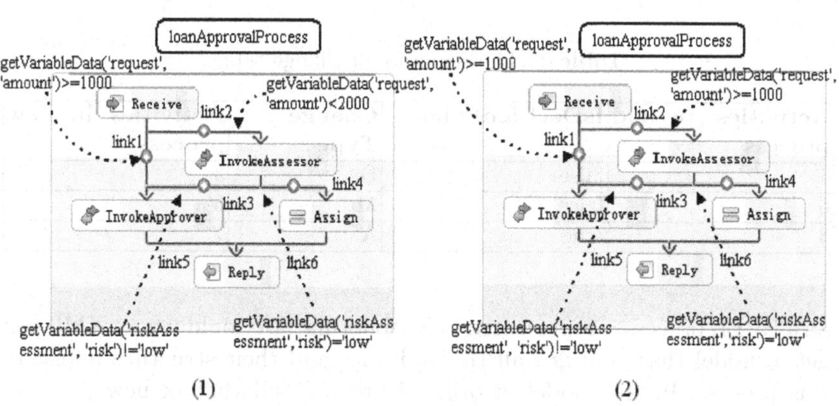

Fig. 3. The modified processes of loan process

Actually, the problems here are caused by the concurrent characteristic of the flow activity. Potentially, all the elements contained in a flow could execute concurrently. Just for the existence of link activities, some activities are prohibited to run, consequently not included in some test paths. For the test path with request.amount >= 1000 in figure 1, as the condition of link 2 is false, both

InvokeAssessor and *Assign* activity are prohibited to be executed, not including in this test path. Further more, the activation of link 2 is related with link 1, consequently the change of link 1 could affect both the test paths covering link 1 and those covering link 2. So, in order to select the modified, obsolete and new-structural paths impacted by a link activity change, we have to solve two problems: 1, analysis the impact of the link activity changes to test paths; 2, select the relevant test paths(modified, obsolete, new-structural paths) from the impacted test paths.

3.2 BPEL Diff

In order to select the impacted test paths, we need firstly identify the changes of a business process upon modification, and by the inclusion relationship between activities and test paths, the impacted test paths could be selected and classified. A change table is used to record all the changed activities here, as is shown in table 1. Therein, each row represents a change item. *IsDecisionPoint* indicates whether the changed activity is a decision point. *ChangeType* indicates the type of the change action: *M*, *D*, and *A*. *M* is modification action, *D* is deletion action, *A* is addition action. *Activities in old process* refers to the changed activity in the original process, and *Activities in new process* refers to the changed activity in the new process. For the deletion action, because the deleted activity does not exist in the new process, the previous activity of the deleted activity is put in *Activities in new process* column. Similarly, for the addition action, *Activities in old process* will point to the previous activity of the added activity. Such as for the process in figure 2, we could get the change table showed as table 1.

Table 1. The structure of change table

Activities in old process	**IsDecisionPoint**	**Change Type**	**Activities in new process**
4	false	D	3
6	false	M	6'
3	true	A	7

As a BPEL process is represented in XML format, we could use an XML parser to get a model that contains all the activities and their structure information of this process. In the model of original process and that of new process, in order to identify the same activity, the activity name is used as the unique identifier in this paper. In the BPEL process model coming from two processes, by comparing the activities in the original and the new process, we could get all the change information, and fill them into the change table. *Link* activity is special as it connects source and target activities. We use the following rules for the comparison of *link* activities. Only when the source activity name, the target activity name and the transition condition of two *links* are all the same, the *link* activities are considered as same. If either the source or the target activities are different, the *link* activities are considered as different entities (this case will be broken down into a *link* delete action and a *link* addition action); if the transition condition is modified, this *link* is considered as modified.

3.3 Path Selection

For the new business process, based on our previous work [8], its test paths can also be generated automatically. So, in this paper, our test path selection algorithm is applied on these two test path sets to classify the reusable, modified, obsolete and new-structural paths. In order to record the relationship between test paths and activities, a test path table is used, as is shown in table 2. Therein, the value in column j and row i represents whether activity j is on test path i. When this value is 1, the activity j is on the test path i; when the value is 0, the activity j is not on the test path i. We call this value as indicator in this paper. Table 2 is the test path table of the loan process in figure 1.

Table 2. The test path table of the loan process

Test Path	Receive	Link1	Link2	Invoke Assessor	Link3	Link4	Invoke Approver	Assign	Link5	Link6	Reply
path 1	1	1	0	0	0	0	1	0	1	0	1
path 2	1	0	1	1	1	0	1	0	1	0	1
path 3	1	0	1	1	0	1	0	1	0	1	1

Impact Analysis for Concurrent Control Structure Change. From the change table, we could get all the change information of a business process, and for the different types of activities, the impact to test paths is definitely different. For a decision point, its deletion will cause all test paths passing this activity in original test path set become obsolete, and at the same time introduces new test paths that could cover the previous activity of this decision point into new path set. The addition of a decision point will generate new paths covering this activity in the new path set, and at the same time could make all test paths containing its previous activity in the original test path set become obsolete paths. For a branch activity of a decision point, its deletion could also make the test paths passing it in the original path set become obsolete, and its addition could generate new-structural paths passing it in the new path set. For a non-decision-point activity, its addition, deletion and modification could only make all test paths passing it become modified paths.

For the change of a *link* activity, the test paths covering the changed *link* activity are only a subset of the impacted test paths. Just as explained in section 3.1, its impact to the test paths is far beyond this. In fact, based on the characteristic of the target activity of a changed *link* activity, there are two types of impact results. One is that the target activity of a changed *link* activity is a start activity of a *flow* activity in the opposite process (we say the original and new process as opposite process), we call this change as first type of *link* change;

the other type is that the target activity is not a start activity, and we call this change as second type of *link* change.

First type of link change: in this type, because in current process, the target activity of the changed *link* activity is a start activity of a *flow* in the opposite process, all test paths passing this flow activity will include the activity. While in current process, for the existence of the *link* activity, only some test paths contain the target activity and it can not be a start activity in the flow activity. So all test paths passing this *flow* in the original and the new process will be impacted by the change. See the example in figure 4, which is another changed process of the loan process. In this process, *link 4* is deleted from the original process, and *Assign* activity becomes the start activity of the *flow* activity (although in semantics, this cannot happen for this process, here we just use it as an example). It could be seen that all the test paths passing the flow activity in the new process have the *Assign* activity as a start activity of this *flow*. While in the original process, no matter for which path, *Assign* activity is not a start activity. That is to say, no matter in the original or the new process, all the paths passing the *flow* activity are impacted.

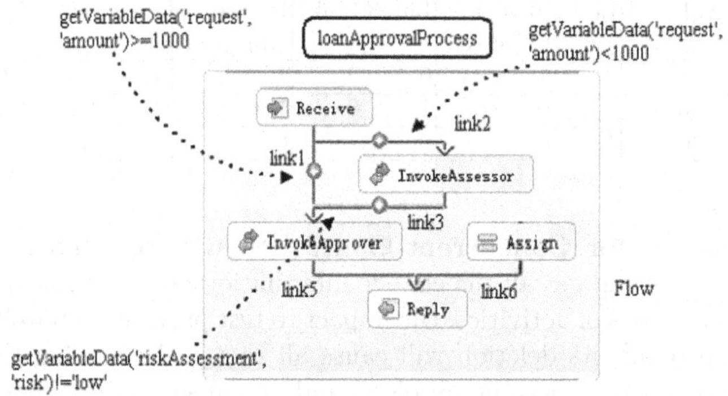

Fig. 4. Another changed process of the loan Process

Second type of link change: in this type, suppose in the original process, the *links* using the source activity of the changed *link* as source activity are link_1, link_2, ... , link_n, and the corresponding transition conditions are C_1, C_2, ... , C_n, the intersections they generate could be expressed as $C_1 \bigcap C_2 \bigcap ... \bigcap C_n$, it is obviously that each branch of this source activity is a region of this expression. For a condition C_i, if it has no intersection with the other conditions C_j(i!=j), its deletion or addition will not impact other regions of this expression, but only reduce or increase one region. See the process showed in figure 1, the transition conditions of link3 and link4 have no intersection, so the deletion of link3 could only reduce the branches of activity *InvokeAssessor* by one. In this case, only the test paths containing the changed *link* activity are impacted. At the other extremity, if C_i has intersection with all the other conditions C_j(i!=j), its deletion or addition definitely can impact all other intersections, such as C_i == true. In this case, all the test paths passing the source activity will be impacted. In general cases, when the *link* transition condition is changed, the impacted test paths will have a scope between the above two extremity cases. In this paper, for this change type, we consider all the test paths covering the source activity as impacted paths.

So, for the changes of *link* activities, an impact analysis rule could be applied to select out all the impacted test paths. This rule can be described as follows. Firstly, based on the information of a changed *link* activity, judge which change type it belongs. Secondly, following the conclusion of relevant impact analysis, select out the impacted test paths caused by the change of this *link* activity. By this rule, we could solve the first problem introduced by concurrent control flow.

Path Selection Based on Test Path Table. Based on the impact analysis, we could get the regression test selection process as follows. Firstly, based on the change table, the non-impacted test paths could be selected as reusable paths. Secondly, the obsolete and new-structural paths caused by general activity changes could be selected out from the original and the new path set. Thirdly, the impacted test paths caused by *link* activity changes could be selected respectively from the original and the new path set. Finally, the remaining paths is modified paths. In this paper, we call the test paths impacted by link activity changes **special path sets**.

In the special path sets, for two test paths p and p' that come from the original path set and the new path set respectively, if p' is modified from p, they must execute the same *link* activities. If in the original path set, there is no test path that could execute the same *link* activities with p', p' must belongs to new-structural path set. Oppositely, if there is no test path that could execute the same *link* activities with p in the new path set, p must belong to obsolete path set. So, for a test path p' in the special path set coming from new path set, following the rule that whether there is a path p in the original path set has the same *link* activities with it, we could decide p' as a modified path or new-structural path. If p' is a modified path, p should also be a modified path. Finally, all the remaining paths in the special path set coming from the original path set are obsolete paths. Consequently, the test paths impacted by the changes of *link* activities could be classified into modified, obsolete, and new-structural paths, solving the second problem introduced by concurrent control flow.

In summary, the path selection algorithm is shown as below. In this algorithm, each path is labeled with a symbol from (*R, M, O, N, R*). In the symbol for path p_i, R represents p_i is reusable, M represents p_i is modified, O represents p_i is obsolete, N represents p_i is new-structural, and S represents p_i belongs special path sets.

PathSelection(Change Table: C, Test Path Table of Original Process: T, Test Path Table of new Process: T')

Label all paths in original and new path set as R

for each modified activity a in C **do**

  get impacted test paths I and I' from T and T'

```
4    if a is a decision point or a branch activity of a decision point
5    label the paths in I as O and the paths I' as N
6    else if a is not a link activity
7      for the paths in I and I' are labeled with R, label them as M
8      else
9        if the change type of a is addition or deletion
10          label all paths containing a in I as O and those in I' as N
11       end if
12       label other impacted test paths being labeled with R or M in I and I' as S
13     end if
14    end if
15  end for
16  classify the test paths are labeled with S into modified, obsolete and new-structural paths.
```

Table 3. The test path table of modified loan process

Test Path	Receive	Link1	Link2	Invoke Assessor	Link3	Link4	Invoke Approver	Assign	Link5	Link6	Reply
path 1	1	1	1	1	1	0	1	0	1	0	1
path 2	1	1	1	1	0	1	1	1	0	1	1

In the identification of the special test path sets, because the paths executing the added or deleted *link* activities have been selected out(shown in the 9 and 10 lines of **PathSelection** algorithm), in the special test path sets, all the *link* activities contained in the paths are modified or non-changed, which exist in original and new process at the same time. We represent this *link* activities set as S_{link}. In the original path table, for a test path in the special test path set, from top to down, all the indicator values of *link* activities contained in S_{link} could form a 0 and 1 string, which in deed indicates the *link* activities that a test path contains. In the new path table, from top to down, by tuning the order of *link* activities contained in S_{link} to keep the same order with that of original path table, for a test path in the special test path set of new path set, all the indicator values of *link* activities contained in S_{link} also could form a 0 and 1 string. By judging whether this string is contained in the 0 and 1 string set of original path set, we could select this path into relevant path set. Finally, all the remaining paths in the special path set in the original path set are obsolete paths. Such as for the original process in figure 1 and the new process in figure 3(2), table 3 shows the test paths of the process in figure 3(2). By impact analysis, we could learn that all test paths in test path table 2 and 3 are special paths. Firstly, we could get the 0 and 1 strings for the special path set of original path set as {path 1: 100010, path 2: 011010, path 3: 010101}(from left to right, the link activities are: link1, link2, link3, link4, link5, link6). The 0 and 1 strings for the special path set of this new process are: {path 1:111010, path 2: 110101}.

Because 111010 and 110101 are neither contained in $\{100010, 011010, 010101\}$, the test paths of table 3 are new-structural paths, and the remaining paths in table 2 are obsolete.

After the test paths are selected, the regression testing actions are taken as follows: the test cases of reusable paths are added to new test case set, those of modified paths are updated, and new test cases are generated for the new-structural paths. Then the updated and new test cases are selected to (re)run.

The tool of this paper is built as an Eclipse plugin tool, making it could easily integrated with other SOA develop or testing tool, such as WebSphere Integration Developer or Rational Architectural Develop.

4 Related Work

Regression testing has been recognized as an effective technology to ensure the quality of software after a system has been changed. Lots of previous work has been done around the regression test selection problem, and the test selection based on control flow is widely applied [7, 4, 9]. In these approaches, after a program has been changed, the control flow graphs of the original and the new program are obtained by analyzing the source codes of original and new program. Based on the control flow graphs, a graph comparison algorithm is used to identify the changed nodes or edges. Consequently, the test cases covering the changed nodes or edges are selected as impacted cases. In the face of the new characteristic introduced by the object-oriented programs and aspect-oriented programs, the control flow graph is extended by [4, 9] respectively to support the new characteristic of new programming language. Then based on the extended control flow graph, the test selection algorithm is applied to select the impacted test cases [4, 9]. So far as we know, [1] is the only work that also selects the impacted test cases under the path coverage criteria. In this paper [1], all test paths are represented by a special expression-algebraic expression. Based on the representation, a test path comparison approach was proposed to select the impacted test cases. However, this approach is limited by the expression capability of test path model, and only could be applied to selected the impacted test cases when the test paths are generated. While the approach of our paper not only could be applied to the select the (re)run test cases via test paths, but also could be applied to select the (re)run test cases when test paths are not generated.

5 Conclusions and Future Work

Service Oriented Architecture (SOA) is recognized as a good solution for the integration of diverse IT systems. BPEL as a standard for the service orchestration has been widely used in SOA to compose multiple services to accomplish a business process. The pivotal role of BPEL in a SOA system makes its reliability become especially critical in the maintenance of a SOA system. Regression testing has been recognized as an effective technology to ensure the quality of modified programs. In this paper, to address the special problems introduced by the concurrent control structure of BPEL, a regression test selection approach for BPEL is proposed. In this approach, the changed activities are identified by BPEL Diff. The impact of concurrent control structure changes to test paths is classified into two types. Based on the analysis for these two types, an impacted analysis rule for the changes of concurrent control flow is proposed. By considering all the *link* activities on a test path, the test paths impacted by a *link* activity changes are classified into modified, obsolete and new-structural paths. Consequently, the reusable, modified, obsolete and new-structural path sets are selected out. Finally the related test cases are selected and updated. In future, we will study a more precise selection algorithm to select the test paths impacted by *link* activity changes, and further validate our technology in more real cases.

References

[1] Benedusi, P., Cimitile, A., Carlini, U.D.: Post-maintenance testing based on path change analysis. In: ICSM' 88. Proceedings of the Conference on Software Maintenance, Scottsdale, AZ, USA, pp. 352–361 (October 1988)

[2] Chen, L., Wassermann, B., Emmerich, W., Foster, H.: Web service orchestration with bpel. In: ICSE'06. Proceeding of the 28th International Conference on Software Engineering, Shanghai, China, pp. 1071–1072 (May 2006)

[3] Vokolos, F.I., Frankl, P.G.: Pythia: A regression test selection tool based on textual differencing. In: ENCRESS' 97. Porceedings of the 3th International Conference on Reliability, Quality, and Safety of Software Intensive Systems, Athens, Greece, pp. 3–21 (May 1997)

[4] Harrold, M.J., Jones, J.A., Li, T., Liang, D.: Regression test selection for java software. In: OOPSLA'01. Proceedings of the ACM Conference on OO Programming, Systems, Languages, and Applications, Tampa Bay, FL, USA, pp. 312–326. ACM Press, New York (October 2001)

[5] Li, Y., Wahl, N.J.: An overview of regression testing. ACM SIGSOFT Software Engineering Notes 24(1), 69–73 (1999)

[6] Li, Z., Sun, W.: Bpel-unit: Junit for bpel processes. In: Dan, A., Lamersdorf, W. (eds.) ICSOC 2006. LNCS, vol. 4294, pp. 415–426. Springer, Heidelberg (December 2006)

[7] Rothermel, G., Harrold, M.J.: A safe, efficient regression test selection technique. ACM Transactions on Software Engineering and Methodology 6(2), 173–210 (1997)

[8] Yuan, Y., Li, Z., Sun, W.: A graph-search based approach to bpel4ws test generation. In: ICSEA'06. Proceedings of the International Conference on Software Engineering Advances, Papeete, Tahiti, French Polynesia, p. 14 (October 2006)

[9] Zhao, J., Xie, T., Li, N.: Towards regression test selection for aspectj programs. In: WTAOP06. Proceedings of the 2nd workshop on Testing Aspect-Oriented Programs, Portland, Maine, pp. 21–26 (July 2006)

Auditing Business Process Compliance

Aditya Ghose and George Koliadis

Decision Systems Laboratory
School of Computer Science and Software Engineering
University of Wollongong, NSW 2522 Australia
{aditya, gk56}@uow.edu.au

Abstract. Compliance issues impose significant management and reporting requirements upon organizations. We present an approach to enhance business process modeling notations with the capability to detect and resolve many broad compliance related issues. We provide a semantic characterization of a minimal revision strategy that helps us obtain compliant process models from models that might be initially non-compliant, in a manner that accommodates the structural and semantic dimensions of parsimoniously annotated process models. We also provide a heuristic approach to compliance resolution using a notion of *compliance patterns*. This allows us to partially automate compliance resolution, leading to reduced levels of analyst involvement and improved decision support.

1 Introduction

Compliance management has become a significant concern for organizations given increasingly onerous legislative and regulatory environments. Legislation such as the Sarbanes-Oxley Act imposes stringent compliance requirements, and organizations are increasingly having to make heavy investments in meeting these requirements (arguably evaluated to approx. US$15 billion in year 2005 US corporate cost and $1.4 trillion in market costs [1]). Thus, we address the problem of auditing business processes for compliance with legislative/regulatory frameworks, as well as the problem of appropriately modifying processes if they are found to be non-compliant. We focus primarily on early-phase analysis and design (or model) time compliance analysis and resolution.

We will use Figure 1: a simple BPMN (see Section 1.2) "Screen Package" process owned by a $CourierOrganization$ as a motivating example. This process is concerned with scanning packages upon arrival to the organization to establish their $Status$ and ensure that they are screened by a $RegulatoryAuthority$ to determine if they should be $Held$. One simple (and critical) compliance rule imposed by a $RegulatoryAuthority$ may state that: (CR_1) *"Packages Known to be Held by a Regulatory Authority must not be Routed by a Sort Officer until the Package is Known to be Cleared by the Regulatory Authority"*.

Our challenge in this paper is to determine whether a process violates compliance requirements and to decide how to modify the process to ensure it complies. Several alternative approaches exist for the former - we therefore devote much of our attention to the latter. In particular we note that ad-hoc changes to processes in the face of non-compliance can lead to significant downsides, including additional inconsistencies,

B. Krämer, K.-J. Lin, and P. Narasimhan (Eds.): ICSOC 2007, LNCS 4749, pp. 169–180, 2007.

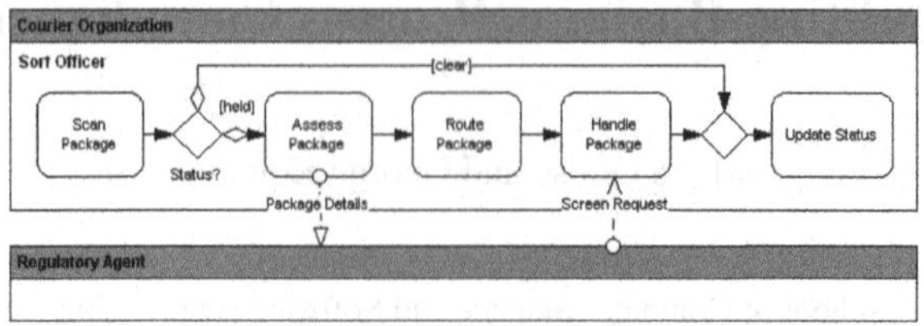

Fig. 1. Package Screening Process (O)

unwarranted side-effects as well as changes within the model and subsequent organization upon deployment.

We provide a conceptual framework that can be relatively easily implemented in decision-support tools that audit process models for compliance and suggest modifications when processes are found to be non-compliant. A key challenge with BPMN is that it provides relatively little by way semantics of the processes being modeled. Another challenge is that there is no consensus on how the semantics of BPMN might be defined, although several competing formalisms have been proposed. Since compliance checking clearly requires more information than is available in a pure BPMN process model, we propose a lightweight, analyst-mediated approach to semantic annotation of BPMN models, in particular, the annotation of activities with effects. Model checking is an alternative approach, but it requires mapping BPMN process models to state models, which is problematic and ill-defined.

We encode BPMN process models into semantically-annotated digraphs called Semantic Process Networks (or SPNets). We then define a class of *proximity relations* that permit us to compare alternative modifications of process models in terms of how much they deviate from the original process model. Armed with these tools we are able to resolve non-compliance by identifying minimally different process models (to the original) that satisfy the applicable compliance requirements. We are also able to focus analyst attention on the minimal sources of inconsistency (with the applicable rules) within a process model - appropriately modifying each of these is an alternative approach to restoring compliance. In addition to laying the semantic groundwork for reasoning about resolutions to process non-compliance, we also introduce the notion of process *compliance patterns*. These patterns provide heuristic guidance for detecting and resolving process non-compliance. This research lays the foundations for a new class of tools that would help analysts determine, using design-time artefacts, whether a process model satisfies the applicable compliance requirements and how best to modify these processes if they are found to be non-compliant.

1.1 Related Work

In [2], logic-based contractual formalisms are provided for specifying and evaluating the conformance of business process designs with business contracts. In comparison, we present a framework that permits the semi-automated alteration of non-compliant process models in a minimal, structure and semantics preserving manner. In [3], an approach for checking semantic integrity constraints within the narrative structure of web documents is proposed. Description logic extensions to Computational Tree Logic (CTL) are provided for specifying a formal model of a documents conventions, criteria, structure and content. In most cases, the 'high-level' nature of most business process models may not lead directly to detailed fine grained execution and interaction models used in model-checking based approaches to static analysis [4]. Furthermore, techniques employing model checking have limited support for localizing errors and inconsistencies to specific (or range of) elements on process models. In [5], an approach for integrating business rule definitions into process execution languages is presented. In addition, [6] have recently proposed a method for verifying semantic properties of a process w.r.t. execution traces once model change operations have been applied. Finally, heuristic change strategies have been used to provide additional guidance for scoping business process change requirements. For example, [7] present approx. thirty workflow redesign heuristics that encompass change in *task assignment*, *routing*, *allocation*, *communication* to guide performance improvement. [6] also define *insertion*, *deletion* and *movement* process change primitives to limit the scope of verifying semantic correctness of models.

1.2 Some Preliminaries

The *Business Process Modeling Notation (BPMN)* has received strong industry interest and support [8], and has been found to be of high maturity in representing the concepts required for modeling business process, apart from some limitations regarding the representation of process state and possible ambiguity of the swim-lane concept [9]. Processes are represented in BPMN using **flows**: *events*, *activities*, and *decisions*; **connectors**: *control flow links*, and *message flow links*; and **lanes**: *pools*, and *lanes* within pools. The process section in Figure 1 shows "Courier Organization" and "Regulatory Agent" participants collaborating to achieve the screening of a package.

Business (or Compliance) Rules (BR) declare constraints governing action, their coordination, structure, assignment and results, as well as the participants, their responsibilities, structure, interactions, rights and decisions. [10] provide a rich taxonomy of business rules that includes: *State Constraints*; *Process Constraints*; *Derivation Rules*; *Reaction Rules*; and, *Deontic Assignments*. In addition, the formal specification of business rules may include additional modal operators signifying the deontic (as in [2]) or temporal (as in [11]) characteristics of desirable properties of the model. For example, the following CTL expression refines the informal rule stated in Section 1:

$$(CR_1)\ \mathbf{AG}[Knows(RegulatoryAgent, Package, Status, Held) \rightarrow \\ \mathbf{A}[\neg Performs(SortOfficer, Route, Package) \\ \mathbf{U}\ Knows(RegulatoryAgent, Package, Status, Clear)]]$$

2 Modeling Business Processes for Compliance Auditing

Compliance of a business process is commonly concerned with the possible state of affairs a business process may bring to bear. *Activities* and *Sub-Processes* (i.e. represented in BPMN as rounded boxes) signify such transition of state, where the labeling of an activity (e.g. 'Register New Customer') abstracts one or more normal/abnormal outcomes. In order to improve the clarity and descriptive capability of process models for testing compliance, we augment state altering nodes (i.e. atomic activities and sub-processes) with parsimonious *effect annotations*. An *effect* is the result (i.e. product or outcome) of an activity being executed by some cause or agent. Table 1 below outlines the immediate effect of the tasks in Figure 1. Effects can be viewed as both: *normative* - as they state required outcomes (e.g. goals); and, *descriptive* Ð in that they describe the normal, and predicted, subset of all possible outcomes. Effect annotations can be *formal* (for instance, in first order logic, possibly augmented with temporal operators), or informal (such as simple English). Many of the examples we use in this paper rely on formal effect annotations, but most of our observations hold even if these annotations were in natural language (e.g. via Controlled Natural Languages - CNL). Formal annotations (i.e. provided, or derived from CNL), e.g. $Performs(Actor, Action, Object)$ / $Knows(Actor, Object, Property, Value)$, permit us to use automated reasoners, while informal annotations oblige analysts to check for consistency between effects.

Table 1. Annotation of Package Screening Process (O) in Figure 1

Scan Package	$Performs(SortOfficer, Scan, Package)$
Assess Package	$Performs(SortOfficer, Assess, Package)$ $\wedge Knows(RegulatoryAgent, Package, Status, Held)$
Route Package	$Performs(SortOfficer, Route, Package)$ $\wedge Knows(SortOfficer, Package, Location, Forwarding)$
Handle Package	$Performs(SortOfficer, Handle, Package)$ $\wedge Knows(RegulatoryAgent, Package, Status, Clear)$
Update Status	$Performs(SortOfficer, Update, PackageStatus)$
General Rule (GR_1)	$\forall a : Actor\ Knows(a, PackageStatus, Held)$ $\Leftrightarrow \neg Knows(a, Package, Status, Cleared)$

An *annotated BPMN model*, for the purposes of this paper, is one in which every task (atomic, loop, compensatory or multi-instance) and every sub-process has been annotated with descriptions of its immediate effects. We verify process compliance by establishing that a business process model is consistent with a set of compliance rules. In general, inconsistencies exist when some domain / process specific rules contradict each other. We evaluate compliance locally at sections of the process where they apply. However, before doing this, we require that an analyst accumulates effects throughout the process to provide a local in-context description of the *cumulative effect* at task nodes in the process. We define a process for *pair-wise effect accumulation*, which, given an ordered pair of tasks with effect annotations, determines the cumulative effect after both tasks have been executed in contiguous sequence. The procedure serves as a methodology for analysts to follow if only informal annotations are available. We assume that the effect annotations have been represented in conjunctive normal form or CNF. Simple techniques exist for translating arbitrary sentences into the conjunctive normal form.

- **Contiguous Tasks:** Let $\langle t_i, t_j \rangle$ be the ordered pair of tasks, and let e_i and e_j be the corresponding pair of (immediate) effect annotations. Let $e_i = \{c_{i1}, c_{i2}, \ldots, c_{im}\}$

and $e_j = \{c_{j1}, c_{j2}, \ldots, c_{jn}\}$ (we can view CNF sentences as sets of clauses, without loss of generality). If $e_i \cup e_j$ is consistent, then the resulting cumulative effect is $e_i \cup e_j$. Else, we define $e'_i = \{c_k | c_k \in e_i \text{ and } \{c_k\} \cup e_j \text{ is consistent}\}$ and the resulting cumulative effect to be $e'_i \cup e_j$. In other words, the cumulative effect of the two tasks consists of the effects of the second task plus as many of the effects of the first task as can be consistently included. We remove those clauses in the effect annotation of the first task that contradict the effects of the second task. The remaining clauses are undone, i.e., these effects are overridden by the second task. In the following, we shall use $acc(e_1, e_2)$ to denote the result of pair-wise effect accumulation of two contiguous tasks t_1 and t_2 with (immediate) effects e_1 and e_2. For example: $acc(\{Knows(RegulatoryAgent, Package, Status, Held)\}, \{Knows(RegulatoryAgent, Package, Status, Clear)\}) = \{Knows(RegulatoryAgent, Package, Status, Clear)\}$ in the case that GR_1 (Table 1) is considered applicable and protected.

Effects are only accumulated within participant lanes. In addition to the effect annotation of each task, we annotate each task t with a cumulative effect E_t. E_t is defined as a set $\{es_1, es_2, \ldots, es_p\}$ of alternative *effect scenarios*. Alternative effect scenarios are introduced by OR-joins or XOR-joins, as we shall see below. Cumulative effect annotation involves a left-to-right pass through a participant lane. Tasks which are not connected to any preceding task via a control flow link are annotated with the cumulative effect $\{e\}$ where e is the immediate effect of the task in question. We accumulate effects through a left-to-right pass of a participant lane, applying the pair-wise effect accumulation procedure on contiguous pairs of tasks connected via control flow links. The process continues without modification over splits. Joins require special consideration. In the following, we describe the procedure to be followed in the case of 2-way joins only, for brevity. The procedure generalizes in a straightforward manner for n-way joins.

- **AND-joins:** Let t_1 and t_2 be the two tasks immediately preceding an AND-join. Let their cumulative effect annotations be $E_1 = \{es_{11}, es_{12}, \ldots, es_{1m}\}$ and $E_2 = \{es_{21}, es_{22}, \ldots, es_{2n}\}$ respectively (where es_{ts} denotes an effect scenario, subscript s within the cumulative effect of some task, subscript t). Let e be the immediate effect annotation, and E the cumulative effect annotation of a task t immediately following the AND-join. We define $E = \{acc(es_{1i}, e) \cup acc(es_{2j}, e) | es_{1i} \in E_1 \text{ and } es_{2j} \in E_2\}$. Note that we do not consider the possibility of a pair of effect scenarios es_{1i} and es_{2j} being inconsistent, since this would only happen in the case of intrinsically and obviously erroneously constructed process models. The result of effect accumulation in the setting described here is denoted by $ANDacc(E_1, E_2, e)$.
- **XOR-joins:** Let t_1 and t_2 be the two tasks immediately preceding an XOR-join. Let their cumulative effect annotations be $E_1 = \{es_{11}, es_{12}, \ldots, es_{1m}\}$ and $E_2 = \{es_{21}, es_{22}, \ldots, es_{2n}\}$ respectively. Let e be the immediate effect annotation, and E the cumulative effect annotation of a task t immediately following the XOR-join. We define $E = \{acc(es_i, e) | es_i \in E_1 \text{ or } es_i \in E_2\}$. The result of effect accumulation in the setting described here is denoted by $XORacc(E_1, E_2, e)$.
- **OR-joins:** Let t_1 and t_2 be the two tasks immediately preceding an OR-join. Let their cumulative effect annotations be $E_1 = \{es_{11}, es_{12}, \ldots, es_{1m}\}$ and $E_2 =$

$\{es_{21}, es_{22}, \ldots, es_{2n}\}$ respectively. Let e be the immediate effect annotation, and E the cumulative effect annotation of a task t immediately following the OR-join. The result of effect accumulation in the setting described here is denoted by $ORacc(E_1, E_2, e) = ANDacc(E_1, E_2, e) \cup XORacc(E_1, E_2, e)$.

We note that the procedure described above does not satisfactorily deal with loops, but we can perform approximate checking by partial loop unraveling. We also note that some of the effect scenarios generated might be infeasible. Our objective is to devise decision-support functionality in the compliance management space, with human analysts vetting key changes before they are deployed.

3 Detecting and Resolving Compliance Issues Within Business Process Models

Compliance detection involves some machinery takes semantically annotated process models and formal representations of compliance requirements, and generates a boolean flag indicating compliance or otherwise. A simple detection procedure in our context would involve exhaustive path exploration through effect-annotated BPMN models, checking for rule violations. Due to space limitations, we do not describe this any further. When a process model is found to violate a set of compliance requirements, it must be modified to ensure compliance. In our semantically annotated example (Figure 1 and Table 1) we can simply determine that the "Route Package" node will induce an effect scenario where both $Knows(RegulatoryAgent, Package, Status, Held) \wedge Performs(SortOfficer, Route, Package)$ is true upon accumulation. It is also easy to see that our aforementioned compliance rule CR_1 is violated. Figures 2 (R_1) and 3 (R_2) describe two simple resolutions of the inconsistent "Screen Package" process in Figure 1 (O). Both these examples illustrate slight consistency preserving alterations to the process models for illustrating how we may automate their selection.

Any approach to revising process models to deal with non-compliance must meet the following two requirements. First, the revised process must satisfy the intent or goals of the original process. Second, it must deviate as little as possible from the original process. The requirement for minimal deviation is driven by the need to avoid designing new processes from scratch (which can require significant additional investment) when an existing process is found to be non-compliant. While the analysis relies exclusively on design-time artefacts, the process in question might have already been implemented or resources might have been allocated/configured to meet the requirements of the original

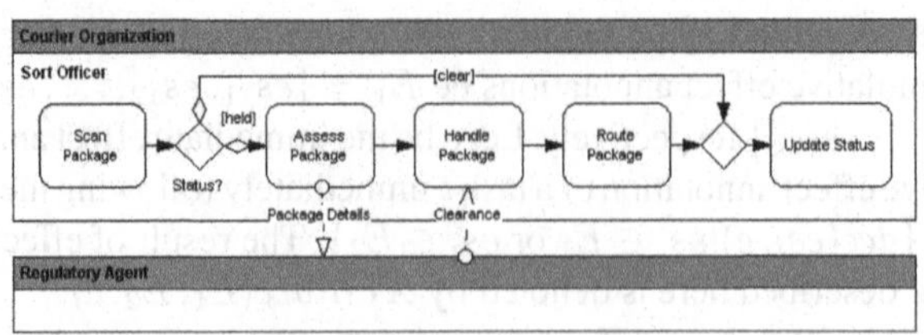

Fig. 2. Resolved Package Screening Process (R_1)

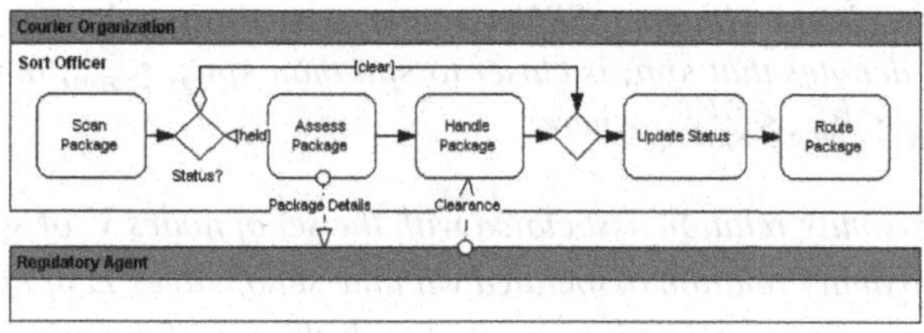

Fig. 3. Resolved Package Screening Process (R_2)

process. By seeking minimally different processes from the original one, we are able to avoid disruptive changes to the organizational context of the process.

We begin by describing what it means for a process model to minimally deviate from another. This task is complicated by the fact that there is no consensus on the semantics for BPMN (our chosen process modeling notation, selected for its widespread use in industry). Little exists in the literature on measures of deviation for process models ([12] provides some similarity measures, but these rely on petri net models of processes). We address this problem by exploiting both the structure of BPMN process models and the lightweight semantic annotations described earlier in the paper. To provide a uniform basis for conjoint structural and semantic comparisons, we encode effect-annotated BPMN models into *semantic process networks* (or SPNets).

Definition 1. *A Semantic Process Network (SPNet) is a digraph (V, E), where:*

- *each node is of the form $\langle ID, nodetype, owner, effect_I, effect_C \rangle$, and*
- *each edge is of the form $\langle \langle u, v \rangle, edgetype \rangle$.*

Each event, activity or gateway in a BPMN model maps to a node, with the nodetype indicating whether the node was obtained from an event, activity or gateway respectively in the BPMN model. The ID of nodes of type event or activity refers to the ID of the corresponding event or activity in the BPMN model. The ID of a gateway type node refers to the condition associated with the corresponding gateway in the BPMN model. The owner attribute of a node refers to the role associated with the pool from which the node was obtained. The $effect_I$ of a node corresponds to the set of sentences describing the immediate effects of that node, and $effect_C$ the cumulative effect at the node within the network - these are only defined for nodes obtained from activities, and are empty in other cases. Note that $effect_I$ is a set of sentences, while $effect_C$ is a set of sets of sentences, with each element of $effect_C$ representing a distinct effect scenario. The edgetype of an edge can be either control *or* message *depending on whether the edge represents a control flow or message flow in the BPMN model.*

We note that a unique SPNet exists for each process model in BPMN. This can be determined objectively by transforming BPMN models into a predetermined normal form. The BPMN notation illustrates how certain modeling patterns can be transformed into equivalent and far less ambiguous format.

Definition 2. *Associated with each SPNet spn is a* proximity relation $\leq_{spn}$ *such that* $spn_i \leq_{spn} spn_j$ *denotes that* spn_i *is closer to spn than* spn_j*.* $\leq_{spn}$*, in turn, is defined by a triple* $\langle \leq^V_{spn}, \leq^E_{spn}, \leq^{EFF}_{spn} \rangle$ *where:*

- $\leq^V_{spn}$ *is a proximity relation associated with the set of nodes V of spn,*
- $\leq^E_{spn}$ *is a proximity relation associated with the set of edges E of spn and*
- $\leq^{EFF}_{spn}$ *is a proximity relation associated with the set of cumulative effect annotations associated with nodes in spn.* $spn_i \leq_{spn} spn_j$ *iff each of* $spn_i \leq^V_{spn} spn_j$, $spn_i \leq^E_{spn} spn_j$ *and* $spn_i \leq^{EFF}_{spn} spn_j$ *holds. We write* $spn_i <_{spn} spn_j$ *iff* $spn_i \leq_{spn} spn_j$ *and at least one of* $spn_i <^V_{spn} spn_j$, $spn_i <^E_{spn} spn_j$ *or* $spn_i <^{EFF}_{spn} spn_j$ *holds.*

The proximity relations $\leq^V_{spn}, \leq^E_{spn}$ and $\leq^{EFF}_{spn}$ can be defined in different ways to reflect alternative intuitions. For instance, the following, set inclusion-oriented definition might be of interest: $spn_i \leq^V_{spn} spn_j$ iff $(V_{spn} \Delta V_{spn_i}) \subseteq (V_{spn} \Delta V_{spn_j})$, where $A \Delta B$ denotes the symmetric difference of sets A and B. An alternative, set cardinality-oriented definition is as follows: $spn_i \leq^V_{spn} spn_j$ iff $|V_{spn} \Delta V_{spn_i}| \leq \left|V_{spn} \Delta V_{spn_j}\right|$ (here $|A|$ denotes the cardinality of set A). Similar alternatives exist for the $\leq^E_{spn}$ relation. Both $\leq^V_{spn}$ and $\leq^E_{spn}$ define the structural proximity of one SPNet to another.

Take R_1 (Figure 2) and R_2 (Figure 3) as examples to illustrate our structural proximity relations. Trivially, R_1 and R_2 share all their nodes with O, and therefore, no comparison can be made across this structural dimension. Next, we determine a significant edge difference between R_1 and O, including the "Handle Package' → 'Route Package' edge. R_2 also differs with O across some edges including "Update Status" → "Route Package". If an inclusion-oriented definition for proximity (i.e. $\leq^E_{spn}$ in Definition 2) were applied, we would not be able to differentiate R_1 and R_2 w.r.t. structural proximity to O. On the other hand, if we choose to apply the cardinality-oriented definition, we'd determine $R_2 \leq^E_{spn} R_1$ as $|R_1 \Delta O| = 6$ and $|R_2 \Delta O| = 4$ (see Table 2). We can comprehend that an inclusion-oriented definition would ensure less commitment and greater control for analysts.

Defining the proximity relation $\leq^{EFF}_{spn}$ is somewhat more complicated, since it explores semantic proximity. One approach is to look at the terminating or leaf nodes in an SPNet, i.e., nodes with no outgoing edges. Each such node might be associated with multiple effect scenarios. The set of all effect scenarios associated with every terminating node in an SPNet thus represents a (coarse-grained) description of all possible end-states that might be reached via the execution of some instance of the corresponding process

Table 2. Edge Difference of R_1 and R_2 w.r.t. O

$R_1 \Delta O$	$AssessPackage \rightarrow HandlePackage\ (R_1), XORjoin \rightarrow RoutePackage\ (R_1)$ $RoutePackage \rightarrow UpdateStatus\ (R_1), XORjoin \rightarrow UpdateStatus\ (O)$ $RoutePackage \rightarrow HandlePackage\ (O), AssessPackage \rightarrow RoutePackage\ (O)$
$R_2 \Delta O$	$AssessPackage \rightarrow HandlePackage\ (R_2), UpdateStatus \rightarrow RoutePackage\ (R_2)$ $AssessPackage \rightarrow RoutePackage\ (O), RoutePackage \rightarrow HandlePackage\ (O)$

model. For an SPNet spn, let this set be represented by $T_{spn} = \{es_1, \ldots, es_n\}$ where each es_i represents an effect scenario. Let $Diff(spn, spn_i) = \{d_1, \ldots, d_m\}$ where d_i is the smallest cardinality element of the set of symmetric differences between $es_i \in T_{spn_i}$ and each $es \in T_{spn}$. In other words, let $S(es_i, T_{spn}) = \{es_i \Delta e \mid e \in T_{spn}\}$. Then d_i is any (non-deterministically chosen) cardinality-minimal element of $S(es_i, T_{spn})$. Then we write $spn_i \leq_{spn}^{EFF} spn_j$ iff for each $e \in Diff(spn, spn_i)$, there exists an $e' \in Diff(spn, spn_j)$ such that $e \subseteq e'$.

The definition of $\leq_{spn}^{EFF}$ above exploited set inclusion. An alternative, cardinality-oriented definition is as follows: $spn_i \leq_{spn}^{EFF} spn_j$ iff

$$\sum_{d \in Diff(spn, spn_i)} d \leq \sum_{d \in Diff(spn, spn_i)} d$$

The two approaches to defining $\leq_{spn}^{EFF}$ presented above focus on the cumulative end-effects of processes, thus ensuring that modifications to processes deviate minimally in their final effects. In some situations, it is also interesting to consider minimal deviations of the internal workflows that achieve the end-effects. In part this is evaluated by the $\leq_{spn}^{V}$ and $\leq_{spn}^{E}$ proximity relations, but not entirely. Analysis similar to what we have described above with end-effect scenarios, but extended to include intermediate effect scenarios, can be used to achieve this. We do not include details here for brevity.

Now, we establish their semantic proximity of R_1 and R_2 w.r.t. O based on the final cumulative effect scenarios at terminating nodes. In the case of the simple annotations defined in Table 1, we can determine that the final cumulative effect of both R_1 and R_2 result in two effect scenarios such that R_1 actually remains identical to O in terms of final state approximation. R_2 on the other hand receives the additional effects of $Performs(SortOfficer, Route, Package) \wedge Knows(SortOfficer, Package, Location, Forwarding)$ on the effect scenario now generated by placing the "Route Package" activity in line with both process trajectories. Therefore, $Diff(O, R_1) = \emptyset$ and $Diff(O, R_2) = \{\{Perf \ldots\}\}$, and R_1 would be nominally chosen over R_2.

Finally, consider a more detailed analysis where, say for instance, we also evaluate non-terminating nodes using the aforementioned cardinality-oriented definition. In this situation, only the cumulative scenario in R_1 at "Handle Package" minimally differs from the scenario in R_2 at the corresponding node by $\{Performs(\ldots, Route, \ldots) \wedge Knows(\ldots, Forwarding)\}$. R_2 on the other hand differs w.r.t. a scenario at "Handle Package" by (2), at a scenario in "Update Status" by (2), and at a scenario in "Route Package" by (2). This in-turn reinforces the selection of R_1.

Definition 3. *A process model m' is R-minimal with respect to another process model m and a set of rules R iff each of the following hold:*

- *m violates R.*
- *m' satisfies R.*
- *There exists no process model m'' such that $spn'' <_{spn} spn'$ and m'' satisfies R, where spn, spn' and spn'' are SPNets corres. to m, m' and m'' respectively.*

The definition of R-minimality above provides a "semantic" yardstick for evaluating whether a process is being minimally modified to restore compliance with a set of rules. It also provides an outline of a procedure for dealing with compliance violations: generate the set of R-minimal process models and select one. The selection process could be analyst-mediated, or might involve the application of extraneously encoded preference criteria. An alternative approach is to identify the minimal sources of inconsistency with a given set of rules, thus focussing analyst attention to the portions of a model that require editing to restore compliance.

Definition 4. *Given a process model m that violates a set of rules R, a* minimal source of inconsistency *with respect to m and R is a process model m' such that each of the following hold:*

- *spn′, (SPNet of m'), is a sub-graph of spn, (SPNet of m).*
- *m' violates R.*
- *m'' does not violate R for any process model m'' whose corresponding SPNet spn″ is a sub-graph of spn′, the SPNet corresponding to m'.*

An obvious modification to restore compliance is to replace the terminal activities of the process models that are minimal sources of inconsistency. Note that in general, every minimal source of inconsistency must be appropriately modified to restore compliance. Useful guidance can be provided to the analyst on what the best modifications might be (given, for instance, a repertoire of possible alternative activities to replace a given activity with), using analysis that involves measuring deviations of effect annotations of activities. We ommit details for brevity. Much of our discussion above assumes only the existence of process models and their analyst-mediated effect annotations. Sometimes, goal-based annotations are also available, which describe the objectives that processes, sub-processes or individual activities are designed to achieve. While effect annotations are descriptive, goal annotations are normative. Goal annotations can impose "hard" constraints on how process models might be modified, given that modifications must still achieve the original goals of a process or its constituent elements, wherever possible. Analysis of the kind that we have discussed above could be performed to support such reasoning, but we ommit details again due to space restrictions.

4 Heuristics for Asserting and Resolving Compliance Issues

In the previous section we have provided a semantic basis for reasoning about alternative resolutions to non-compliant processes. In this section we introduce the notion of a *compliance pattern* as a heuristic basis for supporting (even in partially automated ways) the resolution of non-compliance in process moels. Informally, a compliance pattern captures a commonly occurring mode of compliance violation, including both the compliance requirement that is violated and the actions required to restore compliance. In the following, we summarize the main types of process compliance patterns. Further details have been omitted due to space restrictions.

Structural Patterns

- **Activity/Event/Decision Inclusion.** Activity, event and decision inclusion may be defined against deontic modalities (permitted, mandatory, prohibited) and/or based on path quantifiers (as in CTL). For example: *The action of receiving package details must always occur during the screening of a package.* **Resolution:** Add or remove an activity. This may require co-ordination and assignment change to occur in structured processes.

- **Activity/Event/Decision Coordination.** Activity coordination may be serial, conditional, parallel, and/or repetitive. In the case of branching constructs, CTL [?] assertions provide a natural means to refer to the required temporal relations between activities. Interval algebra [13] is also applicable. For example: *If a package is cleared, then it must have been screened some time in the past*; *If a package is held then it should not be delivered until it is cleared, along all possible paths globally.* **Resolution:** Add or remove an activity. Re-order existing activities.
- **Activity/Event/Decision Assignment.** The assignment of an activity to a role is defined using deontic operators. A statement making an action mandatory for some role may or may not preclude its assignment to other roles, and vice-versa. For example: *Clearing a package must only be assigned to a Regulatory Authority role*; *The customer must provide the details of the package to a Courier role (however the courier is still able to provide package details to another role).* **Resolution:** Add or remove an activity. Re-assign an activity.
- **Actor/Resource Inclusion.** The participation of an actor or availability of a resource within a process may also be defined using deontic operators. An actor's existence in a process model (e.g. using BPMN lanes) will also indicate their participation. For example: *A regulatory authority must be included in the process for screening a package.* **Resolution:** Add or remove a participant/resource. This may require the addition and removal of activities and/or interactions.
- **Actor/Resource Interaction.** The interaction between actors and/or the transfer of resources may be governed by security, privacy or other concerns. For example: *A Customer must never interact with a Regulatory Authority during the screening of a package.* **Resolution:** Add or remove a participant/resource. Add or remove an interaction/transfer.

Semantic Patterns: To resolve the following compliance issues, almost any (or combination of) changes may be required - e.g. Add or remove an action. Add or remove an effect. Re-assign an action. Add or remove an actor. Add or remove an interaction.

- **Effect Inclusion.** An effect may be permitted, mandatory or prohibited to hold at a set of final or intermediate states of the process. For example: *Delivered packages must not be held*; *Delivered packages must be cleared.*
- **Effect Coordination.** The temporal relationship among the effects of a process (i.e. declared discretely in process models such as BPMN) may also be constrained. For example, *In all possible cases, a cleared package must be delivered unless it is held some time after clearance.*
- **Effect Modification.** Temporal rules may also refer to allowable changes upon intermediate effects within a process. For example: *If a package is held, then it cannot be cleared by a delivery process.*

5 Conclusion

We define a novel framework for auditing BPMN process models for compliance with legislative/regulatory requirements, and for exploring alternative modifications to restore compliance in the event that the processes are found to be non-compliant. This lays the foundations for tool support in the area, which we are in the process of implementing, but whose details we have had to omit due to space constraints. Parts of this framework have been empirically validated, but a complete industry-scale validation remains future work.

References

1. Zhang, I.X.: Economic consequences of the sarbanes-oxley act of 2002. AEI-Brookings Joint Center 5 (2005)
2. Governatori, G., Milosevic, Z., Sadiq, S.: Compliance checking between business processes and business contracts. In: Proc. 10th Int. Enterprise Dist. Object Computing Conf. (2006)
3. Weitl, F., Freitag, B.: Checking semantic integrity constraints on integrated web documents. In: Workshop Proc. of ER., pp. 198–209 (2004)
4. Janssen, W., Mateescu, R., Mauw, S., Springintveld, J.: Verifying business processes using spin. In: Holzman, G., Serhrouchni, E.N. (eds.) Proceedings of the 4th International SPIN Workshop, Paris, France, pp. 21–36 (1998)
5. Rosenberg, F., Dustdar, S.: Business rule integration in bpel - a service-oriented approach. In: Proc. of the 7th Int. IEEE Conf. on E-Commerce Technology, IEEE Computer Society Press, Los Alamitos (2005)
6. Ly, L.T., Rinderle, S., Dadam, P.: Semantic correctness in adaptive process management systems. In: Dustdar, S., Fiadeiro, J.L., Sheth, A. (eds.) BPM 2006. LNCS, vol. 4102, Springer, Heidelberg (2006)
7. Reijers, H.A.: Design and Control of Workflow Processes: Business Process Management for the Service Industry. In: van der Aalst, W.M.P., ter Hofstede, A.H.M., Weske, M. (eds.) BPM 2003. LNCS, vol. 2678, Springer, Heidelberg (2003)
8. White, S.: Business process modeling notation (bpmn), Technical report, OMG Final Adopted Specification 1.0 (2006), `http://www.bpmn.org`
9. Becker, J., Indulska, M., Rosemann, M., Green, P.: Do process modelling techniques get better? In: Proc. 16th Australasian Conf. on I.S. (2005)
10. Wagner, G.: How to design a general rule markup language. In: Proc. of the Workshop XML Technologies for the Semantic Web (2002)
11. van Lamsweerde, A.: Goal-oriented requirements engineering: A guided tour. In: Proc. of the Int. Joint Conference on R.E., Toronto, pp. 249–263. IEEE Press, Los Alamitos (2001)
12. Ehrig, M., Koschmider, A., Oberweis, A.: Measuring similarity between semantic business process models. In: Proc. of the Fourth Asia-Pacific Conf. on Conceptual Modelling (2007)
13. Huth, M., Ryan, M.: Logic in Computer Science: Modelling and Reasoning about Systems. Cambridge University Press, Cambridge (2004)
14. Allen, J.F.: Maintaining knowledge about temporal intervals. Communications of the ACM 26(11), 832–843 (1983)

Specification and Verification of Artifact Behaviors in Business Process Models*

Cagdas E. Gerede and Jianwen Su

Department of Computer Science
University of California at Santa Barbara
Santa Barbara, CA 93106
{gerede, su}@cs.ucsb.edu

Abstract. SOA has influenced business process modeling and management. Recent business process models have elevated data representation to the same level as control flows, for example, the artifact-centric business process models allow the life cycle properties of artifacts (data objects) to be specified and analyzed. In this paper, we develop a specification language ABSL based on computation tree logic for artifact life cycle behaviors (e.g., reachability). We show that given a business model and starting configuration, it can be decided if an ABSL sentence is satisfied when the domains are bounded, and if an ABSL-core (sublanguage of ABSL) sentence is satisfied when the domains are totally ordered but unbounded. We also show that if the starting configuration is not given, ABSL(-core) is still decidable if the number of artifacts is bounded with bounded (resp. unbounded but ordered) domains.

1 Introduction

Business process modeling has received considerable attention from research communities in and related to computer science. This is a natural consequence of the trend that computer and software systems have found rapidly increasing usage in all aspects of business process management. The fundamental principle of service oriented architecture (SOA) to design software systems based on composition of a *flexible* assembly of *services* has already influenced many business operations today. We argue that the SOA principle will continue to impact on several key aspects of business process management, including business process modeling, design, integration, and evolution aspects. This paper makes a significant step in advancing SOA techniques for business process management by focusing on how to specify *dynamic* properties on data being processed, and on how to verify these properties.

Business process modeling is a foundation for design and management of business processes. Two key aspects of business process modeling are a formal framework that well integrates both *control flow* and *data*, and a set of tools to assist all aspects of a business process life cycle. A typical business process life cycle includes at least a design phase where the main concerns are around "correct" realization of business logic in a resource constrained environment, and an operational phase where a main objective is to optimize and improve the realization during the execution (operation). Traditional business process models emphasize heavily on control flow, leaving the data design in an

* Supported in part by NSF grants IIS-0415195 and CNS-0613998.

B. Krämer, K.-J. Lin, and P. Narasimhan (Eds.): ICSOC 2007, LNCS 4749, pp. 181–192, 2007.

auxiliary role if not as an afterthought. Recently, it has been argued that the consideration of data design should be elevated to the same level as control flows [14,9,4,11,1]. In our earlier efforts [9,4], we have developed artifact centric business process models and studied verification of ad hoc properties of the models.

Intuitively, *business artifacts* (or simply *artifacts*) are data objects whose manipulations define in an important way the underlying processes in a business model. Not only the past and current practice of business process specification naturally embodies the artifacts, recent engineering and development efforts (e.g., at IBM Services Division) have already adopted the artifact approach in the process of design and analysis of business models[5,12,10]. An important distinction between artifact centric models and traditional data flow (computational) models is that the notion of the life cycle of the data objects is prominent in the former, while not existing in the latter.

In the initial attempt [9], our main focus was on assembling together a business process and analyzing several execution properties including reachability. In doing so, we essentially augmented object oriented classes with states to represent artifact classes, and use guarded finite state automata to capture (the logic of) entities that carry out the work in a business model. In another approach [4], we focus more on the life cycle of artifacts and evolution of business (process) logic. In that study, we used services to model logical activities that can be executed and a declarative approach to represent a business model as a set of business rules. The two models are closely related but different. A detailed comparison of two models can be found in [8].

Business analysts need to verify whether artifact-centric business process models satisfy certain artifact properties. These properties reflect the requirements to meet business needs. Currently, a business analyst takes a process model and a property, and reason about the process model to see if the model satisfies the property. This reasoning process is not only tedious and nontrivial but it is also repetitive and can be automated. To address this problem, in this paper we develop a logic language based on computational tree logic [7], called Artifact Behavior Specification Language (ABSL). We also study the verification of properties specified in ABSL. We use the model of [9] (without finite functions and no "new" action) as the basis for the language, expecting that ABSL and technical results developed here be easily adapted to the model of [4].

The main technical results in this paper include:

1. The temporal logic based language ABSL for specifying life cycle properties of artifacts.
2. Decidability results of ABSL for a given operational model and a starting configuration for bounded domains.
3. Decidability results of ABSL-core (a sublanguage of ABSL) for a given operational model and a starting configuration for unbounded but ordered domains (i.e., with a total order).
4. Decidability results of ABSL (ABSL-core) for a given operational model and a bound for the number of artifacts, with bounded (resp. unbounded ordered) domains.

This paper is organized as follows. In Section 2, we overview artifact-centric operational model proposed in [9]. In Section 3, we propose a language for specifying artifact behaviors (ABSL). In Section 4.1, we show the decidability results of ABSL for bounded domains. In Section 4.2, we show the decidability results of ABSL-core for unbounded but ordered domains. In Section 4.3, we show the decidability results of ABSL (ABSL-core) for bounded (resp., unbounded ordered) domains. We conclude

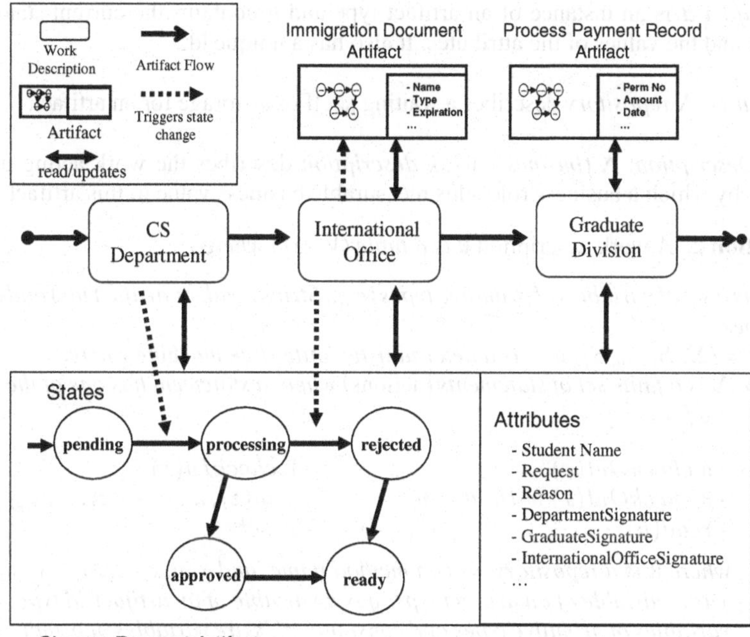

Fig. 1. An artifact-based view of a process model

the paper in Section 5. Due to space limitations, the detailed proofs and some technical definitions are omitted. More detailed discussion can be found in [8].

2 Overview: Artifact-Centric Operational Models

In this section, we briefly describe the terminology and the constructs in artifact-centric modeling. More formal and detailed discussion can be found in [8]. Artifact-centric models consist of 3 key constructs: Business artifacts, business work descriptions, and repositories [13] (In this study, the term task type and the term task are renamed to work description, and work).

Definition 1. *A* (business) artifact type T *is a tuple* (V, P, M) *such that*

- V *is a set of attributes of primitive types (such as String, real, or artifact ids).*
- P *is a set of* methods *with distinct names.*
- M *is a finite state machine and its transitions are labeled with method names from* P.
- *A* method *in* P *is a tuple* (name, I, O, body) *where* I *(*input paremeters*) and* O *(*output parameters*) are pairwise disjoint set of variables of primitive types, and the body is a sequence of statements each is of the form* $x := y$ *where* $x \in V \cup O$, $y \in V \cup I$.

An *artifact* a is an instance of an artifact type and it contains the current state of the artifact and the values of the attributes. It also has a unique id.

Repository: A *repository* describes a waiting shelf or a storage for an artifact.

Work Description: A *(business) work description* describes the work acting upon an artifact by which a business role adds measurable business value to this artifact.

Definition 2. *A* work description W *is a tuple* (V, M) *where*

- V *is a set of variables of primitive types (e.g., String, real, or artifact ids) and artifact types.*
- $M = (\Sigma, S, s_0, S_f, \delta, l)$ *is a deterministic finite state machine where:*
  - Σ *is a finite set of statements* (actions) *where a statement has one of the following forms:*

- R.$checkOut(x)$	- R.$checkIn(x)$
- R.$checkOut(x)$ $with\ id = y$	- $x.m(z_1, ..., z_k \mapsto z'_1, ..., z'_n)$
- $read(u)$	- $reset$

    where R *is a repository,* m *is a method name, and* $x, y, z_i, z'_j, u \in V$ *such that* x *is a variable of an artifact type,* y *is a variable of an artifact-id type,* z_i*'s are variables of primitive types and constants,* z'_j*'s are variables of primitive types,* u *is a variable of scalar types, and* $k \geq 0, n \geq 0$.
  - S *is a set of states,* $S_f \subseteq S$ *is a set of final states,*
  - $s_0 \in S_f$ *denotes the "initial" state,*
  - δ*, the transition relation, is a subset of* $(S \times (\Sigma - \{reset\}) \times S) \cup (S_f \times \{reset\} \times \{s_0\})$*,*
  - $l : \delta \rightarrow G$ *is a labeling function where* G *is a set of guards.*
  - *A* guard *is defined inductively as follows:* false, true *are guards; for every* $x \in V$ *of scalar type (such as String, real), and a constant c, every scalar comparison between* x, c *is a guard (such as* $x > c$*,* $x = c$*,* $x \neq c$*); for every* $x, y \in L$ *of scalar type, every scalar comparison between* x, y *is a guard (such as* $x > y$*,* $x = y$*,* $x \neq y$*;* R.$nonempty$ *is a guard for every repository* R*; and* $g_1 \wedge g_2$ *is a guard for every pair of guards* g_1 *and* g_2.

The type of actions in a work description and their intuitive meaning is provided below:

- R.$checkOut(x)$: check out a (random) artifact from repository R;
- R.$checkOut(x)$ $with\ id = y$: check out an artifact from repository R with id y;
- R.$checkIn(x)$: check an artifact in repostory R;
- $x.m(z_1, \ldots, z_k \mapsto z'_1, \ldots, z'_n)$: invoke the method m of the artifact held by the variable x with the input parameters $z_1, \ldots, z_k$ and expect the output in the variables $z'_1, \ldots, z'_n$;
- *read*(u): read a scalar value (such as String, real) from external environment;
- *reset* : uninitialize the values of all variables.

A *work* w (an instance of a work description) contains the values of work description variables, and the current state of the work. There is one work for each work description at run time.

Operational Model: An *(artifact-centric) operational model* $\mathcal{O}$ is a tuple $(\mathbf{T}, \mathbf{R}, \mathbf{W})$ where $\mathbf{T}$ is a set of artifact types, $\mathbf{R}$ is a set of repositories, $\mathbf{W}$ is a set of work descriptions.

A *configuration* of an operational model can be thought as a snapshot of the process at runtime, and it contains a set of artifacts, a set of work, and a set of repositories. Let $\mathcal{C}, \mathcal{C}'$ be two configurations. We say $\mathcal{C}'$ can be derived from $\mathcal{C}$, denoted as $\mathcal{C}' \rightarrow \mathcal{C}$, if $\mathcal{C}'$ can be produced as a result of a work executing an action.

A *root configuration* is a configuration where all the artifacts are in the repositories, and each work is in its initial state.

An *execution graph* with respect to a root configuration $\mathcal{C}^0$ is a Kripke structure (G^0, G, H) where $G^0 = \{\mathcal{C}^0\}$ is the initial state, G is the set of configurations, and H is the transition relation such that $(\mathcal{C}, \mathcal{C}') \in H$ if $\mathcal{C} \rightarrow \mathcal{C}'$.

Example 1. The scenario in Figure 1 describes an operational model for the processing of the *Student Change Request Artifact*. This artifact is used by students to request various changes such as the addition of an emphasis to the student's degree, or a committee member addition, or extension of a degree deadline. The approval of this artifact requires the signatures of the student's department, the graduate division, and the international office if the student holds a student visa. The processing of this artifact requires the payment of a processing fee which is tracked through *Processing Payment Record Artifact*. In addition, if the student holds a student visa, then the international office requires the verification of the student's the *Immigration Document Artifact* before they approve the change request. In addition, the graduate division and international office partially rely on the decision of the department, therefore, they require the student's department to process the artifact first.

Based on the specification, some of the desirable properties of this process can be enumerated as follows:

- Every approved change request artifact must have Department and Graduate Division signatures. Every change request artifact submitted by international students requires a signature from International Office.
- International Office and Graduate Division should not sign a change request artifact until Department signs it.
- Every change request artifact that Department does not approve should not be approved by Graduate Division or International Office.
- Every change request artifact by students under 18 requires her parents' signature.
- If a change request artifact is rejected by one authority, then the artifact shouldn't be processed any further by any authority.
- Every change request artifact by international students requires an encounter with the student's immigration document artifact at International Office.
- The approval of every change request artifact requires an encounter with a paid processing payment record artifact at Graduate Division.
- When a change request artifact is approved, the next action on the artifact should be the delivery to the student.

The verification of an artifact-centric process model at design time is crucial to avoid higher costs of breakdown, debugging and fixing during runtime. The verification requires a formalism to describe artifact-centric models, and a specification language to describe the properties the model should have. Therefore, in the next section, we propose a language to specify artifact behaviors. We show how to verify an artifact-centric process model with respect to artifact behavior specifications.

3 A Language for Specifying Artifact Behaviors: ABSL

Given an operational model $\mathcal{O} = (\mathbf{T}, \mathbf{R}, \mathbf{W})$, the set of symbols of ABSL consists of, in addition to the standard logical symbols (,), $\wedge$, $\neg$, $\forall$, and constants:

- variables (each is associated with a type in $\mathbf{T}$ or with a scalar type such as String, real);
- propositions, one for each state of a work description
- unary predicate symbols:
  - one for each work description ($\mathtt{W}(x)$ if x is checked out by W);
  - one for each repository ($\mathtt{R}(x)$ if x is checked out by R);
  - one for each state of each artifact type;
  - two for each attribute
    - a *read*-predicate, ($Read_A(x)$ if the attribute A of artifact x is read);
    - a *defined*-predicate ($Defined_A(x)$ if the value of the attribute A of artifact x is defined);
- binary predicates $Equal, NotEqual, GreaterThan, LessThan$ (e.g., $Equal(x, y)$ if x, y are not undefined, and x equals to y);
- 0-ary function symbols one for each work description variable;
- unary function symbols:
  - one for each attribute ($A(x)$ is the value of the attribute A of artifact x);
  - ID ($\mathtt{ID}(x)$ is id of artifact x).

A *term* is a constant, or a variable, or an expression of the form v, or $\mathtt{ID}(x_1)$, or $A(x_2)$ where v is a 0-ary function symbol, A is a unary function symbol, x_1 is a variable of an artifact type, x_2 is a variable of an artifact type containing an attribute A.

An atomic formula is an expression of the following forms:

true	q_{state}	$\mathtt{R}(x)$	$\mathtt{W}(x)$
$p_{state}(x)$	$Read_A(x)$	$Defined_A(x)$	$Equal(t_1, t_2)$
$NotEqual(t_1, t_2)$	$GreaterThan(t_1, t_2)$	$LessThan(t_1, t_2)$	

where q_{state} is a proposition corresponding to the state of a work description; p_{state} is a unary predicate corresponding to the state of an artifact type; x is a variable of an artifact type; t_1, t_2 are terms.

An artifact centric model describes the behaviors of all artifacts related to the underlying business operations that is being designed[13]. The artifact-centric approach reflects itself in the way the desirable process model behaviors are described, and these descriptions "focus" on behaviors of individual artifacts. To capture this requirement in ABSL, we propose a temporal operators based on computational tree logic (CTL) [7] operators (also inspired by the clock operator of the temporal language Sugar[3]):

- $\boldsymbol{EN_{@a}}\psi$ ("Next" w.r.t $\boldsymbol{a}$): requires that the formula ψ holds the next time the artifact $\boldsymbol{a}$ is involved;
- $\boldsymbol{EG_{@a}}\ \psi$ ("Globally" w.r.t. $\boldsymbol{a}$) : requires that the formula ψ holds every time the artifact $\boldsymbol{a}$ is involved,
- $\boldsymbol{E}\psi_1\ \boldsymbol{U_{@a}}\ \psi_2$ ("Until" w.r.t. $\boldsymbol{a}$): requires that there is a time when $\boldsymbol{a}$ is involved and ψ_1 holds, and at all preceeding times that $\boldsymbol{a}$ is involved, ψ_2 holds.

The *family of formulas* in ABSL is the set of expressions such that if ψ_1 and ψ_2 are formulas, then so are

$$\psi_1 \wedge \psi_2, \ \ \neg\psi_1, \ \ \forall x_1\, \psi_1, \ \ \boldsymbol{EN}_{@x}\psi_1, \ \ \boldsymbol{E}\psi_1\boldsymbol{U}_{@x}\psi_2, \ \ \boldsymbol{EG}_{@x}\psi_1$$

where x, x_1 are variables, and the type of the variable x is an artifact type.

The notion of free and bounded variables are defined in the standard manner. A *sentence* is a formula without any free variables.

Example 2. ABSL can formulate all the properties described in Example 1. Here we illustrate some of them. We use $\boldsymbol{F}_{@x}\psi$ to mean *true* $\boldsymbol{U}_{@x}\psi$.

- Every approved change request artifact must have the department signature.
  $\forall x \neg \boldsymbol{EF}_{@x}\ (approved(x) \wedge \neg Defined_{DeptSignature}(x))$
- Any change request artifact that Department does not approve should not be approved by Graduate Division.
  $\forall x\, \neg \boldsymbol{EF}_{@x}(AtDept(x) \wedge Equal(decision, \text{"}reject\text{"}) \wedge \boldsymbol{EF}_{@x} Defined_{DeptSignature}(x))$.
- International Office should not sign a form until Department signs it.
  $\forall x\, \neg \boldsymbol{E}\ \neg Defined_{DeptSignature}(x)\ \boldsymbol{U}_{@x} Defined_{IntOfficeSignature}(x)$
- Any form by international students requires an *encounter* with the student's immigration document at International Office. Let $\psi_1 \vee \psi_2$ represent $\neg(\neg\psi_1 \vee \psi_2)$ and $\exists y$ represent $\neg\forall\neg y$.
  $\forall x Equal(international(x), \text{"}false\text{"})\ \vee (\boldsymbol{EF}_{@x} AtIntOff(x) \wedge \exists y AtIntOff(y) \wedge Equal(immigrationDoc(x), ID(y)))\ \vee\ (\exists y \boldsymbol{EF}_{@y} AtIntOff(x) \wedge AtIntOff(y) \wedge Equal(immigrationDoc(x), ID(y)))$.

Definition 3. ABSL-core *is a sub-language of ABSL consisting of formulas using only variables of artifact types.*

Before we explain the semantics of ABSL, we would like to mention the technical differences of ABSL from computational tree logic (CTL) [7] and the temporal language Sugar [3]. In ABSL, differently from CTL, we have the focus operator @. The focus operator may sound similar to the clock operator of Sugar; however there is a big semantic difference. The clock operator in Sugar causes the projection of execution paths with respect to a clock (causes to consider only the configurations at which the clock holds). On the other hand, the focus operator doesn't modify the original execution path but allows to skip configurations which are not focused.

3.1 Semantics

In order to describe the semantics of ABSL, we extend the concept of a configuration with two more pieces of information. First, we record the artifact an action on which leads to this configuration. This is used to point out the "artifact-focused" configurations. Second, we record the attributes that are read. Intuition behind this is to allow the formulation of the properties about the "usefulness" of attributes during the processing of the artifacts

These are formalized as follows:

Definition 4. (Extended Configuration) For a configuration $\mathcal{C}$ of an operational model $\mathcal{O}$, an *extended configuration* of $\mathcal{O}$ is a tuple $\mathcal{D} = (\mathcal{C}, \alpha, \theta)$ where α is a subset of $\{(\boldsymbol{a}, A) \mid \boldsymbol{a}$ is an artifact in $\mathcal{C}$ and A is an attribute of $\boldsymbol{a}\}$, θ is a constant partial function, and if is defined it is an artifact in $\mathcal{C}$ (Conceptually α represents the set of attributes that are read, and θ represents the artifact such that the configuration is reached as a result of an action on that artifact). An *extended root configuration* $\mathcal{D}^0 = (\mathcal{C}, \alpha, \theta)$ of $\mathcal{O}$ is an extended configuration of $\mathcal{O}$ such that $\mathcal{C}$ is a root configuration of $\mathcal{O}$, and α is empty, and θ is not defined.

Given two configurations $\mathcal{C}_1, \mathcal{C}_2$ such that $\mathcal{C}_2$ can be derived from $\mathcal{C}_1$, we say $\mathcal{C}_2$ *focuses on the artifact* a, if the derivation is due to an action on $\boldsymbol{a}$ (i.e., a check-in or check-out of $\boldsymbol{a}$, or a method invocation on $\boldsymbol{a}$).

Next we extend the concept of derivation to extended configurations. An extended configuration $\mathcal{D}_2 = (\mathcal{C}_2, \alpha_2, \theta_2)$ can be can be *derived* from $\mathcal{D}_1 = (\mathcal{C}_1, \alpha_1, \theta_1)$, denoted as $\mathcal{D}_1 \rightarrow \mathcal{D}_2$, if the configuration $\mathcal{C}_2$ can be derived from the configuration $\mathcal{C}_1$, and α_2 is the union of α_1 and the set of attributes which are read in the derivation, and θ_2 is defined and equals to the artifact that the derivation $\mathcal{C}_1 \rightarrow \mathcal{C}_2$ focuses on We say the derivation $\mathcal{D}_1 \rightarrow \mathcal{D}_2$ *focuses on the artifact* $\boldsymbol{a}$, if θ equals to $\boldsymbol{a}$.

An extended configuration $\mathcal{D}$ is *reachable* from another extended configuration $\mathcal{D}'$ if there exists a finite positive number of extended configurations $\mathcal{D}_1, \ldots, \mathcal{D}_k$ such that $\mathcal{D} \rightarrow \mathcal{D}_1, \mathcal{D}_1 \rightarrow \mathcal{D}_2, \ldots, \mathcal{D}_{k-1} \rightarrow \mathcal{D}_k, \mathcal{D}_k \rightarrow \mathcal{D}'$.

Next we describe the semantics of terms of the language with an example.

Example 3. For an extended configuration $\mathcal{D}$, we describe the semantics of formulas containing no path and temporal operators on a simple example formula $\forall x\ ready(x) \wedge AtStudent(x) \rightarrow \exists y\ Equal(DeptSignature(x), y) \wedge Read_{Reason}(x)$. Assuming that the type of x is a change request artifact, and the type of y is String, x ranges over all change request artifacts in $\mathcal{D}$, and y ranges over all String value domain. Then, for every artifact $\boldsymbol{a}$, $ready(\boldsymbol{a})$ is true when the state of $\boldsymbol{a}$ is "ready"; $AtStudent(\boldsymbol{a})$ is true if $\boldsymbol{a}$ is in the repository $AtStudent$; $DeptSignature(\boldsymbol{a})$, if defined, evaluates to the value of the attribute $DeptSignature$ of $\boldsymbol{a}$; $Equal$ is true there exists a String value that equals to $DeptSignature$ of $\boldsymbol{a}$; $Read_{Reason}(\boldsymbol{a})$ is true if $Reason$ attribute of $\boldsymbol{a}$ is in the read set. $\mathcal{D}$ *satisfies* the formula if the formula evaluates to true.

Definition 5. An *extended execution graph* $\mathscr{E}$ of an operational model $\mathcal{O}$ and an extended root configuration $\mathcal{D}^0$ is a Kripke structure (G^0, G, H) where $G^0 = \{\mathcal{D}^0\}$ is the initial state, G is the set of extended configurations, and H is the transition relation such that $(\mathcal{D}, \mathcal{D}') \in H$ if $\mathcal{D} \rightarrow \mathcal{D}'$, and $(\mathcal{D}, \mathcal{D}) \in H$ if $\neg\exists\ \mathcal{D}'$ s.t. $\mathcal{D} \rightarrow \mathcal{D}'$. A *path* ρ in $\mathscr{E}$ is an infinite sequence of extended configurations $\mathcal{D}_1, \mathcal{D}_2, \ldots$ such that for every $i \geq 0$, $(\mathcal{D}_i, \mathcal{D}_{i+1}) \in H$.

Next, we informally describe the semantics of formulas containing temporal operators. Let $\mathscr{E}$ be an extended execution graph of an operational model $\mathcal{O}$, and an extended root configuration $\mathcal{D}^0$. Also, let $\mathcal{D}$ be an extended configuration in $\mathscr{E}$, and $\boldsymbol{a}$ be an artifact in $\mathcal{D}$. Then, $(\mathscr{E}, \mathcal{D})$ *satisfies*

- $\boldsymbol{EN}_{@\boldsymbol{a}}\psi_1$ if there is a path from $\mathcal{D}$ in $\mathscr{E}$ on which the next $\boldsymbol{a}$-focused extended configuration satisfies ψ_1.
- $\boldsymbol{EG}_{@\boldsymbol{a}}\psi_1$ if there is a path from $\mathcal{D}$ in $\mathscr{E}$ s.t. every $\boldsymbol{a}$-focused extended configuration on the path satisfies ψ_1.
- $\boldsymbol{E}\psi_1\boldsymbol{U}_{@\boldsymbol{a}}\psi_2$ if there is a path from $\mathcal{D}$ in $\mathscr{E}$ s.t. there is an extended configuration satisfies ψ_2, and ψ_1 is true at all preceeding extended configurations.

$(\mathcal{O}, \mathcal{D}^0)$ *satisfies* a formula ψ, denoted as $(\mathcal{O}, \mathcal{D}^0) \models \psi$, if $(\mathscr{E}, \mathcal{D}^0)$ satisfies ψ.

4 Verification of Artifact Behaviors

Verifying artifact behaviors such as reachability is proven to be undecidable with the ability of creating new artifacts[9]. Although decidability result was obtained there when the ability of creating new artifacts is removed, extending the result to ABSL is not obvious because of two main reasons. First, the domains of the artifact attributes, and work description variables can be unbounded. Second, even the number of these attributes and variables are bounded, the work descriptions can read external values and invent infinite number of new values during the computation.

In the following sections, we develop decidability results for different cases.

4.1 Bounded Domains

The main result of this section is:

Theorem 1. *For an operational model $\mathcal{O}$, an ABSL sentence ψ, an extended root configuration $\mathcal{D}^0$ of $\mathcal{O}$, it is decidable to check whether $(\mathcal{O}, \mathcal{D}^0)$ satisfies ψ, when the domains are bounded.*

The rest of this section is devoted to prove this result.

Step 1: Given an ABSL sentence, we first eliminate the variables in the sentence. As an example, let our sentence be $\forall x\ pending(x) \wedge \forall y\ \neg Equal(signature(x), y)$ where x quantifies over artifacts, and y is over scalar domain Eq (e.g. Strings). Let the extended root configuration contains three artifacts $\boldsymbol{a}_1, \boldsymbol{a}_2, \boldsymbol{a}_3$, and let Eq contains two elements c_1, c_2. Then, we eliminate x by replacing it with all possible values, and we take the conjunction of the expression since x is universally quantified. We can eliminate y similarly. The variable eliminated version of the sentence becomes $\bigwedge_{c_1,c_2} \bigwedge_{\boldsymbol{a}_1,\boldsymbol{a}_2}$ $pending(\boldsymbol{a}_i) \wedge \neg Equal(signature(\boldsymbol{a}_i), c_j)$. The approach is extended to the other expressions. The following can be proven:

Lemma 1. *For an operational model $\mathcal{O}$, an extended root configuration $\mathcal{D}^0$ of $\mathcal{O}$, and an ABSL sentence ψ, $(\mathcal{O}, \mathcal{D}^0)$ satisfies ψ iff $(\mathcal{O}, \mathcal{D}^0)$ satisfies the variable eliminated version of ψ.*

Step 2: For a variable eliminated sentence, we define a set of propositions. This set depends on the formula, the operational model, and the root configuration. For instance, for each repository R, for each artifact $\boldsymbol{a}$ appearing in the extended root configuration, we have a proposition $p[\mathtt{R}(\boldsymbol{a})]$ and this proposition is true in an extended configuration if $\boldsymbol{a}$ is located in R in the configuration. For every attribute A, every artifact $\boldsymbol{a}$, and every constant c appearing in the formula or in a work description of the operational model we have a proposition $p[A(\boldsymbol{a}) = c]$ (and $p[A(\boldsymbol{a}) < c]$ if the domain of A is ordered). $p[A(\boldsymbol{a}) = c]$ is true in an extended configuration if the value of A of $\boldsymbol{a}$ in the configuration equals to c (resp., if it is less than c). Also, for every artifact $\boldsymbol{a}$, we have a proposition $p[\boldsymbol{a}]$ and it is true in an extended configuration if the configuration is $\boldsymbol{a}$-focused. The approach is extended to other predicates including artifact states, work description states, and work description variables.

Step 3: We translate a variable eliminated ABSL sentence to a propositional branching temporal logic (CTL) formula. We assume some familiarity with CTL [6]. We, first, replace each atomic formula by a propositional formula. For example, if the atomic formula is $\mathtt{R}(\boldsymbol{a})$ where R is a predicate corresponds to a repository, and $\boldsymbol{a}$ is an artifact, then we replace it with the proposition $p[\mathtt{R}(\boldsymbol{a})]$. The same technique is naturally extended to the other atomic formulas involving unary predicates and binary predicates. For each atomic formula involving a binary predicate, we replace the binary predicate with a propositional formula. For instance, $Equal(A_1(\boldsymbol{a}_1), A_2(\boldsymbol{a}_2))$ is replaced by $p[Defined_{A_1}(\boldsymbol{a}_1)] \wedge p[Defined_{A_2}(\boldsymbol{a}_2)] \wedge p[A_1(\boldsymbol{a}_1) = A_2(\boldsymbol{a}_2)]$.

For the path and temporal operators, we do the following translation:

- $\boldsymbol{EN}_{@\boldsymbol{a}}\, \psi \;\Rightarrow\; \boldsymbol{E}\,\boldsymbol{X}\,\boldsymbol{E}\neg p[\boldsymbol{a}]\,\boldsymbol{U}\,(p[\boldsymbol{a}] \wedge \psi)$
- $\boldsymbol{EG}_{@\boldsymbol{a}}\, \psi \Rightarrow \;(p[\boldsymbol{a}] \wedge \psi \wedge \boldsymbol{EXEG}(p[\boldsymbol{a}] \rightarrow \psi)) \vee$
  $(\neg p[\boldsymbol{a}] \wedge (\boldsymbol{EXE}\neg p[\boldsymbol{a}]\boldsymbol{U}(p[\boldsymbol{a}] \wedge \psi)) \wedge (\boldsymbol{EXEG}(p[\boldsymbol{a}] \rightarrow \psi)))$
- $\boldsymbol{E}\,\psi_1\,\boldsymbol{U}_{@x}\,\psi_2 \Rightarrow \;\boldsymbol{E}\,(p[\boldsymbol{a}] \rightarrow \psi_1)\,\boldsymbol{U}\,(p[\boldsymbol{a}] \wedge \psi_2)$

As a result, we obtain a propositional CTL formula. Then, we create a *labeled* version of the extended execution graph such that each extended configuration $\mathcal{D}$ in the graph is labeled with the set of propositions that hold in $\mathcal{D}$.

We can prove the following:

Lemma 2. *For an operational model $\mathcal{O}$, an extended root configuration $\mathcal{D}^0$ of $\mathcal{O}$, Let $\mathscr{E}$ be the extended execution graph of $\mathcal{O}$ and $\mathcal{D}^0$. For a variable eliminated ABSL sentence ψ, $(\mathscr{E}, \mathcal{D}^0)$ satisfies ψ iff $(\mathscr{E}^L, \mathcal{D}^0)$ satisfies the CTL version of ψ, where $\mathscr{E}^L$ is the labeled version of $\mathscr{E}$.*

Coming back to Theorem 1, the proof idea is as follows: Since the domains are bounded, the size of the extended execution graph is finite. Due to Lemma 1 and Lemma 2, the problem of checking if an extended execution graph satisfies an ABSL sentence can be translated to a CTL model checking problem. The size of the extended execution graph is finite, and the decidability of model checking on finite structures is known[6]; therefore, the verification of an ABSL sentence is decidable.

4.2 Unbounded Domains

The main result of this section is:

Theorem 2. *For an operational model $\mathcal{O}$, an ABSL-core sentence ψ, an extended root configuration $\mathcal{D}^0$ of $\mathcal{O}$, it is decidable to check whether $(\mathcal{O}, \mathcal{D}^0)$ satisfies ψ, when the domains are unbounded.*

The rest of this section is devoted to prove this result.

Given an ABSL-core sentence and an extended root configuration, similar to the bounded domains case, we eliminate the variables from the sentence and obtain a CTL formula. Note that the CTL formula we obtain has a finite length, because the quantifiers in the ABSL-core sentences can only be used over artifact variables and the number of artifacts in the extended root configuration is finite.

The following can be proven:

Lemma 3. *For an operational model $\mathcal{O}$, an extended root configuration $\mathcal{D}^0$ of $\mathcal{O}$, Let $\mathscr{E}$ be the extended execution graph of $\mathcal{O}$ and $\mathcal{D}^0$. For a variable eliminated ABSL-core sentence ψ, $(\mathscr{E}, \mathcal{D}^0)$ satisfies ψ iff $(\mathscr{E}^L, \mathcal{D}^0)$ satisfies the CTL version of ψ where $\mathscr{E}^L$ is the labeled version of $\mathscr{E}$.*

It is not straightforward to obtain a result like Theorem 1, because the domains are not bounded and therefore the size of the extended execution graph is not finite. Interestingly we show that we can obtain a finite abstraction of the infinite space and verify a given sentence on this finite abstraction. In order to do this, we use an approach similar to the region approach used for the decidability results of timed-automata [2]. Timed-automata were introduced to model the behavior of real-time systems, which annotates state-transition graphs with timing constraints using finitely many real-valued clock variables. While in timed-automata, the infiniteness results from incrementing the clocks, in our model, it results from reading values from external environment.

We first define a binary relation among extended configurations. For an extended root configuration $\mathcal{D}^0$, let $R_{\mathcal{D}^0}$ be a binary relation over extended configurations such that two extended configurations are in the relation if they have the same set of artifacts with $\mathcal{D}^0$, and they satisfy the same set of propositions (Conceptually, two configurations obey the same *total ordering* of the artifact attribues and work description variables).

Lemma 4. *For an extended root configuration $\mathcal{D}^0$, $R_{\mathcal{D}^0}$ is an equivalence relation.*

The equivalence class[7] of an extended configuration $\mathcal{D}$, denoted as $[\mathcal{D}]_{\mathcal{D}^0}$, with respect to an extended root configuration $\mathcal{D}^0$ and the relation $R_{\mathcal{D}^0}$, is defined in the standard manner. Note that the number of such equivalence classes is finite.

Lemma 5. *For every pair of extended configurations $\mathcal{D}, \mathcal{D}'$ with $[\mathcal{D}]_{\mathcal{D}^0} = [\mathcal{D}']_{\mathcal{D}^0}$, it is true that for every extended configuration $\mathcal{D}'$ that satisfies $\mathcal{D} \to \mathcal{D}'$, there exists an extended configuration $\mathcal{D}'_1$ that satisfies both $\mathcal{D}' \to \mathcal{D}'_1$ and $[\mathcal{D}']_{\mathcal{D}^0} = [\mathcal{D}]_{\mathcal{D}^0}$.*

Definition 6. For an extended execution graph $\mathscr{E} = (\{\mathcal{D}^0\}, G, H)$, the *region graph* of $\mathscr{E}$ is a Kripke structure $(\{\mathcal{D}^0\}, G', H')$ where G' and H' is defined inductively as follows: $\mathcal{D}^0$ is in G'; for every $\mathcal{D}_1 \in G'$, and for every $\mathcal{D}_2$ such that $(\mathcal{D}_1, \mathcal{D}_2) \in H$, if there does not exist $\mathcal{D}_3$ such that $(\mathcal{D}_1, \mathcal{D}_3) \in H'$ and $[\mathcal{D}_2]_{\mathcal{D}^0} = [\mathcal{D}_3]_{\mathcal{D}^0}$, then $(\mathcal{D}_1, \mathcal{D}_2) \in H'$ and $\mathcal{D}_2 \in G$.

The size of the region graph is finite, because the number of equivalence classes is finite. We extend the region graph to a *labeled region graph* by labeling its configurations with the set of atomic propositions that hold in that configuration.

Based on Lemma 4 and Lemma 5, we can show that there is a bisimulation relation[7] between every labeled execution graph and its corresponding labeled region graph.

Lemma 6. *Given an extended root configuration $\mathcal{D}^0$, $R_{\mathcal{D}^0}$ forms a bisimulation relation between $\mathcal{D}^0$'s (labeled) extended execution graph and $\mathcal{D}^0$'s (labeled) region graph.*

Coming back to Theorem 2, the proof idea is as follows: As it is given in Lemma 6, there is a bisimulation relation between a labeled execution graph and its labeled region region graph. Therefore, a CTL formula is satisfied by a labeled execution graph iff it is satisfied by its labeled region graph[6]. The size of a region graph is finite, and the decidability of the the model checking on finite structures is known. This is combined with Lemma 3 concludes that the verification of an ABSL-core sentence with unbounded domains is decidable.

4.3 Verification with Bounded Number of Artifacts

An extended root configuration $\mathcal{D}^0$ is k-bounded if the number of artifacts in $\mathcal{D}^0$ is at most k, where k is a positive integer. For an operational model $\mathcal{O}$, and a positive integer

k, $(\mathcal{O}, k)$ *satisfies* an ABSL(-core) sentence ψ, if for every extended root configuration $\mathcal{D}^0$, $(\mathcal{O}, \mathcal{D}^0)$ satisfies ψ.

The following can be proven:

Theorem 3. *For an operational model $\mathcal{O}$, a positive integer k,*

- *it is decidable to check whether $(\mathcal{O}, k)$ satisfies an ABSL sentence ψ with bounded domains;*
- *it is decidable to check whether $(\mathcal{O}, k)$ satisfies an ABSL-core sentence ψ with unbounded domains.*

5 Conclusion

In this paper, we proposed a logic language based on computational tree logic [7], to specify artifact behaviors in artifact-centric process models. We showed decidability results of our language for different cases. While we provide key insights on how artifact-centric view can affect the specification of desirable business properties, extensions and refinements of our language and results will be beneficial.

References

1. Aalst, W., Weske, M., Grnbauer, D.: Case handling: a new paradigm for business process support. Data and Knowledge Engineering 53, 129–162 (2005)
2. Alur, R.: Timed automata. In: Halbwachs, N., Peled, D.A. (eds.) CAV 1999. LNCS, vol. 1633, pp. 8–22. Springer, Heidelberg (1999)
3. Beer, I., Ben-David, S., Eisner, C., Fisman, D., Gringauze, A., Rodeh, Y.: The temporal logic sugar. In: Berry, G., Comon, H., Finkel, A. (eds.) CAV 2001. LNCS, vol. 2102, Springer, Heidelberg (2001)
4. Bhattacharya, K., Gerede, C.E., Hull, R., Liu, R., Su, J.: Towards formal analysis of artifact-centric business process models. Business Process Management (BPM) (2007)
5. Bhattacharya, K., Guttman, R., Lymann, K., Heath III, F.F., Kumaran, S., Nandi, P., Wu, F., Athma, P., Freiberg, C., Johannsen, L., Staudt, A.: A model-driven approach to industrializing discovery processes in pharmaceutical research. IBM Systems Journal 44(1), 145–162 (2005)
6. Clarke, E., Grumberg, O., Peled, D.A.: Model Checking. The MIT Press, Cambridge, Massachusetts (2000)
7. Emerson, E.A.: Temporal and modal logic. In: Leeuwen, J. (ed.) Handbook of Theoretical Computer Science, vol. B,ch. 7, pp. 995–1072. North Holland, Amsterdam (1990)
8. Gerede, C.E.: Modeling, Analysis, and Composition of Business Processes. PhD thesis, Dept. of Computer Science, University of California at Santa Barbara (2007)
9. Gerede, C.E., Bhattacharya, K., Su, J.: Static analysis of business artifact-centric operational models. In: SOCA. IEEE International Conference on Service-Oriented Computing and Applications, IEEE Computer Society Press, Los Alamitos (2007)
10. Kumaran, S., Nandi, P., Heath, T., Bhaskaran, K., Das, R.: Adoc-oriented programming. In: Symposium on Applications and the Internet (SAINT) (2003)
11. Liu, R., Bhattacharya, K., Wu, F.Y.: Modeling business contexture and behavior using business artifacts. In: CAiSE. LNCS, vol. 4495, Springer, Heidelberg (2007)
12. Nandi, P., Kumaran, S.: Adaptive business objects a new component model for business integration. In: Int. Conf. on Enterprise Information Systems (2005)
13. Nigam, A., Caswell, N.S.: Business artifacts: An approach to operational specification. IBM Systems Journal 42(3), 428–445 (2003)
14. Wang, J., Kumar, A.: A framework for document-driven workflow systems. In: Business Process Management, pp. 285–301 (2005)

Improving Temporal-Awareness of WS-Agreement*

C. Müller, O. Martín-Díaz, A. Ruiz-Cortés, M. Resinas, and P. Fernández

Dpto. Lenguajes y Sistemas Informáticos
ETS. Ingeniería Informática - Universidad de Sevilla (Spain - España)
41012 Sevilla (Spain - España)
{cmuller, resinas, pablofm, aruiz}@us.es, octavio@lsi.us.es

Abstract. WS-Agreement (WS-Ag) is a proposed recommendation of the Open Grid Forum that provides a schema to describe SLAs and a protocol to create them based on a mechanism of templates. However, although it identifies the necessity of specifying temporal-aware agreement terms (e.g. *the response time is 30 ms from 8:00h to 17:00h and 15 ms from 17:00h to 8:00h*), to the best of our knowledge, there are no existing proposals that deal with that necessity. We propose an extension that gives WS-Ag support to temporality. This allows describing expressive validity periods such as those composed by several periodic or non-periodic intervals and it applies not only to the agreement terms themselves but also to other parts of WS-Ag such as creation constraints and preferences about the service properties. In addition, in this paper we propose a *preference XML schema* to describe preferences over any set of service properties using any kind of utility function. In further research we will study a concrete specification for those utility functions.

Keywords: Temporal-Aware, Quality of Service, Service Level Agreement, WS-Agreement, Utility Functions.

1 Introduction

Service oriented architectures are based on the use of loosely coupled services to support the requirements of business processes and users. In this context, service level agreements (SLAs) [12,13,20] can be used to regulate the execution of the services and to provide guarantees related to them.

A SLA usually specifies "*which*" service is offered and "*how*" it is offered. That is to say, it includes requirements and guarantees about functional, and non-functional properties of the services. However, another important question about services is "*when*". Temporality affects orthogonally all aspects of a SLA because it may refer to the entire agreement (e.g. *the agreement expires on 2007/05/31*); to any functional property of the service (e.g. *this operation of the service is available from 8:00h to 18:00h*); or to any non-functional property

* This work has been partially supported by the European Commission (FEDER) and Spanish Government under CICYT project Web-Factories (TIN2006-00472).

B. Krämer, K.-J. Lin, and P. Narasimhan (Eds.): ICSOC 2007, LNCS 4749, pp. 193–206, 2007.

that appears in the SLA (e.g. *the response time is 30 ms from 8:00h to 17:00h and 15 ms from 17:00h to 8:00h*). Therefore, a temporal-aware SLA allows us to express precisely the periods of time in which its terms are valid.

The most significant language to specify SLAs is WS-Agreement (WS-Ag) [12]. WS-Ag is a proposed recommendation of the Open Grid Forum working group (OGF) that provides a schema for defining SLAs and a protocol for creating them based on a mechanism of templates. For compatibility and complexity, WS-Ag only defines the general structure of the agreement. Other aspects such as defining domain-specific extensions or specific languages for expressing conditions are out of the scope of WS-Ag. For this reason the research community has proposed several WS-Ag extensions like [1] and [21]. This is also the case of temporality: WS-Ag recognizes that it is necessary to include temporality in the agreement terms, but for the above mentioned reasons it does not establish how to specify it. However, as far as we know, there is no existing extension to WS-Ag that tackles the problem of temporality.

In this paper, we propose an extension to give WS-Ag support to temporality. To define it, we build on a previous work [18], in which we presented operational semantics on constraint-based temporal-aware matchmaking. We define a *temporal XML schema* and we describe how this temporal schema can be applied to the different elements of WS-Ag.

The advantages of our approach are the following: (i) we apply temporality not only to the entire agreement and the agreement terms but also to other elements of WS-Ag such as the creation constraints, which are used to create agreements based on templates, and business values, which are used to express preferences about the terms of the agreement; (ii) we support expressive specifications of validity periods such as composed intervals like "*From 8:00h to 14:00h and From 16:00h to 18:00h*" and periodical intervals like "*From Mondays to Fridays, from 8:00 to 18:00*", and (iii) as the extension builds on [18], we have a sound foundation on which to develop a constraint-based implementation to give support to the temporal extension.

Moreover, we also propose a *preference XML schema* to describe preferences over any set of service properties using any kind of utility function instead of the constant float utility function which WS-Ag specifies. The specific language for describing those utility functions is currently open and we will study it in further research.

This paper is structured as follows. Section 2 introduces a case study in which temporality is an important feature. Section 3 presents the WS-Ag structure and its temporal-awareness. Section 4 exposes our proposal of WS-Ag extension on temporal-awareness and on preferences descriptions. Section 5 compares the related proposals. Finally Section 6 exposes our conclusions and future work.

2 A Case Study

In general, temporal issues are present in the majority of agreements in real-world scenarios. In this section we explore a particular case where a provider offers computing services to other organizations; i.e. customers send jobs (data to be processed by a certain algorithm) to be executed in the provider's infrastructure. This specific scenario represents a common situation in research fields with intensive computational requirements [4,15] as it has a wide set of temporal features that can be covered by our model.

In this scenario, a provider is likely to be looking for an optimization in the usage of its resources; that means unused (or underused) resources represent a lack of benefits and, therefore, a low recovery of the initial investment. In doing so, agreement offers should vary in a certain period on the basis of two key elements: (i) The mean time between two consecutive requests (MTBR) in the period and (ii) SLAs already signed with other customers for that period.

Concretely, we focus our case study in the following terms:

- The global validity of the SLA is from october 1/2007 to december 30/2007.
- All Sundays at 23:00h. servers are down for an hour due to maintenance.
- The Provider needs part of its server resources for its own computing necessities from Mondays to Fridays, from 8:00h to 18:00h. Therefore, in such time period, the provider requires that consumers specify in their service requests a MTBR greater or equal to 20 seconds.
- At any other instant, all server resources can be offered to consumers. Thus, at those instants the provider allows more exigent service requests over MTBR from consumers. Concretely the MTBR can be greater or equal to 1 second.
- The service consumer (i.e. the client) must specify in his agreement offer: a request; an algorithm for processing the request; the MTBR; and lastly the temporal execution pattern for the request (that means an estimation about when the service invocations are going to occur).
- The provider prefers receiving demands with a requirement of 20s or more of MTBR from Mondays to Fridays, from 8:00h to 18:00h. Thus, demands which require less MTBR should be satisfied when the provider has all server resources available.
- The provider prefers satisfying only one more exigent demand over MTBR (e.g. only one demand with MTBR=10s) rather than several less exigent demands over MTBR (e.g. 10 demands with 100s of MTBR each one).
- In periods with high MTBR available, the provider prefers customers demanding the *Knapsack algorithm (as first choice), or* Kruskal algorithm (as second choice). In other cases, the provider prefers demands of *Dijkstra algorithm, or* Kruskal algorithm (in this order of preference).

On the consumer side, we consider a case where a certain customer needs to compare two different algorithms with the same requirements on MTBR.

3 WS-Agreement in a Nutshell

3.1 Basic Description of WS-Agreement

In this section we will discuss WS-Ag, a framework for specifying electronic agreements. Concretely, this proposed recommendation specifies an XML-based language and a protocol for advertising the capabilities of service providers, creating agreements based on agreement offers (with the possibility of further agreement compliance monitoring at runtime).

The interaction protocol comprises of two participants: the agreement initiator (that triggers the beginning of the process) and the agreement responder (that reacts to the initiator's requests). The protocol is divided in three main stages namely: (i) the initiator of the agreement process asks for agreement templates to the agreement responder.(ii) The initiator sends to the responder an agreement offer taking into account the agreement variability contained in the template. (iii) The responder accepts or rejects the agreement offer; additionally, if the responder rejects it, the process may start again.

WS-Ag proposes a structure of the agreement with the following elements:

Name: it identifies the agreement and can be used for reference to it.

Context: it includes information such as the name of the parties and their roles of initiator or responder of the agreement. Additionally, it can refer to an agreement template if needed. In this element, an agreement lifetime can be defined by means of an element called "ExpirationTime".

Terms: agreement terms are wrapped by term compositors, which allow simple terms or sets of terms to be denoted by "ExactlyOne", "OneOrMore", or "All". The following are the two main types of terms:

1. Service terms: they provide information to instantiate or identify services and operations involved in the agreement. Additionally, it can comprise information about the measurable service properties.
2. Guarantee terms: they describe the service level objectives (SLO) agreed by the parties. They comprise a SLO specified as a target for a key performance indicator, or as a "CustomServiceLevel" element in a customized way; it also includes the scope of the term (e.g. a certain operation of the service or the whole service itself); a "QualifyingCondition" that specifies the validity conditions under which the term is applied; and information about business properties in the "BusinessValueList" element of the guarantee term such as "Importance", "Penalty" or "Reward" and "Preference" defined as an utility value pointing to a service term.

In order to create agreements, WS-Ag allows to specify templates with the above structure, but including agreement creation constraints that should be taken into account during the agreement creation process. These constraints describe the variability allowed by a party; they can be denoted as general "Constraints", or "Items" pointing to specific locations with their own constraints.

3.2 Temporal-Awareness of WS-Agreement

Concerning temporal issues, WS-Ag identifies two locations to include temporal awareness. On the one hand, lifetime for the entire agreement must be included in

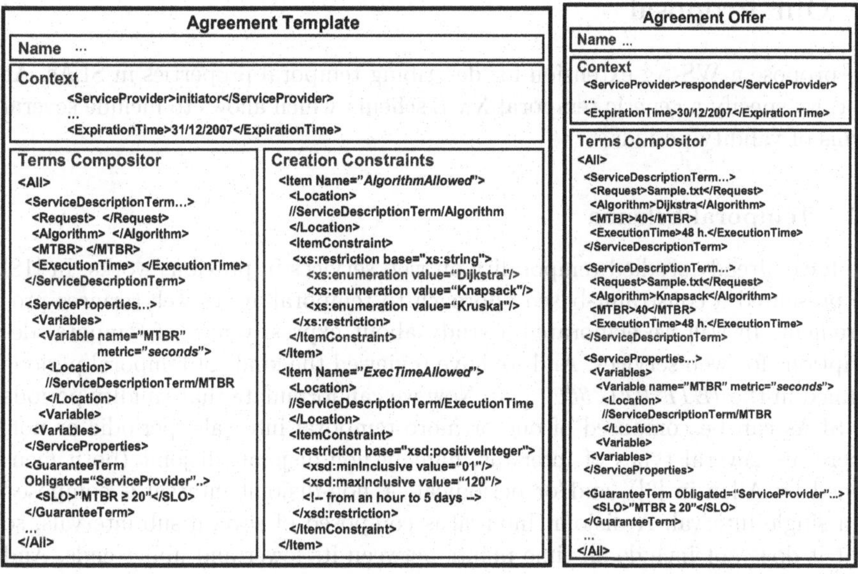

(a) Agreement Template. (b) Agreement Offer.

Fig. 1. An Example of Agreement Template and a possible Agreement Offer

Context into the "ExpirationTime" element (i.e. the last instant where the agreement is valid). On the other hand, WS-Ag recommends the use of "QualifyingCondition" elements for describing validity periods of terms and/or the party preferences. However, the specification document leaves open the specific way these temporal awareness must be exposed for reasons of compatibility and complexity.

The case study presented in the previous section includes several issues with little (or no) support with WS-Ag; in particular, the temporal execution pattern has a high degree of complexity for the WS-Ag recommendation (it includes several temporal expressions) thus we have to reduce it as denoted in the agreement template of Figure 1(a). This implies two main simplifications: (i) specifying the lifetime with an expiration time only (not initial time); (ii) temporal execution pattern for the request (which in the case study is expressed as several validity periods) has to be changed with a simple value of execution time.

Additionally, the need of restarting the server periodically could have been described as creation constraints for the agreement (and thus consumers would have to take these constraints into account in their agreement offers). However, we find that WS-Ag does not allow this temporal description, and therefore we have to reduce the example by restricting only the possible range of execution time in hours (and in addition the algorithms allowed). The possible values for MTBR correspond to the worst case (MTBR≥20s) and the preferences of the provider require the validity period of the case to be included in the example, but for the above reason it is not possible.

Figure 1(b) depicts an offer for such template describing an execution of the same request with two different algorithms with similar MTBR.

4 Our Proposal

We propose a WS-Ag extension for describing temporal properties in SLAs. At first, we specify a generic temporal XML schema which allows to include several forms of validity periods.

4.1 Temporal Schema

We have already studied temporality on web services in previous works. In [18] we presented a constraint-based approach to temporal-aware web services procurement. In [19] we elaborated a study about expressiveness of temporal descriptions for web services. And we have reviewed the kinds of temporal periods defined in the *IETF RFC 3060* [24]. Now we can formulate that validity periods on SLAs can be composed of one or more temporal intervals, periodic or not. There are several types of intervals, namely non-disjoint, disjoint (both mentioned by Allen in [3]), and/or periodical. A non-disjoint interval is composed of a single interval. A disjoint interval is composed of several sub-intervals, so that it does not include all time points between its lower and upper ends. And an interval is periodical if it is repeated regularly.

We have designed an XML schema named "twsag.xsd" for describing these validity periods in practice. An interval is the basic element; different non-disjoint intervals can be grouped together so that more complex intervals can be composed. Several authors [5,17] have proposed a more friendly representation of XML schemas by means of UML class diagrams. Thus, Figure 2 shows an UML class diagram which represents "twsag.xsd"; the three interfaces denote the types of intervals above mentioned: (1) **Interval**: it stands for the basic element; it is comprised of an initial time and a duration (which can be infinite) expressed in seconds, hours, days, or months. (2) **Disjoint**: it stands for disjoint intervals constituted of a set of intervals related by a logic operator (or, and, or xor). (3) **Periodical**: it stands for periodic intervals, be either disjoint or non-disjoint. Its periodicity is comprised of the number of period repetitions (which can be infinite) and a frequency expressed in seconds, hours, days, or months, which denotes the time between two consecutive intervals.

Our proposal allows to include temporality regarding several aspects of agreements. Therefore, we comment them separately: first, temporality on agreement terms and agreement creation constraints in Section 4.2; and later, temporality on preferences in Section 4.3.

4.2 Temporality on Terms and Creation Constraints

Depending on the way validity periods affect the agreement terms, we classify them in two groups: (1) global periods (GP) if validity periods wrap all agreement terms; and (2) local periods (LP) in other cases. We have studied the inclusion of these types of periods in the WS-Ag structure.

WS-Ag specifies the lifetime of agreements by means of an "Expiration Time" in the context. Thus, it only allows a non-disjoint GP, starting from the current

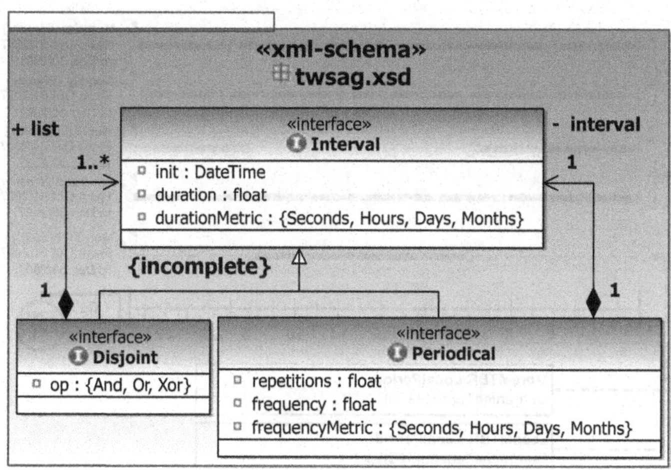

Fig. 2. Schema for Temporal Intervals

date. For a lifetime to be expressed without restrictions, we propose to use the "Any" element, which allows to include any information in the context, for including a new element called "GlobalPeriod" in order to describe it as an "Interval" element of our temporal schema.

WS-Ag recommends to specify temporality regarding agreement terms in the "QualifyingCondition" element. We propose to specify these local periods by means of "Interval" elements of our temporal schema.

Figure 3 shows the global and local periods for the scenario described in Section 2. Figure 4 shows a template and an offer using our WS-Ag extension for describing the validity periods in this case study. In Figure 4(c), note that non-disjoint intervals are put into a single periodical non-disjoint interval which constitutes the agreement offer GP; and periodical disjoint intervals are used to constitute the agreement offer LPs.

It is important to remark that WS-Ag only includes temporal properties in guarantee terms. However, we also need to describe validity periods of service terms. In Figure 4(b), functional properties described in service description terms are active only at specific validity periods (e.g. we must use the service description term with MTBR≥20s, in case of periods with a minimum of 20s of MTBR allowed). Therefore, we make use of term compositors to associate service terms with the guarantee terms which contain the desired validity period.

We also allow to specify temporal properties regarding the agreement creation constraints. There are two ways of describe them: either to allow validity periods on single constraints, e.g. "Provider must allow execution tests with a minimum MTBR of 40s, *48 hours before agreement initiation date*"; or to allow several constraints apart from the validity period definition, e.g. the previous constraints

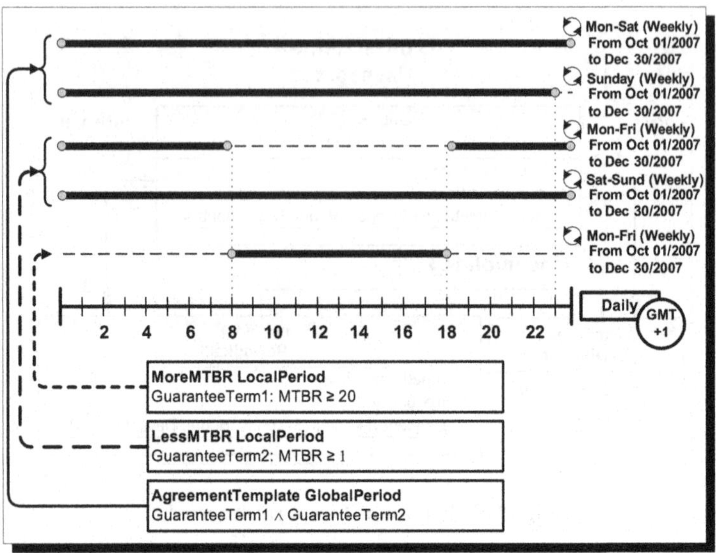

Fig. 3. Global & Local Periods for the Case Study

without validity period: "Provider must allow execution tests with 40s of MTBR", and also "Provider must assure a maximum execution time of 24 hours", both active during the validity period: "*48 hours before agreement initiation date*". For temporality in creation constraints to be allowed, we propose to describe it as an "Interval" element of our temporal schema: (1) a new element under the "Item" of creation constraints, for describing temporal periods on a single constraint (by means of "Any" element of WS-Ag); and (2) the "Constraint" element for temporal periods on several constraints. Figure 5 denotes case (1) with an example of testing requests before an agreement initiation date.

4.3 Temporality on Preferences

In a guarantee term, a validity period described in "QualifyingCondition" involves not only the service level objective, but also the preferences in the "BusinessValueList" element. However, preferences in WS-Ag are described with limitations, because we must specify a float constant value in the "Preference" element in order to describe the utility of a concrete service description term. That forces to define (1) several service description terms with different choices of values in service properties according to preferences, and (2) several guarantee terms, including the constant utility of each service description term on each validity period. Therefore, we obtain constant utility functions anyway.

In order to use any utility function with any number of service properties, we propose to extend the manner of expressing preferences in WS-Ag by using the "CustomBusinessValue" element. Our purpose is to describe the preference

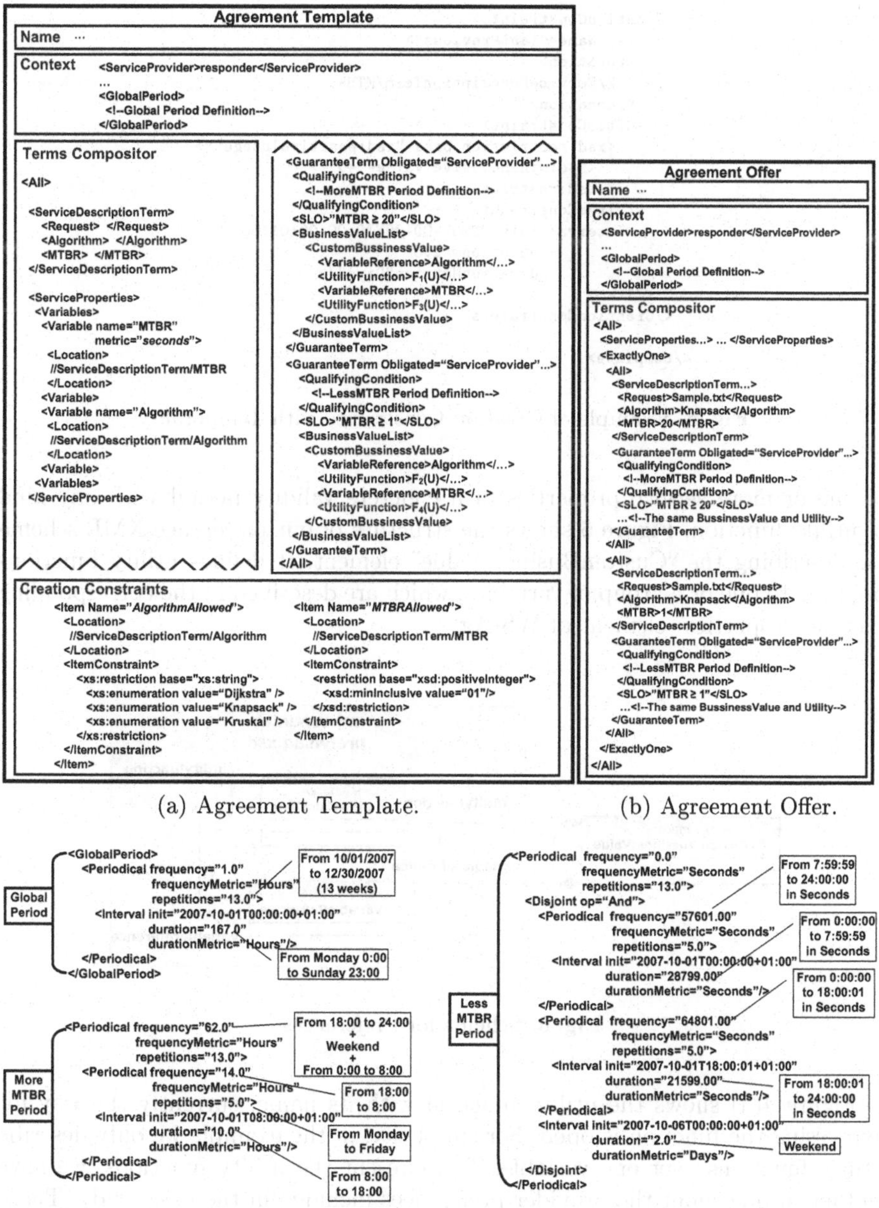

```
Agreement Template
Name ...
Context   <ServiceProvider>responder</ServiceProvider>
          ...
          <GlobalPeriod>
            <!--Global Period Definition-->
          </GlobalPeriod>

Terms Compositor
<All>

 <ServiceDescriptionTerm>
   <Request> </Request>
   <Algorithm> </Algorithm>
   <MTBR> </MTBR>
 </ServiceDescriptionTerm>

 <ServiceProperties>
  <Variables>
   <Variable name="MTBR"
            metric="seconds">
    <Location>
    //ServiceDescriptionTerm/MTBR
    </Location>
   <Variable>
   <Variable name="Algorithm">
    <Location>
    //ServiceDescriptionTerm/Algorithm
    </Location>
   <Variable>
  <Variables>
 </ServiceProperties>

 <GuaranteeTerm Obligated="ServiceProvider"...>
  <QualifyingCondition>
   <!--MoreMTBR Period Definition-->
  </QualifyingCondition>
  <SLO>"MTBR ≥ 20"</SLO>
  <BusinessValueList>
   <CustomBussinessValue>
     <VariableReference>Algorithm</...>
     <UtilityFunction>F1(U)</...>
     <VariableReference>MTBR</...>
     <UtilityFunction>F3(U)</...>
   </CustomBussinessValue>
  </BusinessValueList>
 </GuaranteeTerm>
 <GuaranteeTerm Obligated="ServiceProvider"...>
  <QualifyingCondition>
   <!--LessMTBR Period Definition-->
  </QualifyingCondition>
  <SLO>"MTBR ≥ 1"</SLO>
  <BusinessValueList>
   <CustomBussinessValue>
     <VariableReference>Algorithm</...>
     <UtilityFunction>F2(U)</...>
     <VariableReference>MTBR</...>
     <UtilityFunction>F4(U)</...>
   </CustomBussinessValue>
  </BusinessValueList>
 </GuaranteeTerm>
</All>

Creation Constraints
  <Item Name="AlgorithmAllowed">
   <Location>
    //ServiceDescriptionTerm/Algorithm
   </Location>
   <ItemConstraint>
     <xs:restriction base="xs:string">
       <xs:enumeration value="Dijkstra" />
       <xs:enumeration value="Knapsack" />
       <xs:enumeration value="Kruskal" />
     </xs:restriction>
   </ItemConstraint>
  </Item>
  <Item Name="MTBRAllowed">
   <Location>
    //ServiceDescriptionTerm/MTBR
   </Location>
   <ItemConstraint>
    <restriction base="xsd:positiveInteger">
     <xsd:minInclusive value="01"/>
    </xsd:restriction>
   </ItemConstraint>
  </Item>
```

(a) Agreement Template.

```
Agreement Offer
Name ...
Context
<ServiceProvider>responder</ServiceProvider>
...
<GlobalPeriod>
  <!--Global Period Definition-->
</GlobalPeriod>
Terms Compositor
<All>
 <ServiceProperties...> ... </ServiceProperties>
 <ExactlyOne>
  <All>
   <ServiceDescriptionTerm...>
    <Request>Sample.txt</Request>
    <Algorithm>Knapsack</Algorithm>
    <MTBR>20</MTBR>
   </ServiceDescriptionTerm>
   <GuaranteeTerm Obligated="ServiceProvider"...>
    <QualifyingCondition>
     <!--MoreMTBR Period Definition-->
    </QualifyingCondition>
    <SLO>"MTBR ≥ 20"</SLO>
    ...<!--The same BussinessValue and Utility-->
   </GuaranteeTerm>
  </All>
  <All>
   <ServiceDescriptionTerm...>
    <Request>Sample.txt</Request>
    <Algorithm>Knapsack</Algorithm>
    <MTBR>1</MTBR>
   </ServiceDescriptionTerm>
   <GuaranteeTerm Obligated="ServiceProvider"...>
    <QualifyingCondition>
     <!--LessMTBR Period Definition-->
    </QualifyingCondition>
    <SLO>"MTBR ≥ 1"</SLO>
    ...<!--The same BussinessValue and Utility-->
   </GuaranteeTerm>
  </All>
 </ExactlyOne>
</All>
```

(b) Agreement Offer.

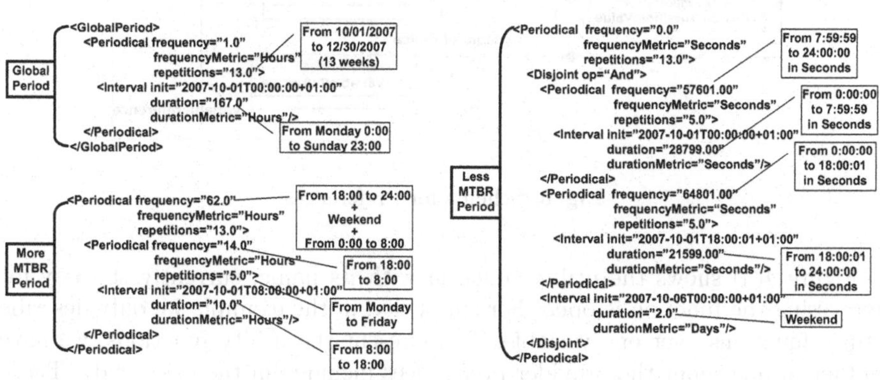

(c) Period Definitions.

Fig. 4. Agreement Template and Agreement Offer

```
<template...>
...
  <CreationConstraints>
    <Item Name="TestPrevious">
      <Location>
        //ServiceDescriptionTerm/MTBR
      </Location>
      <ItemConstraint>
        <xsd:restriction base="xsd:positiveInteger">
          <xsd:minInclusive value="40"/>
        </xsd:restriction>
      </ItemConstraint>
      <Interval init="2007-09-29T00:00:00+01:00"
                duration="2.0"
                durationMetric="Days"/>
    </Item>
  </CreationConstraints>
  ...
</template>
```

Fig. 5. Example of Creation Constraints with Temporality

of one or more service properties in a concrete validity period with any kind of utility function. Figure 6 shows the structure of our preference XML schema for describing the "CustomBusinessValue" element. It defines utility functions pointing to one or a group of variables, which are described in the corresponding "ServiceProperties" element of WS-Ag.

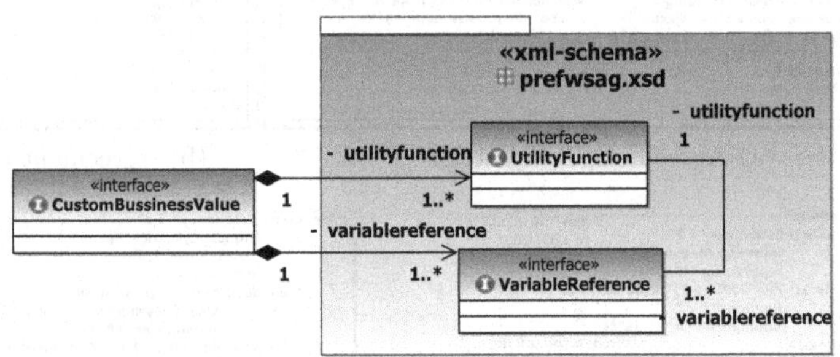

Fig. 6. Schema for Preferences

Figure 4(a) shows the utility function with its name; currently the way for expressing the function is open. For simplicity, in the example we only describe utility functions over one variable. To represent the utility functions, we have to take into account the provider preferences included in the case study. Those preferences are several criteria on the algorithms, on satisfying demands in concrete validity periods, and on satisfying one more exigent demand in MTBR (e.g. a lower value) than several less exigent demands. Figure 7 denotes the utility functions referenced in Figure 4(a).

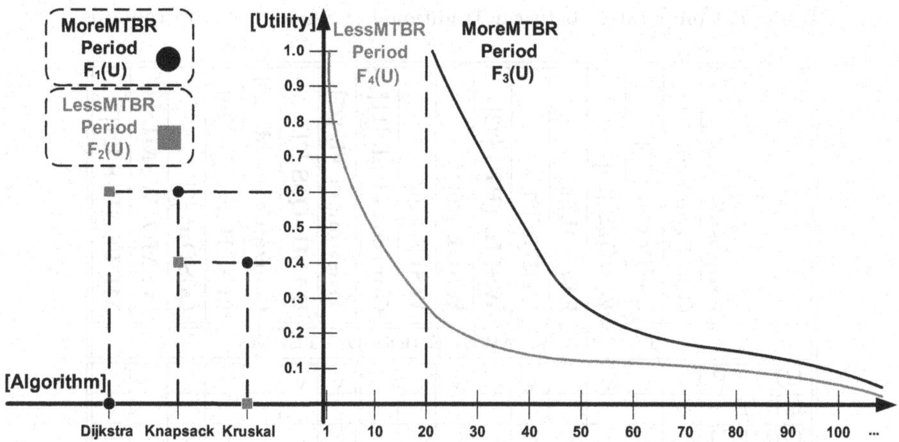

Fig. 7. Utility Functions from the Case Study

5 Related Work

Several authors have studied temporal-awareness on service descriptions. In Table 1 we show a comparative of their proposals, including this paper (those of traditional web at left side, and those of semantic web at right).

Concerning temporal-aware terms, the table denotes that authors who consider GPs, only mention "Non-Periodical" and "Non-Disjoint" intervals, but neither "Periodical" nor "Disjoint" intervals. On the other hand, authors who take into account LPs mention "Periodical" and "Non-Disjoint", but only METEOR-S and WSMO/WSML show interest in "Non-Periodical" intervals. The other authors don't even mention "Non-Periodical" or "Disjoint" intervals in their works. The reason for that lack of "Disjoint" intervals may be due to the fact that they can be expressed by means of several "Non-Disjoint" intervals, though this solution is less expressive. We emphasize WSML(HP) and WSOL because these proposals concern both GPs and LPs in their works. Other proposals like QoSOnt, METEOR-S, and WSMO/WSML have declared that they will study GPs and LPs in their future work.

Only a few of the proposals, among those which are temporal-aware, have taken preferences into account. However, to the best of our knowledge, none of them have studied temporality on preferences and creation constraints. We distinguish two ways to declare the preferences: (1) by comparing the "degree of similarity" between values of service properties from different agreement offers and templates; for example, if a provider specifies in the agreement template that it prefers a value of MTBR of 30s, an agreement offer which requires a MTBR of 32s will be more similar to the template than another offer requiring 20s; and (2) by comparing utility values given by utility functions defined on the service properties, just as we have described above. Both alternatives use weights as a means of incorporating the degree of importance among service properties to the

Table 1. Comparative between Traditional & Semantic Web Proposals

Proposals	Our Proposal.	Lodi et al. [15]	WS-QoS [25]	EWSDL [6]	UDDIe [2]	WSML (HP) [23]	WSOL [26]	WSLA [16]	Gouscos et al. [11]	Trastour et al. [27]	DAML-QoS [7]	Gonzalez. et al. [10]	Li & Horrocks [14]	QoSOnt [9]	WSMO/WSML [8]	METEOR-S [21]
TEMPORAL-AWARENESS ON TERMS																
GP/NP	√	√	√	√	√	√	√			√	√	√	√	~	~	~
GP/P	√															
GP/ND	√	√	√	√	√	√	√			√	√	√	√	~	~	~
GP/D	√															
LP/NP	√													~	~	~
LP/P	√					√	√	√	√							
LP/ND	√					√	√	√	√					~	~	~
LP/D	√															
PREFERENCES																
DoS				√	√							~		~	~	√
UF	√											~			~	~

D=Disjoint, ND=Non-Disjoint, P=Periodical, NP=Non-Periodical
DoS=Degree of Similarity, UF=Utility Functions.
√=feature included, ~=feature identified as future work.

preferences. EWSDL, UDDIe, and METEOR-S have based their preferences on the degree of similarity, whereas other proposals have only mentioned their interest. Regarding utility functions, Gonzalez et al., WSMO/WSML, and METEOR-S are currently working on incorporating this feature to their proposals.

6 Conclusions and Future Work

In this paper, we have shown how a temporal domain-specific language (DSL) can be used to incorporate validity periods into WS-Ag descriptions, such as qualifying conditions associated to SLOs, template creation constraints during agreement creation process, or preferences over service properties. In order to express these validity periods, we have define a schema which includes several kinds of temporal intervals, from disjoint to periodical. Our temporal DSL would have a very large domain of applications, apart from WS-Ag. In addition we propose another schema which allows the definition of preferences over service properties using any utility function instead of constant float functions as described in WS-Ag. Currently, we abstain from defining a specific language for describing the utility functions.

For future work, we are considering several open issues. First, our temporal DSL should be validated in different scenarios to prove its soundness. In order to do so, it would be needed to develop a proof-of-concept prototype from operational semantics on temporal-aware matchmaking defined in previous works [18,22]. Another future improvement would be defining a concrete DSL to specify advanced utility functions, in order to complete our improvement for the preferences description in WS-Ag.

Acknowledgements

The authors would like to thank the reviewers of the 5th International Conference on Service Oriented Computing, whose comments and suggestions improved the presentation substantially.

References

1. Aiello, M., Frankova, G., Malfatti, D.: What's in an Agreement? An Analysis and an Extension of WS-Agreement. In: Benatallah, B., Casati, F., Traverso, P. (eds.) ICSOC 2005. LNCS, vol. 3826, pp. 424–436. Springer, Heidelberg (2005)
2. Ali, A.S., Al-Ali, R., Rana, O., Walker, D.: UDDIe: An Extended Registry for Web Services. In: Proc. of the IEEE Int'l Workshop on Service Oriented Computing: Models, Architectures and Applications at SAINT Conference, IEEE Press, Los Alamitos (2003)
3. Allen, J.F.: Maintaining Knowledge about Temporal Intervals. Communications of the ACM 26(11) (1983)
4. Balaziska, M., Balakrishnan, H., Stonebraker, M.: Contract-Based Load Management in Federated Distributed Systems. In: Proc. of the ACM Symposium on Networked Systems Design and Implementation, San Francisco, California, ACM Press, New York (2004)
5. Bernauer, M., Kappel, G., Kramler, G.: Representing XML Schema in UML - A Comparison of Approaches. In: Koch, N., Fraternali, P., Wirsing, M. (eds.) ICWE 2004. LNCS, vol. 3140, pp. 440–444. Springer, Heidelberg (2004)
6. Chen, Y., Li, Z., Jin, Q., Wang, C.: Study on QoS Driven Web Services Composition. In: Zhou, X., Li, J., Shen, H.T., Kitsuregawa, M., Zhang, Y. (eds.) APWeb 2006. LNCS, vol. 3841, pp. 702–707. Springer, Heidelberg (2006)
7. Chen, Z., Liang-Tien, C., Bu-Sung, L.: Semantics in Service Discovery and QoS Measurement. In: IT Pro - IEEE Computer Society, pp. 29–34 (2005)
8. de Bruijn, J., Feier, C., Keller, U., Lara, R., Polleres, A., Predoiu, L.: WSML Reasoning Survey (November 2005)
9. Dobson, G., Sánchez-Macián, A.: Towards Unified QoS/SLA Ontologies. In: Proc. of the 3rd IEEE International ICWS/SCC Workshop on Semantic and Dynamic Web Processes, Chicago, IL, pp. 169–174. IEEE Press, Los Alamitos (2006)
10. González-Castillo, J., Trastour, D., Bartolini, C.: Description Logics for Matchmaking of Services. Technical Report HPL-2001-265, Hewlett-Packard (2001)
11. Gouscos, D., Kalikakis, M., Georgiadis, P.: An Approach to Modeling Web Service QoS and Provision Price. In: Proc. of the IEEE Int'l Web Services Quality Workshop (at WISE'03), pp. 121–130. IEEE Computer Society Press, Los Alamitos (2003)

12. OGF Grid Resource Allocation Agreement Protocol WG (GRAAP-WG): Web Services Agreement Specification (WS-Agreement) (v. gfd.107) (2007)
13. IBM: Web Service Level Agreement (WSLA) Language Specification (2003)
14. Li, L., Horrocks, I.: A Software Framework for Matchmaking based on Semantic Web Technology. In: Proc. of the 12th ACM Intl. Conf. on WWW, pp. 331–339. ACM Press, New York (2003)
15. Lodi, G., Panzieri, F., Rossi, D., Turrini, E.: SLA-Driven Clustering of QoS-Aware Application Servers. IEEE Transactions on Software Engineering 33(3), 186–196 (2007)
16. Ludwig, H., Keller, A., Dan, A., King, R.P.: A Service Level Agreement Language for Dynamic Electronic Services. Technical Report 22316 W0201-112, IBM (2002)
17. Marcos, E., de Castro, V., Vela, B.: Representing Web Services with UML: A Case Study. In: Orlowska, M.E., Weerawarana, S., Papazoglou, M.M.P., Yang, J. (eds.) ICSOC 2003. LNCS, vol. 2910, pp. 17–27. Springer, Heidelberg (2003)
18. Martín-Díaz, O., Ruiz-Cortés, A., Durán, A., Müller, C.: An approach to temporal-aware procurement of web services. In: Benatallah, B., Casati, F., Traverso, P. (eds.) ICSOC 2005. LNCS, vol. 3826, pp. 170–184. Springer, Heidelberg (2005)
19. Müller, C., Martín-Díaz, O., Resinas, M., Fernández, P., Ruiz-Cortés, A.: A WS-Agreement Extension for Specifying Temporal Properties in SLAs. In: Proc. of the 3rd Jornadas Científico-Técnicas en Servicios Web y SOA (2007)
20. OASIS and UN/CEFAT: Electronic business using XML (ebXML) (2007)
21. Oldham, N., Verma, K., Sheth, A., Hakimpour, F.: Semantic WS-Agreement Partner Selection. In: 15th International WWW Conf., ACM Press, New York (2006)
22. Ruiz-Cortés, A., Martín-Díaz, O., Durán, A., Toro, M.: Improving the Automatic Procurement of Web Services using Constraint Programming. Int. Journal on Cooperative Information Systems 14(4), 439–467 (2005)
23. Sahai, A., Machiraju, V., Sayal, M., Jin, L.J., Casati, F.: Automated SLA Monitoring for Web Services. Research Report HPL-2002-191, HP Laboratories (2002)
24. The Internet Society: Policy Core Information Model - v1 Specification (2001)
25. Tian, M., Gramm, A., Naumowicz, T., Ritter, H., Schiller, J.: A Concept for QoS Integration in Web Services. In: Proc. of the IEEE Int'l Web Services Quality Workshop (at WISE'03), pp. 149–155. IEEE Computer Society Press, Los Alamitos (2003)
26. Tosic, V., Pagurek, B., Patel, K., Esfandiari, B.: Management Applications of the Web Service Offering Language (WSOL). In: I. Systems, pp. 564–586 (2005)
27. Trastour, D., Bartolini, C., González-Castillo, J.: A Semantic Web Approach to Service Description for Matchmaking of Services. Technical Report HPL-2001-183.

Maintaining Data Dependencies Across BPEL Process Fragments

Rania Khalaf[1], Oliver Kopp[2], and Frank Leymann[2]

[1] IBM TJ Watson Research Center, 19 Skyline Drive, Hawthorne, NY 10532, USA
rkhalaf@us.ibm.com
[2] University of Stuttgart, Universitätsstr.38,70569 Stuttgart, Germany
{kopp,leymann}@iaas.uni-stuttgart.de

Abstract. Continuous process improvement (CPI) may require a BPEL process to be split amongst different participants. In this paper, we enable splitting standard BPEL - without any extensions or new middleware. We present a solution that uses a BPEL process, partition information, and results of data analysis to produce a BPEL process for each participant. The collective behavior of these participant processes recreates the control and data flow of the non-split process. Previous work presented process splitting using a variant of BPEL where data flow is modeled explicitly using 'data links'. We reuse the control flow aspect from that work, focusing in this paper on maintaining the data dependencies in standard BPEL.

Keywords: Web services, fragments, business process, BPEL.

1 Introduction

When outsourcing non-competitive parts of a process or restructuring an organization, it is often necessary to move fragments of a business process to different partners, companies, or simply physical locations within the same corporation. We provided a mechanism in [8] that takes a business process and a user-defined partition of it between participants, and creates a BPEL [16] processes for each participant such that the collective behavior of these processes is the same as the behavior of the unsplit one. The process model given as input was based on a variant of BPEL, referred to as BPEL-D, in which data dependencies were explicitly modeled using 'data links'.

Our work in this paper aims to study splitting a process specified in standard compliant BPEL, in which data dependencies are – by definition – implicit. We want to do so while maintaining transparency and without requiring additional middleware. Transparency here means that (1) the same process modeling concepts/language are used in both the main process and the processes created from splitting it; (2) process modifications made to transmit data and control dependencies are easily identifiable in these processes, as are the original activities. This enables the designer to more easily understand and debug the resulting processes, and enables tools to provide a view on each process without the generated communication activities.

B. Krämer, K.-J. Lin, and P. Narasimhan (Eds.): ICSOC 2007, LNCS 4749, pp. 207–219, 2007.

Data analysis of BPEL processes returns data dependencies between activities. On a cursory glance, it seems that it would provide enough information to create the necessary BPEL-D data links. In fact, that was the assumption made in [8] when discussing how the approach could be used for standard BPEL. While for some cases that would be true, section 2 will show that the intricacies of the data sharing behavior exhibited by BPEL's use of shared variables, parallelism, and dead path elimination (DPE) in fact require a more sophisticated approach. DPE [16] is the technique of propagating the disablement of an activity so that downstream activities do not hang waiting for it. This is especially needed for an activity with multiple incoming links, which is always a synchronizing join.

Our work explains the necessary steps required to fully support splitting a BPEL process based on business need without extending BPEL or using specialized middleware. A main enabler is reproducing BPEL's behavior in BPEL itself.

2 Scenario and Overview

Consider the purchasing scenario in Figure 1: It provides a 10% discount to members with 'Gold' status, a 5% discount to those with 'Silver' status, and no discount to all others. After receiving the order (A) and calculating the appropriate discount (C, D, or neither), the order status is updated (E), the order is processed (F), the customer account is billed (G), and a response is sent back stating the discount received (H). We will show how data is appropriately propagated between participant processes, created by splitting this example, using only BPEL constructs.

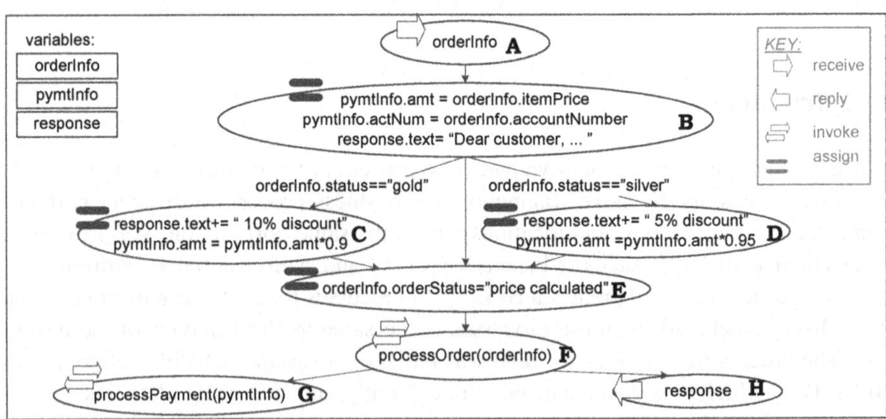

Fig. 1. Sample: an ordering process that provides discounts to Gold and Silver customers

Activity F reads data from A and E. In BPEL-D [8], data links from different activities were allowed to write to the same location of the target activity's input container with a fixed conflict resolution policy of 'random'. Data was considered valid if the activity that wrote it had completed successfully. For cases where data is needed from only one activity (e.g.: A to B, C, D above), data links suffice. However, consider G. It reads *pymtInfo*, whose value of *amt* comes from B, and possibly from C or D. If one had drawn a data link from all three and the *status* is *gold*, then B and C would have run successfully but not D. There would be a race between B and C's writes of *amt*, when only C should have won. A different resolution policy, such as 'last writer wins', is needed here. However, this cannot be realized using the order of the incoming messages carrying the required data: they may get reordered on the network. Even if synchronized clocks [5] are used, BPEL does not have constructs to handle setting variable values based on time stamps.

A high level overview of the approach we propose is: Given a BPEL process, a partition, and the results of data analysis on that process, we produce the appropriate BPEL constructs in the process of each participant to exchange the necessary data. For every reader of a variable, writer(s) in different participants need to send both the data and whether or not the writer(s) ran successfully. The participant's process that contains the reader receives this information and assembles the value of the variable. The recipient uses a graph of receive and assign activities reproducing the dependencies of the original writers. Thus, any writer conflicts and races in the non-split process are replicated.

In more detail, the steps of our approach are: (1) Create a writer-dependency-graph (*WDG*) that encodes the control dependencies between the writers. (2) To reduce the number of messages, use information about a particular partition: Create a participant-writer-dependency-graph (*PWDG*) that encodes the control dependencies between regions of writers whose conflicts can be resolved locally (in one participant). (3) Create *Local Resolvers* (*LR*) in the processes of the writers to send the data. (4) Create a '*receiving flow*' (RF) in the process of the reading activity that receives the data and builds the value of the needed variable.

Criteria: The criteria we aim to maintain is that conflicting writes between multiple activities are resolved in a manner that respects the *explicit control order,* as opposed to runtime completion times, in the original process model.

Restriction: We assume that data flow follows control flow. We disallow splitting processes in which a write and a read that are in parallel write to the same location. BPEL does allow this behavior, but it is a violation of the Bernstein Criterion [1,12]. The Bernstein Criterion states that if two activities are executed sequentially and they do not have any data dependency on each other, they can be reordered to execute in parallel.

3 Background

Our work builds on [8], for which we now provide an overview. We reuse the parts of the algorithm that create the structure of the processes, the endpoint wiring, and splitting of control links. In order to enable splitting *standard* BPEL (i.e. without explicit data links) we need to specify (1) how data dependencies are encoded without appropriate BPEL extensions (see partition dependent graphs introduced below) and (2) how data dependencies are reflected in the generated BPEL processes by using just standard BPEL constructs.

A designer splits a process by defining a partition of the set *A* of all its simple activities. Consider *P*, a set of participants. Every participant, p 2 P, consists of a participant name and a set of one or more activities such that: (i) a participant must have at least one activity, (ii) no two participants share an activity or a name, and (iii) every simple activity of the process is assigned to a participant. The result is one BPEL process and one WSDL file *per participant*, as well as a global wiring definition. Figure 2 shows a partition of the process in Figure 1.

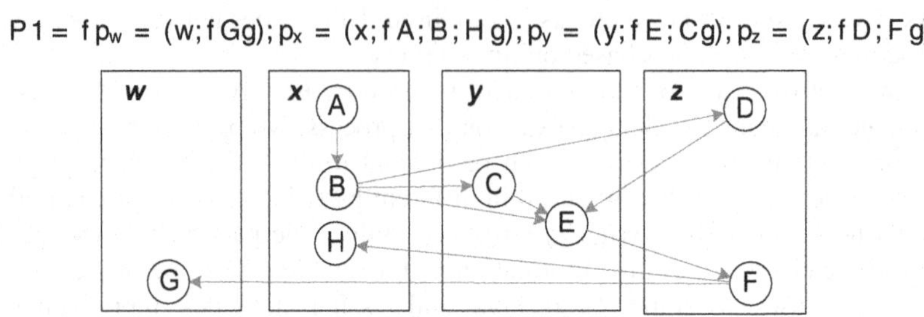

Fig. 2. A partition, P1, of the process in Figure 1

The subset of BPEL constructs that our algorithm, in both [8] and this paper, can actually consume is: (i) processes with 'suppressJoinFailure' set to 'yes' (DPE on), (ii) exactly one correlation set, (iii) any number of partnerLinks, (iv) a single top level 'flow' activity, (v) links, (vi) simple BPEL activities (except 'terminate', 'throw', 'compensate', and endpoint reference copying in an 'assign'). Additionally, (vii) a 'receive' and its corresponding 'reply' are disallowed from being placed in different participants. The single correlation set restriction is to enable properly routing inter-participant messages that transmit control and data dependencies.

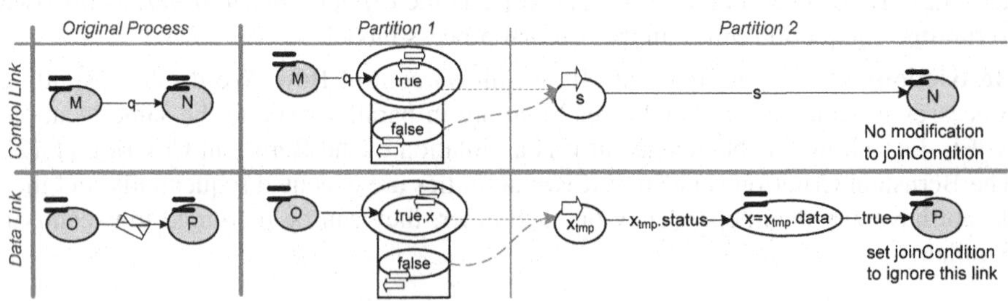

Fig. 3. Summary of link splitting in [8]: the rectangle is a fault handler that catches the BPEL 'joinFailure' fault. Dashed line is a message

The main idea of [8] is to split of control and data links by adding activities in the participant processes as shown in Figure 3. The top row shows splitting a control link with a transition condition q between M and N. To transmit the value of the link to N in participant 2, a scope with a fault handler for 'joinFailure' is used in participant 1. The body of the scope contains an invoke with 'suppressJoinFailure' set to 'no'. The invoke sends 'true()' if the link from M evaluates to true. If not, then that invoke throws a joinFailure, because DPE is off at the invoke (suppressJoinFailure=no). The joinFailure is caught by the fault handler, which contains an invoke that sends 'false()'. Participant 2 receives the value of the link, using a 'receive' activity that is in turn linked to N with a transition condition set to the received value. This is the status, determined at runtime, of the link from M to N in the original process.

The bottom row shows splitting a data link between P and O. We use, in participant 1, a similar construct to that of a split control link. 'true()' is used as the transition condition and the data is sent if O completes successfully. If O fails or is skipped, the invoke in the fault handler sends 'false()' and an empty data item is sent.

In participant 2, a receiving block is created. Such a receiving block consists of (1) a receive activity receiving the data into a uniquely named variable r, (2) an assign activity copying from *r.data* to the desired variable, and (3) a link between them conditional on *r.status*. The message from participant 1 is written in x_{tmp}. If the status is true, the assign writes the data to x. Otherwise the assign is skipped. P must wait for the data but does not depend on whether x was written, so the join condition of P is modified to ignore this new incoming link.

4 Related Work

There is a sizable body of work on splitting business processes, covered in more details in [8]. The most relevant using BPEL is [6] where a process is broken down into several BPEL processes using program analysis and possibly node reordering, with the aim of maximizing the throughput when multiple instances are running concurrently. They claim data analysis on BPEL can lead to enough information to easily propagate data. However, they support a limited set of dependencies because they do not handle faults – in particular those needed for Dead-Path-Elimination.

Alternative approaches for maintaining data dependencies across processes are those that do not require standard BPEL, use new middleware, or tolerate fragmentation obfuscation. In the non-BPEL arena, the most relevant in splitting processes are the use of BPEL-D [8] (explicit data links) which is a simpler case of this paper's algorithms, van der Aalst and Weske's P2P approach [19] for multi-party business processes using Petri Nets, and Muth et. al's work on Mentor [15] using State Charts. In the P2P work, a public workflow is defined as a Petri Net based Workflow Net, with interactions between the parties defined using a place between two transitions (one from each). Then, the flow is divided into one public part per party. Transformation rules are provided to allow one the creation of a private flow from a single party's public one. In Mentor, a state and activity chart process model is split so that different partners can enact its different subsets. Data flow in activity charts, however, is explicitly modeled using labeled arcs between activities - much simpler to split than BPEL's shared variables.

For new middleware instead of our approach, one could explore a wide variety of other ways of propagating data. Examples include: shared data using space-based computing [11]; distributed BPEL engines like the OSIRIS system [18]; modifying a BPEL engine to support using data from partially ordered logical clocks [5] along with write conflict resolution rules.

Dumas et. al [4] translate a process into an event based application on a space-based computing runtime, to enable flexible process modeling. While not created for decomposition, it could be used for it: the process runs in a coordination space and is thus distribution-friendly. The SELF-SERV Project [3] provides a distributed process execution runtime using state-charts as the process model. In both these works, the result is not inline with our goals: the use of a non-BPEL model (UML Activity diagrams, state charts), the requirement of new middleware (coordination space, SELF-SERV runtime), and lack of transparency because runtime artifacts are in a different model (controllers, coordinators) than the process itself.

Mainstream data flow analysis techniques are presented in [14], but BPEL presents special challenges due to parallelism and especially Dead-Path-Elimination. The application of the Concurrent Single Static Assignment Form (CSSA, [10]) to BPEL is shown in [13]. The result of the CSSA analysis is a possible encoding of the use-definition chains, where the definitions (write) of a variable for every use (read) are stated. Thus, the CSSA form can be transformed to provide a set of writers for each reading activity which can be in turn used as one of the inputs to our approach.

We are not aware of any work that propagates data dependencies among fragments of a BPEL process in the presence of dead-path elimination and using BPEL itself.

5 Encoding Dependencies

In this section, we describe how the necessary data dependencies are captured and encoded. The Figure 1 scenario is used throughout to illustrate the various steps. The presented algorithms require the results of a data analysis on the process. In parallel, we are working on such an algorithm (in preparation for publication), optimized for our approach, but whose details are out of scope for this paper. Any data analysis algorithm on BPEL is usable provided it can handle dead path elimination, parallelism, and provide the result (directly or after manipulation) explained below.

One challenging area is in handling writes to different parts of a variable. Our approach handles not only writes to an entire variable, but can handle multiple queries of the form that select a named path (i.e.: (/e)*, called *lvalue* in the BPEL specification) and do not refer to other variables. For example, consider w_1 writes *x.a*, then w_2 writes *x.b*, then r reads *x*; r should get data from both writers and in such a way that *x.b* from w_1 does not overwrite *x.b* from w_2 and vice versa for *x.a*. However, if they had both written to all of *x*, r would need *x* from just w_2. On the other hand, whether an activity reads all or part of a variable is treated the same for the purposes of determining which data to send.

The data algorithm result should provide for each activity *a*, and variable *x* read by *a* (or any of the transition conditions on *a*'s outgoing links), a set $Q_s(a,x)$. $Q_s(a,x)$ groups sets of queries on *x* with writers which may have written to the same parts of *x* expressed in those queries by the time *a* is reached in the control flow. Thus, $\boldsymbol{Q_s(a,x)}$ is a set of tuples, each containing a query set and a writer set. Consider w_1, w_2, and w_3 that write to *x* such that their writes are visible to *a* when *a* is reached. Assume they respectively write to $\{x.b, x.c\}$, $\{x.b, x.c, x.d\}$, and $\{x.d, x.e\}$. Then $Q_s(a,x) = \{(\{x.b, x.c\}, \{w_1, w_2\}), (\{x.d\}, \{w_2, w_3\}), (\{x.e\}, \{w_3\})\}$. Consider $A_d(a,x)$ to provide the set of all writers that *a* depends on for a variable *x* that it reads. In other words, using $\pi_i(t)$ to denote the projection to the ith component of a tuple t, $A_d(a,x) = \bigcup_{q_s \in Q_s(a,x)} \pi_2(q_s)$.

5.1 Writer Dependency Graph (WDG)

We define a *writer dependency graph (WDG)* for activity *a* and variable *x* to be the flow representing the control dependencies between the activities in $A_d(a;x)$. As we are dealing with the subset of BPEL that is a flow with links, the structure is a Directed Acyclic Graph. We have: $WDG_{a;x} = (V;E)$ where the nodes are the writers:

$$V = A_d(a;x) ½ A$$

As for the edges, if there is a path in the process between any two activities in A_d that contains no other activity in A_d, then there is an edge in the WDG connecting these two activities. Consider a function *Paths(a,b)* that returns all paths in the process between *a* and *b*. A path is expressed as an ordered set of activities. Formally, and where $f\, v_1; v_2 g\, 2\, V$:

$$(v_1;v_2)\ 2\ E\ ,\ \ jPaths(v_1;v_2)j > 0 \wedge 8p\ 2\ Paths(v_1;v_2); p \setminus V = f\, v_1; v_2 g$$

A WDG is not dependent on a particular partition. Consider F in Figure 1. $A_d(F; orderInfo) = f\, A; E\, g$. E is control-dependent on A; therefore, $WDG_{F;orderInfo}$ $= (f\, A; E g; f\, (A; E) g)$. Another example is $WDG_{G;pymtInfo} = (f\, B; C; D g; f\, (B; C); (B; D) g)$.

To reduce the number of messages exchanged between partitions to handle the split data, one can: (i) use assigns for writers in the partition of the reader; (ii) join results of multiple writers in the same partition when possible. The next section shows how to do so while maintaining the partial order amongst partitions.

5.2 Partitioned Writer Dependency Graph (PWDG)

The *partitioned writer dependency graph* for a given WDG is the graph representing the control dependencies between the sets of writers of *x* for *a* based on a given partition of the process. A PWDG node is a tuple, containing a partition name and a set of activities. Each node represents a '*region*'. A region consists of activities of the same partition, where no activity from another partition is contained on any path between two of the region's activities. The regions are constructed as follows:

1) Place a temporary (root) node for each partition, and draw an edge from it to every WDG activity having no incoming links in that partition. This root node is needed to build the proper subgraphs in step 2.
2) Form the largest strongly connected subgraphs where no path between its activities contains any activities from another partition.
3) The regions are formed by the subgraphs after removing the temporary nodes.

Each edge in the PWDG represents a control dependency between the regions. The edges of the PWDG are created by adding an edge between the nodes representing two regions, r_1 and r_2, if there exists at least one link whose source is in r_1 and whose target is in r_2.

Consider the partition P1in Figure 2. The PWDG for F and variable *orderInfo*, and the PWDG of G and variable *pymtInfo* would therefore be as follows:

$$PWDG_{F;orderInfo;P1} = (f\, n_1 = (x; f\, A g); n_2 = (y; f\, E g) g; f\, (n_1; n_2) g)$$

$$PWDG_{G;pymtInfo;P1} = (f\, n_1 = (x; f\, B g); n_2 = (y; f\, C g); n_3 = (z; f\, D g) g; f\, (n_1; n_2); (n_1; n_3) g)$$

Next, consider a different partition, P2, similar to P1 except that C is in p_z with D, instead of p_y, then the PWDG of H and response has only two nodes:

PWDG$_{H;response;P2}$ = (f n$_1$ = (x;f B g); n$_2$ = (z;f C; D g)g; f (n$_1$; n$_2$)g)

If all writers and the reader are in the same partition, no *PWDG* is needed or created. Every PWDG node results in the creation of constructs to send the data in the writer's partition and some to receive it in the reader's partition. The former will be the Local Resolvers (section 5.3). The latter will be part of the Receiving Flow for the entire PWDG (section 5.4).

5.3 Sending the Necessary Values and the Use of *Local Resolvers*

A writer sending data to a reader in another participant needs to send both whether or not the writer was successful and if so, also the value of the data. We name the pattern of activities constructed to send the data a *Local Resolver (LR).*

```
CREATE-LOCAL-RESOLVER-MULTIPLE-WRITERS(Node n, String x)
  Q = Qs(n;x)
  If p=pr
      Add b=new empty, v=new variable, v.name = idn(n)
      t = idn(n)
  If jQj = 1, let Q = f qs g
     If p!=pr
         b=CREATE-SENDING-BLOCK(x)
     8w 2 ½(qs)
         Add link l = (w; b; true())
  Else  // more than one query set
     If p!=pr
         Add b = new invoke, v = new variable
         b.inputVariable=v, b.toPart=("data",x), b.joinCondition="true()"
         t=name(v)
     8qs 2 Q
         s = CREATE-ASSIGN-SCOPE(t,qs)
     Add link l1 = (s; b; true())
```

```
CREATE-ASSIGN-SCOPE(String t, Set qs):
   Add s= new scope
   s.addFaultHandler('joinFailure',
                     a_sf=new assign)
   s.setActivity(a_s=new assign),
   a_s.suppressJoinFailure='no'
   a_sf.addCopy(QSTATUS-STR(t,qs),false())
   a_s.addCopy(QSTATUS-STR(t,qs), true())
   8w 2 ½(qs 2 Q)
      Add link l = (w; as; true())
   Return s
```

```
QSTATUS-STR (String t, Set qs)
  Return t + ".status" + id(qs)
```

```
CREATE-SENDING-BLOCK(String x)
   Add s= new scope
   s.addFaultHandler("joinFailure",
                     invf=new invoke)
   Add v = new variable
   invf.inputVariable=v
   invf.toPart=("status",false())
   s.setActivity(inv=new invoke)
   inv.inputVariable=v
   inv.toPart=("status",true())
   inv.toPart=("data",x)
   inv.suppressJoinFailure="no"
   Return inv
```

If there is only one writer in a node of a PWDG, then: if the node is in the same partition as the PWDG, do nothing. Otherwise, the Local Resolver is simply a *sending block* as with an explicit data link (Figure 3, partition 1).

If there is more than one writer, the algorithm below is used. Basically, conflicts between writers in the same PWDG node, $n=(p,B)$, are resolved in the process of p: An activity waits for all writers in n and collects the status for each set of queries.

Assume a PWDG for variable x, and the reader in partition p_r. Consider *id* to be a map associating a unique string for each set of queries in Q, and *idn* to do the same for each PWDG node. For each PWDG node, $n=(p,B)$, *with more than one writer,* add the following activities to the process of participant p:

If the reader is in the same partition as the writers in this node, then we wait with an 'empty' (line 3). If all writers write to the same set of queries, and the node is not in the reader's participant, use a sending block. Create a link from every writer to b, which is either the empty or the sending block's invoke (line 6-9). Figure 4 shows such use of an invoke for C and D in partition y.

If there is more than one query set, the status for each one needs to be written. If the reader is in another participant we create an invoke that runs regardless of the status of the writers (line 11-16). For each query, use a structure similar to a sending block (i.e.: scope, fault handler) to get the writers' status (line 16), but using assigns rather than invokes. The assigns write true or false to a part of the status variable corresponding to the query. Create links from each writer of the query set to the assign in the scope. Create a link (line 17) from the scope to either the empty from line 3 or the invoke from line 12.

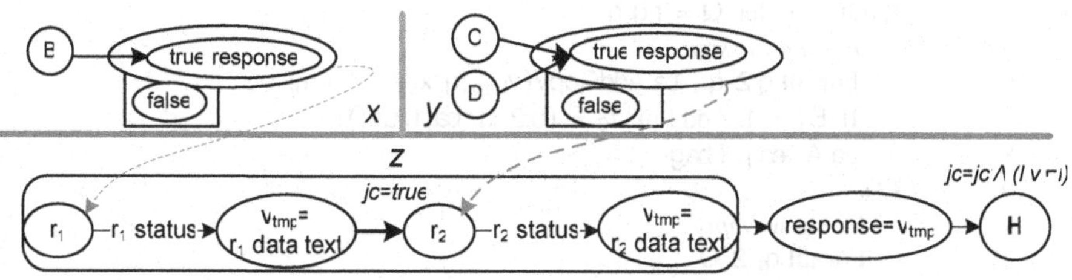

Fig. 4. Snippets from processes from the process in Fig. 1 w/ partition P2

5.4 Receiving Flow (RF)

A Receiving Flow, for a reader a and variable x, is the structure created from a PWDG that creates the value of x needed by the time a runs. It contains a set of receive/assign activities, in a's process, to resolve the write conflicts for x.

Consider *pr* to be the reader's partition, and G to be the PWDG from $WDG(a,x)$. An RF defines a variable, *vtmp,* whose name is unique to the RF. The need for *vtmp* is explained in the next section. A receiving flow is created from G as follows:

```
CREATE-RF(PWDG G)
1   Create a <flow> F
2   For all n = (p; B) 2 ¼1(G)
3       PROCESS-NODE(n)
4   For all e = (n1; n2) 2 ¼2(G)
5       For all d 2 ean1
6           Add a link l=(d, ban2 true())
7   Add af =new assign
8   af :addCopy(vtmp; x)
9   Add links lf = (F; af ; true()) and lr = (af ; a; true())
10  joinCondition(a) = joinCondition(a) ^ (lr _ : lr)
```

Create a flow activity (line 1). For each node (line2-3), we will add a block of constructs to receive the value of the variable and copy it into appropriate locations in a temporary, uniquely named variable $v_{tmp.}$ Link the blocks together (line 4-6) by connecting them based on the connections between the partitions, using *ba* and *ea* as the first and last activities of a block, respectively. The subscript is used to identify which node's block they are for (i.e.: ea_{n1} is the *ea* set created in PROCESS-NODE(n1)). Link the flow to an assign (line 7-9) that copies from v_{tmp} to *x*. Link the assign to *a* and modify *a*'s join condition to ignore the new link's status (line 10).

```
PROCESS-NODE(Node n) //recall n=(p,B)
1       Q = Qs(n; x), ea = ;
2       //All activities added in this procedure are added to F
3       If p = pr
4           If jQj = 1, let Q = f qsg
5               ba =new assign,
6               For all q 2 qs, ba:addCopy(vtmp:q; x + ":" + q)
7               If jBj = 1, Add link l0 = (b2 B; ba; true())
8               ea Ã ea [ f bag
9           Else
10              ba =new empty
11              For all qs 2 Q
12                  CREATE-Q-ASSIGN(qs; "x"; QSTATUS-STR(idn(n); qs))
13          If jBj 6 1
14              Add link l0 = (em; ba; true()), where em=empty from LR
15          joinCondition(ba)=status(l0)
16      Else //p is not pr
17          Add rrb= new receive, joinCondition(rrb)=true(), rrb.variable=ri
18          ba = rrb //note that ea will be created in lines 20,23
19          If jQj = 1, let Q = f qsg
20              CREATE-Q-ASSIGN(qs; "ri:data"; "ri:status")
21          Else
22              For all qs 2 Q
23                  CREATE-Q-ASSIGN(qs; "ri:data"; QSTATUS-STR(ri; qs))
```

And the creation of the assigns for each query is as follows:

```
CREATE-Q-ASSIGN(Set qs, String var, String statusP)
c.1   Add act =new assign
c.2   ea Ã ea[ f actg
c.3   Add link l = (ba; act; statusP)
c.4   For all q 2 qs, act:addCopy(vtmp:q; var + ":" + q)
```

For each node: If the node is in the same participant as *a* and has, one query set, add an assign copying from the locations in *x* to the same locations in v_{tmp} (line 3-6). If the node has only one writer, link from the writer to the assign (line 7). If it has more than one writer, an 'empty' was created in the Local Resolver (LR), so link from *that* empty to the assign (line 13-14). If the node has more than one query set, create an empty instead of an assign and (line 11-12) create one assign per query set. Create links from the empty to the new assigns whose status is whether the query set was successfully written (line c.3). Add a copy to each of these assigns, for every query in the query set, from the locations in *x* to the same locations in v_{tmp} (line c.4). Then, (line 15) set the joinCondition of the empty or assign to only run if the data was valid.

If the node is another partition, create a receiving block (line 17) instead of an assign. Set the joinCondition of the receive to true so it is never skipped. Again copy the queries into a set of assigns (line 19-23).

Figure 5 shows two examples for partition P1 of our scenario. The top creates *pymtInfo* for G: The value of *amt* may come from B,C, or D but *actNum* always from B. The bottom creates *orderInfo* for F. Notice how A's write is incorporated into the RF even though A and F are in the same participant.

Note that receiving flows reproduce the building of the actual variable using BPEL semantics. Thus, the behavior of the original process is mirrored, not changed.

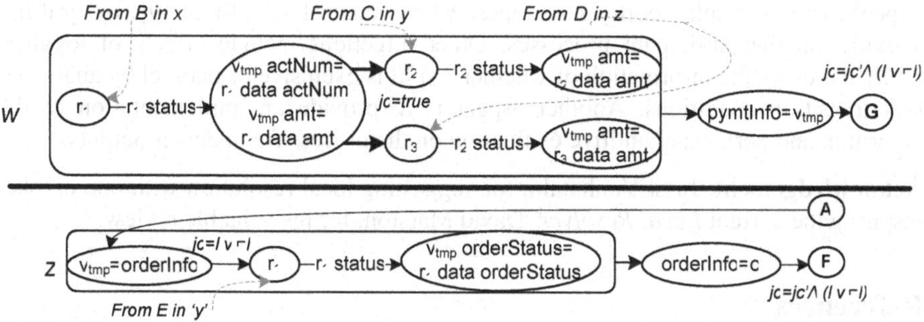

Fig. 5. Two RFs using partition P1. Top: *pymtInfo* to G in w. Bottom: *orderInfo* to F in z.

Multiple RFs and the Trailing Assign

Consider multiple readers of the same variable placed in the same participant Each RF writes to its local temporary variable, and only copies to the shared variable when the trailing assign at the end of the RF is reached. This temporary variable is used so that messages arriving out of order or to multiple RFs concerned with the same variable do not incorrectly overwrite each other's values. The algorithms require that the original process adhere to the Bernstein Criterion; otherwise, one cannot guarantee that RFs with overlapping WDGs don't interfere with each other's writes.

6 Conclusion and Future Work

We provided an algorithm for splitting BPEL processes using BPEL itself for proper data communication between participants; furthermore, splits are transparent, i.e. it is clear where the changes are and they are done in the same modeling abstractions as the main process model. This has been achieved by use of LRs and RFs as long as the original process respects the Bernstein Criterion. If not, one would have to take into consideration actual completion times of activities, which goes beyond BPEL's capabilities. Having placed the activities that handle data and control dependencies at the boundaries of the process and used naming conventions on the operations, we enable graphical/text-based filters to toggle views between the activities of the non-split process and the 'glue' activities we have added. The difficulty in maintaining data dependencies in BPEL is due to unique situations (section 2), such as the ability to 'revive' a dead path with an 'or' join condition, resulting from dead-path elimination and parallelism.

The complexity, in number of messages exchanged and activities added, depends on two factors: The amount of inter-participant data dependencies and the quality of the data algorithm. Poor data analysis leads to larger writer sets. At most one 'invoke' is added for each PWDG node, so the number of message exchanges added is at most the *total* number of PWDG nodes: $O(n_{PWDG}) = O(n)$. For the number of added activities, the upper bound is quadratic, $O(n_{PWDG}$ £ $max(jQ_{s}j)) = O(n^2)$.

Our future work includes optimizations such as merging overlapping RFs and targeted data analysis. A first step for optimization is the application of the work presented in [2,7,17] to BPEL. Also of interest is enabling transmitting (some) data dependencies for split loops and scopes, whose control is split in [9], by grafting activities in the participant processes. Other directions include effects of toggling DPE, and using the information of whether a split is exclusive or parallel by analyzing link transition conditions. Another aspect is to provide an implementation of the algorithm and perform quantitive evaluation on the process fragments it outputs.

Acknowledgement. Jussi Vanhatalo, for suggesting local resolution with one invoke, inspiring the current *Local Resolver*. David Marston, for his valuable review.

References

1. Baer, J. L.: A Survey of Some Theoretical Aspects of Multiprocessing. ACM Computing Surveys, Vol. 5 No. 1 (1973) 31-80
2. Balasundaram, V., Kennedy, Ken: A Technique for Summarizing Data Access and Its Use in Parallelism Enhancing Transformations. In: Proceedings of the ACM SIGPLAN '89 Conference on Programming Language Design and Implementation. SIGPLAN Notices, Vol. 24 No. 7 (1989) 41-53
3. Benatallah, B., Dumas, M., Sheng, Q.Z.: Facilitating the Rapid Development and Scalable Orchestration of Composite Web Services. Journal of Distributed and Parallel Databases, Vol. 17 No. 1 (2005) 5-37

4. Dumas, M., Fjellheim, T., Milliner, S., Vayssiere J.: Event-based Coordination of Process-oriented Composite Applications. Proceedings of the 3rd International Conference on Business Process Management (BPM). Lecture Notes in Computer Science, Vol. 3649. Springer-Verlag, (2005) 236-251
5. Fidge, C.: Logical Time in Distributed Computing Systems. IEEE Computer, Vol. 24 No. 8 (1991) 28-33
6. Gowri, M., Karnik, N.: Synchronization Analysis for Decentralizing Composite Web Services. International Journal of Cooperative Information Systems, Vol. 13 No. 1 (2004) 91-119
7. Kennedy, K., Nedeljkovi'c, N.: Combining dependence and data-flow analyses to optimize communication. In: Proceedings of the 9th International Parallel Processing Symposium (1995) 340-346
8. Khalaf, R., Leymann, F.: Role Based Decomposition of Business Processes Using BPEL. In: Proceeding of the IEEE 2006 International Conference on Web Services (ICWS 2006), Chicago, Il, (2006) 770-780
9. Khalaf, R., Leymann, F.: Coordination Protocols for Split BPEL Loops and Scopes. University of Stuttgart, Technical Report No. 2007/01, March 2007
10. Lee, J., Midkiff, S.P., Padua D.A.: Concurrent Static Single Assignment Form and Constant Propagation for Explicitly Parallel Programs. In: Proceedings of the 10th International Workshop on Languages and Compilers for Parallel Computing. Lecture Notes in Computer Science, Vol. 1366. Springer-Verlag, (1997) 114-130
11. Lehmann, T.J., McLaughry, S.W., Wyckoff, P.:T Spaces: The Next Wave. Proceedings of the 32nd Hawaii International Conference on System Sciences (HICSS '99), Maui, Hawaii, Jan. 1999
12. Leymann, F., Altenhuber, W.: Managing Business Processes as Information Resources, IBM Systems Journal, Vol. 33 No. 2. (1994) 326-348
13. Moser, S., Martens, A., Görlach, K., Amme, W., Godlinski, A.: Advanced Verification of Distributed WS-BPEL Business Processes Incorporating CSSA-based Data Flow Analysis. IEEE International Conference on Services Computing (SCC 2007). (2007) 98-105
14. Muchnick, S.S.: Advanced Compiler Design and Implementation. Morgan Kaufmann. 1997
15. Muth, P., Wodkte, D., Wiessenfels, J., Kotz, D.A., Weikum, G.: From Centralized Workflow Specification to Distributed Workflow Execution, Journal of Intelligent Information Systems, Vol. 10 No. 2 (1998) 159-184
16. OASIS: Web Services Business Process Execution Language Version 2.0, 11 April 2007 Online at http://docs.oasis-open.org/wsbpel/2.0/wsbpel-v2.0.html
17. Sarkar, V.: Analysis and Optimization of Explicitly Parallel Programs Using the Parallel Program Graph Representation. In: Li, Z. et al. (eds.): 10th Workshop on Languages and Compilers for Parallel Computing (LCPC). Lecture Notes in Computer Science, Vol. 1366. Springer-Verlag (1997)
18. Schuler, C., Weber, R., Schuldt, H., Scheck, H.J.: Peer-to-Peer Process Execution with OSIRIS. In: 1st International Conference on Service Oriented Computing (ICSOC 2003). Lecture Notes in Computer Science, Vol. 2910. Springer-Verlag (2003) 483-498
19. van der Aalst, W.M.P., Weske, M.: The P2P Approach to Interorganizational Workflow. In: Proceedings of the 13th International Conference on Advanced Information Systems Engineering (CAiSE 2001). Lecture Notes in Computer Science, Vol. 2068. Springer-Verlag (2001) 140-156.

Supporting Dynamics in Service Descriptions - The Key to Automatic Service Usage

Ulrich Küster and Birgitta König-Ries

Institute of Computer Science, Friedrich-Schiller-Universität Jena
D-07743 Jena, Germany
ukuester,koenig@informatik.uni-jena.de

Abstract. In realistic settings, service descriptions will never be precise reflections of the services really offered. An online seller of notebooks, for instance, will most certainly not describe each and every notebook offered in his service description. This imprecision causes poor quality in discovery results. A matcher will be able to find potentially matching services but can give no guarantees that the concrete service needed will really be provided. To alleviate this problem, a contract agreement phase between service provider and requester following the discovery has been suggested in the literature. In this paper, we present an approach to the automation of this contracting. At the heart of our solution is the possibility to extend service descriptions with dynamically changing information and to provide several means tailored to the abilities of the service provider to obtain this information at discovery time.

1 Introduction

In recent years two trends – the Semantic Web and Web Services – have been combined to form Semantic Web Services, services that are semantically annotated in a way that allows for fully or semi automated discovery, matchmaking and binding. At the core of Semantic Web Services is an appropriate service description language that is on the one hand expressive enough to allow for precise automated matchmaking but on the other hand restricted enough to support efficient processing and reasoning. Several frameworks have been proposed (among them WSMO[1] and OWL-S[2]) but overall there is no consensus about the most suitable formalism yet.

One of the challenges in the design of semantic service description languages and matchmaking tools is the granularity at which services are to be described and thus the precision that can be achieved during discovery. Most efforts describe services at the interface level, e.g. a service that sells computer parts will be described exactly like that. This is fine to service requests that are given at the same level of detail, like *"I'm looking for a service that sells notebooks"*. Such a description is sufficient, if the aim of discovery is to find *potentially* matching services. In this case, the user or her agent will be presented with a list of notebook sellers and will then browse through their inventory or use some other mechanisms to obtain more precise information about available notebooks, their

B. Krämer, K.-J. Lin, and P. Narasimhan (Eds.): ICSOC 2007, LNCS 4749, pp. 220–232, 2007.

configurations and prices. The user will then have to make a decision which notebook to buy and call the service to actually do so. This works fine, as long as the user is in the loop during the process. It does *not* work anymore if complete automation is expected. Take for instance a fine grained and precise request like *"I want to buy a 13 - 14 inch Apple MacBook with at least 1 GB RAM and at least 2.0 GHZ Intel Core 2 Duo Processor for at most $1500"*. Such a request might be posed by a user, but might as well be posed, e.g., by an application run by the purchasing department of a big company with the expectation that matching services will be found, the best one selected and then invoked autonomously by the discovery engine. To handle such requests successfully, detailed information about available products, their properties and their price is needed in the offer descriptions.

In [3] Preist writes about this issue. He distinguishes *abstract, agreed and concrete services.* A concrete service is defined as "an actual or possible performance of a set of tasks [...]" whereas an abstract service is some set of concrete services and described by a machine-understandable description. Ideally, these descriptions are *correct* and *complete. Correct* means that the description covers only elements that the service actually provides. The description "This is a notebook selling service" is *not* correct, since the service will typically not be able to deliver all existing notebooks. *Complete* means, that everything the service offers is covered by the description. While completeness of descriptions is rather easy to achieve, correctness is not. To achieve this characteristic much more information would have to be included in the static descriptions published to the service repositories than is usually feasible for several reasons. Typical services will sell hundreds of products and big players may even sell thousands of thousands of different articles. Regardless of whether one creates few comprehensive descriptions each including many products or many specific descriptions each comprising only few closely related articles: The overall amount of information that needs to be sent to the registry and that needs to be maintained and updated will be forbiddingly big. Scalability issues will become increasingly bad when properties of articles like availability, predicted shipping time or prices change dynamically, which will often be the case. Furthermore, many service providers will not be willing to disclose too much information to a public repository. First, a huge up-to-date database of information about products constitutes a direct marketing value that providers will not be willing to share. Second, information about the availability of items may give bargaining power to potential buyers (think of the number of available seats on a certain flight). In these cases – again – the provider will be unwilling to reveal such information.

Preist suggests a separate contract agreement phase following the discovery to determine whether a matching abstract service is really able to fulfill a given request and to negotiate the concrete service to provide. We argue, that similar to discovery, contracting can be automated, if enough information is made available to the matchmaker. To enable such an extension of a matchmaker, a flexible way to represent dynamically changing information in service descriptions and to obtain this information during discovery is needed. Existing frameworks for semantic web services offer little if any support for this step.

In this paper we extend our previous work on semantic service description languages and semantic service matchmaking in this direction. We propose means to enable fully automated yet flexible and dynamic interactions between a matchmaker and service providers that are used during the matchmaking process to gather dynamic information that is missing in the static service description (like the availability and the current price of certain articles). We then illustrate how this is used to enable contracting within the discovery phase.

The rest of the paper is organized as follows: In Section 2 we provide some background information about the service description language and the matchmaking algorithm used to implement our ideas. Building on that we present the above mentioned extensions to the language and matchmaking algorithm in Section 3. There, we also illustrate and motivate our extensions via a set of examples. In Section 4 we give more details on the implementation of our ideas and how we evaluated it. Finally, we provide an overview of the related work in Section 5 and summarize and conclude in Section 6.

2 DIANE Service Description

In this section we provide some background information about the DIANE Service Description (DSD) that we used to implement our ideas and the DIANE middleware built around it to facilitate the efficient usage of the language.

DSD is a service description language based on its own light-weight ontology language that is specialized for the characteristics of services and can be processed efficiently at the same time. In the following an intuitive understanding of DSD and the DSD matchmaking algorithm is sufficient for this paper. We will therefore include only the necessary aspects of DSD to make this paper self-contained. The interested reader is referred to [4,5,6] for further details. Figure 1 shows relevant excerpts of a DSD request to buy a notebook roughly corresponding to the one mentioned in the introduction in an intuitive graphical notation.

The basis for DSD is standard object orientation which is extended by additional elements, two of which are of particular importance in the context of this paper.

Aggregating Elements: A service is typically able to offer not one specific effect, but a set of similar effects. An internet shop for instance will be able to offer a variety of different products and will ship each order to at least all national addresses. That means, services offer to provide one out of a set of similar effects. In Preist's terminology, these are *abstract* services. Requesters on the other hand are typically looking for one out of a number of acceptable services, but will have preferences for some of these. (Our notebook buyer might prefer a 13-inch, 1.5 GB RAM notebook over a 14-inch, 1 GB RAM notebook – or the other way round.) Thus, DSD is based on the notion of *sets*. Sets are depicted in DSD by a small diagonal line in the upper left corner of a concept. This way, offers

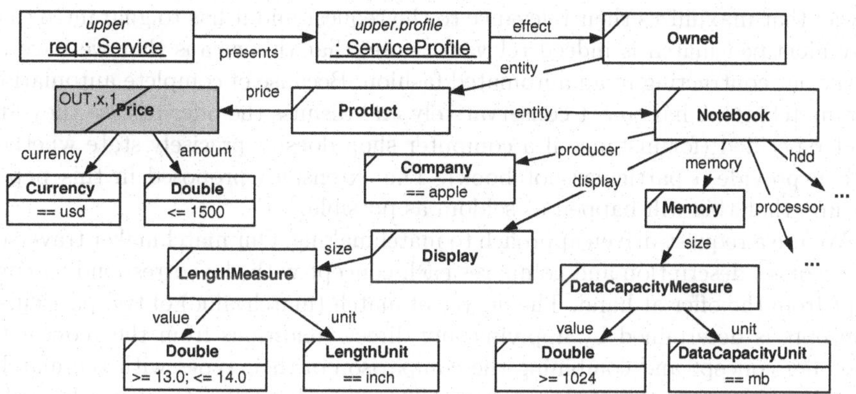

Fig. 1. Simplified DSD request

describe the set of possible effects they can provide and requests describe the set of effects they are willing to accept together with the preference among the elements of this set. Like all DSD concepts sets are declaratively defined which leads to descriptions as trees as seen in Figure 1. This request asks for any one service that sells a notebook that is produced by Apple, has a display size between 13.0 and 14.0 inches, at least one gigabyte RAM and costs at most \$1500. Fuzzy instead of crisp sets may be used in requests to encode preferences, e.g., for more RAM or lower cost or to trade between different attributes, e.g. between cost and memory size [6].

Variables: While a service will offer different effects, upon invocation, the requester needs to choose or at least limit which of these effects the service should provide in this specific instance. This step is referred to by Preist as contract agreement and negotiation. Meanwhile, after service execution the requester might need to receive results about the specific effect performed by the invocation. In DSD, *variables* (denoted by a grayed rectangle) are used to support this. In offers, variables are used to encode input and output concepts, in requests (as in in Figure 1) they can be used to require the delivery of certain outputs of the service invocation (like the exact price of the purchased notebook in the example) or to enable configurable request templates.

In our envisioned setting we use a request-driven paradigm for semantic service discovery and matchmaking and assume the need for complete automation. Service providers publish their offer descriptions to some kind of repository. Service users create request descriptions that describe desired effects. The task to find, bind and execute the most suitable service offer for a given request is then delegated to a fully automated semantic middleware that works on behalf of the requester.

Since the semantic middleware is supposed to work in a fully automated fashion up to the invocation of the most suitable offer (if there is one), matchmaking is not limited to identifying potential matches. Instead it has to prepare the invocation by configuring the offers (i.e. choosing values for all necessary inputs) in a way that maximizes their relevance to the request and it has to guarantee that any identified match is indeed relevant. Note, that this means that we have to carry out contracting in an automated fashion. Because of complete automation the matchmaker has to act conservatively and dismiss the offer in case they are underspecified (for instance if a computer shop doesn't precisely state whether it can provide a particular notebook). The extensions proposed in this paper ensure, that this will happen as seldom as possible.

We use a request-driven approach to matchmaking. Our matchmaker traverses the request description and compares each concept with the corresponding concept from the offer at hand. The degree of match (matchvalue) of two particular concepts is determined by applying any direct conditions from the request to the offer concept and combining the comparison of their types with the matchvalues of the properties of the concepts. These are determined recursively in the same fashion. When the matchmaker encounters a variable in the offer during its traversal of the descriptions it determines the optimal value for this variable with respect to the request. Due to space limitations please refer to [4,6] for further detail.

3 Dynamic Information Gathering for Improved Matchmaking

In this section we will present how we integrated an automated contracting phase into our matchmaking algorithm. We will illustrate our approach by means of offer descriptions for three fictitious providers that are potentially relevant for a user seeking to buy a notebook with particular properties. Note that for reasons of simplicity and due to space limitations all examples shown in this sections have been simplified and show relevant excerpts of the offer descriptions only. In particular all aspects related to actually execute any service operations (grounding to SOAP, lifting and lowering between DSD and XML data, etc.) have been omitted[1].

In order to interact with services, DSD supports a two-phase choreography: An arbitrary number of so-called *estimation steps* is followed by a single *execution step*. The execution step is the final stateful service invocation that is used to create the effect that is desired by the requester. It will be executed for the most suitable offer after the matchmaking is completed. Contrary, the estimation steps will be executed on demand for various offers during the matchmaking process to gather additional information, i.e. to dynamically obtain a more specific and detailed offer description where necessary. Since they may be executed during the matchmaking process for various providers they are expected to be *safe* as defined in Section 3.4. of the Web Architecture [8].

Concepts in an offer description may be tagged as `estimate n out` variables, thereby specifying that they can be concretized and detailed by invoking the

[1] Information about the automated invocation of services described using DSD can be found in [7].

operation(s) associated with the nth estimation step providing the values of the concepts tagged as `estimate n in` variables as input. In order to be able to invoke the corresponding operation, it has to be assured that those variables have already been filled by the matchmaker. Thus our matchmaking algorithm uses a two phase approach[2]:

The first phase is used to filter irrelevant offers, fill variables in the remaining offer descriptions and in particular to collect information about whether a certain estimation step needs to be performed at all. We are able to do this by exploiting the fact that our structured approach to matchmaking (see Section 2) allows us to precisely determine those parts (or aspects) of two service descriptions that did not match. If the matcher encounters a concept that is tagged as `estimate out` variable three cases can be distinguished:

- A perfect match can be guaranteed using the static description alone: A provider states that the shipping time for all offered products does not exceed one week and that the precise shipping time of a particular product can be obtained dynamically. If the request does not require the shipping time to be faster than one week, there is no need to inquire the additional information.
- A total fail is unavoidable from the static description alone: A provider states that the notebooks offered have a price range from \$1500 to \$2500 and that the precise price can be inquired dynamically. If the requester is seeking a notebook for less than \$1500 this offer will not match in any case and may be discarded.
- In all other cases the estimation operation needs to be performed. Even in cases where an imperfect match can be guaranteed based on the static description alone, more precise information obtained dynamically might improve the matchvalue of the service.

After the first phase the necessary estimation operations for all remaining offers will be performed. It is important to stress again that our matchmaking algorithm allows us to determine whether a particular estimation operation offers useful information for a given matchmaking operation. Thus we are able to reduce the expensive execution of estimation operation to the absolute minimum. Once the estimation operation have been executed the corresponding service descriptions will be updated with the newly obtained information. Based on the completed offer descriptions the matchmaker computes the precise matching value of each offer in a second matching phase. This procedure is used in the following example.

Midge, a small internet-based merchant, is specialized on delivering highly customized notebooks. Customers may choose the various components (display, CPU, RAM, HDD, ...) to select a machine that corresponds most closely to their specific requirements. The available components are precisely described in the static offer description but the price depends on the chosen configuration and can be obtained by calling a specific endpoint with the configuration's key data as input.

[2] Actually it uses three phases due to issues related to automated composition but this is not relevant for this paper. Please refer to [6] for further details.

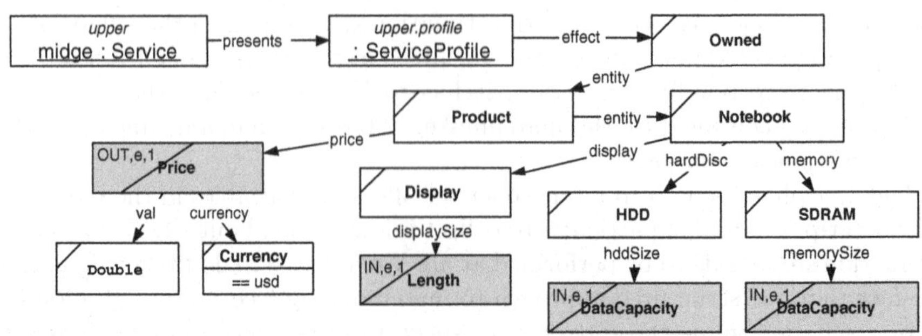

Fig. 2. Relevant parts of Midge's offer description

The relevant part of the offer description of Midge is shown in Figure 2. Midge simply declares the concepts corresponding to the sizes of display, RAM, HDD, ... as `estimate in` variables and the price concept as `estimate out` concept. The matcher will assure to provide single concrete values for the necessary input variables. This way Midge's grounding can be kept extremely simple thereby minimizing the effort involved for Midge to create the service implementation. Note however that the matchmaker will first choose values for display, RAM, HDD, ... and then inquire the corresponding price. Since a general matchmaker does not know typical dependencies between those properties (more RAM usually results in a higher price) it cannot always find the best value for the money. Thus Midge's attempt is lightweight, but not suitable for all cases.

In order to provide greater flexibility and cope with the different requirements of different providers, in this paper, we additionally propose an extended concept of variables to be used in the context of estimation steps. DSD variables – as introduced in [5] – link the inputs and outputs of service operations with concepts in the service descriptions.

For different tasks we suggest four increasingly complex types of binding (or filling) of variables.

- A variable that supports only *simple binding* needs to be filled with a concrete instance value. Examples include the instance *Jena* for a variable of type *Town* or $< P1Y2MT2H >$ for a variable of type *XSD_Duration*.
- A variable that supports *enumerated binding* can be filled with a a *list* of concrete instances.
- A variable that supports *declarative binding* can be filled with a crisp, declarative DSD set like the set of all towns that are at most 300 km away from Jena or the set of notebooks with a 13 inch display, an Intel Duo Core processor and more than one GB RAM.
- A variable that supports *fuzzy declarative binding* can be filled with a *fuzzy* declarative DSD set. This way preferences can be expressed in a variable filling.

Which type of binding is used in a given service description may depend on a number of factors, including the kind of service, the number of instances

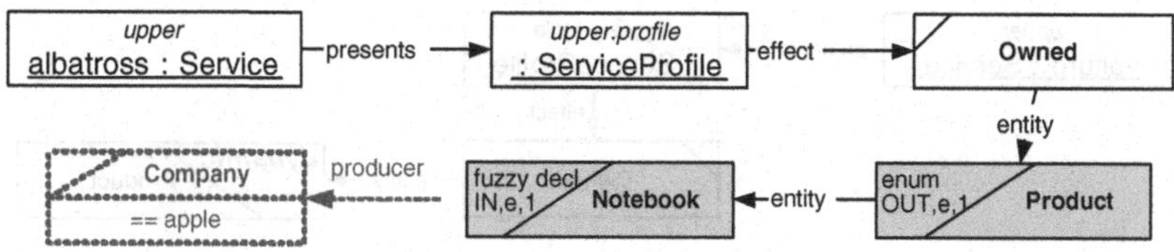

Fig. 3. Relevant parts of Albatross's offer description

associated with certain variables, the willingness of the service provider to share information and its ability to process the more complex bindings. Midge for instance used simple variables, thereby minimizing its effort to create its service implementation but failing to deliver the most suitable offer in all cases. This approach is unsuitable for our next example that will be based on fuzzy declarative and enumerated bindings.

Albatross operates a huge online shop for all kind of electronic products. Including the offers of third party sellers that Albatross's online shop integrates as a broker, hundreds of thousands of articles are available. Human customers can browse the catalogue data through Albatross's website and for the envisioned automated usage Albatross plans to list the most suitable products for a request in a similar fashion. However, in order to limit network bandwidth consumption and to avoid to reveal all the catalogue data, Albatross decided to never list more than thirty items in reply of a single request. It is therefore important for Albatross to carefully select those thirty listings in a way that maximizes the relevance to the request at hand. Since the overall range of available articles is fairly stable, Albatross decided to create a single offer description for each type of article (printer, monitor, notebooks, servers, ...). Depending on the range of articles and the granularity chosen for the descriptions, a fair deal of static information can be included in the descriptions and Albatross's endpoint will not be called for obviously unsuitable requests. To retrieve a maximum of information about the interests of the user, Albatross uses fuzzy declarative binding for the `in` variables of the necessary estimation operation and will retrieve all information available at all about the users preferences. It is up to the implementation of Albatross's endpoint how much of that information is then really evaluated to select the thirty most relevant products (see Section 4 for further detail). The list of these products will be returned in the `out` variable of the corresponding estimation operation, that is therefore declared as an enumerated variable.

The relevant parts of Albatross's offer description for notebooks can be seen in Figure 3. Note that the displayed parts are still very generic. To avoid to be called too many times Albatross could just as well decide to further specialize its descriptions by statically adding further restrictions (e.g. restrict the offer to notebooks produced by Apple as indicated in grey in Figure 3).

One disadvantage of Albatross' descriptions is that due to the broad nature of Albatross' catalogue they can not reveal a whole lot of information statically. This motivated another extension that will be demonstrated with the following example.

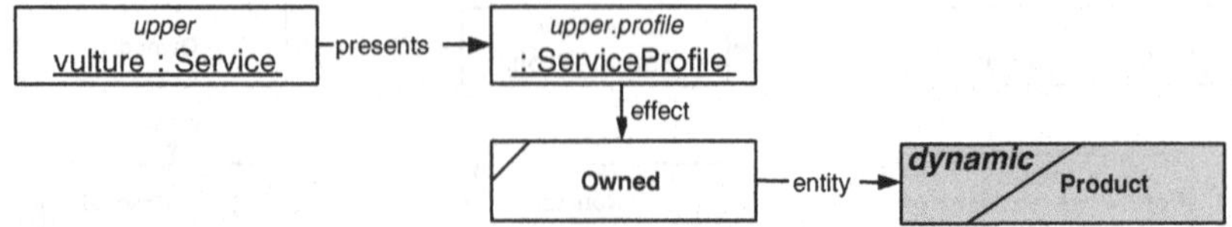

Fig. 4. Relevant parts of Vulture's offer description

Vulture is a reseller of remaining stock and similar extraordinary items. Available items change from day to day and range from hightech servers to wooden lawn seats. Vulture's main interest is to limit maintenance (i.e. programming) cost and to quickly sell any items currently on stock.

The relevant part of the offer description of Vulture is shown in Figure 4. Due to the dynamically changing range of available articles, Vulture cannot provide much information in the static offer description (basically all it states is that Vulture is a vending service). Since such an offer is not very meaningful we created a special operation: Concepts tagged as *dynamic sets* may have an associated estimation operation that will be evaluated right at the beginning of the first phase of the matching process. Since it cannot be assured that input values have been determined by the matchmaker already, the corresponding operation must not have any specific `in` variables. Instead the corresponding concept description from the request will be given as input. In the case of Vulture, Vulture's implementation (see Section 4) simply extracts the type of Product seeked by the requester and returns a listing of all related available products that will be used to complete the offer description during matchmaking. This operation is basically syntactic sugar, the main difference to using standard estimation operations is the time the estimation operation will be evaluated. We chose to add this option since it can pay off to minimize the number of remaining offers early in the matching process (e.g. in cases where automated composition takes place [6]).

4 Implementation and Evaluation

The concepts illustrated above have been implemented in our matchmaker and the supporting DIANE middleware [6]. For the sake of much greater objectiveness we sought to have our ideas and techniques evaluated by a greater community in addition to our own evaluation. We believe the ongoing Semantic Web Services Challenge[3] [9] to be an ideal setting for this task. The challenge presents sets of increasingly difficult problem scenarios[4] and evaluates solutions to these scenarios at a series of workshops. It specifically aims at developing a certification process for semantic service technology.

A basic example similar to the case of Midge has been used in the solutions for the first Shipment Discovery Scenario of the SWS-Challenge to

[3] http://sws-challenge.org

[4] http://sws-challenge.org/wiki/index.php/Scenarios

dynamically obtain the price of a shipping operation depending on the properties of the parcel[10,11]. Our solution including dynamic gathering of the price was successfully evaluated at the second SWS-Challenge workshop in Budva, Montenegro[5]. Since then we improved the integration of the estimation step handling into the matchmaking algorithm in order to avoid the execution of unnecessary estimation operations whereas in our original solution for the SWS-Challenge scenario all available estimation operations were executed. This was motivated by the fact that the inevitable communication cost for the estimation operations quickly dominates the cost of the whole matching process.

We submitted a new scenario[6] to the SWS-Challenge that meanwhile has been accepted as an official scenario by the SWS-Challenge Programm Committee. This scenario deals among other things with the dynamic retrieval of a listing of available products from given web service endpoints to perform service discovery for very specific purchasing requests. We used offer descriptions similar to that of Vulture to model the services and successfully solved the relevant goals A and B of the scenario. At the fourth SWS-Challenge workshop in Innsbruck, Austria our current solution [12] to both scenarios was evaluated as the most complete discovery solution[7]. It can be downloaded from the SWS Challenge web site[8].

To test our solution under more realistic settings in terms of the number of available products we simulated the Albatross service. We gathered about 2500 structured descriptions of notebook offerings with a total of more than 100.000 attributes from the Internet and stored it in a relational product database similar to one that a service like Albatross might have. We created a corresponding offer description and a service implementation that operates on our database. We applied the restriction that no more than thirty offers will be listed for any request and created a grounding of our service description to our implementation that queries our product database and uses the fuzzy information taken from the request to select the thirty notebooks expected to be most relevant. We ran a series of requests against the Albatross offer and measured the time needed to gather the relevant notebooks. We ran the experiment locally and did not measure communication cost. On an Intel Pentium 1.8 GHz machine it took about 500 ms to query the product database and convert *all* 2500 notebook descriptions including their attributes into ontological DSD instances. On average it then took another 950 ms to determine the precise matchvalue of all these notebooks with respect to the fuzzy description taken from the request. Based on that we returned the 30 top-ranked products and could be sure that these were the most relevant with regard to the request as determined by the matchmaker on behalf of the user. These results show the practical applicability of our approach for the given setting. This is particular true since there is much room for optimization left. One could, e.g., include hard restrictions from the

[5] http://sws-challenge.org/wiki/index.php/Workshop_Budva#Evaluation

[6] http://sws-challenge.org/wiki/index.php/Scenario:_Discovery_II_and_Simple_Composition

[7] http://sws-challenge.org/wiki/index.php/Workshop_Innsbruck#Evaluation

[8] http://sws-challenge.org/wiki/index.php/Solution_Jena

request (like a price limit or a limitation to specific brands) in the query to the database, thereby drastically reducing the number of notebooks that need to be converted to DSD instances and dealt with in the first place.

5 Related Work

To the best of our knowledge, none of the matchmaking algorithms based on ontological reasoning like the ones proposed by Kaufer and Klusch [13], Klusch et al. [14], Li and Horrocks [15] or Sycara et al. [16] support an automated contracting phase with dynamic information gathering as we propose in this paper.

Keller et al. [17,18] propose a conceptual model for automated web service discovery and matchmaking that explicitly distinguishes between abstract service discovery and service contracting. The latter refers to inquiring the dynamic parts of service descriptions and negotiating a concrete contract. Unfortunately, only an abstract model is presented and no details or ideas about an implementation are provided.

Similar to our approach [19] acknowledges the need to support highly configurable web services but focuses on algorithms for the optimal preference-based selection of configurations for such web services and not on how to dynamically explore the value space of possible configurations.

As mentioned in Section 4 the two discovery scenarios of the SWS-Challenge require the dynamic inquiry of price information and product listings. At the first workshop in Budva[9] DIANE was the only submission able to dynamically inquire price information. Meanwhile two teams successfully improved their technology to address this issue[10] [20,21]. Both solutions are similar to ours in that they complement service descriptions with information about operations that can be executed in order to dynamically gather additional information. However, both do not automatically evaluate whether a particular information needs to be gathered and therefore execute *all* available information retrieval operations. They are also lacking an equivalent of our concept of binding types for variables to accommodate for different information needs.

The work that is most closely related to the work in this paper is the Web Services Matchmaking Engine (WSME) proposed by Facciorusso et al. [22]. Like our approach, WSME allows to tag properties of a service description as dynamic, to provide means to dynamically update those properties by calling the service provider's endpoint and to pass properties from the request in that call to allow the provider to tailor the response. However, dynamic service properties are always evaluated whereas in our work we are able to detect whether a particular evaluation is needed or not. Furthermore, service descriptions in WSME are flat (based on simple name-value property pairs) and do not support fine-grained ranking as DSD does, therefore the WSME does not aim at complete

[9] http://sws-challenge.org/wiki/index.php/Workshop_Budva#Evaluation

[10] http://sws-challenge.org/wiki/index.php/Workshop_Innsbruck#Evaluation

automation and leaves the user in the loop. To avoid this was one of the main motivations of our work.

6 Summary and Conclusion

In order to allow for fully automated usage of service oriented architectures, it must be possible to automatically select, bind, and invoke appropriate services for any given request. This automation is hampered by the unavoidable imprecision in offer descriptions. Typically, discovery will only be able to find *possibly* matching services. It needs to be followed by a contracting phase that makes sure that the required service can indeed be rendered. In this paper, we have presented an approach that allows for the integration of the contracting into the discovery phase and for its complete automation. The approach is based on augmenting service descriptions with dynamic parts. Information about this parts can be obtained from the service provider at discovery time.

References

1. de Bruijn, J., Bussler, C., Domingue, J., Fensel, D., Hepp, M., Keller, U., Kifer, M., König-Ries, B., Kopecky, J., Lara, R., Lausen, H., Oren, E., Polleres, A., Roman, D., Scicluna, J., Stollberg, M.: Web service modeling ontology (WSMO) (W3C Member Submission June 3, 2005)
2. Martin, D., Burstein, M., Hobbs, J., Lassila, O., McDermott, D., McIlraith, S., Narayanan, S., Paolucci, M., Parsia, B., Payne, T., Sirin, E., Srinivasan, N., Sycara, K.: OWL-S: Semantic markup for web services (W3C Member Submission November 22, 2004)
3. Preist, C.: A conceptual architecture for semantic web services (extended version). Technical Report HPL-2004-215 (2004)
4. Klein, M., König-Ries, B.: Coupled signature and specification matching for automatic service binding. In: Zhang, L.-J(L.), Jeckle, M. (eds.) ECOWS 2004. LNCS, vol. 3250, Springer, Heidelberg (2004)
5. Klein, M., König-Ries, B., Müssig, M.: What is needed for semantic service descriptions - a proposal for suitable language constructs. International Journal on Web and Grid Services (IJWGS) 1(3/4) (2005)
6. Küster, U., König-Ries, B., Klein, M., Stern, M.: Diane - a matchmaking-centered framework for automated service discovery, composition, binding and invocation on the web. International Journal of Electronic Commerce (IJEC), Special Issue on Semantic Matchmaking and Retrieval (2007) (to appear)
7. Küster, U., König-Ries, B.: Dynamic binding for BPEL processes - a lightweight approach to integrate semantics into web services. In: Second International Workshop on Engineering Service-Oriented Applications: Design and Composition (WESOA06) at ICSOC06, Chicago, Illinois, USA (2006)
8. Walsh, N., Jacobs, I.: Architecture of the world wide web, volume one. W3C recommendation, W3C (2004), `www.w3.org/TR/2004/REC-webarch-20041215/`
9. Petrie, C.: It's the programming, stupid. IEEE Internet Computing 10(3) (2006)
10. Küster, U., König-Ries, B., Klein, M.: Discovery and mediation using diane service descriptions. In: Second Workshop of the Semantic Web Service Challenge 2006, Budva, Montenegro (2006)

11. Küster, U., König-Ries, B.: Discovery and mediation using diane service descriptions. In: Third Workshop of the Semantic Web Service Challenge 2006, Athens, GA, USA (2006)
12. Küster, U., König-Ries, B.: Service discovery using DIANE service descriptions - a solution to the SWS-Challenge discovery scenarios. In: Fourth Workshop of the Semantic Web Service Challenge - Challenge on Automating Web Services Mediation, Choreography and Discovery, Innsbruck, Austria (2007)
13. Kaufer, F., Klusch, M.: WSMO-MX: a logic programming based hybrid service matchmaker. In: ECOWS2006. Proceedings of the 4th IEEE European Conference on Web Services, Zürich, Switzerland, IEEE Computer Society Press, Los Alamitos (2006)
14. Klusch, M., Fries, B., Khalid, M., Sycara, K.: OWLS-MX: Hybrid OWL-S Service Matchmaking. In: Proceedings of the First International AAAI Fall Symposium on Agents and the Semantic Web, Arlington, Vriginia, USA (2005)
15. Laukkanen, M., Helin, H.: Composing workflows of semantic web services. In: Workshop on Web Services and Agent-based Engineering, Melbourne, Australia (2003)
16. Sycara, K.P., Widoff, S., Klusch, M., Lu, J.: Larks: Dynamic matchmaking among heterogeneous software agents in cyberspace. Autonomous Agents and Multi-Agent Systems 5(2) (2002)
17. Keller, U., Lara, R., Lausen, H., Polleres, A., Fensel, D.: Automatic location of services. In: Gómez-Pérez, A., Euzenat, J. (eds.) ESWC 2005. LNCS, vol. 3532, Springer, Heidelberg (2005)
18. Fensel, D., Keller, U., Lausen, H., Polleres, A., Toma, I.: WWW or what is wrong with web service discovery. In: W3C Workshop on Frameworks for Semantics in Web Services, Innsbruck, Austria (2005)
19. Lamparter, S., Ankolekar, A., Studer, R., Grimm, S.: Preference-based selection of highly configurable web services. In: WWW2007. Proceedings of the 16th International World Wide Web Conference, Banff, Alberta, Canada (2007)
20. Brambilla, M., Celino, I., Ceri, S., Cerizza, D., Valle, E.D., Facca, F., Tziviskou, C.: Improvements and future perspectives on web engineering methods for automating web services mediation, choreography and discovery: SWS-Challenge phase III. In: Third Workshop of the SWS Challenge 2006, Athens, GA, USA (2006)
21. Zaremba, M., Tomas Vitvar, M.M., Hasselwanter, T.: WSMX discovery for SWS Challenge. In: Third Workshop of the Semantic Web Service Challenge 2006, Athens, GA, USA (2006)
22. Facciorusso, C., Field, S., Hauser, R., Hoffner, Y., Humbel, R., Pawlitzek, R., Rjaibi, W., Siminitz, C.: A web services matchmaking engine for web services. In: EC-Web2003. 4th International Conference on E-Commerce and Web Technologies, Prague, Czech Republic (2003)

Grid Application Fault Diagnosis Using Wrapper Services and Machine Learning

Jürgen Hofer and Thomas Fahringer

Distributed and Parallel Systems Group
Institute of Computer Science, University of Innsbruck
Technikerstrasse 21a, 6020 Innsbruck, Austria
{juergen,tf}@dps.uibk.ac.at

Abstract. With increasing size and complexity of Grids manual diagnosis of individual application faults becomes impractical and time-consuming. Quick and accurate identification of the root cause of failures is an important prerequisite for building reliable systems. We describe a pragmatic model-based technique for application-specific fault diagnosis based on indicators, symptoms and rules. Customized wrapper services then apply this knowledge to reason about root causes of failures. In addition to user-provided diagnosis models we show that given a set of past classified fault events it is possible to extract new models through learning that are able to diagnose new faults. We investigated and compared algorithms of supervised classification learning and cluster analysis. Our approach was implemented as part of the Otho Toolkit that 'service-enables' legacy applications based on synthesis of wrapper service.

1 Introduction

A portion of todays applications used in High-Performance and Grid environments belongs to the class of batch-oriented programs with command-line interfaces. They typically have long lifecycles that surpass multiple generations of Grid and Service environments. Service Oriented Architectures and Web services became a widely accepted and mature paradigm for designing loosely-coupled large-scale distributed systems and can hide heterogeneity of underlying resources. As re-implementation of application codes is frequently too expensive in time and cost, their (semi-)automatic adaptation and migration to newer environments is of paramount importance. We suggest an approach with tailor-made wrapper services customized to each application. Mapping the functionality of applications to wrapper services requires not only to map input and output arguments, messages and files but also to ensure that the applications behavior is well-reflected. For instance the occurrence of faults may lead to errors that need to be detected, diagnosed propagated via the wrapper services interface, such that clients may react appropriately and handled to prevent larger system failures. In order to recover from failures root causes have to be identified, e.g. unsatisfied dependencies, invalid arguments, configuration problems, expired credentials, quota limits, disk crashes, etc. With increasing complexity of Grids

B. Krämer, K.-J. Lin, and P. Narasimhan (Eds.): ICSOC 2007, LNCS 4749, pp. 233–244, 2007.

- growing in size and heterogeneity - this tasks becomes increasingly difficult. Several abstraction layers conveniently shield the user from lower level issues. However these layers also hide important information required for fault diagnosis. Users or support staff are forced to drill down through layers for tracking possible causes. For larger number of failures it then quickly becomes impractical and time-expensive to manually investigate on individual causes by hand.

2 Diagnosing Application Faults

Normally software has been extensively tested before released to production. Nevertheless in large-scale deployments and complex environments such as Grids applications are likely to fail[1]. Common reasons are improper installations or deployments, configuration problems, failures of dependent resources such as hosts, network links, storage devices, limitations or excess on resource usage, performance and concurrency issues, usage errors, etc. Our goal is to provide a mechanism to automatically identify and distinguish such causes. The fault diagnosis process consists of the tasks of error detection, hypothesizing possible faults, identification of actual fault via analysis of application, application artifacts and environment and finally reporting of diagnosis results. Two applications are used throughout this paper: the raytracer POV-Ray [29], an open-source general-purpose visualization application and the GNU Linear Programming Toolkit (GLPK) [28] a software package for solving linear programming and mixed integer programming problems.

2.1 Building Fault Diagnosis Models

Instead of requiring a full formal system specification we provide a set of easy-to-use elements for building fault diagnosis models. They allow developers to describe cases in which their programs may fail and users to describe cases in which their programs have failed in the past. As no knowledge on formal system specification techniques is required we believe our approach is practical and more likely to be applied in the community of Grid users. The diagnosis models are rule-based case descriptions that allow services to perform automated reasoning on the most-likely cause of failures of the wrapped application. Results are then reported to clients. Such diagnosis models are constructed as follows.

1. *Indicators* are externally visible and monitorable effects of the execution of a certain application. We distinguish boolean-valued predicates, e.g. the existence of a certain file or directory, indicators returning strings (StringInd) such as patterns in output, error or log-files, indicators returning reals (RealInd) and indicators performing counting operations (CountInd) such as the number of files in a directory. A few examples are given below

[1] In accordance with Laprie [18] we define a *fault* as the hypothesized or identified cause of an error, e.g. due to a hardware defect; an *error* as a deviation from the correct system state that, if improperly handled or unrecognized, may lead to system *failures* where the delivered service deviates from specified service.

$(\exists file)file$	$extract\_stdout(regexp)$	$extract\_real\_stdout(regexp)$
$(\exists file)dir$	$extract\_file(file, regexp)$	$extract\_real\_stderr(regexp)$
$(\exists regexp)pattern\_stdout$	$count\_pattern\_stdout(regexp)$	$exitCode()$
$(\exists file)((\exists regexp)pattern\_file)$	$count\_files(regexp)$	$wall\_time()$

Next to the set of predefined indicators we allow the use of custom user-provided indicators specific to certain applications, e.g. to verify functional correctness via result checks, error rates, data formats, etc. In some cases runtime argument values are needed as parameters for indicators, e.g. to refer to an output file named via a program argument. Formally we use the $\Theta(argname)$ notation to refer to runtime arguments.

2. A *symptom* is a set of indicators describing an undesirable situation, more concretely the existence of a fault. Symptoms are comparisons of indicators with literal values or comparative combinations of indicators evaluating to boolean values.

$$symptom \vdash CountInd|RealInd\{<|\leq|=|\geq|>\}\{r|r\in\mathbb{R}\}$$
$$symptom \vdash CountInd|RealInd\{<|\leq|=|\geq|>\}CountInd|RealInd$$
$$symptom \vdash StringInd\{=|\neq\}\{s|s\in string\}$$
$$symptom \vdash StringInd\{=|\neq\}StringInd$$
$$symptom \vdash Predicate|\neg symptom|symptom \wedge symptom$$

Examples for symptoms would be if a coredump file was created, occurrence of the string 'Segmentation fault' in stderr, programs exit code other than zero, output values above some threshold, number of output files below a certain number, etc.

3. *Rules* built on the basis of symptoms allow to reason about fault types. We define rules as implications of the form $(s_1 \wedge s_2 \wedge \ldots \wedge s_n) \Rightarrow u$. Example diagnosis rules for the POV-Ray application are given below.

exit=0 $\wedge\exists file(\Theta(\text{sceneout})) \wedge \neg\exists pattern\_stdout(\text{"Failed"}) \Rightarrow$ done_successful
exit=249 $\Rightarrow$ failed_illegal_argument
exit=0 $\wedge\exists file(\Theta(\text{sceneout})) \wedge filesize(\Theta(sceneout)) = 0 \ \wedge$
$\exists pattern\_stdout(\text{"Disk quota exceeded."}) \Rightarrow$ failed_quota
exit=0 $\wedge filesize(\Theta(\text{sceneout})) = 0 \Rightarrow$ failed_disk_quota_exceeded
exit=0 $\wedge\neg\exists file(\Theta(\text{sceneout})) \ \wedge$
$\exists pattern\_stdout(\text{"File Error open"}) \Rightarrow$ failed_file_writing_error
exit=0 $\wedge\exists pattern\_stdout(\text{"Got 1 SIGINT"}) \Rightarrow$ failed_received_sigint
exit=137 $\wedge\exists pattern\_stdout(\text{"Killed"}) \Rightarrow$ failed_received_sigkill
gramExit=1 $\wedge\exists pattern\_gram\_log(\text{'proxy is not valid long enough'}) \Rightarrow$ failed_proxy_expires_soon
gramExit=1 $\wedge\exists pattern\_gram\_log(\text{'couldn't find a valid proxy'})\wedge$
$\exists pattern\_gram\_log(\text{'proxy does not exist'}) \Rightarrow$ failed_no_proxy
gramExit=1 $\wedge\exists pattern\_gram\_log(\text{'proxy does not exist'}) \Rightarrow$ failed_proxy_expired

E.g. the second rule states that the return code 249 unambiguously identifies an illegal argument fault. Failures caused by exceeded disk quota are recognized by an apparently successful return code however in combination with a zero-size outputfile and a certain error message.

4. Finally a set of rules builds a fault diagnosis model. The rules are meant to be evaluated post-mortem, i.e. immediately after the execution terminated, in the specified ordering. If no rule evaluates to true, the fault cannot be identified. Depending on the desired behavior the diagnosis can continue the evaluation if multiple rules are satisfied. The fault is then considered to belong to all found classes.

3 Creating Diagnosis Models Using Machine Learning

With increasing utilization both variety and frequency of faults will increase. Our hypothesis is that given a set of past classified fault events diagnosis models can be learned that are able to correctly classify even unseen novel faults. Fault events are analyzed using he superset of the indicators to build a comprehensive knowledge as trainingset for machine learning. For this purpose an initial set of services is created and deployed. At runtime each fault is analyzed to form a fault event. We investigated on two different learning techniques. In supervised classification learning each fault event in the trainingset has be classified a priori. This is a manual step done by users, service provider or developers. Now the classified training set is used as input to the machine learning procedure that creates new models which are then used to classify faults. The second technique is cluster analysis where the faults do not have to be tagged with class labels but the algorithm partitions the trainingset into groups of fault events that have some degree of similarity.

In order to build the knowledge base each fault incidence has to be analyzed using the superset of indicators. For each detected fault event a tuple of the form $((I \cup T) \times (S \cup F))$ is generated and added to a repository. The tuple contains all relevant information characterizing a certain fault incidence specific to a given application. A set of boolean or numeric indicators $i_i \in I$ such as existence, modification, size, open for reading/writing as detailed above and a set of boolean indicators $t_i \in T$ whether certain regular expression-based patterns (error messages, codes) can be found, are applied to a given set of artifacts created during applications runs. Those artifacts include the standard input/output files associated with each process of and application and the execution environment by $s_i \in S$, i.e. stdout, stderr, system log and log files of resource management system and application-specific input and output files $f_i \in F$. The latter set has to be provided by the user and may be a function of the program arguments.

We selected a set of six well-known supervised classification techniques and three different cluster analysis algorithms [6,21,32] listed in Table 1 and Table 2. The techniques were chosen based on their capabilities to analyze all aspects of

Table 1. Overview on Utilized Classification Techniques

Supervised Classification Learning

OneR (OR)	is an algorithm that produces one-level classification rules based on single attributes. A classification rule consists of an antecedent that applies tests to reason about the consequent.
DecisionStump (DS)	produces simple one-level decision trees. Decision trees follow the divide-and-conquer principle where the problem space is partitioned by outcome of tests until all examples belong to the same class.
Logistic (LG)	is a statistical modeling approach based on logistic regression where coefficient are estimated using the maximum log-likelihood method.
BayesNet (BN)	is a statistical modeling approach producing Bayesian networks in forms of directed acyclic graphs with probabilities over relevant attributes.
DecisionTable (DT)	denotes an algorithm that produces a table consisting of relevant attributes, their values and the prediction class.
J48	is an improved version of the C4.5 decision tree machine learning algorithm. in a decision tree each internal node represents a test on an attribute, branches are the outcomes and leaf nodes indicate the class

Table 2. Overview on Utilized Cluster Analysis Techniques

Cluster Analysis	
k-means (SK)	the number of clusters being sought is defined in the parameter k. then k points are chosen as random cluster centers and instances assigned to closest center. then the new mean is calculated for each cluster. this is repeated until the cluster memberships stop changing.
expectation-minimization (EM)	same basic procedure as k-means algorithm, but calculates the probabilities for each instance to belong to a certain cluster, then calculate the statistical distribution parameters
FarthestFirst (FF)	implements the Farthest First Traversal Algorithm [7] which is a heuristic for approximation of cluster centers designed after procedure of k-means

our trainingsets, their acceptance within the machine learning community and past experience of the authors for similar problems.

4 Implementation

In previous work we discussed the semi-automatic transformation of legacy applications to services for integration into service-oriented environments [8,9,10]. We focused on resource-intensive, non-interactive command-line programs as typically used in HPC and Grid environments and presented the *Otho Toolkit*, a *service-enabler* for *Legacy Applications* $\mathcal{LA}$. Based on formal $\mathcal{LA}$ descriptions it generates tailor-made wrapper services, referred to as *Executor Services* $\mathcal{XS}$. They provide a purely functional interface hiding technical details of the wrapping process on a certain execution platform, the *Backend* $\mathcal{BE}$. Input and output arguments, messages to standard input and output, consumed and produced files are mapped to the $\mathcal{XS}$ interface. Multiple views on the same $\mathcal{LA}$ can be defined to reflect different needs or to ease usage of complex interfaces. The Otho Toolkit generates wrapper service source codes including a build system. Multiple service environments can be targeted and the services may be equipped with application-specific features and generic extensions.

Wrapper services, and especially Executor Services $\mathcal{XS}$ synthesized by the Otho Toolkit, already possess detailed knowledge on the application structure and behavior, control its execution and lifecycle and are aware of input and output arguments, messages and files. Moreover they have the necessary proximity to the execution host for fault investigation. Therefore we chose to address and implement the fault diagnosis as part of the Otho Toolkit and the $\mathcal{XS}$ it creates. All indicators were implemented as generic Bash and Python scripts. We extended Otho Toolkits $\mathcal{LA}$ description to include fault diagnosis models. The Otho Toolkit then generates a custom diagnosis program that evaluates each case using the generic indicator scripts immediately after termination of the application. The diagnosis program evaluates the diagnosis model rule by rule. Indicator results are cached to prevent redundant evaluations. If the $\mathcal{XS}$ uses job submission to a resource management systems the $\mathcal{LA}$ and the fault diagnosis script are submitted as one job to ensure execution on the same resource. In addition to the formal notation introduced before we developed a simple XML-based syntax for representing fault diagnosis models.

```
<fdiag>
  <cause name="successful" status="DONE">
    <exitCode value="0" />
    <fileExists name="|sceneout|" />
    <not><regexpStdout value="Failed" /></not>
  </cause>
  <cause name="illegal argument" status="FAILED">
    <exitCode value="249" />
  </cause>
</fdiag>
```

This shortened example lists two root causes each named and tagged with a post-execution status value. A set of indicators sequentially evaluated with logical conjunction can be given. Elements may be negated by adding a 'not' tag.

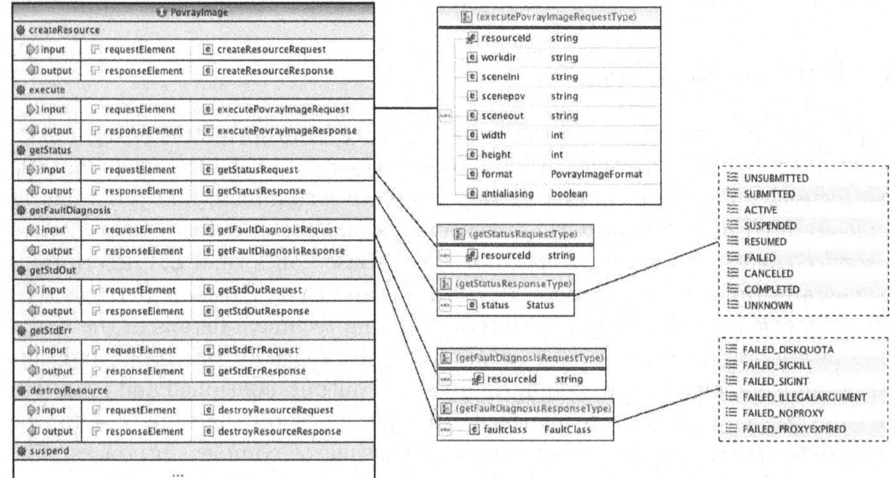

Fig. 1. $\mathcal{XS}$ Interface Adaptations for providing Fault Diagnosis

The fault diagnosis capabilities and states need to be represented in the service interface. Figure 1 shows a partial graphical rendering of the services WSDL interface [31] of synthesized wrapper services for the POV-Ray application and the Axis2 [27] $\mathcal{XS}$ platform. The request type contains the input argument values for the wrapped $\mathcal{LA}$. Operations allow to query service state and fault diagnosis both of which are represented by enumeration values. Obviously the interface differs depending on the service platform used. Axis2 webservice operations for instance carry a job identifier whereas WSRF GT4 services rely on stateful resource properties.

5 Evaluation

For evaluation we used our implementation based on the Otho Toolkit and the $\mathcal{XS}$ it synthesizes. The machine learning techniques described above were implemented as part of $\mathcal{XS}$ using an existing machine learning library [30]. We deployed both case study applications on the AustrianGrid [26] and injected several types of faults. The resulting training set was used in its raw state ('failed noise'), in a cleaned state ('failed clean') and to allow our classifier to also identify correct behaviour with added successful runs ('failed/succ clean').

The performance or accuracy of classifier is commonly evaluated in terms of their success rates which is the proportion of true and false predictions. An important issue in classification is the question about which set of instances to learn from and which set to evaluate against, as classifiers tend to show better performance if evaluated against the training set than against unseen examples. Therefore we applied three evaluation techniques. First we used the full dataset ('ts') for learning and evaluation. Second we used two-third for learning one-third for evaluation ('66-sp'). Third we used 10-fold cross-validation ('10-cv') where metrics are averaged from ten iterations with 9/10 of examples used for training and 1/10 for evaluation. The set of examples not used for training but to which the classifier is tested against represent unseen fault cases. As we had all fault incidences tagged with class labels the evaluation of the clustering techniques was straightforward. During the learning phase we ignored the classes and then compared the instances in a cluster with their labels counting wrong assignments.

Clustering a trainingset with k attributes spawns a k-dimensional space in which aggregation of examples are to be found. Figure 2 depicts a 2-dimensional subspace with two indicators used in the cluster analysis for faults of the POV-Ray application, namely its exit code and whether a certain pattern occurs in stdout. Elements have been slightly scattered for visualization purposes. The plot nicely illustrates four clusters, three of which are homogeneous. Elements aligned at return code of 137 indicate a 'failed_sigkill' or a 'failed_sighup' signal, depending on the outcome of the second indicator. The 'failed_illegalargument' examples group in this particular view around a return code of 249. Contrarily the other fault incidences cannot be clearly assigned to clusters in this subspace. Figure 3 contains parts of the results of our experiments with the classification learning. Vertical axes show the accuracy. In general it can be observed that prediction accuracy for the GLPK application case study were better than those for the POV-Ray application in most cases. The overall quality apparently strongly

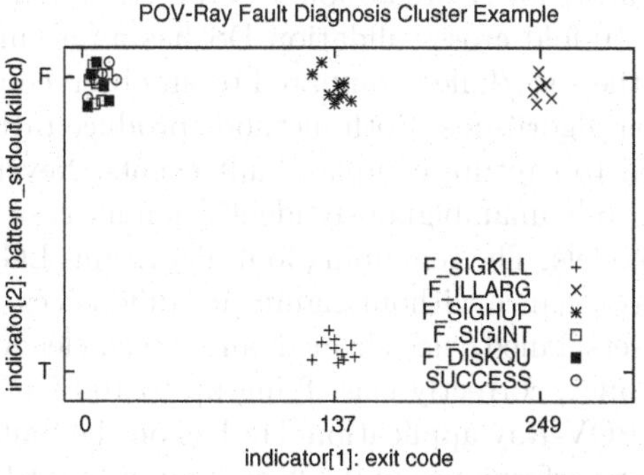

Fig. 2. Visualization of 2-Indicator subspace of SimpleK Means Clustering

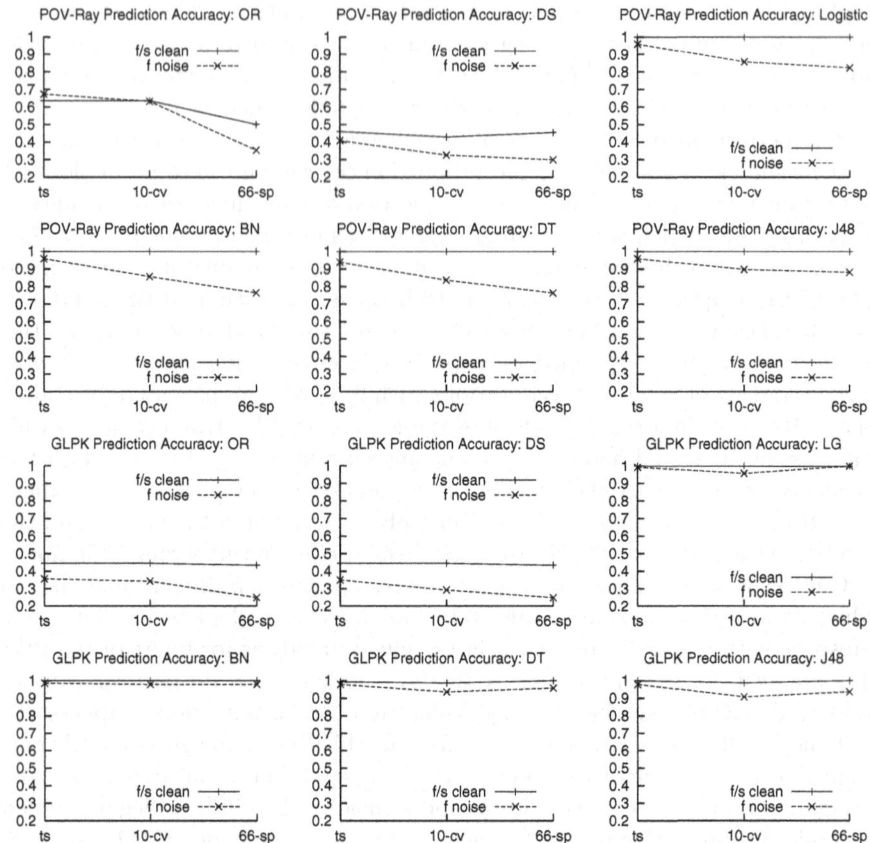

Fig. 3. Evaluation of Machine Learning Algorithms per Algorithm

depends not only on the machine learning technique but also on the concrete application, the indicators used and the corresponding structure of the training set. The second observation is that even on the cleaned datasets the algorithms OR and DS show significantly lower prediction accuracy than LG, DT, BN and J48. For POV-Ray using 10-fold cross-validation DS has an accuracy of only 0.429 and OR of 0.635 on the succ/failed compared to an observed 0.837 lower bound accuracy for the other algorithms. Both methods produce rather simplistic classifier clearly unsuited to capture complex fault events. Nevertheless for trivial diagnostics, e.g. exit code unambiguously identifies fault case, they may be useful as part of meta-models. The remaining four algorithms LG, DT, BN and J48 show comparable performance without significant differences among each other. For the cleaned datasets 'failed/succ cleaned' and 'failed cleaned' all four provide outstanding performance, correctly classifying up to 100% of unseen instances. For instance for the POV-Ray application J48 has on the 'failed uncleaned' raw dataset slightly better performance of 0.898 compared to 0.837 of DT and 0.857 of BN and LG on average on the unseen data. During evaluation we observed

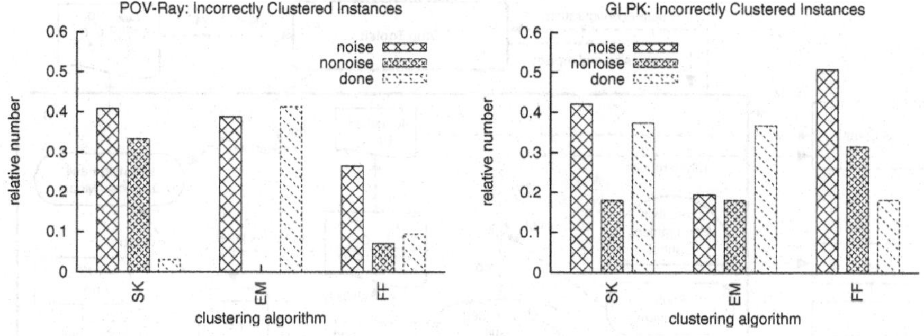

Fig. 4. Evaluation of Clustering Algorithms

that the statistical models BN and LG tend to capture also noise, whereas J48 tree pruning prevented such undesired behavior.

Figure 4 plots some of the results of our evaluation on the clustering algorithms. The plots compares the relative number of incorrectly clustered instances for the algorithms SK, EM and FF for three trainingsets. In general the relative number of errors varied between 0 and 0.5. On the POV-Ray cleaned dataset the EM algorithm was able to perfectly assign all faults to the correct classes. Lower error rates varied up to 0.2. As with our classification algorithms the noisy trainingsets caused major disturbance with error rates between 0.4 and 0.5. In our experiments we could not identify a clustering algorithm significantly outperforming the others. Nevertheless clustering techniques proved to provide good suggestions and valuable guidance for building groups of similar faults. Such otherwise difficult to acquire knowledge and understanding on the nature of faults of applications in a particular setting are of great help to people designing fault-aware application services.

6 Service Evolution for Fault Diagnosis Improvement

The process of lcontinuous diagnosis improvement as realized with the Otho Toolkit and $\mathcal{XS}$ is depicted in Figure 5. Initially a set of services is created and deployed by the Otho Toolkit. At runtime each fault is analyzed, tagged and added to the knowledge base. This is a manual step done by users, service provider or developers. Now the classified training set is used as input to the machine learning procedure that creates new models which enable the classification of unseen fault events that are similar to past faults. The updated or newly learned model is then fed into the Otho Toolkit that creates and redeploys an improved revision of the $\mathcal{XS}$. Additional events are then again collected, learning is re-triggered, followed by synthesis and redeployment and so forth. As the $\mathcal{XS}$ evolves along this cycle its capabilities to diagnose application faults correctly are continuously improved.

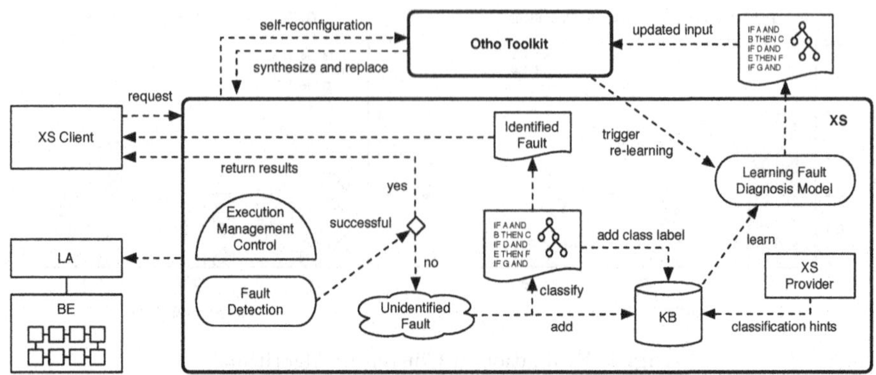

Fig. 5. Service Evolution for Fault Diagnosis Improvement

7 Related Work

Monitoring and failure detection systems [12,14,25] are important Grid components however they discriminate faults no further than into generic task-crashes and per-task exceptions. On the other hand a variety of systems has been suggested for building fault tolerant applications and middleware [13,16] which could benefit from accurate and detailed diagnosis of faults and their causes. Common approaches for fault diagnosis start from formal system specifications [1,15,22] or from its source code [4,17] to derive test cases. Instead neither source code availability nor a formal system specification are prerequisites to our approach. Fault diagnosis in Grids however still is a largely manual time-consuming task. Efforts include an approach for fault localization through unit tests [5] that however requires manual implementation of test cases and frameworks for verification of software stacks and interoperability agreements [24]. Instead we use a model-based description and to automatically generate diagnosis code. The use of machine learning has been successfully applied to many kinds of different classification problems [3,23], e.g. to classify software behavior based on execution data [2] or to locate anomalies in sets of processes via function-level traces [20]. The use of Bayesian Belief Networks for fault localization was proposed [19] but provides neither implementation nor experimental evaluation.

8 Conclusion

With increasing size and complexity of Grids manual application fault diagnosis is a difficult and time-expensive task. We developed a model-based mechanism allowing users, support staff or application developers to formulate precise, rule-based fault diagnosis models evaluated immediately after program termination. Such diagnosis models are used by services to provide accurate and reliable reports. Our approach was implemented as part of application wrapper services synthesized by the Otho Toolkit. In addition we suggest the use of machine learning to semi-automatically create fault diagnosis models based on past classified fault events. Our evaluation showed that the learned diagnosis models were able to classify novel fault situations with high accuracy. The overall performance of the learned classifier was good but depends on the quality of the dataset. We observed significant perturbation caused by noisy or falsely labeled examples. Ideally developers, service providers and knowledgeable users therefore regularly remove unclean examples from the training set. Our results motivate us to continue with the presented work. We plan to use a larger set of applications to get access to a larger variety of faults. Moreover we intend to investigate on overheads and scalability of our fault diagnosis and machine learning approach.

Acknowledgements

This paper presents follow-up work to a preceding workshop contribution [11]. The presented work was partially funded by the European Union through the IST FP6-004265 CoreGRID, IST FP6-031688 EGEE-2 and IST FP6-034601 Edutain@Grid projects.

References

1. Abrial, J.-R., Schuman, S.A., Meyer, B.: A specification language. In: McNaughten, R., McKeag, R.C. (eds.) On the Construction of Programs, Cambridge University Press, Cambridge (1980)
2. Bowring, J., Rehg, J., Harrold, M.J.: Active learning for automatic classification of software behavior. In: ISSTA 2004. Proc. of the Int. Symp. on Software Testing and Analysis (July 2004)
3. Chen, M., Zheng, A., Lloyd, J., Jordan, M., Brewer, E.: Failure diagnosis using decision trees. In: ICAC. Proc. of Int. Conf. on Autonomic Computing, York, NY (May 2004)
4. Millo, R., Mathur, A.: A grammar based fault classification scheme and its application to the classification of the errors of tex. Technical Report SERC-TR-165-P, Purdue University (1995)
5. Duarte, A.N., Brasileiro, F., Cirne, W., Filho, J.S.A.: Collaborative fault diagnosis in grids through automated tests. In: Proc. of the The IEEE 20th Int. Conf. on Advanced Information Networking and Applications, IEEE Computer Society Press, Los Alamitos (2006)
6. Han, J., Kamber, M.: Data Mining: Concepts and Techniques. Morgan Kaufmann, San Francisco (2001)
7. Hochbaum, Shmoys,: A best possible heuristic for the k-center problem. Mathematics of Operations Research 10(2), 180–184 (1985)
8. Hofer, J., Fahringer, T.: Presenting Scientific Legacy Programs as Grid Services via Program Synthesis. In: Proceedings of 2nd IEEE International Conference on e-Science and Grid Computing, Amsterdam, Netherlands, December 4-6, 2006, IEEE Computer Society Press, Los Alamitos (2006)
9. Hofer, J., Fahringer, T.: Specification-based Synthesis of Tailor-made Grid Service Wrappers for Scientific Legacy Codes. In: Grid'06. Proceedings of 7th IEEE/ACM International Conference on Grid Computing (Grid'06), Short Paper and Poster, Barcelona, Spain, September 28-29, 2006 (2006)

10. Hofer, J., Fahringer, T.: The Otho Toolkit - Synthesizing Tailor-made Scientific Grid Application Wrapper Services. Journal of Multiagent and Grid Systems 3(3) (2007)
11. Hofer, J., Fahringer, T.: Towards automated diagnosis of application faults using wrapper services and machine learning. In: Proceedings of CoreGRID Workshop on Grid Middleware, Dresden, Germany, June 25–26, 2007, pp. 25–26. Springer, Heidelberg (2007)
12. Horita, Y., Taura, K., Chikayama, T.: A scalable and efficient self-organizing failure detector for grid applications. In: Grid'05. 6th IEEE/ACM Int. Workshop on Grid Computing, IEEE Computer Society Press, Los Alamitos (2005)
13. Hwang, S., Kesselman, C.: A flexible framework for fault tolerance in the grid. Journal of Grid Computing 1(3), 251–272 (2003)
14. Hwang, S., Kesselman, C.: Gridworkflow: A flexible failure handling framework for the grid. In: HPDC'03. 12th IEEE Int. Symp. on High Performance Distributed Computing, Seattle, Washington, IEEE Press, Los Alamitos (2003)
15. Jones, C.: Systematic Software Development using VDM. Prentice Hall, Englewood Cliffs (1990)
16. Kola, G., Kosar, T., Livny, M.: Phoenix: Making data-intensive grid applications fault-tolerant. In: Proc. of 5th IEEE/ACM Int. Workshop on Grid Computing, Pittsburgh, Pennsylvania, November 8, 2004, pp. 251–258 (2004)
17. Kuhn, D.R.: Fault classes and error detection in specification based testing. ACM Transactions on Software Engineering Methodology 8(4), 411–424 (1999)
18. Laprie, J.-C.: Dependable computing and fault tolerance: Concepts and terminology. In: Proc. of 15th Int. Symp. on Fault-Tolerant Computing (1985)
19. Meshkat, L., Allcock, W., Deelman, E., Kesselman, C.: Fault location in grids using bayesian belief networks. Technical Report GriPhyN-2002-8, GriPhyN Project (2002)
20. Mirgorodskiy, A.V., Maruyama, N., Miller, B.P.: Problem diagnosis in large-scale computing environments. In: Proc. of ACM/IEEE Supercomputing'06 Conference (2006)
21. Mitchell, T.M.: Machine Learning. McGraw-Hill, Boston (1997)
22. Ortmeier, F., Reif, W.: Failure-sensitive Specification - A formal method for finding failure modes. Technical report, University of Augsburg (January 12, 2004)
23. Podgurski, A., Leon, D., Francis, P., Masri, W., Minch, M., Sun, J., Wang, B.: Automated support for classifying software failure reports. In: Proc. of 25th Int. Conf. on Software Engineering, Portland, Oregon, pp. 465–475 (2003)
24. Smallen, S., Olschanowsky, C., Ericson, K., Beckman, P., Schopf, J.M.: The inca test harness and reporting framework. In: Proc. of the ACM/IEEE Supercomputing'04 Conference (November 2004)
25. Stelling, P., Foster, I., Kesselman, C., Lee, C., von Laszewski, G.: A fault detection service for wide area distributed computations. In: Proc. 7th IEEE Symp. on High Performance Distributed Computing, pp. 268–278. IEEE Computer Society Press, Los Alamitos (1998)
26. AustrianGrid, `http://www.austriangrid.at`
27. Apache Axis2, `http://ws.apache.org/axis2/`
28. GNU Linear Programming Kit (GLPK), `http://www.gnu.org/software/glpk/`
29. POV-Ray, `http://www.povray.org`
30. Weka, `http://www.cs.waikato.ac.nz/ml/weka`
31. Web Service Description Language (WSDL), `http://www.w3.org/TR/wsdl`
32. Witten, I.H., Frank, E.: Data Mining: Practical Machine Learning Tools and Techniques with Java Implementations. Morgan Kaufmann, San Francisco (2000)

Stochastic COWS*

Davide Prandi and Paola Quaglia

Dipartimento di Informatica e Telecomunicazioni, Università di Trento, Italy

Abstract. A stochastic extension of COWS is presented. First the formalism is given an operational semantics leading to finitely branching transition systems. Then its syntax and semantics are enriched along the lines of Markovian extensions of process calculi. This allows addressing quantitative reasoning about the behaviour of the specified web services. For instance, a simple case study shows that services can be analyzed using the PRISM probabilistic model checker.

1 Introduction

Interacting via web services is becoming a programming paradigm, and a number of languages, mostly based on XML, has been designed for, e.g., coordinating, orchestrating, and querying services. While the design of those languages and of supporting tools is quickly improving, the formal underpinning of the programming paradigm is still uncertain.

This calls for the investigation of models that can ground the development of methodologies, techniques, and tools for the rigorous analysis of service properties. Recent works on the translation of web service primitives into well-understood formal settings (e.g., [2,3]), as well as on the definition of process calculi for the specification of web service behaviours (e.g., [6,8]), go in this direction. These approaches, although based on languages still quite far from WS-BPEL, WSFL, WSCI, or WSDL, bring in the advantage of being based on clean semantic models. For instance, process calculi typically come with a structural operational semantics in Plotkin's style: The dynamic behaviour of a term of the language is represented by a connected oriented graph (called *transition system*) whose nodes are the reachable states of the system, and whose paths stay for its possible runs. This feature is indeed one of the main reasons why process calculi have been extensively used over the years for the specification and verification of distributed systems. One can guess that the same feature could also be useful to reason about the dynamic behaviour of web services. The challenge is appropriately tuning calculi and formal techniques to this new interaction paradigm.

In this paper we present a stochastic extension of COWS [8] (Calculus for Orchestration of Web Services), a calculus strongly inspired by WS-BPEL which combines primitives of well-known process calculi (like, e.g., the π-calculus [9,16]) with constructs meant to model web services orchestration. For instance, besides

* This work has been partially sponsored by the project SENSORIA, IST-2005-016004.

B. Krämer, K.-J. Lin, and P. Narasimhan (Eds.): ICSOC 2007, LNCS 4749, pp. 245–257, 2007.

the expected request/invoke communication primitives, COWS has operators to specify protection, delimited receiving activities, and killing activities. A number of other interesting constructs, although not taken as primitives of the language, have been shown to be easily encoded in COWS. This is the case, e.g., for fault and compensation handlers [8].

The operational semantics of COWS provides a full qualitative account on the behaviour of services specified in the language. Quantitative aspects of computation, though, are as crucial to SOC as qualitative ones (think, e.g., of quality of service, resource usage, or service level agreement). In this paper, we first present a version of the operational semantics of COWS that, giving raise to finitely branching transition systems, is suitable to stochastic reasoning (Sec. 2). The syntax and semantics of the calculus is then enriched along the lines of Markovian extensions of process calculi [11,5] (Sec. 3). Basic actions are associated with a random duration governed by a negative exponential distribution. In this way the semantic models associated to services result to be Continuous Time Markov Chains, popular models for automated verification. To give a flavour of our approach, we show how the stochastic model checker PRISM [14] can be used to check a few properties of a simple case study (Sec. 4).

2 Operational Semantics of Monadic COWS

We consider a monadic (vs polyadic) version of the calculus, i.e., it is assumed that request/invoke interactions can carry one single parameter at a time (vs multiple parameters). This simplifies the presentation without impacting on the sort of primitives the calculus is based on, and indeed our setting could be generalized to the case of polyadic communications. Some other differences between the operational approach used in [8] and the one provided here are due to the fact that, for the effective application of Markovian techniques, we need to guarantee that the generated transition system is finitely branching. In order to ensure this main property we chose to express recursive behaviours by means of service identifiers rather than by replication. Syntactically, this is the single deviation from the language as presented in [8]. From the semantic point of view, though, some modifications of the operational setting are also needed. They will be fully commented upon below.

The syntax of COWS is based on three countable and pairwise disjoint sets: the set of *names* $\mathcal{N}$ (ranged over by $m, n, o, p, m', n', o', p'$), the set of *variables* $\mathcal{V}$ (ranged over by x, y, x', y'), and the set of *killer labels* $\mathcal{K}$ (ranged over by k, k'). Services are expressed as structured activities built from basic activities that involve elements of the above sets. In particular, request and invoke activities occur at endpoints, which in [8] are identified by both a *partner* and an *operation* name. Here, for ease of notation, we let endpoints be denoted by single identifiers. In what follows, u, v, w, u', v', w' are used to range over $\mathcal{N} \cup \mathcal{V}$, and d, d' to range over $\mathcal{N} \cup \mathcal{V} \cup \mathcal{K}$. Names, variables, and killer labels are collectively referred to as *entities*.

The terms of the COWS language are generated by the following grammar.

$$s ::= u\,!\,w \mid g \mid s \mid s \mid \{\!|s|\!\} \mid \mathbf{kill}(k) \mid [\,d\,]s \mid S(n_1, \ldots, n_j)$$
$$g ::= \mathbf{0} \mid p\,?\,w.\,s \mid g + g$$

where, for some service s, a defining equation $S(n_1, \ldots, n_j) = s$ is given.

A service s can consist in an asynchronous *invoke* activity over the endpoint u with parameter w ($u\,!\,w$), or it can be generated by a guarded choice. In this case it can either be the empty activity $\mathbf{0}$, or a choice between two guarded commands ($g + g$), or an input-guarded service $p\,?\,w.\,s$ that waits for a communication over the endpoint p and then proceeds as s after the (possible) instantiation of the input parameter w. Besides service identifiers like $S(n_1, \ldots, n_j)$, which are used to model recursive behaviours, the language offers a few other primitive operators: parallel composition ($s \mid s$), protection ($\{\!|s|\!\}$), kill activity ($\mathbf{kill}(k)$), and delimitation of the entity d within s ($[\,d\,]s$).

In $[\,d\,]s$ the occurrence of $[\,d\,]$ is a *binding* for d with scope s. An entity is *free* if it is not under the scope of a binder. It is *bound* otherwise. An occurrence of one term in a service is *unguarded* if it is not underneath a request.

Like in [8], the operational semantics of COWS is defined for *closed* services, i.e. for services whose variables and killer labels are all bound. Moreover, to be sure to get finitely branching transition systems, we work under two main assumptions. First, it is assumed that service identifiers do not occur unguarded. Second, we assume that there is no homonymy either among bound entities or among free and bound entities of the service under consideration. This condition can be initially met by appropriately refreshing the term, and is dynamically kept true by a suitable management of the unfolding of recursion.

The labelled transition relation $\xrightarrow{\alpha}$ between services is defined by the rules collected in Tab. 1 and by symmetric rules for the commutative operators of choice and of parallel composition. Labels α are given by the following grammar

$$\alpha ::= \dagger k \mid \dagger \mid p\,?\,w \mid p\,!\,n \mid p\,?\,(x) \mid p\,!\,(n) \mid p \cdot \sigma \cdot \sigma'$$

where, for some n and x, σ ranges over ε, $\{n/x\}$, $\{(n)/x\}$, and σ' over ε, $\{n/x\}$.

Label $\dagger k$ ($\dagger$) denotes that a request for terminating a term s in the delimitation $[\,k\,]s$ is being (was) executed. Label $p\,?\,w$ ($p\,!\,n$) stays for the execution of a request (an invocation) activity over the endpoint p with parameter w (n, respectively). Label $p \cdot \sigma \cdot \sigma'$ denotes a communication over the endpoint p. The two components σ and σ' of label $p \cdot \sigma \cdot \sigma'$ are meant to implement a *best-match* communication mechanism. Among the possibly many receives that could match the same invocation, priority of communication is given to the most defined one. This is achieved by possibly delaying the name substitution induced by the interaction, and also by preventing further moves after a name substitution has been improperly applied. To this end, σ' recalls the name substitution, and σ signals whether is has been already applied ($\sigma = \varepsilon$) or not. We observe that labels like $p \cdot \{(n)/x\} \cdot \sigma'$, just as $p\,?\,(x)$ and $p\,!\,(n)$, have no counterpart in [8]. These labels are used in the rules for scope opening and closure that have no analogue in [8] where scope modification is handled by means of a congruence

Table 1. Operational semantics of COWS

$\mathbf{kill}(k) \xrightarrow{\dagger k} \mathbf{0}$ (*kill*) $\quad p\,?\,w.\,s \xrightarrow{p\,?\,w} s$ (*req*) $\quad p\,!\,n \xrightarrow{p\,!\,n} \mathbf{0}$ (*inv*)

$$\frac{g_1 \xrightarrow{\alpha} s}{g_1 + g_2 \xrightarrow{\alpha} s}\ (choice) \qquad \frac{s \xrightarrow{\alpha} s'}{\{\!|s|\!\} \xrightarrow{\alpha} \{\!|s'|\!\}}\ (prot) \qquad \frac{s_1 \xrightarrow{p\,!\,n} s_1' \quad s_2 \xrightarrow{p\,?\,n} s_2'}{s_1 \mid s_2 \xrightarrow{p\cdot\varepsilon\cdot\varepsilon} s_1' \mid s_2'}\ (com\_n)$$

$$\frac{s_1 \xrightarrow{p\,!\,n} s_1' \quad s_2 \xrightarrow{p\,?\,x} s_2' \quad (s_1 \mid s_2) \not\downarrow_{p\,?\,n}}{s_1 \mid s_2 \xrightarrow{p\cdot\{n/x\}\cdot\{n/x\}} s_1' \mid s_2'}\ (com\_x)$$

$$\frac{s_1 \xrightarrow{p\cdot\sigma\cdot\sigma'} s_1' \quad \sigma' = \{n/x\} \Rightarrow s_2 \not\downarrow_{p\,?\,n}}{s_1 \mid s_2 \xrightarrow{p\cdot\sigma\cdot\sigma'} s_1' \mid s_2}\ (par\_conf) \qquad \frac{s \xrightarrow{p\cdot\{n/x\}\cdot\{n/x\}} s'}{[\,x\,]s \xrightarrow{p\cdot\varepsilon\cdot\{n/x\}} s'\{^n\!/\!_x\}}\ (del\_sub)$$

$$\frac{s_1 \xrightarrow{\dagger k} s_1'}{s_1 \mid s_2 \xrightarrow{\dagger k} s_1' \mid halt(s_2)}\ (par\_kill) \qquad \frac{s_1 \xrightarrow{\alpha} s_1' \quad \alpha \neq p\cdot\sigma\cdot\sigma' \quad \alpha \neq \dagger k}{s_1 \mid s_2 \xrightarrow{\alpha} s_1' \mid s_2}\ (par\_pass)$$

$$\frac{s \xrightarrow{\dagger k} s'}{[\,k\,]s \xrightarrow{\dagger} [\,k\,]s'}\ (del\_kill) \qquad \frac{s \xrightarrow{\alpha} s' \quad d \notin \mathrm{d}(\alpha) \quad s\downarrow_d \Rightarrow (\alpha = \dagger \text{ or } \alpha = \dagger k)}{[\,d\,]s \xrightarrow{\alpha} [\,d\,]s'}\ (del\_pass)$$

$$\frac{s\{^{m_1\ldots m_j}\!/\!_{n_1\ldots n_j}\} \xrightarrow{\alpha} s' \qquad S(n_1,\ldots,n_j) = s}{S(m_1,\ldots,m_j) \xrightarrow{\mathrm{l\_dec}(\alpha)} \mathrm{s\_dec}(\alpha, s')}\ (ser\_id)$$

$$\frac{s \xrightarrow{p\,?\,x} s'}{[\,x\,]s \xrightarrow{p\,?\,(x)} s'}\ (op\_req) \qquad \frac{s_1 \xrightarrow{p\,!\,(n)} s_1' \quad s_2 \xrightarrow{p\,?\,(x)} s_2' \quad (s_1 \mid s_2) \not\downarrow_{p\,?\,n}}{s_1 \mid s_2 \xrightarrow{p\cdot\varepsilon\cdot\{n/x\}} [\,n\,](s_1' \mid s_2'\{^n\!/\!_x\})}\ (cl\_nx)$$

$$\frac{s \xrightarrow{p\,!\,n} s'}{[\,n\,]s \xrightarrow{p\,!\,(n)} s'}\ (op\_inv) \qquad \frac{s_1 \xrightarrow{p\,!\,(n)} s_1' \quad s_2 \xrightarrow{p\,?\,x} s_2' \quad (s_1 \mid s_2) \not\downarrow_{p\,?\,n}}{s_1 \mid s_2 \xrightarrow{p\cdot\{(n)/x\}\cdot\{n/x\}} s_1' \mid s_2'}\ (cl\_n)$$

$$\frac{s \xrightarrow{p\cdot\{(n)/x\}\cdot\{n/x\}} s'}{[\,x\,]s \xrightarrow{p\cdot\varepsilon\cdot\{n/x\}} [\,n\,]s'\{^n\!/\!_x\}}\ (del\_cl) \qquad \frac{s_1 \xrightarrow{p\,!\,n} s_1' \quad s_2 \xrightarrow{p\,?\,(x)} s_2' \quad (s_1 \mid s_2) \not\downarrow_{p\,?\,n}}{s_1 \mid s_2 \xrightarrow{p\cdot\varepsilon\cdot\{n/x\}} s_1' \mid s_2'\{^n\!/\!_x\}}\ (cl\_x)$$

relation. Their intuitive meaning is analogous to the one of the corresponding labels $p \cdot \{n/x\} \cdot \sigma'$, $p\,?\,x$, and $p\,!\,n$. The parentheses only record that the scope of the entity is undergoing a modification.

Notation and auxiliary functions. We use $[\,d_1,\ldots,d_2\,]$ as a shorthand for $[\,d_1\,]\ldots[\,d_2\,]$, and adopt the notation $s\{^{d_1' \cdots d_j'}\!/\!_{d_1 \ldots d_j}\}$ to mean the simultaneous substitution of d_is by d_i's in the term s . We write $s\downarrow_{p\,?\,n}$ if, for some s', an unguarded subterm of s has the shape $p\,?\,n.\,s'$. Analogously, we write $s\downarrow_k$ if some unguarded subterm of s has the shape $\mathbf{kill}(k)$. The predicates $s \not\downarrow_{p\,?\,n}$ and $s \not\downarrow_k$ are used as negations of $s\downarrow_{p\,?\,n}$ and of $s\downarrow_k$, respectively. Function *halt*(_), used to define service behaviours correspondingly to the execution of a kill activity, takes a service s and eliminates all of its unprotected subservices. In detail: $\mathit{halt}(u\,!\,w) = \mathit{halt}(g) = \mathit{halt}(\mathbf{kill}(k)) = \mathbf{0}$, and $\mathit{halt}(\{\!|s|\!\}) = \{\!|s|\!\}$. Function $\mathit{halt}(\_)$ is a homomorphism on the other operators, namely: $\mathit{halt}(s_1 \mid s_2) = \mathit{halt}(s_1) \mid \mathit{halt}(s_2)$, $\mathit{halt}([\,d\,]s) = [\,d\,]\mathit{halt}(s)$, and $\mathit{halt}(S(m_1, \ldots, m_j)) = \mathit{halt}(s\{^{m_1 \cdots m_j}/_{n_1 \ldots n_j}\})$ for $S(n_1, \ldots, n_j) = s$. Finally, an auxiliary function $\mathrm{d}(\_)$ on labels is defined. We let $\mathrm{d}(p \cdot \{n/x\} \cdot \sigma') = \mathrm{d}(p \cdot \{(n)/x\} \cdot \sigma') = \{n, x\}$ and $\mathrm{d}(p \cdot \varepsilon \cdot \sigma') = \emptyset$. For the other forms of labels, $\mathrm{d}(\alpha)$ stays for the set of entities occurring in α.

Tab. 1 defines $\xrightarrow{\alpha}$ for a rich class of labels. This is technically necessary to get what is actually taken as an *execution step* of a closed service:

$$s \xrightarrow{\alpha} s' \text{ with either } \alpha = \dagger \text{ or } \alpha = p \cdot \varepsilon \cdot \sigma'.$$

The upper portion of Tab. 1 displays the monadic version of rules which are in common with the operational semantics presented in [8]. We first comment on the most interesting rules of that portion.

The execution of the $\mathbf{kill}(k)$ primitive (axiom *kill*) results in spreading the killer signal $\dagger k$ that forces the termination of all the parallel services (rule *par_kill*) but the protected ones (rule *prot*). Once $\dagger k$ reaches the delimiter of its scope, the killer signal is turned off to $\dagger$ (rule *del_kill*). Kill activities are executed eagerly: Whenever a kill primitive occurs unguarded within a service s delimited by d, the service $[\,d\,]s$ can only execute actions of the form $\dagger k$ or $\dagger$ (rule *del_pass*).

Notice that, by our convention on the use of meta-entities, an invoke activity (axiom *inv*) cannot take place if its parameter is a variable. Variable instantiation can take place, involving the whole scope of variable x, due to a pending communication action of shape $p \cdot \{n/x\} \cdot \{n/x\}$ (rule *del_sub*). Communication allows the pairing of the invoke activity $p\,!\,n$ with either the best-matching activity $p\,?\,n$ (rule *com_n*), or with a less defined $p\,?\,x$ action if a best-match is not offered by the locally available context (rule *com_x*). A best-match for $p\,!\,n$ is looked for in the surrounding parallel services (rule *par_conf*) until either $p\,?\,n$ or the delimiter of the variable scope is found. In the first case the attempt to establish an interaction between $p\,!\,n$ and $p\,?\,x$ is blocked by the non applicability of the rules for parallel composition.

The rules in the lower portion of Tab. 1 are a main novelty w.r.t. [8]. In order to carry out quantitative reasoning on the behaviour of services we need to base our stochastic extension on a finitely branching transition system. This was not the case for the authors of [8] who defined their setting for modelling purposes, and hence were mainly interested in *runs* of services rather than on the complete description of their behaviour in terms of *graphs*. Indeed, in [8] the operational semantics of COWS is presented in the most elegant way by using both the replication operator and structural congruence. The rules described below are meant to get rid of both these two ingredients while retaining the expressive power of the language.

As said, we discarded the replication operator in favour of service identifiers. Their use, just as that of replication, is a typical way to allow recursion in the language. When replication is out of the language, the main issue about simulating the expressivity of structural congruence is relative to the management of scope opening for delimiters.

As an example, the operational semantics in [8] permits the interaction between the parallel components of service $[n]p!n \mid [x]p?x.\mathbf{0}$ because, by structural congruence, that parallel composition is exactly the same as $[n][x](p!n \mid p?x.\mathbf{0})$ and hence the transition $[n]p!n \mid [x]p?x.\mathbf{0} \xrightarrow{p\cdot\varepsilon\cdot\{n/x\}} [n](\mathbf{0} \mid \mathbf{0})$ is allowed.

Except for rule *ser_id*, all the newly introduced rules are meant to manage possible moves of delimiters without relying on a notion of structural congruence. The effect is obtained by using a mechanism for opening and closing the scope of binders that is analogous to the technique adopted in the definition of the labelled transition systems of the π-calculus.

Both rules *op_req* and *op_inv* open the scope of their parameter by removing the delimiter from the residual service and recording the binding in the transition label. The definition of the opening rules is where our assumption on the non-homonymy of entities comes into play. If not working under that assumption, we should care of possible name captures caused when closing the scope of the opened entity. To be sure to avoid this, we should allow the applicability of the opening rules to a countably infinite set of entities, which surely contrasts with our need to get finitely branching transition systems.

The idea underlying the opening/closing technique is the following. Opened activities can pass over parallel compositions till a (possibly best) match is found. When this happens, communication can take place and, if due, the delimiter is put back into the term to bind the whole of the residual service.

The three closing rules in Tab. 1 reflect the possible recombinations of pairs of request and invoke activities when at least one of them carries the information that the scope of its parameter has been opened. In each case the parameter of the request is a variable. (If it is a name then, independently on any assumption on entities, it is surely distinct from the invoke parameter.) Recombinations have to be ruled out in different ways depending on the relative original positions of delimiters and parallel composition.

Rule *cl_nx* takes care of scenarios like the one illustrated above for the service $[n]p!n \mid [x]p?x.\mathbf{0}$. Delimiters are originally distributed over the parallel operator, and their scope can be opened to embrace both parallel components. The single delimiter that reappears in the residual term is the one for n.

Rule *cl_x* regulates the case when only variable x underwent a scope opening. The delimiter for the invoke parameter, if present, is in outermost position w.r.t. both the delimiter for x and the parallel operator. An example of this situation is $p!n \mid [x]p?x.\mathbf{0}$. The invoke can still find a best matching, though. Think, e.g., of the service $(p!n \mid p?n.\mathbf{0}) \mid [x]p?x.\mathbf{0}$. If such matching is not available, then the closing communication can effectively occur and the variable gets instantiated.

Rule *cl_n* handles those scenarios when the delimiter for the invoke is within the scope of the delimiter for x, like, e.g., in $[x](p?x.\mathbf{0} \mid [n]p!n)$. Communication is left pending by executing $p \cdot \{(n)/x\} \cdot \{n/x\}$ which is passed over possible parallel compositions using the *par_conf* rule. Variable x is instantiated when $p \cdot \{(n)/x\} \cdot \{n/x\}$ reaches the delimiter for x (rule *del_cl*). On the occasion, $[x]$ becomes a delimiter for n.

```
NS(p1,m1) | NS(p2,m2) | ES(p,p1,p2) | US(p,n)
  where
NS(p,m) = [x] p?x. [k,o]( {|NS(p,m)|} | x!m | o!o | o?o. kill(k) )
ES(p,p1,p2) = [y,n1,n2,z1,z2] p?y.
  ( p1!n1 | p2!n2 | n1?z1.(y!z1|ES(p,p1,p2)) + n2?z2.(y!z2|ES(p,p1,p2)) )
US(p,n) = p!n | [z] n?z.0
```

Fig. 1. COWS specification of a news/e-mail service

Rule *ser_id* states that the behaviour of an identifier depends on the behaviour of its defining service after the substitution of actual parameters for formal parameters. The rule is engineered in such a way that the non-homonymy condition on bound entities is preserved by the unfoldings of the identifier. This is obtained by using decorated versions of transition label and of derived service in the conclusion of the *ser_id* rule. Function l_dec(α) decorates the bound name of α, if any. Function s_dec(α, s) returns a copy of s where all of the occurrences of both the bound names of s and of the bound name possibly occurring in α have been decorated. The decoration mechanism is an instance of a technique typically used in the implementation of the abstract machines for calculi with naming and α-conversion (see, e.g., [12,15]). Here the idea is to enrich entities by superscripts consisting in finite strings of zeros, with d staying for the entity decorated by the empty string. Each time an entity is decorated, an extra zero is appended to the string. Entities decorated by distinct strings are different, and this ensures that the non-homonymy condition is dynamically preserved.

Fig. 1 displays the COWS specification of a simple service adapted from the CNN/BBC example in [10]. The global system, which will be used later on to carry on simple quantitative analysis, consists of two news services (`NS(p1,m1)` and `NS(p2,m2)`), the e-mail service `ES(p,p1,p2)`, and a user `US(p,n)`. The user invokes the e-mail service asking to receive a message with the latest news. On its side, `ES(p,p1,p2)` asks them to both `NS(p1,m1)` and `NS(p2,m2)` and sends back to the user the news it receives first. The sub-component `o!o|o?o.kill(k)` of the news service will be used to simulate (via a delay associated to the invoke and to the request over `o`) a time-out for replying to `ES(p,p1,p2)`.

3 Stochastic Semantics

The stochastic extension of COWS is presented below. The syntax of the basic calculus is enriched in such a way that kill, invoke, and request actions are associated with a random variable with exponential distribution. Since exponential distribution is uniquely determined by a single parameter, called *rate*, the above mentioned atomic activities become pairs (μ,r), where μ represents the basic action, and $r \in \mathbb{R}^+$ is the rate of μ. In the enriched syntax, kill activities, invoke activities, and input-guarded services are written:

$$(\mathbf{kill}(k), \lambda) \qquad (u\,!\,w, \delta) \qquad (p\,?\,w, \gamma).\,s$$

Table 2. Apparent rate of a request

$$\texttt{req}(p;(\mathbf{kill}(k),\lambda)) = \texttt{req}(p;(u\,!\,w,\delta)) = \texttt{req}(p;\mathbf{0}) = 0$$

$$\texttt{req}(p;(p'\,?\,w,\gamma).\,s') = \begin{cases}\gamma & \text{if } p = p' \\ 0 & \text{oth.}\end{cases} \qquad \texttt{req}(p;s_1 \mid s_2) = \texttt{req}(p;s_1) + \texttt{req}(p;s_2)$$

$$\texttt{req}(p;g_1 + g_2) = \texttt{req}(p;g_1) + \texttt{req}(p;g_2) \qquad \texttt{req}(p;\{\!|s|\!\}) = \texttt{req}(p;s)$$

$$\texttt{req}(p;[\,d\,]s) = \begin{cases}0 & \text{if } p = d \text{ or } s\downarrow_d \\ \texttt{req}(p;s) & \text{oth.}\end{cases}$$

$$\texttt{req}(p;S(m_1,\ldots,m_j)) = \texttt{req}(p;s\{^{m_1\ldots m_j}/_{n_1\ldots n_j}\}) \qquad \text{if } S(n_1,\ldots,n_j) = s$$

where the metavariables λ, δ and γ are used to range over kill, invoke and request rates, respectively. The intuitive meaning of $(\mathbf{kill}(k),\lambda)$ is that the activity $\mathbf{kill}(k)$ is completed after a delay Δt drawn from the exponential distribution with parameter λ. I.e., the elapsed time Δt models the use of resources needed to complete $\mathbf{kill}(k)$. The meaning of both $(u\,!\,w,\delta)$ and $(p\,?\,w,\gamma)$ is analogous.

Whenever more than one activity is enabled, the dynamic evolution of a service is driven by a *race condition*: All the enabled activities try to proceed, but only the fastest one succeeds. Race conditions ground the replacement of the non-deterministic choice of COWS by a *probabilistic choice*. The probability of a computational step $s \xrightarrow{\alpha} s'$ is the ratio between its rate and the *exit rate* of s which is defined as the sum of the rates of all the activities enabled in s. For instance, service $S = [\,x\,][\,y\,]((p\,?\,x,\gamma_1).\,s_1 + (p\,?\,y,\gamma_2).\,s_2)$ has exit rate $\gamma_1 + \gamma_2$ and the probability that the activity $p\,?\,x$ is completed is $\gamma_1/(\gamma_1+\gamma_2)$.

The exit rate of a service is computed on the basis of the so-called *communication rate*, which is turn is defined in terms of the *apparent rate* of request and invoke activities [13,7]. The apparent rate of a request over the endpoint p in a service s, written $\texttt{req}(p;s)$, is the sum of the rates of all the requests over the endpoint p which are enabled in s. Function $\texttt{req}(p;s)$ is defined in Tab. 2 by induction on the structure of s. It just sums up the rates of all the requests that can be executed in s at endpoint p. As an example, we show in the following the computation of the apparent rate of a request over p for the above service S.

$$\begin{aligned}\texttt{req}(p;S) &= \texttt{req}(p;(p\,?\,x,\gamma_1).\,s_1 + (p\,?\,y,\gamma_2).\,s_2) \\ &= \texttt{req}(p;(p\,?\,x,\gamma_1).\,s_1) + \texttt{req}(p;(p\,?\,y,\gamma_2).\,s_2) = \gamma_1 + \gamma_2\end{aligned}$$

The apparent rate of an invoke over p in a service s, written $\texttt{inv}(p;s)$, is defined analogously to $\texttt{req}(p;s)$. It computes the sum of the rates of all the invoke activities at p which are enabled in s. Its formal definition is omitted for the sake of space. The apparent communication rate of a synchronization at endpoint p in service s is taken to be the slower value between $\texttt{req}(p;s)$ and $\texttt{inv}(p;s)$, i.e. $\texttt{min}(\texttt{req}(p;s),\texttt{inv}(p;s))$.

All the requests over a certain endpoint p in s compete to take a communication over p. Therefore, given that a request at p is enabled in s, the probability that a request $(p\,?\,x,\gamma)$ completes, is $\gamma/\texttt{req}(p;s)$. Likewise, when an invoke at p is enabled in s, the probability that the invoke $(p\,!\,n,\delta)$ completes is $\delta/\texttt{inv}(p;s)$. Hence, if a communication at p occurs in s, the probability that $(p\,?\,x,\gamma)$ and $(p\,!\,n,\delta)$ are involved is $\gamma/\texttt{req}(p;s) \times \delta/\texttt{inv}(p;s)$.

Table 3. Apparent rate of α in service s

$$\sharp(\alpha; s) = \begin{cases} \mathtt{req}(p; s) & \text{if } \alpha = p\,?\,w, p\,?\,(x) \\ \mathtt{inv}(p; s) & \text{if } \alpha = p\,!\,n, p\,!\,(n) \\ [\mathtt{req}(p; s), \mathtt{inv}(p; s)] & \text{if } \alpha = p \cdot \sigma \cdot \sigma' \\ 0 & \text{oth.} \end{cases}$$

The rate of the communication between $(p\,?\,x, \gamma)$ and $(p\,!\,n, \delta)$ in s is given by the following formula:

$$\frac{\gamma}{\mathtt{req}(p; s)} \frac{\delta}{\mathtt{inv}(p; s)} \mathtt{min}(\mathtt{req}(p; s), \mathtt{inv}(p; s)) \tag{1}$$

namely, it is given by the product of the apparent rate of the communication and of the probability, given that a communication at p occurs in s, that this is just a communication between $(p\,?\,x, \gamma)$ and $(p\,!\,n, \delta)$.

The stochastic semantics of COWS uses *enhanced labels* in the style of [4]. An enhanced label θ is a triple (α, ρ, ρ') prefixed by a *choice-address* ϑ. The α component of the triple is a label of the transition system in Tab. 1. The two components ρ and ρ' can both be either a rate (λ, γ, or δ) or a two dimensional vector of request-invoke rates $[\gamma, \delta]$. We will comment later on upon the usefulness of the choice-address component ϑ.

The enhanced label $\vartheta(\alpha, \rho, \rho')$ records in ρ the rate of the fired action. Axioms *kill*, *req*, and *inv* become respectively:

$$(\mathbf{kill}(k), \lambda) \xrightarrow{(\dagger k, \lambda, \lambda)} \mathbf{0} \qquad (p\,?\,w, \gamma) \,.\, s \xrightarrow{(p\,?\,w, \gamma, \gamma)} s \qquad (p\,!\,n, \delta) \xrightarrow{(p\,!\,n, \delta, \delta)} \mathbf{0}\,.$$

The apparent rate of an activity labelled by α is computed inductively and saved in the ρ' component of the enhanced label $\vartheta(\alpha, \rho, \rho')$. Accordingly, rule *par_pass* takes the shape shown below.

$$\frac{s_1 \xrightarrow{\vartheta(\alpha, \rho, \rho')} s_1' \qquad \alpha \neq p \cdot \sigma \cdot \sigma' \qquad \alpha \neq \dagger k}{s_1 \mid s_2 \xrightarrow{\vartheta(\alpha, \rho, \rho' + \sharp(\alpha; s_2))} s_1' \mid s_2} \ (\mathit{par\_pass})$$

Function $\sharp(\alpha; s)$, defined in Tab. 3, computes the apparent rate of the activity α in the service s. If α is a request (an invoke) at endpoint p, then function $\sharp(\alpha; s)$ returns $\mathtt{req}(p; s)$ ($\mathtt{inv}(p; s)$). In case of a communication at p, function $\sharp(\alpha; s)$ returns the vector $[\mathtt{req}(p; s), \mathtt{inv}(p; s)]$ of the request apparent rate and of the invoke apparent rate. Rules *par_conf* and *par_kill* are modified in a similar way.

An example of application of the *par_pass* rule follows.

$$\frac{(p\,!\,n, \delta_1) \xrightarrow{(p\,!\,n, \delta_1, \delta_1)} \mathbf{0} \ (\mathit{inv})}{(p\,!\,n, \delta_1) \mid (p\,!\,m, \delta_2) \xrightarrow{(p\,!\,n, \delta_1, \delta_1 + \sharp(p\,!\,n; (p\,!\,m, \delta_2)))} \mathbf{0} \mid (p\,!\,m, \delta_2)} \ (\mathit{par\_pass})$$

The enhanced label $(p\,!\,n, \delta_1, \delta_1 + \sharp(p\,!\,n; (p\,!\,m, \delta_2)))$ records that the activity $p\,!\,n$ is taking place with rate δ_1, and with apparent rate $\delta_1 + \sharp(p\,!\,n; (p\,!\,m, \delta_2)) = \delta_1 + \delta_2$.

To compute the rate of a communication between the request $(p\,?\,n,\gamma)$ in s_1 and the invoke $(p\,!\,n,\delta)$ in s_2 with apparent rates γ'' and δ'', respectively, the enhanced label keeps track of both the rates γ and δ, and of both the apparent rates $\gamma'' + \sharp(p\,?\,n; s_2)$ and $\delta'' + \sharp(p\,!\,n; s_1)$. Rule *com_n* is modified as follows.

$$\frac{s_1 \xrightarrow{\vartheta(p\,?\,n,\gamma,\gamma'')} s_1' \qquad s_2 \xrightarrow{\vartheta'(p\,!\,n,\delta,\delta'')} s_2'}{s_1 \mid s_2 \xrightarrow{(\vartheta,\vartheta')(p\cdot\varepsilon\cdot\varepsilon,[\gamma,\delta],[\gamma''+\sharp(p\,?\,n;s_2),\delta''+\sharp(p\,!\,n;s_1)])} s_1' \mid s_2'} \ (com\_n)$$

Notice that the enhanced label in the conclusion of rule *com_n* contains all the data needed to compute the relative communication rate which, following Eq. (1), is given by $(\gamma/\gamma')(\delta/\delta')\mathtt{min}(\gamma',\delta')$ where $\gamma' = \gamma'' + \sharp(p\,?\,n; s_2)$ and $\delta' = \delta'' + \sharp(p\,!\,n; s_1)$. From the point of view of stochastic information, rules *com_x*, *cl_nx*, *cl_x*, and *cl_n* behave the same as rule *com_n*. Indeed their stochastic versions are similar to the one of *com_n*.

Rules *prot*, *del_sub*, *del_kill*, *del_pass*, *ser_id*, *op_req*, *op_inv*, and *del_cl* are transparent w.r.t. stochastic information, i.e., their conclusion does not change the values ρ and ρ' occurring in the premise $s \xrightarrow{\vartheta(\alpha,\rho,\rho')} s'$. We report here only the stochastic version of *del_kill*, the other rules are changed in an analogous way.

$$\frac{s \xrightarrow{\vartheta(\dagger k,\rho,\rho')} s'}{[\,k\,]s \xrightarrow{\vartheta(\dagger,\rho,\rho')} [\,k\,]s'} \ (del\_kill)$$

Rule *choice* deserves special care. Consider the service $(p\,!\,n,\delta) \mid (p\,?\,n,\gamma).\mathbf{0} + (p\,?\,n,\gamma).\mathbf{0}$, and suppose that enhanced labels would not comprise a choice-address component. Then the above service could perform two communications at p, both with the same label $(p\cdot\varepsilon\cdot\varepsilon, [\gamma,\delta], [\gamma+\gamma,\delta])$ and with the same residual service $\mathbf{0} \mid \mathbf{0}$. If the semantic setting is not able to discriminate between these two transitions, then the exit rate of the service cannot be consistently computed. This calls for having a way to distinguish between the choice of either the left or the right branch of a choice service. Indeed, the stochastic rules for choice become the following ones.

$$\frac{g_1 \xrightarrow{\vartheta(\alpha,\rho,\rho')} s}{g_1 + g_2 \xrightarrow{+_0\vartheta(\alpha,\rho,\rho'+\sharp(\alpha;g_2))} s} \ (choice_0) \qquad \frac{g_2 \xrightarrow{\vartheta(\alpha,\rho,\rho')} s}{g_1 + g_2 \xrightarrow{+_1\vartheta(\alpha,\rho,\rho'+\sharp(\alpha;g_1))} s} \ (choice_1)$$

By these rules, the above service $(p\,!\,n,\delta) \mid (p\,?\,n,\gamma).\mathbf{0} + (p\,?\,n,\gamma).\mathbf{0}$ executes two transitions leading to the same residual process but labelled by $+_0(p, [\gamma,\delta], [\gamma + \gamma,\delta])$ and by $+_1(p, [\gamma,\delta], [\gamma+\gamma,\delta])$, respectively.

We conclude the presentation of the stochastic semantics of COWS by providing the definition of *stochastic execution step* of a closed service:

$$s \xrightarrow{\vartheta(\alpha,\rho,\rho')} s' \text{ with either } \alpha = \dagger \text{ or } \alpha = p\cdot\varepsilon\cdot\sigma'.$$

4 Stochastic Analysis

The definition of stochastic execution step has two main properties: (*i*) it can be computed automatically by applying the rules of the operational semantics; (*ii*) it is completely abstract, i.e., enhanced labels only collect information about rates and apparent rates. For instance, it would be possible to compute the communication rate using a formula different from Eq. (1). This makes the modelling phase independent from the analysis phase, and also allows the application of different analysis techniques to the same model.

In what follows, we show how to apply Continuous Time Markov Chain (CTMC) based analysis to COWS terms. A CTMC is a triple $\mathcal{C} = (Q, \overline{q}, \mathbf{R})$ where Q is a finite set of *states*, $\overline{q}$ is the *initial state*, $\mathbf{R} : Q \times Q \to \mathbb{R}^+$ is the *transition matrix*. We write $\mathbf{R}(q_1, q_2) = r$ to mean that q_1 evolves to q_2 with rate r. Various tools are available to analyze CTMCs. Among them there are probabilistic model checkers: Tools that allow the formal verification of stochastic systems against quantitative properties.

A service s' is a *derivative* of service s if s' can be reached from s by a finite number of stochastic evolution steps. The *derivative set* of a service s, $\mathtt{ds}(s)$, is the set including s and all of its derivatives. A service s is *finite* if $\mathtt{ds}(s)$ is finite. Given a finite service s, the associated CTMC is $\mathcal{C}(s) = (\mathtt{ds}(s), s, \mathbf{R})$, where $\mathbf{R}(s, s') = \sum_{s \xrightarrow{\theta} s'} \mathtt{rate}(\theta)$. Here the rate of label θ, $\mathtt{rate}(\theta)$, is computed accordingly to Eq. (1):

$$\mathtt{rate}(\theta) = \begin{cases} (\gamma/\gamma')(\delta/\delta')\mathtt{min}(\gamma', \delta') & \text{if} \quad \theta = \vartheta(p, [\gamma, \delta], [\gamma', \delta']) \\ \rho & \text{if} \quad \theta = \vartheta(\dagger, \rho, \rho') \end{cases}$$

After the above definition, we can analyse COWS services exploiting available tools on CTMCs. As a very simple example, we show how the news/e-mail service in Fig. 1 can be verified using PRISM [14], a probabilistic model checking tool that offers direct support for CTMCs and can check properties described in Continuous Stochastic Logic [1]. A short selection of example properties that can be verified against the news/e-mail service follows.

- `P` $\geq$ `0.9[ true U`$\geq$ `60(NS1 | NS2)]`: "With probability greater than 0.9 either `NS(p1,m1)` or `NS(p2,m2)` are activated in at most 60 units of time";

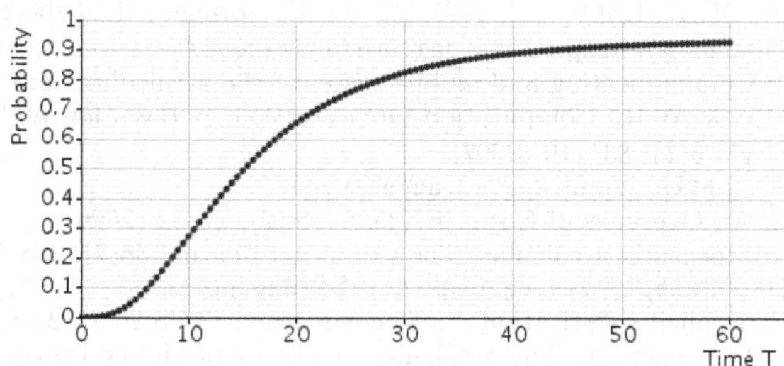

Fig. 2. Probability that `US(p,n)` receives either the message `m1` or `m2` within time `T`

- `P ≥1 [ true U (m1|m2)]`: "The user `US(p,n)` receives either the message `m1` or `m2` with probability 1";
- `P=?[trueU[T,T](m1|m2)]`: "Which is the probability that the user `US(p,n)` receives either the message `m1` or `m2` within time `T`?" Fig. 2 shows a plot generated by PRISM when checking the news/e-mail service against this property.

5 Concluding Remarks

We presented a stochastic extension of COWS, a formal calculus strongly inspired by WS-BPEL, and showed how the obtained semantic model can be used as input to carry on probabilistic verification using PRISM.

The technical approach presented in this paper aims at producing an integrated set of tools to quantitatively model, simulate and analyse web service descriptions.

Acknowledgements. We thank Rosario Pugliese, Francesco Tiezzi, and an anonymous referee for their useful comments and suggestions on a draft of this work.

References

1. Aziz, A., Sanwal, K., Singhal, V., Brayton, R.K.: Model-checking continuous-time markov chains. ACM TOCL 1(1), 162–170 (2000)
2. Bruni, R., Melgratti, H.C., Montanari, U.: Theoretical foundations for compensations in flow composition languages. In: POPL '05, pp. 209–220 (2005)
3. Bruni, R., Melgratti, H.C., Tuosto, E.: Translating Orc Features into Petri Nets and the Join Calculus. In: Bravetti, M., Núñez, M., Zavattaro, G. (eds.) WS-FM 2006. LNCS, vol. 4184, pp. 123–137. Springer, Heidelberg (2006)
4. Degano, P., Priami, C.: Enhanced operational semantics. ACM CS 33(2), 135–176 (2001)
5. Gilmore, S.T., Tribastone, M.: Evaluating the scalability of a web service-based distributed e-learning and course management system. In: Bravetti, M., Núñez, M., Zavattaro, G. (eds.) WS-FM 2006. LNCS, vol. 4184, pp. 214–226. Springer, Heidelberg (2006)
6. Guidi, C., Lucchi, R., Gorrieri, R., Busi, N., Zavattaro, G.: A Calculus for Service Oriented Computing. In: Dan, A., Lamersdorf, W. (eds.) ICSOC 2006. LNCS, vol. 4294, Springer, Heidelberg (2006)
7. Hillston, J.: A Compositional Approach to Performance Modelling. In: CUP (1996)
8. Lapadula, A., Pugliese, R., Tiezzi, F.: Calculus for Orchestration of Web Services. In: Proc. ESOP'07. LNCS, vol. 4421, pp. 33–47. Springer, Heidelberg (2007) (full version available at), `http://rap.dsi.unifi.it/cows/`
9. Milner, R.: Communicating and mobile systems: the π-calculus. In: CUP (1999)
10. Misra, J., Cook, W.R.: Computation Orchestration: A Basis for Wide-area Computing. SoSyM 6(1), 83–110 (2007)
11. PEPA (2007), `http://www.dcs.ed.ac.uk/pepa/`
12. Pottier, F.: An Overview of Caml. ENTCS 148(2), 27–52 (2006)
13. Priami, C.: Stochastic π-calculus. The Computer Journal 38(7), 578–589 (1995)
14. PRISM (2007), `http://www.cs.bham.ac.uk/~dxp/prism/`
15. Quaglia, P.: Explicit substitutions for pi-congruences. TCS 269(1-2), 83–134 (2001)
16. Sangiorgi, D., Walker, D.: The π-calculus: a Theory of Mobile Processes. In: CUP (2001)

Service License Composition and Compatibility Analysis

G.R. Gangadharan[1], Michael Weiss[2], Vincenzo D'Andrea[1], and Renato Iannella[3]

[1] Department of Information and Communication Technology
University of Trento
Via Sommarive, 14, Trento, 38100 Italy
{gr,dandrea}@dit.unitn.it
[2] School of Computer Science, Carleton University
1125 Colonel By Drive, Ottawa, K1S 5B6, Canada
weiss@scs.carleton.ca
[3] National ICT Australia
Level 19, 300 Adelaide Street, Brisbane, Queensland, 4000 Australia
renato@nicta.com.au

Abstract. Services enable the transformation of the World Wide Web as distributed interoperable systems interacting beyond organizational boundaries. Service licensing enables broader usage of services and a means for designing business strategies and relationships. A service license describes the terms and conditions for the use and access of the service in a machine interpretable way that services could be able to understand. Service-based applications are largely grounded on composition of independent services. In that scenario, license compatibility is a complex issue, requiring careful attention before attempting to merge licenses. The permissions and the prohibitions imposed by the licenses of services would deeply impact the composition. Thus, service licensing requires a comprehensive analysis on composition of these rights and requirements conforming to the nature of operations performed and compensation of services used in composition. In this paper, we analyze the compatibility of service license by describing a matchmaking algorithm. Further, we illustrate the composability of service licenses by creating a composite service license, that is compatible with the licenses being composed.

1 Introduction

Service oriented computing (SOC) represents the convergence of technology with an understanding of cross-organizational business processes [1]. Services enhance the World Wide Web not only for human use, but also for machine use by enabling application level interactions. Services have an important advance over stand-alone applications: they intend to make network-accessible operations available anywhere and at anytime. Thus, services deliver complex business processes and transactions, allowing applications to be constructed on-the-fly and to be reused [2].

B. Krämer, K.-J. Lin, and P. Narasimhan (Eds.): ICSOC 2007, LNCS 4749, pp. 257–269, 2007.

In a dynamic market environment, the usage of services is governed by bilateral agreements that specify the terms and conditions of using and provisioning the services. A license is an agreement between parties in which one party receives benefits by giving approximately equal value to the other party in exchange. Licensing [3] includes all transactions between the licensor and the licensee, in which the licensor agrees to grant the licensee the right to use and access the asset under predefined terms and conditions.

The trend of software transforming to a service oriented paradigm demands for a new way of licensing for services [4]. Different types of licenses exist for software. As the nature of services differs significantly from traditional software and components, services prevent the direct adoption of software and component licenses. As services are being accessed and consumed in a number of ways, a spectrum of licenses suitable for services with differing license clauses can be definable. We have formalized the license clauses for services in [5].

As services are composed with one another, the associated service licenses are also to be composed. The license of a composite service should be compatible with the licenses of the services being composed. In this paper, we propose an environment for composing licenses and analyzing the compatibility between the licenses in case of service composition. The salient feature of our approach is a matchmaking algorithm for compatibility analysis of licenses (at license clause level). We also discuss the creation of a composite service license based on the compatibility of candidate service licenses.

The paper is organized as follows: In Section 2, we briefly describe the representation of service licenses using ODRL Service Licensing Profile. Section 3 provides details of a matchmaking algorithm and analyzes the compatibility between licenses at the level of elements. The process of service license composition based on the compatibility of candidate service licenses is illustrated in Section 4. Section 5 discusses related work in this field, showing the distinct contribution of this paper.

2 ODRL Service Licensing Profile (ODRL-S)

A service license describes the terms and conditions that permit the use of and access to a service, in a machine readable way, which services can understand. Licensing of services raises several issues, including:

1. What rights should be associated with services and how should the rights be expressed?
2. How can the composite service license be generated being compatible with the licenses in composition?

We have developed a language ODRL-S [6] by extending the Open Digital Rights Language (ODRL) [7] to implement the clauses of service licensing (see

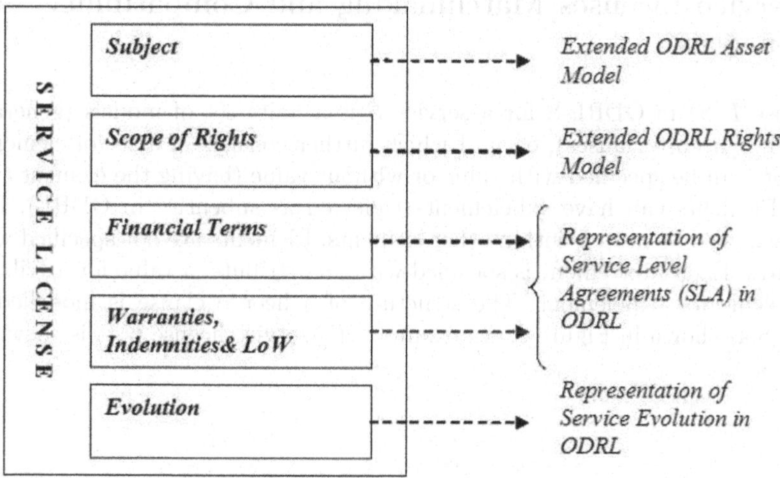

Fig. 1. Conceptual mapping of service license clauses

Figure 1). The complete syntax and semantics of ODRL-S can be found in [6]. The anatomy of a service license in ODRL-S is as follows.

- The *Subject* model of a service license directly adopts the ODRL Asset Model [7]. The subject of the license relates to the definition of the service being licensed. This defines some related information about the service and may include a unique identification code for the service, service name, service location, and other relevant information.
- The *Scope of Rights*, as explained in detail in [5], comprise the extended ODRL Permission, Requirement, and Constraint Models. Composition is the right of execution with the right of interface modification. Derivation is the right of allowing modifications to the interface as well as the implementation of a service. Furthermore, derivation requires independent execution of the service where composition is dependent on the execution of services being composed. Adaptation refers to the right of allowing the use of interface only (independent on the execution of services). ODRL-S reuses the concept of sharealike and non-commercial use from the ODRL Creative Commons profile [8]. Attribution to services is facilitated by the ODRL attribution element.
- We adopt the ODRL payment model for representing the *Financial* model of services. However, Free/Open Services [9] could be represented without a payment model.
- The *WIL* model defines warranties, indemnities and limitation of liabilities associated with services.
- The *Evolution* model specifies modifications in future releases or versions.

3 Service Licenses Matchmaking and Compatibility Analysis

A license $L(S)$ in ODRL-S for a service S is a finite set of models (generally referred as license clauses), each of which further consists of a set of elements. Elements can be specified with value or without value (having the element type only). Elements can have subelements (referred as subentity in ODRL). Elements can also be nested within other elements. Elements are not specified with attributes. Each subelement is specified with an attribute, a value for attribute, and a value for subelement. The structure of a license clause is modelled in ODRL-S as shown in Figure 2. An example of a service license (L_1) is shown in Figure 3.

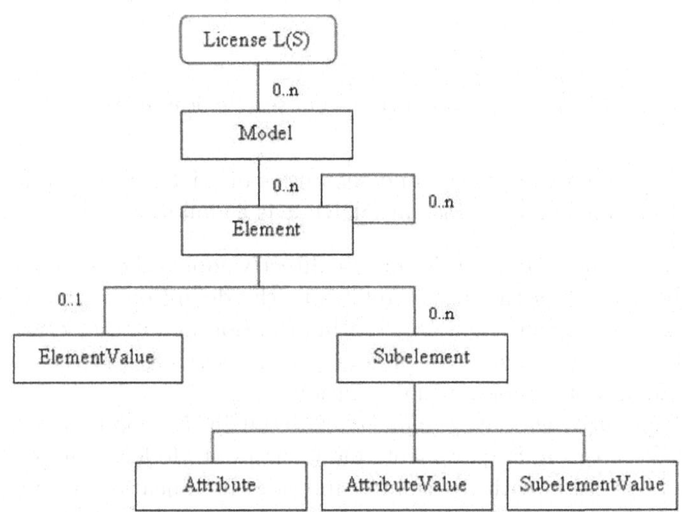

Fig. 2. ODRL-S license clause structure

There are certain elements of licenses which are broader in scope of operation than certain other elements. Assume two services with different license elements say, composition and derivation. If a consumer is looking for a service allowing composition, a service license allowing derivation can also be used, because derivation subsumes composition. For this reason, we say that derivation and composition are compatible. For a complete compatibility analysis, the matchmaking algorithm must know about the possible subsumptions. The concept of subsumption (at the element level) is similar to the concept of redefinition of a method in a sub-class [10]. Subsumption implies a match that should occur, if the given license element is more permissive (accepts more) than the corresponding element in the other license. The subsumption rules for *Scope of Rights* are given below (see Table 1):

Table 1. Subsumption rules over *Scope of Rights* elements

Element1	**Element2**	**Comparison**	**Redefinition**
Composition	Adaptation	Composition $\supset$ Adaptation	Composition
Derivation	Adaptation	Derivation $\supset$ Adaptation	Derivation
	Composition	Derivation $\supset$ Composition	Derivation

There could also be a scenario when analyzing the compatibility of service licenses where one of the licenses contains clauses that the other license does not. In certain cases, the absence of one or several of these clauses does not affect the compatibility with the other license. Table 2 lists rules used by the matchmaking algorithm to determine the compatibility of specified against unspecified ("don't care") elements.

Table 2. Compatibility with unspecified *Scope of Rights* and *Financial Terms* elements

Element1	**Element2**	**Compatibility**	**Rationale**
Adaptation	Unspecified	*Compatible*	Adaptation is the right for interface reuse only.
Composition	Unspecified	*Incompatible*	A license denying composition can not be compatible with a license allowing composition.
Composition	Adaptation	*Compatible*	Based on subsumption (Table 1)
Derivation	Unspecified	*Incompatible*	Derivation requires the source code of interface and implementation to be 'Open'.
Derivation	Adaptation or Composition	*Compatible*	Based on subsumption (Table 1)
Attribution	Unspecified	*Compatible*	The requirement for specification of attribution will not affect the compatibility when unspecified.
Sharealike	Unspecified	*Compatible*	Sharealike affects the composite license requiring that the composite license should be similar to the license having Sharealike element.
Non-CommercialUse	Unspecified	*Incompatible*	Commercial use is denied by Non-CommercialUse.
Payment	Unspecified	*Compatible*	Payment elements do not affect compatibility directly, if unspecified. The license elements related to payment and charging are dependent on service provisioning issues.

The matchmaking algorithm compares a license clause of a license with another license clause of another license. The algorithm analyzes the compatibility of licenses at the element level. The algorithm performs the compatibility analysis between any two given licenses[1] to decide whether they are compatible. A license is compatible with another license if all license clauses are compatible (as defined by the matchmaking algorithm). Service licenses can be combined, if they are found compatible by the matchmaking algorithm, allowing the corresponding services to be composed.

Assuming that semantics inside a license are agreed by service providers and consumers, the algorithm for matching a license SL_α (with subscript α) with another license SL_β (with subscript β) is given as follows. In the following, we use the symbol $\Leftrightarrow$ to denote compatibility. Two licenses are compatible (that is: $SL_\alpha \Leftrightarrow SL_\beta$), if all the respective models in both the licenses are compatible.

$$\begin{array}{lllll} & (\forall m_\alpha : m_\alpha \epsilon SL_\alpha & \exists m_\beta : m_\beta \epsilon SL_\beta & \Rightarrow & (m_\alpha \Leftrightarrow m_\beta)) \\ \wedge & (\forall m_\beta : m_\beta \epsilon SL_\beta & \exists m_\alpha : m_\alpha \epsilon SL_\alpha & \Rightarrow & (m_\alpha \Leftrightarrow m_\beta)) \end{array}$$

A model m_α is compatible with another model m_β, if the model types are same (represented by $\equiv$) and their elements are compatible.

$$\begin{array}{lllll} & & & & (m_\alpha \equiv m_\beta) \\ \wedge & (\forall e_\alpha : e_\alpha \epsilon Elements(m_\alpha) & \exists e_\beta : e_\beta \epsilon Elements(m_\beta) & \Rightarrow & (e_\alpha \Leftrightarrow e_\beta)) \\ \wedge & (\forall e_\beta : e_\beta \epsilon Elements(m_\beta) & \exists e_\alpha : e_\alpha \epsilon Elements(m_\alpha) & \Rightarrow & (e_\alpha \Leftrightarrow e_\beta)) \end{array}$$

Now, an element e_α is compatible with another element e_β, if:

- e_α and e_β have same type (represented by $\equiv$) or e_α can be redefined as e_β using Table 1 or in case of unspecification of either e_α or e_β, use Table 2 for looking the compatible element;
- e_α and e_β have equal value;
- all subelements of e_α and e_β are compatible.
- for all nested elements, corresponding elements are compatible.

$$\begin{array}{lllll} & ((e_\alpha \equiv e_\beta) \quad \vee \quad Redefinition(e_\alpha, e_\beta) & & \vee & Unspecification(e_\alpha, e_\beta)) \\ & & & \wedge & (Value(e_\alpha) = Value(e_\beta)) \\ \wedge & (\forall s_\alpha : s_\alpha \epsilon Subelements(e_\alpha) & \exists s_\beta : s_\beta \epsilon Subelements(e_\beta) & \Rightarrow & (s_\alpha \Leftrightarrow s_\beta)) \\ \wedge & (\forall s_\beta : s_\beta \epsilon Subelements(e_\beta) & \exists s_\alpha : s_\alpha \epsilon Subelements(e_\alpha) & \Rightarrow & (s_\alpha \Leftrightarrow s_\beta)) \\ \wedge & (\forall e_\alpha : e_\alpha \epsilon Elements(e_\alpha) & \exists e_\beta : e_\beta \epsilon Elements(e_\beta)) & \Rightarrow & (e_\alpha \Leftrightarrow e_\beta)) \\ \wedge & (\forall e_\beta : e_\beta \epsilon Elements(e_\beta) & \exists e_\alpha : e_\alpha \epsilon Elements(e_\alpha)) & \Rightarrow & (e_\alpha \Leftrightarrow e_\beta)) \end{array}$$

A subelement s_α is compatible with another subelement s_β, if the values of subelements are equal and if their attributes are of same type (represented by $\equiv$) and the associated values of attributes are equal.

[1] The described algorithm does not support service consumer and service provider relationship between the given licenses, thus bypassing the directional issues of compatibility.

$$
\begin{aligned}
& (Value(Se_\alpha) = Value(Se_\beta)) \\
\wedge \quad & (\forall h_\alpha : h_\alpha \epsilon Attributes(Se_\alpha) \quad \exists h_\beta : h_\beta \epsilon Attributes(Se_\beta) \\
& \Rightarrow \quad (h_\alpha \equiv h_\beta) \wedge (Value(h_\alpha) = Value(h_\beta)) \\
\wedge \quad & (\forall h_\beta : h_\beta \epsilon Attributes(Se_\beta) \quad \exists h_\alpha : h_\alpha \epsilon Attributes(Se_\alpha) \\
& \Rightarrow \quad (h_\alpha \equiv h_\beta) \wedge (Value(h_\alpha) = Value(h_\beta))
\end{aligned}
$$

Consider the example of a restaurant service R, composed of a resource allocation service (I) and a map service (M). Assume that I allows derivation and costs 1 euro per use of the service. Furthermore, the service requires attribution. The license (say $L1$) for the service I is represented in ODRL-S as follows (shown in Figure 3).

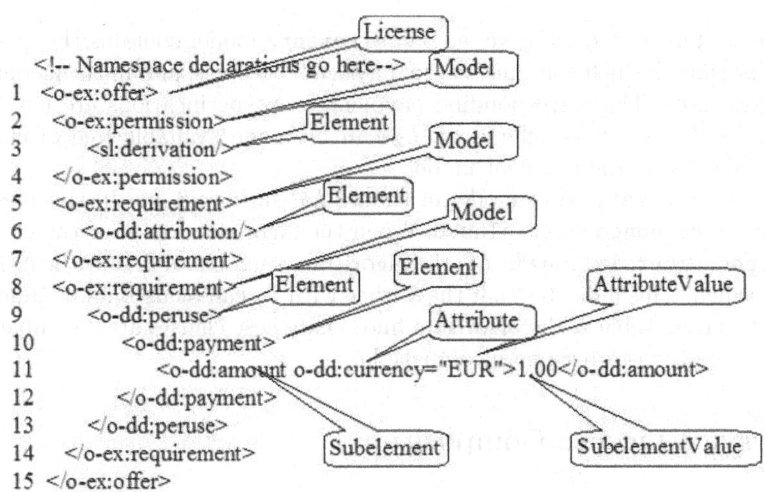

Fig. 3. Example license L_1

Assume that the map service M allows composition and requires attribution. However, this service denies commercial use. The license (say $L2$) for the service M is represented in ODRL-S as follows (shown in Figure 4).

Assume we now want to analyze the compatibility between license L_1 and another license L_2.

Following the matchmaking algorithm, we compare licenses at the model level. Line 2 of both licenses are `<o-ex:permission>` models. The elements in line 3 of L_1 (`<ls:derivation>`) and line 3 of L_2 (`<ls:composition>`) are not of the same type, but we can redefine one (composition) as the other (derivation) by applying a rule from Table 1 (derivation subsumes composition).

In lines 5, 6, and 7 of L_1 and L_2, we compare the model `<o-ex:requirement>` with the element `<o-ex:attribution>`. As the models are of the same type and the elements are of the same type, the model is compatible.

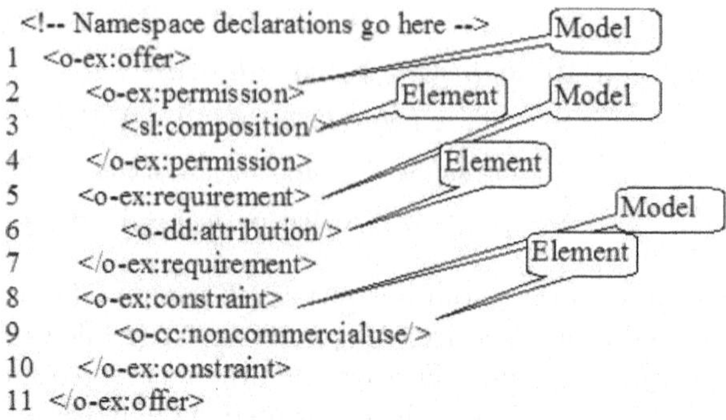

Fig. 4. Example License L_2

Then, in line 8 of L_1, the `<o-ex:requirement>` model contains the element `<o-dd:peruse>`, which contains `<o-dd:payment>` element, and in turn, contains `<o-dd:amount>`. The corresponding payment term specifications are not specified in L_2. (The service offered by L_2 can be made available free of charge, without specifying the payment model.)

The `<o-ex:constraint>` model of license L_2 (in lines 8 and 9) specifies the element `<o-cc:noncommercialuse>`. When the algorithm looks for the element `<o-cc:noncommercialuse>` in L_1, the algorithm is unable to find as the element is unspecified. This indicates that the service with L_1 can be used for commercial purposes. From Table 2, the algorithm finds that these clauses are incompatible, and thus the licenses become incompatible.

4 Service License Composition

Service composition combines of independently developed services into a more complex service. The license of the composite service should be consistent with the licenses of the individual services. Composability of licenses refers to the generation of the composite service license from the given service licenses for the services being composed. A pre-requisite for composability of licenses is that the licenses are to be compatible.

A lookup in a service directory for services with a given functionality may result in multiple candidate services. Each candidate service may be provided under a different license. When the services are composed, there can be several licenses for the composite service. The process of a license selection for a service is depicted in Figure 5. The service consumer/aggregator could manually select one of the services with the desired functionality and the desired license. Otherwise the process assigns a license to the composite service (may be most permissible).

Consider our example of a restaurant service R, composed of a map service and a resource allocation service. The search for a map service in the service directory might return several services with the same functionality, but different licenses, say M, M', and M''. The search for resource allocation results in services

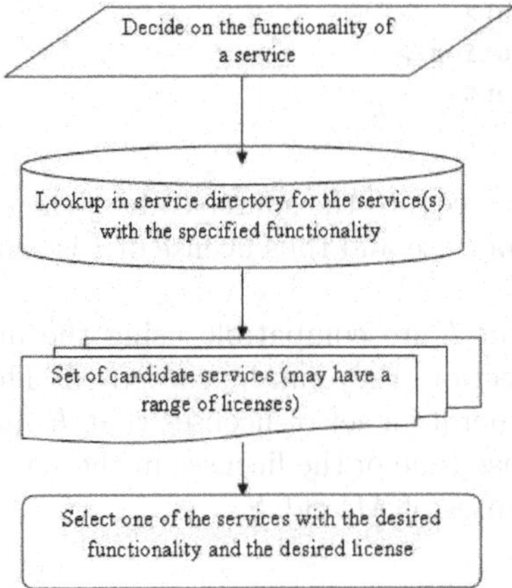

Fig. 5. Process of a service license selection with the service functionality

with different licenses, I, I', and I''. The composite service R could be licensed under a variety of licenses, but then must be compatible with the licenses of M or M' or M'' and I or I' or I'' (see Figure 6). Each combination could lead to the creation of a distinct license for R.

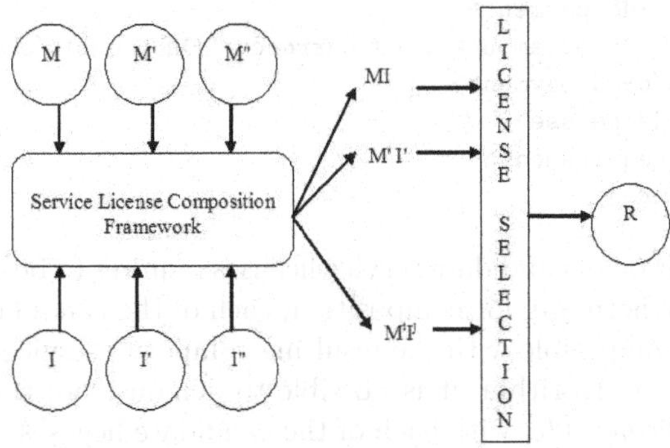

Fig. 6. Service license composition scenario by license generation and selection

Consider the case where M allows composition and requires attribution, when M is used by other services. The license of M in ODRL-S may look like this:

```
<!-- Namespace declarations go here-->
  <o-ex:offer>
     <o-ex:permission>
        <sl:composition/>
     </o-ex:permission>
```

```
    <o-ex:requirement>
        <o-dd:attribution/>
    </o-ex:requirement>
</o-ex:offer>
```

Assume that I allows access to the source code of the service (derivation) and requires a fee of 1 Euro per use and thus license of I is same as the license shown in Figure 3.

As the licenses M and I are compatible using the matchmaking algorithm illustrated in previous section, they can be composed. The composition of these service licenses could generate a set of licenses that R may select. Assume that R has the following license (one of the licenses in the set of compatible licenses), compatible with the licenses of M and I:

```
<!-- Namespace declarations go here-->
<o-ex:offer>
    <o-ex:permission>
        <sl:derivation/>
    </o-ex:permission>
    <o-ex:requirement>
        <o-dd:attribution/>
    </o-ex:requirement>
    <o-ex:requirement>
        <o-dd:peruse>
            <o-dd:payment>
                <o-dd:amount o-dd:currency="EUR">1.00</o-dd:amount>
            </o-dd:payment>
        </o-dd:peruse>
    </o-ex:requirement>
</o-ex:offer>
```

The composition of candidate service licenses requires to be compatible among themselves. Furthermore, for composition, each of the candidate service licenses should also be compatible with the resulting composite service license. Following the matchmaking algorithm, it is possible to demonstrate the compatibility of the composite license (R) with each of the candidate licenses (M and I). Space, however, does not allow us to show the details of executing the matchmaking algorithm for the example.

5 Related Work and Discussion

Though there are examples of service licenses in practical use (by Amazon, Google, Yahoo!), to the best of our knowledge, there appears to be no conceptualization of service licensing in general. The business and legal contractual information are not described at a detailed level by the services research community, either in industry or academia. Though the design of service licenses seems to be an initiative of the software industry, there is no active involvement in this topic by industry. One of the primary causes for this could be fear still faced by industries over the lack of standardization of technologies surrounding service oriented computing. The need for a language defining both the internal business needs of an organization and its requirements on external services, and for a systematic way of linking them to business processes is proposed in [11]. As the mechanism of technology transfer, licensing addresses how a process is related to and affects business requirements and needs, describing the legal requirements. Licenses affect the design of business strategies and relationships, linking the business processes across boundaries.

In the business domain, consumer confidence is established through a contract with the service provider. In SOC, service level agreements (SLA) and policies support these contractual terms. A service license primarily focuses on the usage and provisioning terms of services. A service license may include the SLA terms. Thus, a service license is broader than the scope of SLA, protecting the rights of service providers and service consumers. In general, an agreement is negotiated between the service provider and the service consumer and agree upon a SLA that covers a service (or a group of services). The agreement is terminated when either of the party terminates or violates the agreement. If one of the partners violates the agreement, the agreement might be renegotiated (in case of recoverable violation). In case of a service license, there is a service provider that plays the main role of the licensor. There could be many service consumers (the licensees) binded by the service license. The agreement between the service provider and a consumer is bound to comply with license clauses, but the license itself is generally not part of the negotiation. If a license is modified, it leads to the creation of a new version of the license. A new invocation of a service might use the modified version of the license. However, the unmodified version of the license, if it is implemented and executed by a service, will remain active and will not be overridden by the new version [12].

Current SLA and policies specifications for services (WSLA [13], SLANG [14], WSOL [15], WS-Agreement [16], WS-Policy [17]) define what to measure/monitor and describe payments/penalties. Generally, all the specifications focus on the QoS and the terms and conditions agreed by the provider and consumer. License clauses [18] are unexplored by current service description standards and languages (as mentioned above). We have proposed ODRL-S as a language to represent a service license concretely in a machine interpretable form so that any services can automatically interpret license clauses. Using ODRL-S, a service license can be described in service level and feature level [6].

Compatibility between services is one of the active research areas in service oriented computing. The present researches on the compatibility of services have been focused on the matching of functional properties of services [19,20]. A selection processes for commercial-off-the-shelf components using some of the non-technical features is addressed in [21], vaguely related to our work. An interesting approach for matching non-functional properties of Web services represented using WS-Policy is described in [22]. The most comprehensive work on automated compatibility analysis of WSLA service level objectives is elaborated in [23].

However, license clauses are not simple as in the case of service level objectives of WSLA or policies of WS-Policy and the algorithm presented in [23] can not be parse service license clauses. The problem of licensing compatibility is difficult to resolve automatically as license clauses are generally written in a natural language (like English) and contains highly legalized terms, sometimes even difficult for the end users to understand. A comprehensive semantic approach for digital rights management based on ontologies is proposed in [24]. However, the framework does not describe the rights expression for services and their composition. To the best of our knowledge, there is no research on a framework for composing licenses (at least semi-automatically) for services. Not only have we developed an algorithm for matchmaking of service licenses, but we have also proposed the way of composing candidate service licenses. The illustrated compatibility analysis of service licenses in the element level can be applicable to analyze the compatibility of licenses in any digital assets. We position our work as a complementary approach in service license composition.

6 Concluding Remarks

The full potential of services as a means of developing dynamic business solutions will only be realized when cross organizational business processes can federate in a scale-free manner. Today, services offer programmatic interfaces to applications. However, many available services are not even considered to provide relevant business value. As a way of managing the rights between service consumers and service providers, licenses are of critical importance to services. In this paper, we have analyzed the compatibility between licenses by describing a comprehensive service license matchmaking algorithm. Further, we have described the composition of service licenses. In our ongoing work, we are describing license conflicts during service composition and resolving them by feature interactions.

References

1. Paulson, L.: Services Science: A New Field for Today's Economy. IEEE Computer 39(8), 18–21 (2006)
2. Alonso, G., Casati, F., Kuno, H., Machiraju, V.: Web Services Concepts, Architectures, and Applications. Springer, Heidelberg (2004)
3. Classen, W.: Fundamentals of Software Licensing. IDEA: The Journal of Law and Technology 37(1) (1996)
4. D'Andrea, V., Gangadharan, G.R.: Licensing Services: The Rising. In: ICIW'06. Proceedings of the IEEE Web Services Based Systems and Applications, Guadeloupe, French Caribbean, pp. 142–147. IEEE Computer Society Press, Los Alamitos (2006)
5. Gangadharan, G.R., D'Andrea, V.: Licensing Services: Formal Analysis and Implementation. In: Dan, A., Lamersdorf, W. (eds.) ICSOC 2006. LNCS, vol. 4294, pp. 365–377. Springer, Heidelberg (2006)

6. Gangadharan, G.R., D'Andrea, V., Iannella, R., Weiss, M.: ODRL Service Licensing Profile. Technical Report DIT-07-027, University of Trento (2007)
7. Iannella, R. (ed.): Open Digital Rights Language (ODRL) Version 1.1 (2002), http://odrl.net/1.1/ODRL-11.pdf
8. Iannella, R. (ed.): ODRL Creative Commons Profile (2005), http://odrl.net/Profiles/CC/SPEC.html
9. Gangadharan, G.R., D'Andrea, V., Weiss, M.: Free/Open Services: Conceptualization, Classification, and Commercialization. In: OSS. Proceedings of the Third IFIP International Conference on Open Source Systems, Limerick, Ireland (2007)
10. Jezequel, J.M., Train, M., Mingins, C.: Design Patterns and Contracts. Addison-Wesley, Reading (1999)
11. Papazoglou, M., Traverso, P., Dustdar, S., Leymann, F., Kramer, B.: Service Oriented Computing Research Roadmap. In: Dagstuhl Seminar Proceedings 05462 (SOC) (2006)
12. Gangadharan, G.R., Frankova, G., D'Andrea, V.: Service License Life Cycle. In: CTS 2007. Proceedings of the International Symposium on Collaborative Technologies and Systems, pp. 150–158 (2007)
13. Ludwig, H., Keller, A., Dan, A., King, R., Franck, R.: Web Service Level Agreement (WSLA) Language Specification. IBM Coporation (2003)
14. Skene, J., Lamanna, D., Emmerich, W.: Precise Service Level Agreements. In: ICSE. Proc. of 26th Intl. Conference on Software Engineering (2004)
15. Tosic, V., Pagurek, B., Patel, K., Esfandiari, B., Ma, W.: Management Applications of the Web Service Offerings Language. In: Eder, J., Missikoff, M. (eds.) CAiSE 2003. LNCS, vol. 2681, Springer, Heidelberg (2003)
16. Andrieux, A., Czajkowski, K., Dan, A., Keahey, K., Ludwig, H., Nakata, T., Pruyne, J., Rofrano, J., Tuecke, S., Xu, M.: Web Services Agreement Specification (WS-Agreement) Version 2005/09 (2005), http://www.gridforum.org
17. Vedamuthu, A., Orchard, D., Hirsch, F., Hondo, M., Yendluri, P., Boubez, T., Yalcinalp, U.: Web Services Policy (WS-Policy) Framework (2007), http://www.w3.org/TR/ws-policy
18. World Intellectual Property Organization: WIPO Copyright Treaty (WCT) (1996), http://www.wipo.int/treaties/en/ip/wct/trtdocs_wo033.html
19. Wang, Y., Stroulia, E.: Flexible Interface Matching for Web Service Discovery. In: Proc. of the Fourth Intl. Conf. on Web Information Systems Engineering (2003)
20. Paolucci, M., Kawamura, T., Payne, T., Sycara, K.: Semantic Matching of Web Services Capabilities. In: Horrocks, I., Hendler, J. (eds.) ISWC 2002. LNCS, vol. 2342, Springer, Heidelberg (2002)
21. Vega, J.P.C., Franch, X., Quer, C.: Towards a Unified Catalogue of Non-Technical Quality Attributes to Support COTS-Based Systems Lifecycle Activities. In: ICCBSS. Proc. of the IEEE Intl. Conference on COTS Based Software Systems, IEEE Computer Society Press, Los Alamitos (2007)
22. Verma, K., Akkiraj, R., Goodwin, R.: Semantic Matching of Web Service Policies. In: Second Intl. Workshop on Semantic and Dynamic Web Processes (2005)
23. Yang, W., Ludwig, H., Dan, A.: Compatibility Analysis of WSLA Service Level Objectives. Technical Report RC22800 (W0305-082), IBM Research Division (2003)
24. Garcia, R., Gil, R., Delgado, J.: A Web Ontologies Framework for Digital Rights Management. Journal of Artificial Intelligence and Law Online First (2007), http://springerlink.metapress.com/content/03732x05200u7h27

Dynamic Requirements Specification for Adaptable and Open Service-Oriented Systems

Ivan J. Jureta, Stéphane Faulkner, and Philippe Thiran

Information Management Research Unit, University of Namur, Belgium
iju@info.fundp.ac.be, sfaulkne@fundp.ac.be, pthiran@fundp.ac.be

Abstract. It is not feasible to engineer requirements for adaptable and open service-oriented systems (AOSS) by specifying stakeholders' expectations in detail during system development. Openness and adaptability allow new services to appear at runtime so that ways in, and degrees to which the initial functional and nonfunctional requirements will be satisfied may vary at runtime. To remain relevant after deployment, the initial requirements specification ought to be continually updated to reflect such variation. Depending on the frequency of updates, this paper separates the requirements engineering (RE) of AOSS onto the RE for: individual services (Service RE), service coordination mechanisms (Coordination RE), and quality parameters and constraints guiding service composition (Client RE). To assist existing RE methodologies in dealing with Client RE, the Dynamic Requirements Adaptation Method (DRAM) is proposed. DRAM updates a requirements specification at runtime to reflect change due to adaptability and openness.

1 Introduction

To specify requirements, the engineer describes the stimuli that the future system may encounter in its operating environment and defines the system's responses according to the stakeholders' expectations. The more potential stimuli she anticipates and accounts for, the less likely a discrepancy between the expected and observed behavior and quality of the system. Ensuring that the requirements specification is complete (e.g., [17]) becomes increasingly difficult as systems continue to gain in complexity and/or operate in changing conditions (e.g., [15,10]). Adaptable and open service-oriented systems (AOSS) are one relevant response to such complexity. They are *open* to permit a large pool of distinct and competing services orignating from various service providers to participate. AOSS are *adaptable*—i.e., an AOSS coordinates service provision by dynamically selecting the participating services according to multiple quality criteria, so that the users continually receive optimal results (e.g., [7,8]).

A complete requirements specification for an AOSS would include the description of all relevant properties of the system's operating environment, and of all alternative system and environment behaviors. All services that may participate would thus be entirely known at development time. Following any established

B. Krämer, K.-J. Lin, and P. Narasimhan (Eds.): ICSOC 2007, LNCS 4749, pp. 270–282, 2007.

RE methodology (e.g., KAOS [4], Tropos [3]), such a specification would be constructed by moving from abstract stakeholder expectations towards a detailed specification of the entire system's behavior. As we explain in Section 2, applying such an approach and arriving at the extensive specification of an AOSS is not feasible. In response, this paper introduces concepts and techniques needed to *(1) determine how extensive the initial specification ought to be and what parts thereof are to be updated at runtime to reflect system adaptation*, and *(2) know how to perform such updates.* The specification can then be used to continually survey and validate system behavior. To enable (1), this paper separates the requirements engineering (RE) of AOSS depending on the frequency at which the requirements are to be updated (§2): RE executed for individual services or small sets of services (*Service RE*), RE of mechanisms for coordinating the interaction between services (*Coordination RE*), and RE of parameters guiding the runtime operation of the coordination mechanisms (*Client RE*). To address (2), this paper focuses on Client RE and introduces a method, called Dynamic Requirements Adaptation Method (DRAM) for performing Client RE for AOSS (§3). We close the paper with a discussion of related work (§4), and conclusions and indications for future effort (§5).

Motivation. The proposal outlined in the remainder resulted from the difficulties encountered in engineering requirements for an experimental AOSS, call it TravelWeb, which allows users to search for and book flights, trains, hotels, rental cars, or any combination thereof. Services which perform search and booking originate from the various service providers that either represent the various airlines and other companies, so that TravelWeb aggregates and provides an interface to the user when moving through the offerings of the various providers. Each provider can decide what options to offer to the user: e.g., in addition to the basics, such as booking a seat on an airplane, some airlines may ask for seating, entertainment, and food preferences, while others may further personalize the offering through additional options. We have studied elsewhere [7,8] the appropriate architecture and service composition algorithms for TravelWeb. Here, we focus on the engineering of requirements for such systems.

2 Service, Coordination, and Client RE

To engineer the requirements for TravelWeb, a common RE methodology such as Tropos [3] would start with early and late requirements analyses to better understand the organizational setting, where dependencies between the service providers, TravelWeb, and end users would be identified, along with the goals, resources, and tasks of these various parties. Architectural design would ensue to define the sub-systems and their interconnections in terms of data, control, and other dependencies. Finally, detailed design would result in an extensive behavioral specification of all system components. While other methodologies, such as KAOS [4] involve a somewhat different approach, all move from high-level requirements into detailed behavioral specifications. The discussion below, however, concludes that such an approach is not satisfactory, because:

1) TravelWeb is open. Various hotels/airlines/rental companies may wish to offer or retract their services. Characteristics of services that may participate in TravelWeb at runtime is thus unknown at TravelWeb development time. Individual services are likely to be developed outside the TravelWeb development team, before or during the operation of TravelWeb. It is thus impossible to proceed as described for the entire TravelWeb—instead, it is more realistic to apply an established RE methodology locally for each individual service, and separately for the entire TravelWeb system, taking individual services as black boxes of functionality (i.e., not knowing their internal architecture, detailed design, etc.).

2) Resources are distributed and the system adapts. All services may or may not be available at all times. Moreover, individual services are often not sufficient for satisfying user requests—that is, several services from distinct providers may need to interact to provide the user with appropriate feedback. Adaptability in the case of TravelWeb amounts to changing service compositions according to service availability, a set of quality parameters, and constraints on service inputs and outputs (see, [8] for details). RE specific to the coordination of services carries distinct concerns from the RE of individual services.

3) Quality parameters vary. Quality (i.e., nonfunctional) parameters are used by the service composer as criteria for comparing alternative services and service compositions. Quality parameters are not all known at TravelWeb development time, for different services can be advertised with different sets of quality parameters. As the sets of quality parameters to account for in composing services change, (a) different sets of stakeholders' nonfunctional expectations will be concerned by various service compositions *and* (b) there may be quality parameters that do not have corresponding expectations in the initial specification. Observation (a) entails that initial desired levels of expectations may not be achieved at all times, making the initial specification idealistic. Deidealizing requirements has been dealt through a probabilistic approach by Letier and van Lamsweerde [11] where requirements are combined with probability of satisfaction estimates. In an adaptable system, the probability values are expected to change favorably over time (see, e.g., our experiments on service composition algorithms for AOSS [7,8]), so that updating the initial requirements specification to reflect the changes seems appropriate if the specification is to remain relevant after system deployment. Observation (b) relates to the difficulty in translating stakeholders' goals into a specification: as March observed in a noted paper [12], both individual and organizational goals (which translate into requirements) tend to suffer from problems of relevance, priority, clarity, coherence, and stability over time, all of which relate to the variability, inconsistency, and imprecision, among other, of stakeholder preferences. Instead of assuming that the initial set of expectations is complete, the specification can be updated at runtime to reflect new system behaviors *and* to enable the stakeholders to modify requirements as they learn about the system's abilities and about their own expectations.

Having established that updates are needed, we turn to the question of what to update. A requirements specification for an AOSS involves requirements that are of different variability over time. Our experience with AOSS [7,8] indicates that a particular combination of service-oriented architecture and service coordination algorithm enables adaptability, whereby the architecture and the algorithm act as a cadre in which various requirements can be specified. Since adaptability does not require change in the architecture and algorithm, requirements on these two remain reasonably stable. This observation, along with the localization of service-specific RE to each individual service or small service groups leads to a separation of AOSS RE effort as follows:

Service RE involves the engineering of requirements for an individual service, or a set of strongly related services (e.g., those obtained by modularization of a complex service). Depending on whether the service itself is adaptable, a classical RE methodology such as Tropos or KAOS can be applied. As the coordination mechanism selects individual services for fulfiling user requests, requirements on an individual service do not change with changes in service requests (inputs and/or outputs and constraints on these and quality parameters change with variation in requests).

Coordination RE takes services as self-contained functionality and focuses on the requirements for the coordination of services. In an AOSS, this typically involves the definition of the architecture to enable openness, service interaction, service selection, and service composition for providing more elaborate, composite services to fulfil user requests. As noted above, these requirements vary less frequently than those elicited as a result of Client RE.

Client RE assumes a coordination mechanism is defined and is guided by constraints to obey, and quality parameters to optimize (e.g., QoS, execution time, service reputation). This is the case after a service-oriented architecture is defined in combination with an algorithm for service composition (see, e.g., [7,8]). The aim at Client RE is to facilitate the specification of service requests at runtime. This involves, among other expressing constraints on desired outputs, quality criteria/parameters for evaluating the output and the way in which it is produced. This can be performed by traditional RE methodologies. In addition, Client RE ought to enable the definition of mechanisms for updating the service requests specification according to change in AOSS's behavior at runtime. The set of constraints and quality parameters is likely to vary as new services appear and other become unavailable. Quality parameter values will vary as well, as the system adapts to the availability of the various services and change in stakeholders' expectations.

3 Using DRAM at Client RE

We arrived above at the conclusion that there are two tasks to perform at Client RE: (a) specification of requirements that result in service requests, and (b) the definition of mechanisms for keeping these requirements current with behaviors of the AOSS and degrees of quality it can achieve over the various quality parameters defined in the requirements. We focus now on Client RE, assume the use of an established RE methodology for accomplishing (a), and introduce the

Dynamic Requirements Adaptation Method (DRAM) to perform (b). DRAM is thus not a standalone RE methodology—it does not indicate, e.g., how to elicit stakeholder expectations and convert these into precise requirements. Instead, DRAM integrates concepts and techniques for defining mappings between fragments of the requirements specification produced by an existing RE methodology and elements defining a service request (SReq). Mapping requirements onto SReqs aims to ensure that the stakeholders' expectations are translated into constraints and quality parameters understood by the AOSS. Mapping in the other direction—from SReqs onto requirements—allows the initial (also: static) requirements specification to be updated to reflect runtime changes in the system due to adaptability and openness. The specification obtained by applying DRAM on the initial, static requirements specification is referred to as the *dynamic requirements specification.*

Definition 1. ***Dynamic requirements specification*** *$\mathcal{S}$ is $\langle \mathsf{R}, \mathcal{R}, \mathcal{Q}, \mathcal{P}, \mathcal{U}, \mathcal{A} \rangle$, where: R is the* ***static requirements specification*** *(Def.2); $\mathcal{R}$ the set of* ***service requirements*** *(Def.3); $\mathcal{Q}$ the set of* ***quality parameters*** *(Def.4); $\mathcal{P}$ the* ***preferences specification*** *(Def.5); $\mathcal{U}$ the set of* ***update rules*** *(Def.6); and $\mathcal{A}$ the* ***argument repository*** *(Def.7).*

The aim with DRAM is to build the dynamic requirements specification. Members of R are specifications of nonfunctional and functional requirements, taking the form of, e.g., goals, softgoals, tasks, resources, agents, dependencies, scenarios, or other, depending on the RE methodology being used. Service requests submitted at runtime express these requirements in a format understandable to service composers in the AOSS. Nonfunctional requirements from R are mapped onto elements of $\mathcal{Q}$ and $\mathcal{P}$, whereas functional requirements from R onto service request constraints grouped in $\mathcal{R}$. As equivalence between fragments of R and $\mathcal{R}, \mathcal{Q}, \mathcal{P}$ can seldom be claimed, a less demanding binary relation is introduced: the *justified correspondence* "$\triangleq$" between two elements in $\mathcal{S}$ indicates that there is a *justification* for believing that the two elements correspond in the given AOSS, at least until a defeating argument is found which breaks the justification. In other words, the justified correspondence establishes a mapping between instances of concepts and relationships in the language in which members of R are written and the language in which members of $\mathcal{R}, \mathcal{Q}, \mathcal{P}$ are written. The preferences specification $\mathcal{P}$ contains information needed to manage conflict and subsequent negotiation over quality parameters that cannot be satisfied simultaneously to desired levels. Update rules serve to continually change the contents of R according to system changes at runtime. Finally, the argument repository $\mathcal{A}$ contains knowledge, arguments, and justifications used to construct justified correspondences and at other places in $\mathcal{S}$, as explained below.

$\mathcal{S}$ is continually updated to reflect change in how the service requests are fulfilled. Updates are performed with update rules: an update rule will automatically (or with limited human involvement) change the R according to the quality parameters, their values, and the constraints on inputs and outputs characterizing the services composed at runtime to satisfy service requests. An update rule can thus be understood as a mapping between fragments of R and those of

$\mathcal{R}, \mathcal{Q}, \mathcal{P}$. Consequently, an update rule is derived from a justified correspondence. It is according to the constraints on inputs/outputs and quality parameter values observed at runtime that fragments of requirements will be added or removed to R. Update rules work both ways, i.e., change in R is mapped onto service requests, and the properties of services participating in compositions are mapped onto fragments of R.

Building fully automatic update rules is difficult for it depends on the precision of the syntax and semantics of languages used at both ends, i.e., the specification language of the RE methodology which produces R and the specification language employed to specify input/output constraints on services and quality parameters. Due to a lack of agreement on precise conceptualizations of key RE concepts (e.g., [17]), DRAM makes no assumptions about the languages employed for writing R, $\mathcal{R}$, and $\mathcal{Q}$. Hence the assumption that languages at both ends are ill-defined, and the subsequent choice of establishing a "justified" correspondence (i.e., a defeasible relation) between specification fragments. An unfortunate consequence is that update rules in many cases cannot be established automatically—a repository of update rules is built during testing and at runtime. $\mathcal{S}$ integrates the necessary means for constructing update rules: to build justified correspondences between elements of R and $\mathcal{R}, \mathcal{Q}, \mathcal{P}$, arguments are built and placed in the argument repository $\mathcal{A}$. Update rules are automatically extracted from justified correspondences. As competing services will offer different sets of and values of quality parameters at service delivery, and as not all will be always available, trade-offs performed by the AOSS need to be appropriately mapped to R. Moreover, stakeholders may need to negotiate the quality parameters and their values. $\mathcal{P}$ performs the latter two roles. DRAM proceeds as follows in building the dynamic requirements specification (concepts and techniques referred to below are explained in the remainder).

Building the dynamic requirements specification with DRAM

1. Starting from the static requirements specification R (Def.2), select a fragment $r \in R$ of that specification that has not been converted into a fragment in $\mathcal{R}$ (Def.3), $\mathcal{Q}$ (Def.4), and/or $\mathcal{P}$ (Def.5).
2. Determine the service requirement and/or quality parameter information that can be extracted from r as follows:
   (a) If r is a functional requirement (i.e., it specifies a behavior to perform), focus is on building a justified correspondence (see, Def.6 and Technique 1) between r and elements of service requirements. Consider, e.g., the following requirement: Each user of TravelWeb expects a list of available flights for a destination to be shown within 5 seconds after submitting the departure and destination city and travel dates.

   $$available(depC, depD, arrC, arrD, flight) \wedge correctFormat(depC, depD, arrC, arrD) \Rightarrow \Diamond_{5s}\, shown(searchResults, flight)$$

   Starting from the above functional requirement:

   i. Identify the various pieces of data that are to be used (in the example: $depC, depD, arrC, arrD, flight$) and those that are to be produced ($searchResults$) according to the requirement.

ii. Find services that take the used data as input and give produced data at output (e.g., FlightSearch Serv, s.t. $\{depC, depD, arrC, arrD, flight\} \subseteq I \wedge searchResults \in O$).

iii. Determine whether the service requirements available on inputs justifiably corresponds to the conditions on input data in the requirement, and perform the same for output data (i.e., check if there is a justified correspondence between input/output service requirements and conditions in the relevant requirements in R—i.e., use Def.6 and Technique 1). If constraints do not correspond (justified correspondence does not apply), map the conditions from the requirement in R into constraints on inputs and/or outputs, and write them down as service requirements. If there is no single service that satisfies the requirement (i.e., step 2(a)i above fails), refine the requirement (i.e., brake it down into and replace with more detailed requirements)—to refine, apply techniques provided in the RE methodology.

iv. Use step 2b to identify the quality parameters and preferences related to the obtained service requirement.

(b) If r is a nonfunctional requirement (i.e., describes *how* some behavior is to be performed, e.g., by optimizing a criterion such as delay, security, safety, and so on), the following approach is useful:

i. Find quality parameters (Def.4) that describe the quality at which the inputs and outputs mentioned in a particular service requirement are being used and produced. In the example cited in the DRAM process, the delay between the moment input data is available and the moment it is displayed to the user can be associated to a quality parameter which measures the said time period.

ii. Following Def.4, identify the various descriptive elements for each quality parameter. Use R as a source for the name, target and threshold value, and relevant stakeholders. If, e.g., Tropos is employed to produce R, softgoals provide an indication for the definition of quality parameters.

iii. For each quality parameter that has been defined, specify priority and preferences. Initial preferences data for trade-offs comes from test runs.

3. Write down the obtained $r \in \mathcal{R}$, $q \in \mathcal{Q}$, and/or $p \in \mathcal{P}$ information, along with arguments and justifications used in mapping r into r and/or q. Each justified correspondence obtained by performing the step 2. above is written down as an update rule $u \in \mathcal{U}$.
4. Verify that the new arguments added to $\mathcal{A}$ do not defeat justifications already in $\mathcal{A}$; revise the old justifications if needed.

Definition 2. *The* ***static requirements specification*** *R is the high-level requirements specification obtained during RE before the system is in operation.*

R is obtained by applying a RE methodology, such as, e.g., KAOS [4] or Tropos [3]. The meaning of "high-level" in Def.2 varies accross RE methodologies: if a goal-oriented RE methodology is employed, R must contain the goals of the system down to the operational level, so that detailed behavioral specification in terms of, e.g., state machines, is not needed. If, e.g., KAOS is used, the engineer need not move further than the specification of goals and concerned objects, that is, can stop before operationalizing goals into constraints. If Tropos is used, the engineer stops before architectural design, having performed late requirements analysis and, ideally, formal specification of the functional goals.

Example 1. When a RE methodology with a specification language grounded temporal first-order logic is used[1], the following requirement r ∈ R for TravelWeb states that all options that a service may be offering to the user should be visible to the first time user:

$$\mathsf{1stOpt} \equiv (\mathit{hasOptions}(\mathit{servID}) \wedge \mathit{firstTimeUser}(\mathit{servID}, \mathit{userID}) \\ \Rightarrow \diamond_{1s}\, \mathit{showOptions}(\mathit{all}, \mathit{servID}, \mathit{userID}))$$

Definition 3. *A **service requirement** $r \in \mathcal{R}$ is a constraint on service inputs or outputs that appears in at least one service request and there is a unique* r ∈ R *such that there is a justified correspondence between it and* r*.*

Example 2. Any service that visualizes to the TravelWeb user the options that other services offer when booking obeys the following service requirement:

$$r = (\textbf{input:}\mathsf{servID} \notin \mathsf{userID.visited} \wedge \mathsf{servID.options} \neq \emptyset; \textbf{output:}\mathsf{thisService.show} = \mathsf{servID.options})$$

Definition 4. *A **quality parameter** $q \in \mathcal{Q}$ is a metric expressing constraints on how the system (is expected to) performs. $q = \langle$Name, Type, Target, Threshold, Current, Stakeholder$\rangle$, where Name is the unique name for the metric; Type indicates the type of the metric; Target gives a unique or a set of desired values for the variable; Threshold carries the worst acceptable values; Current contains the current value or average value over some period of system operation; and Stakeholder carries names of the stakeholders that agree on the various values given for the variable.*

Example 3. The following quality parameters can be defined on the service from Example 2:

$$q_1 = \langle \mathsf{ShowDelay, Ratio, 500ms, 1s, 780ms, MaintenanceTeam} \rangle$$
$$q_2 = \langle \mathsf{OptionsPerScreen, Ratio, \{3,4,5\}, 7, (all), UsabilityTeam} \rangle$$
$$q_3 = \langle \mathsf{OptionsSafety, Nominal, High, Med, Low, MaintenanceTeam} \rangle$$
$$q_4 = \langle \mathsf{BlockedOptions, Ratio, 0, (\geq 1), 0, MaintenanceTeam} \rangle$$

As quality parameters usually cannot be satisfied to the ideal extent simultaneously, the preference specification contains information on priority and positive or negative interaction relationships between quality parameters. Prioritization assists when negotiating trade-offs, while interactions indicate trade-off directions between parameters.

---

[1] Assuming, for simplicity, a linear discrete time structure, one evaluates the formula for a given history (i.e., sequence of global system states) and at a certain time point. The usual operators are used: for a history H and time points i, j, $(H, i) \models \circ\phi$ iff $(H, \mathit{next}(i)) \models \phi$; $(H, i) \models \diamond\phi$ iff $\exists j > i, (H, j) \models \phi$; $(H, i) \models \Box\phi$ iff $\forall j \geq i, (H, j) \models \phi$. Mirror operators for the past can be added in a straightforward manner. Operators for eventually $\diamond$ and always $\Box$ can be decorated with duration constraints, e.g., $\diamond_{\leq 5s}\phi$ indicates that ϕ is to hold some time in the future but not after 5 seconds. To avoid confusion, note that $\rightarrow$ stands for implication, while $\phi \Rightarrow \psi$ is equivalent to $\Box(\phi \rightarrow \psi)$. For further details, see, e.g., [16].

Definition 5. *The **preferences specification** is the tuple $\mathcal{P} = \langle \succ, \mathcal{P}^{\succ}, \mathcal{P}^{\pm} \rangle$. "$\succ$" is a priority relation over quality parameters. The set $\mathcal{P}^{\succ}$ contains partial priority orderings, specified as $(q_i \succ q_j, \textsf{Stakeholder}) \in \mathcal{P}^{\succ}$ where q_i carries higher priority than q_j, and* Stakeholder *contains the names of the stakeholders agreeing on the given preference relation. Higher priority indicates that a trade-off between the two quality parameters will favor the parameter with higher priority. The set $\mathcal{P}^{\pm}$ contains interactions. An interaction indicates that a given variation of the value of a quality parameter results in a variation of the value of another quality parameter. An interaction is denoted $(q_1 \overset{b_1 \Rightarrow b_2}{\longleftrightarrow} q_2)@\phi$. $q_1 \overset{b_1 \Rightarrow b_2}{\longleftrightarrow} q_2$ indicates that changing the value of the quality parameter q_1 by or to b_1 necessarily leads the value of the parameter q_2 to change for or to b_2. As the interaction may only apply when particular conditions hold, an optional non-empty condition ϕ can be added to indicate when the interaction applies. The condition is written in the same language as service requirements. When the relationship between the values of two quality parameters can be described with a function, we give that functional relationship instead of $b_1 \Rightarrow b_2$.*

Example 4. Starting from the quality parameters in Ex.3, the following is a fragment of the preferences specification:

$$p_1 = \left(\textsf{OptionsPerScreen} \overset{+1 \Rightarrow +60ms}{\longleftrightarrow} \textsf{ShowDelay}\right) @(\textsf{OptionsPerScreen} > 4)$$

p_1 indicates that increasing the number of options per screen by 1 increases the delay to show options to the user by 60ms, this only if the number of options to show is above 4.

Definition 6. *A **justified correspondence** exists between $\phi \in R$ and $\psi \in \mathcal{R} \cup \mathcal{Q} \cup \mathcal{P}$, i.e., $\phi \triangleq \psi$ iff there is a justification $\langle P, \phi \triangleq \psi \rangle$.*

Recall from the above that the justified correspondence is a form of mapping in which very few assumptions are made on the precision and formality of the languages being mapped. This entails the usual difficulties (as those encountered in ontology mapping, see, e.g., [9]) regarding conversion automation and the defeasibility of the constructed mappings, making DRAM somewhat elaborate to apply in its current form. Defeasibility does, however, carry the benefit of flexibility in building and revising mappings.

Definition 7. *A **justification** $\langle P, c \rangle$ is an argument that remains undefeated after the justification process.*[2]

[2] Some background [14]: Let A a set of agents (e.g., stakeholders) and the first-order language $\mathcal{L}$ defined as usual. Each agent $a \in A$ is associated to a set of first-order formulae K_a which represent knowledge taken at face value about the universe of discourse, and Δ_a which contains defeasible rules to represent knowledge which can be revised. Let $K \equiv \bigcup_{a \in A} K_a$, and $\Delta \equiv \bigcup_{a \in A} \Delta_a$. "$\mid\!\sim$" is called the *defeasible consequence* and is defined as follows. Define $\Phi = \{\phi_1, \ldots, \phi_n\}$ such that for any $\phi_i \in \Phi$, $\phi_i \in K \cup \Delta^{\downarrow}$. A formula ϕ is a defeasible consequence of Φ (i.e., $\Phi \mid\!\sim \phi$) if

Up to this point, the concepts needed in DRAM have been introduced. The remainder of this section describes the techniques in DRAM that use the given concepts in the aim of constructing the dynamic requirements specification.

Technique 1. The *justification process* [14] consists of recursively defining and labeling a *dialectical tree* $\mathcal{T}\langle P, c\rangle$ as follows:

1. A single node containing the argument $\langle P, c\rangle$ with no defeaters is by itself a dialectical tree for $\langle P, c\rangle$. This node is also the root of the tree.
2. Suppose that $\langle P_1, c_1\rangle, \ldots, \langle P_n, c_n\rangle$ each defeats[3] $\langle P, c\rangle$. Then the dialectical tree $\mathcal{T}\langle P, c\rangle$ for $\langle P, c\rangle$ is built by placing $\langle P, c\rangle$ at the root of the tree and by making this node the parent node of roots of dialectical trees rooted respectively in $\langle P_1, c_1\rangle, \ldots, \langle P_n, c_n\rangle$.
3. When the tree has been constructed to a satisfactory extent by recursive application of steps 1) and 2) above, label the leaves of the tree *undefeated* (U). For any inner node, label it undefeated if and only if every child of that node is a *defeated* (D) node. An inner node will be a defeated node if and only if it has at least one U node as a child. Do step 4 below after the entire dialectical tree is labeled.
4. $\langle P, c\rangle$ is a *justification* (or, P justifies c) iff the node $\langle P, c\rangle$ is labelled U.

Example 5. Fig.1 contains the dialectical tree for the justified correspondence $\mathsf{1stOpt} \triangleq r$, where r is from Ex.1 and r from Ex.2. To simplify the presentation of the example, we have used both formal and natural language in arguing. More importantly, notice that the correspondence $\mathsf{1stOpt} \triangleq r$ is unjustifed, as it is defeated by an undefeated argument containing information on a quality parameter and a fragment of the preferences specification. A justified correspondence such as, e.g., *firstTimeUser(servID, userID)* $\triangleq servID \notin userID.visited$, becomes an update rule, i.e., (*firstTimeUser(servID, userID)* $\triangleq servID \notin userID.visited) \in \mathcal{U}$. Having established that justified correspondence, the service requirement is taken to correspond to the given initial requirement until the justified correspondence is defeated. Elements of the argument repository correspond to the argument structure shown in Fig.1.

---

and only if there exists a sequence $B_1, \ldots, B_m$ such that $\phi = B_m$, and, for each $B_i \in \{B_1, \ldots, B_m\}$, either B_i is an axiom of $\mathcal{L}$, or B_i is in Φ, or B_i is a direct consequence of the preceding members of the sequence using modus ponens or instantiation of a universally quantified sentence. An argument $\langle P, c\rangle$ is a set of consistent premises P supporting a conclusion c. The language in which the premises and the conclusion are written is enriched with the binary relation $\hookrightarrow$. The relation $\hookrightarrow$ between formulae α and β is understood to express that "reasons to believe in the antecedent α provide reasons to believe in the consequent β". In short, $\alpha \hookrightarrow \beta$ reads "α is reason for β" (see, [14] for details). Formally then, P is an argument for c, denoted $\langle P, c\rangle$, iff: (1) $K \cup P \mathrel{|\!\sim} c$ (K and P derive c); (2) $K \cup P \not\mathrel{|\!\sim} \bot$ (K and P are consistent); and (3) $\nexists P' \subset P, K \cup P' \mathrel{|\!\sim} c$ (P is minimal for K).

[3] Roughly (for a precise definition, see [14]) the argument $\langle P_1, c_1\rangle$ *defeats at* c an argument $\langle P_2, c_2\rangle$ if the conclusion of a subargument $\langle P, c\rangle$ of $\langle P_2, c_2\rangle$ contradicts $\langle P_1, c_1\rangle$ and $\langle P_1, c_1\rangle$ is more specific (roughly, contains more information) than the subargument of $\langle P_2, c_2\rangle$.

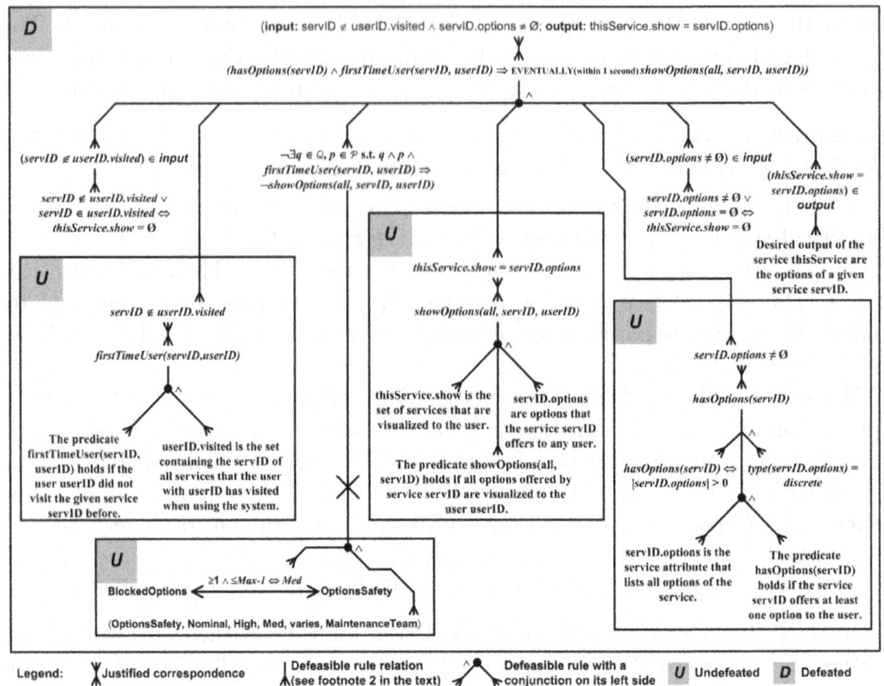

Fig. 1. Output of the justification process related to Examples 1 and 2

4 Related Work

Engineering requirements and subsequently addressing completeness concerns for AOSS has only recently started to receive attention in RE research. Berry and colleagues [1] argue in a note that, while much effort is being placed in enabling adaptive behavior, few have dealt with how to ensure correctness of software before, during, and after adaptation, that is, at the RE level. They recognize that RE for such systems is not limited to the initial steps of the system development process, but is likely to continue in some form over the entire lifecycle of the system. Zhang and Cheng [19] suggest a model-driven process for adaptive software; they represent programs as state machines and define adaptive behaviors usually encountered in adaptable systems as transitions between distinct state machines, each giving a different behavior to the system. Being situated more closely to the design phase of development than to RE, Zhang and Cheng's process has been related [2] to the KAOS RE methodology by using A-LTL instead of temporal logic employed usually in KAOS. In the extended KAOS, a requirement on adaptation behavior amounts to a goal refined into two sequentially ordered goals, whereby the first in the sequence specifies the conditions holding in the state of the system before adaptation while the second goal gives those to hold in the state after adaptation. This paper differs in terms of concerns being addressed and the response thereto. The suggested separation onto Service, Coordination, and Client RE for AOSS usefully delimits the concerns and focus when dealing with AOSS. The notion of dynamic requirements specification, along with the associated concepts and techniques is novel with regards to the cited research.

5 Conclusions and Future Work

This paper presents one approach to addressing the difficulties in the RE of AOSS. We argued that the RE of AOSS involves the specification of requirements that may vary at runtime. We consequently identified the most variable class of AOSS requirements and proposed DRAM, a method for specifying these within dynamic requirements specifications. The method has the benefit that it can be combined to any RE methodology. Its principal limitation at this time is the lack of automated means for defining or facilitating the definition of update rules. Automation of the DRAM process by reusing results in defeasible logic programming is the focus of current work.

References

1. Berry, D.M., Cheng, B.H., Zhang, J.: The four levels of requirements engineering for and in dynamic adaptive systems. In: REFSQ'05 (2005)
2. Brown, G., Cheng, B.H.C., Goldsby, H., Zhang, J.: Goal-oriented Specification of Adaptation Semantics in Adaptive Systems. In: SEAMS@ICSE'06 (2006)
3. Castro, J., Kolp, M., Mylopoulos, J.: Towards requirements-driven information systems engineering: the Tropos project. Info. Sys. 27(6) (2002)
4. Dardenne, A., van Lamsweerde, A., Fickas, S.: Goal-directed requirements acquisition. Sci. Comp. Progr. 20 (1993)
5. Jennings, N.R.: On Agent-Based Software Engineering. Artif. Int. 117 (2000)
6. Jureta, I.J., Faulkner, S., Schobbens, P.-Y.: Justifying Goal Models. In: RE'06 (2006)
7. Jureta, I.J., Faulkner, S., Achbany, Y., Saerens, M.: Dynamic Task Allocation within an Open Service-Oriented MAS Architecture. In: AAMAS'07 (2007) (to appear)
8. Jureta, I.J., Faulkner, S., Achbany, Y., Searens, M.: Dynamic Web Service Composition within a Service-Oriented Architecture. In: ICWS'07 (2007) (to appear)
9. Kalfoglou, Y., Schorlemmer, M.: Ontology Mapping: The State of the Art. In: Dagstuhl Seminar Proceedings (2005)
10. Kephart, J.O., Chess, D.M.: The vision of autonomic computing. Computer 36(1), 41–52 (2003)
11. Letier, E., van Lamsweerde, A.: Reasoning about partial goal satisfaction for requirements and design engineering. ACM Sigsoft Softw. Eng. Notes 29(6) (2004)
12. March, J.: Bounded Rationality, Ambiguity, and the Engineering of Choice. The Bell J. Econonomics 9(2) (1978)
13. Papazoglou, M.P., Georgakopoulos, D.: Service-Oriented Computing. Comm. ACM 46(10) (2003)
14. Simari, G.R., Loui, R.P.: A mathematical treatment of defeasible reasoning and its implementation. Artif. Int. 53 (1992)

15. Tennenhouse, D.: Proactive Computing. Comm. ACM 42(5) (2000)
16. van Lamsweerde, A., Letier, E.: Handling Obstacles in Goal-Oriented Requirements Engineering. IEEE Trans. Softw. Eng. 26(10) (2000)
17. van Lamsweerde, A.: Goal-Oriented Requirements Engineering: A Guided Tour. In: RE'01 (2001)
18. Zhang, J., Cheng, B.H.C.: Specifying adaptation semantics. In: Dehne, F., López-Ortiz, A., Sack, J.-R. (eds.) WADS 2005. LNCS, vol. 3608, Springer, Heidelberg (2005)
19. Zhang, J., Cheng, B.H.C.: Model-Based Development of Dynamically Adaptive Software. In: ICSE'06 (2006)

High Performance Approach for Multi-QoS Constrained Web Services Selection

Lei Li[1,2], Jun Wei[1], and Tao Huang[1,2]

[1]Institute of Software, Chinese Academy of Sciences, Beijing, China
[2]University of Science and Technology of China, Anhui Hefei, China
{lilei,wj,tao}@otcaix.iscas.ac.cn

Abstract. In general, multi-QoS constrained Web Services composition, with or without optimization, is a NP-complete problem on computational complexity that cannot be exactly solved in polynomial time. A lot of heuristics and approximation algorithms with polynomial- and pseudo-polynomial-time complexities have been designed to deal with this problem. However, they suffer from excessive computational complexities that cannot be used for service composition in runtime. In this paper, we propose a high performance approach for multi-QoS constrained Web Services selection. Firstly, a correlation model of candidate services are established in order to reduce the search space efficiently. Based on the correlation model, a heuristic algorithm is then proposed to find a feasible solution for multi-QoS constrained Web Services selection with high performance and high precision. The experimental results show that the proposed approach can achieve the expecting goal.

1 Introduction

With the integration of Web services as a business solution in many enterprise applications, the QoS presented by Web services is becoming the main concern of both service providers and consumers. Providers need to specify and guarantee the QoS in their Web services to remain competitive and achieve the highest possible revenue from their business. On the other hand, consumers expect to have a good service performance. A service composition system that can leverage, aggregate and make use of individual component's QoS information to derive the optimal QoS of the composite service is still an ongoing research problem.

Since many available Web Services provider overlapping or identical functionality, albeit with different QoS, a choice needs to be made to determine which services are to participate in a given composite service. In general, multi-QoS constrained Web Services selection, with or without optimization, is an NP-complete problem that cannot be exactly solved in polynomial time [1], [2]. Heuristics and approximation algorithms with polynomial- and pseudo-polynomial-time complexities are often used to deal with this problem. However, existing solutions suffer from excessive computational complexities, and cannot be used for dynamic service selection at runtime. The complexity of multi-QoS constrained Web Services selection problem is reflected by the following factors:

B. Krämer, K.-J. Lin, and P. Narasimhan (Eds.): ICSOC 2007, LNCS 4749, pp. 283–295, 2007.

(i) the huge number of the atomic candidate services that may be available to use; (ii) the large number of QoS constrained required by user; (iii) the different possibilities of composing an individual service into a service set which can satisfy the user's demand. The above difficulties make the problem very hard to solve.

In this paper, we propose a high performance approach for multi-QoS constrained Web Services composition. The correlations of all the candidate services are collected to construct a constrained model, which can reduce the search space efficiently. By using the constrained model, we propose a heuristic algorithm to find the feasible solution with high performance and high precision. We performed experiments to evaluate the validity and efficiency of the model in the final of the paper.

The remainder of the paper is organized as follows: Section 2 provides an overview of the related works. A service correlation model is then presented in Section 3. Section 4 proposes our algorithm and experimental results are shown in Section 5. Section 6 concludes the paper and introduces our future work.

2 Related Works

QoS support for Web services is among the hot topics attracting researchers from both academia and industry. Until recently, considerable efforts have been conducted to work on QoS for Web services. Multi-QoS constrained selection is a typical problem in many other research areas.

2.1 QoS Routing

QoS routing is very similar to multi-QoS constrained Web Services selection problem. In the last ten years, large numbers of studies have been proposed to address this issue. [3], [4], [5], [6] all present their approaches to solve this problem. In essential, the QoS routing problem is to create a feasible path from a given node to the destination so that the QoS requirements of the path are satisfied and the cost of the path is minimized. [5] proposes several optimal and heuristic algorithms for QoS partitioning, which assume that all nodes in the network have full topology and cost information, and then apply approximation algorithms to realize QoS partitioning. Though QoS routing is similar to multi-QoS constrained Web Services selection problem, there still remains tremendous distinction between the two. Compare to QoS routing multi-QoS constrained Web Services selection problem is based on the workflow model and the topology is immutable, consequently we only need to select a candidate service from each task node to keep user-defined constraints satisfied and make the QoS of the selected services optimal.

2.2 Multi-QoS Constrained Web Services Selection

QoS support in Web Services plays a great role for the success of this emerging technology. Essentially, the Multi-QoS Constrained Web Services Selection is an NP-complete problem that cannot be exactly solved in polynomial time. If the QoS attributes are all multiplicative or minimal attributes, the multi-QoS constrained services selection can be solved in polynomial time [8]. Hence, in order to simplify the problem, we only discuss the additive QoS attributes in this paper. Before analyzing,let's give a formal description of the problem.

Multi-QoS Constrained Web Services Selection(MCWS). For a composite service *CS*, its structure is specified as $CS \triangleq (N, E)$, where N is the set of task nodes and E is the set of edges. Each task node $n_i \in N$ has $|n_i|$ candidate services and each candidate services s_j has K additive attributes which value is denoted as w_k^j, $k \in [1,K]$. Given K constraints $\{c_k,\ k \in [1,K]\}$, the problem is to select one service from each task node and aggregate all the selected services to form a specific service set S, *c(S)* is a cost function about S, S should satisfy the following two constraints:
(i) $w_k^S \leq c_k, w_k^S = \sum_{s_i \in S} w_k^i, k \in [1, K]$
(ii) $\forall\ S'$, $c(S) \leq c(S')$, S' is also a selected service set

The above problem is known with NP-complete computational complexity. In [7], [8], the authors propose a quality driven approach to select component services during execution of a composite service. They consider multiple QoS attributes such as price, duration, reliability, take into account of global constraints, and use the integer linear programming method to solve the service selection problem, which is too complex for run time decisions. [1] defines the problem as a multi-dimension multi-choice 0-1 knapsack problem or the multi-constraint optimal path problem. [2] describes an approach for QoS-aware service composition, based on composition of the QoS attributes of the component services and on genetic algorithms. Similar to [2], [9] uses genetic algorithms to determine a set of concrete services to be bound to abstract services contained in a orchestration to meet a set of constraints and to optimize a fitness criterion on QoS attributes. Compared with linear Integer Programming, GA can deal with QoS attributes with non-linear aggregation functions. [10] proposes an approach to trigger and perform composite service replanning during execution.

These studies can solve the Multi-QoS Constrained Web Services Selection problem; however, they suffer from excessive computational complexities, which make these solutions infeasible in many scenarios. Moreover, most of these studies assume that the same service interface definition is used by all atomic service candidates for a specific service component, i.e. these studies are not concerned about the compatibility issue among services. However, whether services are compatible is a major issue in the automatic composition of Web Services.

3 Service Correlation Model

A variety of approaches have been proposed to solve multi-QoS constrained service selection problem. As we mentioned, whether services are compatible is a major issue in the automatic composition of Web Services. Because incompatibility can lead to some collaboration mistakes, if the selected services are not compatible to each other, the service set can not be a feasible solution even though its overall QoS value is optimal. Moreover, the correlation of services is very useful in the search space reduction. Therefore, the correlation of services is very useful to improve the precision and performance of the selected services. In this section, we will describe our service correlation model and illuminate how to use it to reduce the search space.

3.1 Analysis of Correlations

There are lots of researches focusing on analysis of compatibility of Web Services interface [11], [12], seldom considering the multifaceted service correlation, which may lead to mistake in some situations. For example, s_i is a service to book a ticket. s_n and s_m are Visa and Master credit card payment services respectively. Service s_i can only be paid by Master, i.e. s_i is mutually exclusive to s_n. Our approach is to specify not only the interface compatibility but also more relations between services, and utilize these relations to reduce the search space.

Borrowing from some temporal operators defined in [13], we define that operator $X(s)$ outputs the service set next to s, operator $F(s)$ outputs the service set following s in the future. The operator $comp(x, y)$ means x and y are interface compatible.

Definition 1 (Sequence Relation). If $s_j \in X(s_i)$, then s_i and s_j have the sequence relation, $seq(s_i, s_j)$.
Definition 2 (Fork Relation). If $(s_j \notin F(s_i)) \vee (s_i \notin F(s_j))$, then s_i and s_j have the fork relation, $Fork(s_i, s_j)$.
Definition 3 (Adjoined Compatibility Relation). If $seq(s_i, s_j) \wedge comp(s_i, s_j)$, then s_i and s_j have the adjoined compatibility relation, $adj\_comp(s_i, s_j)$.
Definition 4 (Mutually Exclusion Relation). If s_i has been executed, s_j should never be executed and vice verse, then s_i and s_j have the mutually exclusion relation, $MuExcl(s_i, s_j)$.

The above correlation between services must be analyzed before selecting the composite services, because these analyses can help program to avoid choosing some incompatible services. Moreover, these analyses can help program to accelerate the selection. There are also many other correlations, however in this paper we do not enumerate them all.

3.2 Service Correlation Model

Definition 5 (Incompatible Service set, ISS). Each service s_i has an incompatible service set $S_i^{\varnothing}$, which means if the service s_i has been selected, then any service in $S_i^{\varnothing}$ should not be selected at the same time. How to construct the incompatible service set will be described below.

R1: If $s_j \in X(s_i) \wedge \neg adj\_comp(s_i, s_j)$ then $S_i^{\varnothing} \leftarrow S_i^{\varnothing} \cup \{s_j\}$

Rule 1 means if s_j is the next service executed after s_i and s_i is incompatible with s_j, then s_j will be included in $S_i^{\varnothing}$.

R2: If $s_j \in F(s_i) \wedge MuExcl(s_i, s_j)$ then $S_i^{\varnothing} \leftarrow S_i^{\varnothing} \cup \{s_j\}$

Rule 2 means if s_j will be executed after s_i and s_j is mutually exclusive to s_i, then s_j will be included in $S_i^{\varnothing}$.

R3: If $Fork(s_i, s_j)$ then $S_i^{\varnothing} \leftarrow S_i^{\varnothing} \cup \{s_j\}$

Rule 3 means if s_i and s_j have fork relation, then s_j will be included in $S_i^{\varnothing}$.

Rules 1-3 are backward compatible, which guarantee the service s_j executed after s_i should be compatible to s_i. Using rules 1-3, we can construct an incompatible service set of s_i.

Assuming algorithm is considering selecting a candidate service from the task node n_j. Let $S^{\varnothing}$ be the incompatible services found in selecting round, i.e. $S^{\varnothing} = \bigcup_{1 \leq i < j} S_i^{\varnothing}$. Obviously if $|S^{\varnothing}| = 0$, then every service is available to be selected. We can create the overall incompatible service set by the following rules. Assuming S_{n_i} is the service set bound to task node n_i.

R4: $\forall s \in S_{n_i}$, If $s \in S^{\varnothing}$, then set s_j as the unavailable service.

Rule 4 means that a service is unavailable service when it is in the incompatible service set.

R5: If $((\forall s \in S_{n_i}) \rightarrow (s \in S^{\varnothing}))$, then no available service can be selected.

Rule 5 means if all the services belong to task node n_i are in $S^{\varnothing}$, then the selecting program will terminate the searching of current round and begin a new round searching.

The incompatible service set $S^{\varnothing}$can be created within $O(\sum_{1 \leq i < j} |n_i|)$ time . $S^{\varnothing}$ can help algorithm to reduce the search space efficiently and in the next subsection, we will analyze the efficiency of the correlation model. The efficiency of this model is determined by the size of incompatible service set, i.e. the bigger the size of incompatible service set, the more space reduction we can get.

4 The Proposed Algorithm

In this section, we present our proposed algorithm H_MCWS, which attempts to find a feasible service set subject to K additive user's constraints and minimize the cost of that service set.

4.1 Theoretical Foundation

First, we design a nonlinear cost function to evaluate the QoS value of the selected service set. The same nonlinear cost function was also used in [3] and [14] to develop algorithm for the Multiple Constrained Path problem. Assuming S is the selected service set. Consider the following cost function for S.

$$g_\lambda(S) = \left(\frac{w_1^S}{c_1}\right)^\lambda + \left(\frac{w_2^S}{c_2}\right)^\lambda + ... + \left(\frac{w_K^S}{c_K}\right)^\lambda, \ where \ \ \lambda \geq 1 \qquad (1).$$

From the cost function, we can get the following theorems. (Other characteristics of the nonlinear function can be found in [3])

Theorem 1: If λ=1, the minimal $g_1 S$ can be found in polynomial time.

Proof: When λ=1, then the cost function is $g_1(s) = (\frac{w_1^S}{c_1}) + (\frac{w_2^S}{c_2}) + ... + (\frac{w_K^S}{c_K})$. Hence, we only need to select a service with the minimal cost from each node. Therefore, the complexity is $\sum_{n_i \in N} |n_i|$, *i.e.* $O(|S|)$. □

Theorem 2: When λ is close to ∞, it is guaranteed to find a feasible service set if one exists.

Proof: Let S be a service set that minimizes the cost function $g_{\lambda \to \infty}$. Assuming there is a feasible service set S_*. Therefore, $g_{\lambda \to \infty}(S) \leq g_{\lambda \to \infty}(S_*)$. If S is not a feasible service set, then $\exists k \in [1, K]$, $w_k^S > c_k$. When $\lambda \to \infty$, $g_{\lambda \to \infty}(S)$ is dominated by the largest term. Hence, $g_{\lambda \to \infty}(S) \to \infty$ and $g_{\lambda \to \infty}(S_*) \to 0$, i.e. $g_{\lambda \to \infty}(S) > g_{\lambda \to \infty}(S_*)$. Since this contradicts, we must have $w_k^S \leq c_k$ for each k. Therefore, S is a feasible service set. □

When we set λ=1, the algorithm can find the minimal cost in polynomial time. But unfortunately, the selected service set may not be the feasible service set. Theorem 2 can guarantee to find a feasible service set when $\lambda \to \infty$. But unfortunately, when $\lambda \geq 2$, it is impossible to provide an exact polynomial time algorithm. So, a heuristic algorithm must be proposed to solve this problem.

4.2 Proposed Algorithm

In this section, we present our algorithm H_MCWS, which attempts to find a feasible service set which satisfies all the users' constraints and simultaneously minimize the cost of that service set. H_MCWS is similar to the H_MCOP [3]. The differences of them are that H_MCWS is used to select the composite services and faster than H_MCOP. First, H_MCWS traverses all the services to eliminate the service which does not satisfy the multiplicative attributes and minimal attributes and create incompatible service set for each candidate service. This traversing process will be completed with $O(|S|)$ complexity. Second, the algorithm first finds the best service set with g_1. If the service set satisfies all the constraints, it is exactly the result and will be returned to user. Otherwise, H_MCWS finds the best temporary service set from each task node n_u to n_t. It then starts from task node n_s and discovers each task node n_u based on the minimization of $g_\lambda(S)$, where the service set S is from task node n_s to n_t and passing through task node n_u. S is determined at task node n_u by concatenating the already traveled segment from task node n_s to n_u and the estimated remaining segment from task node n_u to n_t. A pseudo code of H_MCWS is shown below. n_s represents the start task node, n_t represents the end task node and n_u represents the middle task node.

H_MCWS Algorithm

1. Deal_non_additive_Attributes(N)
2. Create_ISS_Set(N)
3. Reverse_Relax(N,n_t)
4. if $\forall s_i \in S_{n_s}$, t[s_i] $>K$, then return error
5. Look_Ahead(N)
6. if $\exists s_i \in S_{n_t}, G_k[s_i] \leq c_k, k \in [1, K], then\ return\ this\ services\ set$
7. return error

The algorithm uses the following notations. $t[n_u]/t[s_i]$ represent the minimal cost of the selected services from task node n_u/service s_i to n_u. Notation $R_k[n_u]$, $k{\in}[1,K]$ represents the individually accumulated link weights along the above selected services. Notation $g[n_u]$ represents the cost of a foreseen complete service set that goes from task node n_s to n_t. Notation $G_k[n_u]$, $k{\in}[1,K]$ represents the individually accumulated cost of services weights from task node n_s to n_u. $c[n_u]$ represents the cost along the already selected segment of this service set from task node n_s to n_u. Deal_non_additive_Attributes(N algorithm is used to handle the non-additive QoS attributes and Create_ISS_Set(N) algorithm is used to create the incompatible service set for each candidate services. There are two directions in H_MCWS: backward to estimate the cost of the remaining segment using λ=1 and forward to find the most promising service set in terms of feasibility and optimality using λ >1. The backward algorithm and forward algorithm are shown in Reverse_Relax algorithm and Look_Ahead algorithm respectively.

Reverse_Relax(n_u, n_v) Algorithm

1. t[n_u]=t[n_v]+$min_{1\leq i\leq |n_u|}\{\sum_{1\leq k\leq K} \frac{w_k^i}{c_k}\}$
2. t[s_i]=t[n_v]+c[s_i] (for i=1 to $|\ n_u\ |, s_i \in n_u$)
3. $R_k[n_u]$=$R_k[n_v]$+$min_{1\leq i\leq |n_u|}\{w_k^i\}$ (for k=1 to K)
4. $R_k[s_i]$=$R_k[n_v]$+w_k^i (for k=1 to K)

Look_Ahead(n_u) Algorithm

1. for each service $s_i \in n_u$ begin
2. if$s_i \in S^{\varnothing}$ then continue
3. if$\lambda < \infty$ then $g[s_i] = max\{\frac{G_k[\pi_p[n_u]]+w_k^i+\pi_s[n_u]}{c_k},\ k \in [1, K]\}$
4. $G_k[s_i] = G_k[\pi_p[n_u]] + w_k^i$ (for k=1 to K)
5. $R_k[s_i]$=$R_k[\pi_s[n_u]]$+w_k^i (for k=1 to K)
6. $s_b = Choosing\_Best\_Service(n_u)$
7. $c[n_u] = c[\pi_p[n_u]] + c[s_b]$
8. end

In the backward direction, the Reverse_Relax algorithm finds the optimal service set from every task node n_u to n_t using λ. The complexity of the backward direction is $O(|\ S\ |)$. $\pi_p[n_u]$ and $\pi_s[n_u]$ represent the predecessor and successor of task node n_u respectively. Look_Ahead algorithm is executed in the forward direction. This procedure uses the information provided by the Reverse_Relax algorithm. Look_Ahead algorithm explores the whole workflow by choosing the next services in specific task nodes based on the rule below.

Choosing_Best_Service(n_u) Algorithm

---

1. Let s_v be a virtual service in n_u
2. c[s_v]=∞, $G_k[s_v] = \infty$, $R_k[s_v] = \infty$
3. for each service $s_i \in n_u$ begin
4.   if $(c[s_i] < c[s_v]) \& (\forall k(G_k[s_i] + R_k[s_i]) \leq c_k), then$
5. $s_v = s_i, c[s_v] > c[s_i], G_k[s_v] = G_k[s_i], R_k[s_v] = R_k[s_i]$
6.   else if $(c[s_i] > c[s_v]) \& (\forall k(G_k[s_v] + R_k[s_v]) \leq c_k), then\ continue$
7.   else if $g[s_i] < g[s_v]$ *then*
8. $s_v = s_i, c[s_v] = c[s_i], G_k[s_v] = G_k[s_i], R_k[s_v] = R_k[s_i]$
9. end
10. return s_v

The above preference rule can choose the best service from the specific task node n_u. In the end, H_MCWS returns a service set using $\lambda > 1$. As λ increases, the likelihood of finding a feasible service set also increases. When λ is close to ∞, H_MCWS can guarantee to find a feasible service set if one exists.
Lemma 1: If there are one additive QoS attributes, we can find k-minimal cost services set with the complexity $O(k| S |)$.

Proof: If there are only one additive QoS attributes, we can get the best candidate services from each node by $| n_i |$ comparisons. So, we can find the best services set within $\sum_{1 \leq i \leq |N|} | n_i |$ comparisons, i.e. $O(|S|)$. Let w(s) represent the additive QoS value of service s. Assuming s_i is the selected service from task node n_i, $s_i \in S$ and $s_i^{'}$ represent the service with the second minimal QoS value, i.e. if $(\forall s_i^*, s_i^* \neq s_i)$, then $w(s_i^*) \geq w(s_i^{'})$. Assuming $s_j^{'}$ satisfies the following rule: if $\forall s_i, s_i^{'} \in n_i$, then $(w(s_i^{'}) - w(s_i)) \geq (w(s_j^{'}) - w(s_j))$. Let $S^{'} = S - \{s_j\} \cup \{s_j^{'}\}$, then $S^{'}$ is the second minimal cost services set. Finding the specific service $s_j^{'}$ needs $O(|S|)$ times comparisons at the worst case. Hence, we can find 2 minimal cost services set with the complexity $O(2|S|)$. According to the same procedure, we can find k-minimal cost services set with the complexity $O(k| S |)$. □

Theorem 3: The MCWS problem can be solved by H_MCWS algorithm in time $O((k+1)|S|)$.

Proof: The algorithm can be executed within . Similar to H_MCOP, the forward direction of H_MCWS can also be used with the k-shortest algorithm (in MCWS problem, the algorithm is k-minimal cost service set algorithm). As we proved in lemma 1, it needs time to find k-minimal cost service set. Hence, the overall complexity of H_MCWS algorithm is $O((k+1)| S |)$. □

Although H_MCWS is similar to H_MCOP, it is more efficient to solve the MCWS problem. Theorem 3 did not consider the influence of the correlation of services. In real practice, H_MCWS can get more performance improvement.

5 Experiments and Evaluation

In this section, we investigate the performance of H_MCWS algorithm and compare it to the most promising algorithms selected from the ones surveyed in section 2. The simulations environments are: Pentium IV 2.8G CPU, 1024M RAM, and the operation system is Windows XP SP2. In our study, two important aspects are considered, one is computation time and the other is the excellence in approximating the optimal solution.

5.1 Comparison of H_MCWS with H_MCOP

To study the performance of H_MCWS, we randomly create a composite services structure with 20 task nodes and each node has several candidate services. We analyze the impact of i) varying the number of constraints; (ii) varying the number of candidate services. In these test groups, we did not consider the influence of the correlation of services.

(i) Analysis the impact of the number of constraints

In this test case, we generate 30 candidate services for each task node, and we set the number of additive constraints from 2 to 10 and use $\lambda = 20$.

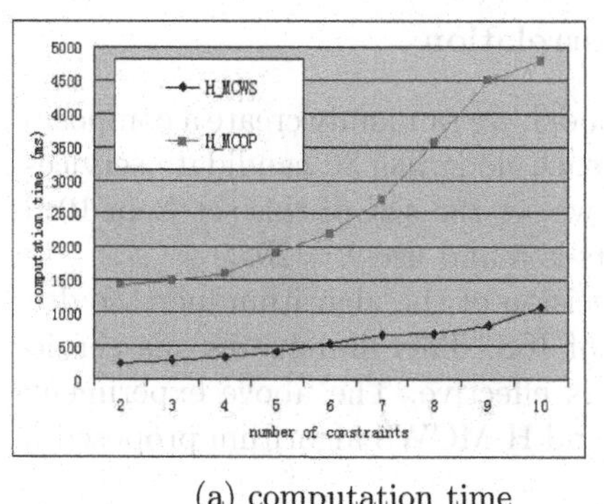

(a) computation time

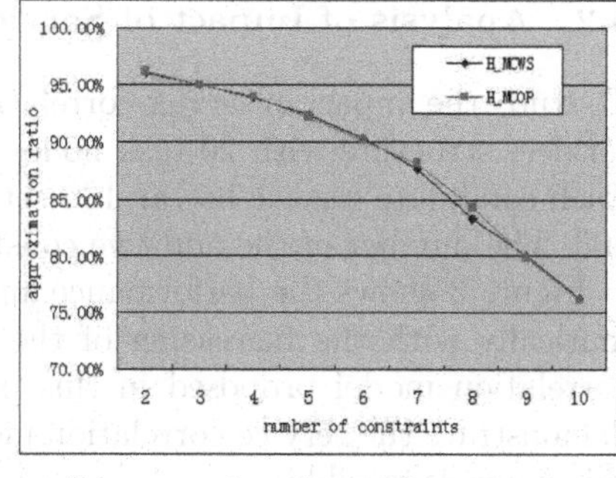

(b) approximation ratio

Fig. 1. Impact of the Number of Constraints

From Figure 1(a) we can find that H_MCWS performs much better than H_MCOP. Figure 1(b) demonstrates the probabilities of finding optimal service set for the two algorithms with the different number of constraints. This experiment results show H_MCWS achieves higher performance while keeping approximately the same precision comparing to H_MCOP.

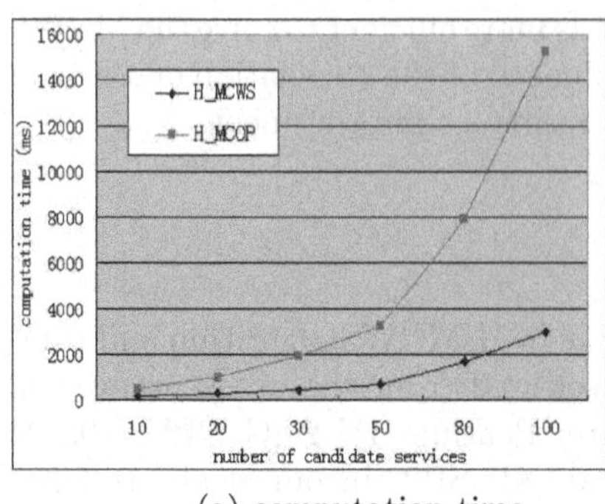

(a) computation time

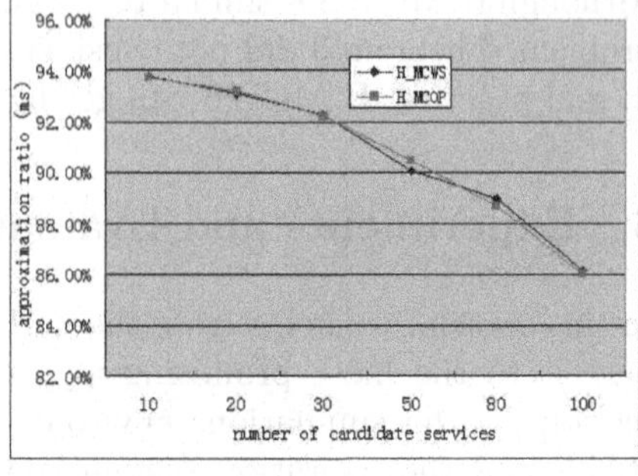

(b) approximation ratio

Fig. 2. Impact of the number of candidate services

(ii) Analysis of the impact of the number of candidate services

In this test case, we generate [10, 100] candidate services for each task node. The number of the additive constraints is 5 and use $\lambda = 20$.

Figure 2 depicts that with the increase of the number of candidate services, the precision and performance of the algorithm drop slightly. For H_MCOP algorithm, the complexity is $O(n\log(n)+km\log(kn)+(k^2+1)m)$, where n represents the number of task nodes and m is the number of links. In MCWS problem, the $m = \prod_{1\leq i\leq |N|} \mid n_i \mid$, which is a very huge number. For example, if there are 20 task nodes and each node has 20 candidate services, then m=20^{20}. Therefore, H_MCOP is not suitable to solve this problem directly.

5.2 Analysis of Impact of Service Correlation

To study the impact of service correlation model, we randomly create a composite services structure with 20 task nodes and each node has 30 candidate services. Each candidate service has an ISS set and we set the size of this set from 10 to 100. The number of the additive constraints is 5 and use $\lambda = 20$.

Figure 3 shows the performance and precision of the algorithm increase dramatically with the increasing of the size of ISS. This illuminates the service correlation model proposed in this paper is effective. The above experiments demonstrate the service correlation model and H_MCWS algorithm proposed in this paper is feasible.

5.3 Evaluation and Comparison

In this subsection, we analyze and compare four different algorithms: Integer Programming in [7], WS_HEU in [15], Genetic Algorithm in [9] and our approach H_MCWS. Figure 4 presents the comparison results.

From Figure 4, we can see that four different algorithm have the different properties and are suitable to the different scenarios. Integer programming is one

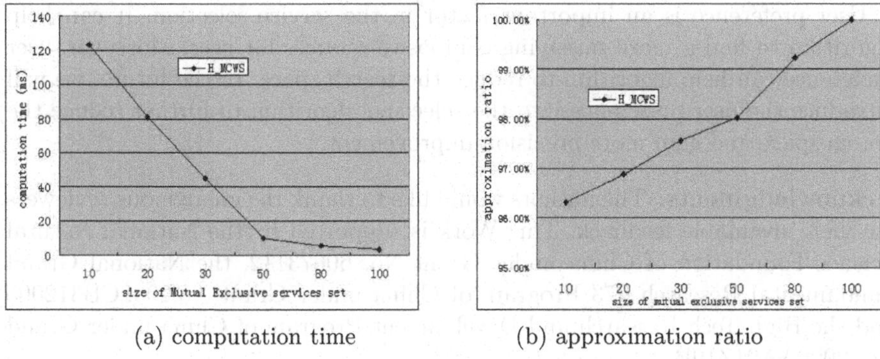

(a) computation time (b) approximation ratio

Fig. 3. Impact of the service correlation

	IP	WS_HEU	GA	H_MCWS
Running Time	very slow	fast	slow	fast
Optimality	optimal	near-optimal	near-optimal	near-optimal
Complexity	—	$O(N^2(l-1)^2 m)$	—	$O((k+1)\|S\|)$
Algorithm Usage	very small size problem	no limitations	small size problem	no limitations

Fig. 4. Comparison of Algorithms

of the most adopted tools to solve a QoS-aware composition problem. Integer programming can find the optimal solution, but unfortunately the running time is very slow which makes it only can be used in very small size problem. Genetic algorithm can represent a more scalable choice and are more suitable to handle generic QoS attributes. However, the genome size of GA is bound to the number of services, which makes GA slow when the number of candidate services is large. WS_HEU and H_MCWS have no limitations and can be used in every situation. H_MCWS consider the correlation of service and use it to reduce the search space. Hence, although it is near-optimal, it performs very well in practice.

6 Conclusions and Future Work

Web Services selection subject to multi-QoS constraints is an NP-complete problem. Previously proposed algorithms suffer from excessive computational complexities and are not concerned about the compatibility issue among services, which makes that these approaches can not be used in many applications. In this paper, we proposed an efficient approach for Web Services selection with multi-QoS constraints. The complexity of the algorithm is lower and the simulation results show the algorithm can find the feasible solution with high performance and high precision. We believe the proposed models and algorithms provide a useful engineering solution to multi-constrained Web Services selection problem.

User preference is an important factor in the service selection. It can help algorithm to find a more satisfying composite services for user. Moreover, user preference can help algorithm to reduce the search space. In the future, we will introduce the user preference into the selecting algorithm to further reduce the search space and gain more precision improvement.

Acknowledgments. The authors would like to thank the anonymous reviewers for their invaluable feedback. This Work is supported by the National Natural Science Foundation of China under Grant No. 60673112, the National Grand Fundamental Research 973 Program of China under Grant No.2002CB312005 and the High-Tech Research and Development Program of China under Grand No. 2006AA01Z19B.

References

1. Yu, T., Lin, K.-J.: Service Selection Algorithms for Composing Complex Services with Multiple QoS Constraints. In: Benatallah, B., Casati, F., Traverso, P. (eds.) ICSOC 2005. LNCS, vol. 3826, pp. 130–143. Springer, Heidelberg (2005)
2. Canfora, G., Di Penta, M., Esposito, R., Villani, M.L.: A lightweight approach for QoS-aware service composition. In: ICSOC (2004)
3. Korkmaz, T., Krunz, M.: Multi-Constrained Optimal Path Selection. In: INFOCOM 2001. Proceeding of 20th Joint Conf. IEEE Computer and Communications, pp. 834–843 (2001)
4. Wang, B., Hou, J.: Multicast routing and its QoS extension: Problems, algorithms, and Protocols. IEEE Network 14(1), 22–36 (2000)
5. Vogel, R., et al.: QoS-based routing of multimedia streams in computer networks. IEEE Journal on Selected Areas in Communications 14(7), 1235–1244 (1996)
6. Lorenz, D.H., Orda, A., Raz, D., Shavitt, Y.: Efficient QoS partition and routing of unicast and multicast. In: Proc. IEEE/IFIP IWQoS, pp. 75–83 (2000)
7. Zeng, L., Benatallah, B., Dumas, M., Kalagnanam, J., Sheng, Q.Z.: Quality driven web services composition. In: WWW. Proc. 12th Int'l Conf. World Wide Web (2003)
8. Liang-Zhao, Z., Boualem, B., et al.: QoS-aware middleware for web services composition. IEEE Transactions on Software Engineering 30(5), 311–327 (2004)
9. Canfora, G., Di Penta, M., Esposito, R., et al.: An Approach for QoS-aware Service Composition based on Genetic Algorithms. In: GECCO'05 (2005)
10. Liu, Y., Ngu, A.H., Zeng, L.: QoS computation and policing in dynamic web service selection. In: WWW. Proceedings of the 13th International Conference on World Wide Web, pp. 66–73. ACM Press, New York (2004)
11. Megjahed, B., Bouguettaya, A., Elmagarmid, A.K.: Composing Web Services on the semantic Web. The VLDB Journal (2003)
12. Lamparter, S., Ankolekar, A., Grimm, S.: Preference-based Selection of Highly Configurable Web Services. In: WWW. Proceedings of International Conference on World Wide Web (2007)
13. Huth, M., Ryan, M.: Logic in Computer Science: Modeling and Reasoning about Systems, 2nd edn. Cambridge University Press, Cambridge (2004)
14. De Neve, H., Van Mieghem, P.: A multiple quality of service routing algorithm for PNNI. In: Proceedings of the ATM Workshop, pp. 324–328. IEEE Press, Los Alamitos (1998)
15. Yu, T., Zhang, Y., Lin, K.-J.: Efficient Algorithms for Web Services Selection with End-to-End QoS Constraints. ACM Transaction on Web (May 2007)

Negotiation of Service Level Agreements: An Architecture and a Search-Based Approach

Elisabetta Di Nitto[1], Massimiliano Di Penta[2], Alessio Gambi[1], Gianluca Ripa[1], and Maria Luisa Villani[2]

[1] CEFRIEL - Politecnico di Milano
Via Fucini, 2 20133 Milano
[2] RCOST - Research Centre on Software Technology
University of Sannio – Palazzo ex Poste, Via Traiano 82100 Benevento, Italy
dinitto@elet.polimi.it, dipenta@unisannio.it, alessiogambi@gmail.com, ripa@cefriel.it, villani@unisannio.it

Abstract. Software systems built by composing existing services are more and more capturing the interest of researchers and practitioners. The envisaged long term scenario is that services, offered by some competing providers, are chosen by some consumers and used for their own purpose, possibly, in conjunction with other services. In the case the consumer is not anymore satisfied by the performance of some service, he can try to replace it with some other service. This implies the creation of a global market of services and poses new requirements concerning validation of exploited services, security of transactions engaged with services, trustworthiness, creation and negotiation of Service Level Agreements with these services. In this paper we focus on the last aspect and present our approach for negotiation of Service Level Agreements. Our architecture supports the actuation of various negotiation processes and offers a search-based algorithm to assist the negotiating parts in the achievement of an agreement.

Keywords: Quality of Service, Service Level Agreements, Negotiation, Optimization Heuristics.

1 Introduction

Software systems built by composing existing services are more and more capturing the interest of researchers and practitioners. The envisaged long term scenario is that services, offered by some competing providers, are chosen by some consumers and used for their own purpose, possibly, in conjunction with other services. If the consumer is not anymore satisfied by the performance of some service, s/he can try to replace it with some other service. This implies the creation of a global market of services and poses new requirements concerning validation of exploited services, security of transactions engaged with services, trustworthiness, creation and negotiation of Service Level Agreements (SLAs).

This paper focuses on SLA negotiation. While this issue has been deeply studied within the domain of e-commerce, there are not many approaches that

B. Krämer, K.-J. Lin, and P. Narasimhan (Eds.): ICSOC 2007, LNCS 4749, pp. 295–306, 2007.

focus specifically on the domain of services. In such a context, the subject of the negotiation is the definition of so called SLAs, that is, more or less formal contracts that discipline the way services are provided to consumers and, in turn, the obligations to be fulfilled by the consumer in order to obtain the service. Such SLAs can either be negotiated on a per service usage basis, or they can have a longer term validity. This last one is actually the most common situation, but the other should be possible as well, even if to be effective it requires a fast execution of negotiation.

Negotiation can either be performed directly by the interested stakeholders or it can be automatic. In this second case, human beings are replaced by automated negotiators that try to achieve the objective that has been suggested to them. Automated negotiation is particularly important when the consumer of a service is a software systems that has to negotiate on the fly (part) of the SLA with the service. In the following we present our approach for negotiation of SLAs. Our architecture supports the actuation of various negotiation processes (one to one negotiations, auctions, many-to-many negotiations) and offers an efficient search-based algorithm to assist the negotiating parts in the achievement of an agreement.

The paper is structured as follows. Section 2 provides some definitions that will be used through the rest of the paper. Section 3 presents an overview of the architecture of our system. Section 4 focuses on the negotiation search-based approach while Section 5 presents some preliminary simulation results that show the advantages of this approach. Finally, Section 6 provides a comparison with the related literature and Section 7 draws the conclusions.

2 Definitions

According to Jennings *et al.* [6], a negotiation can be defined as: *"the process by which a group of agents come to a mutually acceptable agreement on some matter"*. We argue that a negotiation process requires the following key elements:

1. *The negotiation objectives*, i.e., the set of parameters over which an agreement must be reached. These can include the price of the service usage, its availability, the nature of the operations the service will make available, etc.
2. *The negotiation workflow*, i.e., the set of steps that constitute the negotiation; they depend on the kind of negotiation that is actually executed (bilateral bargaining, auctions, reverse auctions, etc).
3. *The negotiation protocol*, i.e., the set of conditions that indicate the validity of all information concerning the negotiation and provided by the negotiation participants. For instance, if the adopted negotiation process is an English auction, the negotiation protocol will define as acceptable only those offers that improve the values associated to the negotiation objectives.
4. *The agent decision model*, i.e., the decision making apparatus the participants employ to act in line with the negotiation protocol in order to achieve their objectives. For example, this can be based on (i) the acceptable ranges for the negotiation parameters (definition of sub-domains); (ii) functions to

evaluate the offers; (iii) the goal to pursue, e.g., maximize one ore more utility functions; and (iv) a strategy to pursue that goal, that is, the algorithm to decide the moves, in reply to the move by some other participant.

The agents may use both a *cooperative* or *competitive* approach to come to an agreement. This is determined by the kind of the interdependence of the respective interests [5] and has an impact on the process they follow to come to an agreement.

In a Service Oriented Architecture (SOA) context, the negotiation participants are essentially service providers and service consumers, although an overparts mediator could be included to provide conciliation mechanisms or help setting up cooperative strategies. In automated negotiations, (part of) these participants are replaced by software agents that act on behalf of them.

Negotiation objectives, workflow, protocol, and decision models depend on the multiplicity of the participating agents:

- **1-1:** it is the most known approach and requires that a consumer bargains with a provider for the definition of the SLA of the specific service;
- **1-N:** a consumer bargains with a set of providers. These providers can either compete among each other to reach the agreement with the consumer (this approach is applicable when the consumer needs to obtain a binding to a single service) or they can cooperate to share the service provisioning, e.g., for example, split the service availability interval.
- **M-1:** several consumers bargain with a single provider. Consumers in this case can either compete to acquire an SLA with the provider (in an auction style) or they can obtain a single SLA with the provider to share its resources (e.g., the bandwidth).
- **M-N:** combining the previous two multi-party negotiation types, at one side, service providers could cooperate to reach an integrated SLA. On the other side, consumers may fight to get the best Quality of Service (QoS) guarantees for that service.

Differently from many works in literature that support specific negotiation processes, we aim at developing an infrastructure that can be tailored depending on the multiplicity, workflow, protocol, and decision model that fit a specific application domain. Furthermore, we exploit optimization techniques to speed up the search for agreements in (semi)automatic negotiations.

3 Negotiation Architecture

The architecture of our negotiation framework, shown in Figure 1, is composed of a *Marketplace* and various *Negotiation MultiAgent Systems*, each associated with a specific negotiation participant, and including various *Negotiators*, one for each negotiation that involves the participant at that given time. Negotiators either interface human beings with the negotiation framework through proper GUIs that allow him/her to place offers and counter offers, or they encapsulate

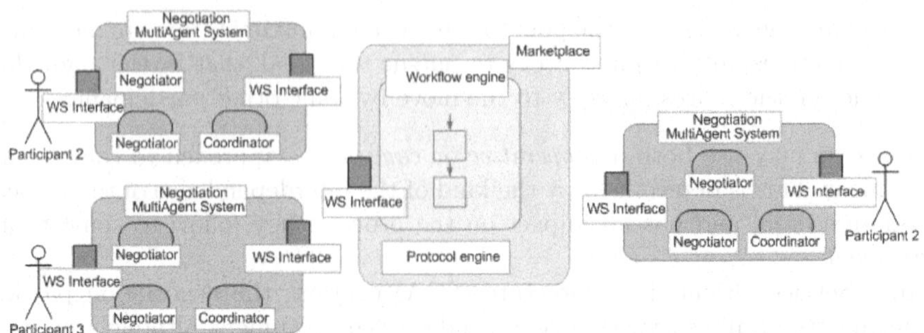

Fig. 1. The negotiation framework architecture

a decision model (see Section 4) that enables automatic negotiation to be executed. This allows us to support not only manual or automatic negotiations, but also hybrid negotiations where some participants are represented by automated agents, and some others are human beings.

Given that each negotiation participant has limited resources available, the result of one negotiation can impact on the participant ability to place an offer in another negotiation. For instance, if a telecom provider is negotiating with a consumer a high availability of its services, it might not be able to offer high availability to other consumers with which it has engaged other negotiations. In turn, if a consumer that is composing several services is accepting low level of performance from a service, it should be careful not to accept low level of performance from other services as well, otherwise the whole QoS of the resulting composition could become lower than required. In order to regulate these kinds of situations, each participant may exploit a *Negotiation Coordinator* that has the role of coordinating the action taken by the various Negotiators of the same participant. As regular Negotiators, the Negotiation Coordinator has a decision model that allows it to take decision at a higher level of abstraction.

The Marketplace defined in our framework is composed of two main parts, one taking care of the execution of the negotiation workflow and the second one controlling the correctness of the negotiation protocol. In particular, the Marketplace acts as an intermediary in all interactions among the participants, providing validity checks for the offers exchanged (through the *Protocol Engine*), based on their structure and the current state of the negotiation workflow. To make the search for agreements more efficient, the Marketplace is enhanced with a mediation function to guide the generation of the offers towards convergence of the individual objectives, based on the reactions of the participants. For example, in the one-to-one bargaining process whose implementation is described in Section 4, the mediator iteratively issues proposals to the parties. At each step, the given proposal is evaluated by the Negotiators, and if it is accepted by both, the negotiation ends successfully. Otherwise, a new proposal is generated based on the Negotiators evaluation. The mediator is implemented by an optimization algorithm, which will stop when no joint improvement is observed, i.e., at convergence to some offer, or if interrupted by the negotiation timeout.

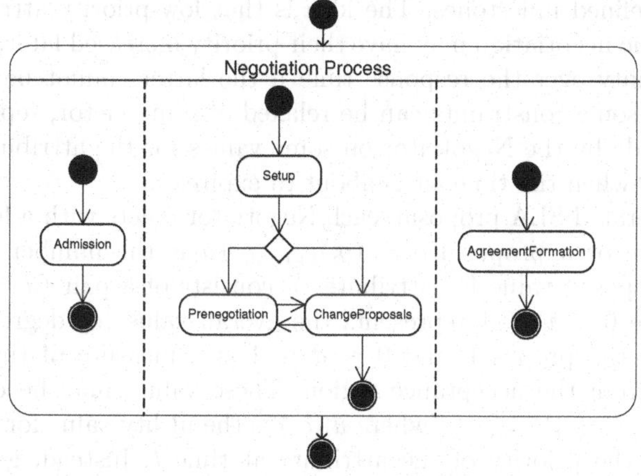

Fig. 2. The generic negotiation workflow

Our negotiation framework allows designers of negotiation to define the negotiation workflow as a Statechart using ArgoUML, and the negotiation protocol as a set of rules in the JBoss[1] Rule sintax. Figure 2 shows the Statechart associated to the most generic negotiation workflow. It can of course be replaced by more specific definitions. The framework, besides offering some predefined implementations of the decision model for Negotiators and Negotiator Coordinators, also allows the designer to define new decision models and to execute them. In the following sections we describe how the search-based optimization technique can be used to mediate one-to-one negotiation processes, and present an agent decision model.

4 Search-Based Negotiation Approach

As we have mentioned in the previous section, each Negotiator implements some decision model of the negotiation party, which can be arbitrarily configured beforehand. This usually implies to:

- define QoS attribute boundaries, expressed by constraints;
- identify the objectives to pursue, e.g., maximize one ore more utility functions expressed in terms of QoS attributes;
- prioritize the objectives and evaluate possible trade-offs among them;
- decide what information to make public, e.g., one of the above.

Negotiators may be equipped with a strategy, i.e., the algorithm to decide the reaction to a received offer at the given stage of the negotiation. In our approach, the strategy defines whether and how some of the above decision data, like the priorities of the attributes or the constraints, must change during the negotiation

[1] *http://www.jboss.org/*

at some pre-defined milestones. The idea is that low-priority attributes at the beginning of the negotiation may have their priority increased later, for example, prefer availability over the response time if the latter cannot be improved so far. Similarly, some constraints can be relaxed of some factor, representing the concession made by the Negotiator on some values for the attributes, to try to achieve a SLA when the timeout is about to expire.

Over a generated SLA proposal, each Negotiator reacts with a feedback. The feedback value for a proposal $o = (o_i)_{i=1,\dots n}$ (n is the number of attributes and o_i the proposed value for attribute i), consists of a pair ($u = U(o,t), d = D(o,t)$), where $0 \leq u \leq 1$ represents the overall value (or degree of satisfaction) given to the proposal, and $0 \leq d \leq 1$ is a measure of the distance of the proposal from the acceptance region. These values may be computed as: $U(o,t) = (p_i(t) \cdot u_i(o_i))_{i=1,\dots,n}$, where $u_i(o_i)$ is the utility value for the attribute i and $p_i(t)$ is the priority of the attribute at time t. Instead, given the constraint set at time t, represented as $cl_i(g,t) \leq 0$, $i = 1,\dots,n$, the *distance from constraint satisfaction*, is:

$$D(g,t) = \sum_{i=1}^{n} cl_i(g,t) \cdot y_i, \tag{1}$$

where: $y_i = 0$ if $cl_i(g,t) \leq 0$ and $y_i = 1$ if $cl_i(g,t) > 0$.

In case of the one-to-one negotiation exploiting the mediation capabilities of the Marketplace (see Section 3), when the negotiation starts, the number of attributes and their domains are specified to identify the search space. Hence, according to the protocol in place, the mediation algorithm produces one or more proposals, to which fitness values will be attached. For the purpose of experimentations presented in this paper, the following fitness function (to be minimized) has been considered: $F(o,t) = eu \cdot (1 + e^{d1 \cdot d2})$, where, if $(u1, d1)$ and $(u2, d2)$ are the feedback values for offer o at time t received from the Negotiators 1 and 2, eu represents the Euclidean distance of $u1$ and $u2$. The rationale of this fitness is to equally accommodate the Negotiators preferences and to impose the offer to fall into the intersection area of the acceptance regions of the two Negotiators.

For the optimization problem, we propose to use meta-heuristic search algorithms, such as Hill-Climbing, Genetic Algorithms, and Simulated Annealing (SA). From the experiments we conducted, the latter outperformed the others, above all in terms of number of solutions required to converge. SA is a variant of the hill-climbing local search method (further details on these heuristics can be found in [8]). The SA approach constructed for the negotiation algorithm proposed in this paper works as follows: (i) it starts from a random solution; (ii) a neighbor solution of the current one is selected, by randomly choosing one QoS attribute and randomly changing its value within the admissible domain. The solution is then accepted if $p < m$, with: p a random number in the range $[0 \dots 1]$, and $m = e^{\Delta fitness/T}$. The temperature T was chosen as:

$$T = T_{max} \cdot e^{-j \cdot r},$$

T_{max} being the maximum (starting) temperature, r the *cooling factor* and j the number of iterations. The process iterates until $T < T_{min}$.

5 Empirical Study

This section reports the empirical assessment of the search-based negotiation approach described in Section 4. In particular, the empirical study aims at answering the following research questions:

1. **RQ1:** To what extent the proposed negotiation approach is able to achieve feasible solutions for the different stakeholders?
2. **RQ2:** How do results vary for different QoS range overlaps?
3. **RQ3:** How do results vary for different utility functions?
4. **RQ4:** Are the performance of the proposed approach suitable for a run-time negotiation?

In the following we describe the experimentation context and setting, and then we report and discuss the obtained results.

5.1 Context and Settings

To assess the proposed negotiation approach, we set up a number of mediated one-to-one negotiation scenarios between a service provider and a consumer, bargaining over the average values of: price, response time and availability of a service. Although an SLA is usually concerned with ranges of values for each attribute, the empirical study focuses on negotiation of single values (representing the average, least, or maximum values), typical scenario that can be envisaged for the run-time binding of a service composition. Of course, our approach is also applicable to searching for agreements on QoS ranges, by specifying, in that case, the variability domains for the minimum and maximum values for each range or else the length of such ranges.

For these experiments, the global domain for the optimization algorithm was specified as in Table 1 (Domain column), where the price is expressed in Euro, the response time in seconds and the availability as a percentage. This domain may be agreeded by the Negotiators beforehand to limit the automatic generation of offers within realistic values, based on the type of service. We set up three different negotiation scenarios with different QoS acceptance sub-domains for the participating Negotiators, so to have sub domains of different negotiating agents — in particular of three providers negotiating with a consumer — overlapping by 80%, 50%, and 20%. An example of such a setting is given in Table 1.

Having fixed a negotiation timeout to a maximum 1200 generated offers, SA was configured as follows: $T_{max} = 0.30$, $T_{min} = 0.01$, $r = 0.0025$, Number of restarts = 3. For the fitness, we used the function $F(0, t)$ described in Section 4, which was reformulated in order to be maximized (e.g, replacing each constraint distance d_i with $1 - d_i$ and eu with $\sqrt{3} - eu$). As the focus of this empirical evaluation is on the effectiveness of the search-based approach, we considered

Table 1. Search domain and constraints of the negotiating agents

	Domain		Consumer		$Provider_1$		$Provider_2$		$Provider_3$	
	Min	Max	Min	Max	Min	Max	Min	Max	Min	Max
Price	0.10	5.50	0.10	3.40	0.76	4.06	1.75	5.05	2.74	5.50
Response Time	1.50	120.00	32.00	65.99	38.80	72.79	48.99	82.98	59.20	93.18
Availability	50.00	99.90	0.70	0.99	0.64	0.93	0.55	0.84	0.50	0.76

Table 2. Offers variability according to constraints overlapping percentage

	80% Overlap			50% Overlap			20% Overlap		
	Min	Max	Av	Min	Max	Av	Min	Max	Av
Price	1.63	1.66	1.64	1.75	1.77	1.76	2.74	2.76	2.74
Response Time	38.73	38.93	38.84	48.71	49.60	49.11	59.07	59.46	59.24
Availability	0.75	0.75	0.75	0.75	0.75	0.74	0.75	0.75	0.74

(i) the Negotiator's feedback functions as fixed during the negotiation, with a priority vector $[p_{price}, p_{rtime}, p_{availability}] = [0.4, 0.4, 0.2]$ for both providers and Consumer and (ii) fixed constraints. In this model, the feedback value of an offer from each Negotiator consists of a pair (u, d) where u is the vector of the attributes utility values, normalized in the interval [0,1] with respect to the overall domain of Table 1, and d is the normalized distance from constraints satisfaction. Experiments were performed on a Intel Core Duo T2500 2.0 GHz machine, with 1 GB of RAM. To avoid bias introduced by randomness, analyses were performed by replicating each run 10 times. Finally, a random search algorithm (i.e., offers are randomly generated) has been implemented in order to perform a sanity check of the SA-based approach.

5.2 Results

Question **RQ1** is concerned with the capability of the search-based approach to find one (or a set of) sub-optimal solution(s), according to the offer evaluating functions and constraints of the two Negotiators. Given the constraints setting of Table 1, the negotiation has been executed between Consumer and $Provider_1$, Consumer and $Provider_2$, and Consumer and $Provider_3$, using linear utility functions. Figure 3 reports, for each negotiation scenario, the fitness function evolution for SA (averaged over 10 runs), for each negotiation scenario. For these runs, we computed that 99% of the maximum fitness value was reached, respectively, after: 155, 137 and 200 generated offers in the worse case. The outcome of negotiations for different levels of overlap between the QoS admissible ranges of Provider and Consumer, is shown in Table 2. The final offers, although significantly different (according to the Kruskal-Wallis test, p-value$=2.5 \cdot 10^{-6}$), satisfy both negotiating agents' constraints and, when the overlap between Provider and Consumer domains decreases, the Consumer must expect higher cost and response times and lower availability (this answers to **RQ2**).

To answer **RQ3**, negotiation runs between Consumer and $Provider_1$ have been performed by using different utility function shapes, i.e., linear, exponential, and logarithmic. Minimum, maximum and average of the QoS attributes negotiated values with respect to the utility shapes are shown in Table 3.

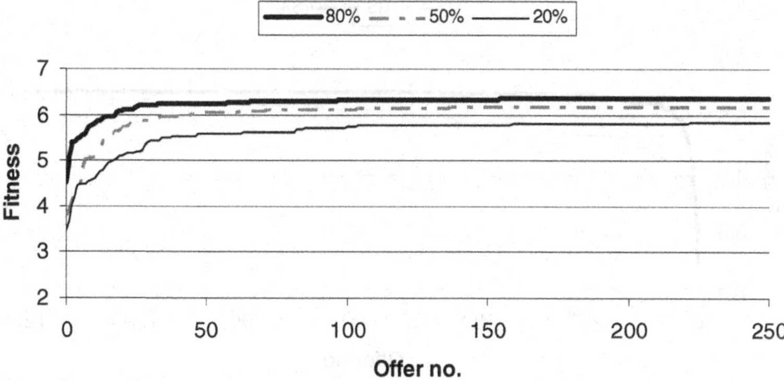

Fig. 3. Evolution of the negotiation for different overlap percentages of the QoS domains

Table 3. Offers variability according to utility shapes

	Linear			Exponential			Logarithmic		
	Min	Max	Av	Min	Max	Av	Min	Max	Av
Price	1.63	1.66	1.64	3.38	3.40	3.39	0.80	0.84	0.82
Response Time	38.73	38.93	38.84	40.03	65.49	55.24	38.74	39.00	38.85
Availability	0.75	0.75	0.75	0.78	0.78	0.78	0.73	0.734	0.732

In the exponential case, convergence is towards the boundary values of the Consumer's subdomain. Indeed, the Consumer's utility-based evaluations of the offers in the specified domain are much higher (for response time and cost, lower for availability) than those by the Provider (for response time, these could only be higher for values greater than the intersection point of the two utility curves, which is about of 119.30 s), and the Euclidean distance is minimal at the boundaries. Also, quite a high variation of the resulting response time can be observed across the different runs, as the normalized Consumer feedback values (which lead the fitness improvement as just explained) of offers of that region are all close to 1.0, thus they are all equally acceptable solutions.

Finally, to answer **RQ4**, we compared the performance of SA with that of a random-search (RS) algorithm. From all our experiments, it turned out that SA is both more efficient (in terms of best fitness reached) and faster. Also, we could observe that the difference increases for lower size acceptance sub-domains on the search space and/or low overlapping percentage. Figure 4 shows the outcomes of SA and RS when carrying out negotiations with a domain overlap of 20%. Although both SA and RS reach very similar values (SA final value is only 3% of that of RS), SA was able to converge significantly quicker to the 99% of the final value (p-value=0.0001 according to the Mann-Whitney test). Also, for random search, Negotiators' constraints were met only for the 30% of the runs, against 100% of SA. This indicates the soundness of choosing SA to drive the automatic, search-based SLA negotiation.

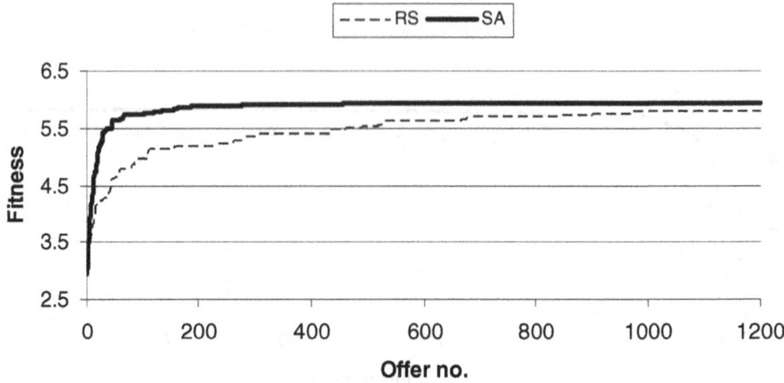

Fig. 4. Performance of SA vs Random Search (RS)

6 Related Work

Research works on automated negotiation are mainly related to architectural solutions for negotiation or algorithms and models for protocols and Negotiators strategies. In [3] a multi-agent framework with a two-layered architecture is presented, where local QoS negotiations for finding a binding to the same invoke activity are coordinated to satisfy global QoS constraints of a composition. Local constraints have to be inferred from the global ones and from the workflow topology. The model presented in [4] consists of a negotiation broker carrying out one-to-one negotiations on behalf of both service consumers and providers. The decision model of the negotiators is expressed by a hard-coded parametric function, which needs to be instantiated by the parties before negotiation starts. Instead, a marketplace-based architecture is presented in [12], where the marketplace mediates all the communication among negotiation parties, but it does not take part, itself, in the negotiations. In [9], the multi-agent system paradigm is combined with the web service technology to enable distributed online bargaining applications. However, only two negotiation processes are supported, bilateral and trilateral. The last uses a third entity to authenticate the trading agents and to validate the deals.

On the negotiation algorithms side, the existing approaches are generally concerned with two aspects: definition of decision models for the agents, and search for the near-optimal strategy, i.e., leading to Pareto optimal solutions. In [7] a strategy is defined as a weighted sum of tactics. Also, machine learning techniques can be used by the agents to learn decision rules from historical negotiation data ([10]). With respect to finding the optimal strategy, in [1], the Q-learning algorithm is used to select strategies as linear combinations of tactics, and convergence to optimality is proved to be reached after each action has been tried sufficiently often. Instead, in [11] Genetic Algorithms are used to evolve strategies whose fitness is computed according to their outcomes in negotiation runs. Finally, in [2], evolutionary methods are combined with cooperative game theory to first explore possible agreements spaces and then to distribute the payoffs and find an optimized point.

In our work, we focus on the applicability of automated negotiation approaches to the web services world. We use heuristic-based optimization algorithms to try to speed up the process of finding possible agreements. Our approach can be integrated with other decision models and strategy evolution methods as part of the agents' implementations. Moreover, we present a strategy model, taylored for negotiation to support the dynamic binding of a composition, so that the single negotiation objectives can be tuned on the run, to try to obtain the best possible QoS at global level.

7 Conclusions

In this paper we have presented an architecture that supports the actuation of various negotiation processes and offers an efficient search-based algorithm to assist the negotiating parts in the achievement of an agreement. The interesting aspect of the architecture is the possibility of instantiating negotiation workflows and protocols defined by the designer as well as various decision models for Negotiators. As future work we plan to perform more experiments with different workflows, protocols (including also optimization strategies), and decision models to try to understand which of them is more interesting in the specific application domains we are considering in the SeCSE project. Also, we plan to experiment with real SLAs that will be provided by our industrial partners in the project.

Acknowledgments

This work is framed within the European Commission VI Framework IP Project SeCSE (Service Centric System Engineering) (*http://secse.eng.it*), Contract No. 511680.

References

1. Cardoso, H., Schaefer, M., Oliveira, E.: A Multi-agent System for Electronic Commerce including Adaptive Strategic Behaviours. In: Barahona, P., Alferes, J.J. (eds.) EPIA 1999. LNCS (LNAI), vol. 1695, pp. 252–266. Springer, Heidelberg (1999)
2. Chen, J.-H., Chao, K.-M., Godwin, N., Soo, V.-W.: A Multiple-Stage Cooperative Negotiation. In: EEE'04. Proc. International Conference on e-Technology, e-Commerce and e-Service, Taipei, Taiwan, pp. 131–138. EEE (March 2004)
3. Chhetri, M., Lin, J., Goh, S., Zhang, J., Kowalczyk, R., Yan, J.: A Coordinated Architecture for the Agent-based Service Level Agreement Negotiation of Web service Composition. In: ASWEC'06. Proc. of the Australian Software Engineering Conference, Washington, DC, USA, pp. 90–99. IEEE Computer Society Press, Los Alamitos (2006)

4. Comuzzi, M., Pernici, B.: An Architecture for Flexible Web Service QoS Negotiation. In: EDOC'05. Proc. of the Ninth IEEE International EDOC Enterprise Computing Conference, Washington, DC, USA, pp. 70–82. IEEE Computer Society Press, Los Alamitos (2005)
5. Deutsch, M.: Cooperation and competition. The Handbook of Conflict Resolution: Theory and Practice (22), 21–40 (2000)
6. Jennings, N., Faratin, P., Lomuscio, A., Parsons, S., Wooldridge, M., Sierra, C.: Automated Negotiation: Prospects Methods and Challenges. Group Decision and Negotiation 10(2), 199–215 (2001)
7. Matos, N., Sierra, C., Jennings, N.: Determining Successful Negotiation Strategies: An Evolutionary Approach. In: ICMAS 1998. Proc. 3rd International Conference on Multi-Agent Systems, Paris, FR, pp. 182–189. IEEE Press, Los Alamitos (1998)
8. Michalewicz, Z., Fogel, D.B.: How to Solve It: Modern Heuristics, 2nd edn. Springer, Berlin (2004)
9. Ncho, A., Aimeur, E.: Building a Multi-Agent System for Automatic Negotiation in Web Service Applications. In: Proc. of the Third International Joint Conference on Autonomous Agents and Multiagent Systems, New York, pp. 1466–1467. IEEE Computer Society Press, Los Alamitos (2004)
10. Oliveira, E., Rocha, A.: Agents Advanced Features for Negotiation in Electronic Commerce and Virtual Organisations Formation Processes. In: Sierra, C., Dignum, F.P.M. (eds.) Agent Mediated Electronic Commerce. LNCS (LNAI), vol. 1991, pp. 78–97. Springer, Heidelberg (2001)
11. Oliver, J.: On Artificial Agents for Negotiation in Electronic Commerce. PhD thesis, Univ. of Pennsylvania (1996)
12. Rolli, D., Luckner, S., Momm, C., Weinhardt, C.: A Framework for Composing Electronic Marketplaces - From Market Structure to Service Implementation. In: WeB 2004. Proc. of the 3rd Workshop on e-Business, Washington, DC, USA (2004)

Byzantine Fault Tolerant Coordination for Web Services Atomic Transactions*

Wenbing Zhao

Department of Electrical and Computer Engineering
Cleveland State University, Cleveland, OH 44115
wenbing@ieee.org

Abstract. In this paper, we present the mechanisms needed for Byzantine fault tolerant coordination of Web services atomic transactions. The mechanisms have been incorporated into an open-source framework implementing the standard Web services atomic transactions specification. The core services of the framework, namely, the activation service, the registration service, the completion service, and the distributed commit service, are replicated and protected with our Byzantine fault tolerance mechanisms. Such a framework can be useful for many transactional Web services that require high degree of security and dependability.

Keywords: Reliable Service-Oriented Computing, Service-Oriented Middleware, Distributed Transactions, Byzantine Fault Tolerance.

1 Introduction

The bulk of business applications involve with transaction processing and require high degree of security and dependability. We have seen more and more such applications being deployed over the Internet, driven by the need for business integration and collaboration, and enabled by the latest service-oriented computing techniques such as Web services. This requires the development of a new generation of transaction processing (TP) monitors, not only due to the new computing paradigm, but because of the untrusted operating environment as well.

This work is an investigation of the issues and challenges of building a Byzantine fault tolerant (BFT) [1] TP monitor for Web services, which constitutes the major contribution of this paper. We focus on the Web services atomic transaction specification (WS-AT) [2]. The core services specified in WS-AT are replicated and protected with BFT mechanisms. The BFT algorithm in [3] is adapted for the replicas to achieve Byzantine agreement. We emphasize that the resulting BFT TP monitor framework is not a trivial integration of WS-AT and the BFT algorithm. As documented in detail in later sections, we proposed a number of novel mechanisms to achieve BFT with minimum overhead in the

* This work was supported in part by Department of Energy Contract DE-FC26-06NT42853, and by a Faculty Research Development award from Cleveland State University.

B. Krämer, K.-J. Lin, and P. Narasimhan (Eds.): ICSOC 2007, LNCS 4749, pp. 307–318, 2007.

context of distributed transactions coordination, and the experimental evaluation of a working prototype proves the optimality of our mechanisms and their implementations.

2 Background

2.1 Byzantine Fault Tolerance

Byzantine fault tolerance refers to the capability of a system to tolerate Byzantine faults. It can be achieved by replicating the server and by ensuring all server replicas reach an agreement on the input despite Byzantine faulty replicas and clients. Such an agreement is often referred to as Byzantine agreement [1].

The most efficient Byzantine agreement algorithm reported so far is due to Castro and Liskov (referred to as the BFT algorithm) [3]. The BFT algorithm is executed by a set of $3f + 1$ replicas to tolerate f Byzantine faulty replicas. One of the replicas is designated as the primary while the rest are backups. The normal operation of the BFT algorithm involves three phases. During the first phase (called pre-prepare phase), the primary multicasts a pre-prepare message containing the client's request, the current view and a sequence number assigned to the request to all backups. A backup verifies the request message and the ordering information. If the backup accepts the message, it multicasts to all other replicas a prepare message containing the ordering information and the digest of the request being ordered. This starts the second phase, *i.e.*, the prepare phase. A replica waits until it has collected $2f$ matching prepare messages from different replicas before it multicasts a commit message to other replicas, which starts the third phase (*i.e.*, commit phase). The commit phase ends when a replica has received $2f$ matching commit messages from other replicas. At this point, the request message has been totally ordered and it is ready to be delivered to the server application. To avoid possible confusion with the two phases (*i.e.*, the prepare phase and the commit/abort phase) in the two-phase commit (2PC) protocol [4], we refer the three phases in the BFT algorithm as ba-pre-prepare, ba-prepare, and ba-commit phases in this paper.

2.2 Web Services Atomic Transactions Specification

In WS-AT [2], a distributed transaction is modelled to have a coordinator, an initiator, and one or more participants. WS-AT specifies two protocol (*i.e.*, the 2PC protocol and the completion protocol), and a set of services. These protocols and services together ensure automatic activation, registration, propagation, and atomic termination of Web-services based distributed transactions. The 2PC protocol is run between the coordinator and the participants, and the completion protocol is run between the initiator and the completion service. The initiator is responsible to start and end a transaction. The coordinator side consists of the following services:

- *Activation Service*: It is responsible to create a coordinator object (to handle registration, completion, and distributed commit) and a transaction context for each transaction.
- *Registration Service*: It is provided to the transaction participants and the initiator to register their endpoint references for the associated participant-side services.
- *Coordinator Service*: This service is responsible to run the 2PC protocol to ensure atomic commitment of a distributed transaction.
- *Completion Service*: This service is used by the transaction initiator to signal the start of a distributed commit.

The set of coordinator services run in the same address space. For each transaction, all but the Activation Service are provided by a (distinct) coordinator object. The participant-side services include:

- *CompletionInitiator Service*: It is used by the coordinator to inform the transaction initiator the final outcome of the transaction, as part of the completion protocol.
- *Participant Service*: The coordinator uses this service to solicit votes from, and to send the transaction outcome to the participants.

The detailed steps of a distributed transaction using a WS-AT conformant framework are shown with a banking example (adapted from [5] and used in our performance evaluation) in Fig. 1. In this example, a bank provides an online banking Web service that a customer can access. The transaction is started due to a single Web service call from the customer on the bank to transfer some amount of money from one account to the other.

3 System Models

We consider a composite Web service that utilizes Web services provided by other departments or organizations, similar to the example shown in Fig. 1. We assume that an end user uses the composite Web service through a Web browser or directly invokes the Web service interface through a standalone client application. In response to each request from an end user, a distributed transaction is started to coordinate the interactions with other Web services. The distributed transactions are supported by a WS-AT conformant framework such as [5].

For simplicity, we assume a flat distributed transaction model. We assume that for each transaction, a distinct coordinator is created. The lifespan of the coordinator is the same as the transaction it coordinates.

The composite Web service provider serves as the role of the initiator. We assume that the initiator is stateless because it typically provides only a front-end service for its clients and delegates actually work to the participants. All transactions are started and terminated by the initiator. The initiator also propagates the transaction to other participants through a transaction context included in the requests.

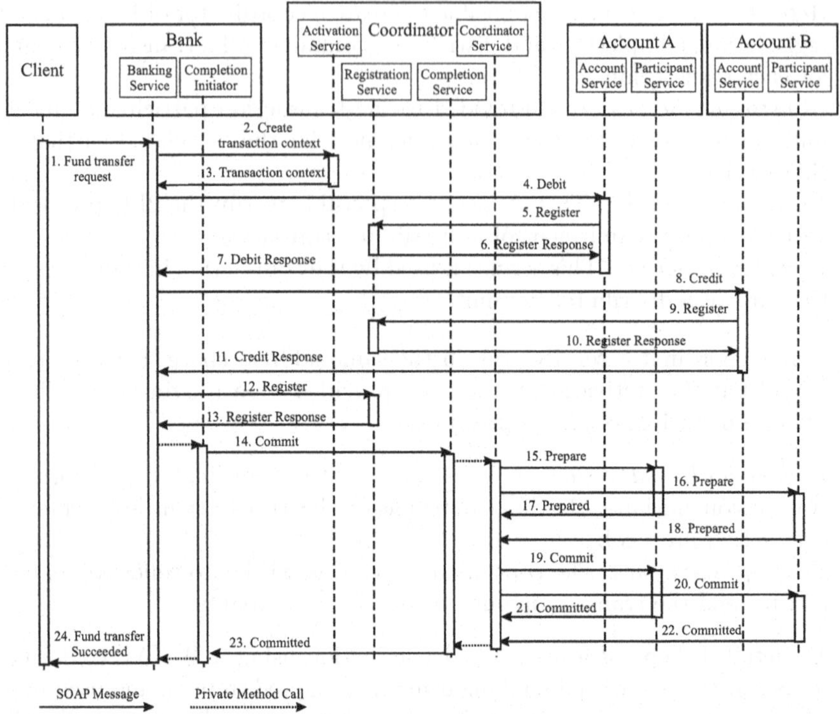

Fig. 1. The sequence diagram of a banking example using WS-AT

We assume that the transaction coordinator runs separately from the initiator and the participants.[1] Both the coordinator and the initiator are replicated. For simplicity, we assume that the participants are not replicated. We assume that $3f + 1$ coordinator replicas are available, among which at most f can be faulty during a transaction. Because the initiator is stateless, we require only $2f + 1$ initiator replicas to tolerate f faulty initiator replicas. There is no limit on the number of faulty participants.

We call a coordinator/initiator replica correct if it does not fail during its lifetime, *i.e.*, it faithfully executes according to the protocol prescribed from the start to the end. However, we call a participant correct if it is not Byzantine faulty, *i.e.*, it may be subject to typical non-malicious faults such as crash faults or performance faults.

[1] Even though it is a common practice to collocate the initiator with the coordinator in the same node, it might not be a desirable approach, due to primarily two reasons. First, collocating the initiator and the coordinator tightly couples the business logic with the generic transaction coordination mechanism (also observed in [6]), which is desirable neither from the software engineering perspective (it is harder to test) nor from the security perspective (it is against the defence-in-depth principle). Second, the initiator typically is stateless, which can be rendered fault tolerant fairly easily, while the coordination service is stateful. This naturally calls for the separation of the initiator and the coordinator.

The coordinator and initiator replicas are subject to Byzantine faults, *i.e.,* a Byzantine faulty replica can fail arbitrarily. For participants, however, we have to rule out some forms of Byzantine faulty behaviors. A Byzantine faulty participant can always vote to abort, or it can vote to commit a transaction, but actually abort the transaction locally. It is beyond the scope of any distributed commit protocol to deal with these situations. Rather, they should be addressed by business accountability and non-repudiation techniques. Other forms of participant faults, such as a faulty participant sending conflicting votes to different coordinator replicas, will be tolerated.

All messages between the coordinator and the participants are digitally signed. We assume that the coordinator replicas and the participants each has a public/secret key pair. The public keys of the participants are known to all coordinator replicas, and vice versa, while the private key is kept secret to its owner. We assume that the adversaries have limited computing power so that they cannot break the encryption and digital signatures of correct coordinator replicas.

4 Byzantine Fault Tolerance Mechanisms

4.1 Activation

Figure 2 shows the mechanisms for the activation process. Upon receiving a request from a client, the initiator starts a distributed transaction and sends an activation request to the activation service. The client's request has the form $<\text{CREQ}, o, t, c>_{\sigma_c}$, where o is the operation to be executed by the initiator, t is a monotonically increasing timestamp, c is the client id, and σ_c is the client's digital signature for the request. A correct client sends the request to all initiator replicas. An initiator accepts the request if it is properly signed by the client, and it has not accepted a request with equal or larger timestamp from the same client. If the request carries an obsolete timestamp, the cached reply is retransmitted if one is found in the reply log.

The activation request has the form $<\text{ACTIVATION}, v, c, t, k>_{\sigma_k}$, where v is the current view, k is the initiator replica id. The request is sent to the primary replica of the activation service. The primary initially logs the activation request if the message is correctly signed by the initiator replica and it has not accepted a request with equal or larger timestamp from the initiator in view v. Only when $f+1$ such messages are received from different initiator replicas with matching c and t, does the primary accept the activation request. This is to ensure the request comes from a correct initiator replica. The primary then sends a ba-pre-prepare message to the backup replicas. The ba-prepare message has the form $<\text{BA-PRE-PREPARE}, v, r, uuid_p, p>_{\sigma_p}$, where r is the content of the activation request, p is the primary id, $uuid_p$ is a universally unique identifier (UUID) proposed by the primary.

The UUID is used to generate the transaction id, which will be used to identify the transaction and its coordinator object. To maximize security, the UUID should be generated from a high entropy source, which means the activation operation is inherently nondeterministic, and the UUID proposed by one replica cannot be

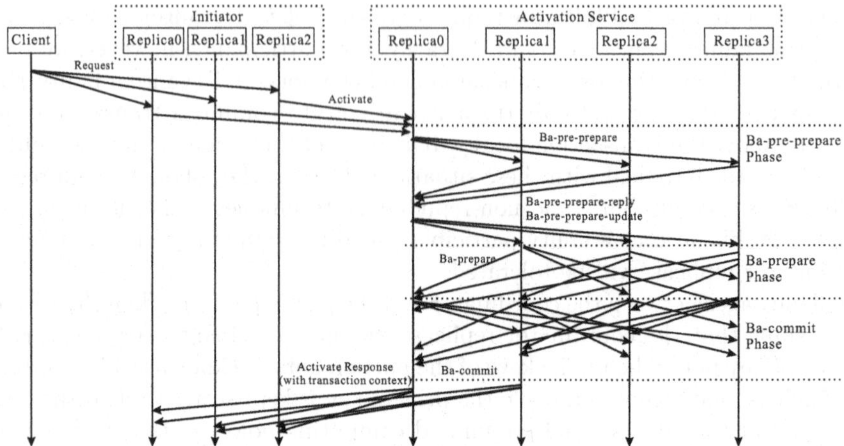

Fig. 2. Byzantine fault tolerance mechanisms for the activation of a transaction

verified by another. This calls for the collective determination of the UUID for the transaction.[2] This is achieved during the ba-pre-prepare phase.

A backup activation replica accepts the ba-prepare message if it is in view v, the message is properly signed, r is a correct activation request, and it has not accepted the same message before. The backup then sends a ba-pre-prepare-reply message in the form $<$BA-PRE-PREPARE-REPLY$, v, d, uuid_i, i>_{\sigma_i}$ to all replicas, where d is the digest of the ba-prepare message, i is the replica id and $uuid_i$ is i's UUID proposal. When the primary collects $2f$ ba-prepare-reply messages from different backups, it sends a ba-prepare-update message in the form $<$BA-PRE-PREPARE-UPDATE$, v, d, U, p>_{\sigma_p}$ to the backup replicas, where U is the collection of the digests of the $2f$ ba-pre-prepare-reply messages.

A backup accepts a ba-pre-prepare-reply message if it is in view v, the message is properly signed and d matches the digest of the ba-pre-prepare message. It accepts the ba-pre-prepare-update message if it is in view v, d matches that of the ba-pre-prepare message, and the digests in U match that of the ba-pre-prepare-reply messages. It is possible that a backup has not received a particular ba-pre-prepare-reply message, in which case, the backup asks for a retransmission from the primary. Upon accepting the ba-pre-prepare-update message, a backup sends a ba-prepare message to all replicas. The message has the form $<$BA-PREPARE$, v, d, uuid, i>_{\sigma_i}$, where $uuid$ is the final UUID computed deterministically based on the proposals from the primary and $2f$ backups (we choose to use the average of the group of UUIDs as the final UUID, but other computation method is possible). A replica accepts a ba-prepare message if it is in view v, the

[2] One might attempt to replace the high entropy source with a deterministic source to ensure the replica consistency. However, doing so might result in an easy-to-predict transaction identifier, which opens the door for replay attacks. An alternative to our approach is the coin-tossing scheme [7], however, it requires an additional phase to securely distribute the private key shares to the replicas.

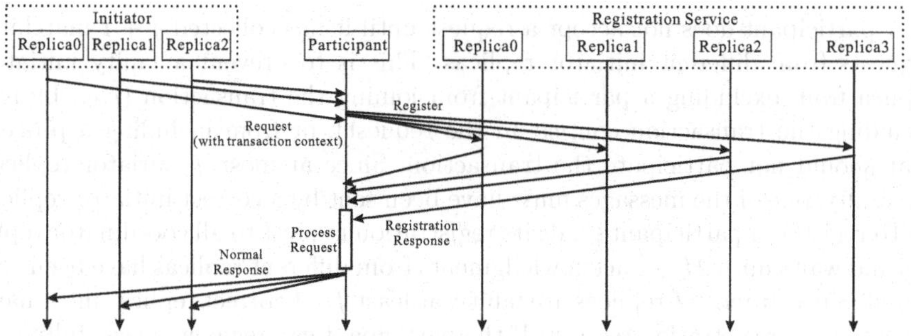

Fig. 3. Byzantine fault tolerance mechanisms for the registration of a participant

message is properly signed, d is the digest of the ba-pre-prepare message, and *uuid* matches its own.

When an activation replica has accepted $2f$ ba-prepare messages from different replicas (including the message it sent), in addition to the ba-pre-prepare and ba-pre-prepare-update messages it has accepted or has sent (if it is the primary), it sends a ba-commit message in the form $<\text{BA-COMMIT}, v, d, uuid, i>_{\sigma_i}$ to all other replicas. The verification of the ba-commit message is similar to that of the ba-prepare message. When a replica accepts $2f + 1$ matching ba-commit messages from different replicas (including the message it has sent), it calculates (deterministically) the transaction id *tid* based on *uuid*, creates a coordinator object with the *tid*, and sends the activation response to the initiator replicas. The response has the form $<\text{ACTIVATION-RESPONSE}, c, t, C, i>_{\sigma_i}$, where c and t are the client id and the timestamp included in the activation request, C is the transaction context. Note that if the primary is faulty, it can prevent a correct replica from completing the three phases, in which case, the replica suspects the primary and initiates a view change.

An initiator replica logs the activation response if it is properly signed, and c and t match those in its activation request. The replica accepts the message if it has collected $f + 1$ matching responses from different activation service replicas.

4.2 Registration and Transaction Propagation

To ensure atomic termination of a distributed transaction, it is essential that all correct coordinator replicas agree on the set of participants involved in the transaction. This can be achieved by running a Byzantine agreement algorithm among the coordinator replicas whenever a participant registers itself. However, doing so might incur too much overhead for the coordination service to be practical. In this work, we defer the Byzantine agreement on the participants set until the distributed commit stage and combine it with that for the transaction outcome. This optimization is made possible by the mechanisms shown in Fig. 3. In addition, we assume that there is proper authentication mechanism in place to prevent a Byzantine faulty process from illegally registering itself as a participant at correct coordinator replicas.

A participant does not accept a request until it has collected $f+1$ matching requests from different initiator replicas. This is to prevent a faulty initiator replica from excluding a participant from joining the transaction (*e.g.*, by not including the transaction context in the request), or from including a process that should not participate the transaction. Since at most f initiator replicas are faulty, one of the messages must have been sent by a correct initiator replica.

To register, a participant sends its registration request to all coordinator replicas and waits until $2f+1$ acknowledgments from different replicas have been collected. Since at most f replicas are faulty, at least $f+1$ correct replicas must have accepted the registration request. If the participant can register successfully and complete its execution of the initiator's request, it sends a normal reply to the initiator replicas. Otherwise, it sends an exception back (possibly after recovery from a transient failure). If an initiator replica receives an exception from a participant, or times out a participant, it should choose to abort the transaction.

The initiator replicas also register with the coordinator replicas prior to the termination of the transaction. It follows a similar mechanism as that of the participants. Because at most f initiator replicas are faulty, at least $f+1$ replicas can finish the registration successfully.

4.3 Completion and Distributed Commit

The Byzantine fault tolerant transaction completion and distributed commit mechanisms are illustrated in Fig. 4. When an initiator replica completes all the operations successfully within a transaction, it sends a commit request to the coordinator replicas. Otherwise, it sends a rollback request. A coordinator replica does not accept the commit or rollback request until it has received $f+1$ matching requests from different initiator replicas.

Upon accepting a commit request, a coordinator replica starts the first phase of the standard 2PC protocol. However, at the end of the first phase, a Byzantine agreement phase is conducted so that all correct coordinator replicas agree on the same outcome and the participants set for the transaction. This will be followed by the second phase of the 2PC protocol. If a rollback request is received, the first phase of 2PC is skipped, but the Byzantine agreement phase is still needed before the final decision is sent to all participants. When the distributed commit is completed, the coordinator replicas inform the transaction outcome to the initiator replicas. An initiator replica accepts such a notification only if it has collected $f+1$ matching messages from different coordinator replicas. Similarly, a participant accepts a prepare request, or a commit/rollback notification only if it has collected $f+1$ matching messages for the same transaction from different coordinator replicas. Again, this is to ensure the request or notification comes from a correct replica.

As shown in Fig. 4, the Byzantine agreement algorithm used for distributed commit is similar to that in Sect. 4.1, except that no ba-pre-prepare-reply and ba-pre-prepare-update messages are involved and the content of the messages are different. Due to space limitation, we only describe the format and the verification criteria for each type of messages used.

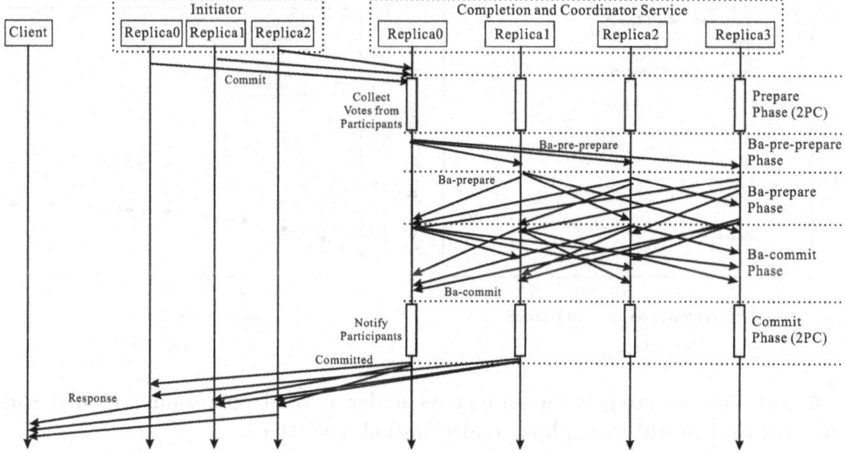

Fig. 4. Byzantine fault tolerance mechanisms for completion and distributed commit

The ba-pre-prepare message has the form <BA-PRE-PREPARE, v, tid, o, C>$_{\sigma_p}$, where o is the proposed transaction outcome (*i.e.*, commit or abort), C is the decision certificate, and σ_p is the primary's signature for the message. The decision certificate contains a collection of records, one for each participant. The record for a participant j contains a signed registration $R_j = (tid, j)_{\sigma_j}$ and a signed vote $V_j = (tid, vote)_{\sigma_j}$ if a vote from j has been received by the primary. The *tid* is included in each registration and vote record so that a faulty primary cannot reuse an obsolete registration or vote record to force a transaction outcome against the will of some correct participants.

A backup accepts a ba-pre-prepare message provided it is in view v, it is handling *tid*, the message is signed properly, the registration records in C are identical to, or form a superset of, the local registration records, and it has not accepted another ba-pre-prepare message for *tid* in view v. It also verifies that every vote record in C is properly signed by its sending participant and the *tid* in the record matches that of the current transaction, and the proposed decision o is consistent with the registration and vote records.

The ba-prepare message takes the form <BA-PREPARE, v, t, d, o, i>$_{\sigma_i}$, where d is the digest of the decision certificate C. A coordinator replica accepts a ba-prepare message provided it is in view v, it is handling *tid*, the message is correctly signed by replica i, the decision o matches that in the ba-pre-prepare message, and the digest d matches that of the decision certificate in the accepted ba-pre-prepare message.

The ba-commit message has the form <BA-COMMIT, v, tid, d, o, i>$_{\sigma_i}$. The ba-commit message is verified using the same criteria as those for ba-prepare messages. When a replica collects $2f + 1$ matching ba-commit messages from different replicas, it sends the decision o to all participants of transaction *tid*. If a replica i could not reach an agreement, it initiates a view change when a timeout occurs.

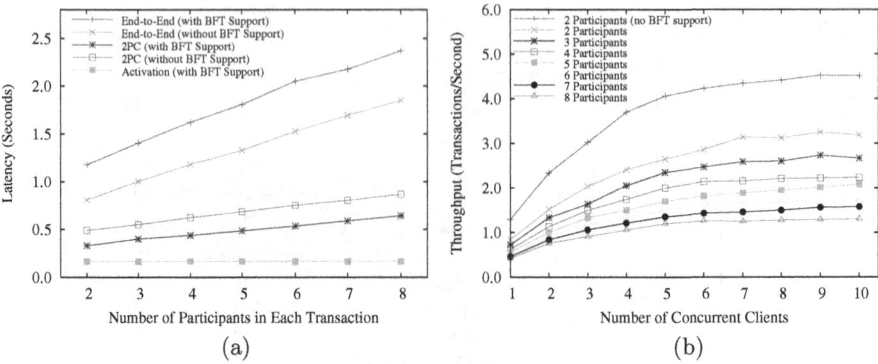

Fig. 5. (a) Various latency measurements under normal operations (with a single client). (b) End-to-end throughput under normal operations.

5 Implementation and Performance Evaluation

We have implemented the core Byzantine fault tolerance mechanisms (with the exception of the view change mechanisms) and integrated them into Kandula [5], a Java-based open source implementation of WS-AT. The extended framework also uses WSS4J (an implementation of the Web Services Security Specification) [8], and Apache Axis (SOAP Engine) 1.1 [9]. Due to space limitation, the implementation details are omitted.

Our experiment is carried out on a testbed consisting of 20 Dell SC1420 servers connected by a 100Mbps Ethernet. Each server is equipped with two Intel Xeon 2.8GHz processors and 1GB memory running SuSE 10.2 Linux.

The test application is the banking Web services application described in Sec. 2.2. The initiator is replicated across 3 nodes, and the coordination services are replicated on 4 nodes. The participants and the clients are not replicated, and are distributed among the remaining nodes. Each client invokes a fund transfer operation on the banking Web service within a loop without any "think" time between two consecutive calls. In each run, 1000 samples are obtained. The end-to-end latency for the fund transfer operation is measured at the client. The latency for the transaction activation and distributed commit are measured at the coordinator replicas. Finally, the throughput of the distributed commit service is measured at the initiator for various number of participants and concurrent clients.

As can be seen in Fig. 5(a), the end-to-end latency for a transaction is increased by about 400-500 ms when the number of participants varies from 2 to 8. The increase is primary due to the two Byzantine agreement phases in our mechanisms (one for activation, the other for 2PC). The latencies for transaction activation and for 2PC are also shown in Fig. 5(a). While the latency for 2PC increases with the number of participants, the activation latency remains constant because the participants are not involved with activation. As shown in Fig. 5(b), the throughput for transactions using our mechanisms is about 30% to 40% lower than those without replication protection, which is quite moderate considering the complexity of the BFT mechanisms. (To avoid cluttering, only the 2-participants case is shown for the no-replication configuration.)

6 Related Work

There are a number of system-level work on fault tolerant TP monitors, such as [10,11]. However, they all use a benign fault model. Such systems do not work if the coordinator is subject to intrusion attacks. We have yet to see other system-level work on Byzantine fault tolerant TP monitors. The work closest to ours is Thema [12], which is a BFT framework for generic multi-tiered Web services. Even though some of the mechanisms are identical, our work contains specific mechanisms to ensure atomic transaction commitment.

The problem of BFT distributed commit for atomic transactions has been of research interest in the past two decades [13,14]. The first such protocol is proposed by Mohan et al. [13]. In [13], the 2PC protocol is enhanced with a Byzantine agreement phase on the transaction outcome among the coordinator and all participants in the root cluster. This approach has several limitations. First, the atomicity of a transaction is guaranteed only for participants residing in the root cluster under Byzantine faults. Second, it requires every participant within the cluster knows the cluster membership, which may not be applicable to Web services atomic transactions because a participant is not obligated to know all other participants. Our work, on the other hand, requires a Byzantine agreement only among the coordinator replicas and hence, allows dynamic propagation of transactions. Rothermel *et al.* [14] addressed the challenges of ensuring atomic distributed commit in open systems where participants may be compromised. However, [14] assumes that the root coordinator is trusted. This assumption negates the necessity to replicate the coordinator for Byzantine fault tolerance. Apparently, this assumption is not applicable to Web services applications.

7 Conclusion and Future Work

In this paper, we presented Byzantine fault tolerance mechanisms for distributed coordination of Web services atomic transactions. We focus on the protection of the basic services and infrastructures provided by typical TP monitors against Byzantine faults. By exploiting the semantics of the distributed coordination services, we are able to adapt Castro and Liskov's BFT algorithm [3] to ensure Byzantine agreement on the transaction identifiers and the outcome of transactions fairly efficiently. A working prototype is built on top of an open source distributed coordination framework for Web services. The measurement results show only moderate runtime overhead considering the complexity of Byzantine fault tolerance. We believe that our work is an important step towards a highly secure and dependable TP monitor for Web services.[3] We are currently working on the implementation of the view change mechanisms and conducting experiments in the wide-area network configurations.

Acknowledgement. We wish to thank the anonymous reviewers for their insightful comments on an earlier draft of this paper.

References

1. Lamport, L., Shostak, R., Pease, M.: The Byzantine generals problem. ACM Transactions on Programming Languages and Systems 4(3), 382–401 (1982)
2. Cabrera, L., et al.: WS-AtomicTransaction Specification (August 2005)
3. Castro, M., Liskov, B.: Practical Byzantine fault tolerance and proactive recovery. ACM Transactions on Computer Systems 20(4), 398–461 (2002)
4. Gray, J., Reuter, A.: Transaction Processing: Concepts and Techniques. Morgan Kaufmann, San Mateo, CA (1983)
5. Apache Kandula project, `http://ws.apache.org/kandula/`
6. Erven, H., Hicker, H., Huemer, C., Zapletal, M.: Web Services-BusinessActivity-Initiator (WS-BA-I) Protocol: an extension to the Web Services-BusinessActivity specification. In: Proceedings of the IEEE Internaltion Conference on Web Services, Salt Lake City, Utah (July 2007)
7. Cachin, C., Kursawe, K., Shoup, V.: Random oracles in Constantinople: Practical asynchronous Byzantine agreement using cryptography. In: Proceedings of the 19th ACM Symposium on Principles of Distributed Computing, pp. 123–132. ACM Press, New York (2000)
8. Apache WSS4J project, `http://ws.apache.org/wss4j/`
9. Apache Axis project, `http://ws.apache.org/axis/`
10. Frolund, S., Guerraoui, R.: e-Transactions: End-to-end reliability for three-tier architectures. IEEE Transactions on Software Engineering 28(4), 378–395 (2002)
11. Zhao, W., Moser, L.E., Melliar-Smith, P.M.: Unification of transactions and replication in three-tier architectures based on CORBA. IEEE Transactions on Dependable and Secure Computing 2(2), 20–33 (2005)
12. Merideth, M., Iyengar, A., Mikalsen, T., Tai, S., Rouvellou, I., Narasimhan, P.: Thema: Byzantine-fault-tolerant middleware for web services applications. In: Proceedings of the IEEE Symposium on Reliable Distributed Systems, pp. 131–142. IEEE Computer Society Press, Los Alamitos (2005)
13. Mohan, C., Strong, R., Finkelstein, S.: Method for distributed transaction commit and recovery using Byzantine agreement within clusters of processors. In: Proceedings of the ACM symposium on Principles of Distributed Computing, Montreal, Quebec, Canada, pp. 89–103. ACM Press, New York (1983)
14. Rothermel, K., Pappe, S.: Open commit protocols tolerating commission failures. ACM Transactions on Database Systems 18(2), 289–332 (1993)

[3] In the current stage, due to the high redundancy level required and the high degree of complexity imposed by the BFT mechanisms, the solutions proposed in this paper are useful only for those applications that are so mission critical that the cost of doing so is well justified.

Syntactic Validation of Web Services Security Policies

Yuichi Nakamura[1], Fumiko Sato[1], and Hyen-Vui Chung[2]

[1] IBM Research, Tokyo Research Laboratory
1623-14 Shimo-tsuruma, Yamato, Kanagawa
242-0001 Japan
{nakamury, sfumiko}@jp.ibm.com
[2] IBM Software Group, Web Service Security Development
11501 Burnet Road, Austin, TX
78758-3400 USA
hychung@us.ibm.com

Abstract. The Service-Oriented Architecture (SOA) makes application development flexible in such a way that services are composed in a highly distributed manner. However, because of the flexibility, it is often hard for users to define application configurations properly. Regarding the security concerns we address in this paper, though WS-SecurityPolicy provides a standard way to describe security policies, it is difficult for users to make sure that the defined policies are valid. In this paper, we discuss the validation of WS-SecurityPolicy in the context of Service Component Architecture, and propose a method called *syntactic validation*. Most enterprises have security guidelines, some of which can be described in the format of Web services security messages. There also exist standard profiles for Web services such as the WS-I Basic Security Profile that also prescribes message formats. Since those guidelines and profiles are based on accepted best practices, the syntactic validation is sufficiently effective for practical use to prevent security vulnerabilities.

1 Introduction

Many enterprises are undertaking development using the Service-Oriented Architecture (SOA) [1] because their business models are changing more frequently. SOA makes application development easier because technology-independent services can be coupled over intranets and via the Internet. Meanwhile, the underlying computing environments on which the applications are running are becoming complex, because computers can be networked in complicated topologies, including firewalls and intermediate servers. Consequently, the proper configuration of non-functional aspects such as security requires a fairly deep understanding of such complex environments.

We believe that security must be unified with the software engineering process from the beginning, and thus security engineering [2, 3] is important. Unfortunately, security is considered as an afterthought in most actual development in the sense that security is added after the functional requirements are implemented. It is well known that finding defects downstream greatly increases the costs of removal and repair.

Recently, Service Component Architecture (SCA) [4] is being standardized as a component model for SOA. More importantly, the SCA Policy Framework [5] is also being discussed in which intentions for non-functional requirements such as security

B. Krämer, K.-J. Lin, and P. Narasimhan (Eds.): ICSOC 2007, LNCS 4749, pp. 319–329, 2007.

and transaction are specified at an abstract level, and the intentions are later mapped onto concrete policies such as WS-SecurityPolicy [6]. The concept of the SCA Policy Framework is quite similar that of the Model-Driven Security (MDS) architecture we have been developing [7, 8]. Where we added security intentions to UML [9] constructs such as classes and methods in MDS, we instead add intentions to SCA components and composites.

In this paper, we describe *syntactic validation* of WS-SecurityPolicy in the context of the SCA Policy Framework. According to the SCA Policy, we need to prepare in advance a collection of WS-SecurityPolicy documents so that we will retrieve the policies from the security intentions attached to the SCA composites. Therefore, it is important to define *valid* policy documents. Most enterprises have security guidelines, some of which can be described in the format of Web services security messages. There also exist standard profiles on Web services security [10] such as WS-I Basic Security Profile [11] that also prescribe message formats. Based on those guidelines and profiles, we think that we can prevent the security vulnerabilities in a highly practical way by means of syntactic validation which performs syntax checks of policies against guidelines and profiles.

Our main contribution is to show a practical way to validate WS-SecurityPolicy based on a solid foundation of predicate logic. While semantic validation which includes formal security analysis is often too complicated for practical situations, syntactic validations based on best practices can be realistic and sufficiently useful in many situations. We also describe a framework to transform WS-SecurityPolicy into predicate logic rules in an orderly fashion.

The rest of this paper is organized as follows: Section 2 introduces Web services security and Web services security policy, and discusses the problems in defining security policies. In Section 3, we begin by SCA Policy Framework, and describe the details of syntactic validation and show examples. Section 4 discusses related work. In Section 5, we conclude this paper.

2 Reviewing Web Services Policy

Here we introduce Web policy (WS-Policy) [12] and discuss the issues of defining WS-Policy, mainly focusing on Web services security (WSS) [10]. We begin by introducing WSS, giving a summary of the concepts and showing its XML message format. Then WS-Policy is presented, including a security-specific policy language called WS-SecurityPolicy [6]. Since the message format of WSS is complex, WS-SecurityPolicy naturally tends to become complex. As a result, it is often hard for policy developers to define security policies using WS-SecurityPolicy. Some problems are discussed in more detail in Section 2.3.

2.1 Web Services Security

The WSS specification [10] defines a format including security tokens and mechanisms to protect SOAP messages. Digital signatures serve as integrity checks to ensure message protection, and encryption guarantees confidentiality. In addition, WS-Security provides a flexible mechanism to include various claims in SOAP messages using security tokens. With message protection and security tokens, WSS can provide a basis for other specifications such as WS-Trust [13] and WS-SecureConversation [14].

WSS messages includes three types of elements: a Signature element (defined in the XML Digital Signature specification [15]), an encryption-related element such as EncryptedKey (defined in the XML Encryption specification [16]), and security tokens such as UsernameToken (defined in WSS UsernameToken Profile [17]). Listing 1 shows an example of a WSS message that includes an X.509 certificate as a security

Listing 1. WSS Message Example. In this example, we omit namespace declarations, and use abbreviated notations for URIs such as algorithm names in order to save space

```
<soap:Envelope>
<soap:Header>
 <wsse:Security>
  <wsse:BinarySecurityToken
   ValueType="X509v3" wsu:Id="X509Token" EncodingType="Base64Binary">
    MIIEZzCCA9CgAwIBAgIQEmtJZc0rqrKh5i...
  </wsse:BinarySecurityToken>
   <ds:Signature>
      <ds:SignedInfo>
         <ds:CanonicalizationMethod Algorithm="xml-exc-c14n"/>
          <ds:SignatureMethod Algorithm=" rsa-sha1"/>
       <ds:Reference URI="#body">
       <ds:Transforms>
           <ds:Transform
              Algorithm=" xml-exc-c14n"/>
       </ds:Transforms>
       <ds:DigestMethod
              Algorithm="sha1"/>
       <ds:DigestValue>LyLsF094hPi4wPU...</ds:DigestValue>
     </ds:Reference>
  </ds:SignedInfo>
  <ds:SignatureValue>Hp1ZkmFZ/2kQLXDJbchm5gK...</ds:SignatureValue>
  <ds:KeyInfo>
     <wsse:SecurityTokenReference>
         <wsse:Reference URI="#X509Token"/>
     </wsse:SecurityTokenReference>
  </ds:KeyInfo>
 </ds:Signature>
 </wsse:Security>
</soap:Header>
 <soap:Body wsu:Id="body">
  <tru:StockSymbol xmlns:tru="http://fabrikam123.com/payloads">
     QQQ
  </tru:StockSymbol>
</soap:Body>
</soap:Envelope>
```

2.2 WS-Policy and WS-SecurityPolicy

WS-Policy [12] provides a framework to describe policies which are associated with particular services. It defines a set of logical operators such as conjunction, All[. . .], and disjunction, OneOrMore[. . .] so as to formulate domain-specific assertions. WS-SecurityPolicy is a domain-specific language to represent policies for message protection based on WSS and SSL. For example, we can describe our desired policy in such a way that a signature is required on a particular element or so that a particular element must be encrypted.

Listing 2 shows an example of WS-SecurityPolicy [6] that can be used for verifying or generating the WSS message shown in Listing 1. WS-SecurityPolicy has a number of sections for integrity and confidentiality assertions, bindings, and supporting tokens. Integrity and confidentiality assertions indicate which particular parts of the message should be signed and encrypted, respectively. A binding specifies detailed information to sign and encrypt some parts of messages such as signatures and gives encryption algorithms, security token information, and a layout for the WSS elements. Supporting tokens are additional tokens that are not described in a binding section. Listing 2 only includes an integrity assertion which appears as a SignedParts element, and a binding section which appears as an AsymmetricBinding element.

Listing 2. WS-SecurityPolicy Example. Actual representation requires inserting logical operators such as All and ExactlyOne that are all omitted here

```
<sp:AsymmetricBinding>
  <sp:InitiatorToken>
    <sp:X509Token sp:IncludeToken="AlwaysToRecpt">
      <sp:WssX509V3Token10/>
    </sp:X509Token>
  </sp:InitiatorToken>
  <sp:RecipientToken> ..... </sp:RecipientToken>
  <sp:AlgorithmSuite>
    <sp:Basic256/>
  </sp:AlgorithmSuite>
  <sp:Layout>
    <sp:Strict/>
  </sp:Layout>
</sp:AsymmetricBinding>

<sp:SignedParts>
 <sp:Body/>
</sp:SignedParts>
```

2.3 Issues in Defining Policies

Since WS-SecurityPolicy is extremely flexible, it is often hard for users to define *valid* policies with it. We can consider two kinds of validations: *syntactic* and *semantic* validations. Syntactic validation is concerned with validating the format of the messages. For example, we may have a syntactic rule such that a BinarySecurityToken must appear before Signature element. On the other hand, semantic validation means formal methods prove that the defined policy ensures no security vulnerability exists. For example, we may want to guarantee that attackers cannot alter messages during message transmission.

In our research, we focus on syntactic validation. Obviously, semantic validation is important since one of the ultimate goals is to prevent security vulnerabilities in a systematic manner. However, considering the complexity of WS-SecurityPolicy, it is hard to establish a theoretical foundation for semantic validation. In contrast, while syntactic validation does not provide security analysis in a theoretical sense, it can still be useful for security validation in real situations.

Most enterprises have security guidelines, which often describe detailed security requirements. For example, a requirement might say that when customer information is sent over a network, it should be encrypted with the RSA Encryption Standard Version 1.5 using a 1,024-bit key. This rule can be checked against the WS-SecurityPolicy by checking a certain element. Also, the format of WSS will be included in such guidelines, again taking account of various security considerations. With a good set of rules for WSS formats, syntactic validation can be sufficiently effective.

WS-I Basic Security Profile (BSP) provides several good examples. The following is one of them, C5543:

- When the signer's SECURITY_TOKEN is an INTERNAL_SECURITY_TOKEN, the SIGNED_INFO MAY include a SIG_REFERENCE that refers to the signer's SECURITY_TOKEN in order to prevent substitution with another SECURITY_TOKEN that uses the same key

This indicates that Listing 1 may not be secure since the BinarySecurityToken is not signed. This rule can be checked with syntactic validation.

In addition to security checking based on guidelines, interoperability is a major concern for WSS. Since WS-I BSP provides a set of rules for message formats, we can also improve interoperability by means of syntactic validation.

3 Policy Validation

Here, we describe syntactic policy validation. We first introduce a framework for developing applications for the Service Component Architecture (SCA), and explain how policies are defined and used in the framework. Then we discuss a theoretical foundation for performing syntactic validation using WS-SecurityPolicy. In our research, we use predicate logic to represent WS-SecurityPolicy, profiles such as WS-I BSP, and security guidelines. On the basis of the predicate logic, we can perform validations as inferences over the predicates. In this framework, we must transform WS-SecurityPolicy expressions to predicates, so the transformation is also described.

3.1 Policy Development for Service Component Architecture

Security should be considered from the beginning, though in most actual development it is considered as an afterthought. Our thesis is that users should be able to specify abstract security intentions at an initial stage, and the intentions can be refined toward a detailed security policy. This idea can be easily implemented based on the Service Component Architecture (SCA) [4] and the SCA Policy Framework [5].

Figure 1 illustrates how abstract policies are specified and refined. The assembler creates the SCA composite, combining the primitive components, and adds the abstract security intentions such as confidentiality and integrity to that composite. Policy developers define concrete policies typically represented in WS-Policy, specifying which intentions can be realized with each concrete policy. In our framework, a Policy deployer deploys the concrete policies to the SCA runtime in advance. When the SCA composites are deployed in the SCA runtime, appropriate concrete policies are retrieved based on the intentions attached to the SCA composites..

In our framework, it is important to make sure that valid concrete policies are deployed on the SCA runtime. Otherwise, even if the security intentions are appropriately added to SCA composite, the intentions will no be realized correctly, and security vulnerabilities may result.

3.2 Validation Based on Predicate Logic

We understand that a WS-Policy document prescribes a set of Web services messages based on predicate logic. For example, the WSS message in Listing 1 is a representative of the WSS messages that are prescribed by the WS-SecurityPolicy in Listing 2. Extending this notion, we see that security guidelines and profiles can be represented using predicate logic, and thus we can prescribe sets of messages.

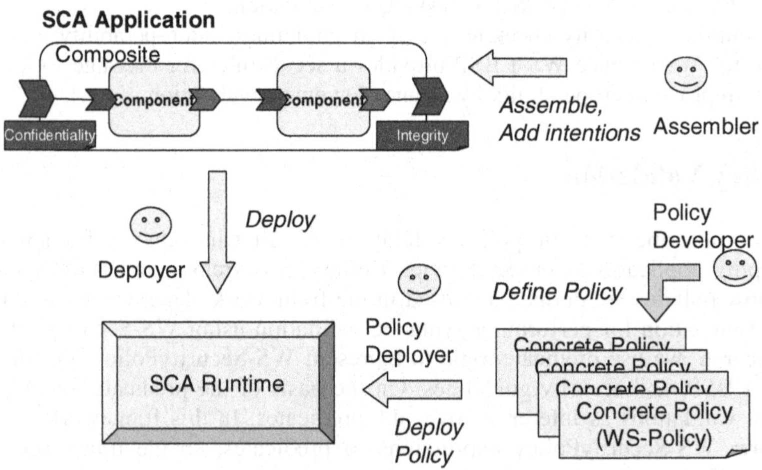

Fig. 1. Policy Configuration and Development for SCA

Figure 2 shows that validation can be viewed as a set operation between predicates. In the figure, WSSP1, WSSP2, and WSSP3 are WS-SecurityPolicy documents. Because the sets of WSSP1 and WSSP2 are both included in the set of BSP, we can say that WSSP1 and WSSP2 conform to BSP. In contrast, WSSP3 does not conform to BSP, since WSSP3 is not included in BSP.

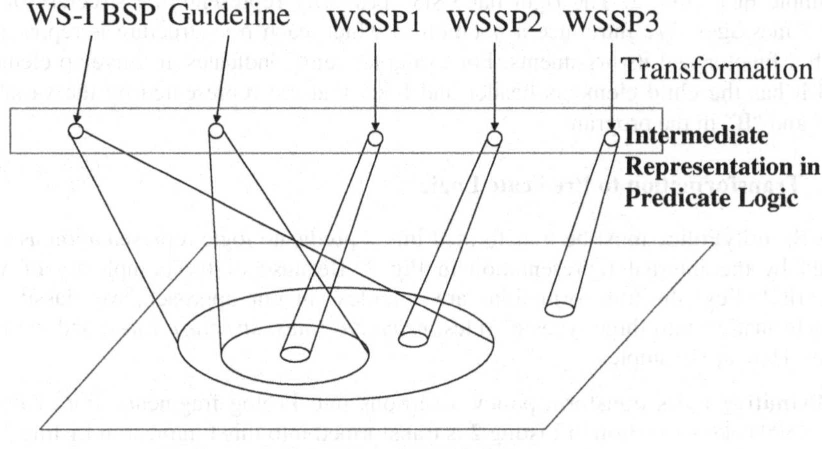

Fig. 2. Concept of WS-Policy Formalization Based on Predicate Logic

In our approach, WS-SecurityPolicy is represented using predicate logic, and threfore we can adopt Prolog [12] as a concrete representation and a calculation foundation. Listing 3 shows a Prolog program that is equivalent to the WS-SecurityPolicy

Listing 3. Prolog Program for a WS-SecurityPolicy Document

```
myPolicy0(E):-
    E=env(H,B),
    H=h(Sec),
    Sec=
    sec(
        bst('@ValueType'('#X509v3'),
        '@EncodingType'('#Base64Binary'),
        '@id'(TokenID),
        bstValue),
        sig(
        sigInfo(
        c14nMethod('@Algorithm'('xml-exc-c14n#')),
        sigMethod('@Algorithm'('xmldsig#rsa-sha1')),
        ref('@URL'(BodyID),
            transforms(
              transform(
              '@Algorithm'('xml-exc-c14n#')),
              digestMethod('@Algorithm'('xmldsig#sha1')),
              digestValue(dVal))),
      sigValue(sVal),
      keyInfo(
        str(reference('@URI'(TokenID))))))),
  B=body('@id'(BodyID),bodyValue).
```

example in Listing 2. The right hand side primarily represents the structure of the WSS messages. We introduce a notation in which each tree structure is represented with a functor and its arguments. For example, "env" indicates an Envelop element, and it has the child elements header and body that are represented by the variables "H" and "B" in the program.

3.3 Transformation to Predicate Logic

WS-SecurityPolicy must be transformed into a predicate logic representation as indicated by the internal representation in Fig 2. Because of the complexity of WS-SecurityPolicy, the transformations are complex. In our approach, we classify the transformation into three types of rules, *primitive rules*, *structure rules*, and *merging rules*. Here are examples:

Primitive rules transform policy assertions into Prolog fragments. For example, the X509Token assertion in Listing 2 is transformed into this fragment in Listing 3:

```
bst('@ValueType'('#X509v3'),
    '@EncodingType'('#Base64Binary'),
    '@id'(TokenID),
    bstValue),
```

In the same manner, SignedPart assertion is transformed into "sig" and its child elements in Listing 3.

Structure rules order the elements of the header elements, and optionally change the order of processing. For example, a Layout assertion defines the order of elements in a SOAP header, and an EncryptBeforeSigning assertion requires that encryption must be performed before signing.

Merging rules define how to merge the Prolog fragments created by primitive rules. With only primitive and structure rules, the constructed messages may have redundant elements or may lack necessary associations between elements. Figure 3 illustrates how a transformation is performed. The Primitive rules for X509Token and SignedPart construct "bst" and "sig" elements, respectively. In addition, two merging rules are applied. First, Basic256 under AlgorithmSuite is used to specify an algorithm in the signature. Second, we associate an X.509 token and the signature, applying the rule that the signature element created by SignedPart must refer to a token created by InitiatorToken.

We have defined a set of rules classified into these three categories. Using these rules, we can transform WS-SecurityPolicy documents into our internal representation as Prolog programs.

3.4 Performing Validation

Since profiles and guidelines can be represented in Prolog, validation can be performed by executing the Prolog formulas. Let's consider C5443 of WS-I BSP as introduced in Section 2.3. Listing 4 shows a Prolog program for C5443. Since this is similar to Listing 3, most of it is omitted and the crucial difference is emphasized in bold. The key difference is that C5443 requires signing on a security token, and therefore the reference to the token is included in the signature element.

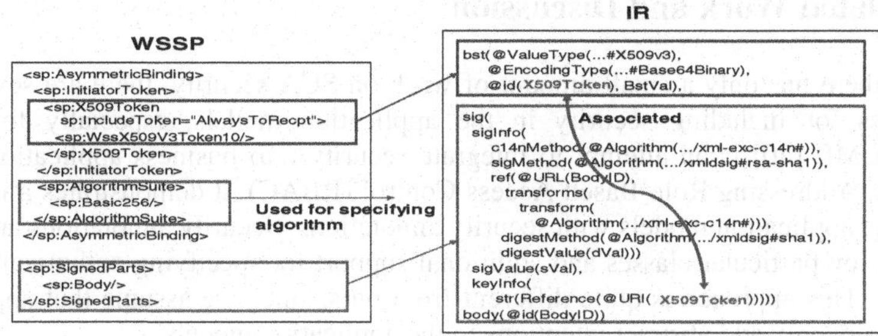

Fig. 3. Merging Token and Signature Elements

Listing 4. Predicate for the C5443 of WS-I BSP

```
c5443(E):-
   ....
   sec(
      sig(...
         ref('@URL'(BodyID), ...)
         ref('@URL'(TokenID), ..)
         ....
      ),
   B=body('@id'(BodyID),bodyValue).
```

Let us consider validation using myPolicy0 in Listing 3 and c5443 in Listing 4. One of the easiest ways is to perform the following formula:

~c5443(E),myPolicy0(E).

The result must always be "false" if myPolicy0 conforms to C5443. This formula indicates that there exists an envelope E that does not satisfy C5443, but satisfies myPolicy0. In this way, once the predicates have been represented as Prolog, the validations can be performed easily.

In addition to the validations, we can derive counterexamples by executing the formula. If the formula returns true, we should receive a substitution value, an envelope instance. The returned envelope is a counterexample in the sense that it can be derived from myPolicy0, but does not conform to C5443. As we mentioned, it is difficult for users to check if a WS-SecurityPolicy document is valid. On the other hand, counterexamples are often helpful for users seeking to understand the nature of bugs in the policy definitions.

Here is an example of how a user might apply this function. Listing 1 is shown as a counterexample and the user is informed that C5443 is not satisfied. When she compares the listing and C5443, she can see that the security token is not signed. In order to fix the bug, she needs to add a ProtectToken assertion that indicates the security token should be signed. Though we cannot yet programmatically offer suggestions about how to fix problems, such counterexamples can be good hints for users to help them fix such bugs by themselves.

4 Related Work and Discussion

While there has only a small amount of work on SCA security, there are several approaches for including security in the application models, especially for UML. SecureUML [20] is an attempt to integrate security into business application development. Addressing Role-Based Access Control (RBAC), it demonstrates a means to combine application models with security annotations. Security annotations are access controls on particular classes and additional support for specifying authorization constraints. This approach is quite different from ours, since we assume that application developers only add abstract intentions to the application models.

Deubler et al. [21] proposed an interesting approach to developing secure SOA applications. Using state transition diagrams and system structure diagrams (both similar to UML diagrams), they built application models, including security functions such as authentication. Then they perform model checking [22] to find security problems. Compared to our approach, they represent the mechanisms for security explicitly. For example, authentication and permission services are defined, specifying their behaviors. On the other hand, we think that such detailed security mechanisms should not be a concern of the application developers. In our tooling architecture, application developers only add security intentions that are associated with detailed security policies during deployment.

Bhargavan et al. [23] proposed formal semantics for WS-SecurityPolicy[1]. Concerned with XML rewriting attacks, their tool can automatically check whether or not the security goals of the formal model are vulnerable to any XML rewriting attacks. We regard such validation as semantic validation, since the model represents how to send, receive, and process security primitives such as tokens, timestamps, nonces, signatures, and encryption requests. While such semantic validation can prove that a given policy is secure, there are limitations in practical situations. For example, a formal model may address only limited types of security attacks, or may not represent all of the semantics of the security processing due to the complexity of WSS. As long as we cannot provide a complete solution, we think that the syntactic validation we are proposing should be useful. Since they provide a collection of guidelines and profiles, we can leverage them in order to reduce security risks.

5 Concluding Remarks

Since applications are becoming more complex in the SOA environment, it is becoming harder to configure their security. Addressing this issue, we introduced a security configuration framework based on the SCA policy concept, and discussed how to define valid WS-SecurityPolicy documents, since such valid definitions are critical when preparing valid security policies.

Syntactic validation of WS-SecurityPolicy is the key idea in this paper. Since most enterprises have security guidelines and best practices, we can leverage them to validate the security policies. Because guidelines can be described in the format of Web services security messages, we can eliminate security vulnerabilities in a highly practical way by means of syntax checking of the security policies against the guidelines, what we call syntactic validation. We can implment this idea using predicate logic,

[1] This work is based on an older version of WS-SecurityPolicy [24].

where the policies and guidelines are represented as Prolog programs. We also have described a framework to transform WS-SecurityPolicy into predicate logic rules in an orderly fashion.

While semantic validation is effective in theory, it requires formal security analysis that is often too complicated for practical situations. Still, syntactic validations based on best practices can be realistic and sufficiently useful in many situations. We will continue investigating this approach, accumulating and representing more guidelines using predicate logic.

References

1. A CBDI Report Series – Guiding the Transition to Web Services and SOA, http://www.cbdiforum.com/bronze/downloads/ws_roadmap_guide.pdf
2. Devanbu, P., Stubblebine, D.: Software Engineering for Security: a Roadmap. In: ICSE 2000 (2000)
3. Anderson, R.: Security Engineering: A Guide to Building Dependable Distributed Systems. Wiley, Chichester (2001)
4. SCA Service Component Architecture: Assembly Model Specification, Version 1.00, (March 15, 2007)
5. SCA Policy Framework: Version 1.00 (March 2007)
6. WS-SecurityPolicy v1.2, Committee Specification (April 30, 2007), http://www.oasis-open.org/committees/download.php/23821/ws-securitypolicy-1.2-spec-cs.pdf
7. Tatsubori, M., Imamura, T., Nakamura, Y.: Best Practice Patterns and Tool Support for Configuring Secure Web Services Messaging. In: ICWS 2004 (2004)
8. Nakamura, Y., Tatsubori, M., Imamura, T., Ono, K.: Model-Driven Security Based on a Web Services Security Architecture. In: International Conference on Service Computing (2005)
9. Unified Modeling Language, http://www.omg.org/technology/documents/formal/uml.htm
10. Web Services Security: SOAP Message Security 1.1
11. Basic Security Profile Version 1.0, Final Material (March 30, 2003)
12. W3C Candidate Recommendation "Web Services Policy 1.5 –Framework" (February 28, 2007), http://www.w3.org/TR/2007/CR-ws-policy-framework-20070228/
13. WS-Trust 1.3 OASIS Standard (March 19, 2007)
14. WS-SecureConversation 1.3 OASIS Standard (March 1, 2007)
15. Eastlake, D., Solo, J.R., Bartel, M., Boyer, J., Fox, B., Simon, E.: XML Signature Syntax and Processing, W3C Recommendation (February 12, 2002)
16. XML Encryption Syntax and Processing, W3C Recommendation (December 10, 2002)
17. Web Services Security, UsernameToken Profile 1.1
18. Web Services Security: X.509 Certificate Token Profile 1.1
19. Prolog :- tutorial, http://www.csupomona.edu/~jrfisher/www/prolog_tutorial/contents.html
20. Lodderstedt, T., Basin, D., Doser, J.: SecureUML: A UML-Based Modeling Language for Model-Driven Security. In: Proceedings of UML2002 (2002)
21. Deubler, M., Grünbauer, J., Jürjens, J., Wimmel, G.: Sound Development of Secure Service-based Systems. In: ICSOC (2004)
22. McMillan, K.: Symbolic Model Checking. Kluwer Academic Publishers, Boston (1993)
23. Bhargavan, K., Fournet, C., Gordon, A.D.: Verifying policy-based security for web services. In: CCS '04. Proceedings of the 11th ACM conference on Computer and communications security, pp. 268–277. ACM Press, New York (2004)
24. Web Services Security Policy Language (WS-SecurityPolicy) (December 18, 2002) http://www-106.ibm.com/developerworks/library/ws-secpol/

An Agent-Based, Model-Driven Approach for Enabling Interoperability in the Area of Multi-brand Vehicle Configuration*

Ingo Zinnikus[2], Christian Hahn[2], Michael Klein[1], and Klaus Fischer[2]

[1] CAS Software AG, Karlsruhe (Germany)
michael.klein@cas.de
[2] DFKI GmbH, Saarbrücken (Germany)
{ingo.zinnikus, christian.hahn, klaus.fischer}@dfki.de

Abstract. With the change of EU regulations in the automotive market in 2002, multi-brand car dealers became possible. Despite the high economical expectations connected with them, the existing IT infrastructure does not provide satisfying support for these changes as it had been developed independently by each brand for many years. In this paper, we describe a solution which supports rapid prototyping by combining a model-driven framework for cross-organisational service-oriented architectures (SOA) with an agent-based approach for flexible process execution. We discuss advantages of agent-based SOAs and summarize the lessons learned.

1 Introduction

In cross-organisational business interactions such as multi-brand vehicle configuration, the most desirable solution for integrating different partners would suggest to integrate their processes and data on a rather low level. However, the internal processes and interfaces of the participating partners are often pre-existing and have to be taken as given. Furthermore, in cross-organisational scenarios partners are typically very sensitive about their product data and the algorithms that process it. In many cases, private processes are only partially visible and hidden behind public interface descriptions [1]. This imposes restrictions on the possible solutions for the problems which occur when partner processes are integrated.

Thus, a service-oriented architecture (SOA) is the most appropriate approach. It enables partners to offer the functionality of their systems via a public service interface (WSDL) and hide the sensitive parts behind it. As usual in a SOA, the communication is performed by the exchange of messages between the partners.

A very important second advantage of SOA is the possibility of a loose coupling of partners. New partners can enter the system with little effort whereas

* The work published in this paper is (partly) funded by the E.C. through the ATHENA IP. It does not represent the view of E.C. or the ATHENA consortium, and authors are solely responsible for the paper's content.

B. Krämer, K.-J. Lin, and P. Narasimhan (Eds.): ICSOC 2007, LNCS 4749, pp. 330–341, 2007.

obsolete partners are able to leave it easily. Especially in the case where additional smaller non-OEM manufacturers providing vehicle parts like radios or tires are integrated in the sales process, the system needs to become robust against temporary unavailable partners.

Despite the advantages of a SOA, several difficulties arise especially in the case where the systems of the partners have evolved independently for several years:

- The *philosophies* of the systems differ, e.g. one partner service uses a strict sequential run through the product space whereas another service allows e.g. randomly browsing through the products and product features.
- The *granularity* of operations of the various partner services differs.
- *Non-functional aspects* such as exception handling, session management, transactional demarcation, which differ from partner to partner, supersede the core functionality of the services.
- *Structural differences* in the payload data of the exchanged messages stemming from data models used by the different partners' sites are present.
- *Semantical misunderstandings* within the exchanged messages may arise due to different tagging of business data, different conventions etc.

The European project ATHENA (Advanced Technologies for interoperability of Heterogeneous Enterprise Networks and their Applications) provides a comprehensive set of methodologies and tools to address interoperability problems of enterprise applications in order to realize seamless business interaction across organizational boundaries. In this paper, we present the results of a pilot application of the ATHENA approach to interoperability and the supporting technology in a real-world scenario of a multi-brand vehicle dealer.

The paper is organized as follows. In Section 2 we will sketch the business case of our pilot application and discuss the current and the to-be scenario for multi-brand vehicle dealers. Sections 3 and 4 are devoted to our technical approach. Here, we present the approach developed in ATHENA and used within our pilot for the integration of cross-organizational processes. We discuss the advantages of this approach in Section 5 and conclude the paper by taking a look at the lessons learned in Section 7.

2 Scenario

In 2002, due to new laws in EU legislation, the market of car distribution changed fundamentally. Instead of being limited to selling only one brand, vending vehicles of different brands under one roof was facilitated. Dealers now can reach a broader audience and improve their business relations for more competitiveness. As a consequence, many so-called *multi-brand dealers* have appeared.

Today, multi-brand dealers are confronted with a huge set of problems. Rather than having to use the IT system of one specific car manufacturer, multi-brand dealers are now faced with a number of different IT systems from their different manufacturers. One specific problem is the integration of configuration, customization and ordering functionality for a variety of brands into the IT landscape of a multi-brand dealer.

In this paper, the business cases we are looking at are such multi-brand dealers. Multi-branding seamlessly offers products of different brands in one coherent sales process. This establishes a certain level of comparability among products of different brands and provides added value to the customers, thus strengthens the competitiveness of multi-brand dealers. However, multi-branding calls for an increased level of interoperability among the dealer on one side and the different manufacturers on the other side.

Today, however, systems for car configuration and order processing of different car manufacturers are isolated systems and not integrated into the dealer specific IT landscape. Thus, multi-brand dealers are faced with a simple multiplication of IT systems to support their pre-sales, sales and after-sales processes. As a consequence, one of the desired advantages of multi-branding, namely to seamlessly offer cars of different car manufactures and to establish comparability among the different products is seriously put at stake. We rather observe the phenomenon of what we call *early brand selection*, i.e. a customer has to choose his desired brand at the beginning and than go all the way through its brand-specific product configuration and order process. Changing the brand later means starting the process all over from the beginning.

In this paper, we propose an integrated scenario, where multi-brand dealers use services provided by the different car and non-OEM manufactures and plug them into an integrated dealer system. In the following section, we will describe our solution in more detail.

3 Our Solution

The desired to-be-scenario with its general architecture is depicted in Figure 1. The solution consists of two parts which are necessary to provide an integrated solution for a multi-brand dealer:

– *An integration of the manufacturers* (lower part of the figure). The systems of the different car and non-OEM manufacturers are integrated via an integrator component. This integrator enables the dealer to access the software

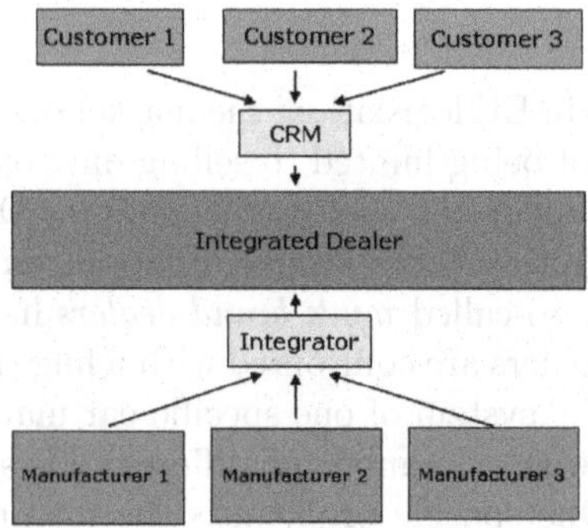

Fig. 1. Overview over the architecture of the solution

of the manufacturers in a uniform manner. For the sake of the pilot application, the car configurator CAS MERLIN by CAS Software AG currently used for order processing and sales support applications by a leading German car manufacturer was used.
- *An integration of the customers* (upper part of the figure). The interaction of customers and the dealer is harmonized by integrating their different processes within a CRM system. In the pilot setting, the CRM system CAS GENESISWORLD was used.

In the following, we give an overview of our approach of the pilot application. However, the paper will focus on the manufacturer integration (see Section 3 and 4) and present the model-driven, agent-based integration approach for cross-organizational processes modeling. The customer integration has already been presented in detail in [2].

Manufacturer Integration

The integrator in the overall architecture in Figure 1 can be seen as a service integrator performing message transformations.

The messages that are exchanged between the dealer and the manufacturers are (conceptually) transformed in three steps. The resulting three layers of the architecture of our service integrator are shown in Figure 2 (left hand side).

In the top most component, a message entering the component from the dealer is analyzed by the CAS Instance Distributor and routed to the set of manufacturers that need to process this request. If the dealer e.g. wants to find a suitable family car for his customer, typically all (or many) of the manufacturers will receive the message. If the dealer however wants to configure and order a car of a certain brand, only this specific system will be addressed. In the inverse direction, i.e. when the results of the different manufacturers reach the component, the CAS Instance Aggregator comes into play: by applying metrics of equality, similarity

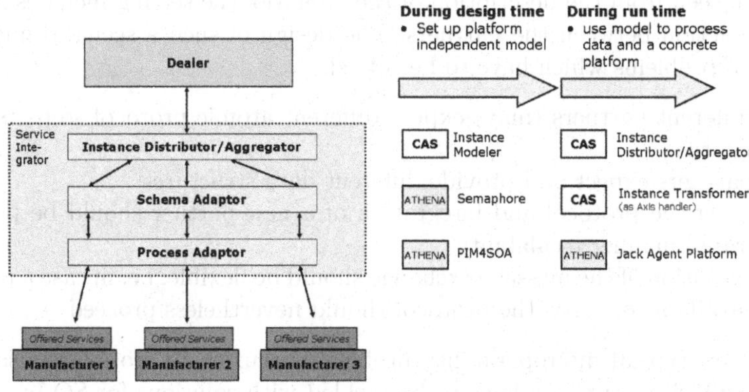

Fig. 2. Integration of car and non-OEM manufacturers

and equivalence, it tries to combine the different partial results to one meaningful integrated result.

The middle layer is responsible for harmonizing the data models of the different manufacturers with the common data model of the dealer. Thus, the business objects extracted from the incoming messages are remodeled and put into the outgoing messages. It is important to mention that for this step in certain cases several messages must be processed together in order to be able to rebuild a business object and its dependent objects.

The task of the lower layer is to mediate between the integrator and the different processes offered by the manufacturers, i.e. to adapt the sequence of messages that is expected by a manufacturer system with the sequence that is sent out by the dealer. Furthermore, the process adaptor reacts to unavailable services e.g. by invoking alternative services.

All three components have been developed with a model-driven approach. In a first step during design-time, platform independent models have been created for each component. E.g., for the process adaptor, the metamodel PIM4SOA (Platform Independent Model for Service Oriented Architectures) [3] was used to define a connection between the processes of the dealer and manufacturer; for the schema adaptor, Semaphore[1] was used to graphically map the entities and attributes of one data model to the corresponding entities and attributes in the other model. From these models, executables were generated, which have been applied in a second step during run-time to process the data on a concrete platform. E.g., for the process adaptor, the generated process models are executed as software agent on Jack [4], an agent platform based on the BDI-agent theory (*belief-desire-intention*, [5]).

In the following, we will describe this approach in detail and discuss advantages and problems.

4 Mediating Services for Cross-Organisational Business Processes

As can be seen from the description of the scenario, the setting includes a complex interaction between the partners. The design of such a scenario implies a number of problems which have to be solved:

- the different partners (may) expect different atomic protocol steps (service granularity)
- the partners expect and provide different data structures
- changing the protocol and integration of a new partner should be possible in a rapid manner (scalability)
- the execution of the message exchange should be flexible, i.e. in case a partner is unavailable or busy, the protocol should nevertheless proceed

These are typical interoperability problems occuring in cross-organisational scenarios which in our case have to be tackled with solutions for SOAs. A core

[1] `http://www.modelbased.net/semaphore`

idea in the ATHENA project was to bring together different approaches and to combine them into a new framework: a modelling approach for designing collaborative processes, a model-driven development framework for SOAs and an agent-based approach for flexible execution. It turned out that these approaches fit nicely together, as e.g. the PIM4SOA metamodel and the agents' metamodel bear a striking resemblance to each other.

Hence, the first problem is solved by specifying a collaborative protocol which allows adapting to different service granularities. The mediation of the data is tackled with transformations which are specified at design-time and executed at run-time by transforming the exchanged messages based on the design-time transformations.

Scalability is envisaged by applying a model-driven approach: the protocol is specified on a platform-independent level so that a change in the protocol can be made on this level and code generated automatically.

Finally, flexibility is achieved by applying a BDI agent-based approach. BDI agents provide flexible behaviour for exception-handling in a natural way (compared to e.g. BPEL4WS where specifying code for faults often leads to complicated, nested code).

PIM4SOA: A Platform-Independent Model for SOAs

The PIM4SOA is a visual platform-independent model (PIM) which specifies services in a technology independent manner. It represents an integrated view of SOAs in which different components can be deployed on different execution platforms. The PIM4SOA model helps us to align relevant aspects of enterprise and technical IT models, such as process, organisation and products models. The PIM4SOA metamodel defines modelling concepts that can be used to model four different aspects or views of a SOA:

Services are an abstraction and an encapsulation of the functionality provided by an autonomous entity. Service architectures are composed of functions provided by a system or a set of systems to achieve a shared goal. The service concepts of the PIM4SOA metamodel have been heavily based on the Web Services Architecture as proposed by W3C [6].

Information is related to the messages or structures exchanged, processed and stored by software systems or software components. The information concepts of the PIM4SOA metamodel have been based on the structural constructs for class modelling in UML 2.0 [7].

Processes describe sequencing of work in terms of actions, control flows, information flows, interactions, protocols, etc. The process concepts of the PIM4SOA metamodel have been founded on ongoing standardization work for the Business Process Definition Metamodel (BPDM) [8].

Non-functional aspects can be applied to services, information and processes. Concepts for describing non-functional aspects of SOAs have been based on the UML Profile for Modeling Quality of Service and Fault Tolerance Characteristics and Mechanisms [9].

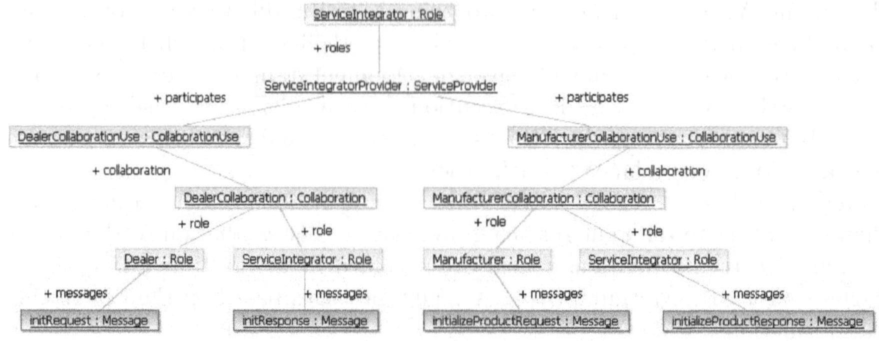

Fig. 3. PIM4SOA Model for Pilot (part)

Via model-to-model transformations, PIM4SOA models can be transformed into underlying platform-specific models (PSM) such as XSD, Jack BDI-agents or BPEL.

The business protocol between dealer (dealer software), integrator and manufacturers is specified as PIM4SOA model (see Figure 3). In order to execute collaborative processes specified on the PIM level, the first step consists of transforming PIM4SOA models to agent models that can be directly executed by specific agent execution platforms. In our case, the Jack Intelligent agent framework is used for the execution of BDI-style agents. The constructs of the PIM4SOA metamodel are mapped to BDI-agents represented by the Jack metamodel (JackMM). For detailed information on JackMM we refer to [10].

In this service-oriented setting, the partners provide and exhibit services. Partner (manufacturer etc.) services are described as WSDL interfaces. The WSDL files are used to generate integration stubs for the integrator. We use a model-driven approach for mapping WSDL concepts to agent concepts, thereby integrating agents into a SOA and supporting rapid prototyping.

The partner models are transformed to a Jack agent model with the model-to-model transformation developed in ATHENA. The following sketch outlines the metamodel mappings (see Figure 4, for more details, cf. e.g. [10]).

A *ServiceProvider* (i.e. ServiceIntegratorProvider in Figure 3) is assigned to a *Team* (which is an extension of an *Agent*). The name of the *ServiceProvider* coincides with the name of the *Team*, its roles are the roles the *Team* performs. Furthermore, the team makes use of the roles specified as bound roles in the *CollaborationUse* (i.e. Dealer and Manufacturer), in which it participates. For each of these roles, we additionally introduce an atomic *Team*. The *Process* of the *ServiceProvider* is mapped to the *TeamPlan* of the non-atomic *Team*. This *TeamPlan* defines how a combined service is orchestrated by making use of the services the atomic *Teams* (i.e. ManufacturerTeam and DealerTeam in Figure 5) provide. Finally, *Messages* that are sent by the roles we already have transformed are mapped to *Events* in JackMM.

The process integrator and the manufacturers are modelled as Web services. Their interface is described by WSDL descriptions publishing the platform as

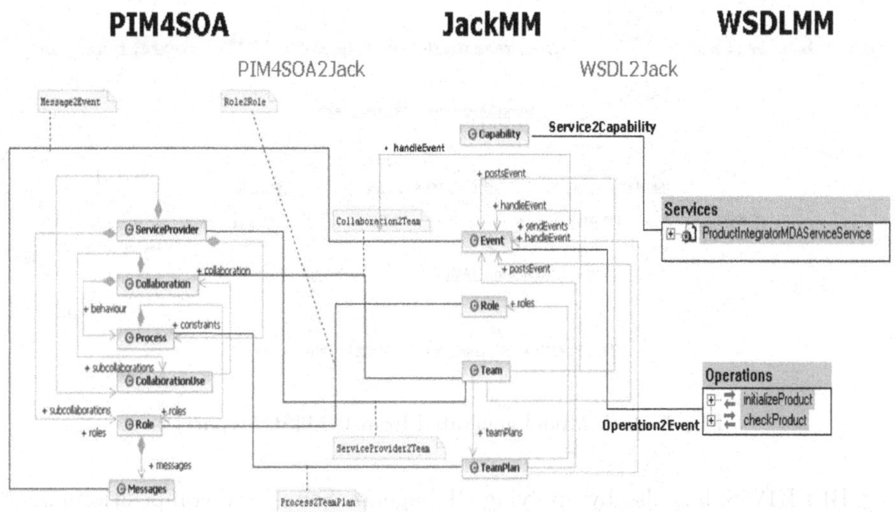

Fig. 4. PIM4SOA and WSDLMM to JackMM transformation

Web service. In the pilot, only the process integrator is executed by Jack agents which are wrapped by a Web service, whereas the manufacturers and other partner services are pure Web services. For integrating Web services into the Jack agent platform, we map a service as described by a WSDL file to the agent concept *Capability* which can be conceived of as a module. A capability provides access to the Web services via automatically generated stubs (using Apache Axis). A capability comprises of plans for invoking the operations as declared in the WSDL (it encapsulates and corresponds to commands such as invoke and reply in BPEL4WS).

By executing the model transformations we automatically derive the JackMM model illustrated in Figure 5 (for more details, cf. [10]). It should be stressed that these model transformations and the respective code generation can be done automatically if (i) the PIM4SOA model is defined properly and (ii) the WSDL descriptions are available. The only interventions necessary for a system designer are the insertion of the proper XSLT transformations and the assignment of the capabilities to the agents/teams responsible for a specific Web service invocation.

5 Advantages of Agent-Based SOAs

The similarities between agent architectures and SOAs have already been recognized (e.g. [11]). In fact, the strong correspondence between the PIM4SOA and the JackMM confirms this observation. In the following we will briefly discuss advantages of applying BDI-agents in a service-oriented environment.

In order to compare an agent-based approach with other standards for Web service composition, the distinction introduced in [12] between *fixed*, *semi-fixed*, and *explorative composition* is useful. Fixed composition can be done with

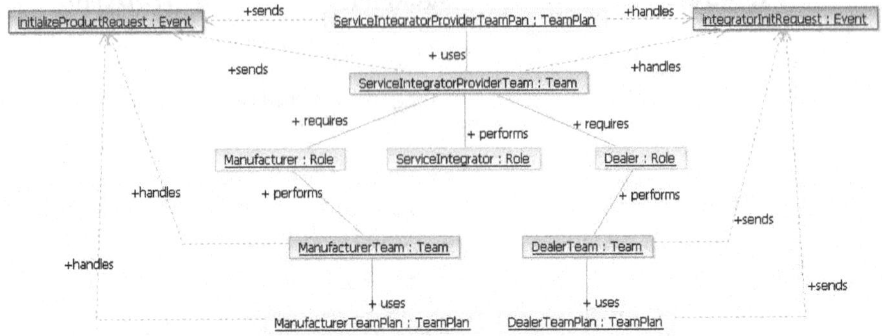

Fig. 5. Jack Model generated from PIM4SOA (part)

e.g. BPEL4WS, but also by applying BDI agents. Semi-fixed composition might also be specified with BPEL4WS: partner links are defined at design-time, but the actual service endpoint for a partner might be fixed at run-time, as long as the service complies with the structure defined at design-time. Late binding can also be done with the Jack framework. The service endpoint needs to be set (at the latest) when the actual call to the service is done. Explorative composition is beyond of what BPEL4WS and a BDI-agent approach offer (at least if they are used in a 'normal' way). To enable explorative composition, a general purpose planner might be applied which dynamically generates, based on the service descriptions stored in a registry, a plan which tries to achieve the objective specified by the consumer [13].

It might seem as if BPEL4WS and BDI-style agents offer the same features. However, there are several advantages of a BDI-style agent approach. An important question is how the availability of a partner service is detected. This might be checked only by actually calling the service. If the service is not available or does not return the expected output, an exception will be raised. BPEL4WS provides a fault handler which allows specifying what to do in case of an exception. Similarly, an agent plan will fail if a Web service call raises an exception, and execute some activities specified for the failure case.

However, the difference is that a plan is executed in a context which specifies conditions for plan instances and also other applicable plans. The context is implicitly given by the beliefs of an agent and can be made explicit. If for a specific goal several options are feasible, an agent chooses one of these options and, in case of a failure, immediately executes the next feasible option to achieve the desired goal. This means that in a given context, several plan instances might be executed, e.g. for all known services of a specific type, the services are called (one after another), until one of the services provides the desired result. An exception in one plan instance then leads to the execution of another plan instance for the next known service. Additionally, BDI-style agents permit 'meta-level reasoning' which allows choosing the most feasible plan according to specified criteria.

In our car configuration scenario, agents have to react to service unavailability and the protocols for e.g. selecting a non-OEM supplier involve auctions or *first come - first served* mechanisms which can be modelled in an very elegant manner with a BDI-agent approach. The BDI-agent approach supports this adaptive behaviour in a natural way, whereas a BPEL4WS process specification which attempts to provide the same behaviour would require awkward coding such as nested fault handlers etc.

Furthermore, since it is in many cases not possible to fully specify all necessary details on the PIM level, a system engineer must add these details on the PSM level. Hence, *customizing* the composition is facilitated since the different plans clearly structure the alternatives of possible actions. Since the control structure is implicit, changes in a plan do not have impact on the control structure, reducing the danger of errors in the code. Another advantage is that *extending* the behaviour by adding a new, alternative plan for a specific task is straightforward. The new plan is simply added to the plan library and will be executed at the next opportunity.

Finally, business process notations allow specifying unstructured processes. To execute these processes with BPEL, unstructured PIM4SOA process descriptions normally are transformed to block-structured BPEL processes. In doing so, most approaches restrict the expressiveness of processes by only permitting acyclic or already (block-)structured graphs [14]. In the case that any unstructured processes shall be executed, an approach like described in [15] has to be followed. The idea is to translate processes with arbitrary topologies to BPEL by making solely use of its Event Handler concept. The result is again cumbersome BPEL code, whereas the Jack agent platform naturally supports event-based behaviour.

6 Related Work

Apart from the wealth of literature about business process modelling, enterprise application integration and SOAs, the relation between agents and SOAs has already been investigated. [11] cover several important aspects, [16] propose the application of agents for workflows in general. [17] and [18] present a technical and conceptual integration of an agent platform and Web services. However, the model-driven approach and the strong consideration of problems related to cross-organisational settings have not been investigated in this context. Furthermore, our focus on tightly integrating BDI-style agents fits much better to a model-driven, process-centric setting than the Web service gateway to a JADE agent platform considered by e.g. [17].

7 Conclusions and Summary

From a research transfer point of view, the following lessons could be learned:

- Evidently, a model based approach is a step in the right direction as design-time tasks are separated from run-time tasks which allows performing them

graphically. Moreover, it is easier to react to changes of the different interacting partners as only the models have to be adapted but not the run-time environment.
- The PIM4SOA metamodel is sufficient for modelling basic exchange patterns but needs to be more expressive.
- A model-driven, agent-based approach offers additional flexibility and advantages (in general and in the scenario discussed) when agents are tightly integrated into a service-oriented framework.

In this paper, we presented a pilot developed within the EU project ATHENA in the area of multi-brand automotive dealers. For its realization, several integration problems on different levels had to be solved. We described a solution which supports rapid prototyping by combining a model-driven framework for cross-organisational service-oriented architectures with an agent-based approach for flexible process execution. We argued that agent-based SOAs provide additional advantages over standard process execution environments.

References

1. Schulz, K., Orlowska, A.: Facilitating cross-organisational workflows with a workflow view approach. Data and Knowledge Engineering 51(1), 109–147 (2004)
2. Klein, M., Greiner, U., Genßler, T., Kuhn, J., Born, M.: Enabling Interoperability in the Area of Multi-Brand Vehicle Configuration. In: I-ESA 2007. 3rd International Conference on Interoperability for Enterprise Software and Applications (2007)
3. Benguria, G., Larrucea, X., Elvesæter, B., Neple, T., Beardsmore, A., Friess, M.: A Platform Independent Model for Service Oriented Architectures. In: I-ESA 2006. 2nd International Conference on Interoperability of Enterprise Software and Applications (2006)
4. JACK Intelligent Agents: The Agent Oriented Software Group (AOS) (2006), `http://www.agent-software.com/shared/home/`
5. Rao, A.S., Georgeff, M.P.: Modeling Rational Agents within a BDI-Architecture. In: Allen, J., Fikes, R., Sandewall, E. (eds.) KR91. 2nd International Conference on Principles of Knowledge Representation and Reasoning, pp. 473–484. Morgan Kaufmann publishers Inc., San Mateo, CA, USA (1991)
6. W3C: Web Services Architecture, World Wide Web Consortium (W3C), W3C Working Group Note (February 11, 2004), `http://www.w3.org/TR/2004/NOTE-ws-arch-20040211/`
7. OMG: UML 2.0 Superstructure Specification, Object Management Group (OMG), Document ptc/03-08-02 (August 2003), `http://www.omg.org/docs/ptc/03-08-02.pdf`
8. IBM: Adaptive, Borland, Data Access Technologies, EDS, and 88 Solutions, "Business Process Definition Metamodel - Revised Submission to BEI RFP bei/2003-01-06", Object Management Group (OMG), Document bei/04-08-03 (August 2004), `http://www.omg.org/docs/bei/04-08-03.pdf`
9. OMG: UML Profile for Modeling Quality of Service and Fault Tolerance Characteristics and Mechanisms, Object Management Group (OMG), Document ptc/04-09-01 (September 2004), `http://www.omg.org/docs/ptc/04-09-01.pdf`

10. Hahn, C., Madrigal-Mora, C., Fischer, K., Elvesæter, B., Berre, A.J., Zinnikus, I.: Meta-models, Models, and Model Transformations: Towards Interoperable Agents. In: Fischer, K., Timm, I.J., André, E., Zhong, N. (eds.) MATES 2006. LNCS (LNAI), vol. 4196, Springer, Heidelberg (2006)
11. Singh, M., Huhns, M.: Service Oriented Computing: Semantics, Processes, Agents. John Wiley & Sons, Chichster, West Sussex, UK (2005)
12. Yang, J., Heuvel, W., Papazoglou, M.: Tackling the Challenges of Service Composition in e-Marketplaces. In: RIDE-2EC 2002. 12th International Workshop on Research Issues on Data Engineering: Engineering E-Commerce/E-Business Systems (2002)
13. Sirin, E., Parsia, B., Wu, D., Hendler, J.A., Nau, D.S.: HTN planning for Web Service composition using SHOP2. J. Web Sem. 1, 377–396 (2004)
14. Mendling, J., Lassen, K., Zdun, U.: Transformation Strategies between Block- Oriented and Graph-Oriented Process Modelling Languages. In: Lehner, F., Nekabel, H., Kleinschmidt, P. (eds.) Multikonferenz Wirtschaftsinformatik 2006 (MKWI 2006), Berlin (2006)
15. Ouyang, C., Dumas, M., Breutel, S., ter Hofstede, A.H.M.: Translating Standard Process Models to BPEL. In: Dubois, E., Pohl, K. (eds.) CAiSE 2006. LNCS, vol. 4001, Springer, Heidelberg (2006)
16. Vidal, J.M., Buhler, P., Stahl, C.: Multiagent systems with workflows. IEEE Internet Computing 8(1), 76–82 (2004)
17. Greenwood, D., Calisti, M.: Engineering Web Service – Agent Integration. In: IEEE Systems, Cybernetics and Man Conference, the Hague, Netherlands, October 10-13, 2004, pp. 10–13. IEEE Computer Society Press, Los Alamitos (2004)
18. Dickinson, I., Wooldridge, M.: Agents are not (just) web services: Considering BDI agents and web services. In: SOCABE. AAMAS 2005 Workshop on Service-Oriented Computing and Agent-Based Engineering (2005)

User-Driven Service Lifecycle Management – Adopting Internet Paradigms in Telecom Services

Juan C. Yelmo[1], Rubén Trapero[1], José M. del Álamo[1], Juergen Sienel[2], Marc Drewniok[2], Isabel Ordás[3], and Kathleen McCallum[3]

[1] DIT, Universidad Politécnica de Madrid, Ciudad Universitaria s/n, 28040 Madrid, Spain
{jcyelmo, rubentb, jmdela}@dit.upm.es
http://www.dit.upm.es

[2] Alcatel-Lucent Deutschland AG, 70435 Suttgart, Germany
{Juergen.Sienel, Marc.Drewniok}@alcatel-lucent.de
www.alcatel-lucent.com

[3] Telefónica I+D, Emilio Vargas 6, 28043 Madrid, Spain
{ioa, kmc352}@tid.es
http://www.tid.es

Abstract. The user-centric service creation paradigm set out in Web 2.0 technologies on the Internet allows users to define and share their new content and applications. Open services and interfaces provided by Google et al can be used to build easily, and quickly deploy exciting applications. User-centric service creation provides a cheap solution in contrast with the huge engineering effort that has to be spent both on development and marketing in order to get a new telecom service running and deployed in the market. Adopting Internet paradigms in telecom services requires major flexibility and dynamicity in managing service lifecycle compared to current service management systems.

This paper proposes an approach to user-centric service lifecycle management in telecom-oriented platforms. It allows users to drive their services' lifecycle, e.g. when and for how long they must be available, as well as automating the process between the creation and the execution of the services.

1 Introduction

In an IP world, new competitors such as mobile virtual network operators (MVNO) or Internet companies threaten the traditional business models of telecom operators by providing their services directly to the operators' customers. They use the operator's network as a kind of bit pipe [1], without returning any benefit to it in exchange for the use of those services.

Moreover, end users are also putting on pressure by increasingly requiring innovative and attractive new services: They would like to have the advanced model they use on the Internet which allows users to define new contents and applications

B. Krämer, K.-J. Lin, and P. Narasimhan (Eds.): ICSOC 2007, LNCS 4749, pp. 342–352, 2007.

(mashups) using open services and interfaces that could be quickly and easily built and deployed e.g. Yahoo Pipes [2].

User-centric service creation refers to this process. It enables end-users (not necessarily the very technically skilled) to create their own services and manage the lifecycle of those services autonomously. It also allows users to share these services within a community which will promote the most interesting ones at a minimum cost (viral marketing[1]).

In order to support the aforementioned approach, it has become imperative for telcos to change their rigid business and provisioning models, replacing them with much more agile processes. This could be accomplished by identifying the operators' assets that can be provided only in the core network such as end-user location and presence information, and then abstract and offer them through well defined interfaces. Users may use these resources to create new or personalized services, thus generating a powerful and self-increasing ecosystem around the telecom operators' core business - their networks.

Service Oriented Architecture (SOA) is the main approach to opening up these network resources with initiatives such as ParlayX [3] or Open Mobile Alliance (OMA) enablers [4], which converge in the use of Web Services as the middleware allowing third parties to access and control network resources.

Nonetheless, operators still have to cope with some difficulties that arise from the openness of their networks and the reduction of the time to market in the lifecycle of new services. Furthermore, in order to apply the user-centric model telcos must also deal with a huge set of short-lived user-generated services each one having its own user-driven lifecycle and orchestrating a subset of telecom based services.

The Open Platform for User-centric service Creation and Execution (OPUCE) [5] allows users to create, manage and use their own telecom-based services in an Internet style. In this article we introduce some of the early results within the OPUCE project, focusing on the lifecycle of these services. We pay special attention to user-driven lifecycle management of user-centric services as well as the automation of the related processes.

The following sections introduce the fundamentals of the OPUCE project stressing the importance of having a structured way of describing user-generated services and their lifecycles in such an open service ecosystem. The paper continues by setting out the model that supports user-driven service lifecycles in a user-centric telecom environment. Section 5 concludes the paper.

2 The OPUCE Project

The OPUCE project is a research project within the European Union Sixth Framework Programme for Research and Technological Development. OPUCE aims to bridge advances in networking, communication and information technology

[1] Viral marketing refers to marketing techniques that use pre-existing social networks to produce increases in brand awareness, through self-replicating viral processes, analogous to the spread of pathological and computer viruses. It can be word-of-mouth delivered or enhanced by the network effects of the Internet. [Source: Wikipedia].

services towards a unique service environment where personalized services are dynamically created and provisioned by the end-users themselves.

The general objective of OPUCE is to leverage the creation of a user-centric service ecosystem giving users the chance to create their own personalized services as is currently done on the Internet.

Within this approach, service concepts are redefined. In OPUCE, services are envisioned as short-lived telecom services that end-users will create by orchestrating simpler services called base services. Base services are considered as functional units deployed by the operator or authorized third parties, available at the OPUCE platform and offered to end users through Web Services interfaces.[2]

Figure 1 introduces a detailed diagram of the OPUCE architecture. Its main elements are:

- A *Service Creation Environment* with a set of tools to be used by people or third parties to dynamically create services [6]. It can be seen as a portal through which users can create, deploy and share services. It consists on two portals: a user portal, to manage social networks, service subscriptions and configurations, etc; and a service portal, to manage the service edition, test, simulation, monitoring, etc. The Service Creation Environment also includes other general functions (access control, registration) and administration tools.
- A *Context Awareness* module to manage the adaptation and customization of services to the users' ambience conditions. In OPUCE two types of context aware adaptations are supported: explicit, when it is the service creator who specifies the service behavior taking into account user context information; and implicit, when the platform itself analyzes the service and adapts dynamically the execution.
- A *User Information Management* module to control the user's personal information (agenda, buddy list, presence information, device capabilities, potential use of certain services, etc.) identity management and AAA.
- A *Subscription Management* module to keep control of the user subscriptions to services. The information that this module stores is mainly consumed by other OPUCE modules (such as the context awareness or the user information modules).
- A *Service Lifecycle Manager* module which manages the lifecycle of all services created within the OPUCE platform. Section 4 describes in depth this module.
- A *Service Execution Environment* which manages the execution of services and orchestrates base services following the logic created by the users when composing them. A BPEL (Business Process Execution Language) [7] engine is used to orchestrate them, thus it is necessary to wrap those base services with Web Services interfaces. This module also supports events, managed by an event handler. Those events are generated by other OPUCE modules, such as the context awareness module.

---

[2] This definition is still coherent with the extended idea of service: Services are autonomous, platform-independent computational elements that can be described, published, discovered, orchestrated and programmed using standard protocols for the purpose of building networks of collaborating applications distributed within and across organizational boundaries. [Source: ICSOC 2005].

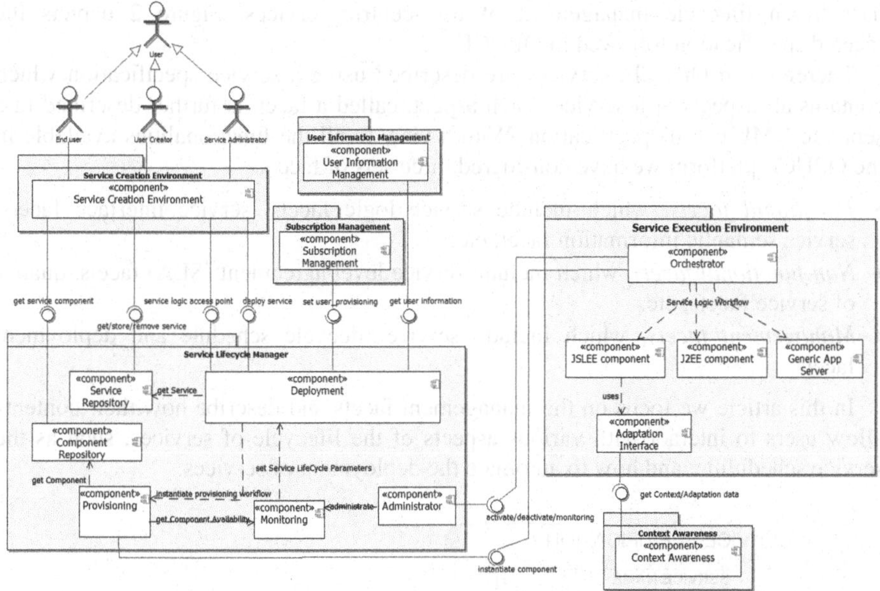

Fig. 1. The OPUCE architecture

This architecture has been validated with the creation of an intelligent email service. It forwards an incoming email according to the situation of the user and the device he has connected to the platform. For example, if the user is driving the service will set-up a call to read the email. If the user is not logged in his office PC, the service may also send an SMS containing the email subject and sender. The base services combined by the user creator are an email service, an SMS service, a text-to-speech call service and a user-context service.

Since this paper is focused on the service lifecycle of these user-centric services, we concentrate on both the Service Lifecycle Manager and the Service Execution Environment. The following sections will detail how user's can indirectly interact with these platform modules when creating services.

3 Supporting User-Centric Services: Service Description

A user-centric based service ecosystem requires major flexibility and dynamicity in managing service lifecycle compared to current service management systems. In order to automate the process between the creation and the execution of the services, the OPUCE platform needs a common way to completely describe the services.

The concept of service description has already been addressed in projects such as SPICE [8] and SeCSE [9]. Some of the results of these projects have been considered in OPUCE to create a service specification model completely. More precisely, the faceted approach [10] of the service description defined by the SeCSE project has been extended to support the user-centric features of OPUCE services, including the user-driven lifecycle management of user-centric services. Figure 2 depicts the faceted specification followed in OPUCE.

Therefore, in OPUCE, services are described using a service specification which contains all aspects of a service. Each aspect, called a facet, is further described in a separate XML-based specification. With a view to all the functionalities available in the OPUCE platform we have considered three sets of facets:

- *Functional facets*, which include service logic facets, service interface facets, service semantic information facet, etc.
- *Non-functional facets*, which include service level agreement (SLA) facets, quality of service facets, etc.
- *Management facets*, which include service lifecycle schedule and deployment facets.

In this article we focus on the management facets and describe how their contents allow users to interact with various aspects of the lifecycle of services, such as the service scheduling, and how to automate the deployment of services.

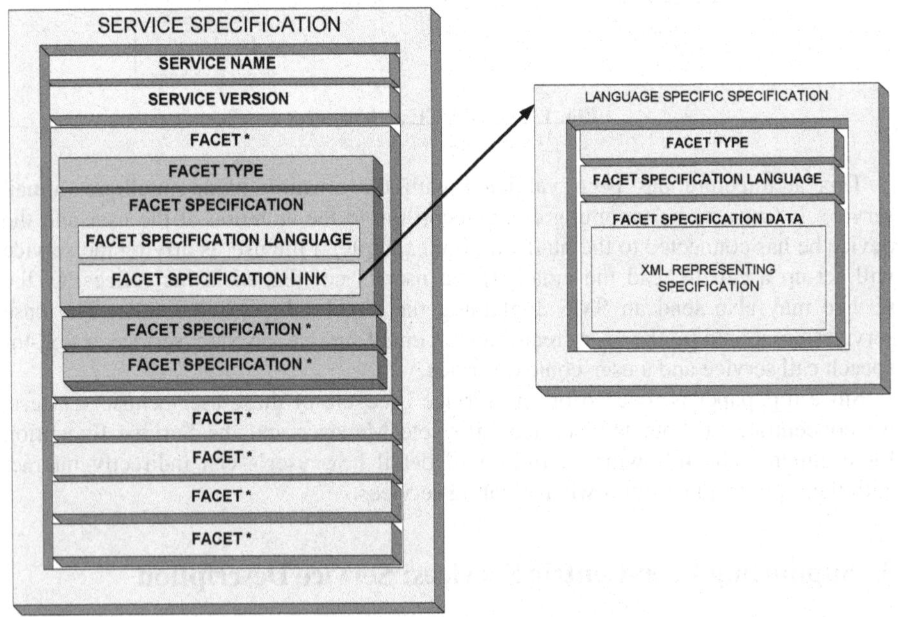

Fig. 2. Faceted approach used to describe services

4 Service Lifecycle Management in User-Centric Telecom Platforms

One of the major constraints in today's telecommunication services is the huge engineering effort that has to be spent both on development and marketing, in order to get a service running and deployed in the market. On the other hand, the Internet model provides a quite different and cheaper approach through user-centric service creation, e.g. mashups and viral marketing.

In order to transfer the advantages of the Internet model to telecom environments the platform must be able to cope with a huge set of user generated services each one orchestrating a subset of telecom-oriented base services. The requirements for the lifecycle management of these new services are:

1. to allow users to decide when and for how long their services must be available i.e. the lifecycle schedule. Since we encourage end-users to create services, the lifetime of services may be very short including even a one-time usage of a service. This means the overheads for users and platform administrators to deploy the services must be limited to an absolute minimum, which brings us to the second requirement;
2. to be able to provision base services and platform elements automatically, and to register and publish new services in order to be available to end-users.

As each service is compound of a different subset of base services and has its own dynamicity, lifecycle management processes in user-centric telecom platforms cannot be completely set beforehand and will depend both on the base services used and the user needs. However, there is at least one set of common activities a service always goes through in a telecom platform: creation, deployment, maintenance, and withdrawal.

- *Service Creation.* End users compose their own services by orchestrating a set of telecom base services. At the end of this process a service description is generated and stored in a service repository.
- *Service Deployment.* This is a platform supported process to make a service available in the communications environment. It usually includes physical installation, provisioning, registration, publication and activation. These tasks must be carried out in a given order. Whenever something fails, the steps already carried out must be undone. Deployment finishes when the service is up and running and ready to be subscribed to by end users.
- *Service Maintenance.* After the service has been properly deployed, this step will help the service provider to analyze the service execution status. This information will help to improve the service based on monitoring and usage statistics, to optimise the resource usage spent on that service and to identify errors and other runtime problems.
- *Service Withdrawal.* If the service is going to be substituted or evolved, or will not be used for a while, it must be stopped. Then, when it is no longer needed it must be cleared up from the platform. Service withdrawal consists of undoing the steps carried out during deployment phase; i.e. deactivation, withdraw the publication (unpublishing), deregistration, unprovisioning and physical uninstallation. Again, these tasks must be carried out in a given order.

The whole process a service goes through during its lifecycle can be formalized in a UML state diagram (Figure 3). Within OPUCE we consider that the execution platform exists and provides enough resources to provision all components and deploy the service. For this reason the physical installation and uninstallation will not be taken into account. For later stages of the project we will provide virtualized resources which can be set-up on demand with appropriate functionality. This virtualisation will provide not only the means to adapt the platform dynamically to the specific needs of the services running on top, but also provide a secured sand-box for testing and running services in a separate environment.

The activities associated to the other sub-states within the service deployment and service withdrawal depend on the base services used and the one that is composed: reservation of network resources, provision of base services, deployment of the new service, and so on. This information is implicitly obtained during the creation process. Therefore once the platform knows the set of base services that are used, and how the creator orchestrates them, it automatically generates the description of the activities associated to the management of the service lifecycle. Finally this information is stored as a set of facets within the service description: deployment and provisioning facets.

On the other hand, in order to allow users to drive the lifecycle of their new services, the Service Creation Environment explicitly collects information about the desired activation and deactivation events. This information, which allows the schedule of the service to be known, is also stored as a facet within the service description: lifecycle schedule facet.

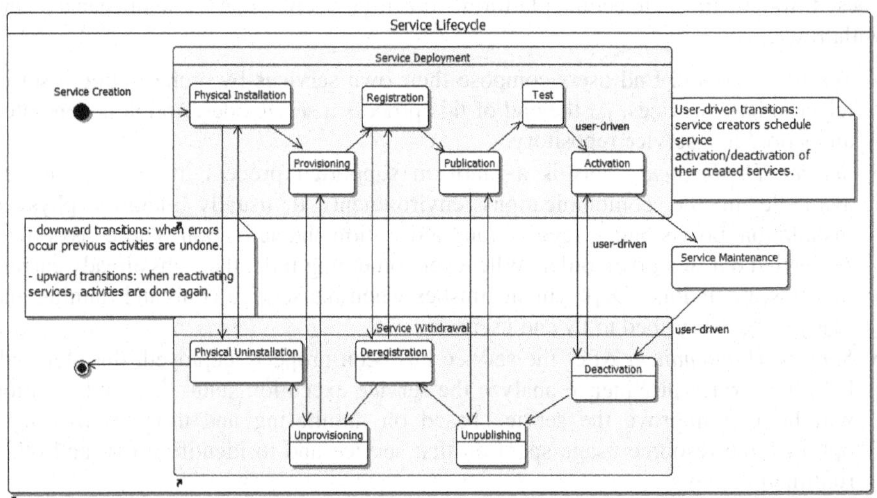

Fig. 3. The Service Lifecycle in OPUCE

Therefore, the service description includes all the information needed to carry out automated user-driven service lifecycle in its facets.

The following subsections detail this service lifecycle. First we explain how service creators can modify some aspects of the service lifecycle, scheduling the activation and deactivation of services. Then, the deployment process is described and how the service description contributes to making this process automatic. Finally, we close with the description of the lifecycle detailing the service withdrawal.

4.1 User-Driven Service Lifecycle

Within a user-centric service lifecycle model, users would like to decide, depending on their own preferences, when, where and how their services must be active. For example, an SMS service sending messages of the results of the local football team should only be available every weekend from Friday afternoon to Sunday evening, or a personal friend finder will be activated based on the location context.

Since activation in telecom platforms means the real allocation of resources, and therefore expenses to the platform providers, the deployment activities must be planned based on the initial schedule that the creator has decided for the service. On the other hand, at the end of the lifecycle the operator needs to be sure that all allocated resources are released and can be re-used for other services. Therefore withdrawal activities must be carried out after the service has been deactivated, whether the service is going to be activated again (following the user schedule) or if it is going to be definitely removed.

Within the OPUCE architecture the entity that controls and monitors the lifecycle activities is the Service Lifecycle Manager. This subsystem knows the current state of a service lifecycle, how to make a transition, and how to carry out the activities inside each transition. This entity also knows the user-driven transitions, monitors their occurrence, and triggers the related events. This entity must also set the policy for the other events within the lifecycle.

4.2 Service Deployment

Automatic deployment is nothing new in the Telco world, however the traditional deployment, automatic or not, has always been instigated and determined by operators. In OPUCE we go a step further; letting the service creators (the users) take control of some aspects of the deployment, such as the service scheduling.

There are more aspects that make the difference between OPUCE deployment concepts and traditional ones: the nature of the services. It is the user himself who triggers the deployment of the services until it is activated and finally available to users. In OPUCE, services are also created from outside the operator's administration domain, either from a computer, PDA or cellular phone and from different places such as the users' living room, a taxi or from their workplace.

Therefore, in OPUCE there is no human intervention from the operator either when triggering the service deployment process or during the deployment itself. Thus the service description must contain all the data that is necessary to deploy the service in each of the activities that make up the service deployment. As we will see, with the faceted approach the information needed to be handled by each activity can be clearly separated.

In the intelligent email service, once the creator has finished the composition the service must be deployed and provisioned to the platform. The Service Creation Environment will generate the service description including the facets needed for the deployment, i.e. service logic description, service deployment facet, service provisioning facet and the service lifecycle schedule. The deployment process is initialized and the following steps are executed in the OPUCE Platform:

- *Service Provisioning.* In OPUCE service provisioning is carried out automatically contrary to traditional provisioning which often requires a manual participation to create accounts for users, reserve resources, etc. We have identified three provisioning tasks, each one affecting different elements of the OPUCE architecture.
  - *Component Provisioning*, which considers the provisioning tasks to be done in those base services that the user creator has combined. These activities include the reservation of resources or configuration of permissions to use the base services. In the intelligent mail service, one of the component provisioning tasks is the creation of an email account for the user in the email base service.
  - *Platform Provisioning*, which considers the provisioning tasks to be carried out in the OPUCE platform components such as updating billing systems, updating service repository. These tasks are common for all the services created.
  - *User Provisioning*, which considers the provisioning tasks to be carried out on the user side at subscription time, such as installing a dedicated application in the user's mobile device. In our example, the user context base service requires that a module for generating the location information is provisioned on the client device. This provisioning task also involves the Subscription Management module to control subscriptions of end-users to services.

Each type of provisioning is a compound of different tasks. Thus separate facets for each type of provisioning are nested within the provisioning facet so as to be easily separated and distributed to the provisioning module within the Service Lifecycle Manager. Figure 4 depicts the service description structure for this facet and the relationship of each type of provisioning with the corresponding OPUCE architecture module.

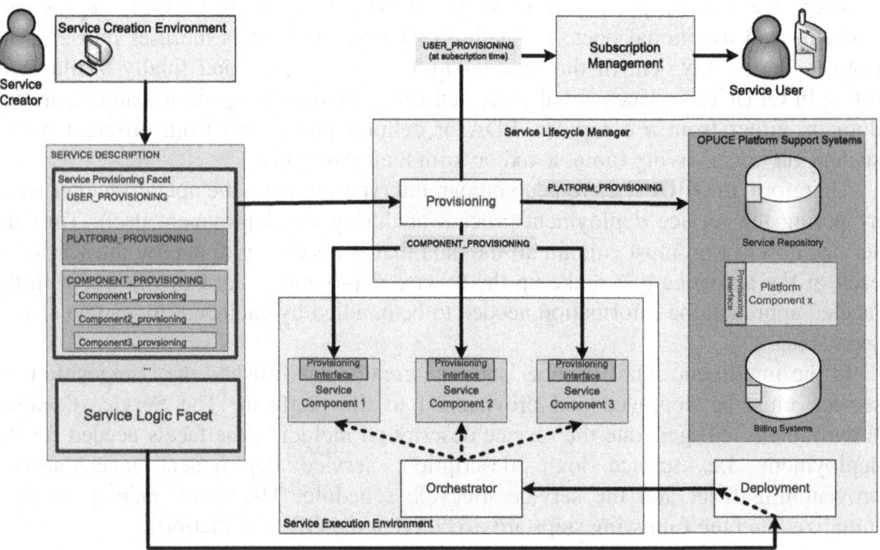

Fig. 4. Service provisioning and deployment in OPUCE

- *Service Registration.* In this activity the platform registers all the information needed to access the service once activated, such as endpoints if it is a Web Services-based access. In our service prototype, it consists of registering the email address as the way to access to the service.
- *Service Publication.* In this activity the service is officially published including all associated attributes, e.g. service type, descriptions, terms and conditions of use, etc, making service discovery easier. Some of these data are taken from the service description, such as the service name, the semantic facet, etc. Publication is done via a service advertiser to which other users can subscribe specific keywords describing the service instance like "intelligent email", "email forward" or "email reading".
- *Service Test.* The aim of this activity is to ensure that a new service is ready to be subscribed to and consumed by end-users. Nonetheless, this activity has not been considered in the first stages of the OPUCE project. It might be included in the second iteration of the project.
- *Service Activation.* This is the last step of the service deployment process. Once the service has been activated it becomes publicly available and ready for subscription. This activity is triggered by using the information included within the service lifecycle schedule facet of the service description. This is done by connecting the email system to forward the emails to our receiving component and thus initializing the service logic flow. So it can be configured that the service is only active Monday to Friday between 8 am and 8 pm.

4.3 Service Withdrawal

Basically, the service removal consists of undoing the steps carried out while deploying the service (except for testing the service). Most of them are automatic, and there is no intervention from the user. As well as the service description containing information on the correct deployment and provisioning of a service, it also contains information about the undeployment and unprovisioning activities. This information is automatically included in the service description by the service creation environment.

On the other hand, the user-centricity capabilities of OPUCE services imply that the service description must also include some information about when the users would like the services to be deactivated. Just as with the activation activity, this information is explicitly introduced by the service creator when scheduling the service from the service creation environment and is stored in the lifecycle schedule facet.

5 Conclusions

The user-centricity of services is gaining momentum in the current opening up of telecom service ecosystems. Within this approach, services are created and managed by the end-users themselves, even if they are not technically skilled.

The OPUCE project aims to create a complete platform to support the creation, management and execution of user-centric services. Its initial results have been summarized in this paper, especially those focused on the service lifecycle management of user-centric services and the architecture that supports it. This service lifecycle is also driven by users since service creators can interact with some of its aspects: they trigger the deployment process and can schedule the activation and deactivation of the services they have created.

The role of the service description in such an automatic and customizable lifecycle has also been described. We have used a faceted service specification to describe different aspects of the service: the deployment tasks, the scheduling of services, etc. Each one is used at a certain stage of the lifecycle and by a specific architecture module of the platform.

In order to validate the suitability of the service description in conjunction with the user-driven service lifecycle considered in OPUCE, we have developed a simple, but realistic and relevant, prototype. It consists of a simple service which orchestrates several base services (an email service, messaging service, a text to speech service and a user context service). It allows users to receive the content of an incoming email either as an SMS or as a voice message, depending on user's situation. This prototype validates the service description and some stages of the service lifecycle, such as the user-driven automatic deployment.

Further work considers a potential contribution to the OMA Service Provider Environment specification [11], which is currently under development, with some aspects of this user-driven lifecycle of user-centric services.

Acknowledgments

This work is framed within the IST European Integrated Project OPUCE (*Open Platform for User-centric service Creation and Execution*), 6th Framework Programme, Contract No. 34101. We thank all our partners in the project for their valuable comments and proposals aiming at improving the conceptual model.

References

1. Cuevas, A., Einsiedler, H., Moreno, J.I., Vidales, P.: The IMS Service Platform: A Solution for Next-Generation Networks Operators to Be More than Bit Pipes. IEEE Commun. Mag. 44(8), 75–81 (2006)
2. Yahoo Pipes Website (2007), http://pipes.yahoo.com/pipes
3. ETSI Standard: Open Service Access (OSA); Parlay X Web Services; Part 1: Common (Parlay X 3). ES 202 504-01 (2007)
4. OMA Specification: OMA Web Services Enabler (OWSER): Core Specification. Version 1.1 (2006)
5. OPUCE Website (2007), http://www.opuce.eu
6. Caetano, J., et al.: Introducing the user to the service creation world: concepts for user centric creation, personalization and notification. International Workshop on User centricity – state of the art. Budapest, Hungary (2007)
7. Andrews, T., et al.: Business Process Execution Language for Web Services. Version 1.1 (2003)
8. SPICE Website (2007), http://www.ist-spice.org
9. SeCSE Website (2007), http://secse.eng.it
10. Sawyer, P., Hutchison, J., Walkerdine, J., Sommerville, I.: Faceted Service Specification. In: Proceedings of Workshop on Service-Oriented Computing Requirements, Paris, France (2005)
11. OMA Specification: OMA Service Provider Environment Requirements. Candidate Version 1.0 (2005)

Run-Time Monitoring for Privacy-Agreement Compliance*

S. Benbernou, H. Meziane, and M.S. Hacid

LIRIS, University Claude Bernard Lyon1, France
{sbenbern,mshacid}@liris.univ-lyon1.fr,meziane_has@yahoo.fr

Abstract. This paper addresses the problem of monitoring the compliance of privacy agreement that spells out a consumer's privacy rights and how consumer private information must be handled by the service provider. A state machine based model is proposed to describe the Private Data Use Flow (PDUF) toward monitoring which can be used by privacy analyst to observe the flow and capture privacy vulnerabilities that may lead to non-compliance. The model is built on top of (i) properties and timed-related privacy requirements to be monitored that are specified using LTL (Linear Temporal logic) (ii) a set of identified privacy misuses.

1 Introduction

Numerous web services targeting consumers have accompanied the rapid growth of the Internet. Web services are available for banking, shopping, learning, healthcare, and government online. Most of these services require the consumer's personal information in one form or another which makes the service provider in the possession of a large amount of consumer private information along with the accompanying concerns over potential loss of consumer privacy. While *access control* aspect of security and privacy is well understood, it is unclear of how to do *usage control*. In response to the privacy concerns quoted above, in [4] we proposed a *privacy agreement* model that spells out a set of requirements related to consumer's privacy rights in terms of how service provider must handle privacy information. The properties and private requirements can be checked at a design time prior to execution, however, the monitoring of the requirements at run-time has strong motivations since those properties can be violated at run time. Thus, checking at run-time the compliance of the requirements defined in the privacy agreement is a challenging issue. That issue must be properly addressed otherwise it could lead to agreement breaches and to lower service quality. Indeed, the private data use flow must be observed which means monitoring the behaviour of the privacy agreement. From the results of the observations, analysis can be done to come up to an understanding, why the non-compliance took place and what remedy will be provided enhancing the privacy agreement.

* This work is partially supported by the French National Research Agency (ANR) - Program "Jeunes chercheurs:Servicemosaic" a part of the international project ServiceMosaic; http://servicemosaic.isima.fr/.

B. Krämer, K.-J. Lin, and P. Narasimhan (Eds.): ICSOC 2007, LNCS 4749, pp. 353–364, 2007.

The common approach developed to support requirements monitoring at run-time assumes that the system must identify the set of the requirements to be monitored. In fact, as part of the privacy agreement model, the set of privacy requirements to be monitored are needed from which *monitoring private units* are extracted and their occurrences at run-time would imply the violation of the requirements. Besides the functional properties (e.g operations of the service), the time-related aspects are relevant in the setting of the privacy agreement. In addition, the non-compliance or failing to uphold the privacy requirements are manifested in terms of vulnerabilities must be identified.

In this paper, we propose an approach for the management of privacy data terms defined in the privacy agreement at run-time. The approach features a model based on state machine which is supported by *abstractions* and *artifacts* allowing the run-time management. Our contribution articulates as follows:

1. From the privacy requirements defined in the privacy agreement, we extract a set of *monitoring private units* specified by the means of Linear Temporal logic (LTL) formulas,
2. The set of privacy misuses is most likely met throughout the private data use is provided. That set is not limited and can be enriched by those promptly revealed when they occur in run-time and captured by the analysis,
3. A state machine based model is provided in order to describe the activation of each privacy agreement clauses, that is, it spells out the Private Data Use Flow (PDUF). The state machine supports abstractions and by the means of previous artifacts, the behaviour observations are expressed. It will *observe* which and when a clause is activated, or which and when a clause is violated and what types of vulnerabilities happened, or which clause is compliant and etc. Such observations lead to do reasoning to enhance the privacy agreement and enrich the knowledge on misuses.

The remainder of the paper is structured as follows. We start by presenting an overview of the privacy agreement developed in our previous work in Section 2. In Section 3, we describe the architectural support for privacy data use flow monitoring. Section 4 proposes an LTL-based approach to specify the monitoring private units and presents a set of privacy misuses. In Section 5, we present the private data use flow model. We discuss related work in Section 6 and conclude with a summary and issues for future work in Section 7.

2 Privacy Agreement Model

To make the paper self containing, in this section we recall the privacy agreement model specified in our previous work [4,5]. We proposed a framework for privacy management in Web services. A privacy policy model has been defined as an agreement supporting a lifecycle management which is an important deal of a dynamic environment that characterizes Web services based on the state machine, taking into account the flow of the data use in the agreement. Hence, WS-Agreement has been extended including privacy aspects. In this setting, the features of the framework are:

- The privacy policy and data subject preferences are defined together as one element called *Privacy-agreement*, which represents a contract between two parties, the service customer and the service provider within a validity. We provided abstractions defining the expressiveness required for the privacy model, such as rights and obligations.
- The framework supports lifecycle management of privacy agreement. We defined a set of events that may occur in the dynamic environment, and a set of change actions used to modify the privacy agreement. An *agreement-evolution* model is provided in the privacy-agreement.
- An *agreement-negotiation protocol* is provided to build flexible interactions and conversations between parties when a conflict happens due to the events occurring in the dynamic environment of the Web service.

Informally speaking the abstraction of privacy model is defined in terms of the following requirements:

- *data-right*, is a predefined action on data the data-user is authorized to do if he wishes to.
- *data-obligation*, is the expected action to be performed by service provider or third parties (data- users) after handling personal information in data-right. This type of obligation is related to the management of personal data in terms of their selection, deletion or transformation.

Formally speaking, we defined **data-right** r_d as a tuple (u, d, op_d, p_d), with $u \subseteq \mathcal{U}$ and $d \subseteq \mathcal{D}$ and $op_d \subseteq \mathcal{PO}$ and $\mathcal{R}^d = \{\{r_d^i\}_j \;/\; i > 0\; j > 0\}$, where $\mathcal{U}$ is the ontology of data users and $\mathcal{D}$ is the ontology of personal data and $\mathcal{PU}$ is the ontology of purposes $\mathcal{PO}$ is the set of authorized operations identifying purposes of the service and p_d is the period of data retention (the data-right validity), and $\mathcal{R}^d$ is the set of data-rights.

We defined **data-obligation** o_d as a tuple (u, d, a_d, μ_d) with $u \subseteq \mathcal{U}$ and $d \subseteq \mathcal{D}$ and $a_d \in \mathcal{A}_o$ and $\mathcal{O}^d = \{\{o_d^i\}_j \;/\; i > 0\; j > 0\}$, where $\mathcal{U}$ is the ontology of data users and $\mathcal{D}$ is the ontology of personal data and $\mathcal{A}_o$ a set of actions that must be taken by the data user and μ_d is an activated date of the obligation, and $\mathcal{O}^d$ is the set of data-obligations.

Based on those requirements, we formalized a privacy data model $\mathcal{P}^d$ as a couple $< \mathcal{R}^d, \mathcal{O}^d >$, where $\mathcal{R}^d$ is the set of data-rights and $\mathcal{O}^d$ is the set of data-obligations. By means the proposed privacy model, we extended current WS-Agreement specifications which do not support the privacy structure and do not include the possibility to update the agreement at runtime. The proposed extension is reflected in a new component in a WS-Agreement called ***Privacy-agreement***,

A privacy-agreement structure is represented in two levels :

(1) *policy level*, it specifies the *Privacy-Data term* defined as a set of *clauses* of the contract denoted by $\mathcal{C}$ between the provider and the customer. The description of the elements defined in the privacy-data model is embedded in this level, including guarantees dealing with privacy-data model.

(2) *negotiation level*, it specifies all possible events that may happen in the service behavior, thus evolving the privacy guarantee terms defined in the policy level. Negotiation terms are all possible actions to be taken if the guarantee of privacy terms is not respected, then a conflict arises. They are used through a negotiation protocol between

the service provider and the customer. We also defined in this level the validity period of the privacy agreement and a set of penalties when the requirements are not fulfilled. In the rest of the paper, we are interested by the first level. We will present a way to observe the use of the private data throughout the run time, and how to capture the compliance of the agreement related in the privacy data terms.

3 Overview of the Monitoring Framework

We devise a privacy-compliance architecture for monitoring. It incorporates three main components discussed in this paper, they are depicted in Figure1 and are namely a *private requirements specification*, a *PDUF Observer*, a *monitor*. The figure assumes the web service executes a set of operations using private data. While executing the operations of the service, the process generates events stored in a database as logs.

In order to check the privacy compliance, the monitoring private units are extracted from the *private requirements specification* defined in the privacy agreement. Monitoring private units are specified by the means of LTL formulas taking into account the privacy time-related requirements using a set of clocks.

The *monitor* collects the raw information to be monitored regarding the monitoring private units from the event logs database. The collected data and private data misuses stored in a database are fitted together in the *PDUF Observer* component in order to check the non-compliance.

The PDUF observer observes the behaviour of the private data use flow. The privacy agreement clauses are observed, which means, when a clause is activated, or which

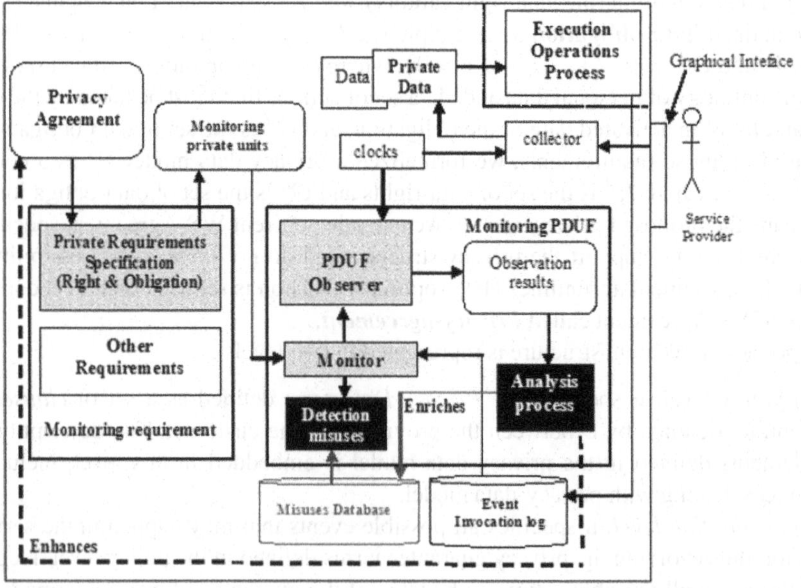

Fig. 1. Monitoring framework

and when a clause is violated and what types of vulnerabilities happened, or which clause is compliant etc. A model to represent such behaviour is provided. At the end of the observations the *observation results* report is generated to the Analysis process depicted in the figure.

From the previous observed results and reasoning facilities, the analysis process will provide diagnosis of violations, for instance understanding why the non-compliance took place and what remedy will be provided enhancing the privacy agreement. It can also enrich the database of misuses by those promptly revealed when they occur at run-time. Finally, the detection misuses component consumes the misuses recorded in the database and identify the violation types from compliant usage behaviour. We will not give more details about the analysis and detection components, they are out of the scope of the paper.

4 Requirements for Monitoring Privacy

One of the key aspects for the reliability of the service is the trustworthiness of the compliance of its collected private data use to the agreement. To ensure the privacy agreement compliance, the observation of the service behaviour and its private data use becomes a necessity. For making the compliance happen, keep track of all uses is a fact, that is, from the result of the observations, if needed when violations are detected, the revision of the agreement can be held and relaxed. Indeed, to make the observation effective, two essential ingredients are required, we need to define what kind of knowledge must be monitored and the knowledge which makes the agreement not compliant. In this section we discuss the two aspects.

4.1 Monitoring Units for Privacy

We distinguish four types of unit to be monitored: *private data unit*, *operation unit*, *temporal unit* and *role unit*.

• *Private data unit.* The private data unit d is the core of our monitoring framework. In fact, from the log, we need to observe only the private data and its behaviour.

• *Operation unit.* We distinguish two types of actions (i) actions used to complete the service activity for the current purpose for which it was provided and are denoted by $Op_{current}$ (ii) actions used by a service to achieve other activities than those for which they are provided, called $Op_{extra-activity}$. Those two kinds of operations are proposed in order to know when a compliance is compromised, while the service is running for which it was provided or for some operations else. The set of the operations is denoted Op.

• *Role unit.*We need to observe who will use the private data.

• *Temporal unit.* The analysis of time-related aspects of the privacy monitoring requires the specification of operation durations and timed requirements. The instance monitor i.e. temporal unit is defined as a temporal formula using Linear Temporal Logic (P,S,H, operators) [10]. We identify four types of temporal units, and we denote the set of temporal units by $\mathcal{T}$:

Definition 1. ***(Right triggering time).*** *For each collected private data d, the right triggering time denoted ϵ is the activation time of the operation associated to the right:* $\forall R^i_d \in \mathcal{C} \rightarrow \exists \epsilon^i_d \in T \mid (op^i_d.R^i_d)^{\epsilon^i_d}$ *is activated, where i is the i th right associated to the private data d, $\mathcal{C}$ is a set of clauses in the agreement, and T is a domain of time values, and the LTL formula using P the past temporal operator is* $\models_{\epsilon^i_d} P\ op^i_d.R^i_d$, *which means in the past at ϵ^i_d time the operation is true.*

Definition 2. ***(Right end time).*** *For each collected private data d, the right end time denoted β is the end time of the data use (operation) associated to the right:* $\forall R^i_d \in \mathcal{C} \rightarrow \exists \beta^i_d \in T \mid (op^i_d.R^i_d)^{\beta^i_d}$ *is finished, and the LTL formula is* $\models_{\beta^i_d} P\neg op^i_d.R^i_d$ *at β time the operation is not valid.*

Definition 3. ***(Obligation triggering time).*** *For each collected private data d, the obligation triggering time denoted μ is the activation time of the action associated to the obligation:* $\forall O_d \in \mathcal{C} \rightarrow \exists \mu_d \in T \mid (a_d.O_d)^{\mu_d}$ *is activated, the LTL formula using S since operator,* $\models_{\mu_d} (a_d.O_d)S(\neg op_d.R_d)$, *which means $a_d.O_d$ is true since $\neg op_d.R_d$ (The formula is valid for the last occurrence of each right in which the obligation is associated to).*

Definition 4. ***(Obligation end time).*** *For each collected private data d, the obligation end time denoted α is the end time of the action associated to the obligation:* $\forall O_d \in \mathcal{C} \rightarrow \exists \alpha_d \in T \mid (a_d.O_d)^{\alpha_d}$ *is ended, the LTL formula is* $\models_{\alpha_d} P\ \neg a_d.O_d$ *at α time the action is not valid.*

4.2 Privacy Misuses

In this section, we identify the non-compliance or failing to uphold the agreement manifested in terms of vulnerabilities or misuses. We provide a privacy misuses which is most likely met throughout the private data use. We have classified them into two classes *explicit* and *implicit misuses*. The former one can be visualized in our private data use flow model whereas the latter can not be identified. For instance, *security on data, accountability* can not be identified in our model, so it is not in the scope of the paper. We classified three types of explicit misuses, *Temporal misuses*, *operation misuses* and *role misuses*. Table 1 summarizes such misuses. However, the listed misuses are not unique, while run-time, some new misuses can be detected and come to enrich the misuse database. How to detect such misuses is not discussed in this paper.

5 Monitoring Private Data Use Flow

In order to describe the lifecycle management privacy data terms defined in the agreement, we need to *observe* the data use flow. Such observations will allow us to make analysis, diagnosis and to provide reasoning on violations, for instance why the violations happen, what we can improve in the agreement for making the compliance of the agreement happens etc. The analysis aspect is not handled in this paper.

We propose to express the Private Data Use Flow (PDUF) as a state machine because of its formal semantic, well suited to describe the activation of different clauses of the

Table 1. Misuses identification through privacy data use flow

Requirement	Compliance Category	Misuses	Type of misuses
Data-right	Use	no-authorized operation op_d *[wrong-use]*; the misuse happens when the following formula is not valid: $\not\models Hop_d.R_d$, in all the past op_d is not admitted.	Explicit
	Retention time	violation of data retention period: the misuse happens when the formula $\models P\left((\beta_d - \epsilon_d) > p_d\right)$ is valid.	Explicit
	Disclose-To	a *[wrong collector]* as third party; the following formula is not valid: $\not\models Hu_d.R_d$, in all the past u_d is a wrong user.	Explicit
Data-obligation	Obligation Activation date	violation of the obligation activation, the misuse happens when the formula $\models P(\beta_d > \mu_d)$ is valid.	Explicit
	Security on data (delete, update, hide, unhide,...)	Lack or failure of mechanism or procedure.	Implicit
Security	/	1)loss of confidentiality and integrity of data for flows from the Internet, 2) external attacks on the processes and platform operating systems since they are linked to the Internet, 3) external attacks on the database,...	Implicit

privacy agreement. It is an effective way to identify privacy vulnerabilities, where a service 's compliance to privacy regulations may be compromised. It will show *which* and *when* a clause is activated toward the monitoring or which and when a clause is violated. The time-related requirement properties set in the agreement are depicted explicitly in the state machine. It will specify the states of each activated clause in the policy level. The semantic of the state machine is to define all the triggered operations involving private data from the activation of the agreement (initial state) to the end of the agreement (final state) . We need to keep track of all private data use with or without violations. Figure 2 shows an example of the privacy data term activation for the purchase service provider.

We have identified several abstractions in relation to private data flow, *private data use* abstractions and *authorization* abstractions. The first abstractions describe the different states in which the agreement is -which private data is collected and when it is used and for what and who use it- . The authorization abstractions provide the conditions that must be met for transitions to be fired.

In this formalism, the fact that the private data has a time retention for a right (respectively the activation time of an obligation) called *fixed guard time*, the private data use time is represented by time increment in the state, followed by the end of the right (respectively obligations) with success or a violation of that time. Intuitively, PDUF is a

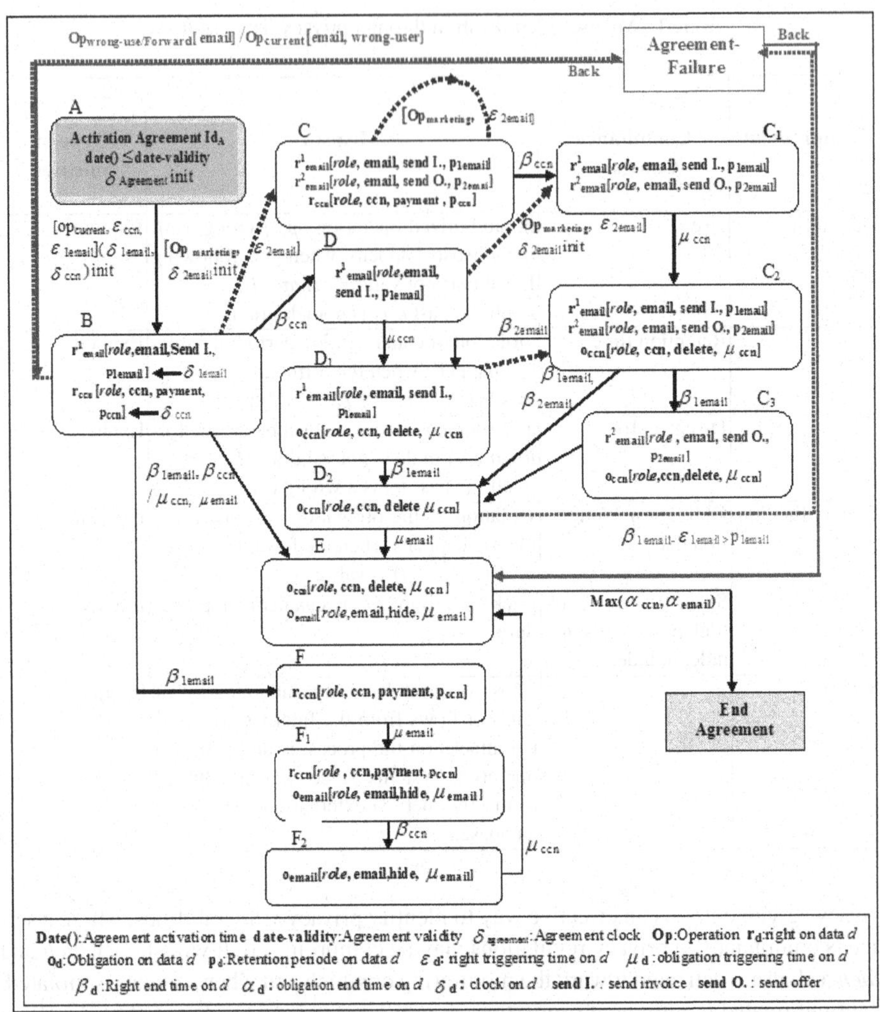

Fig. 2. Private Data Use Flow (PDUF)

finite state machine for which a set of clock variables is assigned denoted by Δ. A variable is assigned for each activation of the clauses (rights and obligations). The values of these variables increase with passing the time. The transition will take place when an operation is activated or monitoring time units are triggered. If the temporal units are compliant to the guard times, it will happen the transition will take place with success and no violation is recorded in that state. However, if non-compliance is detected, the transition will take place with violation, then the state is marked as violated.

Definition 5. ***(PDUF.)*** *A PDUF is a tuple* $(\mathcal{S}, s_0, s_f, \mathcal{M}, \mathcal{R}, \mathcal{Q})$

- $\mathcal{S}$ *is a set of states;*
- $s_0 \in \mathcal{S}$ *is the initial state, and* $s_f \in \mathcal{S}$ *is the final state ;*

- *$\mathcal{M}$ is a set of monitoring private units: set of triggered operations and/or set of temporal units, $\mathcal{M} = \{\mathcal{OP}, \mathcal{T}\}$;*
- *$\mathcal{R} \subseteq \mathcal{S}^2 \times \mathcal{M} \times 2^{\Delta}$ is a set of transitions with a set of operations or a set of triggering time and a set of clocks to be initialized $\delta_{d-init} \in \Delta$;*
- *$\mathcal{Q} : \mathcal{S} \rightarrow \{\delta_i \mid \delta_i \in \Delta, i \geq 1\}$ assigns a set of clocks to the states.*

The effect of each transition $\mathcal{R}(s, s^{'}, m, c)$ from the source state s to the target state $s^{'}$ is to set a status of the clauses in the agreement which means to perform an operation $op \in \mathcal{OP}$ using a private data or a monitoring time unit $t \in \mathcal{T}$ is activated.

Let's define the semantic of PDUF through the following example for the agreement with a set of clauses (rights and obligations).

Example 1. Let us consider the example of a purchase service without giving details about transactions between the customer and the service. An agreement has been signed between them setting up a set of clauses with a validity period denoted by *validity-date*. Those clauses are specified as follows: at the date *date()* the agreement is activated and the service collects email address (email) and Credit card number (ccn). Those private data are used for two types of operations **(1)** to complete the service activity for the current purpose i.e. the email is used to send invoices and Credit card number for the payment of invoices. The operation are expressed by the following rights $r^1_{email}(role, email, send\ \ invoice, p_{1email})$ and $r_{ccn}(role, ccn, payment\ \ invoice, p_{ccn})$ **(2)** to achieve other activities than those for which they are provided, for instance marketing purpose i.e. the email is used to send the available products and their prices, that clause is expressed by the right $r^2_{email}(role, email, send\ offer, p_{2email})$.

When the retention times of the private data email and ccn $(\beta_{1email}, \beta_{2email}, \beta_{ccn})$ are elapsed, the corresponding obligations are triggered, $O_{email}(role, email, hide, \mu_{email})$ and $O_{ccn}(role, ccn, delete, \mu_{ccn})$. Those obligations specifying the role must hide (respectively delete) as soon as the activation date μ_{email} (respectively μ_{ccn}) is reached.

In what follow, due to the space limitation we will not comment on all the state machine, and for the sake of clarity, we omit some details about it, such as the clocks on the states and all the misuses etc.

States: we define four types of states:

- The initial state s_i represents the activation of the agreement where the first private data of the customer is collected. In Figure 2, s_i is defined by A.
- The intermediary states represent the flow of the collected private data use. By entering a new state, a private data is used.
  - to complete the activity of the service for which it was provided, identified in Figure 2 by $Op_{current}$. In the state B, the current operations are *SendInvoice* and *payment.* In this state, the clocks δ_{1email} and δ_{ccn} are activated respectively to r^1_{email} and r_{ccn} and incremented passing the time.
  - and/or to achieve an extra activity as depicted in Figure 2 by $Op_{marketing}$. The right r^2_{email} is activated in the state C as soon as the marketing operation is triggered. The same operation can be activated as many times as the data time retention p_{email} is valid. It is represented by a *loop* in the state C. The privacy agreement remains in the same state.

  - and the data use is finished (the right). For instance, the agreement will be in the state C_1 since the data retention guard time is reached, which means the finishing time of the right is over and is denoted by β_{ccn}.
  - and/or to activate an operation dealing with the security (e.g. obligations) when the retention time of the private data defined as a fixed time in the right is elapsed and the time for triggering the obligations starts. For instance, such case is depicted in Figure 2 in the state C_2, where o_{ccn} is activated when the usage time of the date β_{ccn} is reached and the obligation time starts defined in the transition by μ_{ccn}.
- The *virtual* state labeled *Failure agreement* will be reached when a private data is used to achieve the operation misuse, and/or role misuse and/or time misuse happens regarding the clock variable values and fixed times. For instance, the first type of misuse is identified by $Op_{wrong-use/Forward}[email]$ between state B and Failure agreement state. We call this state as a virtual state because it is considered only like a flag of misuses.
- The final state s_f represents the end of the agreement which means the validity of the agreement is over, and either the data use in all its shapes is compliant to the agreement or the agreement is not respected due to the misuses. The best case is to reach the end of the agreement without any misuses as depicted in the figure from the state E to the end-agreement state.

Transitions: Transitions are labeled with conditions which must be met for the transition to be triggered. We have identified three kinds of authorization abstractions:

- Activation conditions. We define two types of activation (i) an operation has the authorization to collect private data to achieve the current aim of the service, for instance, $op_{current}$ condition on the transition from the state A to the state B, an operation dealing with an extra activity of the service has the authorization to be triggered. For instance, the operation $op_{marketing}$ from the state B to the state C.
- Temporal conditions. The transition is called *timed transition*. Regarding the temporal monitoring unit, we define four types of timed transitions (1) *right triggering time* ϵ, for instance from the state B to the state C the timed transition is labeled by ϵ_{2email} along with the activation of the clock δ_{2email} assigned to the right r^2_{email} (2) *Right end time* β, from the state C to state C_1 the transition is labeled β_{ccn}, which means the ccn use is over (3) *Obligation triggering time* μ, the authorization to keep the private data is finished and the obligation is triggered, for instance from the state C_1 to C_2, the transition is labeled μ_{ccn}, the operation of security must be fired (4) *Obligation end time* α, the obligation is over, for instance from the state E to the end-agreement state, we calculate the maximum of the two end times α_{email} and α_{ccn}, in our case it is the best way to finish the compliance of the agreement.
- Misuse Conditions. The transition can be labeled by all the misuses identified in section 4.2. For the misuse dealing with the operations , the target state of the transition is *failure-agreement* and *Back* to the previous state, for instance, the operation $op_{wrong-use/forward}$ on the transition between the state B and the failure-agreement state, and back to the state B. For the temporal misuse the target state of the transition is *failure-agreement* and no back to the previous state rather to the

next state, for instance, a time violation happens in D_2 and the system passes to the next state E.

6 Related Work

The literature is very scarce on works dealing with monitoring the privacy compliance in web service. However, the problem of web services and distributed business processes monitoring is investigated in the works [2,3,9,12,1,7]. The research in [9,12] is focusing on monitoring of service-based software (SBS) systems specified in BPEL. They use event calculus for specifying the requirements that must be monitored. The run-time checking is done by an algorithm based on integrity constraint checking in temporal deductive databases. Barezi et al in [2,3], developed a tool that instruments the composition process of an SBS system in order to make it call external monitoring services that check assertions at runtime. The work in [1] is close to the previous works, the authors present a novel approach to web services described as BPEL processes. The approach offers a clear separation of the service business logic from the monitoring functionality. Moreover, it provides the ability to monitor both the behaviours of single instances of BPEL processes, as well as behaviours of a class of instances. Lazovik et al. [8] propose an approach based on operational assertions and actor assertions. They are used to express properties that must be true in one state before passing to the next, to express an invariant property that must be held throughout all the execution states, and to express properties on the evolution of process variables. While providing facilities for the verification of processes these approaches do not take privacy requirements into account.

In terms of privacy compliance, there exist few works including [6,13,11]. In [6], the authors examine privacy legislation to derive requirements for privacy policy compliance systems. They propose an architecture for a privacy policy compliance system that satisfies the requirements and discuss the strengths and weaknesses of their proposed architecture. In [13] the author proposes a graphical visualization notation to facilitate the identification of private information vulnerabilities that can lead to privacy legislation non-compliance. In [11], the authors automate the management and enforcement of privacy policies (including privacy obligations) and the process of checking that such policies and legislation are indeed complied with. This work is related to enterprise. While providing tools for privacy compliance in the previous works, however, these approaches do not take private data use flow into account and no formal method along with reasoning and also no time-related properties are discussed.

7 Conclusion

This work has proposed an effective and formal approach to observe and verify the privacy compliance of web services at run-time. We have emphasized private data use flow monitoring of privacy-agreement requirements, which is an important issue to date has not been addressed. It is a state machine based approach, that allows to take into account the timed-related properties of privacy requirements and to facilitate the identification of private information misuses. The privacy properties to be monitored are specified in LTL. The monitored units are extracted from the privacy agreement requirements. The approach supports the monitoring of a set of identified misuses that lead to non-compliance, and which can be enriched from the observation diagnosis. The approach is still under development. Our ongoing work and a promising area for the future include: (1) The development of reasoning facilities to provide a diagnosis of misuses, (2) The development of tools for detecting the misuses (3) The development of tools along with metrics for enhancing the privacy-agreement from the observations (4) Expanding the approach to handle the composition of the services.

References

1. Barbon, F., Traverso, P., Pistore, M., Trainotti, M.: Run-time monitoring of instances and classes of web service compositions. In: ICWS'06. Proceedings of the IEEE International Conference on Web Services, pp. 63–71. IEEE Computer Society Press, Chicago (2006)
2. Baresi, L., Ghezzi, C., Guinea, S.: Smart monitors for composed services. In: ICSOC '04. Proceedings of the 2nd international conference on Service oriented computing (2004)
3. Baresi, L., Guinea, S.: Towards dynamic monitoring of ws-bpel processes. In: Benatallah, B., Casati, F., Traverso, P. (eds.) ICSOC 2005. LNCS, vol. 3826, pp. 269–282. Springer, Heidelberg (2005)
4. Benbernou, S., Meziane, H., Li, Y.H., Hacid, M.: A privacy agreement model for web services. In: SCC'07. IEEE International Conference on Service Computing, IEEE Computer Society Press, Salt Lake City, USA (2007)
5. Guermouche, N., Benbernou, S., Coquery, C.E, Hacid, M.: Privacy-aware web service protocol replaceability. In: ICWS'07. IEEE International Conference on Web Services, IEEE Computer Society Press, Salt Lake City, USA (2007)
6. Yee, G., Korba, L.: Privacy policy compliance for web services. In: ICWS'04. Proc. of the IEEE International Conference on Web Services, IEEE Computer Society Press, San Diego, USA (2004)
7. Kazhamiakin, R., Pandya, P., Pistore, M.: Representation, verification, and computation of timed properties in web. In: ICWS'06. Proceedings of the IEEE International Conference on Web Services, IEEE Computer Society Press, Los Alamitos (2006)
8. Lazovik, A., Aiello, M., Papazoglou, M.: Associating assertions with business processes and monitoring their execution. In: ICSOC '04. Proceedings of the 2nd international conference on Service oriented computing (2004)
9. Mahbub, K., Spanoudakis, G.: Run-time monitoring of requirements for systems composed of web-services: Initial implementation and evaluation experience. In: ICWS. 2005 IEEE International Conference on Web Services, IEEE Computer Society Press, Orlando, Florida, USA (2005)
10. Manna, Z., Pnueli, A.: The Temporal Logic of Reactive and Concurrent Systems:Specification. Springer, Heidelberg (1992)
11. Mont, M.C., Pearson, S., Thyne, R.: A systematic approach to privacy enforcement and policy compliance checking in enterprises. In: Fischer-Hübner, S., Furnell, S., Lambrinoudakis, C. (eds.) TrustBus 2006. LNCS, vol. 4083, pp. 91–102. Springer, Heidelberg (2006)
12. Spanoudakis, G., Mahbub, K.: Non intrusive monitoring of service based systems. International Journal of Cooperative Information Systems (2006)
13. Yee, G.: Visualization for privacy compliance. In: VizSEC '06. Proceedings of the 3rd international workshop on Visualization for computer security, Fairfax, USA (2006)

Task Memories and Task Forums: A Foundation for Sharing Service-Based Personal Processes

Rosanna Bova[1,2], Hye-Young Paik[3], Boualem Benatallah[3], Liangzhao Zeng[4], and Salima Benbernou[1]

[1] LIRIS, University of Lyon 1, France
{rosanna.bova,sbenbern}@liris.cnrs.fr
[2] LIESP, University of Lyon 1, France
[3] CSE, University of New South Wales, Australia
{hpaik,boualem}@cse.unsw.edu.au
[4] IBM T. J. Watson Research Center Yorktown Heights, NY 10598
lzeng@us.ibm.com

Abstract. The growing number of online accessible services call for effective techniques to support users in discovering, selecting, and aggregating services. We present WS-Advisor, a framework for enabling users to capture and share task memories. A task memory represents knowledge (e.g., context and user rating) about services selection history for a given task. WS-Advisor provides a declarative language that allows users to share task definitions and task memories with other users and communities. The service selection component of this framework enables a user agent to improve its service selection recommendations by leveraging task memories of other user agents with which the user share tasks in addition to the local task memories.

1 Introduction

The recent advances in ICT comprising Web services, pervasive computing, and Web 2.0 promise to enable interactions and efficiencies that have never been experienced before. Users will have ubiquitous access to a network of services along with computing resources, data sources, and user friendly tools [1]. The concerted advances in services oriented computing [2] and pervasive systems [1] provide the foundations for a holistic paradigm in which users, services, and resources can establish on-demand interactions, possibly in real-time, to realize useful and context-aware experiences.

Service oriented architecture and Web services propose abstractions, frameworks, and standards to facilitate integrated access to heterogeneous applications and resources. There has been major progress in terms of services description, interaction protocols, services discovery and composition [2]. More specifically, services composition languages and frameworks foster agile integration by simplifying integration at the communication, data or business logic layers. Furthermore, by leveraging efforts in semantic web services [3], service composition frameworks made a forward step in enabling automated support for service description matching [3].

B. Krämer, K.-J. Lin, and P. Narasimhan (Eds.): ICSOC 2007, LNCS 4749, pp. 365–376, 2007.

Although existing composition techniques have produced promising results that are certainly useful, they are primarily targeted to professional programmers (e.g., business process developers). Composition languages are still procedural in nature and composition logic is still hard to specify [4]. Specifying even simple personal processes is still time consuming. Most of the time, if the needed integrated service is not available, users need to access various individual services to become self-supported. For example, a driver might need to use several services including location, travel route computation, traffic information, and road conditions services to get timely information regarding a trip in progress [1].

The emerging wave of innovations in Web 2.0 promotes a new paradigm in which both providers and end users (including non-expert users) can easily and freely share information and services over the Web [5]. For instance, users publish and share information (e.g., URLs, photos, opinions) via personal blogs, social networks and Web communities. Portals such as YouTube, Flickr and Delicious flourished over the years as user-centric information sharing systems. These systems offer more simple and ad-hoc information sharing techniques (e.g., free tagging and flexible organization of content) [6]. We argue that applying such easy-and-free style of information sharing to service oriented paradigm would offer tremendous opportunities for automating information management, in particular for the area of managing data from a variety of end-user processes (or referred to as *personal processes* [16]). Such processes are apparent in office, travel, media, or e-government. For example, travellers will script personal travel arrangement tasks and office workers will script purchasing processes, etc.

In this direction, we propose the WS-Advisor framework. WS-Advisor provides a declarative language and an agent-based architecture for sharing task definitions and services selection recommendations among users.

In our previous work [7,8], we proposed *task memories*. In a nutshell, a task memory represents the knowledge about services that have been selected in past executions of the task and contexts in which these services have been selected (i.e, the information about the contexts in which certain combination of services were considered most appropriate by users). Task memories are used during service selection to recommend most relevant candidate services. By applying continuous feedback on the on-going usage of services, the system is able to maintain and evolve the task memories, resulting in more fine-tuned service selection.

In this paper, we focus on task definitions and task memories sharing in the WS-Advisor framework. More specifically, we make the following contributions:

- To simplify task information sharing, WS-Advisor provides a metadata model and a declarative (SQL-like) language. Together, they provide an effective management platform for a task repository. The language is used for specifying *task sharing policies.* which includes what a user is willing to share about a task repository and with whom.
- We propose the concept of *task forums* to maintain task repositories (e.g., task definitions and task memories) that may be of interests to several individuals or communities. Essentially a task forum provides a means to collect

and share domain specific task definitions and task memories among users. This allows users to reuse and customize shared definitions instead of developing definitions of tasks from scratch. In addition a task forum uses publish/subscribe interaction model to support service selection recommendations for the "masses".

We briefly overview the basic concepts in Section 2. Section 3 introduces the meta-data model and task sharing policies. Section 4 presents task forums. Section 5 describes the implementation architecture and finally discussion and concluding remarks are presented in Section 6.

2 Preliminaries

In this section, we summarize some background concepts used in the remainder of this paper, namely *task, task memories* and *context summary queries*, to keep the paper self-contained. Details about these concepts are presented in [7,8].

Task Definition. A task in WS-Advisor represents a set of coordinated *activities* that realize *recurrent needs.* For example, a frequent business travel task may include activities such as hotel booking, car rental, flight reservation, meeting scheduling and attendee's notification. We assume a service ontology in which service categories, service attributes and operations for each service category are defined. A task is described in terms of services ontologies and is defined using UML state charts. A state can be basic or composite. Each basic state is labeled with an activity that refers to either an operation or a service. A task definition can be translated to executable processes such BPEL. Also, the administrator associates each task with its relevant contexts (e.g., for a travel booking task, the user's timezone, local currency, smoking preferences, type of Web browser, may be relevant). Therefore, when a user chooses a task, any relevant contexts can be determined. This enables WS-Advisor to consider context information during service selection and such context forms the basis for making recommendations.

Context Summary Queries. A context summary query (CSQ) represents a context to be considered by the service selection process. It is specified using a conjunctive query of atomic comparisons involving context attributes, service attributes, service operation inputs/outputs, and constants. How the context summary queries are generated and associated with a task is explained in [7]. For example, for a flight booking task, relevant context attributes may be `origin`, `destination`, `price`, `seat class`, `currency`, etc. and a CSQ for a task could be expressed as a set of pairs `(c,v)` where `c` is an context attribute and `v` is the value (e.g., {(origin, "Sydney"),(destination,"Paris"),(seat class, "Economy")}).

Task Memory. A *task memory* is a data structure which captures the information about the contexts and combinations of services that have been successfully used in the past to execute a given task. The service selection process considers task memories so that the selection is not only based on the description or content of services but also on how likely they will be relevant in a given context.

The design of task memories is independent of the different service selection strategies as presented in [8]. A task memory is associated with each task and is gradually built overtime using the context and service selection history.

3 Metadata Model for Sharing Tasks and Task Memories

We first present a set of metadata abstractions designed for sharing tasks, task memories and task categories, as well as a simple declarative SQL-like language for manipulating them. Most attributes of metadata are self-explanatory. Hence, we will mainly elaborate the ones that need clarifications.

3.1 Representing Task Categories, Tasks and Task Memories

Users: `Users` represent a group of contacts with whom a single user maintains some relationships. Each user has their own `Users` table which contains information about his her contacts. We assume that the user will add/delete contacts from this table as appropriate [1].

Users.

user_id	**user_relationship**	**user_type**
Luc	friend	individual
Jazz_music	common_interest	group

user_relationship specifies the nature of relationships. Possible values are `business`, `family`, `friend`, `common_interest`. user_type specifies the type of user_id which can be either `individual` or `group` (i.e, a community of users with special interests).

Tasks: As metadata for managing task definitions, we define `Tasks` with the attributes shown below. task_annotation_tags represents a collection of keywords that characterize a task. The attribute task_query_schema is a collection of attributes that could be used to query a task. For example, attributes origin, destination, travel_start, travel_end could be the ones for the Sydney trip plan task.

Tasks.

task_name	**task_annotation_tags**	**task_query_schema**
Sydney_Trip	sydneytrip, australia, 2007trip, holiday	origin,destination, travel_start, travel_end
Visa_Trip	international, 2006trip, business	origin, destination, period, VISA_number

Task Memories: We represent task memories with the attributes: tm_name, context_summary and recommendations.

[1] This is very much like the way Internet users are finding their "friends" in social networks.

Task Memory.

tm_name	context summary	recommendations
biz_tripAug06	{(origin,"Lyon"), (destination,"London"), (price, <500)}	{[(AustrianAirline, Ibis), 0.7, Luc]; [(Qantas, Hilton),0.5, Moby]}
hol_tripApr07	{(origin,"Lyon"), (destination, "Sydney"), (price, >1000 && <2000)}	{[(VirginAirline, Stamford), 0.8, Luc]; [(Qantas, Ibis),0.4, Luc]}

We have explained context summary earlier. The attribute recommendations represents the most preferred combinations of services to execute a given task. In fact, for each context summary query, the task memory maintains the $K(K >= 0)$ most preferred services to execute for the given activity. Each service is associated with a positive weight value, called `Global Affinity` (`GA`), exceeding a predefined threshold [1]. The global affinity of a service measures the relevance of the service in performing the activity in the given context in the task. More precisely, this value represents a weighted average of the values that measures the level of satisfaction of users, about the service, with respect to all the possible services that have been selected in that context[2].

We represent recommendations as a set of triple (sc, score, p), where sc is itself a combination of web services, score represents GA for the combination and p denotes the provenance of the recommendation which references the user or group `Users`. The issue of trusting the provenance of a recommendation and whether a user is allowed to share outsourced recommendations is interesting by itself and is outside the scope of this paper.

Task Categories: For intuitive manipulation, browsing, and querying of tasks we provide the notion of task category (similar to folders and files abstractions desktop user interfaces). A task category is defined as a view (in the database terminology) over tasks and other task categories.

Task_Category.

category name	category_tags	sub_categories	tasks
Travel	Q2, Q3, trip, tourism, travelogue, lodging	International_Travel	Visa_Trip, Sydney_Trip

```
Q2: SELECT  task_annotation_tags FROM Task
WHERE task_name = 'Sydney_Trip'
Q3: SELECT  task_annotation_tags FROM Task
WHERE task_name = 'Visa_Trip'
```

The attribute category_tags represents a collection of keywords that characterize a category (e.g. for the category *Travel*, the keywords can be, trip, lodging etc). The attribute sub_categories represents a collection of categories that are linked

[1] This could be a parameter set by a system administrator.

[2] How to compute GA is presented in [9].

to a category via the specialization relationship (e.g., for the category *Travel*, one sub_category can be International_Travel). Each tuple of this relation is a container of tasks (and categories) of a specific domain. Some attributes of this table may be explicitly provided by the user of specified using relational views (e.g., Q2 and Q3).

Task Repositories: With the metadata described aboved, WS-Advisor can provide what we refer to as *Task Repository*, that is, a repository of tasks, task memories and task categories. Users can interact with the task repository in a number of ways. This includes:

- *Task Repository Browsing*: The task query language of WS-Advisor allows a user to browse a task repository. Users can navigate through the task categories hierarchy, select, a display information about specific categories and tasks.
- *Task Repository Querying*: The task query language of WS-Advisor supports both SQL-like querying over the schema of the task repository (i.e, Tasks, Task_Categories, Task_Memories, and Users relations) and keywords based querying. It also supports task signature queries. Task signature queries are useful to find tasks that can accept given input or output parameters (i.e, queries over task schemas).
- *Task Repository Sharing*: The task definition language of WS-Advisor supports the definition of views for sharing information about tasks (e.g, task categories, task definitions, and task memories) of a given task repository with users in social networks. It also supports the definition views for outsourcing information from other task repositories which are accessible through user social networks. We will illustrate the main features of this language through examples in the next Section.

3.2 Representing Sharing Policies

Besides the metadata representation needed for the sharing, there is a need for a simple and effective language for specifying the "sharing policies" for a task repository. We propose the following set of metadata for the purpose: Shared_Categories, Shared_Tasks, and Shared_Recommendations. One thing to note is that the values of the attributes in the metadata are both conventional data types and "query-types". That is, the values of the attributes may be queries which are to be evaluated[3].

Shared Categories: This includes the attributes C_To_Share and C_With. A tuple (cq,uq) of Shared_Categories is created by two queries:

- cq is a query over Task_Category and selects a collection of categories to be shared
- uq is a query over Users and selects a set of users who will have access to the categories selected by cq.

[3] This is similar to the work proposed in [10].

Shared Tasks: It is defined to define tasks to be shared. It has attributes T_To_Share and T_With. A tuple (tq,uq) of Shared_Tasks is created by tq which is a query over Tasks and selects a collection of tasks which are to be shared. Same as Shared_Categories, uq represents a query over Users.

In fact, Shared_Tasks enables the user to refine the sharing policies in the sense that s/he can identify a subset ot tasks within a category for sharing instead of all tasks in a shared category.

Shared Recommendations: To share task memories, we use the attributes R_To_Share and R_With. A tuple (rq,uq) in Shared_Recommendations is created by rq is a query over Task_Memories and selects task memories to be shared and uq is a query over Users.

3.3 Importing and Mapping Views

Similar to browsing task repositories, a user can browse and search the views created by other users. Once a user finds a view that is useful to fulfilling her task, she can do one of the followings:

Remote View Importation: View importation provides a means for users to copy task categories and task definitions from the shared views of other users. Definitions can be imported and stored in Imported_Categories and Imported_Tasks tables. The schema of the Imported_Categories (respectively, Imported_Tasks) includes the following attributes: I_Categories (respectively, I_Tasks) and I_User. The attribute I_Categories (I_Tasks) represents a collection of categories (respectively, tasks) that are imported from the repository of the user identified by the attribute I_User. Defining new tasks could be demanding to end users. This allows users to share, not only recommendations, but also definitions of tasks. More, importantly the importation provides a practical means for easy definitions of tasks.

View Mapping and Query Forwarding: In addition to directly importing a shared view, users can also create a mapping between a local repository and a remote repository. Via the mapping, a query (i.e., query over task categories, tasks or task memories) can be forwarded from one to another. In order to forward queries, there is a need to align the terminologies used in these repositories so that queries expressed over one repository could be translated to queries expressed over the other repository. For such mapping, we presented a peer-to-peer schema mapping approach in [11]. The mapping can be complete (that is, all attributes in shared categories, tasks and task memories views are mapped) or partial (that is, only some of the attributes in the views are mapped. For the ones without mapping, synonyms are to translate the terms). The complete description of the mapping and query forwarding process is outside the scope of this paper.

4 Task Forums

In WS-Advisor, a user forms "links" with other users based on the sharing policies they create (i.e., sharing tasks and task memories). These links can be considered as *views* over remote task repositories and can used to forward queries for the purpose of outsourcing service selection recommendations (i.e., obtaining recommendations from remote task repositories).

Based on the foundation of sharing tasks, in this section, we put forward a concept of *Task Forums* to promote what we call "mass sharing". Creating or importing views provide a mechanism for sharing tasks among a relatively small number of individuals (e.g., friends in your Skype contact list). Task forums aim to take the paradigm to a larger scale.

To explain the idea behind the task forums, we would like to draw an analogy from the Internet user groups (e.g., Google groups). In user groups, users share the same domain of special interests. They come to the group with different levels of skills and expertise in the domain. Inside an active group, we would see a novice user posting questions like "How do I do X", "Where can I find X" or "What is X", etc., and experts providing answers or appropriate recommendations. There would be some feedback mechanism to keep track of the quality of the answers or recommendations. Therefore, overtime, the wealth of high quality knowledge is accumulated and shared by the users in the group.

Task forums operate on the similar idea, but they provide a unique and innovative concept in that their focus is on facilitation of sharing recurrent personal processes (i.e., tasks) and recommendations for services that realise such processes. We envisage that a community of individuals or interest groups will form a task forum, which is specialised in a particular domain and various tasks within it (e.g., task forum of travel plans, task forum of small businesses or task forum of financial plans). Each task forum has a set of peers who are task forums themselves, forming a network of task forums.

In each task forum, there are task definitions, task memories and a set of metadata for storing necessary mapping data for querying peer task forums. Expert users can provide various task definitions and even bind them to a specific execution language such as BPEL. For example, a task forum for small businesses may have task definitions such as *issuing a business registration number*, *filing an insurance claim*, *search for a tax agent near your area*, etc. A novice user can easily import such task definitions and execute them in her own task execution engine. The users can discover and import tasks from other forums and provide mappings so that queries can be forwarded.

Although users can browse and search task definitions and task memories for recommendations, there is a need for effectively managing the communication of interests (similar to posting a question and providing an answer). Inside a task forum, users can use a query publication/subscription mechanism to manage the communication.

Query Publication and Subscription: The concept of shared views allows peers (individuals or communities) to publish information that they are willing to share and with whom. This mechanism allows for importation and query forwarding as discussed earlier. In addition, we use the concept of *query subscription* to allow a peer to receive relevant recommendations from other peers in a proactive manner. This is similar to the concept of continuous queries in publish/subscribe systems [12]. While, any peer can use the mechanism of query subscriptions, we will focus on how a community exploit this mechanism to provide a kind of a mass sharing of service selection recommendations. In order to facilitate such sharing, WS-Advisor models subscriptions using a relation called Query_Subscriptions. This relation includes the following attributes: S_Query, Publishers, S_Mode. The S_Query attribute represents a query over a task schema or a context summary query as in the Task_Memories relation. The attribute Publishers represents a collection of peers (e.g.,community members) with whom the query is subscribed. The S_Mode attribute represents the subscription mode. Currently, our approach supports two subscription modes: push mode and pull mode. In a push mode, a peer identifies the publishers and explicitly subscribe by specifying the relevant subscription queries. In a push mode, a peer in fact publish a subscription and other members register for it. For instance, a community may use an internal monitoring mechanism to identify relevant query or context summary query and publish them. Members of a community may subscribe to provide recommendations about these queries.

In a nutshell, a pull subscription query has the same meaning as a subscription in traditional publish-subscribe systems. A push subscription query is in fact a publication of subscription query. We assume that peers also forward feedback to each other and this especially important for communities, but this issue is outside the scope of this paper.

5 Implementation Aspects

It should be noted, that a detailed description of the WS-Advisor framework and the supporting platform is outside the scope of this paper. Here, we briefly overview the system architecture and describe components that support the concepts and techniques presented in this paper. We adopt a layered architecture for the design and implementation WS-Advisor system. Figure 1 shows the elements of this architecture. The user layer consists of three components. The task manager allows expert users to create task definitions using a state-chart based modelling notation or directly using BPEL. The implementation of this component relies on the services composition editor of the Self-Serv platform [13]. The view manager allows both expert users and non experts users to share information about their task repositories. It also allows users to reuse both task definitions and task memories from task repositories of other users or task forums. The query manager allows users to browse and query task repositories as well as executing individual tasks. The agent layer consists of three agents, namely; the advisor, builder and social network agents. These agents implements the processes related to providing service selection recommendations, building task memories, and maintaining the relationships that a user may have with other users and task forums. More detailed description of this agents is presented in [8].

The service layer consists a gateway to access underlying meta-data and services from both user and agent layers. It provides a number of infrastructure

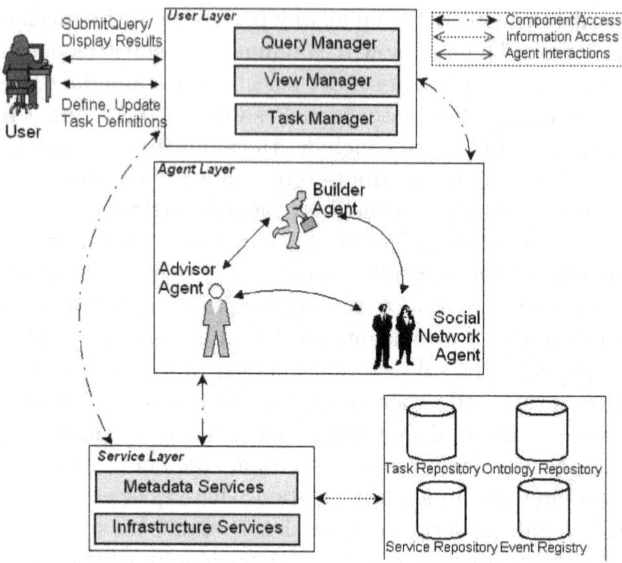

Fig. 1. Implementation Architecture

services that we reuse from our existing work on Web services platforms including service discovery and context management engines [13]. In addition to that, to support the task representation and manipulation facilities presented in this paper, we propose the use of data services as a foundation to access the information required to manage task repositories. These data services provide operations to query, browse, and update task repositories and event buses. These also provide operations to query and browse service ontologies and service registries. In order to support the publish and subscribe model of task forums, the data services rely on a semantic publish subscribe event bus. The event bus allows social network agents representing individuals or task forums to: (i) publish requests for service selection recommendations, (ii) register with other agents and notify them when relevant service selection recommendations become available, (iii) subscribe with other agents for relevant service recommendation recommendations, (iv) send notifications about relevant service selection recommendation to interested agents. The implementation of the service bus is in progress and will rely on the *Semantic Pub/Sub* techniques developed in [12].

6 Discussion and Conclusions

Our work builds upon results in services oriented architectures and semantic Web services to provide a foundation for sharing personal processes. We leverage techniques from the areas of services discovery and composition to cater for the specification and provisioning of user tasks. We leverage results in ontologies and schema mapping in peer-to-peer architectures [11] to support interaction among different task repositories. The above techniques are used in a composition framework called WS-Advisor to allow experienced users to define tasks and build mappings among different and possibly related task repositories. In our previous work [8], we presented an agent-based framework that leverages knowledge about past experiences to improve the effectiveness of Web service selection.

Inspired by advances in Web 2.0 and personal information management and sharing [14,15,5], the WS-Advisor framework aims at providing a foundation for easy sharing of users tasks and task memories (i.e, knowledge about past services selection experiences) among individual users and communities. Work in personal data management and sharing [14,15] focuses on uniform management and sharing of personal data stored in files and databases. As mentioned in the introduction of this paper, systems such such as Flickr and Delicious allow easy and ad-hoc sharing of information such as URLs and photos over the Web [5]. To the best of our knowledge there is no previous work that focuses on sharing personal processes. [6] introduces the concept of service clubs as service-based middleware for accessing e-market places. The Self-Serv framework [13] features the concept of service communities as a mechanism for integrating a large number of possibly dynamic services. Early work on personal processes [16] focuses on providing modelling notations and operators for querying personal processes. This work focuses specifically on catering for the requirements of travelling users when accessing personal processes. Although these efforts produced results that are certainly useful for sharing services and specifying tasks, more advanced techniques that cater for simple and declarative exploration and sharing of task repositories are needed. These techniques are necessary to transition composition systems from the realm a static and elite developer type of business processes to composition systems which are end user-centric.

Our work builds upon these efforts and provides complementary and innovative contributions to facilitate personal processes sharing. We provided a meta-data model and declarative language for sharing task repositories. The meta-data model captures a minimal set of abstractions that are useful for representing tasks, task memories, and user relationships. The proposed language hides the complexity of managing processes by providing an SQL-like language and a number of pre-defined functions for browsing, querying, and sharing task repositories. We proposed the concept of task forums to facilitate the sharing of task definitions and task memories. Task forums act as containers of task definitions and task memories for a specific domain. Non experienced users can outsource task definitions from task forums by using simple importation mechanism (aka file copying). Task forums also provide means for gathering and dissemination of task memories among individual users or communities. We rely on data services to provide uniform access to task repositories. These data services are used to develop applications and interfaces for main functionality of the WS-Advisor (i.e, services selection, personal processes management and sharing). The proposed framework is an important step toward easy and effective sharing of personal processes. Ongoing work includes developing case studies in specific domains such as travel and personal finance to further study the added value of the proposed foundation.

References

1. Coutaz, J., Crowley, J.L., Dobson, S., Garlan, D.: Context is key. CACM 48(3), 49–53 (2005)
2. Alonso, G., et al.: Web services: Concepts, Architectures, and Application. Springer, Heidelberg (2004)
3. Paolucci, M., Kawamura, T., Payne, T.R., Sycara, K.P.: Semantic Matching of Web Services Capabilities. In: Horrocks, I., Hendler, J. (eds.) ISWC 2002. LNCS, vol. 2342, pp. 333–347. Springer, Heidelberg (2002)
4. Carey, M.J.: Data delivery in a service-oriented world: the BEA aquaLogic data services platform. In: SIGMOD, pp. 695–705 (2006)
5. Ankolekar, A., Krotzsch, M., Tran, T., Vrandecic, D.: The two cultures: Mashing up Web 2.0 and the Semantic Web. WWW, position paper (2007)
6. Tai, S., Desai, N., Mazzoleni, P.: Service communities: applications and middleware. In: SEM, pp. 17–22 (2006)
7. Bova, R., Paik, H.Y., Hassas, S., Benbernou, S., Benatallah, B.: On Embedding Task Memory in Services Composition Frameworks. In: ICWE (2007) (to appear)
8. Bova, R., Paik, H.Y., Hassas, S., Benbernou, S., Benatallah, B.: WS-Advisor: A Task Memory for Service Composition Frameworks. In: IC3N (2007) (to appear)
9. Bova, R., Hassas, S., Benbernou, S.: An Immune System-Inspired Approach for Composite Web Service Reuse. In: Workshop on AI for Service Composition (in conjunction with ECAI 2006)
10. Srivastava, D., Velegrakis, Y.: Intentional Associations Between Data and Metadata. In: SIGMOD (2007) (to appear)
11. Benatallah, B., Hacid, M.S., Paik, H.Y., Rey, C., Toumani, F.: Towards semantic-driven, flexible and scalable framework for peering and querying e-catalog communities. Inf. Syst. 31(4-5), 266–294 (2006)
12. Zeng, L., Lei, H.: A Semantic Publish/Subscribe System. In: Proc. of the International Conference on E-Commerce Technology For Dynamic E-Business (2004)
13. Sheng, Z., Benatallah, B., Dumas, M., Mak, E.: SELF-SERV: A Platform for Rapid Composition of Web Services in a Peer-to-Peer Environment. In: VLDB, pp. 1051–1054 (2002)
14. Geambasu, R., Balazinska, M., Gribble, S.D., Levy, H.M.: HomeViews: Peer-to-Peer Middleware for Personal Data Sharing Applications. In: SIGMOD (2007) (to appear)
15. Dittrich, J.P., Salles, M.A.V.: IMEX: iDM: A Unified and Versatile Data Model for Personal Dataspace Management. In: VLDB, pp. 367–378 (2006)
16. Hwang, S.Y., Chen, Y.F.: Personal Workflows: Modeling and Management. In: Chen, M.-S., Chrysanthis, P.K., Sloman, M., Zaslavsky, A. (eds.) MDM 2003. LNCS, vol. 2574, pp. 141–152. Springer, Heidelberg (2003)

Addressing the Issue of Service Volatility in Scientific Workflows

Khalid Belhajjame

School of Computer Science
University of Manchester
Oxford Road, Manchester, UK
Khalid.Belhajjame@cs.man.ac.uk

Abstract. Workflows are increasingly used in scientific disciplines for modelling, enacting and sharing *in silico* experiments. However, the reuse of an existing workflow is frequently hampered by the volatility of its constituent service operations. To deal with this issue, we propose in this paper a set of criteria for characterising service replaceability using which substitute operations can be automatically located for replacing unavailable ones in workflows.

1 Introduction

The wide adoption of web services, as a means for delivering both data and computational analysis, together with the use of workflow technology, as a mechanism for loosely aggregating services, has dramatically revolutionised the way many scientists conduct their daily experiments. Using a workflow, a scientific experiment is defined as a series of analysis operations connected together using links that specify the flow of data between them. Enacting the specified workflows allows scientists to gather evidence for or against a hypothesis or demonstrate a known fact. Once tried-and-tested, the specifications of scientific workflows can be, just like with web services, stored in public repositories to be shared and reused by other scientists. For example, the *myExperiment* project[1], launched recently, aims to provide a public repository for sharing workflows (and thus the experiments these workflows model) between life scientists.

In practice, however, the reuse of an existing workflow is frequently hampered by the fact that certain of its constituent service operations are no longer available. Because of this, the workflow cannot be executed nor used as a building block for composing new experiments. This is not surprising; the service operations composing the workflows are supplied by independent third party providers and there is no agreement between service providers and users that compel the providers to continuously supply their services.

A solution that can be adopted to deal with the issue described above would consist in substituting each of the unavailable operations with an operation that is able to fulfil the same role as the unavailable one within the workflow. This

[1] http://myexperiment.org/

B. Krämer, K.-J. Lin, and P. Narasimhan (Eds.): ICSOC 2007, LNCS 4749, pp. 377–382, 2007.

raises the key question as to *what operation is suitable for substituting a given unavailable one*. In this paper, we formally characterise service operation replaceability in workflows. We begin (in Section 2) by presenting the semantic annotations of web services that are used for characterising service replaceability. We then present the criteria that we identified for characterising service replaceability in Section 3 and conclude in Section 4.

2 Semantic Annotations for Characterising Replaceability

For the purposes of this work, we use the workflow definition that we adopted in an earlier work for the detection of mismatches [4]. We define a scientific workflow *wf* as a set of operations connected together using data links. Formally $wf = \langle nameWf, OP, DL \rangle$, where *nameWf* is a unique identifier for the workflow, *OP* is the set of operations from which the workflow is composed, and *DL* is the set of data links connecting the operations in *OP*.

A service operation is associated with input and output parameters. A parameter is defined by the pair $\langle op, p \rangle$, where *op* denotes the operation to which the parameter belongs and *p* is the parameter's identifier (unique within the operation). An operation parameter is characterised by a data type. We assume the existence of the function *type()*, which given a parameter returns its data type.

A data link describes a data flow between the output of one operation and the input of another. Let *IN* be the set of all input parameters of all operations present in the workflow *wf* and *OUT* the set of all their output parameters. The set of data links connecting the operations in *wf* must then satisfy, $DL \subseteq OUT \times IN$. In the rest of the paper, we use *OPS* to denote the domain of service operations, *INS* the domain of input parameters and *OUTS* the domain of output parameters.

To be able to locate the service operations able to substitute an unavailable one, we need information that explicitly describes, amongst others, the task performed by the unavailable service operation and the semantics of its input and outputs. This information is commonly encoded in the form of annotations that relates the service elements (i.e., operation, inputs and outputs) to concepts from ontologies that specify the semantics of the service elements in the real world. An ontology is commonly defined as an explicit specification of a conceptualisation [6]. Formally, an ontology θ can be defined as a set of concepts, $\theta = \{c1,\ldots,cn\}$. The concepts are related to each other using the sub-concept relationship, which links general concepts to more specific ones. For example, *ProteinSequence* is a sub-concept of *Sequence*, for which we write *ProteinSequence* $\sqsubseteq$ *Sequence*. The concepts can also be connected by other binary relationships, depending on the specific semantics encoded by the ontology.

To characterise service replaceability we assume that the web services are annotated using the following ontologies.

Task ontology, θ_{task}: This ontology captures information about the action carried out by service operations within a domain of interest. In bioinformatics, for instance, an operation is annotated using a term that describes the *in silico* analysis it performs. Example of bioinformatics analyses include *sequence alignment* and *protein identification.* To retrieve the task annotation of service operations we consider the function *task()* defined as follows: *task: OPS* $\rightarrow \theta_{task}$.

Resource ontology, $\theta_{resource}$: This ontology contains concepts that denotes public bioinformatics data sources used by analysis operation for performing their task. For example, the bioinformatics service operation *getUniprotEntry()* provided by the *DDBJ*[2] uses the *Uniprot*[3] database for fetching the protein entry having the accession number given as input. From the point of view of replaceability, it is sometimes important to specify the external data source used by the operation as well as its task. Two operations that perform the same task can deliver different outputs depending on the underlying data source they are using. Therefore, the user should be informed with this difference before taking the decision of whether to accept the located operation as a substitute of the unavailable one or not. To know the resource used by a given service operation we use the function *resource()*: *resource: OPS* $\rightarrow \theta_{resource}$

Domain ontology, θ_{domain}: This ontology captures information about the application domains covered by the operations, and enables us to describe the real world concepts to which each parameter corresponds. An example of such an ontology is that developed by the TAMBIS project [2] describing the domain of molecular biology. Examples of domain concepts include *Protein*, *DNA* and *RNA*. In this work, we assume the existence of a function *domain()* with the following signature: *domain:* $(INS \cup OUTS) \rightarrow \theta_{domain}$

3 Service Operation Replaceability

The semantic annotations of service operations presented in the previous section can be used to deal with the problem of service unavailability in workflows by supporting the user in the task of locating the service operations candidates for substituting the unavailable ones. We will use an example of a real *in silico* experiment that we have developed in ISPIDER, and e-Science project[4]. The experiment is used for performing value-added protein identification in which protein identification results are augmented with additional information about the proteins that are homologous to the identified protein [3]. Figure 1 illustrates the workflow that implements this experiment.

The workflow consists of three operations. The *IdentifyProtein* operation takes as input peptide masses obtained from the digestion of a protein together with an identification error and outputs the Uniprot accession number of the *"best"* match. Given a protein accession, the operation *GetHomologous* performs a homology search and returns the list of similar proteins. The accessions of the homologous proteins are then used to feed the execution of the *GetGOTerm*

---

[2] DNA Data Bank of Japan

[3] http://www.pir2.uniprot.org/

[4] http://www.ispider.man.ac.uk/

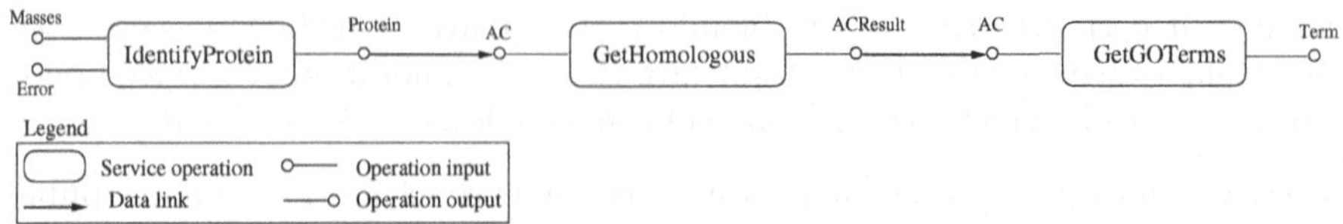

Fig. 1. Example workflow

operation to obtain their corresponding gene ontology term[5]. We have constructed this workflow two years before the time of writing. Recently, we received a request from a bioinformatician to use the workflow. However, because the operation *GetHomologous* that we used for performing the protein homology search does no longer exist, the user was unable to execute the workflow. Therefore, we had to search for an available web service that performs homology searches and that we can use instead. This operation turned out to be time consuming. We found several web services for performing homology searches and that are provided by the DNA Databank of Japan[6], the European Bioinformatics Institute[7] and the National Centre for Biotechnology Information[8]. Nonetheless, we had to try several service operations before locating an operation that can actually replace the *GetHomologous* operation within the protein identification workflow. The reason is that even though the service operations we found fulfil the task that the unavailable one does (i.e., protein homology search), they require and deliver parameters different from those that the unavailable operation has: some of the operations that we tried to use have input and output parameters that are mismatching with the input of *IdentifyProtein* operation and the input of the operation *GetGOTerm*. Moreover, some of the candidate operations were found to be using data sources that are different from that required by the unavailable operation and as a such were judged inappropriate. For example, we were unable to use the *Blastx* operation provided by the NCBI as it uses a nucleotide sequence data sources whereas the unavailable operation relies on a protein database for identifying similar proteins.

To support the user and facilitate the process of locating the service operations able to substitute the unavailable operations in a workflow (as illustrated in the example workflow presented above), we use the replaceability criteria presented in the following.

Task Replaceability. In order for an operation *op2* to be able to substitute an operation *op1*, *op2* must fulfil a task that is equivalent to or subsumes the task *op1* performs. Formally, $task(op1) \sqsubseteq task(op2)$.

For instance, in the protein identification workflow illustrated in Figure 1, the unavailable operation *GetHomologous* performs a protein sequence alignment. An example of an operation that can replace *GetHomologous* in terms of task is the

[5] http://www.geneontology.org/
[6] http://www.ddbj.nig.ac.jp/
[7] http://www.ebi.ac.uk/
[8] http://www.ncbi.nlm.nih.gov/

operation *SearchSimple* provided by the DDBJ and which aligns bioinformatics sequences: *ProteinSequenceAlignment* $\sqsubseteq$ *BioinformaticsSequenceAlignment.*

Resource Replaceability. If an operation uses an external data source for performing its task, then the operation that replaces it within the workflow must uses the same data source. Formally, an operation *op2* can replace an operation *op1* in terms of resource iff *resource(op1)* = *resource(op2)*

Resource replaceability can be of extreme importance when locating substitutes for a service operation in scientific workflows. Indeed, workflows are being recognised as a mean for validating the results claimed by their authors (scientists) and which may, for instance, be demonstrating a certain scientific fact. To verify the claims of the authors of the workflow, other scientists execute the same workflow and examine the execution results to see whether it is compatible with the authors' conclusions or not. Therefore, it is important that the workflow execution reproduces the same results as those obtained by the authors of the workflow in the first instance. For the workflow execution to reproduce the same results, the substitute operations in the workflow should use the same resource as their counterpart unavailable operations.

Parameter Compatibility. When substituting an operation *op1* in a workflow *wf* with another operation *op2*, new data links must be defined to connect the input and output parameters of *op2* to operation parameters that were previously connected to *op1*'s parameters within the workflow *wf*. These data links are established by using parameter compatibility rules that ensure that a defined data link connects an output parameter to an input able to consume the data produced by that output. We adopt two parameter compatibility rules that we used in a previous work to identify mismatches in workflows [4].

Data type. Two connected output and input parameter are compatible in terms of data type iff the data type of the output is the same as or a subtype of the data type required by the input parameter. Formally, the output *(op,o)* is compatible with the input *(op',i)* in terms of data type iff[9]: *type(op,o)* $\preceq$ *type(op',i)*

Domain compatibility. In order to be compatible, the domain of the output must be equivalent to or a sub-concept of the domain of the subsequent input. Formally, the output parameter *(op,o)* is domain compatible with the input parameter *(op',i)* iff: *domain(op,o)* $\sqsubseteq$ *domain(op',i)*

The parameter compatibility criteria just presented are used to draw the correspondences between the parameters of the operation *op2*, a candidate for substituting an operation *op1* in a workflow *wf*, and the operations parameters previously connected to *op1* in *wf*. If for every mandatory input of *op2*, there exists a corresponding operation output in the workflow *wf*, and for every output parameter that were previously connected to the unavailable operation *op1*, there exists a corresponding operation input in the workflow *wf*, then the operation *op2* is added to the list of substitutes of *op1* in the workflow *wf*.

[9] The symbol $\preceq$ stands for subtype of.

4 Conclusions

The volatility of web services is one of the main issues that hinder the sharing and the reuse of scientific workflows. To our knowledge, there does not exist any work that attempted to address this issue. However, there are some proposals that address problems that are closely related. For example, Benatallah *et al* presents replaceability as a means for adapting a web service to different applications [5]. The problem they tackle is, however, different from ours: they focus on the replaceability of a web service from the business protocol perspective (i.e., the series of interactions with the service operations). Akram *et al* defined a framework for detecting changes in web services and reacting to those changes by redirecting the requests to the unavailable service to another service [1]. Using this framework, however, the discovery query used for locating the substituting service is manually specified by the service user. The method presented here compile the aspects considered by these proposals for characterising service operations and considers additional characteristics that are peculiar to the analysis operations that compose scientific workflows, e.g., the data source used by the service operation for performing the analysis.

References

1. Akram, M.S., Medjahed, B., Bouguettaya, A.: Supporting dynamic changes in web service environments. In: Orlowska, M.E., Weerawarana, S., Papazoglou, M.M.P., Yang, J. (eds.) ICSOC 2003. LNCS, vol. 2910, pp. 319–334. Springer, Heidelberg (2003)
2. Baker, P.G., Goble, C.A., Bechhofer, S., Paton, N.W., Stevens, R., Brass, A.: An ontology for bioinformatics applications. Bioinformatics 15(6), 510–520 (1999)
3. Belhajjame, K., Embury, S.M., Fan, H., Goble, C.A., Hermjakob, H., Hubbard, S.J., Jones, D., Jones, P., Martin, N., Oliver, S., Orengo, C., Paton, N.W., Poulovassilis, A., Siepen, J., Stevens, R., Taylor, C., Vinod, N., Zamboulis, L., Zhu, W.: Proteome data integration: Characteristics and challenges. In: UK All Hands Meeting (2005)
4. Belhajjame, K., Embury, S.M., Paton, N.W.: On characterising and identifying mismatches in scientific workflows. In: Leser, U., Naumann, F., Eckman, B. (eds.) DILS 2006. LNCS (LNBI), vol. 4075, pp. 240–247. Springer, Heidelberg (2006)
5. Benatallah, B., Casati, F., Grigori, D., Nezhad, H.R.M., Toumani, F.: Developing adapters for web services integration. In: Pastor, Ó., Falcão e Cunha, J. (eds.) CAiSE 2005. LNCS, vol. 3520, pp. 415–429. Springer, Heidelberg (2005)
6. Gruber, T.: A translation approach to portable ontology specifications. Knowledge Acquisition 5(2), 199–220 (1993)

Facilitating Mobile Service Provisioning in IP Multimedia Subsystem (IMS) Using Service Oriented Architecture

Igor Radovanović[1], Amit Ray[2], Johan Lukkien[1], and Michel Chaudron[1]

[1] Technische Universiteit Eindhoven, Den Dolech 2, 5600MB Eindhoven, The Netherlands
[2] Atos Origin Technical Automation Nederland B.V., De Run 1121, 5503LB Veldhoven, The Netherlands
{i.radovanovic,j.j.lukkien,m.r.v.chaudron}tue.nl
amit.ray@atosorigin.com

Abstract. This paper presents an extension of the IMS software architecture using a service orientation, which provides flexibility of mobile service provisioning. The suggested extension facilitates composition of new mobile services in run-time based on the existing services and enables the end users to become mobile service providers. Moreover, it enables addition of new mobile services with plug-n-play similar to an addition of an end user device to the network. With this extension, the core system architecture of IMS is not affected. The extension is realized by introducing Web services in combination with the SIP protocol. Using SIP will enable operators to remain in control of mobile service provisioning as they are the owners of the IMS networks. This property of the extension may also facilitate its acceptance by the operators. A proof-of-concept prototype is discussed to demonstrate feasibility of the proposed extension.

Keywords: Service Oriented Architecture, IP Multimedia Subsystem, SIP, Web services.

1 Introduction

The mobile systems beyond 3G in Europe are aiming at providing enhanced user experience using various mobile applications anytime, anyplace using any type of end user devices [1]. The main motivation is to meet user's wishes to be able to choose among variety of mobile services (applications) and to communicate in an intuitive way.

However, the new systems will also give a boost to operators as their networks will not be used as bit pipes only by the service providers providing the mobile applications. With the new system in place, they will get the possibility to provide mobile applications to the end users as well. These mobile applications comprise the information retrieval services (e.g. weather forecast, stock reports and car navigation), the multimedia services (e.g. video-on-demand) and the communication services (e.g. messaging, voice).

B. Krämer, K.-J. Lin, and P. Narasimhan (Eds.): ICSOC 2007, LNCS 4749, pp. 383–390, 2007.

To enhance the user experience, operators intend to introduce and exploit the IP Multimedia Subsystem (IMS) SIP-based technology [2,3] that provides flexible IP media management and a session control platform, which they can lay on top of their current IP-based and (virtual) circuit-switched infrastructures. In Fig. 1, the basic elements of the IMS architecture are shown [4]. The SIP

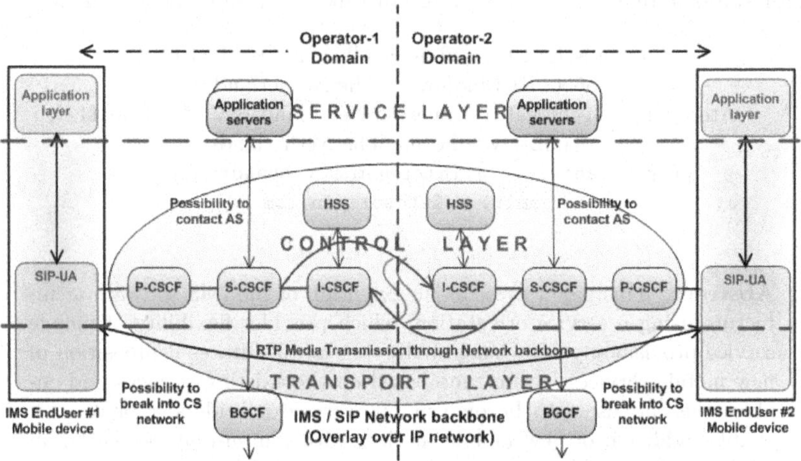

Fig. 1. The IMS system architecture

signalling is used during session establishment, maintenance and termination. The application servers (AS) provide mobile applications to the end users and the other AS's belonging to the same network administrative domain. The CSCF (Call Session Control Function) elements play a role during a user registration and a session establishment and form a SIP routing machinery in IMS. The HSS (Home Subscriber Server) is the main data storage for all subscriber- and service-related data of IMS in an operator's network. BGCF (Border Gateways) are used for connecting IMS to the circuit-switched telephone network. Other elements of the IMS infrastructure (like Resource List Server, Presence Server etc.) are not shown for the sake of clarity of representation.

2 The Effect of Limitations of the IMS Architecture

A lack of the proposed IMS architecture is that it does not provide remote access to mobile services provided by the third parties from a different administrative domain as the interfaces for using those mobile services are not standardized across different network administrative domains and there is no standard way of publishing these services. This is also important if the mobile services offered to the end users are to be built from other mobile services at run-time. For example, if we consider a car navigation service, it could be possible that an operator providing this service to the end users actually needs to compose it from other services like a location service and a map service, possibly offered by the operators in different network domains.

One consequence of these drawbacks is the loss of revenue for the operators that lose opportunity to offer enabling services to other operators. Another one is a limited possibility to enhance user's experience as the system is unable to provide the tailor-made services to the end users that are particularly suitable to support their needs. Finally, a mobile service user might have a different experience when using mobile services provided in different network domains.

The current IMS architecture also fails to provide end users with a possibility to share their services over the network, just like they can do that over the Internet (e.g. using peer-to-peer technology [5]). The cellular terminals are mostly statically provisioned with a fixed number of services, and there is little possibility for an easy upgrade of services, which is traditionally done in the Internet. Another drawback of the current IMS architecture is that information conveyed in the SIP protocol does not inherently provide separation of mobile services and devices on which those are running.

To overcome these drawbacks, an architecture that (1) increases flexibility of mobile service provisioning, (2) allows end users to become service providers and (3) incrementally extends the IMS architecture, should be used. A solution in this paper is based on using a Service Oriented Architecture overlayed on the existing IMS infrastructure. By introducing web services on top of the SIP protocol, it is shown that new mobile services could be dynamically introduced from an end user device and that these services could easily become accessible outside the operators' domain. The operators still retain control of the system, owing to their ownership of the respective SIP based networks. This work is an extension of the work done by other authors ([6], [7]) who discussed combining SIP protocol (a part of IMS technology) with Web services, but not in the context of IMS.

3 Extended Software Architecture

Fig. 2 shows that a new Web service layer is placed between the top Application layer and the SIP connection layer. This results in a slightly modified software architecture in the end user devices. The Web service layer will represent the mobile services from a remote AS. In cases when the end user also acts as an AS, the Application layer will have its own web service part, which will expose its local services to the Web service layer. The Web service layer will in turn, expose the local services to the outside world by sending out the WSDL information through the NOTIFY (or PUBLISH) message of the SIP stack. For the SOAP request messages received from the Application layer, the Web service layer will forward these SOAP requests through the SIP stack. With this architecture, the services from a value added AS (VAS) would be available to users outside the operators domain. However, usage of the services of an existing AS would still be restricted, and might be used primarily for control of the network by the operator. The IMS core network infrastructure is not affected by this proposed

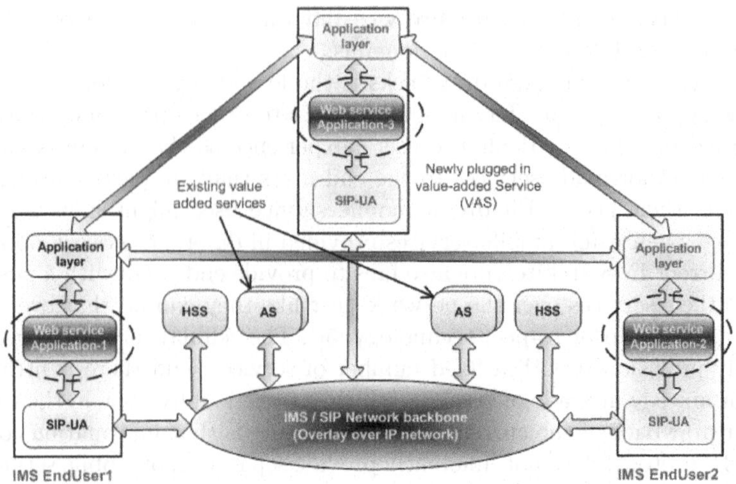

Fig. 2. A modified end-user software architecture in SOA-enabled IMS

architecture. However, if there are services provided by the existing ASs that are not used for network control purposes, these might better be moved over to the plug-n-play VASs under the operators control. This way the services would be available to a broader section of users.

4 Implementation

The interaction between the Application layer and the Web service layer will be in both directions. The Application layer asks for remote services from the Web service layer and the Web service layer asks for local services from the Application layer. In addition to the usual service and proxy components in the Application and the Web service layers, the Web service layer contains elements for (un-) wrapping the SOAP messages (from) to the SIP messages. For this, the design from [6] is extended to suit the proposed IMS architecture.

In the representation of the IMS end user in Fig. 3, the "Proxy for Remote services" in the Application layer is an object locally representing web services from the Web service layer. There is a corresponding object in the Web service layer representing the service(s) from the remote AS, and it acts like a call forwarder by forwarding all SOAP requests from the end user to the remote AS. The "SOAP message constructor" component in the Web service layer remembers the origin of the SOAP requests and the WSDL messages by maintaining a table of remote AS versus a SIP message ID. Additionally, this component has the responsibility to combine the received WSDL messages from various external sources and present a composite web service interface for the currently available remote services. There are tools available to build the proxy class automatically from the WSDL description of a web service. For example, in Microsoft's ASP.NET, a tool named WSDL.exe can build the proxy class. However, to realize

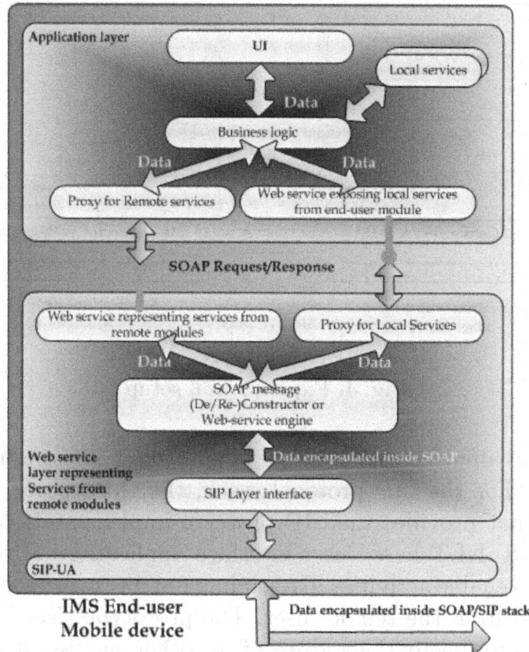

Fig. 3. The IMS End-user Module

the availability feature to its full potential, it is required that update of service states is done at run-time. In order to have this feature, the relevant components in the Application layer and the Web service layer should be dynamically updated based on the WSDL from the Web service layer. The dynamic creation and update of classes is possible with many of today's high level programming languages (.NET, Java) using a feature called "Reflection". A general guideline from [8] is adapted here for implementing this with Microsoft's .NET framework tool for ASP.NET development.

There are 3 implantation constraints at the terminal. The terminal should be equipped with all the features required to communicate as an IMS end user device (SIP-UA). Additionally, it must contain a running web server that can send and receive http messages and it must have the run-time environment for a high level language that supports reflection (e.g. Java runtime, .NET Framework).

5 Experiments

As a proof of concept, we built two software based IMS end user modules (UserA and UserB) with layered structures, similar to that shown in Fig. 3. Both modules offer a "Text" (i.e. messaging) service that can be turned on and off through a checkbox control in the UI. Although, this is a very simplistic interpretation of the "Text" service, this is done in order to simplify the implementation of the

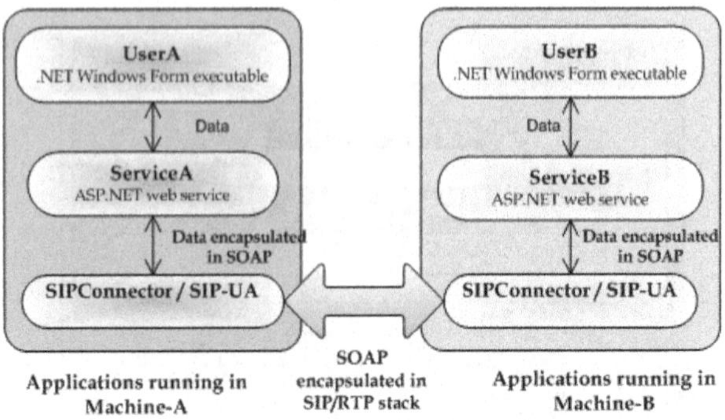

Fig. 4. Experimental setup

prototype without diluting the concept behind it. The experimental set-up is shown in Fig. 4. For the SIP protocol stack, the third party freeware named PJSIP is used, that provides the SIP protocol implementation in a C library. The two Microsoft .NET based user interface applications (UserA and UserB) are also created to enable activities like sending out a text message and displaying messages received from the remote user. The prototype User Interface (Fig. 5) has the text boxes to specify the address of the other end user it wants to connect to. A green color button indicates the availability of the "Text" service at the other end. If UserA starts to type in some characters in the box "Msg to User X" (X being either A or B), the same characters start to appear in the box "Msg to User Y" (Y being either B or A) at the UI on the other machine. In the meanwhile, the boxes designated "SIP messages sent" and "SIP messages recd" display the SIP message exchanges between the two ends. The SIP message "MESSAGE" is used here to send text messages to the other user.

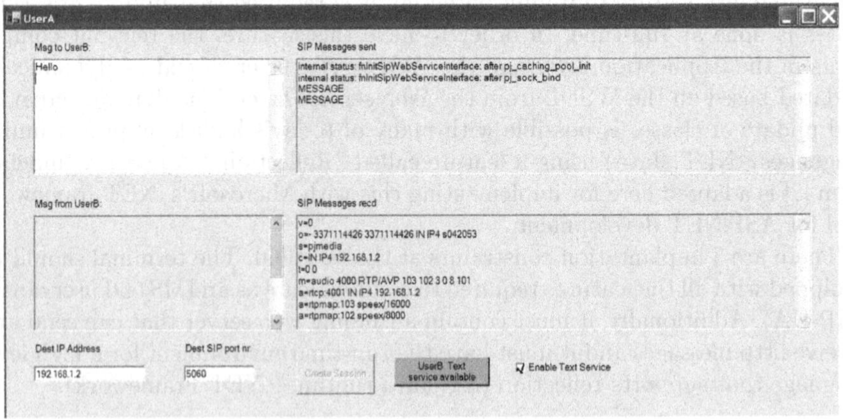

Fig. 5. An UserA console

The "SIP messages recd" box shows the media type information received from the other user (User B) in SDP protocol format. The experiments are performed with the simple text here, but the same could be extended to any data, including video. When the check-state of the "Enable Text Service" checkbox of a user is changed, the other user's UI immediately reflects this changed service availability state. This illustrates the possibility of service *availability* as opposed to device availability only. Fig. 6 shows the scenario for the experimental set-up. Note that

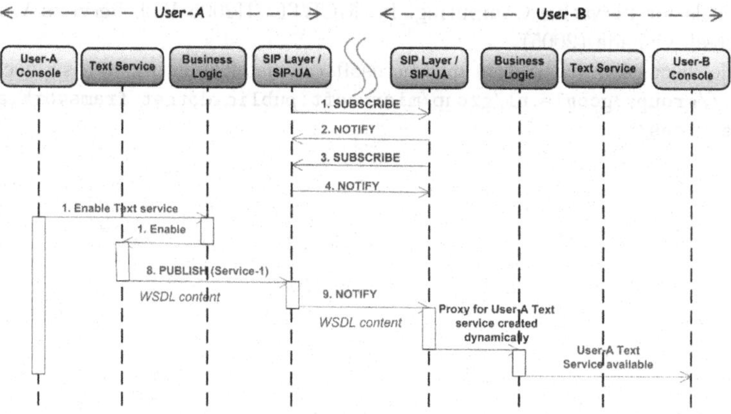

Fig. 6. A scenario for the experimental setup

there is no distinction made between an end user and an Application server. From the principle of web service applications, a web service from an end user can be reused by other web service applications. Moreover, a new end user (with a new web service) could be added to the service infrastructure as easily (flexibly) as plugging in a new IMS end user device to the network.

6 Conclusions

The extension of the IMS capabilities through a service orientation presented facilitates composition of new mobile services from the existing ones and introduction of new mobile and enabling services. It also enables the end users to become service providers. The new IMS software architecture does not require changes in the core IMS architecture, and provides a solution to the SIP message extension, including SIP version mismatch.

References

1. COnverged MEssaging Technology (2007), https://www.comet-consortium.org
2. SIP Architecture: (2007), http://www.protocols.com/pbook/sip_arch.htm
3. IETF working group on SIP/SIMPLE web page (2007), http://www.ietf.org/html.charters/simple-charter.html

4. Poikselkä, M., Mayer, G., Khartabil, H.: Niemi: The IMS – IP Multimedia Concepts and Services, 2nd edn. John Wiley & Sons, Ltd., West Sussex, England (2006)
5. Milojicic, D.S., et al.: Peer-to-Peer Computing, tech. report HPL-2002-57, Hewlett-Packard Laboratories, Palo Alto, Calif. (2002)
6. Liu, F., et al.: WSIP – Web Service SIP Endpoint for Converged Multimedia/Multimodal Communication over IP. In: ICWS'2004. Proceedings of IEEE International Conference on Web Services, pp. 690–697. IEEE Computer Society Press, Los Alamitos (2004)
7. Liscano, R., Dersingh, A.: Projecting Web Services using Presence Communication Protocols for Pervasive Computing. In: MCETECH2005 Web Services Workshop, Montreal, Canada (2005)
8. Google discussion group item on Microsoft dot net framework web service (2007), `http://groups.google.nl/group/microsoft.public.dotnet.framework.aspnet.webservices/`

eServices for Hospital Equipment

Merijn de Jonge[1], Wim van der Linden[1], and Rik Willems[2]

[1] Healthcare Systems Architecture
Philips Research, The Netherlands
[2] Strategy and Innovation Management/Technical Infrastructure
Philips Corporate IT, The Netherlands
Merijn.de.Jonge@philips.com, Wim.van.der.Linden@philips.com
Rik.Willems@philips.com

Abstract. In this paper we explore the idea that by combining different sources of information in a hospital environment, valuable e-services can be developed for reducing cost and improving quality of service.

Companies, like Philips Medical Systems, may have a competitive advantage, because they have a large installed base which may provide valuable information already, and because they can change their products to provide additional information.

To optimally benefit from this advantage, we created a platform that enables quick development of e-services. The platform enables uniform access to data, combines static with live data, and supports transparent composition of existing, into new services.

We discuss the requirements, design, and implementation of the platform, and we show its use in a case study that addresses asset management and utilization services for mobile medical equipment.

1 Introduction

E-services for hospital equipment are a means to add functionality on top of existing products. They can serve to improve the operation of individual devices, to improve the cooperation between devices, or to analyze/improve hospital workflow in general. They are promising because they can help to reduce cost (e.g., by increasing patient throughput) and to improve quality of service (including improving patient safety).

Promising in e-services is that with Philips we expect quick return on investment (because developing a service is far less expensive than developing e.g., an MR scanner), and that the value of e-services can be increased by combining different sources of information (e.g., equipment data, log data, workflow data, etc.). Threats are that we expect a significant need for change (to make services fit smoothly in different hospital environments), a strong competition, and quick market changes. Hence, there is a clear potential for flexible e-services, which combine different information sources, have a manageable development process, and a short time to market.

Services in hospital environments operate by processing and analyzing information. This information can come from equipment itself or from other information sources, like databases. By having more, diverse data available, more

B. Krämer, K.-J. Lin, and P. Narasimhan (Eds.): ICSOC 2007, LNCS 4749, pp. 391–397, 2007.

intelligent services can be offered. By integrating multiple information sources, the value of services can therefore be increased. Philips has a large hospital installed base. Via its diverse product portfolio, many different forms of information can be produced that can be used for innovative e-services. Philips can therefore take a strong position in developing e-services for hospital equipment.

Philips already collects information for (some of) its medical products. Although this information is not used for e-services yet, it forms a huge source of information, ready to be used. Most equipment, however, does not provide equipment data. Although this equipment might contain valuable information, it is simply not prepared for exposing it. The aim of our project is therefore to expose information from equipment and from (existing) data sources, and in combining these into discrimating e-services.

To that end, we have developed a platform for hospital equipment services. It has a service oriented architecture (SOA) that combines state of the art web services and thin client technology. The platform is structured around *push data* (events generated by equipment), *pull data* (information stored in databases), and *data filters* (which massage data for different use). In a case study we demonstrate the development of value added services for mobile medical equipment.

This article is structured as follows. In Sections 2 and 3 we discuss different forms of data sources and how they can be massaged by data filters. In Sections 4 and 5 we discuss the architecture and implementation of our platform. In Section 6 we address service development for mobile medical equipment. In Section 7 we discuss our results and contributions, and we mention directions for future research.

2 Equipment Data

We realized that existing data sets may contain valuable information for other purposes than maintenance, for which they where intended, and that our equipment could be extended to produce additional valuable information. We therefore distinguish two kinds of data: i) data that is already available in some database, ii) data that is produced by particular devices. We called these *pull data* and *push data*, respectively.

Pull data. Pull data is static data that is stored in e.g. a database. It is typically log-type information that serves maintenance activities. It is called pull data, because the data needs to be pulled out of the corresponding databases. This data might be very useful for developing new e-services. However, there are two bottlenecks for efficiently using this data: i) data access is difficult because data models are implicit and not standardized within and across products; ii) data processing is inefficient because data sets are huge. In section 4 we describe how we address these bottlenecks in our architecture for e-services development.

Push data. At any moment in time a device can inform the environment about itself. We call this *push data*, because the device takes the initiative to provide information, rather than a service having to ask for it. All equipment data originates from push data, but once it is stored in e.g., a database it becomes pull data.

Push data fits in an event driven environment and enables real time responses to events, for instance in case of critical errors. In addition to maintenance related data (e.g. log messages), equipment can be adapted to provide other kinds of push data as well. This may give rise to numerous new services (see Section 6).

3 Data Filters

In Section 2 we argued that pull data is difficult to access because data sets are huge and have implicit data models. To address these problems, we introduce the concept of data filters. Data filters are elements in our architecture, which i) provide a consistent interface to data sets; ii) control data visibility; iii) provide virtual databases; iv) improve overall performance. These roles will be discussed below.

Explicit data models. Data filters can transform data from one format into another. One key application of a filter is to transform an unstructured data set into a structured data set, according to an explicit data model.

Control data visibility. Incorporating existing data sets for the development of (new) e-services, should not imply that all data is exposed, or that arbitrary data can be modified. To that end, we do not support direct access to databases (e.g., by supporting direct SQL queries). Instead, data filters precisely define which data is exposed by means of explicit interfaces.

Virtual databases. A filter implements a particular query on one or more databases. The resulting data set is a derived database, with its own data model. Filters can be seen as virtual databases, because they appear as ordinary databases, although they are created on the fly.

Performance. Filters can be used to optimize data for particular services, which can then operate more efficiently (e.g., because they have to process less data, or queries on the data become simpler). This form of optimization, creates particular views on data sets. Additionally, performance can be improved by caching. Instead of executing filters real time when the data is needed, they are executed at particular moments in time. The resulting data sets are stored for later access. This enables balancing resource consumption, and can lead to an improved and predictable overall performance.

4 Architecture

The architecture for our platform is designed to support push and pull data, to enable connectivity between equipment, and to support operation heterogeneous hospital environments.

Hospital environments are highly distributed environments, which bring together a huge variety of products and vendors. The market of e-services for medical equipment is quickly emerging. To efficiently deal with these complicating factors, we adopt a service oriented architecture (SOA) [7]. All parts of our architecture are services and have well-defined interfaces to the environment.

Data from databases is also made available through services. Observe that this gives a transparent view on data and data composition because databases and filters cannot be distinguished. The architecture supports push data in the form of events together with a subscribe mechanism (see Section 5).

Services are accessed from different types of terminal devices and from different locations. Consequently, we can make little assumptions about the equipment from which services are accessed and about the type of connection of this equipment to the hospital network. To that end, e-services are accessed via web applications, separating resource-intensive computations from user interaction. Only a web-browser is needed to make use of our e-services.

5 Implementation

For the implementation of our platform, we adopt state of the art technology. We base our SOA on web services [11] and use SOAP [10] as messaging framework. We used Java as programming language, but this is no prerequisite.

Web services are defined in terms of the Web Services Description Language (WSDL) [6]. Axis2 [4] is the SOAP stack for web services. Axis2 uses AXIOM [3] as object model, which performs on demand object building using pull parsing [9] technology. Both techniques significantly improve performance and reduce memory foot print, which is important for processing huge hospital data sets.

We use the Extensible Messaging and Presence Protocol (XMPP) as eventing mechanism [12]. XMPP serves as a distributed message broker. Event groups are defined for particular types of messages, such as for equipment status information. Events are generated by sending messages to these communities. Joining a group implies subscribing to corresponding events. Any entity in our architecture can create or receive events.

The Google Web Toolkit (GWT) is used for web applications development. GWT [8] enables programming AJAX [2] based web applications (almost) purely in Java. This significantly simplifies web application development.

We use the Central Authentication Service (CAS) system from Yale University [5] as the Single Sign On (SSO) solution for web applications. The CAS system enables users to log in once from their web browser, and be automatically authenticated to all web portals and web applications.

6 Case Study

In this section we discuss the development of a particular class of e-services for hospital equipment: web based asset management and utilization services for mobile equipment. These services build on top of existing asset tracking

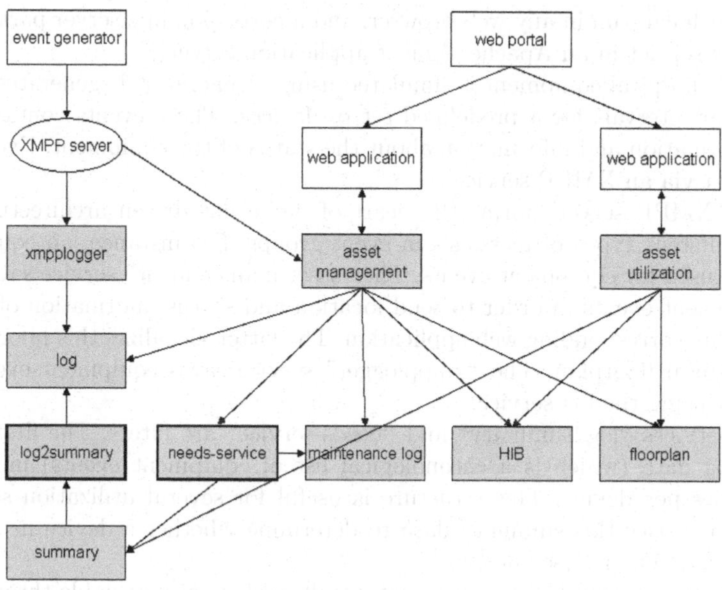

Fig. 1. Architecture of asset management and utilization services

technology, which is becoming a common technique in hospitals to monitor the location of (mobile) equipment. One promising technology for asset tracking is based on WiFi connectivity. Based on signal strength at multiple WiFi receivers, an accurate location of a device can be determined. Since WiFi is entering the hospital environment anyway, this tracking technology is relatively cheap and can easily be integrated and adopted. There are already several commercial solutions to asset tracking available (see e.g. [1]). Therefore, we do not concentrate on asset tracking itself, but we show that the combination with additional equipment data is a big step forward and significantly improves the usability of services for mobile equipment.

To that end, we develop services that combine location information, equipment data, and data from databases. The demonstrator shows how realistic services can be developed with our platform, although equipment is still simulated and data is generated. We focus on asset management and utilization services.

6.1 Implementation

In Figure 1, the structure of the demonstrator is depicted. Grey boxes denote web services, arrows indicate directions of method invocation, boxes with a thick border indicate data filters. The demonstrator consists of a web portal with two web applications, an event generator (which simulates mobile medical equipment), an XMPP server, and a number of web services.

The first web application provides asset management services. The second web application provides utilization services. The applications consist of a client part, which can run in any web browser, and a corresponding server part, which runs as a servlet in an Apache Tomcat application server.

Mobile hospital equipment is simulated using a generator. It generates events at regular intervals for a predefined set of devices. These events contain location information and information about the status of the equipment. Events are broadcast via an XMPP service.

The "XMPP server" forms the heart of our event driven architecture. We group different types of messages in event groups. For instance, an equipment group is used for equipment events. The "asset management" service subscribes to equipment events in order to send location and status information of equipment to its corresponding web application. The latter visualizes this information in a hospital floorplan. The "xmpplogger" service saves equipment events for later use using the log service.

The services "log2summary" and "needs-service" are filters. The first transforms log data (which is a chronological list of equipment events) into daily summaries per device. This structure is useful for several utilization services. The second uses this summary data to determine whether a device needs preventive maintenance (see below).

Static information about equipment and floorplans are available through the "HIB" (Hospital Installed Base) and the "floorplan" services, respectively.

6.2 Asset Management and Utilization Services

The collection of services and the XMPP event mechanism depicted in Figure 1 form the ingredients for building services that go beyond plain asset tracking services. The real time status information that equipment provides in the form of XMPP messages is used directly in the "asset management" application to display equipment status. For instance, the load information of a device forms an indicator whether the device is available for use. The "log" service stores equipment events over time. This data is used for utilization services. For instance, we synthesize in what areas of a hospital particular equipment is used, how equipment is moved around, and what the average load of each device is. The "needs-service" is an example of a composite service. To determine whether a device needs preventive maintenance, the summaries of a device are analyzed to synthesize the uptime of a device, its average load, and its quality of service. Together with information about when it was last serviced (available through the "maintenance log" service), the predicate "needs service" can be derived.

7 Concluding Remarks

This article addressed e-services for hospital equipment. E-services provide functionality on top of or cross cutting existing equipment. We focused on e-services combining different information sources, such as databases with logging type of information, or equipment providing real time device and location information.

Contributions. We explained that by having access to large and diverse data sets and by having control over which data is provided by equipment, companies like Philips may take a lead in e-service development. We identified two sources of information: information stored in databases (which we called pull data), and real time data generated by equipment (which we called push data). Further, we proposed data filters to combine data sources, and to control what data comes available and in what structure. Next, we discussed the design and implementation of a platform for e-services, which adopts state of art technology. Finally, we performed a case study where we developed e-services for mobile medical equipment. In particular, we focused on asset management and utilization services for mobile medical equipment. The case study showed that the combination of information (i.e., location information, log type information, and equipment information) enables more advanced services than plain equipment tracking services can offer today.

Future work. We are in discussion of using our technology in a concrete pilot using real, instead of simulated equipment. Furthermore, together with our product groups we have plans to further explore the area of asset management and utilization services. Next, we can extend our approach for hospital equipment to also include people, enabling patient tracking and throughput services. Finally, we want to explore the options to enable third party integration, e.g., by corporatively defining a standard for e-services in hospital environments.

References

1. AeroScout (2007), Available at: `http://www.aeroscout.com/`
2. AJAX – asynchronous JavaScript and XML (2007), Available at: `http://en.wikipedia.org/wiki/AJAX`
3. Apache axiom (2007), Available at: `http://ws.apache.org/commons/axiom/`
4. Apache Axis2 (2007), Available at: `http://ws.apache.org/axis2/`
5. Central authentication service: single sign-on for the web (2007), Available at: `http://www.ja-sig.org/products/cas/`
6. Christensen, E., Curbera, F., Meredith, G., Weerawarana, S.: Web services description language (WSDL) 1.1 (2001), Available at `http://www.w3.org/TR/wsdl`
7. Erl, T.: Service-Oriented Architecture: Concepts, Technology, and Design. Prentice-Hall, Englewood Cliffs (2005)
8. Google Web Toolkit (2007), Available at: `http://code.google.com/webtoolkit/`
9. Slominski, A.: Design of a pull and push parser system for streaming XML. Technical Report 550, Indiana University, Bloomington, Indiana (May 2001)
10. Simple object access protocol (SOAP) (2003), Available at: `http://www.w3.org/TR/soap/`
11. Web services activity (2007), Available at: `http://www.w3.org/2002/ws/`
12. XMPP standards foundation (2007), Available at: `http://www.xmpp.org/`

Using Reo for Service Coordination

Alexander Lazovik* and Farhad Arbab

CWI, Amsterdam, Netherlands
{a.lazovik,farhad.arbab}@cwi.nl

Abstract. In this paper we address coordination of services in complex business processes. As the main coordination mechanism we rely on a channel-based exogenous coordination language, called Reo, and investigate its application to service-oriented architectures. Reo supports a specific notion of composition that enables coordination of individual services, as well as complex composite business processes. Accordingly, a coordinated business process consists of a set of web services whose collective behavior is coordinated by Reo.

1 Introduction

The current set of web service specifications defines protocols for web service interoperability. On the base of existing services, large distributed computational units can be built, by composing complex compound services out of simple atomic ones. In fact, composition and coordination go hand in hand. Coordinated composition of services is one of the most challenging areas in SOA. A number of existing standards offer techniques to compose services into a business process that achieves specific business goals, e.g., BPEL. While BPEL is a powerful standard for composition of services, it lacks support for actual coordination of services. Orchestration and choreography, which have recently received considerable attention in the web services community and for which new standards (e.g., WS-CDL) are being proposed, are simply different aspects of coordination. It is highly questionable whether approaches based on fragmented solutions for various aspects of coordination, e.g., incongruent models and standards for choreography and orchestration, can yield a satisfactory SOA. Most efforts up to now have been focused on statically defined coordination, expressed as compositions, e.g., BPEL. To the best of our knowledge the issues involved in dynamic coordination of web services with continuously changing requirements have not been seriously considered. The closest attempts consider automatic or semi-automatic service composition, service discovery, etc. However, all these approaches mainly concentrate on how to compose a service, and do not pay adequate attention to the coordination of existing services.

In this paper we address the issue of coordinated composition of services in a loosely-coupled environment. As the main coordination mechanism, we rely

* This work was carried out during the tenure of an ERCIM "Alain Bensoussan" Fellowship Programme.

B. Krämer, K.-J. Lin, and P. Narasimhan (Eds.): ICSOC 2007, LNCS 4749, pp. 398–403, 2007.

on the channel-based exogenous coordination language Reo, and investigate its application to SOA. Reo supports a specific notion of composition that enables coordinated composition of individual services as well as composed business processes. In our approach, it is easy to maintain loose couplings such that services know next to nothing about each other. It is claimed that BPEL-like languages maintain service independence. However, in practice they hard-wire services through the connections that they specify in the process itself. In contrast, Reo allows us to concentrate only on important protocol decisions and define only those restrictions that actually form the domain knowledge, leaving more freedom for process specification, choice of individual services, and their run-time execution. In a traditional scenario, it is very difficult and cost-ineffective to make any modification to the process, because it often has a complex structure, with complex relationships among its participants. We believe having a flexible coordination language like Reo is crucial for the success of service-oriented architectures.

The rest of the paper is organized as follows. In Section 2 we consider Reo as a modeling coordination language for services. A discussion of coordination issues, together with a demonstrating example and tool implementation discussion appears in Section 3. We conclude in Section 4, with a summary of the paper and a discussion of our further work.

2 The Reo Coordination Language

The Reo language was initially introduced in [1]. In this paper, we consider adaptation of general exogenous coordination techniques of Reo to service-oriented architecture. In our setting, Reo is used to coordinate services and service processes in an open service marketplace.

Reo is a coordination language, wherein so-called *connectors* are used to coordinate components. Reo is designed to be exogenous , i.e. it is not aware of the nature of the coordinated entities. Complex connectors are composed out of primitive ones with well-defined behavior, supplied by the domain experts. *Channels* are a typical example for primitive connectors in Reo. To build larger connectors, channels can be attached to nodes and, in this way, arranged in a circuit. Each channel type imposes its own rules for the data flow at its ends, namely synchronization or mutual exclusion. The ends of a channel can be either source ends or sink ends. While source ends can accept data, sink ends are used to produce data. While the behavior of channels is user-defined, nodes are fixed in their routing constraints. It it important to note, that the Reo connector is stateless (unless we have stateful channels introduced), and its execution is instantaneous in an all-or-none matter. That is, the data is transferred from the source nodes to sink nodes without ever being blocked in the middle, or not transferred at all. Formally, a Reo connector is defined as follows:

Definition 1 (Reo connector). *A* connector $\mathcal{C} = \langle \mathcal{N}, \mathcal{P}, E, node, prim, type \rangle$ *consists of a set* $\mathcal{N}$ *of* nodes, *a set* $\mathcal{P}$ *of* primitives, *a set* E *of* primitive ends *and functions:*

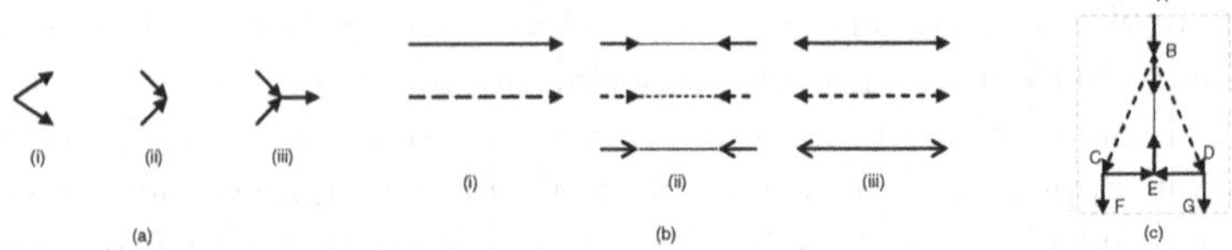

Fig. 1. Reo elements: (a)–nodes; (b)–primitive channels; (c)–XOR connector

- *prim* : $E \rightarrow \mathcal{P}$, *assigning a primitive to each primitive end,*
- *node* : $E \rightarrow \mathcal{N}$, *assigning a node to each primitive end,*
- *type* : $E \rightarrow \{src, snk\}$, *assigning a type to each primitive end.*

Definition 2 (Reo-coordinated system). $\mathcal{R} = \langle \mathcal{C}, \mathcal{S}, serv \rangle$, *where:*

- $\mathcal{C}$ *is a Reo connector;*
- $\mathcal{S}$ *is a set of coordinated services;*
- $serv : \mathcal{S} \rightarrow 2^E$ *attaches services to primitive ends* E *of the connector* $\mathcal{C}$.

Services represent web service operations in the context of Reo connectors. Services are black boxes, Reo does not know anything about their internal behavior except the required inputs and possible outputs that are modeled by the *serv* function. By this definition, services are attached to a Reo connector through primitive ends: typically to write data to source ends, and read from sink ends. Note that although we consider services as a part of a coordinated system, they are still external to Reo. Services are independent distributed entities that utilize Reo channels and connectors to communicate. The service implementation details remain fully internal to individual elements, while the behavior of the whole system is coordinated according to the Reo circuit.

Nodes are used as execution logical points, where execution over different primitives is synchronized. Data flow at a node occurs, iff (i) at least one of the attached sink ends provides data and (ii) all attached source ends are able to accept data. Channels represent a communication mechanism that connects nodes. A channel has two ends which typically correspond to in and out. The actual channel semantics depends on its type. Reo does not restrict the possible channels used as far as their semantics is provided. In this paper we consider the primitive channels shown in Figure 1-(b), with (i)–communication channels; (ii)–drain channels; and (iii)–spout channels. The top three channels represent synchronous communication. A channel is called *synchronous* if it delays the success of the appropriate pairs of operations on its two ends such that they can succeed only simultaneously. The bottom three channels (visually represented as dotted arrows) are *lossy* channel, that is, communication happens but the data can be lost if nobody accepts it. For a more comprehensive discussion of various channel types see [1]. It is important to note that channels can be composed into a connector that is then used disregarding its internal details. An example of such composed connector is a XOR element shown in Figure 1-(c). It is built out of five sync channels, two lossy sync channels, and one sync drain. The intuitive behavior of this connector is that data obtained as input through A is delivered to one of the output nodes F or G. If both F and G is willing to accept data then node E non-deterministically selects which side of the connector will succeed in passing the data. The sync drain channel B-E and the two C-E, D-E channels ensure that data flows at only one of C and D, and hence F and G.

More details on the intuitive semantics of Reo is presented in [1] and in an extended version of this paper [5]. Various formal semantics for Reo are presented elsewhere, including one based on [2], which allows model checking over possible executions of Reo circuit, as described in [3].

3 Building Travel Package in Reo

To illustrate our ideas we use a simple example that is taken from the standard travel domain. We consider reserving a hotel and booking transportation (flight or train in our simplified setting). This process is simple, and works for most users. However, even typical scenarios are usually more complicated with more services involved. Our simple process may be additionally enriched with services that the average user may benefit from, e.g., restaurants, calendar, or museum services. However, it is difficult to put all services within the same process: different users require different services sharing only a few common services.

Traditionally, when a process designer defines a process specification, he must explicitly define all steps and services in their precise execution order. This basically means offering the same process and the same functionality to all users that potentially need to travel. This makes it difficult to add new services, since only a limited number of users are actually interested in the additional services. We first consider some particular user's travel expectations:

> *A trip to Vienna is planned for the time of a conference; a hotel is desired in the center or not far from it; in his spare time, the client wishes to visit some museums; he prefers to have a dinner at a restaurant of his choice on one of the first evenings.*

Hard-coded business process specifications cannot be used effectively for such a complex yet typical goal with a large number of loosely coupled services. The problem is that the number of potential additional services is enormous, and every concrete user may be interested in only a few of them. Having these considerations in mind, the business process is designed to contain only basic services with a number of external services (or other processes) that are not directly a part of the process, but a user may want them as an added value, e.g., museum and places to visit, or booking a restaurant.

One of the possible Reo representations is provided in Figure 2. Box A corresponds to the process with basic functionality. The client initiates the process by issuing a request to the hotel service. If there are no other constraints, the process non-deterministically either reserves a flight or a train and proceeds to payment. Note, that the hotel service is never blocked by the location synchronization channels (between the hotel and the XOR (see Figure 1-(c)) element) since they all are connected by lossy channels. In Figure 2 the flight service is

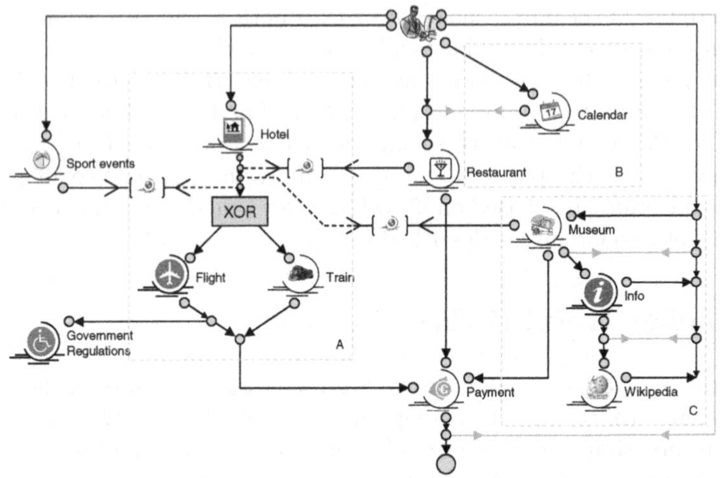

Fig. 2. A travel example in Reo

additionally monitored by a government service, that is, a flight booking is made only if the government service accepts the reservation.

Box *B* corresponds to the user request for visiting a restaurant located not far from the hotel. It is modeled as follows. The restaurant service itself is connected to the hotel using the location synchronization channel, that is, the restaurant service is invoked *only* if the hotel location is close. The location synchronization channel is a domain-specific example of a primitive channel supplied by the domain designers. It models a synchronization based on a physical location [5]. The synchronization is unidirectional: the hotel is reserved even if there are no restaurants around. We also use a calendar service to check if the requested time is free, and if it is, then the calendar service fires an event, that is, through the synchronization channel, enables the restaurant service.

Box *C* shows a possible interactive scenario for requesting a museum visit. If the user issues the corresponding request, the museum service is checked if it is close to the hotel. Then it may show additional information from the tourist office, or, if the user is interested, point to corresponding information from the Wikipedia service. User interaction is modeled via a set of synchronization channels, each of which defines whether the corresponding service is interesting to the user. Finally the payment service is used to order the requested travel package. In this example the payment service is used as many times as it has incoming events. For the real world application, it is practical to change the model to enable the user to pay once for everything.

Using our example, we have just shown how Reo can be used to coordinate different loosely-coupled services, and, thereby, extending the basic functionality of the original basic process. An advantage of Reo is that it allows modeling to reflect the way that users think of building a travel package: for each goal, we just have to add a couple of new services, add some constraints in terms of channels and synchronizations, and we have a new functionality available.

The Reo coordination tool [4] is developed to aid process designers who are interested in complex coordination scenarios. It is written in Java as a set of plug-ins on top of the Eclipse platform (`www.eclipse.org`). Currently the framework consists of the following parts: (i) graphical editors, supporting the most common service and communication channel types; (ii) a simulation plug-in, that generates Flash animated simulations on the fly; (iii) BPEL converter, that allows conversion of Reo connectors to BPEL and vice versa; (iv) java code generation plug-in, as an alternative to BPEL, represents a service coordination model as a set of java classes; (v) validation plug-in, that performs model checking of coordination models represented as constraint automata.

4 Conclusions and Future Work

In this paper we presented an approach for service coordination based on the exogenous coordination language Reo. It focuses on only the important protocol-related decisions and requires the definition of only those restrictions that actually form the domain knowledge. Compared to traditional approaches, this leaves much more freedom in process specification. Reo's distinctive feature is a very liberal notion of channels. New channels can be easily added as long as they comply with a set of non-restrictive Reo requirements. As a consequence of the compositional nature of Reo, we have convenient means for creating domain-specific language extensions. This way, the coordination language provides a unique combination of language mechanisms that makes it easy to smoothly add new language constructs by composing existing language elements.

In this paper we assumed that services support a simplified interaction model. While this is acceptable for simple information providers such as map or calendar services, this assumption is not true in general. We plan to investigate the possibility of using Reo in complex scenarios where services have extended lifecycle support. Reo is perfect in defining new domain-specific language extensions. However, we lack specific extensions to the coordination language that support various issues important to services, e.g., temporal constraints, preferences, and extended service descriptions.

References

1. Arbab, F.: Reo: a channel-based coordination model for component composition. Math. Structures in CS 14(3), 329–366 (2004)
2. Baier, C., Sirjani, M., Arbab, F., Rutten, J.: Modeling component connectors in Reo by constraint automata. Sci. Comput. Program. 61(2), 75–113 (2006)
3. Klueppelholz, S., Baier, C.: Symbolic model checking for channel-based component connectors. In: FOCLASA'06 (2006)
4. Koehler, C., Lazovik, A., Arbab, F.: ReoService: coordination modeling tool. In: ICSOC-07, Demo Session (2007)
5. Lazovik, A., Arbab, F.: Using Reo for service coordination. Technical report, CWI (2007)

A Context-Aware Service Discovery Framework Based on Human Needs Model

Nasser Ghadiri, Mohammad Ali Nematbakhsh, Ahmad Baraani-Dastjerdi, and Nasser Ghasem-Aghaee

Department of Computer Engineering,
University of Isfahan
Isfahan, Iran
{ghadiri, nematbakhsh, ahmadb, aghaee}@eng.ui.ac.ir

Abstract. In this paper we have proposed an approach to extend the existing service-oriented architecture reference model by taking into consideration the hierarchical human needs model, which can help us in determining the user's goals and enhancing the service discovery process. This is achieved by enriching the user's context model and representing the needs model as a specific ontology. The main benefits of this approach are improved service matching, and ensuring better privacy as required by users in utilizing specific services like profile-matching.

1 Introduction

During the past few years, semantic web services have been a major research area for making service-oriented architecture (SOA) more usable in real applications. Numerous efforts are undergoing both research and standardization, including OWL-S, WSMO, WSDL-S, IRS-III, SWSF [5,6] and SAWSDL [14]. Their common goal is exposing the capabilities of web services in a machine-understandable way, by annotating and adding semantics to web services advertisements, to be used by other services and clients for automated service discovery and composition.

However, automated composition of services is in its early stages. More adaptation to changes in customers and more dynamic service composition methods are required [13]. One of the primary reasons of service-orientation is fulfillment of the user's requirements. From the SOA point of view, user's goals, motivations and requirements are important factors to be taken into account. In the SOA reference model [12], these aspects form a major part of the architecture (Figure 1). This model says SOA is not done in isolation but must account for the goals, motivation, and requirements that define the actual problems being addressed. Also in OWL-S, user's goals are considered as a part of service profile [2], and in WSMO, user's desires are taken into account, but working on the user's needs, desires and expectations and mapping them to goal descriptions is a difficult step and is mostly neglected in the current web service discovery models [4].

The main question here is how user's needs are to be satisfied by selecting and composing the semantically annotated services? So we will require a deeper insight

B. Krämer, K.-J. Lin, and P. Narasimhan (Eds.): ICSOC 2007, LNCS 4749, pp. 404–409, 2007.

into user's needs, desires and goals, generally as the user's behavioral context, to improve the overall service matching quality. Although many of existing approaches towards service composition largely neglect the context in which composition takes place [13], two types of context-orientation in web services have been proposed: service context [8] which is used for orchestration of distributed services in service composition, and user context [5], which is discussed and extended in this paper.

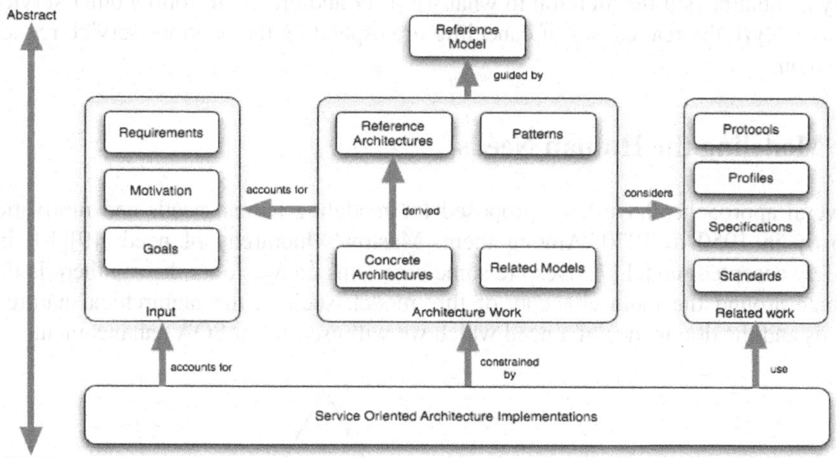

Fig. 1. Goals and motivation in SOA reference model [12]

The rest of the paper is organized as follows. Section 2 motivates the reader with giving a couple of example scenarios which demonstrate the need to model the user's needs. Section 3 introduces the human needs model. Our service discovery model based on human needs is presented in section 4. Section 5 contains some use cases and application areas, followed by a conclusion in section 6.

2 Motivating Examples

For a better understanding of the role of human needs, imagine these scenarios.

• *Scenario 1*: The need for security can be seen as an emerging dominant need. Suppose that you are using a virtual travel agency (VTA) [4] as a service-oriented application to plan your vacation by giving your preferences and constraints for selecting the most suitable services that fit your conditions. Meanwhile, suppose a security problem, for example a credit card fraud happens to you. It will draw all your attention to solving it first. You will probably suspend your travel planning, since the credit card problem is more important to you. You next efforts will be dominated by your personal criteria for selecting services that will potentially help you to solve the fraud problem. You will suspend your travel planning until returning to your secure position that was satisfying you before.

• *Scenario 2*: Finding a good job and keeping it. If the user or service requester is unhappy with his/her job, detected explicitly or implicitly by the service-oriented application, the service composition must be switched to a context for ensuring the user of his/her job security, as it might be more important than other needs, at least in current context of the user.

We can see that knowing more about the user's needs, might help us to understand why a client pays little attention to what we offer and prefers to follow other services, or to analyze the real causes of canceling or suspending the previous service requests an so on.

3 Modeling the Human Needs

Several approaches have been proposed for modeling human needs and motivation, mostly in 1950 to 1970. Among them, Maslow's hierarchy of needs [9][10] is a widely accepted model [7]. Despite some criticisms on Maslow's theory, there is little debate around the main concepts of this model, such as the hierarchical nature of needs and the dominance of a need which we will use for our SOA enhancement.

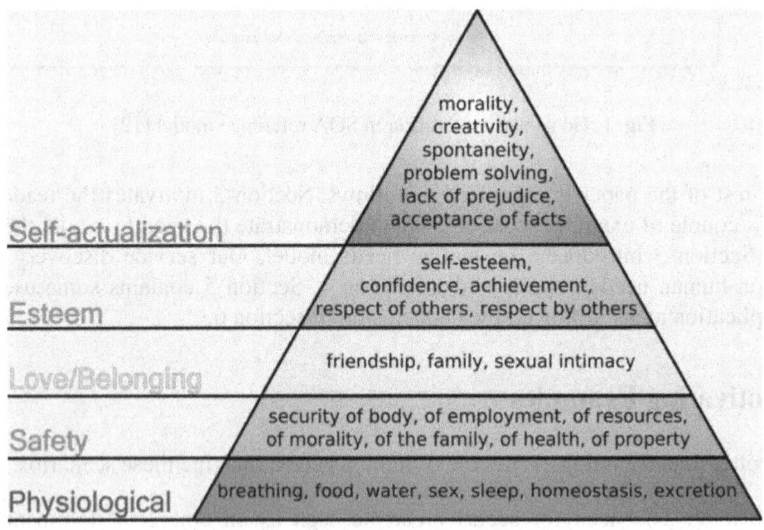

Fig. 2. Maslow's hierarchy of needs [11]

According to Maslow, human needs arrange themselves in hierarchies of prepotency. That is to say, the appearance of one need usually rests on the prior satisfaction of another, more prepotent need [9]. Maslow's hierarchical classification is consisted of five layers as presented in Figure 2. There are at least five sets or layers of needs, which are grouped as physiological, safety, love, esteem, and self-actualization needs. The lowest layer represents our physiological needs such as warmth, shelter, food, etc. The next layer contains safety needs or security needs which means protection from danger. Social needs such as love, friendship and comradeship are above it and the fourth layer is about esteem needs for self-respect, or self-esteem, and for the esteem of others. When lower layer needs are satisfied to an acceptable level, higher layer needs will emerge. The highest layer contains self-actualization needs, which are also called growth needs. Growth needs are satisfied by finding the way to "What a man can be, he must be" [9].

A nice and complex feature of human needs is the dynamic behavior which governs our needs. According to Maslow, as higher priority needs (lower level in hierarchy) are emerging, these needs will *dominate* our behavior until they are satisfied. If all the needs are unsatisfied, and the human is then dominated by the physiological needs, all other needs may become simply *non-existent* or be *pushed into the background*. A similar concept to dominance of a need is *context dominance*, which describes the concept of ordering context information according to importance, and is expressed as a set of rules that are restricted to a device, a user, or are globally applied to all participating services involved in fulfilling a given task [3]. The needs model can be used as those set of rules which restrict a user in context dominance, i.e. dominance of a need can determine context dominance from a user's perspective.

4 Service Discovery Model Based on Human Needs

Our user context model is the result of extending the object-oriented context model in [5]. The proposed context model is depicted in Figure 3. The general context includes location or spatial context, time or temporal context, environment context, device context user context, etc. Our proposed needs context is part of the *user context*, reflecting those parameters which directly present the user's needs and desires. As noted above, the other parts of context may also affect needs context. For instance, being in a certain geographic location, defined as part of spatial context, might trigger some of our needs, or educating as an undergraduate student, defined as part of temporal context, can be a basis for user needs model to be copied from a generic needs context of such a student.

We also briefly introduce our work towards formalizing the needs model for handling this extended user context. For *knowledge representation* about the needs model, we defined an ontology for needs. We used Protégé to build the required ontology based on the Maslow's hierarchical model. Our needs ontology defines every layer in Maslow's model as a class, with different types of needs in each layer as the subclasses. The ontology is designed to support other models of needs as well. The concept of satisfiers is also defined, as the services and others entities which can fulfill the needs and the relationship between needs and satisfiers are modeled by using attributes.

For *reasoning* based on the above representation, we propose using the service matchmaking algorithm in [1], slightly modifying it to handle the needs context. Considering their matchmaking algorithm, we can add the layers in Maslow's needs hierarchy at each layer with $\Sigma_{li}(a_1, a_2, \ldots, a_n)$ which means the activities in layer *i* can be done in any order.

Doing the matchmaking this way, ensures a match adapted with user's current status of satisfaction of needs, which is a more stable matching and closer to the goals and requirements of the user.

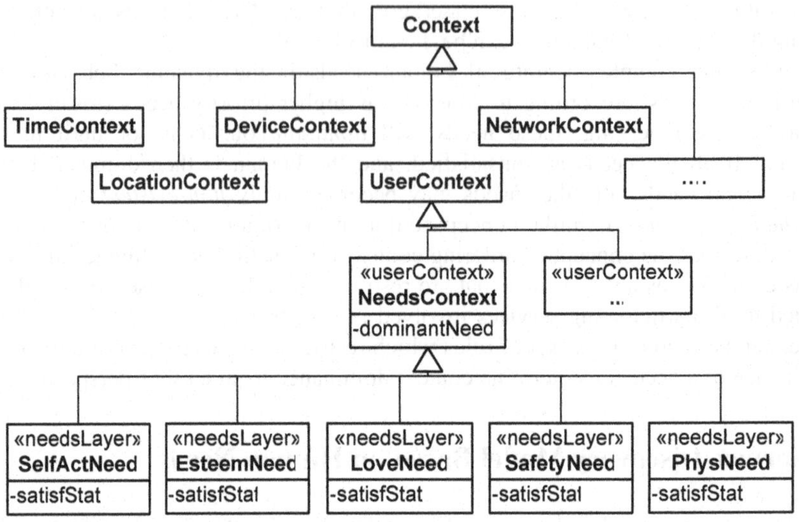

Fig. 3. Partial hierarchy of context focusing on needs as a part of user context

5 Applications Areas

Service composition process can be improved by using the needs model. Discovering the pre-requisites of each service is an important step in service composition. Based on our model, before executing any service for a user, all services which can satisfy lower layer needs must be selected and executed. The human needs model also can improve *web service personalization* process [6] by increasing the quality of similarity measurement. In other words, two users with similar status of their hierarchy of needs, might have similar contexts, which makes the personalization and recommendation more efficient. Another application area is *profile matching*, for example between two or more mobile users, which can be improved by taking the human needs model into account. Profile matching is generally based on comparing the contexts of users which are geographically or temporally near to each other, and ranking the potential users for establishing a relationship and so on. This process can use an enriched profile similarity measure, by taking into account the needs status of parties. The main benefits of adding the needs dimension to context-aware profile matching for the user are:

- Enhanced matchmaking, due to higher quality matching based on needs and filtering out those services which are far from current user's needs context
- Better privacy, by rejecting the people with unmatched needs from accessing user's profile and other private context information.

6 Conclusion and Future Work

In this paper we introduced an approach to extend current service selection methods by using the human needs model. The main contribution of this work is adding a new dimension to context-aware service selection and composition, by presenting a model which enables service selection algorithms to consider human behavior, needs and motivations in the reasoning process. Our approach is based on extending an object-oriented context model by Maslow's hierarchy of needs, which potentially can be used in every semantic web services model. Modeling the human's core needs, could also be a sound conceptual integration point between the different available semantic web services models.

Our future works will include building a proof-of-concept prototype for our proposed architecture and evaluating the modified matchmaking algorithm. We also plan to improve our approach by using inexact reasoning, since the needs model is an aspect of human behavior, which inherently contains some type of uncertainty and will benefit from inexact knowledge representation and reasoning techniques.

References

1. Agrawal, S., Studer, R.: Automatic Matchmaking of Web Services. In: ICWS '06. Proceedings of the International Conference on Web Services, pp. 45–54 (2006)
2. Davis, J., Suder, R., Warren, P.: Semantic Web Technologies: Trends and Research in Ontology-based Systems. John Wiley & sons ltd, West Sussex, England (2006)
3. Dorn, C., Dustdar, S.: Sharing hierarchical context for mobile web services. Distributed Parallel Databases 21, 85–111 (2007)
4. Fensel, D., Lausen, H., Polleres, A., Bruijn, J.d., Stollberg, M., Roman, D., Domingue, J.: Enabling Semantic Web Services. Springer, Heidelberg (2007)
5. Hofer, T., Schwinger, W., Pichler, M., Leonhartsberger, G., Altmann, J.: Context-Awareness on Mobile Devices - the Hydrogen Approach. In: HICSS'03. Proceedings of 36th Annual Hawaii International Conference on System Sciences, pp. 292–302 (2003)
6. Huhns, M.N., Singh, M.P.: Service-Oriented Computing- Key Concepts and Principles. IEEE Internet Computing 9(1), 75–81 (2005)
7. Lee, A.: Psychological Models in Autonomic Computing Systems. In: DEXA. Proceedings of the 15th International Workshop on Database and Expert Systems Applications (2004)
8. Maamar, Z., Mostefaoui, S.K., Yahyaoui, H.: Toward an agent-based and context-oriented approach for Web services composition. IEEE Transactions on Knowledge and Data Engineering 17(5), 686–697 (2005)
9. Maslow, A.H.: A Theory of Human Motivation. Psychological Review 50, 370–396 (1943)
10. Maslow, A.H.: Motivation and Personality, 2nd edn. Harper & Row, New York (1970)
11. Maslow's Hierarchy of Needs, http://en.wikipedia.org/wiki/Maslow's_hierarchy_of_needs
12. OASIS Org. : Reference Model for Service Oriented Architecture 1.0, Committee Specification 1, http://www.oasis-open.org
13. Papazoglou, M.P., Traverso, P., Dustdar, S., Leyman, F.: Service-Oriented Computing Research Roadmap, Report/vision paper on Service oriented computing EU-IST (2006)
14. Verma, K., Sheth, A.: Semantically Annotating a Web Service. IEEE Internet Computing 11(2), 83–85 (2007)

Weight Assignment of Semantic Match Using User Values and a Fuzzy Approach

Simone A. Ludwig

Department of Computer Science
University of Saskatchewan
Canada
ludwig@cs.usask.ca

Abstract. Automatic discovery of services is a crucial task for the e-Science and e-Business communities. Finding a suitable way to address this issue has become one of the key points to convert the Web into a distributed source of computation, as it enables the location of distributed services to perform a required functionality. To provide such an automatic location, the discovery process should be based on the semantic match between a declarative description of the service being sought and a description being offered. This problem requires not only an algorithm to match these descriptions, but also a language to declaratively express the capabilities of services. The proposed matchmaking approach is based on semantic descriptions for service attributes, descriptions and metadata. For the ranking of service matches a match score is calculated whereby the weight values are either given by the user or estimated using a fuzzy approach.

1 Introduction

Dynamic discovery is an important component of Service Oriented Architecture (SOA) [1]. At a high level, SOA is composed of three core components: service providers, service consumers and the directory service. The directory service is an intermediary between providers and consumers. Providers register with the directory service and consumers query the directory service to find service providers. Most directory services typically organize services based on criteria and categorize them. Consumers can then use the directory services' search capabilities to find providers. Embedding a directory service within SOA accomplishes the following, scalability of services, decoupling consumers from providers, allowing updates of services, providing a look-up service for consumers and allowing consumers to choose between providers at runtime rather than hard-coding a single provider.

However, SOA in its current form only performs service discovery based on particular keyword queries from the user. This, in majority of the cases leads to low recall and low precision of the retrieved services. The reason might be that the query keywords are semantically similar but syntactically different from the terms in service descriptions. Another reason is that the query keywords might be syntactically equivalent but semantically different from the terms in the service description.

B. Krämer, K.-J. Lin, and P. Narasimhan (Eds.): ICSOC 2007, LNCS 4749, pp. 410–415, 2007.

Another problem with keyword-based service discovery approaches is that they cannot completely capture the semantics of a user's query because they do not consider the relations between the keywords. One possible solution for this problem is to use ontology-based retrieval.

A lot of related work on semantic service matching has been done [2,3,4,5,6] however, this approach takes not only semantic service descriptions into account but also context information. Ontologies are used for classification of the services based on their properties. This enables retrieval based on service types rather than keywords. This approach also uses context information to discover services using context and service descriptions defined in ontologies.

The structure of this paper is as follows. The next section describes in detail the matching algorithm, match score calculation with weight values and the fuzzy weight assignment. In section 3, a summary of the findings and directions for future work are described.

2 Matching Algorithm

The overall consideration within the matchmaking approach for the calculation of the match score is to get a match score returned which should be between 0 and 1, where 0 represents a "mismatch", 1 represents a "precise match" and a value in-between represents a "partial match". The matchmaking framework [3] relies on a semantic description which is based on attributes, service descriptions and metadata information. Therefore, the overall match score consists of the match score for service attributes, service description and service metadata respectively:

$M_O = \frac{M_A + M_D + M_M}{3}$, whereby M_O, M_A, M_D, M_M are the overall, attribute, description and metadata match scores respectively.

Looking at the service attributes first, it is necessary to determine the ratio of the number of service attributes given in the query in relation to the number given by the actual service. To make sure that this ratio does not exceed 1, a normalization is performed with the inverse of the sum of both values. This is multiplied by the sum of the number of service attributes matches divided by the number of actual service attributes shown below. Similar equations were derived for service descriptions and service metadata respectively. The importance of service attributes, description and metadata in relation to each other is reflected in the weight values.

$$M_A = \frac{w_A}{(n_{AQ} + n_{AS})} \cdot \frac{n_{AQ}}{n_{AS}} \cdot \frac{n_{MA}}{n_{AS}}, \quad M_D = \frac{w_D}{(n_{DQ} + n_{DS})} \cdot \frac{n_{DQ}}{n_{DS}} \cdot \frac{n_{MD}}{n_{DS}},$$

$$M_M = \frac{w_M}{(n_{MQ} + n_{MS})} \cdot \frac{n_{MQ}}{n_{MS}} \cdot \frac{n_{MM}}{n_{MS}}$$

whereby w_A, w_D and w_M are the weights for attributes, description and metadata respectively; n_{AQ}, n_{AS} and n_{MA} are the number of query attributes, service attributes and service attribute matches respectively; n_{DQ}, n_{DS} and n_{MD} are the number of query descriptions, service descriptions and service description matches respectively;

n_{MQ}, n_{MS} and n_{MM} are the number of query metadata, service metadata and service metadata matches respectively.

Match Score with User Weight Assignment (UWA)
The user defines the weight values for service attributes, descriptions and metadata respectively, based upon their confidence in the "search words" used.

Match Score with Fuzzy Weight Assignment (FWA)
Fuzzy weight assignment allows for uncertainty to be captured and represented, and helps the automation of the matching process.

Fuzzy logic is derived from fuzzy set theory [7,8,9,10] dealing with reasoning that is approximate rather than precisely deduced from classical predicate logic. It can be thought of as the application side of fuzzy set theory dealing with well thought out real world expert values for a complex problem. [11]. Fuzzy logic allows for set membership values between and including 0 and 1, and in its linguistic form, imprecise concepts like "slightly", "quite" and "very". Specifically, it allows partial membership in a set.

A fuzzy set A in a universe of discourse U is characterized by a membership function $\mu_A : U \rightarrow [0,1]$ which associates a number $\mu_A(x)$ in the interval [0,1] with each element x of U. This number represents the grade of membership of x in the fuzzy set A (with 0 meaning that x is definitely not a member of the set and 1 meaning that it definitely is a member of the set).

This idea of using approximate descriptions of weight values rather than precise description is used in this approach. First, we have to define a membership function each for w_A, w_D and w_M. The fuzzy subset of the membership function for service attributes can be denoted as such $A = \{(x, \mu_A(x)\}$ $x \in X, \mu_A(x) : X \rightarrow [0,1]$. The fuzzy subset A of the finite reference super set X can be expressed as $A = \{x_1, \mu_A(x_1)\}, \{x_2, \mu_A(x_2)\}, ..., \{x_n, \mu_A(x_n)\}$; or $A = \{\mu_A(x_1)/x_1\}, \{\mu_A(x_2)/x_2\}, ..., \{\mu_A(x_n)/x_n\}$ where the separating symbol / is used to associate the membership value with its coordinate on the horizontal axis. The membership function must be determined first. A number of methods learned from knowledge acquisition can be applied here. Most practical approaches for forming fuzzy sets rely on the knowledge of a single expert. The expert is asked for his or her opinion whether various elements belong to a given set. Another useful approach is to acquire knowledge from multiple experts. A new technique to form fuzzy sets was recently introduced which is based on artificial neural networks, which learn available system operation data and then derive the fuzzy sets automatically.

Fig. 1 shows the membership functions for service attributes, description and metadata respectively. The comparison of the three membership functions shows that it is assumed that service attributes are defined in more detail and therefore there is less overlapping of the three fuzzy sets weak, medium and strong. However, for service description and also metadata the overlap is significantly wider allowing the user a larger "grey area" where the weight values are defined accordingly.

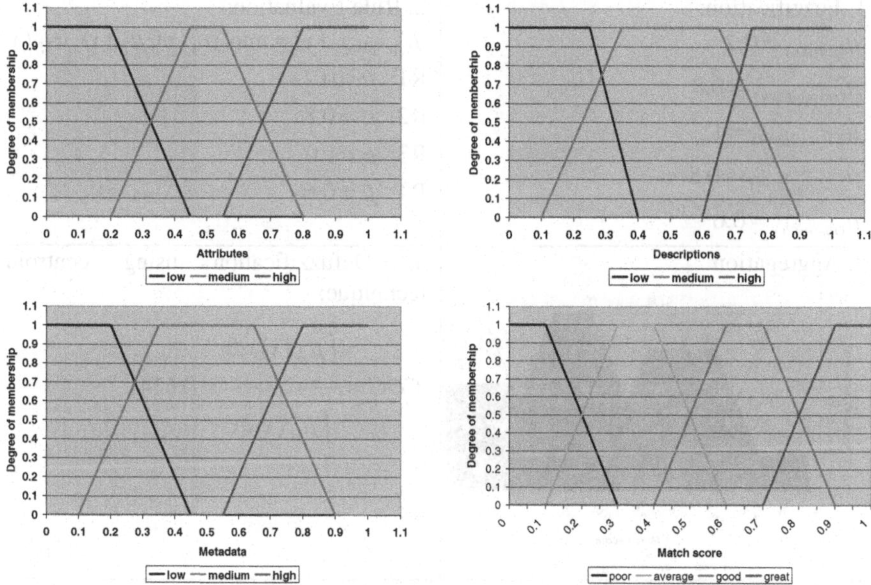

Fig. 1. Membership function of the fuzzy sets for service attributes, descriptions, metadata and match score

In order to do the mapping from a given input to an output using the theory of fuzzy sets, a fuzzy inference must be used. There are two fuzzy inference techniques – Mamdani [12] and Sugeno [13]. The Mamdani method is widely accepted for capturing expert knowledge. It allows describing the expertise more intuitive. However, Mamdani-type inference entails a substantial computational burden. On the other hand, the Sugeno method is computationally effective and works well with optimization and adaptive techniques, which makes it very attractive in control problems. For this investigation, the Mandami inference was chosen because of the fact that it better captures expert knowledge. In 1975, Mandami built one of the first fuzzy systems to control a steam engine and boiler combination by applying a set of fuzzy rules supplied by experienced human operators. The Mamdani-style inference process is performed in four steps which are fuzzification of the input variables, rule evaluation, aggregation of the rule outputs and finally defuzzification.

The four fuzzy rules for service attributes (A), description (D), metadata (M) and match score (MS) are defined as:

R1: IF *A=low* AND *D=low* AND *M=low* THEN *MS=poor*
R2: IF A=medium AND D=low AND M=medium THEN MS=average
R3: IF A=medium AND D=medium AND M=medium THEN MS=good
R4: IF A=high AND D=high AND M=high THEN MS=great

Let us assume a user's query results in the match values M_A=0.4, M_D=0.5 and M_M=0.7 with $w_A = w_D = w_M$ =1.

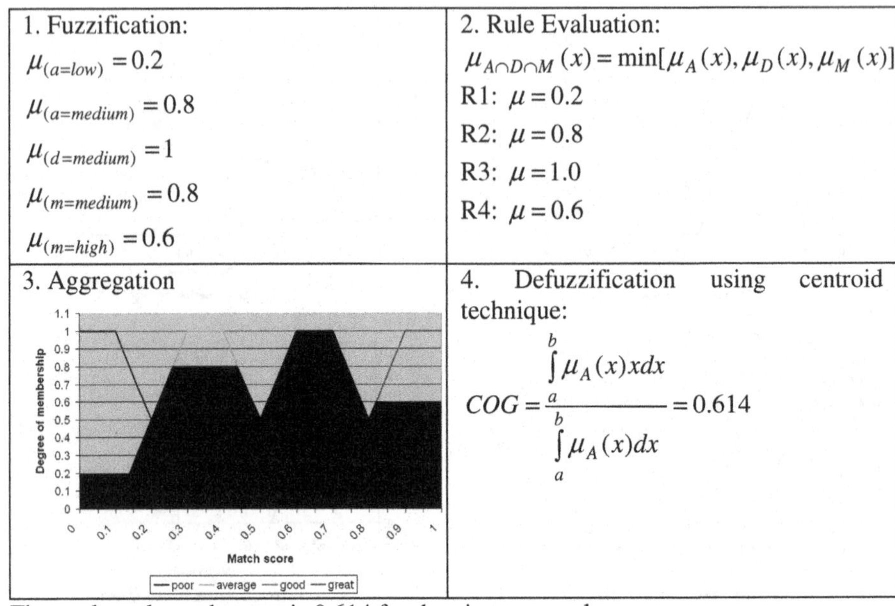

1. Fuzzification:	2. Rule Evaluation:
$\mu_{(a=low)} = 0.2$ $\mu_{(a=medium)} = 0.8$ $\mu_{(d=medium)} = 1$ $\mu_{(m=medium)} = 0.8$ $\mu_{(m=high)} = 0.6$	$\mu_{A \cap D \cap M}(x) = \min[\mu_A(x), \mu_D(x), \mu_M(x)]$ R1: $\mu = 0.2$ R2: $\mu = 0.8$ R3: $\mu = 1.0$ R4: $\mu = 0.6$
3. Aggregation	4. Defuzzification using centroid technique: $COG = \frac{\int_a^b \mu_A(x)xdx}{\int_a^b \mu_A(x)dx} = 0.614$

The evaluated match score is 0.614 for the given example.

3 Conclusion

The contextual information enhances the expressiveness of the matching process, i.e. by adding semantic information to services, and also serves as an implicit input to a service that is not explicitly provided by the user. The introduction of match scores serves as a selection criterion for the user to choose the best match. Two different approaches to calculate the match score were shown whereby one used precise weight values assigned to service attributes, description and metadata, and the second approach showed the usage of fuzzy descriptions for the weight values. The first approach is semi-automatic as the user needs to provide the weight values by entering the query, resulting in a confidence value of how good the user thinks the entered query attributes were chosen. The second approach with the fuzzy weight assignment allows for uncertainty to be captured and represented. The benefit of the second approach is that user intervention is not necessary anymore which helps the automation of the matching process.

For further research, an evaluation will be conducted by an experiment to calculate precision and recall rates for both approaches. Furthermore, an investigation will be done to compare how predefined and hard coded weight values influence the precision and recall values. In addition, due to the computational burden of the Mamdani inference, the Sugeno inference might work better in this area where quick response times are important. However, the advantage of capturing expert knowledge might be compromised. This also needs to be explored further.

References

1. McGovern, J., Tyagi, S., Stevens, M., Mathew, S.: The Java Series Books - Java Web Services Architecture, Ch. 2, Service Oriented Architecture (2003)
2. Tangmunarunkit, H., Decker, S., Kesselman, C.: Ontology-based Resource Matching in the Grid - The Grid meets the Semantic Web. In: Proceedings of the International Semantic Web Conference, Budapest, Hungary (May 2003)
3. Ludwig, S.A., Reyhani, S.M.S.: Semantic Approach to Service Discovery in a Grid Environment. Journal of Web Semantics 4(1), 1–13 (2006)
4. Bell, D., Ludwig, S.A.: Grid Service Discovery in the Financial Markets Sector. Journal of Computing and Information Technology 13(4), 265–270 (2005)
5. Ludwig, S.A., Rana, O.F., Padget, J., Naylor, W.: Matchmaking Framework for Mathematical Web Services. Journal of Grid Computing 4(1), 33–48 (2006)
6. Gagnes, T., Plagemann, T., Munthe-Kaas, E.: A Conceptual Service Discovery Architecture for Semantic Web Services in Dynamic Environments. In: Proceedings of the 22nd International Conference on Data Engineering Workshops (April 2006)
7. Zadeh, L.A.: Fuzzy sets. Information and Control 8, 338–383 (1965)
8. Cox, E.: The Fuzzy Systems Handbook, AP Professional (1995)
9. Tsoukalas, L.H., Uhrig, R.E.: Fuzzy and Neural Approaches in Engineering. John Wiley & Sons Inc., New York (1996)
10. Kosko, B.: Fuzzy Engineering. Prentice Hall, Upper Saddle River, New Jersey (1997)
11. Klir, G.J., St. Clair, U.H., Yuan, B.: Fuzzy Set Theory: Foundations and Applications. Prentice-Hall, Englewood Cliffs (1997)
12. Mamdani, E.H., Assilian, S.: An experiment in linguistic synthesis with a fuzzy logic controller. International Journal of Man–Machine Study, 1–13 (1975)
13. Sugeno, M.: Industrial Applications of Fuzzy Control. North-Holland, Amsterdam (1985)

Grounding OWL-S in SAWSDL

Massimo Paolucci[1], Matthias Wagner[1], and David Martin[2]

[1] DoCoMo Communications Laboratories Europe GmbH
{paolucci,wagner}@docomolab-euro.com
[2] Artificial Intelligence Center, SRI International
martin@ai.sri.com

Abstract. SAWSDL and OWL-S are Semantic Web services languages that both aim at enriching WSDL with semantic annotation. In this paper, we analyze the similarities and differences between the two languages, with the objective of showing how OWL-S annotations could take advantage of SAWSDL annotations. In the process, we discover and analyze representational trade-offs between the two languages.

1 Introduction

Semantic Web services have emerged in the last few years as an attempt to enrich Web services languages with ontological annotations from the Semantic Web. Overall, the goal of such efforts is to facilitate Web services interaction by lowering interoperability barriers and by enabling greater automation of service-related tasks such as discovery and composition. A number of proposals, such as OWL-S 0, WSMO 0 and WSDL-S 0, have been on the table for some time. They provide different perspectives on what Semantic Web services ought to be, and explore different trade-offs. Each of these efforts is concerned with supporting richer descriptions of Web services, but at the same time each has made an effort to tie in with WSDL, and through it to Web service technology. In the case of OWL-S, an ontology-based *WSDL Grounding* is provided, which relates elements of an OWL-S service description with elements of a WSDL service description.

Recently, Semantic Web services reached the standardization level with SAWSDL 0, which is closely derived from WSDL-S. A number of important design decisions were made with SAWSDL to increase its applicability. First, rather than defining a language that spans across the different levels of the WS stack, the authors of SAWSDL have limited their scope to augmenting WSDL, which considerably simplifies the task of providing a semantic representation of services (but also limits expressiveness). Second, there is a deliberate lack of commitment to the use of OWL 0 or to any other particular semantic representation technology. Instead, SAWSDL provides a very general annotation mechanism that can be used to refer to any form of semantic markup. The annotation referents could be expressed in OWL, in UML, or in any other suitable language. Third, an attempt has been made to maximize the use of available XML technology from XML schema, to XML scripts, to XPath, in an attempt to lower the entrance barrier to early adopters.

B. Krämer, K.-J. Lin, and P. Narasimhan (Eds.): ICSOC 2007, LNCS 4749, pp. 416–421, 2007.

Despite these design decisions that seem to suggest a sharp distinction from OWL-S, SAWSDL shares features with OWL-S' WSDL grounding: in particular, both approaches provide semantic annotation attributes for WSDL, which are meant to be used in similar ways. It is therefore natural to expect that SAWSDL may facilitate the specification of the Grounding of OWL-S Web services, but the specific form of such Grounding is still unknown, and more generally a deeper analysis of the relation between SAWSDL and OWL-S is missing. To address these issues, in this paper we define a SAWSDL Grounding for OWL-S. In this process we try to identify how different aspects of OWL-S map into SAWSDL. But we also highlight the differences between the two proposals, and we show that a mapping between the two languages needs to rely on fairly strong assumptions. Our analysis also shows that despite the apparent simplicity of the approach, SAWSDL requires a solution to the two main problems of the semantic representation of Web services: namely the generation and exploitation of ontologies, and the mapping between the ontology and the XML data that is transmitted through the wire.

The result of this paper is of importance for pushing forward the field of Semantic Web services by contributing to the harmonization of two proposals for the annotation of Web services. In the paper, we will assume some familiarity with OWL-S and SAWSDL, neither of which is presented. The rest of the paper is organized as follows. In section 2 we will analyze the similarities and differences between OWL-S and SAWSDL. In section 3, we will introduce an OWL-S grounding based on SAWSDL, with analysis of its strengths and weaknesses. In section 4 we will discuss the finding and conclude.

2 Relating SAWSDL to OWL-S

The first step toward the definition of a SAWSDL Grounding for OWL-S is the precise specification of the overlap between the two languages. Since the two languages have a very similar goal: provide semantic annotation to WSDL, they have some similarities. The first one is that both OWL-S and SAWSDL express the semantics of inputs and outputs of WSDL operations. SAWSDL does it via a direct annotation of the types and elements while the OWL-S Grounding maps the content of inputs and outputs to their semantic representation in the Process Model. The second similarity is that both languages support the use of transformations, typically based on XSLT, to map WSDL messages to OWL concepts. These transformations allow a level of independence between the message formats and the semantic interpretation of the messages, allowing developers to think of the implementation of their application independently of the semantic annotation that is produced. The third similarity is that both OWL-S and SAWSDL acknowledge the importance of expressing the category of a service within a given taxonomy. SAWSDL provides category information by annotating interface definitions. OWL-S provides this information in the Profile through its `type` specification or through the property `serviceCategory`.

Despite their similarities, the two languages have also strong differences. The first one is in the use of WSDL. OWL-S uses WSDL exclusively at invocation time; therefore the WSDL description relates directly to atomic processes in the Process

Model; hence, in OWL-S, there is no direct relation between WSDL and the service Profile, which is used during the discovery phase. Instead SAWSDL uses WSDL both at both discovery and invocation time. Therefore, SAWSDL needs to relate to both the OWL-S Profile and the Process Model. The distinction is important since WSDL and the OWL-S Profile express two very different perspectives on the service: WSDL describes the operations performed by the service during the invocation; on the other hand, the OWL-S Profile takes a global view of the service independent of how this function is realized by the service. From the WSDL perspective, the Profile compresses the Web service to only one operation and it does not specify how this operation can be decomposed to more refined ones. The second difference is in SAWSDL agnostic approach toward semantics. In contrast to OWL-S, which is very committed to OWL and Semantic Web technology, SAWSDL does not make any commitment regarding the representational framework for expressing semantics. The authors of the SAWSDL specification explicitly state that semantics can be expressed in many different ways and languages. Such an agnostic approach extends the applicability of SAWSDL at cost of creating interoperability problems by mixing different annotation frameworks. The third difference is that SAWSDL, on the opposite of OWL-S, allows partial annotation of services. For example, it is possible to annotate the semantics of the attributes of a message, but not the semantics of the whole message. In turn the corresponding OWL-S Grounding will have to define the semantics of the elements that were not described.

Because of these differences, in order to be able to exploit the SAWSDL semantic annotations in the OWL-S Grounding we need to make three assumptions. The first one is that SAWSDL annotations are in OWL since OWL-S does not handle any other type of semantic annotation. The second assumption is that the semantic type of the complete message types is specified. This assumption is required since SAWSDL supports the specification of a schema mapping without a `modelReference.` In such a case, it may be known how to perform the mapping, but not the semantic type of the input or output. Finally, whole description needs to be semantically annotated. If these conditions are violated, then the semantic annotation of parts of the WSDL description will not be available, and therefore the grounding will have to be compiled manually.

3 Grounding OWL-S in SAWSDL

When the previous three assumptions are satisfied, we can take advantage of the SAWSDL semantic annotations in the definition of the mapping of the OWL-S Grounding. To define the OWL-S Grounding, we first need to specify which element of OWL-S maps to the corresponding element in SAWSDL. The class `WsdlAtomicProcessGrounding,` see Figure `2,` specifies the correspondence between the Atomic Process and the WSDL operations through the two properties `owlsProcess` and `wsdlOperation`. The two properties `inputMap` and `outputMap` map the inputs and the outputs of OWL-S processes and WSDL operations.

```
<owl:Class rdf:ID="ModelRefMap">
  <owl:Restriction>
    <owl:onProperty rdf:resource="owlsParameter"/>
    <owl:cardinality rdf:datatype="&xsd;nonNegativeInteger"> 1
    </owl:cardinality>
  </owl:Restriction>
  <owl:Restriction>
    <owl:onProperty rdf:resource="modelRef"/>
    <owl:cardinality rdf:datatype="&xsd;nonNegativeInteger"> 1
    </owl:cardinality>
  </owl:Restriction>
  <owl:Restriction>
    <owl:onProperty rdf:resource="mapParam"/>
    <owl:cardinality rdf:datatype="&xsd;nonNegativeInteger"> 1
    </owl:cardinality>
  </owl:Restriction>
</owl:Class>

<owl:datatypeProperty rdf:ID="owlsParameter">
  <rdfs:domain rdf:resource="#ModelRefMap"/>
  <rdfs:range rdf:resource="&xsd;#anyURI"/>
</owl:datatypeProperty>

<owl:datatypeProperty rdf:ID="modelRef">
  <rdfs:domain rdf:resource="#ModelRefMap"/>
  <rdfs:range rdf:resource="&xsd;#anyURI"/>
</owl:datatypeProperty>

<owl:datatypeProperty rdf:ID="mapParam">
  <rdfs:domain rdf:resource="#ModelRefMap"/>
  <rdfs:range rdf:resource="&xsd;#literal"/>
</owl:datatypeProperty>
```

Fig. 1. Definition of ModelRefMap

As first approximation, OWL-S inputs and outputs can be mapped directly to the results of the concepts representing the semantics of the message types. This way we can take advantage of the lifing elements of SAWSDL. The class `ModelRefMap`, shown in Figure 1 performs this mapping by defining the two properties `owlsParameter` and `modelRef`. The first property specifies the OWL-S parameter to be used, the second property points to the URI of the semantic markup of the message type. One complicating factor in the input and output mapping is that whereas a WSDL operation has only one input and one output, the corresponding Atomic Process in OWL-S may have multiple inputs and outputs. Therefore the straightforward mapping defined above needs a mechanism to select the portions of the input or output that derive from the semantic markup of the message. This can be achieved with rules that specify how the modelRef of a message type maps to and from an OWL-S Parameter. Such a rule could be expressed in a rule language such as SWRL 0. The property `mapParam` of `ModelRefMap` is defined to store such a rule. The cardinality restriction of at most 1 allows for the property not to be used in the grounding, in such case the mapping between the OWL-S parameter and the SAWSDL message is expected to be 1:1.

The last aspect of the grounding is to deal the SAWSDL annotation on the interface. Unlike the previous mappings, in this case there is no need to explicitly add information to the Grounding because first, the expression of service categories is

```
<owl:Class rdf:ID="WsdlAtomicProcessGrounding">
  <owl:Restriction>
    <owl:onProperty rdf:resource="owlsProcess"/>
    <owl:cardinality rdf:datatype="&xsd;nonNegativeInteger">1
    </owl:cardinality>
  </owl:Restriction>
  <owl:Restriction>
    <owl:onProperty rdf:resource="wsdlOperation"/>
    <owl:cardinality rdf:datatype="&xsd;nonNegativeInteger">1
    </owl:cardinality>
  </owl:Restriction>
</owl:Class>

<owl:objectProperty rdf:ID="owlsProcess">
  <rdfs:domain rdf:resource="#WsdlAtomicProcessGrounding"/>
  <rdfs:range rdf:resource="&owlsProcess;#AtomicProcess"/>
</owl:objectproperty>

<owl:datatypeProperty rdf:ID="wsdlOperation">
  <rdfs:domain rdf:resource="#WsdlAtomicProcessGrounding"/>
  <rdfs:range rdf:resource="&xsd;#anyURI"/>
</owl:datatypeProperty>

<owl:objectProperty rdf:ID="inputMap">
  <rdfs:domain rdf:resource="#WsdlAtomicProcessGrounding"/>
  <rdfs:range rdf:resource="#ModelRefMap"/>
</Owl:objectproperty>

<owl:objectProperty rdf:ID="outputMap">
  <rdfs:domain rdf:resource="#WsdlAtomicProcessGrounding"/>
  <rdfs:range rdf:resource="#ModelRefMap"/>
</Owl:objectproperty>
```

Fig. 2. SAWSDL to OWL-S Grounding

equivalent in OWL-S and SAWSDL; and second, the Profile of the service can be found through the Service specification of OWL-S. Therefore, it is possible to stipulate a fixed mapping between the two service descriptions. Such mapping first identifies the Profile corresponding to the Grounding under definition, and then proceeds with a one-to-one mapping between the interface annotation in SAWSDL and the ServiceCategory of OWL-S.

4 Conclusions

The analysis performed in this paper reveals the relation between OWL-S and SAWSDL with the objective of deriving automatically OWL-S Grounding from SAWSDL annotations. The results of our analysis is that whereas in principle such derivation is possible, a number of assumptions on the use of WSDL and the style of annotations are satisfied. When the assumptions are not satisfied, the Grounding can still be defined, but such a mapping has to be derived manually by programmer that understands the semantics of the WSDL specification.

The result of the derivation is a skeletal OWL-S specification that contains a Process Model in which only the atomic processes are specified, and a Profile in which only the service category is specified. The atomic processes themselves will also be partially specified since SAWSDL does not provide any information on their preconditions and effects. An additional modeling problem is the handling of WSDL faults. In principle, they can be represented in OWL-S with conditional results, but the problem is that there is no knowledge in SAWSDL of what are the conditions of a fault since SAWSDL specifies only the annotation of the semantics of content of the message, instead of the conditions under which the fault occurs. These problems could be addressed by adding a specification of preconditions and effects to SAWSDL.

References

1. Akkiraju, R., Farrell, J., Miller, J., Nagarajan, M., Schmidt, M.T., Sheth, A., Verma, K.: Web Service Semantics - WSDL-S. Technical report, W3C Member (submission November 7, 2005) (2005)
2. Farrell, J., Lausen, H.: Semantic Annotations for WSDL and XML Schema, W3C Candidate Recommendation (January 26, 2007), http://www.w3.org/TR/sawsdl/
3. Horrocks, I., Patel-Schneider, P., Boley, H., Tabet, S., Grosof, B., Dean, M.: SWRL: A semantic Web rule language combining OWL and RuleML
4. Lausen, H., Polleres, A., Roman, D.: Web Service Modeling Ontology (WSMO). W3C Member (2005) (submission), http://www.w3.org/Submission/WSMO/
5. Martin, D., Burstein, M., Hobbs, J., Lassila, O., McDermott, D., McIlraith, S., Narayanan, S., Paolucci, M., Parsia, B., Payne, T., Sirin, E., Srinivasan, N., Sycara, K.: OWL-S: Semantic Markup for Web Services. W3C Member Submission (2004)
6. McGuinness, D.L., Harmelen, F. v.: OWL Web Ontology Language overview – W3C recommendation (February 10, 2004)

A Declarative Approach for QoS-Aware Web Service Compositions*

Fabien Baligand[1,2], Nicolas Rivierre[1], and Thomas Ledoux[2]

[1] France Telecom - R&D / MAPS / AMS,
38-40 rue du general Leclerc, 92794 Issy les Moulineaux, France
{fabien.baligand,nicolas.rivierre}@orange-ftgroup.com
[2] OBASCO Group, EMN / INRIA, Lina
Ecole des Mines de Nantes,
4, rue Alfred Kastler, F - 44307 Nantes cedex 3, France
thomas.ledoux@emn.fr

Abstract. While BPEL language has emerged to allow the specification of Web Service compositions from a functional point of view, it is still left to the architects to find proper means to handle the Quality of Service (QoS) concerns of their compositions. Typically, they use ad-hoc technical solutions, at the message level, that significantly reduce flexibility and require costly developments. In this paper, we propose a policy-based language aiming to provide expressivity for QoS behavioural logic specification in Web Service orchestrations, as well as a non-intrusive platform in charge of its execution both at pre-deployment time and at runtime.

1 Introduction

BPEL language provides abstractions and guarantees to easily specify safe service compositions, but its expressivity is limited to functional concerns of a composition, implying that architects have to handle other concerns, such as QoS management, by other means. QoS management, in the context of Web Services, relates to a wide scope of properties such as performance, availability, price or security. To guaranty the QoS of a relationship between a customer and a service provider, a Service Level Agreement (SLA) that contains guarantees and assumptions is negotiated.

Dealing with QoS in service compositions faces numerous challenges both at pre-deployment time and at runtime. At pre-deployment time, architects have to guaranty the QoS properties of the composite services and have to find local services whose QoS satisfies to the global QoS. As discussed in [5], dealing with the QoS properties combinatory is a complex task. Current works [2,4] focus either on a bottom-up approach, that deduces the QoS of the composite service out of local services QoS and the composition structure, either on a top-down approach, that aims to find a set of local services satisfying to the QoS of the

* This work was partially supported by the FAROS research project funded by the French RNTL.

B. Krämer, K.-J. Lin, and P. Narasimhan (Eds.): ICSOC 2007, LNCS 4749, pp. 422–428, 2007.

composite. However, both ways do not take into account architects advanced requirements. For instance, the architects may want to specify QoS of some parts of their orchestrations and may require that some local services are discovered to match the global QoS. At runtime, QoS of local services is likely to vary, and the orchestration client may use various paths in the BPEL flow execution. Such variations lead to QoS variations of the composite service that need to be dynamically counterbalanced. Also, QoS mechanisms such as security, reliable messaging or transaction, which rely on WS-* protocols, are major features that must be addressed.

Because BPEL language does not provide expressivity for QoS management, architects cannot easily specify QoS requirements and behavioural logic in their orchestrations. Instead, they handle QoS management at the message level, using different frameworks and languages: some specific platforms take care of SLA documents, while SOAP filters contain QoS mechanisms implementation and that BPEL engines may offer basic QoS features. Making all these frameworks work together leads to code that lacks flexibility and portability, that decreases loose coupling nature of the composition, and which is error-prone. To provide the required expressivity for QoS management at the composition level, we propose a language accurately targeting parts of the BPEL orchestrations.

In this paper, we present our approach that aims to be non-intrusive with already existing infrastructures and languages. This approach offers a policy-based language, called "QoSL4BP" (Quality of Service Language for Business Processes), and a platform, namely "ORQOS" (ORchestration Quality Of Service). The latest version of ORQOS platform has not been fully implemented yet, but already existing components of previous versions have been used for proof of concept purposes. The remainder of the paper is organized as follows: Section 2 describes QoSL4BP language structure and primitives, Section 3 details the three steps of ORQOS platform process, Section 4 illustrates our approach with a scenario and Section 5 discusses the related works.

2 QoSL4BP Language

Design. To allow a seamless integration with BPEL language, and to increase reusability and portability of our language, QoSL4BP language was designed as a policy-based language. A policy consists in a declarative unit containing the adaptation logic of a base process. It is commonly agreed that a policy contains objectives to reach and actions to perform on a system. In our context, the BPEL orchestration is divided into sub-orchestrations (called scopes), each scope being addressed by a specific QoSL4BP policy, in order to allow the architect to address well-delimited systems of the orchestration, to decompose the QoS aggregation computation problem (described in section 3), and also to increase policies reusability. Thus, QoSL4BP policies contain both static and dynamic QoS behavioural logic, hence allowing architect to specify QoS constraints and adaptation logic over scopes of the orchestration.

Structure. The structure of a QoSL4BP policy is composed of three sections, as shown on Figure 1: The "SCOPE" section specifies the BPEL activity (basic or structured) targeted by the policy, "INIT" section contains the initial QoS settings of the scope, used at pre-deployment time, and "RULE" section embodies Event-Condition-Action (ECA) rules. This section is performed at runtime while the composition performs within the scope targeted by the policy.

```
POLICY policy_name = {
    SCOPE = { BPEL activity targeted by the policy }
    INIT = { scope initial QoS settings }
    RULE = {
        (Condition)? -> (Action)+
    }
}
```

Fig. 1. QoSL4BP Policy Template

Primitives. QoSL4BP language offers a limited set of context access and action primitives, as illustrated on Figure 4. Conditions of rules are formed by testing the context access primitives and can be composed with the usual boolean operators. Context access primitives returns QoS data collected both at the service and at the composition levels: **REQUIRE** and **PROVIDE** primitives give information about the QoS mechanisms required and provided by a service; **SLAVIOLATION** and **SCOPEVIOLATION** primitives respectively detect if a SLA is violated and if the scope QoS initial settings are violated; **USER**, **EXCEPTION**, **RATE** and **LOOP** primitives respectively returns information about the user, QoS exceptions, branch rate of use in a switch activity, and number of loops in a while activity. Action primitives allow the architect to specify QoS behavioural logic of the orchestration: **PERFORM** and **PROCESS** primitives enforce QoS mechanisms for outbound and inbound SOAP messages; **SELECT**, **RENEGOTIATE** and **REPLANNING** primitives respectively enable to select a concrete service to use for an abstract service, to renegotiate a concrete service to match an abstract service, and to perform QoS replanning to satisfy to the scope QoS initial settings; **FAIL** and **THROW** primitives allow to throw QoS exceptions to the customer and inside the orchestration.

3 ORQOS Platform Process

ORQOS platform process includes three steps. First, ORQOS platform statically singles out a set of concrete services to match the abstract services of the orchestration whose QoS aggregation satisfies to the SLA of the composite service, then it modifies the BPEL document to introduce monitoring activities at pre-deployment time, and finally ORQOS performs QoS adaptation at runtime.

QoS Planning. Let k be the number of services of the orchestration, and let n be the number of potential concrete services that can implement each of services of the orchestration, then the number of potential configurations to evaluate is n^k, making the problem NP-hard [5]. To bring answers to these issues, ORQOS decomposes, using policies scopes, the computation of the composite service into multiple computations at some "sub-composite" levels, and recomposes the solutions afterwards. For decomposition, QoS initial settings of QoSL4BP policies are considered both as expectations (for the local services contained in policies scopes) and as guarantees (when evaluating the global QoS of the orchestration). Thus, as shown in Figure 2, smaller aggregations are tested against the QoS initial settings of QoSL4BP policies, then the QoS aggregations of sub-composite services are tested against the SLA of the composite service. Therefore, let p be the number of policies, let $c_i (i \in [1;p])$ be the number of services included in the scope of policy i, and let c_0 be the number of services which are not included in any scope of policies, then the number of potential configurations ORQOS has to evaluate is $\sum_{i=0}^{p} n^{c_i}$, which is in $\Theta(n^{max(c_i)})$, meaning that, with a set of appropriate scopes, testing each configuration with aggregation techniques, such as presented in [2], becomes affordable.

Monitoring Sensors Insertion into BPEL. The second step of ORQOS platform processing consists in inserting sensor activities at relevant places into the BPEL document, to monitor performance of orchestration scopes and to inform ORQOS at runtime. Such sensors are standard "invoke" activities that monitor scope QoS, BPEL execution paths, and exceptions. They call an ORQOS sensor manager interface, hence allowing ORQOS to collect data at runtime. As shown on Figure 2, sensors are inserted into the BPEL document according to the instructions specified in the "RULE" section of QoSL4BP policies. After this transformation step, the BPEL document can be deployed on any BPEL engine.

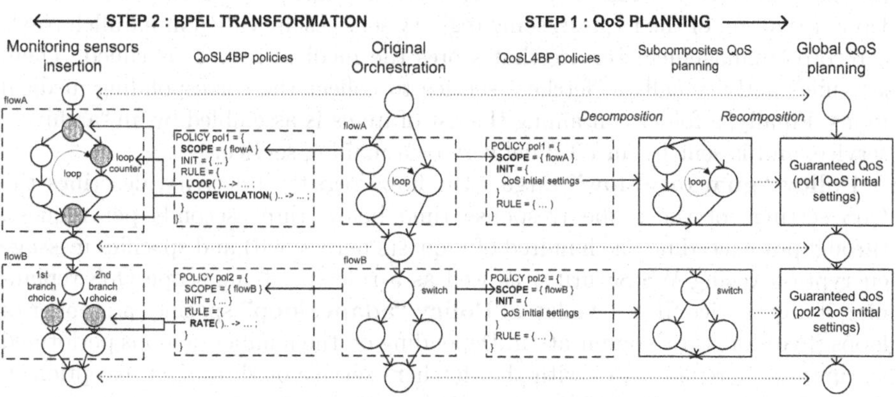

Fig. 2. Pre-deployment Process Steps

QoS Adaptation at Runtime. Once the orchestration is deployed, the BPEL engine exposes both a WSDL interface and an SLA offer for customers to invoke the composite service. As can be seen on Figure 3, a proxy layer has been added for SLA monitoring, for WS-* mechanisms enactment, and for flexible dynamic service binding. Thus, the proxy acts both as a sensor and an actuator in partnership with ORQOS platform. Meanwhile, ORQOS platform is in charge of processing the rules contained in QoSL4BP policies. It receives information both from the proxy (SLA violation, usage of orchestration customers) and from the BPEL engine via the sensors inserted at pre-deployment time . Upon satisfaction of any of the rules conditions, the corresponding actions are performed, hence allowing QoS to be readjusted at runtime.

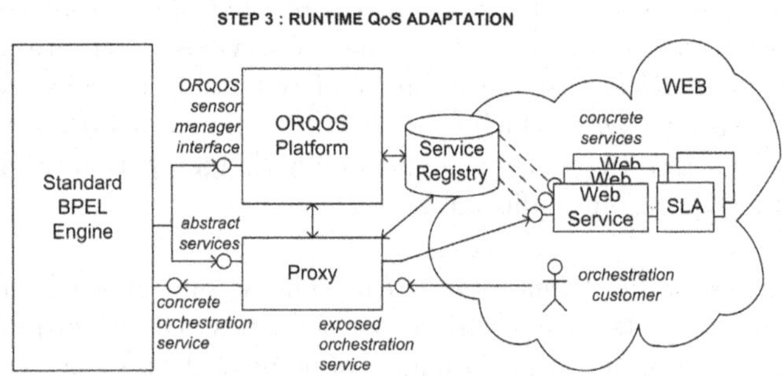

Fig. 3. Runtime QoS Adaptation Step

4 Illustrative Scenario

Depicted in Figure 4, the "Personal Medical Records" scenario illustrates a Web Service orchestration called by a doctor to get medical records of a patient. Upon reception of the request, some registry services are called in parallel. Next, a records management service that stores the medical records is called. Then, a "while" activity calls a "fetcher" service to collect the corresponding medical items. Finally, a folder containing the list of items is assembled by an "archiver" service, and is sent by an FTP delivery or a mailing service.

Policy "guarantyFlow" targets the flow("registry") activity, describes the QoS settings of the scope (response time below three seconds per request, throughput exceeding one hundred of requests per second) and specifies message encryption (using WS-Security) as well as a rule specifying scope QoS replanning if any service SLA is violated. **Policy "adapt2loop"** specifies a number of loops (five) for static computation. Depending on the number of loops performed at runtime, it renegotiates with the "fetcher" service or throws an exception in the orchestration. The "archiver" service can be implemented by two services ("ZIPService" and "RARService") that do not come with SLA. **Policy "noSLA"** specifies the expected QoS for static computation, and implements the service selection logic ("ZIPService" can hold a forty requests per second throughput

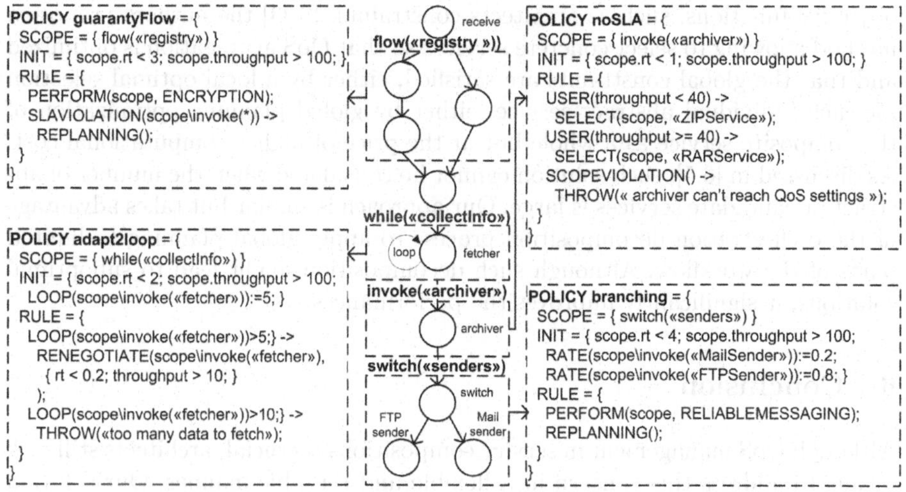

Fig. 4. "Personal Medical Records" Orchestration and QoSL4BP Policies

while "RARService" shows better performance) depending on the usage of orchestration customers. Also, it specifies that an exception should be thrown if the static QoS properties are violated. **Policy "branching"** contains the initial rates of use of the "switch" branches for static computation ("FTPSender" service is initially called four times more than the "MailSender" service). At runtime, WS-ReliableMessaging protocol is specified for each service of the scope and the QoS of services has to readjust according to the rates of use of the branches.

5 Related Works

In [3], the authors have elaborated a language named "Aspect Oriented for Business Process Execution Language" (AO4BPEL) that allows BPEL aspects specification calling non functional mechanisms, such as security (using infrastructural services that modify SOAP messages). This work is different from ours because the framework requires a purposely built BPEL engine, it uses an imperative language to specify extra-functional requirements, and it does not address performance requirements. In [1] the authors propose a policy assertion language, "WS-CoL" (Web Services Constraint Language), based on WS-Policy and specifically designed to be used in monitoring BPEL processes. The approach is similar to ours in that a non intrusive manager, in charge of the evaluation of policies, is called by standard BPEL invoke activities. However, the authors focus on monitoring and only consider security assertions (WS-SecurityPolicy).

In [2] the authors propose a QoS prediction algorithm consisting of a set of graph reduction rules applied to the composite constructs of a workflow. Upon only one atomic service remains, QoS properties corresponding to the process are exposed. We use a similar reduction approach as it enables fast workflow QoS estimation, but we adapt it to take into account dynamic replanning and objective functions, such as architects constraints. In [4] the authors propose a method allowing to select concrete services so that QoS aggregation is optimized and that the global constraints are satisfied, either by a local optimal selection for each individual abstract service, either by global planning optimization of the composite service as a whole but at the price of higher computational cost. As discussed in [6,5], such solution cannot be considered when the number of abstract or candidate services is large. Our approach is similar but takes advantage of the orchestration decomposition process to apply global planning to limited parts of the workflow. Although such decomposition might lead to suboptimal solutions, it significantly improves the performances.

6 Conclusion

Although QoS management in service compositions is crucial, architects still lack means to address this concern in a flexible and reusable manner. Our solution aims to provide expressivity to address the QoS management concerns of service compositions. Our first contribution is the QoSL4BP language, allowing to specify QoS policies over scopes of BPEL orchestrations. Execution of the QoSL4BP language is performed by the ORQOS platform, designed to be non intrusive with already existing infrastructures. At pre-deployment time, ORQOS guarantees the static QoS properties of the orchestration and singles out a relevant set of concrete services. At runtime, ORQOS platform monitors the execution environment and processes policies rules enabling QoS mechanisms management, SLA renegotiation and QoS exception handling.

References

1. Baresi, L., Guinea, S., Plebani, P.: Ws-policy for service monitoring. In: Bussler, C., Shan, M.-C. (eds.) TES 2005. LNCS, vol. 3811, pp. 72–83. Springer, Heidelberg (2006)
2. Cardoso, J., Sheth, A.P., Miller, J.A., Arnold, J., Kochut, K.: Quality of service for workflows and web service processes. J. Web Sem. (2004)
3. Charfi, A., Schmeling, B., Heizenreder, A., Mezini, M.: Reliable, secure, and transacted web service compositions with ao4bpel. In: ECOWS. Proceedings of the 4th IEEE European Conference on Web Services, December 2006, IEEE Computer Society Press, Los Alamitos (2006)
4. Zeng, L., et al.: Qos-aware middleware for web services composition. IEEE Trans. Softw. Eng. 30(5), 311–327 (2004)
5. Jaeger, M.: Optimising Quality-of-Service for the Composition of Electronic Services. PhD thesis, Berlin University of Technology (January 2007)
6. Yu, T., Lin, K.-J.: Service selection algorithms for web services with end-to-end qos constraints. In: CEC'04. CEC '04: Proceedings of the IEEE International Conference on E-Commerce Technology, Washington, DC, USA, pp. 129–136. IEEE Computer Society Press, Los Alamitos (2004)

Supporting QoS Negotiation with Feature Modeling

Marcelo Fantinato[1], Itana Maria de S. Gimenes[2], and Maria Beatriz F. de Toledo[1]

[1] Institute of Computing, University of Campinas, Brazil
[2] Department of Computer Science, University of Maringá, Brazil
mfantina@ic.unicamp.br, itana@din.uem.br, beatriz@ic.unicamp.br

Abstract. Feature modeling is a technique that has been widely used for capturing and managing commonalities and variabilities of product families in the context of software product line. This paper presents a feature-based approach to be applied in QoS negotiation during the establishment of a Web services e-contract. Its motivation is that the e-negotiation process, aiming at defining attributes and levels for QoS – in a particular business domain, usually involves a set of well-defined common and variation points.

Keywords: e-contracts; Web services; QoS; information reuse; features.

1 Introduction

E-contracts are used to describe details of the supply and the consumption of e-services within a business process [1], [2]. An important part of e-contracts are the levels for QoS attributes agreed between the involved parties [3], [4]. The current complexity involved in e-contract establishment and QoS negotiation include aspects such as: great amount of necessary information; increasing number of parameters to be considered; potential long-duration of e-negotiations; and involvement of different profiles (business and development teams) of distinct organizations.

In order to overcome these drawbacks, it is necessary to tackle information structuring and reuse, which is normally tried using e-contract templates [2], [5]–[10]. Templates are commonly treated as simple documents that have empty fields to be fulfilled with some value, usually from a pre-defined list. In general, existing template approaches do not offer suitable mechanisms to manage common and variable elements in similar e-contracts. Therefore, they provide a limited potential for information reuse between similar e-contracts.

In this paper, a new approach to reduce the complexity of QoS negotiation, inside a process to establish e-contracts for Web services, is proposed. It is based on the feature modeling technique [11], which was developed inside the software product line (PL) [12]-[13] context. Its major contribution is to offer a systematic and efficient way for information structure and reuse, thus optimizing the QoS negotiation process. The approach provides a mean to represent QoS attributes and levels, besides other e-contract elements, in feature models that can be transformed into e-contract templates. This paper extends two previous works on e-contract establishment [14], [15] with: a new e-contract metamodel and emphasis on QoS negotiation.

B. Krämer, K.-J. Lin, and P. Narasimhan (Eds.): ICSOC 2007, LNCS 4749, pp. 429–434, 2007.

In brief, the proposed approach consists of a set of five stages. Feature modeling allows the representation of abstract e-services and possible levels for QoS attributes. The activities of the e-contract establishment process, including QoS negotiation, will be oriented by the feature model and feature model configurations. The generic contracted e-services will be mapped to the Web services implementing them, in a one-to-one relationship. These Web services will be referred to in the resulting e-contract, for which specific levels for some QoS attributes can be defined.

This paper covers the following information: e-contract and feature modeling background concepts; proposed approach; related work; conclusions and references.

2 Electronic Contracts

A contract is an agreement between two or more parties interested in creating mutual relationships on business or legal obligations. It defines an activity set to be carried out by each party, which must satisfy a set of terms and conditions – known as contract clauses. An e-contract is an electronic document used to represent an agreement between organization partners carrying out business using the Internet, in which the negotiated services are e-services, currently implemented as Web services.

An e-contract consists of [2]: *parties* – representing the organizations involved in a business process; *activities* – representing e-services to be executed throughout the e-contract enactment; and *contractual clauses* – describing constraints to be satisfied throughout the e-contract enactment. Contractual clauses can represent three different types of constraints [1]: *obligations* – what parties should do; *permissions* – what parties are allowed to do; and *Prohibitions* – what parties should not do.

Obligations include QoS clauses associated with e-services which define attributes related to non-functional properties. They affect the definition and execution of an e-service, regarding to, for example: availability, integrity, reliability, performance, security and reply time [3], [4], [10]. For each QoS attribute, a value must be defined to be used as a tolerable level (e.g. a minimum, a maximum or an exact value).

3 Feature Modeling

Feature modeling is a type of computing ontology that has been applied for capturing and managing commonalities and variabilities in software PL [12]. It was originally proposed in the domain engineering context, as part of the Feature-Oriented Domain Analysis (FODA) [11], and has been applied in a range of domains including telecom systems, template libraries, networks protocols and embedded systems.

In general, a feature model is a description of the relevant characteristics of some entity of interest. A feature can be defined as a system property that is relevant to some stakeholder and is used to capture commonalities or discriminate systems in a family. They may denote any functional or non-functional characteristic at the requirement, architectural, component, platform, or any other level. According to the original FODA method, features can be mandatory, optional or alternative.

A feature model describes the configuration space of a system family. A member of the family can be specified by selecting the desired features from the feature model within the variability constraints defined by the model. This process is called feature configuration. The rules to elaborating features models or diagrams can be specified by feature metamodels. The one being used here is proposed by Czarnecki at. al. [12].

Features can be organized in a feature diagram, which is a tree-like structure where each node represents a feature and each feature may be described by a set of sub-features represented as children nodes. Feature diagrams offer a simple and intuitive notation to represent variation points without delving into implementation details. The diagrams are especially useful to drive the feature configuration process.

4 QoS Negotiation and e-Contracts Establishment

This section presents the process to negotiate QoS attributes, inside a global process to establish WS-contracts (Web services e-contract) between two organizations. The global process consists of five stages, adapted from the FORM method [13]:

1. Feature model elaboration: two feature models are elaborated to represent the e-services and QoS attributes from each organization;
2. WS-contract template creation: having two feature model as the basis, a WS-contract template is created;
3. Web services development and publication: Web services that implement the e-services must be developed and published – which is out of this paper scope;
4. Feature model configuration: the two feature models are then configured to represent the exact e-services and QoS levels for a particular business process;
5. WS-contract establishment: a WS-contract is produced by refining the WS-contract template, based on the previously defined pair of feature model configurations.

Fig. 1 represents, as a class diagram, the artifacts produced throughout the stages above. The *feature model* is the basic artifact from which a unique *WS-contract template* is generated and one or more *feature model configurations* are derived. For each *feature model configuration*, a particular *WS-contract* is established. The *WS-contracts* are established based on the same *WS-contract template*. Each `Web` *service* implementing an abstract e-service of the feature model is referred to by the *WS-contract template*. Only the `Web` *services* implementing e-services of the feature model configuration are referred to by the corresponding *WS-contract*.

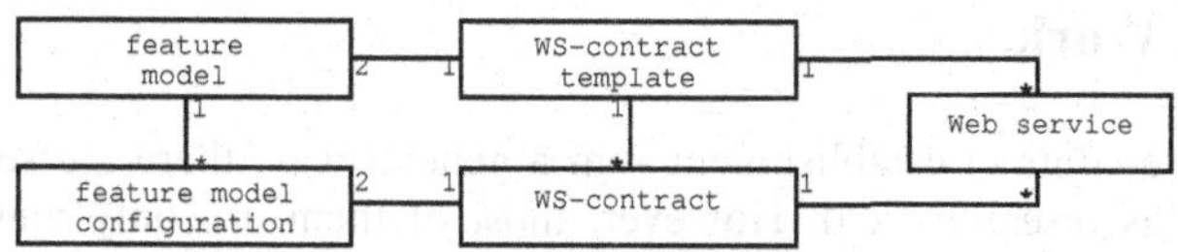

Fig. 1. Artifacts relationship

The QoS attributes, associated to the e-services, are treated as common points and variabilities in feature models. They can be specified by mandatory, alternative and optional features. A feature metamodel [12] was chosen to drive the modeling of this information as features. And a specific feature diagram structure for e-services and QoS attributes representation is being developed, since the inherent flexibility of the metamodel would allow the definition QoS attributes in too many ways.

A WS-contract metamodel was defined to represent rules to create both WS-contracts and templates. The metamodel was created by unifying the main concepts related to: (i) Web services – described by WSDL language; (ii) business processes involving Web services – described by WS-BPEL language; and, (iii) QoS of Web services – described by WS-Agreement language.

The creation of the WS-contract template is carried out in two steps: at first, the WSDL and WS-Agreement sections are created directly from the e-services feature models. For the first step, there is a mapping from elements of the feature metamodel to elements of the WS-contract metamodel. In the second step, the WS-BPEL section is created from WSDL definitions and further information is defined during this stage.

To enable contract instantiation, the WS-contract template is instrumented with a set of annotations linking the contract elements to the respective features used as basis for its creation. During contract instantiation, the feature model configurations are used by a parser in a removal process. This process is driven by the mandatory features and the optional/alternative features that have been selected or not.

A support tool is being developed to aid the proposed process. The tool, named FeMoWS-Contract (Feature Modeling WS-Contract establishment tool), includes a series of software components related to different stages of the approach. One of the component part of the tool is FeaturePlugin tool [16], used for specification of feature models and support theirs configurations.

An approach evaluation was undertaken on a pseudo-scenario to evaluate the approach proposed here. It is concerned with the integration between two business and operation support systems, in the telecom context: customer relationship management (CRM) and dunning systems. The success on its has made possible to demonstrate the feasibility of the approach.

As a result from the approach evaluation, some developed artifacts are presented. Fig. 2 presents an example of a feature model configuration for a system providing information for another one. The right side of the figure models some e-services whereas the left side of it models some levels for a QoS attribute. In both cases, a set of optional features is already selected. Fig. 3 presents a part of the WS-contract template related to this features model. Since only the level "15" was chosen during configuration, all the other options will be removed from the contract model to instantiate the resulting WS-contract – through a annotation removal process.

5 Related Work

In relation to e-contract establishment – in a general way, there are several projects involved in this research field. However, most of them use only metamodels as a basic and limited way to achieve information reuse. In some few cases, they also use e-contract templates as a more efficient way to achieve information reuse. Examples of such projects are [2], [5]–[9]. There are also some projects that work directly with QoS attributes, including [3], [4], [10].

Some works focus on the negotiation phase before specifying the business process, but they are commonly concerned with the process to be followed and the tools to be used during the negotiation between the parties. Some projects related to e-negotiation are presented in [17]–[20]. In these and other similar approaches, there is little emphasis in information reuse compared to the approach proposed by this work.

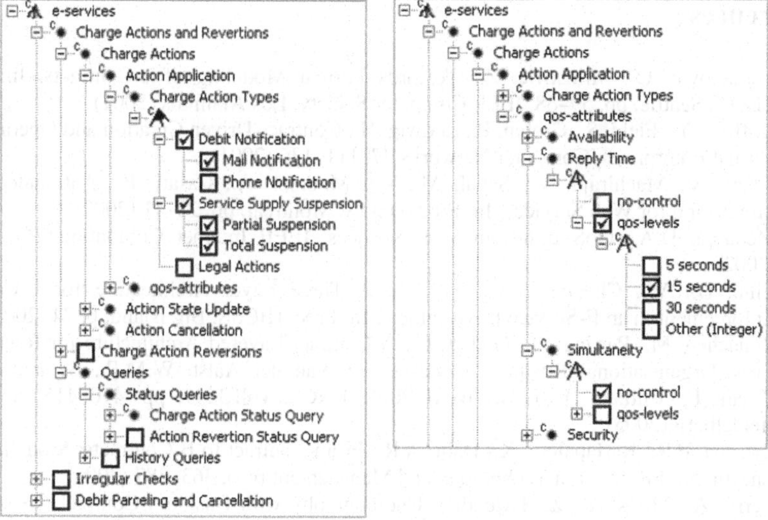

Fig. 2. Example of feature model configuration

```
<wsag:GuaranteeTerm Obligated="ServiceProvider">
  <wsag:ServiceScope ServiceName="applyChargeAction">
  </wsag:ServiceScope>
  <wsag:QualifyingCondition>…</wsag:QualifyingCondition>
  <wsag:ServiceLevelObjective>
    replayTimeSecond IS_LESS_INCLUSIVE
                None  <!-- f:Reply_Time_No_Control_ID -->
                5     <!-- f:Reply_Time_level_5_ID -->
                15    <!-- f:Reply_Time_level_15_ID -->
                30    <!-- f:Reply_Time_level_30_ID -->
                Other <!-- f:Reply_Time_level_Other_ID -->
  </wsag:ServiceLevelObjective>
  <wsag:BusinessValueList>…</wsag:BusinessValueList>
</wsag:GuaranteeTerm>
```

Fig. 3. Example of WS-contract template

6 Conclusions and Future Work

In this paper, a new approach to support QoS negotiation, as a step for establishing e-contracts for Web services, is proposed. Its main contribution is allowing a better management of common and variable points found in similar WS-contracts, including the QoS attributes and levels for different e-services; and information structure and reuse in a systematic way. Such improvement is achieved by the use of e-contract templates associated with feature models representing e-services and QoS attributes.

Future work includes: (i) finishing the development of a prototype tool to automate the establishment of WS-contract templates and resulting WS-contracts; (ii) searching for new ways to analyze the proposed approach effectiveness and compare it to other approaches to establish WS-contracts and QoS negotiation; and (iii) evaluating the approach extension for QoS negotiation between more than two parties.

References

[1] Marjanovic, O., Milosevic, Z.: Towards Formal Modeling of e-Contracts. In: Proc. EDOC, Seattle, pp. 59–68. IEEE Computer Society, Los Alamitos (2001)

[2] Hoffner, Y., Field, S., Grefen, P., Ludwig, H.: Contract-Driven Creation and Operation of Virtual Enterprises. Computer Networks 37, 111–136 (2001)

[3] Sahai, A., Machiraju, V., Sayal, M., van Moorsel, A., Casati, F.: Automated SLA Monitoring for Web Services. In: Proc. DSON, Montreal, pp. 28–41 (2002)

[4] Menasce, D.A.: QoS Issues in Web Services. IEEE Internet Computing 6(6), 72–75 (2002)

[5] Chiu, D.K.W., Cheung, S.-C., Till, S.: A Three Layer Architecture for E-Contract Enforcement in an E-Service Environment. In: Proc. HICSS, Big Island, p. 74 (2003)

[6] Rouached, M., Perring, O., Godart, C.: A Contract Layered Architecture for Regulating Cross-Organisational Business Processes. In: van der Aalst, W.M.P., Benatallah, B., Casati, F., Curbera, F. (eds.) BPM 2005. LNCS, vol. 3649, pp. 410–415. Springer, Heidelberg (2005)

[7] Krishna, P.R., Karlapalem, K., Dani, A.R.: From Contract to E-Contracts: Modeling and Enactment. Information Technology and Management 6(4), 363–387 (2005)

[8] Berry, A., Milosevic, Z.: Extending Choreography with Business Contract Constraints. IJCIS journal 14(2/3), 131–179 (2005)

[9] Hoffner, Y., Field, S.: Transforming Agreements into Contracts. IJCIS journal 14(2/3), 217–244 (2005)

[10] Keller, A., Ludwig, H.: The WSLA Framework: Specifying and Monitoring Service Level Agreements for Web Services. JNSM journal 11(1), 57–81 (2003)

[11] Kang, K., Cohen, S., Hess, J., Novak, W., Peterson, A.: Feature-Oriented Domain Analysis (FODA) Feasibility Study, Tech. Report CMU/SEI-90-TR-021, SEI/CMU (1990)

[12] Czarnecki, K., et al.: Staged Configuration through Specialization and Multi-Level Configuration of Feature Models. Software Proc.: Improv. and Prac. 10(2), 143–169 (2005)

[13] Kang, K.C., et al.: FORM: A Feature-Oriented Reuse Method with Domain-Specific Reference Architectures. Annals of Software Engineering 5, 143–168 (1998)

[14] Fantinato, M., de Toledo, M.B.F., Gimenes, I.M.S.: A Feature-based Approach to Electronic Contracts. In: Proc. IEEE CEC EEE, San Francisco, pp. 34–41 (2006)

[15] Fantinato, M., Gimenes, I.M.S., de Toledo, M.B.F.: Web Services E-contract Establishment Using Features. In: Dustdar, S., Fiadeiro, J.L., Sheth, A. (eds.) BPM 2006. LNCS, vol. 4102, pp. 290–305. Springer, Heidelberg (2006)

[16] Antkiewicz, M., Czarnecki, K.: FeaturePlugin: Feature Modeling Plug-in for Eclipse. In: Proc. eTX workshop, Vancouver, pp. 67–72. ACM Press, New York (2004)

[17] Streitberger, W.: Framework for the Negotiation of Electronic Contracts in E-Business on Demand. In: Proc. IEEE CEC, Munich, pp. 370–373. IEEE Computer Society, Los Alamitos (2005)

[18] Rinderle, S., Benyoucef, M.: Towards the Automation of E-Negotiation Processes Based on Web Services - A Modeling Approach. In: Ngu, A.H.H., Kitsuregawa, M., Neuhold, E.J., Chung, J.-Y., Sheng, Q.Z. (eds.) WISE 2005. LNCS, vol. 3806, pp. 443–453. Springer, Heidelberg (2005)

[19] Jertila, A., Schoop, M.: Electronic Contracts in Negotiation Support Systems: Challenges, Design and Implementation. In: Proc. IEEE CEC, Munich, pp. 396–399 (2005)

[20] Kaminski, H., Perry, M.: SLA Automated Negotiation Manager for Computing Services. In: Proc. IEEE CEC EEE, San Francisco, pp. 47–54 (2006)

[21] Andrieux, A., et al.: Web Services Agreement Specification (WS-Agreement), http:// www. ogf.org/Public_Comment_Docs/Documents/Oct-2006/WS-AgreementSpecification

A Multi-criteria Service Ranking Approach Based on Non-Functional Properties Rules Evaluation

Ioan Toma[1], Dumitru Roman[1], Dieter Fensel[1], Brahmanada Sapkota[2], and Juan Miguel Gomez[3]

[1]DERI Innsbruck, University of Innsbruck, Austria
firstname.lastname@deri.at
[2] DERI Galway, National University of Ireland, Galway, Ireland
brahmananda.sapkota@deri.org
[3] Carlos III University, Madrid, Spain
juanmiguel.gomez@uc3m.es

Abstract. Service oriented architectures (SOAs) are quickly becoming the defacto solutions for providing end-to-end enterprise connectivity. However realizing the vision of SOA requires, among others, solutions for one fundamental challenge, namely service ranking. Once a set of services that fulfill the requested functionality is discovered, an ordered list of services needs to be created according to users preferences. These preferences are often expressed in terms of multiple non-functional properties (NFPs). This paper proposes a multi-criteria ranking approach for semantic web services. We start by briefly introducing ontological models for NFPs. These models are used to specify rules which describe NFP aspects of services and goals/requests. The ranking mechanism evaluates these NFPs rules using a reasoning engine and produces a ranked list of services according to users preferences.

1 Introduction

Service-Oriented Architectures (SOAs) are becoming a widespread solution for realizing distributed applications. Empowered by semantic technologies these solutions are evolving in what is known as Semantically Enabled Service Oriented Architectures (SESAs) [1] bringing more automatization and accuracy to various service related tasks, such as discovery, composition, ranking and selection. Among these tasks discovery, ranking and selection are core building blocks. As with most of the search products available on the market, it is not only important to determine the relevant results, but it is as well extremely important to provide the results in a relevant order. This is exactly the purpose of service ranking process, which complements the discovery process.

While problems such as discovery([6], [9], etc.) and composition([2], etc.) for Semantic Web Services have been intensively studied, the service ranking problem, has rather gathered not so much attention. However, we argue that service ranking in an important task in the overall service usage process and thus it needs to be treated accordantly. Any solution for this task is directly influence by how services are described. Three different aspects must be considered when describing a service: (1) *functional*, (2) *behavior* and (3) *non-functional*. The *functional* description contains the formal specification of

B. Krämer, K.-J. Lin, and P. Narasimhan (Eds.): ICSOC 2007, LNCS 4749, pp. 435–441, 2007.

what exactly the service can do. The *behavior* description contains the formal specification of how the functionality of the service can be achieved. Finally, the *non-functional descriptions* captures constraints over the previous two [3]. Among these aspects, non-functional properties need to be addressed given the high dynamism of any SOA- and SESA- based system. Furthermore, these descriptions are highly relevant for many of the service related tasks. For *ranking* especially, they are fundamental input data that need to be considered when building sorted sets of services. In this paper we present a service ranking approach which uses semantic descriptions of non-functional properties.

The paper is organized as follows: Section 2 briefly introduces our approach for modeling and attaching non-functional properties descriptions to services along with concrete examples. This solution is an integrated part of the Web Service Modeling Ontology (WSMO) [7] and its language Web Service Modeling Language (WSML) [4]. Section 3 provides a detailed description of the proposed service ranking approach. Section 4 presents initial experimental results and finally, Section 5 concludes the paper and points out perspectives for future research.

2 Non-Functional Properties

This section briefly introduce our approach on how to semantically describe NFPs of services. Furthermore concrete examples from a shipping scenario are provided. As a model and language for semantically describe services we adopt the Web Service Modeling Ontology (WSMO) [7], respectively Modeling Language (WSML) [4], due to its clean modeling solution and rule-based support.

The core of our modeling approach is a set of ontologies[1], in WSML, based on the models provided in [5]. These ontologies, provide the NFP terminology, used to specify NFPs aspects of services. Once otological models for NFPs are available, a second challenge that has to be address is how to attach NFPs descriptions to services and goals. Non-functional properties of services or goals are modelled in a way similar to which capabilities are currently modelled in WSMO/WSML [7]. Non-functional properties are defined using logical expressions same as pre/post-conditions, assumptions and effects are being defined in a capability. The terminology needed to construct the logical expressions is provided by non-functional properties ontologies (c.f. [8]).

For exemplification purposes we use services and goals from the SWS Challenge[2] Shipment Discovery scenario. We have extended the initial scenario by augmenting services description with non-functional properties aspects such as discounts and obligations[3]. The shipping services allows requestors to order a shipment by specifying, senders address, receivers address, package information and a collection interval during which the shipper will come to collect the package.

Listing 2 displays a concrete example on how to describe one non-functional property of a service (i.e Runner), namely obligations. Due to space limitations the listing contains only the specification of obligations aspects without any functional, behavioral or any other non-functional descriptions of the service. In an informal manner, the service

[1] http://www.wsmo.org/ontologies/nfp/

[2] http://sws-challenge.org/

[3] http://wiki.wsmx.org/index.php?title=Discovery:NFPUseCase

obligations can be summarized as follows: (1) in case the package is lost or damaged Runner's liability is the declared value of the package but no more than 150$ and (2) packages containing glassware, antiques or jewelry are limited to a maximum declared value of 100$.

Listing 1.1. Runner's obligations

```
namespace {_"WSRunner.wsml#",
   runner _"WSRunner.wsml#", so _"Shipment.wsml#",
   wsml _"http://www.wsmo.org/wsml/wsml-syntax/", up _"UpperOnto.wsml#"}

webService runnerService
   nonFunctionalProperty obligations
    definition
     definedBy
       //in case the package is lost or damaged Runners liability is
       //the declared value of the package but no more than 150 USD
       hasPackageLiability(?package, 150):- ?package[so\#packageStatus hasValue ?status] and
        (?status = so\#packageDamaged or ?status = so\#packageLost) and
        packageDeclaredValue(?package, ?value) and ?value>150.

       hasPackageLiability(?package, ?value):- ?package[so\#packageStatus hasValue ?status] and
         (?status = so\#packageDamaged or ?status = so\#packageLost) and
         packageDeclaredValue(?package, ?value) and ?value =< 150.

       //in case the package is not lost or damaged Runners liability is 0
       hasPackageLiability(?package, 0):- ?package[so\#packageStatus hasValue ?status] and
       ?status != so\#packageDamaged and ?status != so\#packageLost.

       //packages containing glassware, antiques or jewelry
       //are limited to a maximum declared value of 100 USD
       packageDeclaredValue(?package, 100):-
        ?package[so\#containesItemsOfType hasValue ?type, so\#declaredValue hasValue ?value] and
        (?type = so\#Antiques or ?type = so\#Glassware or ?type = so\#Jewelry) and ?value>100.

       packageDeclaredValue(?package, ?value):-
        ?package[so\#containesItemsOfType hasValue ?type, so\#declaredValue hasValue ?value] and
        ((?type != so\#Antiques and ?type != so\#Glassware and ?type != so\#Jewelry) or ?value<100).

    capability runnerOrderSystemCapability
    interface runnerOrderSystemInterface
```

Following our model for NFPs, Runner's obligations are expressed as logical rules in WSML. In a similar way other non-functional properties can be described. Further on, consider the concrete goal of shipping one package (GumblePackage) to a specified address (GumbleAddress) of a specific receiver (Gumble). A goal in WSMO is described in a similar manner to a Web service. Our concrete goal is specified in Listing 2.

User preferences are part of the goal. For example the user can specify which non-functional property will be used as a ordering dimension during the ranking process. In this case the ordering dimension is the obligations non-functional property (`up#nfp hasValue obl#Obligation`). Furthermore the user can specify how the results should be ordered (i.e. ascending or descending), in this case ascending (`up#order hasValue pref#ascending`), the importance of the non-functional properties e.g. for a user the price is less important than the execution time and the number of best services to be selected (`up#top hasValue "1"`). The background knowledge used during the selection and ranking process is usually extracted from the capability section of the goal.

Listing 1.2. Goal description

```
namespace {_"Goal.wsml#",
 so _"Shipment.wsml#",up _"UpperOnto.wsml#", pref _"Preferences.wsml#",
 obl _"http://www.wsmo.org/ontologies/nfp/obligationsNFPOntology.wsml}

goal Goal1
 annotations
    up#order hasValue pref#ascending
    up#nfp hasValue obl#Obligation
    up#top hasValue "1"
 endAnnotations

 capability requestedCapability
  postcondition
   definedBy
    ?order[so#to hasValue Gumble,so#packages hasValue GumblePackage] memberOf so#ShipmentOrder and
    Gumble[so#firstName hasValue "Barney", so#lastName hasValue "Gumble",
    so#address hasValue GumbleAddress] memberOf so#ContactInfo and
    GumbleAddress[ so#streetAddress hasValue "320 East 79th Street",
    so#city hasValue so#NY, so#country hasValue so#US] memberOf so#Address and
    GumblePackage[so#length hasValue 10, so#width hasValue 2, so#height hasValue 3,
    so#weight hasValue 10, so#declaredValue hasValue 150] memberOf so#Package.
```

3 Ranking Services

Service Ranking is the process which generates an ordered list of services out of the candidate services set according to user's preferences. As ranking criteria, specified by the user, various non-functional properties such as Service Level Agreements (SLA), Quality of Services (QoS), etc. can be obtained from the goal description. On the service side the requested non-functional properties values are either directly specified in the service description or are provided (computed or collected) by a monitoring tool. Non-functional properties specified in goal and service descriptions are expressed in a semantic language (i.e WSML), by means of logical rules using terms from NFP ontologies.

Our solution for service ranking combines two aspects types of ranking, namely semantic ranking and multi-criteria ranking. By semantic ranking we understand any ranking mechanism which uses ontological representations of non-functional properties aspects. A multi-criteria ranking mechanism on the other hand considers multiple non-functional properties dimensions.

Non-functional properties of services and goals used in the prototype are semantically described as presented in Section 2. The logical rules used to model NFPs of services are evaluated, during the ranking process, by a reasoning engine. Additional data is required during the rules evaluation process. This data represents mainely user preferences and includes: (1) which NFPs user is interested, (2) the level of importance of each of these NFPs, (3) how the list of services should be ordered (i.e. ascending or descending) and (4) concrete instances data extracted from the goal description. The NFPs values obtained by evaluating the logical rules are sorted and the order list of services is built.

The algorithm for multi-criteria ranking based on non-functional properties is presented in listing Algorithm 1.

```
     Data: Set of services S_Ser, Goal G.
     Result: Order list of services L_Ser.
0.1  begin
0.2      Ω ⟵ ∅, where Ω is a set of tuples [service,score];
0.3      λ = extractNFPs(G), where λ is a set of tuples [nfp, importance];
0.4      G_Know = extractInstancesKnowledge(G);
0.5      d = extractOrderingSense(G);
0.6      β ⟵ ∅, is a set of quadruples [service,nfp,nfpvalue,importance];
0.7      for s ∈ S_Ser do
0.8          for nfp ∈ λ do
0.9              imp = lambda.getImportance(nfp);
0.10             if nfp ∈ s.nfps then
0.11                 rule = extract(nfp, s);
0.12                 nfpvalue = evaluateRule(rule, G_Know);
0.13                 β = β ∪ [s, nfp, nfpvalue, imp];
0.14             end
0.15             else
0.16                 β = β ∪ [s, nfp, 0, 0];
0.17             end
0.18         end
0.19     end
0.20     for s ∈ β do
0.21         score_s = 0;
0.22         for nfp ∈ β do
0.23             nfpvalue = β.getNFPValue(s, nfp);
0.24             nfpvalue_max = max(β.npf);
0.25             score_s = score_s + imp * nfpvalue / nfpvalue_max;
0.26         end
0.27         Ω = Ω ∪ [s, score_s];
0.28     end
0.29     L_Ser ⟵ sort(Ω, d);
0.30 end
```

Algorithm 1. Multi-criteria ranking

First a set of tuples containing non-functional properties and their associated importance is extracted out of the goal description (line 0.3). Considering the goal example provided in Listing 2 the list contains only one non-functional property, namely *obligations*. If no importance is specified the default value is consider to be 0.5 which specify a moderate interest in the non-functional property. The importance is a numeric value ranging from 0 to 1, where 1 encodes the fact that the user is extremely interested in the non-functional property and 0 encodes the fact that the non-functional property is not of interest for the user. Further on instance data from the goal is extracted (line 0.4) and a knowledge base is created. In our example the extracted instance data containers information about the receiver, the package and the destination address. The last step in extracting relevant information for the ranking process is to identify how the results should be ordered i.e. ascending or descending (line 0.5).

Once the preprocessing steps are done, each service is checked if the requested non-functional properties specified in the goal are available in service description. In case of a positive answer the algorithm the corresponding logic rules are extracted (line 0.11) and evaluated (line 0.12) using a reasoning engine which support WSML rules (e.g. MINS[4], KAON2[5] or IRIS[6]). A quadruple structure is built (line 0.13 and 0.16) containing for each service and non-functional property the computed value and the its importance. An aggregated score is computed for each service by summing the normalized values (line 0.24) of non-functional weighted by importance values (line 0.25). The results are collected in a set of tuples, where each tuple contain the service id and the computed score(line 0.27). Finally the scores values are sorted according to the ordering sense extracted from the goal and the final list of services is returned(line 0.29).

4 Experiments

To evaluate the ranking algorithm proposed in Section 3 we have implemented it as part of the WSMX [7] execution environment. The ranking of services is performed on two NFP dimensions: *obligations* and *discounts*, but it can easily support a higher number of NFPs. The set of services used in the experiments are from SWS Challenge.

Table 1. Experimental Results

NFP/WebService	**Weasel**	**Walker**	**Muller**	**Racer**	**Runner**
Obligation	0.66	0.00	0.93	0.81	0.57
Discounts	0.0	0.23	0.85	0.47	0.64
Total Score	0.71	0.19	1.76	1.16	1.03

A set of 50 goals having the same structure with the goal presented in Section 2, but with randomly generated concrete values which influence obligations and discounts values have been used to test the algorithm. Table 1 shows the average score results obtained by running the algorithm with the given input data. An empiric comparison of sample results with ideal results shows a good behavior of our algorithm.

5 Conclusions and Future Work

In this paper a service ranking approach based on semantic descriptions of services non-functional properties was proposed. We briefly introduce our approach for modeling and attaching non-functional properties descriptions to services and goals. The proposed

[4] http://tools.deri.org/mins/
[5] http://kaon2.semanticweb.org/
[6] http://sourceforge.net/projects/iris-reasoner/
[7] http://www.wsmx.org

ranking mechanism makes use of logical rules describing non-functional properties of services and evaluates them using a reasoning engine. As a last step it builds an ordered list of services considering the values computed during the rules evaluation step.

As future work we plan to specify and implement other types of ranking approaches namely social and context-aware ranking. Further on, a set of open issues and improvements need to be addressed and integrated with the current ranking solution. These include but are not limited to: how to integrate non-functional properties values collected by monitoring tools with the service ranking, how to predict non-functional values of services, which are the best solutions to collect and incorporate user feedback and last but not least to consider trust and reputation issues.

References

1. Anicic, D., Brodie, M., de Bruijn, J., Fensel, D., Haselwanter, T., Hepp, M., Heymans, S., Hoffmann, J., Kerrigan, M., Kopecky, J., Krummenacher, R., Lausen, H., Mocan, A., Scicluna, J., Toma, I., Zaremba, M.: A semantically enabled service oriented architecture. In: WImBI 2006. WICI International Workshop on Web Intelligence (WI) meets Brain Informatics, Beijing, China (December 2006)
2. Cardoso, J., Sheth, A.P.: Introduction to semantic web services and web process composition. In: Cardoso, J., Sheth, A.P. (eds.) SWSWPC 2004. LNCS, vol. 3387, pp. 1–13. Springer, Heidelberg (2005)
3. Chung, L.: Non-Functional Requirements for Information Systems Design. In: Andersen, R., Solvberg, A., Bubenko Jr., J.A. (eds.) CAiSE 1991. LNCS, vol. 498, pp. 5–30. Springer, Heidelberg (1991)
4. de Bruijn, J., Lausen, H., Krummenacher, R., Polleres, A., Predoiu, L., Kifer, M., Fensel, D., Toma, I., Steinmetz, N., Kerrigan, M.: The Web Service Modeling Language WSML. Technical report, WSML, WSML Final Draft D16.1v0.3 (2007), `http://www.wsmo.org/TR/d16/d16.1/v0.3/`
5. O'Sullivan, J., Edmond, D., ter Hofstede, A.H.M.: Formal description of non-functional service properties. Technical report, Queensland University of Technology, Brisbane (2005), Available from `http://www.service-description.com/`
6. Paolucci, M., Kawamura, T., Payne, T., Sycara, K.: Semantic matching of web services capabilities. In: Horrocks, I., Hendler, J. (eds.) ISWC 2002. LNCS, vol. 2342, pp. 333–347. Springer, Heidelberg (2002)
7. Roman, D., Lausen, H., Keller, U. (eds.): Web service modeling ontology (WSMO). Working Draft D2v1.4, WSMO (2007), Available from `http://www.wsmo.org/TR/d2/v1.4/`
8. Toma, I., Foxvog, D.: Non-functional properties in Web services. Working draft, Digital Enterprise Research Insitute (DERI) (August 2006), Available from `http://www.wsmo.org/TR/d28/d28.4/v0.1/`
9. Verma, K., Sivashanmugam, K., Sheth, A., Patil, A.: Meteor-s wsdi: A scalable p2p infrastructure of registries for semantic publication and discovery of web services. Journal of Information Technology and Management (2004)

A Development Process for Self-adapting Service Oriented Applications

M. Autili, L. Berardinelli, V. Cortellessa, A. Di Marco, D. Di Ruscio, P. Inverardi, and M. Tivoli

Dipartimento di Informatica
Università degli Studi di L'Aquila,
67100 L'Aquila, Italy
{autili,berardinelli,cortelle,dimarco,diruscio,inverard, tivoli}@di.univaq.it

Abstract. Software services in the near ubiquitous future will need to cope with variability, as they are deployed on an increasingly large diversity of computing platforms, operate in different execution environments, and communicate through Beyond 3G (B3G) networks. Heterogeneity of the underlying communication and computing infrastructure, physical mobility of platform devices, and continuously evolving requirements claim for services to be adaptable according to the context changes without degrading their quality. Supporting the development and execution of software services in this setting raises numerous challenges that involve languages, methods and tools. However these challenges taken in isolation are not new in the service domain. Integrated solutions to these challenges are the main targets of the IST PLASTIC project.

In this paper we introduce the PLASTIC development process model for self-adapting context-aware services, in which we propose model-based solutions to address the main issues of this domain in a comprehensive way. We instantiate the process model by providing methodologies to generate Quality of Service models and adaptable code from UML service models. All these methodologies are supported by an integrated framework which is based on an UML profile that we have defined for the PLASTIC domain.

1 Introduction

Nowadays, software services need to cope with variability, as services get deployed on an increasingly large diversity of computing platforms and operates in different execution environments. Heterogeneity of the underlying communication and computing infrastructure, mobility inducing changes to the execution environments (and therefore changes to the availability of resources) and continuously evolving requirements require services to be *self-adaptive* according to the context changes. At the same time, a service should be *dependable* in the sense that it should meet the user's Quality of Service (QoS) requirements and needs. Moreover, satisfying user expectations is made more complex given the highly dynamic nature of service provision.

B. Krämer, K.-J. Lin, and P. Narasimhan (Eds.): ICSOC 2007, LNCS 4749, pp. 442–448, 2007.

Supporting the development and execution of such adaptable services raises numerous challenges that involve models, methods and tools. However these challenges, taken in isolation, are not new in the service domain. Integrated solutions to these challenges are the main targets of the IST PLASTIC project, whose main goal is the rapid and easy development/deployment of self-adapting services for B3G networks [20].

Broadly speaking, a "standard" development process focuses on activities that are traditionally divided into *development-*, *deployment-* and *run-time* activities. Each activity works on suitable system artifacts, which can be coupled with models suitable for development purposes. The evolutionary nature of services in the near ubiquitous future makes unfeasible a standard development process since dealing with self-adaptiveness would require to predict the functional and non-functional system behavior before the system is in execution. Whenever a change occurs, if service evolution has to be supported by means of adaptation, all the artifacts/models might be exploited also by the deployment and run-time activities, hence leading to a "non-standard" development process view. Thus, the main challenges in this direction are related to the support that can be offered to service developers to satisfy the user expectations in a such heterogeneous and dynamic environment.

In this paper we introduce the PLASTIC development process that relies on model-based solutions to build self-adapting context-aware services. The introduced process encompasses methodologies to generate QoS models and adaptable code from UML-based specifications. All these methodologies are supported by an integrated framework which is based on an UML profile of the PLASTIC domain.

The work described in this paper relates to multiple research areas of the existing literature, that are: (i) web-service development technologies, (ii) model-driven development, (iii) performance and reliability analysis techniques, and (iv) (self-)adapting software. For sake of space, we obviously cannot address all the recent related work in the above areas, thus in the following we shortly discuss and provide major references for each area.

Current (web-)service development technologies, e.g. [7,8,19,22,23] (just to cite some), address only the functional design of complex services, that is they do not take into account the extra-functional aspects (e.g., QoS requirements) and the context-awareness. Our process borrows concepts from these well assessed technologies and builds on them to make QoS issues clearly emerging in the service development, as well as to take into account context-awareness of services for self-adaptiveness purposes.

The PLASTIC development process adheres to the Model Driven Development (MDD) approach which claims to shift the focus of software development from coding to modeling [21]. In this respect, problems can be precisely described using specific terms and concepts more familiar to experts working in the considered domain and technological details which are unnecessary for the service description can be neglected. Model transformations are devised in our process in two directions: (i) to glue the different levels of abstractions and, by encoding the knowledge about the technological assets, to permit the automated generation of the service code, (ii) to generate QoS models, at the same level of abstraction of the service models, that allow to validate extra-functional issues during the service development.

With regard to the latter point, up today performance and reliability models have been integrated in the PLASTIC process to support QoS validation. In this domain interesting progresses have been made in the last ten years due to the introduction of automated techniques and tools that allow to generate extra functional models from annotated software models (see, for example, [3] for performance and [6] for reliability). We have embedded some of these techniques in our service development process. Obviously some effort has been necessary to adapt the techniques to the specific domain of context-aware self-adapting services.

This work exploits also notions and concepts in the area of (self-)adaptation of software entities and self-healing system development, spanning adaptation of communication/interaction [15], performance [11], real-time behaviours [5], and synthesis of coordination/composition behaviour among semantic services [13].

The remainder of the paper is structured as follows: Sect. 2 describes the proposed development process and outlines the adopted technologies supporting it. Sect. 3 draws some conclusions and perspective works.

2 PLASTIC Development Process

In this section we introduce the PLASTIC development process for self-adapting context-aware services. By recalling Section 1, the main issues that this process addresses are: (a) service self-adaptiveness and context-awareness, and (b) service satisfaction of QoS requirements.

To address the former, at design time the possible contexts in which the service will run are specified. Models for context description are introduced to support this activity. At development time, the context specification is exploited to automatically derive, through model-to-code transformation, "generic" code that embodies a certain variability degree. Hereafter, we refer to it as adaptable code. Obviously, only the skeleton is automatically derived, i.e., its logic has to be coded by hand. At deployment time the adaptable code is processed to automatically extract, through adaptable code instantiation, the code that better fits a certain context.

The latter is addressed in two steps: (i) by allowing the designer to annotate the service model with QoS related information (i.e. QoS parameters and requirements), and (ii) by elaborating the annotated information at both design- and run-time through analysis tools whose aim is to predict and solve QoS models within the possible different contexts. The adopted QoS analysis tools use a large variety of models, from behavioral to stochastic, that can represent the system at very different levels of abstraction from requirements specification to code.

As already anticipated in Section 1, the ever growing complexity of software has exacerbated the dichotomy development/static/compile time versus execution/dynamic/interpret time thus concentrating as many analysis and validation

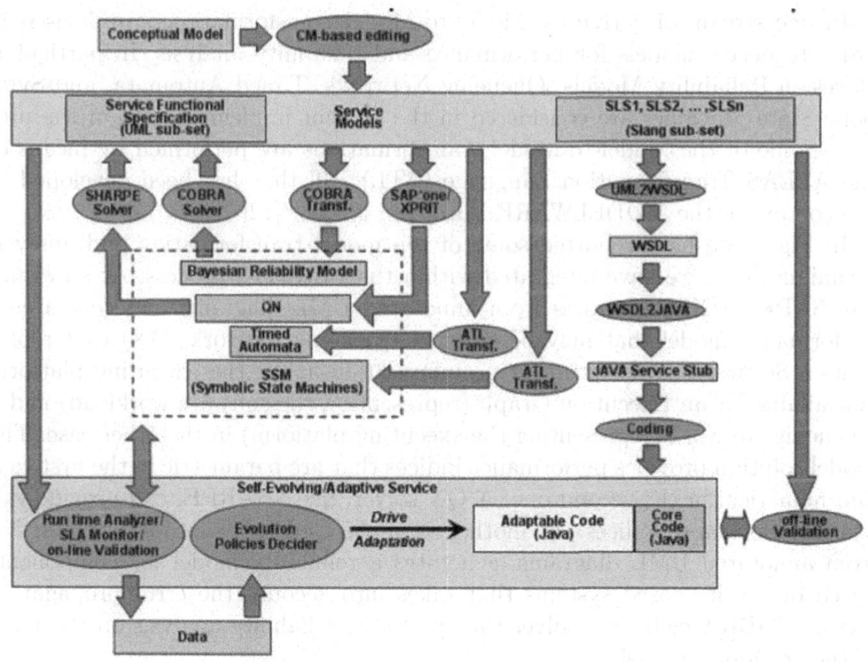

Fig. 1. The PLASTIC process for service development

activities as possible at development time. As opposite, if QoS has to be preserved through adaptation whatever the change mechanism is, at the time the change occurs, a validation mechanism must be devised at run-time. This means that models used at development time to support design decisions must be available at run-time for additional validation activities.

In Fig. 1 we illustrate the PLASTIC development process, where square boxes represent software artifacts/models and ellipses represent activities. Lifecycle time goes from the top to the bottom of the figure. All the process activities originate from a Conceptual Model where entities and relationships of the context-aware service domain are defined [2,16]. Based on these entities, a Service Model can be specified in terms of its Functional Specification and its Service Level Specification (SLS). The former describes behavioral aspects of the modelled service, whereas the latter its QoS characteristics.

The Service Model is specified by means of a UML2 [14] profile whose aim is to extend UML2 to cope with adaptable, context aware and component based software services both from structural and behavioral viewpoints along the entire software lifecycle, from requirements specification to deployment. This profile is an implementation of the Conceptual Model, and it is supported by the customization of an UML 2 tool environment (i.e. *Magic Draw*) that we have developed and described in [17]. For the sake of space, we do not describe here the profile.

Two main streams of activities originate from a Service Model, each addressing one of the issues introduced above.

In one stream of activities, Model-to-Model transformations are devised in order to derive models for performance and reliability analysis. In particular, Bayesian Reliability Models, Queueing Networks, Timed Automata, and Symbolic State Machines are considered in the current implementation of the process. Some of the Model-to-Model transformations are performed by means of the ATLAS Transformation Language (ATL) [10] that has been developed in the context of the MODELWARE European project [12].

In Fig. 1 we have reported some of the model transformation and analysis techniques that we have integrated within the PLASTIC process. As an example, SAP•one/XPRIT starts from annotated UML diagrams and generates a performance model that may be either a Queueing Network (QN) that represents a Software Architecture, if no information about the executing platform is available, or an Execution Graph (representing the software workload) and a Queueing Network (representing the executing platform) in the other case. The model solution provides performance indices that are parametric in the first case and numerical in the second one. A QN solver, like SHARPE, can provide values of performance indices. As another example, COBRA is a tool that, starting from annotated UML diagrams, generates a reliability model for component-based or service-based systems that takes into account the error propagation factor. COBRA embeds a solver that performs reliability analysis on the basis of the generated model.

Bayesian Reliability Models and Queueing Networks can also be analyzed at development time to refine/validate the Service Model characteristics that the analysis addresses. Timed Automata, Symbolic State Machines (SSM), and possibly the previous models will be made available at deployment- and run-time to allow the adaptation of the service to the execution context and for service validation. In particular, we are able to perform two kinds of validations, i.e., on-line and off-line validation (see [18] for details). Off-line validation is performed to generate test cases, before the service execution, by taking into account both the service model (in particular its SSM) and the service code. On-line validation is performed whilst the service is running and uses the generated test cases.

In the other stream of activities, Model-To-Code transformations are used to build both the core and the adaptable code of a service. The core code is the frozen unchanging portion of the service. The adaptable code portion can evolve in the sense that, basing on contextual information and possible changes of the user needs, the variability can be solved with a set of alternatives. A particular alternative might be suitable for a particular execution context and specified user needs. Each alternative can be selected by exploiting the analysis models available at run-time and the service capabilities performing the Run time Analysis/SLA Monitoring and the Evolution Policies Selection (see Fig. 1). When a service is invoked, the run-time analysis is performed (on the available models) and, basing on the analysis results, a new set of alternatives is synthesized and a new alternative is selected. The development of the adaptable service code is based on CHAMELEON [9], that is a resource-aware framework for adaptable Java applications.

Model-To-Code transformations are performed by means of a code generator based on the *Eclipse Java Emitter Template framework* (part of the EMF framework [4]). JSP-like templates explicitly define the code structure and get the data they need from the UML model of the specified service exported into EMF. With this generation engine, the generated code can be customized and then re-generated without losing already defined customizations.

We like to remark that one of the main novelties of this process is to consider SLS as part of a Service Model, as opposite to existing approaches where SLS consists, in best cases, in additional annotations reported on a (service) functional model. This peculiar characteristic of our process brings several advantages: (i) SLS embedded within a Service Model better supports the model-to-model transformations towards analysis models (in particular, the target model parametrization) and, on the way back, better supports the feedback of the analysis (i.e., reporting the analysis results on the Service Model); (ii) in the path to code generation, the SLS can drive the adaptation strategies.

3 Conclusions and Future Work

This paper proposed a development process defined in the context of the IST EU PLASTIC project [20] which aims at offering a comprehensive provisioning platform for context-aware and adaptable software services deployed over B3G networks. In particular, this work describes the instantiation of the process within an UML world. Models and techniques for developing, in UML, adaptable code of context-aware services which have to show optimal QoS within different contexts have been integrated. The approach is supported by languages and tools conceived to increase the automation in all the process steps. Service modeling is based on a PLASTIC UML profile that we have defined and whose main concepts have been inherited from other existing UML profiles and meta-models (e.g. see [1]).

Due to space limitation, in this paper, we have given an overall description of the thorough approach that supports the whole service lifecycle. The approach has been applied to a real-life example concerning the service-oriented development of an e-Health system. The treatment of this example is described in [17].

The instantiation of our process within UML can be improved by integrating a wider number of analysis techniques that may address other dimensions of QoS, such as availability and security. Besides, from a functional viewpoint, we intend to study how to tackle dynamic composition of context-aware services. We are also investigating the usage of non-UML methodologies and tools within the process, such as formal (functional and non-functional) specification of services. This would allow us to introduce in the process formal refinement and analysis techniques, such as model checking.

The application of the approach other real world case studies would obviously allow us to refine and validate the whole framework.

Acknowledgments. This work has been partially supported by the IST EU project PLASTIC (www.ist-plastic.org).

References

1. SeCSE Project, http://secse.eng.it
2. Autili, M., Cortellessa, V., Di Marco, A., Inverardi, P.: A Conceptual Model for Adaptable Context-aware Services. In: WS-MATE (2006)
3. Bernardi, S., Donatelli, S., Merseguer, J.: From uml sequence diagrams and statecharts to analysable petri net models. In: 3rd ACM Workshop on Software and Performance, ACM Press, New York (2002)
4. Budinsky, F., Steinberg, D., Merks, E., Ellersick, R., Grose, T.J.: Eclipse Modeling Framework. Addison-Wesley, Reading (2003)
5. Cortadella, J., Kondratyev, A., Lavagno, L., Passerone, C., Watanabe, Y.: Quasi-static scheduling of independent tasks for reactive systems. IEEE Transactions on Computer-Aided Design of Integrated Circuits and Systems 24(10) (2005)
6. Cortellessa, V., Singh, H., Cukic, B., Gunel, E., Bharadwaj, V.: Early reliability assessment of uml based software models. In: 3rd ACM Workshop on Software and Performance, ACM Press, New York (2002)
7. Eclipse.org. Eclipse Web Standard Tools, http://www.eclipse.org/webtools
8. IBM. BPEL4WS, Business Process Execution Language for Web Services, version 1.1 (2003)
9. Inverardi, P., Mancinelli, F., Nesi, M.: A Declarative Framework for adaptable applications in heterogeneous environments. In: ACM SAC, ACM Press, New York (2004)
10. Jouault, F., Kurtev, I.: Transforming Models with ATL. In: Bruel, J.-M. (ed.) MoDELS 2005. LNCS, vol. 3844, Springer, Heidelberg (2006)
11. Menascé, D.A., Ruan, H., Gomaa, H.: A framework for QoS-aware software components. In: WOSP '04, ACM Press, New York (2004)
12. ModelWare: IST European project 511731, http://www.modelwareist.org
13. Nezhad, H.R.M., Benatallha, B., Martens, A., Curbera, F., Casati, F.: Semi-automated adaptation of service interactions. In: WWW 2007 Web Services Track (2007)
14. OMG: UML 2 Superstructure. formal/2007-02-03 (February 2007)
15. Passerone, R., de Alfaro, L., Heinzinger, T., Sangiovanni-Vincentelli, A.L.: Convertibility verification and converter synthesis: Two faces of the same coin. In: Proc. of ICCAD 2002 (2002)
16. PLASTIC IST STREP Project: Deliverable D2.1: SLA language and analysis techniques for adaptable and resource-aware components, http://www-c.inria.fr/plastic/deliverables/plastic-d2_1-finalpdf.pdf/download
17. PLASTIC IST STREP Project: Deliverable D2.2: Graphical design language and tools for resource-aware adaptable components and services, http://www-c.inria.fr/plastic/deliverables/plastic-d2_2-finalpdf.pdf/download
18. PLASTIC IST STREP Project: Deliverable D4.1: Test Framework Specification and Architecture, http://www-c.inria.fr/plastic/deliverables/plastic_d4_1final.pdf/download
19. A-MUSE Project: Methodological Framework for Freeband Services Development (2004), https://doc.telin.nl/dscgi/ds.py/Get/File-47390/
20. PLASTIC Project: Description of Work (2005), http://www.ist-plastic.org
21. Selic, B.: The Pragmatics of Model-driven Development. IEEE Software 20(5), 19–25 (2003)
22. W3C: Web Service Definition Language, http://www.w3.org/tr/wsdl
23. Yun, H., Kim, Y., Kim, E., Park, J.: Web Services Development Process. In: PDCS (2005)

Automated Dynamic Maintenance of Composite Services Based on Service Reputation

Domenico Bianculli[1], Radu Jurca[2], Walter Binder[1], Carlo Ghezzi[3], and Boi Faltings[2]

[1] Faculty of Informatics – University of Lugano
via G. Buffi 13 - CH-6900, Lugano, Switzerland
domenico.bianculli@lu.unisi.ch, walter.binder@unisi.ch

[2] Artificial Intelligence Lab – Ecole Polytechnique Fédérale de Lausanne
Station 14 - CH-1015, Lausanne, Switzerland
radu.jurca@epfl.ch, boi.faltings@epfl.ch

[3] Dipartimento di Elettronica e Informazione – Politecnico di Milano
Via Ponzio 34/5, I-20133, Milano, Italy
ghezzi@elet.polimi.it

Abstract. Service-oriented computing promotes the construction of applications by composing distributed services that are advertised in an open service market. In such an environment, individual services may change and evolve dynamically, requiring composite services to adapt to such changes. The prevailing strategy is to react on failures and replace the defective component of the composite service. However, this reactive approach does not fully exploit the opportunities of a dynamic market where older services may be replaced by better ones.

In this paper we promote a novel architecture for automated, dynamic, pro-active, and transparent maintenance and improvement of composite services. We leverage fine-grained client-side monitoring techniques to generate information regarding functional and non-functional properties of service behavior. A reputation manager is responsible for collecting and aggregating this information, and provides economical incentives for honest sharing of feedback. Composite services can thus use reliable reputation information to pro-actively improve their aggregate performance.

1 Introduction

The need for businesses to integrate corporate resources in a flexible and efficient way can be addressed by designing complex software solutions as collaboration of contractually defined services. Building applications by integrating standardized services promises to bring many benefits, such as reduced development effort and cost, ease of maintenance, extensibility, and reuse of services. Service-oriented architectures (SOAs) maximize decoupling between services and create well-defined interoperation semantics based on standard protocols.

In the following we consider service-oriented applications built from web services.[1] The composition of individual services into an added-value, composite

[1] In this paper, we use the terms *web service* and *service* interchangeably.

B. Krämer, K.-J. Lin, and P. Narasimhan (Eds.): ICSOC 2007, LNCS 4749, pp. 449–455, 2007.

service is usually represented as a workflow. We assume that service compositions are described in BPEL [1], the *de-facto* standard for web service orchestrations.

Web services support a dynamic architectural style where the binding among components may change at runtime. New services may be developed and published in registries, and then discovered by possible clients. Previously available services may disappear or become unavailable. This situation has been characterized by the term *open-world software* [2], describing a situation where applications are composed out of parts that may change unpredictably and dynamically. It has been observed that open-world software introduces the requirement of continuous validation. Since a software architecture evolves dynamically, validation must extend from development time to runtime.

In order to ensure that composite services are executing as expected, it is necessary to monitor the interactions of individual services within a workflow. Monitoring involves both service functional behavior and non-functional properties, such as Quality-of-Service (QoS) parameters. If services are advertised by Service-Level Agreements (SLAs) that regulate service cost and QoS (e.g., maximum response time), monitoring delivered QoS allows clients to verify that they actually receive the QoS they are expecting and paying for.

When clients executing workflows observe failures or SLA violations of individual services, they have to replace the failing or badly behaving services. However, finding a replacement may take some time, resulting in reduced availability of the composite service. Moreover, there are no guarantees that the replacement will work better than the replaced service.

In this paper, we promote the sharing of service monitoring information amongst clients in order to enable the *pro-active replacement of misbehaving services* in workflows. The original contribution of the paper is an integrated infrastructure for service monitoring and maintenance of composite services. We promote novel techniques for monitoring composite services and introduce an incentive-compatible Reputation Manager (RM) to share reliable service quality information among clients. The RM is integrated with a UDDI service directory and employs a publish/subscribe mechanism to disseminate reputation information to clients.

RMs have emerged as efficient tools for service discovery and selection [3]. When electronic contracts cannot be enforced, users can learn to trust good providers by looking at their past behavior [4]. Maximilien and Singh [5] describe a conceptual model for reputation using which reputation information can be organized and shared and service selection can be facilitated and automated. Lie et al. [6] present a QoS-based selection model that takes into account the feedback from users as well as other business related criteria. Both [7] and [8] propose concrete frameworks for service selection based on the reputation of the service provider.

Several works (see [9] for a detailed comparison of the approaches) have investigated monitoring of service compositions. However, to the best of our knowledge, this is the first attempt to use the result of observations deriving from monitoring to build service reputations and make use of the latter to dynamically maintain service compositions.

2 Architecture

In this section we focus on the interaction between clients and services, on the collection of data about the behavior of services, and on the dissemination of information on service reputation from the registry to the clients. The architecture illustrated in Fig. 1 describes a client workflow which monitors the behavior of the invoked services and communicates the results of monitoring to the registry. The registry comprises the following components:

- *Reputation Manager (RM)*: its task is to collect feedback reports from the clients, to aggregate them, and to compute an estimate of the reputation of a service.
- *Subscription Manager*: this component handles dissemination of the information provided by the RM. We choose to design the communication infrastructure of our architecture using a publish/subscribe mechanism. Services may subscribe to two different kinds of events:
  - Notification by the RM when the reputation of a given service falls under a certain threshold;
  - Notification that a better service has become available, having either the same interface (exact-match) or a compatible interface (plugin-match) w.r.t. a given service.
- *Extended Service Directory*: with respect to its standard counterpart, this directory extends the registry by including information on the current estimated reputation of each registered service, as conveyed by the RM. Furthermore, the directory service is in charge to notify the *Subscription Manager* about the registration of new services.[2] We have explored techniques for efficient matchmaking in service directories in prior work [10].

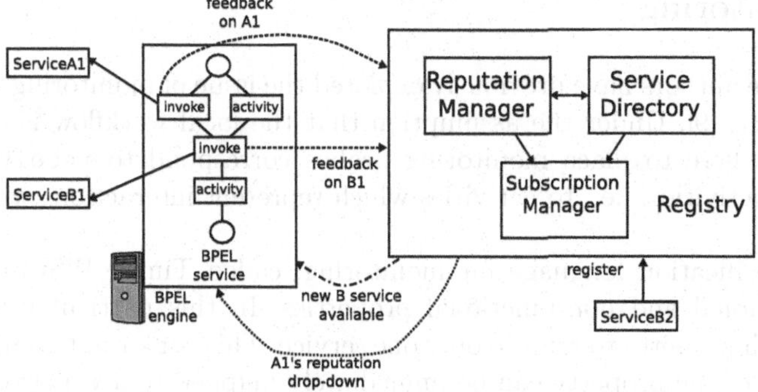

Fig. 1. System architecture

[2] Note that for a newly registered service, the RM will not publish an associated reputation value before sufficient client feedback has been collected.

Figure 1 illustrates a BPEL service, sketched in the figure as a workflow containing two `invoke` activities, each one interacting with an external service, ServiceA1 (assumed to implement interface A) and ServiceB1 (assumed to implement interface B). The architecture also shows three kinds of message exchanged between the components:

- After each invocation of an external service, the BPEL service sends a feedback message back to the RM, which collects feedback from all the clients of a certain service. This message is labelled "feedback on `service-name`" and it is drawn in the figure by using a dashed line.
- Whenever the RM computes a new value of the reputation of a service, the Subscription Manager notifies all the subscribed clients if the reputation of the service dropped below the threshold set by each client. In our example, we assume that the BPEL service has subscribed to the drop-down of the reputation of the two used services and we show the case of A1's reputation drop-down. This message is labelled "`service-name` reputation drop-down" and it is depicted in the figure by using a dotted line.
- A third type of message, labelled "new `interface-name` service available", notifies all interested clients that a new service implementing a certain interface and with a better reputation became available. In the figure, a dash/dotted line depicts a message that notifies the client that a service implementing the interface B (in the example, ServiceB2), and having a better reputation, has been published in the directory.

The frequency of both monitoring and feedback reporting to the RM can be selected and tuned by the client. For simplicity, the architecture illustrated in Fig. 1 ignores how the workflow can dynamically adapt to the changes in service reputation through dynamic binding.

3 Monitoring

Some of the authors have previously explored the issue of monitoring web service compositions [9]. Under the assumption that the local workflow is correct, the *hot spots* where to place monitoring probes correspond to `receive`, `invoke`, and `pick` activities, i.e., to activities which represent interactions with external services.

Our specification language for monitoring, called Timed WSCoL, supports both functional and non-functional properties. In this particular context, we require each property to refer to only one service. This constraint guarantees that a violation of the property can be immediately mapped to a violation/failure of the service involved in the property.

Our monitoring infrastructure is based on an open-source BPEL engine, ActiveBPEL[3]. We have extended the engine using an aspect-oriented programming (AOP) approach [11], by implementing all the monitoring logic using AspectJ.

[3] http://www.activebpel.org

The architecture of the monitoring infrastructure includes (1) a data collector and aggregator, which gathers sequences of timestamped messages from the interactions with external services, and (2) a Timed WSCoL analyzer, which is actually in charge of checking the validity of a property. The output of this analyzer is binary, stating if the property has been violated or not. This output is then sent to the RM, together with the identifier of the service being "evaluated".

AOP is also used to instrument the engine to perform subscription to messages delivered by the Subscription Manager, each time an instance of a BPEL process is started. For each service x the BPEL service interacts with, it can make two subscriptions: (1) notification upon drop-down of the reputation of service x below a certain threshold τ_x, and (2) notification of the availability of new services with an interface equal or compatible to the one of service x.

A third instrumentation is required to make the BPEL workflow respond to reputation notifications. We achieve this by modifying how the engine behaves when a new BPEL process is deployed into it. The basic requirement is that the BPEL process should be able to bind dynamically a *partner link* to a new service, either because of a misbehavior of the service it is currently bound to or because a new service with a better reputation became available. Dynamic binding is achieved by updating the end-point reference of a partner link. Our AOP-based instrumentation of the engine modifies the BPEL process by inserting an event handler in the global scope (or by modifying the handler, if it already exists) for the two kinds of message that the Subscription Manager can send. Message "new service available" triggers the handler to update the end-point reference of the partner link representing the service to be replaced, whereas message "reputation drop-down" triggers a query to the registry to retrieve a substitute service with better reputation.

4 The Reputation Manager

The Reputation Manager is an important component of our framework, that collects feedback from the clients, and output quality measurements for the web services. Clients are required to submit a binary report: positive if the service met the quality constraints set in the SLA, negative otherwise. The reports submitted by the clients also contain the timestamp of the interaction with the service.

We model the behavior of web services by a Hidden Markov Model with two states: the *good* state describing the normal functioning mode when client requests are successfully satisfied with the unknown probability p_G, and the *bad* state describing a failure mode where the quality of the service is very low. The probability of transition from the good state into the bad state is assumed fixed and known, characterizing the different hazards the service is subject to.

Given the sequence of N binary feedback reports, $(r_i)_{i=1...N}$, about the same web service, the RM can (a) estimate the parameter p_G of the web service, and (b) output the probability $Pr[B|(r_i)]$ that the web service is in the bad state. p_G is computed by likelihood maximization, while the probability that the service is in the bad state can be computed using standard HMM tools like the Viterbi algorithm [12]. As the quality can change in time, the RM only uses the most recent N feedback reports. The estimates published by the RM can be used by future clients to optimize their workflows, or to dynamically replace defective services.

An important requirement for the reputation manager is to ensure honest feedback. Since clients may tamper with the default monitoring code in order to manipulate reputation information, special incentives must guarantee that lying, even if technically feasible, is economically uninteresting. The RM pays submitted reports an amount that depends on the feedback provided by other clients about the same web service. The payments can be designed such that truthful reporting maximizes the expected revenue (due to feedback payments) of a client, and honesty thus becomes an equilibrium of the mechanism. The budget for these payments can be raised by the RM from fixed participation fees that service providers and/or clients have to pay.

For example, a report is being paid only if it has the same value as another randomly chosen report. Intuitively, this simple mechanism encourages honest reporting because the private experience of a client changes her belief regarding the reputation of the service, and consequently, her expectation for the value of the report used to compute her payment. If the experience is positive, the client expects with slightly higher probability to be rewarded for a matching positive report. Likewise, if the experience is negative, the client expects with slightly higher probability to be rewarded for a matching negative report. This asymmetry in beliefs can be used to scale the payments for matching positive or negative reports so that honesty becomes optimal. The formal details and algorithms for computing these reward mechanisms are given in [13]. In the same time, measures can be taken to discourage collusion.

5 Conclusions

In this paper we have presented an architecture supporting automated, dynamic, pro-active, and transparent maintenance and improvement of composite services. Our architecture leverages monitoring techniques in order to generate feedback on the quality of service (from both a functional and a non-functional point of view) perceived by clients. This feedback is collected and aggregated by a reputation manager which computes services reputation; information on the reputation is then transmitted to clients that can pro-actively maintain and improve their composite services. Our reputation manager provides economical incentives for honest sharing of feedback.

We are currently focusing on optimizing our registry for queries involving functional properties (to support selecting plugin matches) and non-functional properties (to support ranking according to a user-defined utility function involving QoS parameters, services cost, and service reputation). Future work includes 1) verification of the approach, in terms of measurements of improvement by deployment and simulation; 2) the development of a new model that considers more precise reports on QoS observations (e.g., a response time violated within a 10% bound may concur in a minor way to a decrease of the service reputation); 3) investigation on behavioral reflection mechanisms for workflow languages so as to better support dynamic re-binding within BPEL processes.

Acknowledgements. Part of this work has been supported by the EU project "PLASTIC" (contract number IST 026995), and the EU project "Knowledge Web" (FP6-507482).

References

1. Andrews, T., Curbera, F., Dholakia, H., Goland, Y., Klein, J., Leymann, F., Liu, K., Roller, D., Smith, D., Thatte, S., Trickovic, I., Weerawarana, S.: Business Process Execution Language for Web Services, Version 1.1 (2003)
2. Baresi, L., Di Nitto, E., Ghezzi, C.: Towards Open-World Software. IEEE Computer 39, 36–43 (2006)
3. Singh, M.P., Huhns, M.N.: Service-Oriented Computing. Wiley, Chichester (2005)
4. Zacharia, G., Maes, P.: Trust management through reputation mechanisms. Applied Artificial Intelligence (14), 881–907 (2000)
5. Maximilien, E.M., Singh, M.P.: Conceptual model of web service reputation. SIGMOD Rec. 31(4), 36–41 (2002)
6. Liu, Y., Ngu, A.H., Zeng, L.Z.: Qos computation and policing in dynamic web service selection. In: WWW Alt. '04. Proceedings of the 13th international World Wide Web conference on Alternate track papers & posters, pp. 66–73. ACM Press, New York, NY, USA (2004)
7. Maximilien, E.M., Singh, M.P.: Toward autonomic web services trust and selection. In: ICSOC '04. Proceedings of the 2nd international conference on Service oriented computing, pp. 212–221. ACM Press, New York, NY, USA (2004)
8. Alunkal, B., Veljkovic, I., Laszewski, G., Amin, K.: Reputation-Based Grid Resource Selection. In: Proceedings of AGridM (2003)
9. Baresi, L., Bianculli, D., Ghezzi, C., Guinea, S., Spoletini, P.: A timed extension of WSCoL. In: ICWS 2007. Proceedings of the IEEE International Conference on Web Services, pp. 663–670. IEEE Computer Society Press, Los Alamitos (2007)
10. Constantinescu, I., Binder, W., Faltings, B.: Flexible and efficient matchmaking and ranking in service directories. In: ICWS 2005. Proceedings of the IEEE International Conference on Web Services, pp. 5–12. IEEE Computer Society Press, Los Alamitos (2005)
11. Kiczales, G., Lamping, J., Mendhekar, A., Maeda, C., Lopes, C.V., Loingtier, J., Irwin, J.: Aspect-oriented programming. In: Aksit, M., Matsuoka, S. (eds.) ECOOP 1997. LNCS, vol. 1241, pp. 220–242. Springer, Heidelberg (1997)
12. Forney, G.: The Viterbi algorithm. Proceedings IEEE 61, 268–278 (1973)
13. Jurca, R., Faltings, B., Binder, W.: Reliable QoS monitoring based on client feedback. In: WWW '07. Proceedings of the 16th international conference on World Wide Web, pp. 1003–1012. ACM Press, New York, NY, USA (2007)

Verifying Temporal and Epistemic Properties of Web Service Compositions*

Alessio Lomuscio, Hongyang Qu, Marek Sergot, and Monika Solanki

Department of Computing, Imperial College London, UK
{alessio, hongyang, mjs, monika}@doc.ic.ac.uk

Abstract. Model checking Web service behaviour has remained limited to checking safety and liveness properties. However when viewed as a multi agent system, the system composition can be analysed by considering additional properties which capture the knowledge acquired by services during their interactions. In this paper we present a novel approach to model checking service composition where in addition to safety and liveness, *epistemic* properties are analysed and verified. To do this we use a specialised system description language (ISPL) paired with a symbolic model checker (MCMAS) optimised for the verification of temporal and epistemic modalities. We report on experimental results obtained by analysing the composition for a Loan Approval Service.

1 Introduction

Web services are now considered as one of the key paradigms underlying application integration. Several research efforts – both from industry and academia – have addressed varied aspects of service composition including verification via model checking. Most of the approaches [11, 13] take BPEL [9] as the language for development and use model checkers such as SPIN [6] and NuSMV [3] for checking safety and liveness properties. These model checkers are limited to temporal modalities in the scope of properties they can analyse. However as we argue below, in addition to verifying temporal properties it is also necessary to predict and verify the knowledge gained by services during the composition.

In this paper we propose an alternative yet complementary approach to verifying service behaviour. As proposed by the W3C consortium: " A Web service is an abstract notion that must be implemented by a concrete **agent**. The agent is the concrete piece of software or hardware that sends and receives messages.", a composition of Web services can be viewed as a multi agent system [12].

There is a tradition in the multi agent systems (MAS) community to use rich logic-based languages to analyse the behaviour of agents in the system. In particular not only is temporal logic used but also, among others, epistemic (to reason about knowledge of the processes), deontic (to reason about obligation of the processes), cooperation (to reason about strategies of the agents) modalities.

* The research described in this paper is partly supported by the European Commission Framework 6 funded project CONTRACT (IST Project Number 034418).

B. Krämer, K.-J. Lin, and P. Narasimhan (Eds.): ICSOC 2007, LNCS 4749, pp. 456–461, 2007.

These logic-based languages can be used to specify formally and unambiguously the behaviour of the system. Recent developments in the verification of MAS via model checking techniques [10, 2] allow for the first time the verification of not only plain temporal languages but also a variety of modalities describing the informational and intentional state of the agents. In particular reasoning about the agents' knowledge is demonstrably of interest in a variety of applications, including coordination, security, communication, fault-diagnosis, networking, etc. This work has not yet been extended to the challenges of service composition. The aim of this paper is to make a step in this direction. In particular in this paper we show how MCMAS [8] can be used to model check rich specifications based on temporal-epistemic logic representing compositions of web-services.

The rest of the paper is organised as follows. In Section 2 we introduce the trace-based semantics of interpreted systems. Section 3 introduces a motivating example and some of its key specifications. In Section 4 we introduce MCMAS, a symbolic model checker for semantics of interpreted systems. The encoding of the example in a specialised language is also shown in this section, its key properties are checked automatically, and experimental results are discussed. We discuss related work in Section 5 and conclude in Section 6.

2 Preliminaries

The first class citizen within an interpreted system as applied to Web services is an agent that represents the concrete counterpart of a service in the composition. Below we summarise the framework of interpreted systems [4] as implemented in MCMAS. Every agent i ($i \in \{1, \ldots, n\}$) is characterised by a finite set of local states L_i for the service and a finite set of actions Act_i that the agent performs on behalf of the service. A Protocol defines the actions that may be performed by an agent in each of its local states and is defined as $P_i : L_i \rightarrow 2^{Act_i}$. The environment is modelled as a special agent with a set of local states (L_e), a set of actions (A_e) and a protocol (P_e). The set of global states of the composition can be defined as a non-empty subset of the Cartesian product $L_1 \times L_2 \times L_3 \ldots \times L_n \times L_e$. A global state of the system at a particular instant in time is therefore represented by a tuple $(l_1, l_2, \ldots l_n, l_e)$.

The evolution (transition) of the agents' local states is described by a function $t_i : L_i \times \ldots \times L_n \times L_e \times Act_i \times \ldots \times Act_n \times Act_e \rightarrow L_i$ that defines the next local state of an agent given the current local state and the action(s) that are performed in that state as per the protocol. The evolution of all the agents' local states describes a set of runs over the set of reachable states. It is assumed that in every state the agents perform simultaneous actions. Note that some agents may perform "null" actions. The evolution of the global states of the system is described by a function $t : S \times Act \rightarrow S$ where $S = L_1 \times \ldots \times L_n \times L_e$ and $Act = Act_1 \times \ldots \times Act_n \times Act_e$. Given a set $I \subseteq S$ of possible initial global states, the set $G \subseteq S$ of reachable global states is generated by all possible runs of the system. Finally, the definition includes a set of atomic propositions AP together with a valuation function $h : AP \rightarrow S$.

We adopt the syntactical constructs and semantic model for the interpretation of temporal-epistemic formulae in interpreted systems as presented in [8] to analyse composite Web services. Of particular interest to us is the formula $K_i\varphi$ for expressing epistemic properties. The formula is read as "Agent i knows φ". Epistemic properties capture knowledge that the agents and their environment acquire as the system evolves. Verification of epistemic properties ensures the correctness of this knowledge at various states within the system as interaction progresses. In terms of verification via model checking, in our approach, this can be defined as establishing whether or not $M_s \models K_i\varphi$. We can also verify complex specifications like $K_iK_j\varphi$ which informally expresses "Agent i knows that agent j knows φ".

3 A Motivating Example

We take as our reference example a composition of services for Loan Approval as outlined in the WSBPEL specification [9]. Figure 1 shows the interaction protocols for the various services. At a high level of abstraction, these protocols can be viewed as individual BPEL representations of the processes. For simplicity in this paper, we do not model explicit communication between the agents. We assume that the underlying network for sending and receiving messages is reliable, communication is synchronous and message delivery is instantaneous. Asynchronous communication can be easily modelled by allowing the agents to

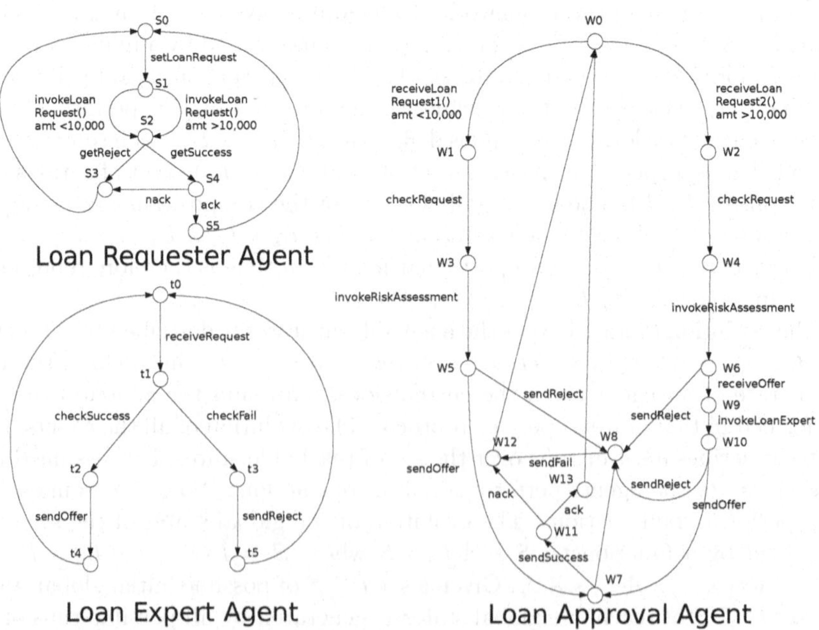

Fig. 1. Protocols for Agents in the Loan Approval Service

"wait" or do "nothing". It is also possible in our framework to model channels as environment for the agents in the systems and reason about their correct behaviour for e.g. coordination and synchronisation. However in this paper we abstract from modelling these.

3.1 Formalisation

We represent the above example using the formalism of interpreted systems. In order to verify a system with MCMAS, we need to translate the system into a model written in ISPL, which includes the following components:

- The definition of agents which describes the local behaviour of every agent, such as states, actions and protocols.
- The global evaluation function of the system which define atomic propositions held over global states, the combinations of local states.
- The local initial state of agents.
- Specifications to be checked. They are expressed as temporal-epistemic formulae.

In the example, we define four agents "Loan Requester (LRA)", "Loan Service (LSA)","Risk Assessor (RAA)" and "Loan Expert (LEA)". Each of them is modelled using their local states, local actions, protocols and transition functions.

For example, for the LRA the local states are $\{s_0, s_1, s_2, s_3, s_4, s_5\}$. The set of actions for the LRA includes *setLoanRequest*, *invokeLoanRequest1*, *invokeLoanRequest2*, *ack*, *nack*, *nothing*, *return1*, among which *invokeLoanRequest1* represents a request with amount less than 10,000 GBP, *invokeLoanRequest2* one with amount greater than 10,000 GBP, *nothing* is just a dummy action (corresponding to no-op) and *return1* is used to move to the initial state. The Protocol function in the definition explicitly specifies possible actions at each state: for example, at state s_1, only *invokeLoanRequest1*, *invokeLoanRequest2* are possible. If no action can be enabled, *nothing* is assigned to the state.

Finally the evolution function defines the behaviour of the agent, i.e., when and how the agent moves to another state. For example, LRA proceeds to the state s_1 if and only if it is in the state s_0 and executes the action *setLoanRequest.* In addition, the agent can jump to other states without firing a "local" action. This is done by following actions of other agents. For instance, LRA moves to state s_3 from state s_2 when agent LSA executes action *sendFail.* In this way, we can easily model synchronisation between agents. A typical scenario of synchronisation is when an agent sends a request to another and the latter has to receive it. Moreover, this mechanism allows us to reduce the total number of actions and thus the number of Boolean variables needed to encode the system which speeds up the verification. Asynchronous communication can be easily modelled as explained earlier. The Loan Service may choose not to receive the request sent by the Loan requester till the send operation is complete. In this case, the transition of the Loan service from state w_0 to state w_1 happens only after the transition *invokeLoanRequest1* of the loan requester from state s_1 to state s_2.

As observed, the evolution function provides a simple means of modelling coordination and synchronisation/asynchronisation between agents for the purposes of the paper. It also allows us to reduce complexity, while focusing on our core objective of verifying temporal-epistemic properties. More elaborate models of coordiantion and synchronisation are possible but will not be presented here.

4 Model Checking the Loan Approval Composition

MCMAS [8] is an OBDD based symbolic Model Checker for Multi Agent Systems. In addition to temporal modalities MCMAS allows the verification of epistemic, correctness and cooperation modalities. Input to the model checker is defined in ISPL. The evaluation function in ISPL maps atomic propositions to states, which specifies for every atomic proposition the set of states in which the proposition holds. For example the proposition *loanApproved* holds if the loan requester is in state s_4 or it is in state s_5.

We check the following epistemic properties: (1) if the loan request is approved by LAA, then LRA *knows* the fact that LSA *knows* that the request of LRA has low risk; (2) if the amount of the loan requested is greater than 10,000, the customer *knows* that his request will be directed to a Loan Expert. They are formalised as follows:

$$\begin{aligned} AF\ loanApproved \rightarrow\ & (amountLess10000 \rightarrow K_{LRA}K_{LSA}LowRisk1) \\ & \wedge(amountGreater10000 \rightarrow K_{LRA}K_{LSA}LowRisk2) \end{aligned}$$

$$AF\ amountGreater10000 \rightarrow K_{LRA}expertInvoked$$

We also tested two CTL formulae: $AF\ (loanFail \vee loanSucceed)$, which stands for eventually in all paths, a loan request would fail or succeed, i.e., LSA must make decision for every load request, and $AF\ amountGreater10000 \rightarrow EF\ loanReject$ which means that for all paths in which the loan amount is greater than 10,000 GBP, the request would fail in some paths.

MCMAS used 13 Boolean variable to encode local states, 12 for actions. It returned the result immediately, as the model is not complex. It is obvious that the four properties are true for the model. It is easy to produce a false property as well, for example, change "EF" into "AF" in the fourth formula. Due to space restrictions we do not present the complete ISPL code for the example; it is available on request.

5 Related Work

Several research efforts have addressed the problem of model checking Web service specification, however to the best of our knowledge this is one of the first papers to address the verification of epistemic properties of agents that represent Web services. Pistore et al [11] present a technique based on "Planning as Model Checking" for planning under uncertainty for composition and monitoring of BPEL4WS processes. The Model checking approach uses the MBP

Planner [1]. Fu et al [5] presents a framework where BPEL specifications are translated to an intermediate representation, using guarded automata as XPath expressions. This is followed by the translation of the intermediate representation to a verification language "Promela", input language of the model checker SPIN. Hu Huang et al [7] presents an approach using the BLAST model checker to verify the process models of OWL-S

6 Conclusions

In this paper we show that along with temporal modalities, epistemic properties for agents representing the services can be verified. We use the symbolic model checker MCMAS and verify temporal-epistemic properties for Loan Approval composition. As part of our future work we intend to investigate the explicit modelling of coordination and synchronisation between agents which are abstracted in this paper.

References

1. Bertoli, P., Cimatti, A., Pistore, M., Roveri, M., Traverso, P.: MBP: a model based planner. In: Proc. of the IJCAI'01 (2001)
2. Bordini, R., Fisher, M., Pardavila, C., Visser, W., Wooldridge, M.: Model checking multi-agent programs with CASP. In: Hunt Jr., W.A., Somenzi, F. (eds.) CAV 2003. LNCS, vol. 2725, pp. 110–113. Springer, Heidelberg (2003)
3. Cimatti, A., Clarke, E., Giunchiglia, F., Roveri, M.: NuSMV: A new symbolic model verifier. In: Halbwachs, N., Peled, D.A. (eds.) CAV 1999. LNCS, vol. 1633, pp. 495–499. Springer, Heidelberg (1999)
4. Fagin, R., Halpern, J.Y., Moses, Y., Vardi, M.Y.: Reasoning about Knowledge. MIT Press, Cambridge (1995)
5. Fu, X., Bultan, T., Su, J.: Analysis of interacting BPEL web services. In: WWW'04, pp. 621–630. ACM Press, New York (2004)
6. Holzmann, G.J.: The model checker SPIN. IEEE Trans. on Software Eng. 23(5), 279–295 (1997)
7. Huang, H., Tsai, W.-T., Paul, R., Chen, Y.: Automated model checking and testing for composite web services. In: ISORC '05, pp. 300–307. IEEE Computer Society, Los Alamitos (2005)
8. Lomuscio, A., Raimondi, F.: MCMAS: A model checker for multi-agent systems. In: Hermanns, H., Palsberg, J. (eds.) TACAS 2006 and ETAPS 2006. LNCS, vol. 3920, pp. 450–454. Springer, Heidelberg (2006)
9. OASIS Web service Business Process Execution Language (WSBPEL) TC: Web service Business Process Execution Language Version 2.0 (2007)
10. Penczek, W., Lomuscio, A.: Verifying epistemic properties of multi-agent systems via bounded model checking. Fundamenta Informaticae 55(2), 167–185 (2003)
11. Pistore, M., Barbon, F., Bertoli, P., Shaparau, D., Traverso, P.: Planning and monitoring web service composition. In: AIMSA, pp. 106–115 (2004)
12. Wooldridge, M.: An introduction to multi-agent systems. John Wiley, England (2002)
13. Fu, X., Bultan, T., Su, J.: Conversation Protocols: A Formalism for Specification and Verification of Reactive Electronic Services. In: Ibarra, O.H., Dang, Z. (eds.) CIAA 2003. LNCS, vol. 2759, pp. 188–200. Springer, Heidelberg (2003)

Research and Implementation of Knowledge-Enhanced Information Services

Bo Yang[1], Hao Wang[1], Liang Liu[1], Qian Ma[1], Ying Chen[1], and Hui Lei[2]

[1] IBM China Research Laboratory, Beijing, 100094, China
{yangbbo, wanghcrl, liuliang, maqian, yingch}@cn.ibm.com
[2] IBM T. J. Watson Research Center, Hawthorne, NY, USA
hlei@us.ibm.com

Abstract. Information isolation has been identified as a big challenge in IT Service Management (ITSM). Existing ITSM practices mostly rely on configuration information and are geared towards individual applications and processes. However, information available in complicated IT infrastructure goes beyond data from the configuration management domain. How to efficiently extract and integrate the hidden knowledge from a wide variety of information sources is a major pain point for ITSM. In this paper, a threading strategy (TS) with KPI mark and knowledge-enhanced information services is proposed to improve ITSM quality. The essential contribution of this work is to organize the highly complex IT service information with KPI mark and to build a knowledge repository for accumulateing and reusing experts' knowledge. In addition, a prototype called BIANCHIN is implemented to explore this knowledge-enhanced information services framework. Finally, a real business application of Cisco VoIP system is used as a case study for evaluating the effectiveness and efficiency of the knowledge-enhanced information services framework.

Keywords: IT service management, information services, configuration management database, knowledge database.

1 Introduction

Information services are critical to IT infrastructure management. They provide diverse information to users or other service components in an IT service management (ITSM) environment [1]. Information services constitute a new level of services that offer added value to information contained in data sources across an organization [2]. They integrate information to provide a unified view of information, add business context to raw information, and expose insightful relationships in information that in turn facilitate better decision-making.

Treating information as a service, organizations can improve the relevance and cost effectiveness of their information by reusing integration logic, making information available to people, processes and applications across the business, and improving the operational impact of information on driving innovation.

B. Krämer, K.-J. Lin, and P. Narasimhan (Eds.): ICSOC 2007, LNCS 4749, pp. 462–473, 2007.

Many approaches have been proposed to improve the utility of information services. Jie, W. et al.[3] proposed an information service architecture model for information management in a Grid Virtual Organization, which is a hierarchical structure that consists of a VO layer, a site layer and a resource layer. In order to satisfy customers' individual demands based on their personal differences, Wang, J. et al. introduced a decision-tree approach of data mining to get special information demands, used agent technology to establish the model of an information service terminal and defined the functions of the components [4]. Zou, H. et al.[5] proposed a hybrid resource information service architecture based on the grid-monitoring architecture to promote the validity of the resource information service with low system cost. Lu, X.D. proposed a distributed information service system architecture [6]; Lu also defined the ratio of correlation and the degree of satisfaction and proposed the autonomous integration and optimal allocation of information services for heterogeneous Faded Information Fields. Zang, T. et al. presented an architecture of the information service and the models of information organization [7]. The main functionality of this information service is the provisioning of information essential to applications running in a distributed environment such as resource information, job status, resource workload, service meta-information, and queue status.

However, information management and organization in complicated ITSM environments with frequent changes is a challenging issue [8]. Information coming from different sources is characterized as diverse, dynamic, heterogeneous, and geographically distributed. In IT infrastructure management, change is much more accelerated, and what actually defines an enterprise is indeed morphing, becoming more fractured and distributed, engaging more third parties and stakeholders within their respective business value chains expanding across the globe. Effective collaboration within and beyond the various information has become both necessary and more difficult to manage. Information as a service needs to be more readily accommodated in an integrated and proactive fashion rather than via one-off efforts.

Our work focuses on a high-level information service which is enhanced by introducing key performance indicator (KPI) mark and knowledge database (KDB). It provides information essential to applications running in a complex IT infrastructure environment including resource information, service status and service dependence. This information is organized in relational models based on a threading strategy with time thread. The information service works with data capture and analysis systems to support resource discovery, job scheduling, and management visibility.

The rest of the paper is organized as follows. The problems confronted by information services are analyzed in Section 2. In Section 3, we illustrate the framework of our Threading Strategy for ITSM (TS-ITSM). Section 4 describes the implementation issues. An experiment with a real application is discussed in Section 5. Finally, the conclusions and future work are presented in Section 6.

2 Problem Analysis

ITSM has received growing attention from both the academia and the industry. An important and challenging subject in ITSM is information as a service. Information services are characterized by their wide distribution, high fault tolerance and dynamic functions as well as diversified forms.

A recent survey by IDC with corporate executives reveals that the executives require access to trusted and reliable information in a timely manner [8]. However, most enterprises are flooded with large scale data and content scattered in many systems and sources, and in multiple forms. The volume and variability of such information continues to increase, including application configurations, network configurations, OS configurations, service status, CPU usage, memory usage, transaction workload, transaction response time, etc. Sharing information and ensuring that the most appropriate views are discovered and used for their intended and changing purposes can be daunting given the many layers of hard-coded and semantic dependencies built within typical applications and systems. Furthermore, it is quite inefficient and disconcerting that different applications apply their respective approaches in a very fragmented, redundant, and inconsistent manner.

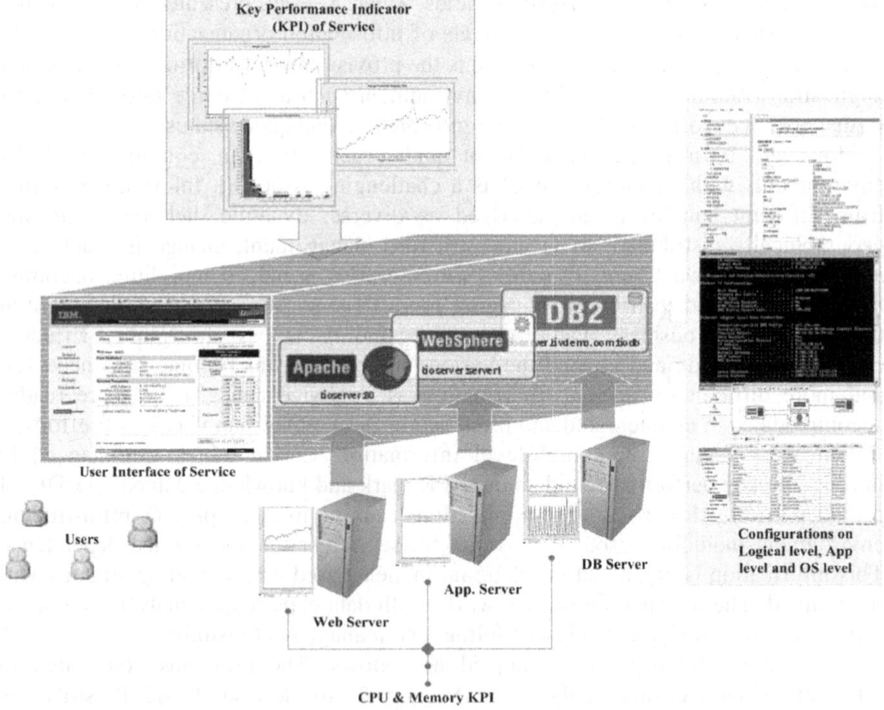

Fig. 1. Typical IT information architecture of distributed business applications

A critical step towards improving ITSM involves creating solutions geared for discrete applications or processes, this evaluation involves creating and instantiating the core elements and functions of the business in a fashion where they can be utilized in multiple ways. It allows one to view all of the components of the environment in a logical organization, as shown in Fig. 1, that is not constrained by any particular physical implementation or use scenario. To maintain an application, all related information need to be captured for performance analysis or problem diagnosis. Each information source is useful in context to its particular initial use case yet can potentially provide tremendous added value when it is combined and utilized for multiple purposes.

For centralizing configurations control, the configuration management database (CMDB) [9-11] has been proposed that focuses on how organizations are positioned to extract value and raise competencies to address their unique information requirements. The concepts underlying CMDB include information governance, change management, as well as the development and maintenance of a flexible information infrastructure. CMDB is intended to be an infrastructure approach to coordinating data-oriented service and integration functions in a dedicated fashion. It provides connectivity to a vast amount of data and delivers relevant information, consolidating these functions in a unified fashion as shown in Fig. 2.

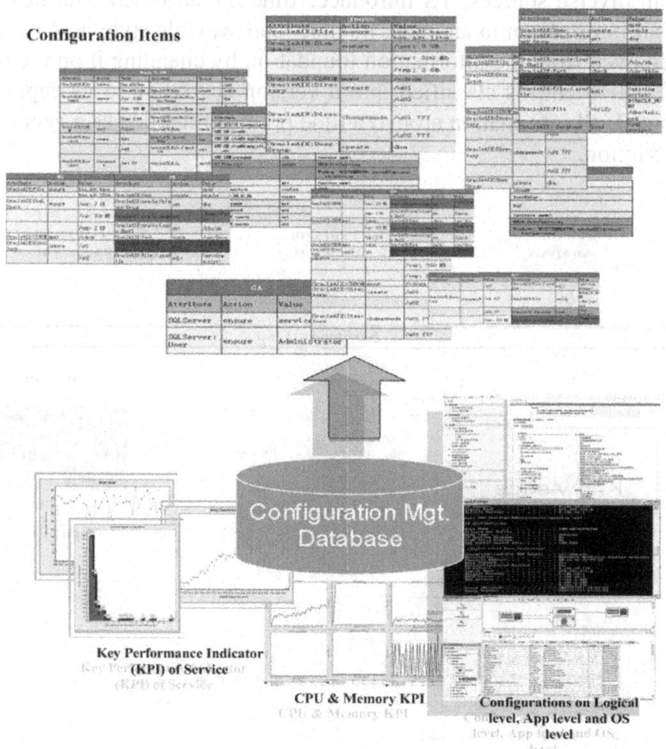

Fig. 2. Configurations management database for information service

However, applying a common form to all information sources within an enterprise is an impossible task, especially in large and changing environments [8]. Given uncertainties on the exact information that may be needed in the future, who will need it, and how it will be used, it is critical to build an information foundation that is open, flexible, and scalable. Furthermore, it is not sufficient simply to record all the information on systems and operations in CMDB. Without the assistance of domain knowledge, ITSM personnel can easily get confused and be lost in low-level redundant details.

3 Threading Strategy for ITSM

When studying how to provide real-time information, we must consider how to satisfy diverse demands from disparate applications. The concept of advanced information services has been put forward from the aspect of services. Without a common foundation of usable information, service-oriented architecture is just a loose confederation of abstract business processes.

Since information from a complicated IT infrastructure is not the only data needed for configuration management, in this paper, we advocate a threading strategy (TS) with KPI mark and knowledge-enhanced information services. The KPI mark represents the performance status of system. To organize a large body of information coming from diverse sources, TS introduces time-thread based data management to coordinate all information in an open, flexible, and scalable style. Each source can be added or removed from the information foundation by changing it on the time thread. Every information chip is classified into a version according to its capture time. As shown in Fig. 3, all information around a time point is regarded as a version of related system description.

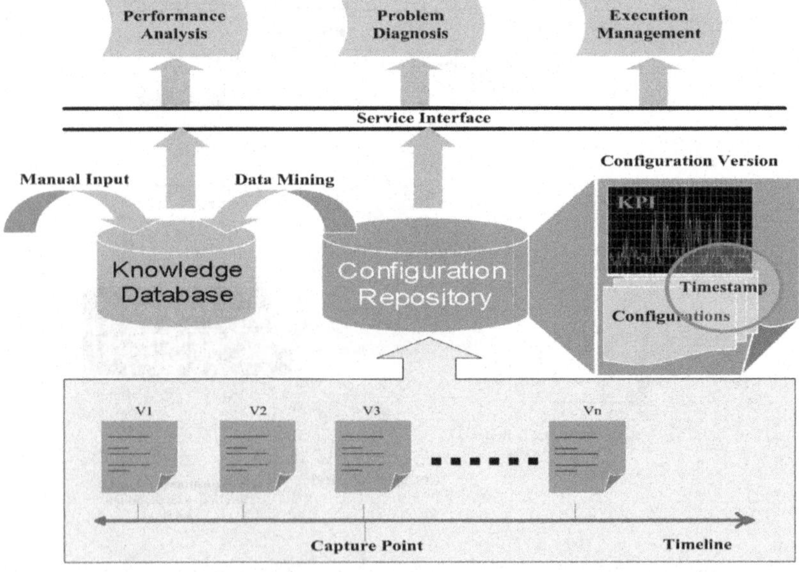

Fig. 3. Threading strategy with KPI mark and knowledge-enhanced information services

In particular, for a version, the KPI mark of the system performance provides tremendous added value to other application services such as capability planning, performance analysis and problem diagnosis etc. It is almost impossible for a traditional CMDB containing only configuration information to provide such added value. KPI mark also provides the change trace of system performance, which can indicate what configurations should be used to meet special business requirements when the KPI mark is combined with configuration information.

Moreover, a knowledge database is introduced to store not only the KPI rank of system versions, but also extended patterns and rules that ITSM operators define in the course of their work. In a distributed environment, this strategy enables ITSM operators to share their domain knowledge for different application services. The reuse of experts' knowledge will be effective in reducing the labor cost for complicated IT service management.

4 Implementation of the Information Service

In this section, a proof of concept (POC) project BIANCHIN is developed to validate the Threading Strategy for information services. It is built on the Eclipse Toolkit with Java technology, and implements a container for information capture, data organization, pattern definition, rule and policy definition, and the GUI of using knowledge.

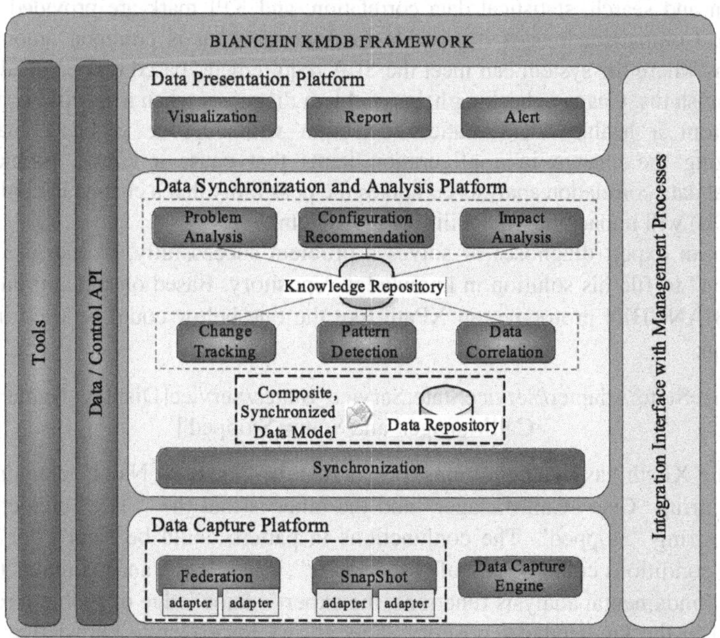

Fig. 4. Prototype framework about knowledge enhanced information service

In the following subsections, we will discuss some key issues involved in the implementation of our information service. These issues include the implementation of the information capture mechanism, the implementation of the data organization mechanism, the implementation of the knowledge accumulation and so on.

4.1 Threading Strategy for Information Coordination

The framework of BIANCHIN is shown in Fig. 4, in which a data capture platform, a data synchronization & analysis platform, and a data presentation platform are constructed to provide information services.

After data is captured from target systems, it needs to be coordinated to represent the target systems. For data coming from diverse sources with different capture schedule, a loose composite data model is proposed to synchronize data by timeline, compose the diverse data, and store the composed data in a data repository. A synchronized data model in xml is introduced in the prototype. All of the data in a version represents the system status at the time point. Thus it provides a comprehensive, synchronized view of the target business-IT infrastructure by aligning diverse information.

4.2 Knowledge-Enhanced ITSM

Moreover, and most importantly, the knowledge repository provides fundamental analysis functions upon the synchronization of data to facilitate knowledge generation. Frequently used data analysis functions such as comparison and change tracking, pattern detection and search, statistical data correlation, and KPI mark are provided as utility libraries. Comparison makes it possible to discover what is common among all the situations where the system can meet the SLA requirement, based on historical versions of system status. Change checking helps problem diagnosis when a specific service goes down from a healthy state. Pattern detection will improve problem analysis by recognizing the change in configuration items that cause a known problem. And statistical data correlation analysis computes the possibility that a change in configuration items (CIs) will impact the availability of the system.

When an expert diagnoses or solves a problem successfully, he can use "pattern definition" to file his solution in knowledge repository. Based on the xml data model in the BIANCHIN prototype, an XPath like the one below could be used in pattern definition:

```
//ServiceState:Adapter/ServiceState:Service_States/Service[Display_Name='Cisco
CallManager' and State='Stopped']
```

where the XPath has two conditions: one is that the "Display_Name" element should equal a string "Cisco CallManager" and the other is that the "State" element should equal a string "Stopped". The conjunctions in pattern could be "and", "or", or "!". And the conditions could be any of "=", ">", "<", ">=", ">=", and "contains ()".

With fundamental analysis functions, the expert's knowledge of problem resolution is stored in the knowledge repository. This allows for effective knowledge reuse on performance analysis, configuration recommendation and problem diagnosis etc., and will add business value to other information services.

In our system, data analysis not only can track system status changes in the form of a configuration change, but also those in the form of KPI fluctuation at business level. That will be powerful to analyze the relationships between IT infrastructure and business requirement, and will be helpful to diagnose a problem's root cause.

5 Experiment Result and Analysis

The purpose of the experiments is to evaluate the efficiency of problem determination using Threading Strategy for ITSM, when TS is used for problem diagnosis on a real business application of Cisco VoIP system. The VoIP system contains a complicated services topology, as shown in Fig. 5, where the system is supported by VoIP application services, database application services and OS services. And there are many relationships between services; for example, Cisco CDR Insert (CCI) service and Cisco Database Layer Monitor (CDLM) service depend on MSSQLSERVER service, Distributed Transaction Coordinator (DTC) service and Remote Procedure Call (RPC) service. Any related service that is blocked will influence the performance of the overall VoIP system. The information sources in our experiment include VoIP application configurations, OS configurations and services status.

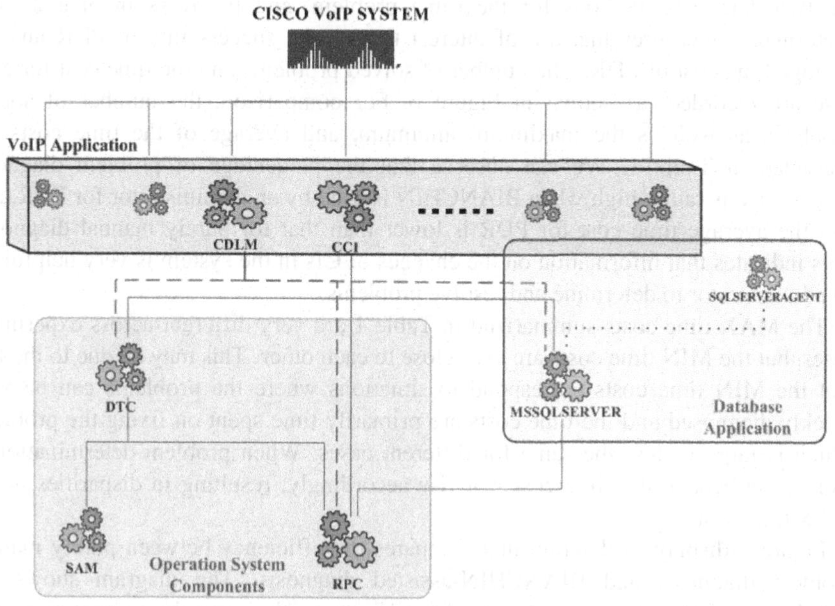

Fig. 5. Part of service relationships in the Cisco VoIP system

The experiment is designed to include 15 troubleshooting cases, Part of the cases are frequent cases cited in the Cisco CallManager trouble-shooting manual [12] and the others are summarized by experienced VoIP administrators. The cases covered both system problems, such as service operation error, and VoIP configuration problems such as improper device settings.

For each case, we examined the efficiency of Problem Determination and problem Remediation (PDR)[13-15] efficiency. The efficiency was measured in terms of the time cost of PDR. For comparative analysis, each troubleshooting case is performed using two methods: one is the traditional method which is purely manual diagnosis by a VoIP system administrator, and the other is diagnosis with assistance from our TS-ITSM prototype system, BIANCHIN. The experiments results are summarized in Table 1 and Figure 6.

Table 1. Summary of all the experiment results

	PURE MANUAL DIAGNOSIS	DIAGNOSIS WITH BIANCHIN
UNSOLVED PROBLEMS	3	0
SUCCESS RATES (%)	80	100
MAX PDR TIME (MIN)	55.63	18.1
MIN PDR TIME (MIN)	1.13	1.12
AVERAGE TIME (MIN)	20.46	7.82

Table 1 summarizes the respective experiment results of problem diagnosis by a VoIP administrator with and without the use of BIANCHIN. The columns represent the two diagnosis methods for the same problem, and the rows involve 2 main performance measures that are of interest to us: the success rate of PDR and the average time cost of PDR. The number of solved problems and the time cost for each case are recorded, as shown in Figure 6. For comparison, the number of solved problems as well as the maximum, minimum, and average of the time costs are presented in Table 1. We can observe that the percentage of problem diagnosis success rate is rather high when BIANCHIN is used by an administrator for PDR, and that the average time cost for PDR is lower than that for purely manual diagnosis. This indicates that information on the changes of CIs in the system is very helpful for an administrator to determine and resolve problems.

The MAX time costs summarized in Table 1 are very different across experiment cases, but the MIN time costs are very close to each other. This may be due to the fact that the MIN time costs correspond to situations where the problems can be very quickly diagnosed and the time costs are primarily time spent on fixing the problem, which is more or less the same for different cases. When problem determination is more complicated, the time cost will rise accordingly, resulting in disparities in the MAX time costs.

Figure 6 displays a diagram that compares the efficiency between purely manual problem diagnosis and BIANCHIN-assisted diagnosis. The diagram shows the distribution of the time cost for each of the 15 cases. The cases that cannot be solved in 1 hour (3600 seconds) were marked as unsolved problems in the experiments.

As shown in Figure 6 and summarized in Table 1, 3 problems cannot be resolved in purely manual diagnosis experiments, which are cases No. 11, No. 14 and No. 15. In comparison, the root cause of the problems was successfully determined and the problem resolved with BIANCHIN. Note that although the change management of CIs improves the success rate of problem determination (PD), it does not always improve the efficiency of PD. Cases 5, 8, 9, 12 and 13 indicate that the change management of CIs may increase the time cost of PD for an experienced administrator because he has to analyze a large amount of information about configuration changes to determine which change is the right root cause for the current problem. This process could be time-consuming. However, the cases can be solved efficiently when patterns of the problem has been accumulated in the knowledge repository, such as in case 2, 3 and 15. In those cases, BIANCHIN determined the problem root cause accurately according to pre-defined problem patterns, and provided refined information to the administrator leading to very efficient PDR.

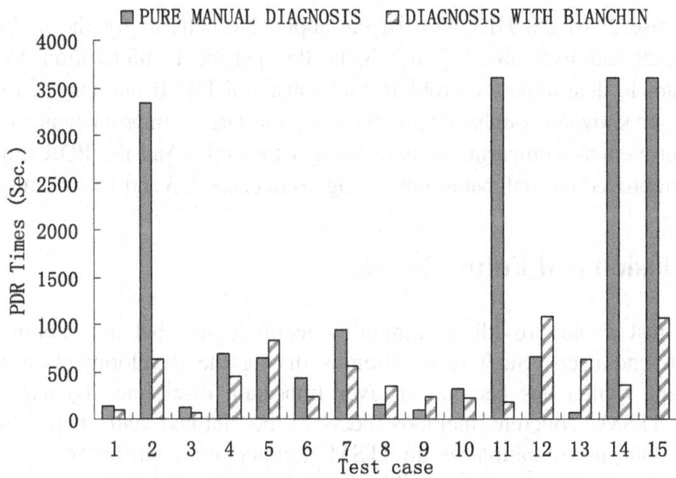

Fig. 6. PDR time cost for each tested case

Among the successfully resolved problems, case 2 is the most time-consuming one. It is a problem where services of VoIP such as CCM, CTI Manager, Extended Functions, and Voice Media Streaming have failed. When such a problem occurs, a VoIP phone user only observes that the IP phone is not working; and a VoIP administrator may observe that the administration page of VoIP does not display and some services cannot be started. In general, there are 3 possibles causes for such symptoms: the system user SQLSvc has been deleted unexpectedly, the password of user SQLSvc has been changed, or the hostname of the VoIP server has been changed.

In purely manual diagnosis, the administrator had to check every cause for PDR because there was no change management tool available to track changes of CIs. Unfortunately, testing SQLSvc password change was a long operation in the VoIP system. And it turned out that the real reason was that hostname of the VoIP server had been changed. It also took some time for the administrator to determine the changes on hostname as the difference between the names was subtle.

When there is no prior knowledge in the knowledge base as is the case with traditional ITSM, the administrator will be presented with excessive change information to make his decision. The information includes the states of services that are different, the change of application functions for the applications depending on the services, the error and warning events recorded in system and application log files, and of course, the configuration change of the hostname. Such information is useful to the administrator for PDR, but it is not time or cost efficient to manually extract the problem root cause from the large volume of information.

Given the same problem, BIANCHIN provides a more advanced approach to leveraging experts' knowledge. There are often repetitive use cases in the experiments. Patterns are defined in the knowledge base when the problem has been resolved successfully or when the case reveals critical insight on troubleshooting. In our experiment, the case about hostname change and its symptoms has been defined as a pattern in the BIANCHIN knowledge base. When the pattern about hostname change occurs in case 2, BIANCHIN will list the applicable patterns for the problem in the control panel automatically. It highlights the pertinent information to help the administrator to determine the problem root cause quickly. If the unsolved problem is excluded, our knowledge-enhanced method has the largest improvement in case 2, an 81.2% improvement comparing to pure manual method. And the PDR time cost has also been improved through pattern matching, as in cases 2, 3 and 15 shown in Figure 6.

6 Conclusion and Future Work

IT is not just about providing computing technologies, but also about providing services to end users. Such recognition is drving the development of IT service management, which has become an ever important discipline. To materialize the notion of ITSM, concrete methods need to be defined and their effectiveness evaluated. Our investigation of an ITSM architecture contributes to this rapidly growing area and suggests new possible research directions.

In this paper, we have analyzed and evaluated the performance of ITSM when it is used in problem determination. From the problem-determination experiments on the VoIP system, we can conclude that knowledge-enhanced ITSM is effective and efficient, and provides significant improvent on experts knowledge reuse and problem root-cause determination. Once the information analysis phase has been completed, additional knowledge is available to suggest solutions for other services. When a special business requirement entails a change of configurations, a version of the configurations will be extracted from the configuration repository if the KPI is likely to meet the requirement. This method could also be used for system disaster recovery, where the system is restored to a specific state in history that is stable and controllable.

Moreover, for those more complicated problems that reference a large amount of configuration data, TS-ITSM may be suitable to filter out information irrelevant for system diagnosis and remediation. Obviously, knowledge-enhanced ITSM needs to be further developed and refined for applications in a wide variety of cases. This paper represents our initial effort. Further investigation will be conducted and reported in the future.

Acknowledgments. This work was developed in the Distributed Computing and System Management department of IBM China Reseach Lab. The authors would like to thank Kewei Sun, Xuefeng Tang and Jian Ma for their comments and support on the experiments in this paper.

References

1. Information Technology Service Management (ITSM) (2005), Available: http://www.cce.umn.edu/professionalcertification/itil/
2. IBM Information On Demand - The Role of Information in a Service Oriented Architecture: IBM Global CFO Study (2006), Available: http://www-306.ibm.com/software/data/information-on-demand

3. Jie, W., Hung, T., Turner, S.J., Cai, W.: Architecture Model for Information Service in Large Scale Grid Environments. In: Sixth IEEE International Symposium on Cluster Computing and the Grid, vol. 1, pp. 107–114. IEEE Computer Society Press, Los Alamitos (2006)
4. Wang, J., Ding, Z.F., An, S.: An agent-based study on personalized travel information service. In: 1st International Symposium on Systems and Control in Aerospace and Astronautics, p. 4 (2006)
5. Zou, H., Jin, H., Han, Z.F., Shi, X.H., Chen, H.H.: HRTC: hybrid resource information service architecture based on GMA. In: IEEE International Conference on e-Business Engineering, pp. 541–544. IEEE Computer Society Press, Los Alamitos (2005)
6. Lu, X.D., Mori, K.: Autonomous information services integration and allocation in agent-based information service system. In: IEEE/WIC International Conference on Intelligent Agent Technology, pp. 290–296 (2003)
7. Zang, T.Y., Jie, W., Hung, T., Lei, Z., Turner, S.J., Cai, W.T.: The design and implementation of an OGSA-based grid information service. In: IEEE International Conference on Web Services, pp. 566–573. IEEE Computer Society Press, Los Alamitos (2004)
8. Rogers, S.: Information as a Service to the Enterprise. White paper (December 2006)
9. Van Bon, J., Kemmerling, G., Pondman, D.: IT Service Management: An Introduction, Van Haren Publishing (September 1, 2002)
10. Berkhout, M., Harrow, R., Johnson, B., Lacy, S., Lloyd, V., Page, D., van Goethem, M., van den Bent, W.G.: Service Support: Service Desk and the Process of Incident Management, Problem Management, Configuration Management, Change Management and Release Management, London: The Stationery Office (2000)
11. Chen, P.Y., Kataria, G., Krishnan, R.: On Software Diversification, Correlated Failures and Risk Management. SSRN (April 8, 2006), Available: http://ssrn.com/abstract=906481
12. Troubleshooting Guide for Cisco CallManager, Release 4.2, Corporate Headquarters, Cisco Systems, Inc. (2006)
13. Chen, M.Y., Kiciman, E., Fratkin, E., Fox, A., Brewer, E.: Pinpoint: problem determination in large, dynamic Internet services. In: International Conference on Dependable Systems and Networks, pp. 595–604 (2002)
14. Hoi, C., Kwok, T.: An Autonomic Problem Determination and Remediation Agent for Ambiguous Situations Based on Singular Value Decomposition Technique: In: International Conference on Intelligent Agent Technology, pp. 270–275 (2006)
15. Agarwal, M.K., Gupta, V.M., Sachindran, N., Anerousis, N., Mummert, L.: Problem Determination in Enterprise Middleware Systems using Change Point Correlation of Time Series Data. In: Network Operations and Management Symposium, pp. 471–482 (2006)

A Model and Rule Driven Approach to Service Integration with Eclipse Modeling Framework

Isaac Cheng, Neil Boyette, Joel Bethea, and Vikas Krishna

IBM Almaden Research Center, 650 Harry Road, San Jose, CA 95120, U.S.A
{isaacc, nboyette, bethea, vikas}@us.ibm.com

Abstract. BPEL is fast becoming the most widely-adopted standard for business processes involving web services; however BPEL is geared mainly at the higher level processes and is not well suited for the lightweight, short-lived "micro-processes" that share the same service space. Such processes require the advantages of interoperability and asynchronicity offered by an SOA approach but at a more granular logical level. This paper details a way to use a declarative approach to define the micro-processes that occur in the services called by an SOA based application. Using the context of a global call center workflow application framework named CCF, for Custom Call Flows, this paper describes how micro-processes (call flows) can be defined, and how declaratively defined rules can be used to integrate these micro-processes with other services to build a flexible service system.

Keywords: architecture, call center, call flow, script, CRM, IT, Web, labor, asset, business transformation, customer, enterprise, global, infrastructure, inference, integrate, internet, leverage, logic, management, offshore, outsource, reasoning, rich client, rule, thin client, workflow, worldwide, support, EMF, XML, UML, BPEL, SOA.

1 Introduction

In an engagement with the call management team of a global enterprise, the authors introduced the Custom Call Flow (CCF) framework that enabled the enterprise to compose services from legacy mainframe-based back-ends to newly introduced third-party systems in a service-oriented architecture (SOA). Using this framework, business analysts can visually design models and declarative rules without requiring any programming skills. At the time application programmers can develop applications independent of business processes and workflows. CCF enables businesses and technical people to work independently and productively. It also enables enterprises to strategically outsource and offshore efficiently and effectively.

The first real-world deployment of CCF was for improving a call center, where customers call for services. A call flow, a special type of workflow, describes the steps that systematically guide a call-taker to solve a customer problem in multiple scenarios. Call flows are essential to enable customer service representatives to

B. Krämer, K.-J. Lin, and P. Narasimhan (Eds.): ICSOC 2007, LNCS 4749, pp. 474–484, 2007.

support products, and as the products evolve, the associated call flows need to be updated with an authoring tool (see Fig. 1). In the existing Call Management System, the authoring tool was tightly coupled with the rest of the system, which posed significant challenges both in evolving the tool and updating the call flows themselves. In particular, enabling the authoring tool to keep up with the current user-interface (UI) technologies proved to be extremely difficult due to the interconnected nature of the UI with the rest if the system. This lack of a modern UI in turn made it hard for a business architect to get a holistic view of a call flow to understand the design. Since the information that can be displayed on the UI is extremely limited (see Fig. 1), the business architect is likely to make local changes that may have unexpected side effects globally. Therefore, updating call flows using the existing tool was often error-prone as each change required both a business analyst to define the change, and a programmer to implement the change in code. Finally, there were also limitations in the proprietary protocol used between the authoring tool and the call flow repository, which made supporting foreign languages and cultural information impossible.

The runtime components also suffered from problems stemming from the tightly coupled nature of the architecture. Similar to the authoring tool, the runtime UI could not keep up with modern technologies which resulted in usability problems., In addition, changing or upgrading algorithms used in the call flows such as those used for business-rule inference, was quite difficult, if not impossible.

```
 9404      NAPRD    B1  FP 130  Trunc=130 Size=295 Line=18 Col=1 Alt=0
====>
       T....+....1....+....T....+....3....+....4....+....5....+....6....+....7...
00018
00019     | DESC/CUST NAME: AS/400 LOW END PROCESSOR
00020     | PROFILE TYPE:
00021     |    x PRODUCT
00022     |
00023     |                              TARGET HOURS    00 : 00          (HH:
00024     | PRODUCT INFORMATION:            ERROR CODE MASK:YYYYYYYYNNNNNNNN
00025     | Product Code 00E00400IHILH072     Provider of Default Support Serv
00026     | "NOF" OR DEFAULT SVC IOR-T&M          FLD x P/S _ RTS _ RSC   OPS _
00027     | ERROR CODES USED IN NSS?   N  (Y|N)   ENTITLEMENT SUPPORT?        Y
00028     | NEDB LOOK UP?              Y  (Y|N)   SERIAL NUMBER REQUIRED?     Y
00029     | S/N LOCAT'N  WHITE BOX-ON FRONT COVER UNDER CONTROL PANEL.
00030     |              BLACK BOX-ON FRONT COVER LOWER LEFT CORNER.
00031     |              XX-XXXXX GATHER ALL 7 DIGITS, INCLUDE THE DASH, USA ON
00032     |                        **DO NOT USE DASH FOR CANADIAN CUSTOMERS**
00033     µ""""""""""""""""""""""""""""""""""""""""""""""""""""""""""""""""""""
00034
00035     Ð Q001 xxxxxxxxxxxxxxxxxxxxxxxxxxxxxxxxxxxx CALL xxxxxxx          Ð H001
00036     ³ CALL = PRDWS3SET                                      ³         ³ SETS
PF:1/13 SAVE    2/14 TOP    3/15 QQUIT    4/16 SPLIT    5/17 JOIN    6/18 TAB
PF:7/19 BACK    8/20 FWD    9/21 BOT     10/22 LEFT    11/23 RIGHT  12/24 FILE
MA    b                                                              02/007
```

Fig. 1. The Authoring Tool of the Existing Call Management System

2 Related Work

In the service-oriented computing (SOC) area, frameworks and adaptation technologies have been developed for composing and integrating heterogeneous services and processes [2], [7], [11]. A model-driven development approach and its technology elements for SOA were described in [6]. A state-of-the-art model-based framework for developing and deploying data aggregation services was described in [10]. The design of this framework hides the complexity of web-service development, but nevertheless requires programming skills to use. Many people we worked with who compose services and design business processes do not have programming skills. To address their business needs, we introduced the CCF framework [3], which is based on the Eclipse Modeling Framework [5]. The CCF architecture features an authoring environment based on Eclipse Rich Client Platform which allows business users to design, test, and deploy workflows visually using a subset of Unified Modeling Language without requiring any traditional programming. The runtime component provides agility by making it possible for business processes to change independent of application changes. The work described in this paper focuses on how a variety of BPEL and non-BPEL processes can integrate seamlessly using the CCF framework.

In the service-rule processing area, a rule driven approach for service development for collaboration exists [9]. Facilitated by the Business Collab175oration Development Framework, our authoring tool allows business users to specify rules in the service design perspective and the task design facet. An intelligent runtime for rule processing using Agent Building and Learning Environment is described in [4]. A declarative pattern-based approach is introduced in [8] that supports the specification and use of service interaction properties in the service description and composition process. We also found that a declarative pattern-based approach is more natural to business users than a procedural program-based approach. However, unlike in [8], the pattern part of our service rules is data-oriented rather than operation-oriented.

3 System Architecture

The software system that implements the CCF framework consists of four major components: an authoring tool, an administration tool, a repository, and a runtime environment.

The authoring tool allows a business analyst to create, modify and test call flows. Call flows are presented in a graphical workflow editor which allows non-programmers to easily work with the call flow objects. The (integrated) administration tooling lets administrators manage call flows. Both tools communicate with a call flow repository via a web service. The repository stores the call flows and provides an interface to search, publish and retrieve the call flows. The runtime consists of an ABLE-based execution engine which provides an API for clients to retrieve and execute call flows from the repository.

Fig. 2 describes the CCF system architecture. A typical scenario would begin with a call flow author using the authoring tool to create or update a call flow. The administrator would then publish this call flow in the repository, making it available to the runtime. An end user can contact the service center in a number of ways including voice (telephone), email, web, etc. The end-user can interacts with the runtime engine through either a self-help application or a customer service representative who interacts with a call management application instead. The runtime environment interacts with the repository to retrieve, display, and execute the appropriate call flows to the end users. As shown in Fig. 2, the ABLE [1] based runtime component enables the runtime to interact with other services by dynamically generating the required web service client interfaces. These interfaces are then used to communicate over the Enterprise Service Bus. This loose coupling allows the business processes and rules to evolve over time without requiring code changes.

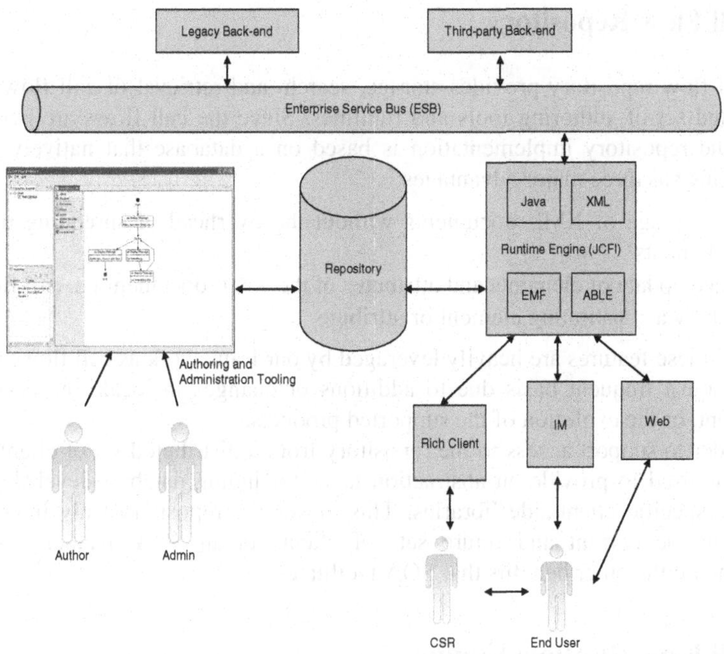

Fig. 2. CCF Architecture

4 Call Flow Authoring Tool

The Call Flow Architect (CFA) tool enables the authoring and administration of call flows. The tool allows business analysts to work with the call flows without requiring any programming skills. The main interface used by a call flow author is the call flow editor which visually displays a given call flow. CFA also provides an interface for searching and browsing the repository, which enables existing call flows (including all versions and locales) to be checked out for editing.

To integrate call flows with external services the CFA application provides a UI to define service rules. A service rule describes a service to be called, as well as the conditions that should be satisfied before calling the service. Each time a field in a call flow's dataset is changed, the CCF runtime examines the available service rules, and if one's conditions are satisfied it automatically calls the specified service.

Once the user has submitted the call flow to the repository, it enters a draft state. An administrator verifies the call flow and then publishes it. Published call flows can now be activated and thus become available to the runtime. Before a call flow can transition to a new state (except rejected or deleted) it will first undergo syntactic and semantic validation by the system. This ensures that the collection of call flows remains valid.

5 Call Flow Repository

The call flow repository provides storage, search, and retrieval of call flows from a distributed set of authoring tools and runtimes. Since the call flows are persisted in XML, the repository implementation is based on a database that natively supports XML. This has three major advantages:

- Direct storage of XML documents without the overhead of shredding them into data elements
- In-place update of elements and attributes of the XML document i.e. call flow
- Search by a constituting element or attribute

All of these features are heavily leveraged by our framework as call flows are often updated on a frequent basis due to additions or changes in locale or service level agreement, or the evolution of the supported products.

In order to support access to the repository from a distributed set of clients, a web service is used to provide an abstraction layer for hiding database level details and database specific client-side libraries. This makes the repository truly interoperable with both the current and future sets of clients in an SOA manner along with providing all the other benefits that SOA facilitates

6 Call Flow Runtime Engine

The runtime engine executes call flows. A major advantage of the runtime engine is agility. As shown in Fig. 2, the runtime engine leverages the fact that the call flows do not contain any UI information (or assume any UI knowledge for that matter) by using the Java Call Flow Interface (JCFI) API. In applying the classic Model-View-Controller design pattern to this system, the call flow is the Model; the client application is the View; and the CCF runtime engine is the Controller. JCFI is the programming interface between the View and the Controller. This UI agnostic design enables a wide variety of applications to invoke the runtime engine. These applications can in turn implement various user interfaces. The advantage is similar to that of decoupling application development from data management. CCF decouples process management from application development resulting in process independence. This greatly enhances the agility of the service system by enabling business analysts to work productively independent of application developers.

7 Call Flow Runtime Sample Applications

A few client applications have been developed to explore the opportunities presented by this design. Each application is independent of the business process under which it is used and demonstrates the agility that results from process independence.

7.1 Web Client

Web clients demonstrate the traditional thin-client model by providing access to the powerful features in the runtime engine via a Web browser.

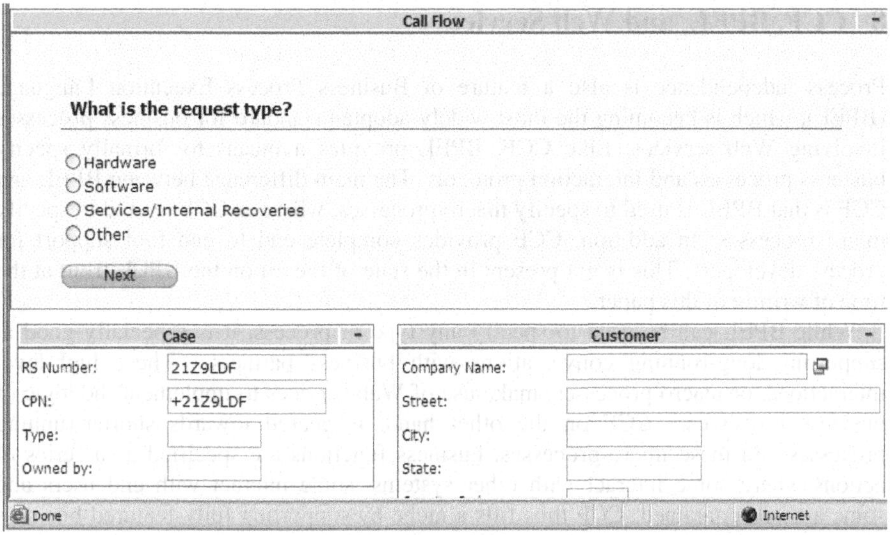

Fig. 3. A Web-based User Interface

7.2 Instant Messaging Client

Instant messaging clients (also known as chat programs) can be used to have a text-based conversation in real-time. Usually the conversation is between two humans, but there are also applications which can provide automated information. These are known as chat bots. In this case, a chat bot is used as the interface to the runtime engine, translating call flow prompts into chat responses in real-time.

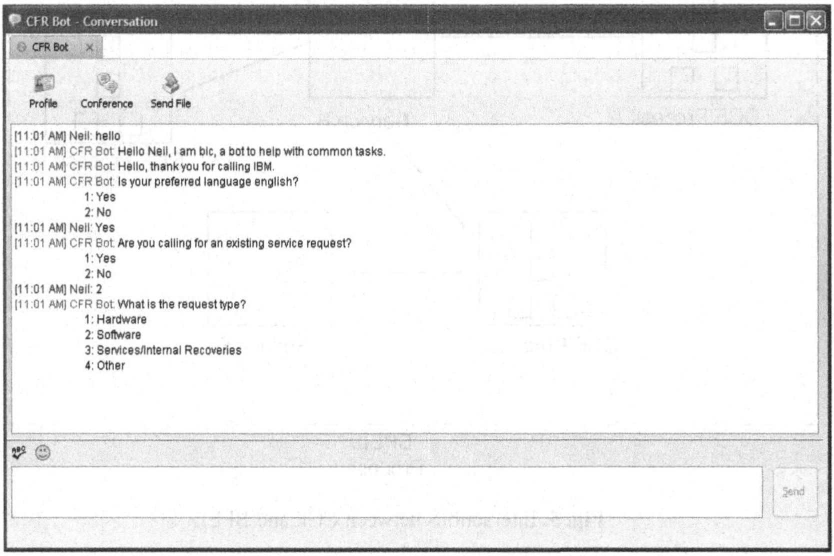

Fig. 4. An Instance Messaging (IM) User Interface

8 CCF, BPEL, and Web Services

Process independence is also a feature of Business Process Execution Language (BPEL), which is becoming the most widely-adopted standard for business processes involving Web services. Like CCF, BPEL provides a means to formally specify business processes and interaction protocols. The main difference between BPEL and CCF is that BPEL is used to specify macro processes, where as CCF is used to specify micro processes. In addition, CCF provides complete end to end tool support for process developers. This is not present in the state of the art on the BPEL front at the time of writing of this paper.

While BPEL can be used to specify any type of process, it is especially good at supporting long-running conversations with business partners. These high-level interactions, or macro processes, make use of Web services to implement the logic of business processes. CCF on the other hand, is geared towards shorter-running processes. In these micro-processes, business functions are specified as a series of actions where some interact with other systems, some interact with end users and some are self contained. CCF thus fills a niche by supporting fully-featured business processes at a smaller granularity of logic.

With this relationship CCF and BPEL complementing each other, they can be used together when building larger frameworks. BPEL is used to define the overall architecture and interaction between different functions/services. CCF is used to define how a given business function accomplishes its task. CCF in turn can interact with the BPEL defined process by exposing itself as a service and call other services in the BPEL process when needed.

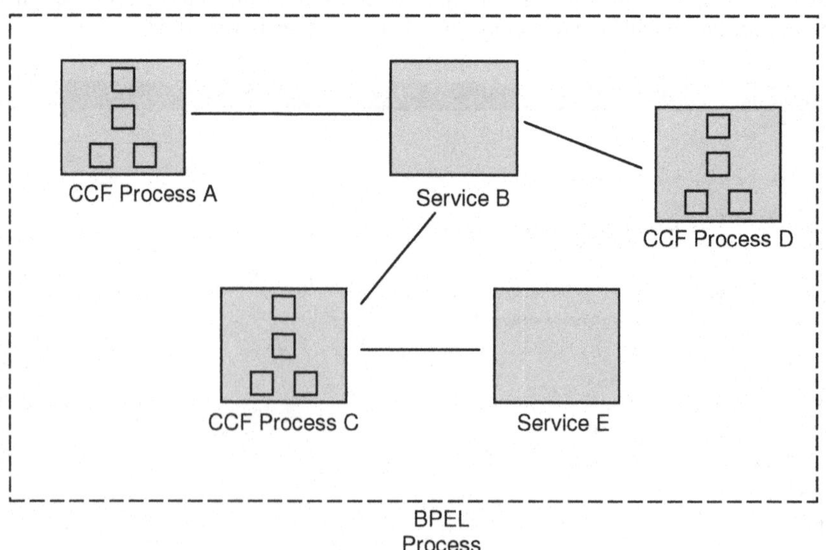

Fig. 5. Interactions between CCF and BPEL

The relationship between CCF and BPEL is analogous to other technologies that partially overlap but still complement each other. An example would be Bluetooth and Wifi wireless technologies. Both can be used to wirelessly connect two devices, but each has its own unique strengths. Wifi is faster but requires more electrical and processing power on the device. Bluetooth is more efficient in terms of electrical and processing power but has a slower speed. The two technologies co-exist because they complement each other. For instance a remote control can connect to a receiver using Bluetooth to request a song. The receiver then connects using Wifi to a home media server to retrieve the song and play it. The remote could have connected using Wifi to the receiver and the receiver could have connected using Bluetooth to the home media server, but that would not have been the most efficient use of technologies.

In a call center scenario, BPEL can be used to specify the interaction between all the services. When for example it requires a customer's information it can contact a CCF service. The CCF service would then gather the information in different ways for different customers. For instance, for preferred customers it may only ask for a customer number; then contact another service (using the BPEL framework) to retrieve the customer data from a database. For new customers it may ask a series of questions to gather the name, address, etc. Using a BPEL process to ask a series of questions is not very efficient so delegating to a CCF service is preferred. Conversely, using a CCF process to orchestrate connections between a set of services is not very efficient either, so having it call a service in the BPEL process is preferred.

In the call center engagement the difference between the CCF micro-processes and BPEL's macro processes was especially evident. This call center had in excess of 80.000 customizations to the standard process in just the United States. In addition hundreds of these customizations are changing every day; new customizations are added, others are removed and others again are changed. The system has to be flexible enough to handle both this level of customizations and this level of daily changes, without effecting system performance and without requiring a large workforce to manage the changes. The current state of BPEL application servers simply can not handle this. Updating the servers with the daily changes would be a full-time job for several people. Alternatively, the CCF framework loosely couples the call flows together to make up the larger process. As it is geared for micro-processes it is designed from the start to support large quantities of smaller processes, while still allowing integration into the larger BPEL processes. The CCF framework also allows changes to be made and call flows to be activated or deactivated by the business analysts themselves. As there is no complex deployment, supporting hundreds, even thousands of changes daily poses no significant workload.

9 Composing Heterogeneous Services with Declarative Rules

One of the challenges in our deployment was that there are many database back-ends. Many of them come from the legacy system, and some of them are newly acquired from third-party vendors. In the original system, supporting such a broad and ever changing collection of data sources proved to be extremely difficult, as call flows essentially were hard-coded at design time with decision-making for invoking every possible operation. This difficulty was then compounded further by the tightly-coupled nature of the call flow and UI displayed on the runtime client, which entangled call flow logic with UI logic, and frustrated efforts to update the existing UI or support additional types of client application.

With CCF, one possible solution to this problem involved granting call flow authors the ability to minimize decision-making complexity by encapsulating the invocation of operations as script nodes. This would then allow client UI applications to avoid the headache of hard-coding service invocation by instead designing the call flow to instead link to pre-defined script nodes. This approach still has the drawback however, that the call flow author is forced to predict in advance exactly when each particular service operation needs to be invoked within a call flow. Since there can often be many places within a call flow where it might be appropriate to invoke a given operation (or combination of operations), this approach makes the call flows complex, inflexible, and hard to maintain.

To address this issue, CFA provides a better alternative in the form of service rules. These service rules allow specific conditions to be linked to an operation, such that when the conditions are satisfied the operation is invoked. At design time, call flow authors specify conditions declaratively as if-then rules in a view separate from the call flow. The exact point of invocation within a call flow is then determined at runtime as guided by the design rules. This method is further enhanced by the use of a reasoning engine. When executing a call flow, the CCF runtime engine infers knowledge behind the scenes by sending the rules and its currently known facts to a forward-chaining reasoning engine, which has been implemented efficiently by scaleable Rete-style pattern matching in ABLE [1]. Although a Prolog-style backward-chaining reasoning engine may be more efficient, it would force the author to come up with a search goal per rule set at design time. This is often a difficult task because it is unlikely that the author can predict what knowledge will be useful to be inferred until runtime. In contrast, a forward-chaining engine can infer new facts based on the currently known facts and a set of rules. This desirable characteristic allows CCF to optimize the execution paths of call flows intelligently at runtime, removing the burden from the call flow authors and client application developers, and making it possible to keep the call flows and the client applications as reusable and maintainable as possible. Another advantage is that since the CCF runtime is determining when service rules are called, it can optimize this behavior and the system would not experience slow downs because of the business analysts adding too many rule calls at once, or in the non-optimal location. The call center owners can be assured that business analysts are shielded to an extent from specifying low-level execution details that do not carry out their intent. This is especially important as the call flows are componentized and thus a business analyst may not be aware of all the contents in which a particular call flow may execute, but the call flow runtime engine will be.

Although getting business owners to accept runtime choices may appear to be challenging when one looks at it in the abstract, it can be quite straightforward in many cases in practice. For instance, consider the service rule in Figure 6. It is straightforward for a business owner to specify that if any of the attributes, such as a customer's phone number and email is set at runtime, invoke the web service SearchForContact. It would be more difficult for the business owner to specify particular points in a call flow at which the web service needs to be invoked. With CCF, business owners still have the control of making important business decisions, such as the conditions by which certain services should be invoked. The runtime system executes the business decisions by employing an efficient pattern-matching algorithm to perform logical inference on the rules.

Service rules consist of the description of the service to be called, the mapping of the service's parameters to data elements in the call flow, and the specification of the condition that governs the rule's execution. As the authoring tool is geared towards business analysts (i.e., non-programmers), service rules are configured in an intuitive and easy to understand UI as shown below in Figure 6.

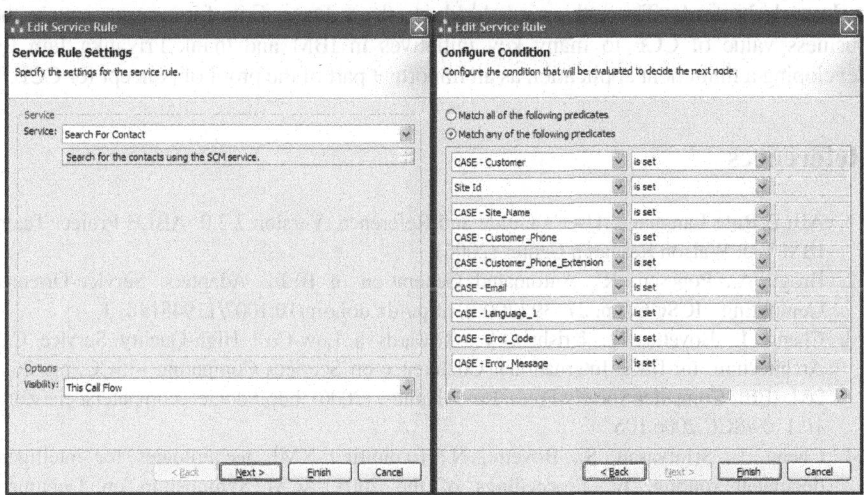

Fig. 6. Editing a Service Rule with CFA

Since CCF allows for the componentization of call flows, this concept was also extended to the service rules. Each service rule has an associated visibility which acts as the scope the service rule is valid for. Visibility can be set only for the call flow which specifies it, for the call flow and any call flows that it references, or for the entire session. The runtime engine takes the visibility into account when it generates the code used by the forward-chaining reasoning engine. The advantage of using componentization in this manner is that different rules can be applied at different times in the problem resolution session. Some rules may only apply during a given call flow, whereas others may apply during the whole session. For instance, the call flow may have a rule which looks up the address information based on the customer's last name. If the name is changed anytime during the session, the address information should be updated.

10 Conclusion

As an initial technology deployment, 40.000 users will use the suggested framework to process 10.000.000 service requests annually. The current systems for defining and handling call flows and supporting calls are mainframe based. This requires mainframe programmers to maintain the calls flows and a certain degree of mainframe expertise on the part of customer service representatives to handle the calls. Both of these factors result in huge costs to the corporation to maintain skills in these areas. The new CCF framework moves the definition and handling of the call flows to the easier to use graphically driven Eclipse platform. With the CCF framework, a system has been designed to handle more than 80.000 customizations to each standard process per country when hundreds of these customizations are changing every day. This is beyond the limit that the current state of BPEL application servers can practically handle. The transformation will result in significant cost savings to the enterprise in managing and running its call centers.

Acknowledgments. The authors would like to thank Dawn Fritz for communicating the business value of CCF to many key initiatives in IBM and thank Priyanka Jain for developing a thin-client application as an important part of the proof of concept for CCF.*

References

1. ABLE Rule Language: User's Guide and Reference, Version 2.3.0. ABLE Project Team, IBM T. J. Watson Research Center (2006)
2. Brogi, A., Popescu, R.: Automated Generation of BPEL Adapters. Service-Oriented Computing - ICSOC, pp. 27–39 (2006), http://dx.doi.org/10.1007/11948148_3
3. Cheng, I., Boyette, N., Krishna, V.: Towards a Low-Cost High-Quality Service Call Architecture. In: IEEE International Conference on Services Computing – SCC, pp. 261–264. IEEE Computer Society Press, Los Alamitos (2006), http://doi.ieeecomputersociety.org/10.1109/SCC.2006.106
4. Cheng, I., Srinivasan, S., Boyette, N.: Exploiting XML technologies for intelligent document routing. In: Proceedings of the 2005 ACM Symposium on Document Engineering, Bristol, United Kingdom, November 02 - 04, 2005, pp. 26–28. ACM Press, New York, NY (2005), http://doi.acm.org/10.1145/1096601.1096609
5. EMF: Eclipse Modeling Framework (2006), http://www.eclipse.org/emf/
6. Johnson, S., Brown, A.: A Model-Driven Development Approach to Creating Service-Oriented Solutions. In: Dan, A., Lamersdorf, W. (eds.) ICSOC 2006. LNCS, vol. 4294, pp. 624–636. Springer, Heidelberg (2006), http://dx.doi.org/10.1007/11948148_60
7. Kongdenfha, W., Saint-Paul, R., Benatallah, B., Casati, F.: An Aspect-Oriented Framework for Service Adaptation. In: Dan, A., Lamersdorf, W. (eds.) ICSOC 2006. LNCS, vol. 4294, pp. 15–26. Springer, Heidelberg (2006), http://dx.doi.org/10.1007/11948148_2
8. Li, Z., Han, J., Jin, Y.: Pattern-Based Specification and Validation of Web Services Interaction Properties. In: Benatallah, B., Casati, F., Traverso, P. (eds.) ICSOC 2005. LNCS, vol. 3826, pp. 73–86. Springer, Heidelberg (2005), http://dx.doi.org/10.1007/11596141_7
9. Orriens, B., Yang, J., Papazoglou, M.: A Rule Driven Approach for Developing Adaptive Service Oriented Business Collaboration. In: Benatallah, B., Casati, F., Traverso, P. (eds.) ICSOC 2005. LNCS, vol. 3826, pp. 61–72. Springer, Heidelberg (2005), http://dx.doi.org/10.1007/11596141_6
10. Soma, R., Bakshi, A.K.V., Da, W.: A Model-Based Framework for Developing and Deploying Data Aggregation Services. In: Dan, A., Lamersdorf, W. (eds.) ICSOC 2006. LNCS, vol. 4294, pp. 227–239. Springer, Heidelberg (2006), http://dx.doi.org/10.1007/11948148_19
11. Zhao, H., Doshi, P.: A Hierarchical Framework for Composing Nested Web Processes. In: Dan, A., Lamersdorf, W. (eds.) ICSOC 2006. LNCS, vol. 4294, pp. 116–128. Springer, Heidelberg (2006), http://dx.doi.org/10.1007/11948148_10

Semantic Web Services in Action - Enterprise Information Integration

Parachuri Deepti and Bijoy Majumdar

Setlabs, Infosys Technologies Ltd., Bangalore
{Deepti_parachuri and Bijoy_majumdar}@infosys.com

Abstract. With the development and maturity of Service Oriented Architectures (SOA) to support business-to-business transactions, enterprises are using Web services to expose the public functionalities associated with internal systems and business processes. Semantic Web service infrastructure achieves automatic data integration to enable enterprises to collaborate and compete effectively in a dynamic global environment. In this paper, we deal with two important aspects of enterprise information integration, namely process integration and data convergence. This paper talks about solution strategies for global enterprise system which provides unified information and agile solution with greater ease and simplicity. Today's Web data lacks machine understandable semantics making it impossible to achieve data integration with the Web service. Hence, the semantic Web services in action to overcome the limitations of information finding, information extracting, information representing, information interpreting and information maintaining. This paper takes you through a case study simulating semantic Web paradigm (and semantic Web services) over a leasing business system. It also portrays the various advantages and explains the hurdles in accepting the semantic Web technology.

Keywords: Semantic Web, Web Services, RDF, OWL, OWL-S, Agent Technologies, SOA, Information Integration, Semantic Web Services.

1 Introduction

Machines cannot easily make sense of most of the information on the Web. Web data is chiefly designed for human consumption. Almost all metadata (e.g., HTML) describing Web documents is about where and how to present a piece of information. Many attempts have been made to automate and improve the gathering and use of information (by means of "spiders" and "wrappers") on the Web, but these technologies still only scratch the surface.

With the evolution of SOA and semantic Web services, automated processing and integration of data and application became easier. Externalization of atomic business capabilities is achieved through Web services by making the business interfaces transparent. Effective and automatic communication with in and between the organizations also raised the need for Web services. The mandate for the semantic data and Web services is the onset of distributed computing model SOA, to provide seamless integration not just for the services but also for the information sent across.

B. Krämer, K.-J. Lin, and P. Narasimhan (Eds.): ICSOC 2007, LNCS 4749, pp. 485–496, 2007.

Current business scenario needs a global enterprise system which provides unified and required information with a greater ease and simplicity. And also should be able to cater the requirements of a constantly changing environment (business environment changes, user requirement changes and technical environment changes etc.) which is the major drawback in traditional data integration systems [1, 2, 3] and data warehouses [4, 2]. Many organizations use Web services for managing distributed applications, such as health care, agricultural management system, insurance claim processing, etc.

Using software as a service helps in sharing of resources in the constantly sharing environment. Web Services (WS) evolved as a solution for publishing, discovering and invoking the software component as services. WS help in integrating interoperable distributed heterogeneous Web services. WS and Service-oriented architecture (SOA) are emerging distributed computing paradigms and are well suited for enterprise information integration. SOA is software architecture which provides interoperable integration of scattered services by using services as components. WS are based on standard internet protocol like XML for data representation, WSDL for binding and to define interface, UDDI for discovery and SOAP for message exchange and are accessible with the help of wide range of computing devices [5, 6]. Beside these advantages it also has drawbacks such as standards and specifications are syntax based, not matured enough, not machine process able, and not sufficient for certain kinds of applications where composition, security, state, transaction management and scalability are highly recommended [7,8].

Semantic [10] is a solution for finding meaningful information and integrating with related information. Semantic approach helps in searching, discovery, selection, composition and integration of WS and also in automation of invocation, composition and execution of services. Ontology [9] is the key technology behind Semantic Web for making information more meaningful, by adding more knowledge. Rules are the next development area in semantic Web to specify declarative knowledge, constraints and to enforce policy. Delivery of personalized context and location based information [11].

The major motivation behind this paper is to organize data of an enterprise in a well defined manner thereby enabling the machines to understand, interact and retrieve the content with a greater ease. In our work, we present a case study on *Leasing Business Enterprise* wherein we model the data using semantic technologies, RDF and OWL, at the *data level*. Next we model a *service level* using OWL-S, which can be processed by machine automatically. Interaction between services is provided using agent technologies.

2 Gaps Resulted by Distributed Computing

Many traditional solutions are available for information integration. One such solution is shown in Fig. 1. An enterprise consists of various processes and when the communication is between few processes then the existing framework catered the needs of the enterprise. But with the advent of business and technology, the need to interact with customers became important, existing solutions failed to handle the complexity in real time. Some of the shortcomings of the existing solutions are mentioned below.

- Integration is performed in the applications
  - Embedded, peer-to-peer integration
  - No reuse
- The integration process is heavy
  - Low reactivity to changes in requirements and processes
  - Low reactivity to changes in data sources
- Information is locked into proprietary formats
  - Difficult to integrate with external applications
- Integration is performed asynchronously
  - Out-of-date data
  - No access to operational data

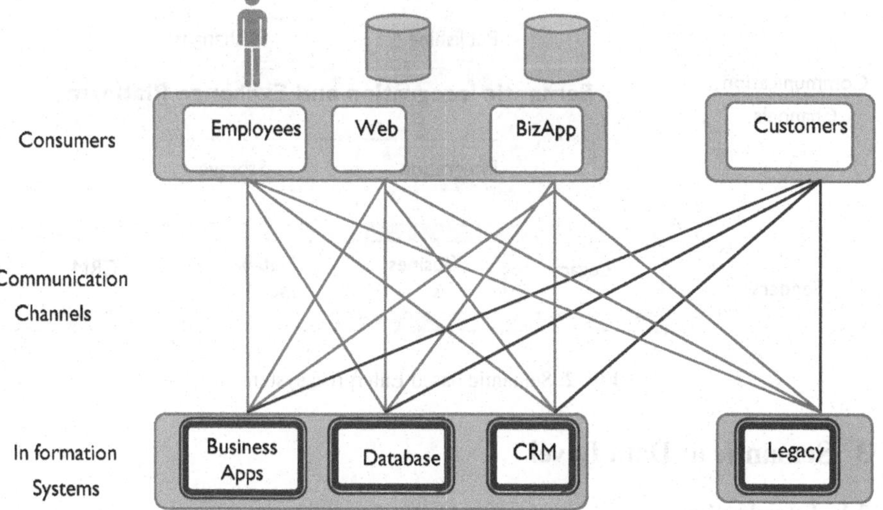

Fig. 1. Information Exchange across the Enterprise

About 80% of the Information Systems in Production Suffer from the following drawbacks

- Require IT assistance for end-user access
- Difficult for end users to identify relevant information
- Overload of information delivery
- Provide only partial answers to questions
- Often present out-of-date information
- Contain enormous amounts of redundant information
- Expensive to develop and maintain

We were delivering data but not information which can be consumed directly with out requirement of any processing.

The architectural framework of the proposed information integration as shown in Fig. 2 adopts a mediated ontology approach to data integration in which each data source is described by its own ontology and translations between different ontologies are by means of mediation.

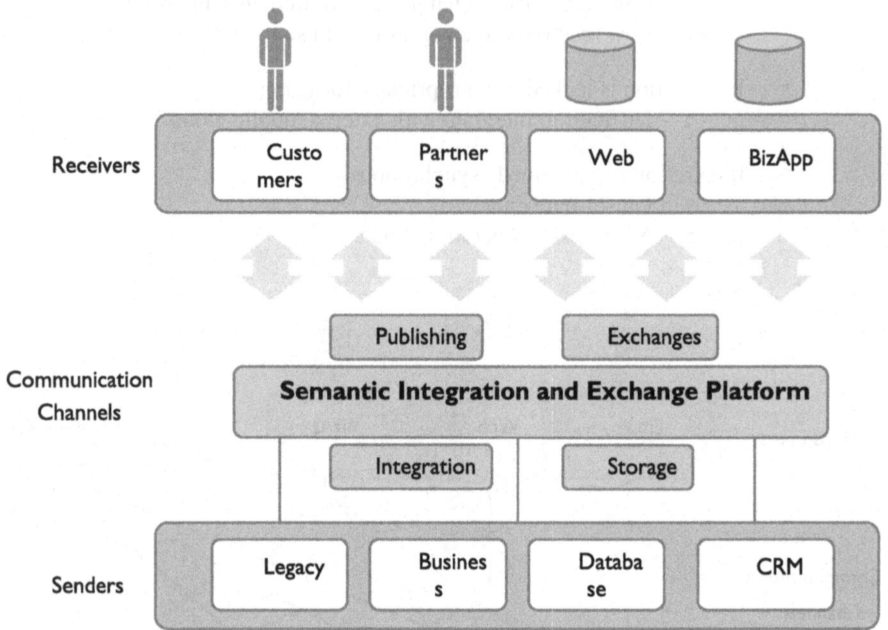

Fig. 2. Semantic based Enterprise system

3 Semantic at Data Level

3.1 Introduction

The semantic Web service has the potential of becoming the most powerful technology for information integration. It deals with two important and complementary aspects of information integration, namely data integration and service integration for effective discovery, automation, integration and reuse across various applications. Automatic data integration on a global scale is important for enterprises operating in a dynamic global market. The large number of data sources needed to access for an application and the changing business requirements make manual integration of data infeasible. With the use of Web services the data is made available for public access. But today's Web is human interpretable not machine understandable. Web data lacks machine understandable semantics making it impossible to achieve data integration with the Web service. Hence, the semantic Web services in action to overcome the limitations.

The idea of the Semantic Web is to refine the existing Web incrementally, inserting machine-readable "semantic" tags into Web documents or other data-streams. These tags are supposed to provide more information regarding the concepts within the data and their relationships to each other. The implications of such added semantic information could be far-reaching: Rather than being restricted to the Web, it would encompass virtually every aspect of life. "The two major business benefits are the promise for **tremendously improved search capabilities** and — in the long term — **improved systems interoperability**, potentially enabling machines to reach new levels of automation." [Berners-Lee,2001] Such semantic tags will be increasingly used across many domains, but whether this will stretch across the whole Web in the near- to mid-term is still uncertain.

3.2 Advantages

The key standards for the development of semantic Web are RDF, RDF-S and OWL. Many resemblances have been noted between RDF and ER diagrams. When entities can be represented by URIs, RDF makes ideal candidate for storing ER diagram as machine readable text. RDF is actually more flexible than classical ER diagrams, because in RDF we can make one of the relationships that is one of the predicates as represented by its URI the subject or object of triples. The ability to treat predicates as first-class objects provides advantages. By using the W3C's Web Ontology Language (OWL), equivalences between predicates makes it easier to combine databases without revising one database to have the same schema as the other. For example, if product_id and product_code are defined as equivalent, a search on products with product_id value of 101 will also get the details written under product_code value 101. This feature of RDF is an attractive approach to aggregating distributed data not controlled by a central authority. If we can define ontology to manage data then RDF triples are the best way to track entries into the ontology.

3.3 Challenges

Semantic technologies drive business value by providing superior capabilities (increased capacity to perform) in five critical areas [14]:

- **Development** — Semantic automation of the "business-need-to capability-to-simulate-to-test-to-deploy to-execute" development paradigm solves problems of complexity, labor-intensively, time-to-solution, cost, and development risk.
- **Infrastructure** — Semantic enablement and orchestration of core resources for transport, storage, and computing helps solve problems of infrastructure scale, complexity, and security.
- **Information** — Semantic interoperability of information and applications in context, powered by semantic models makes "killer apps" of semantic search, semantic collaboration, semantic portals and composite applications.
- **Knowledge** — Knowledge work automation and knowledge worker augmentation based on executable knowledge assets enable new concepts of operation, super-productive knowledge work, enterprise knowledge-superiority, and new forms of intellectual property.

➢ **Behavior** — Systems that learn and reason as humans do, using large knowledge bases, and reasoning with uncertainty and values as well as logic enable new categories of hi-value product, service, and process.

4 Semantic at Service Level

4.1 Introduction

The major motivation for using Web services is to reduce cost, effort and time in integrating enterprise applications but Web service usability and integration needs to be inspected manually. There is no semantically marked up content / services. Only syntactical descriptions are present. Hence requires people to locate services and create interfaces. Semantic Web Services emerged as integrated solution for realizing the vision of the next generation of the Web. Service ontologies provide a way to automatically integrate and manage the integration thereby reducing the total cost of integration.

DAML-S (OWL-S) is a DAML+OIL-based Web service ontology, which supplies Web service providers with a core set of markup language constructs for describing the properties and capabilities of their Web services in unambiguous, computer-interpretable form. DAML-S markup of Web services facilitates the automation of Web service tasks including automated Web service discovery, execution, composition and interoperation. In particular, it provides language primitives for technical, business-related and process-based facts about services. Thus, DAML-S can be regarded as a semantics-based substitution of the above-mentioned Web service languages for service description, service publication, and service flow.

4.2 Advantages

Semantic Web would provide greater access to not only content but also services on the Web. Users and software agents can discover, invoke, compose and monitor Web resources offering particular services and properties.

4.3 Challenges

A service ontology language should enable the following tasks

1. Automatic Web service discovery
2. Automatic Web service invocation
3. Automatic Web service composition and interoperation
4. Automatic Web service execution monitoring

5 Case Study

5.1 Overview

The case study used here, to depict the various challenges and semantic strategies, is the process driven in leasing business for a multi region and multi vendor system.

Fig 3 shows the process flow across various departments and systems that not only spans the organization but also other vendor entities. Applications that need to merge or synchronized with other exiting applications in different administrative domains require complying with the semantic platform to have a robust and agile business system. The lease process is defined in brief in the figure with the various business products and data being passed across systems.

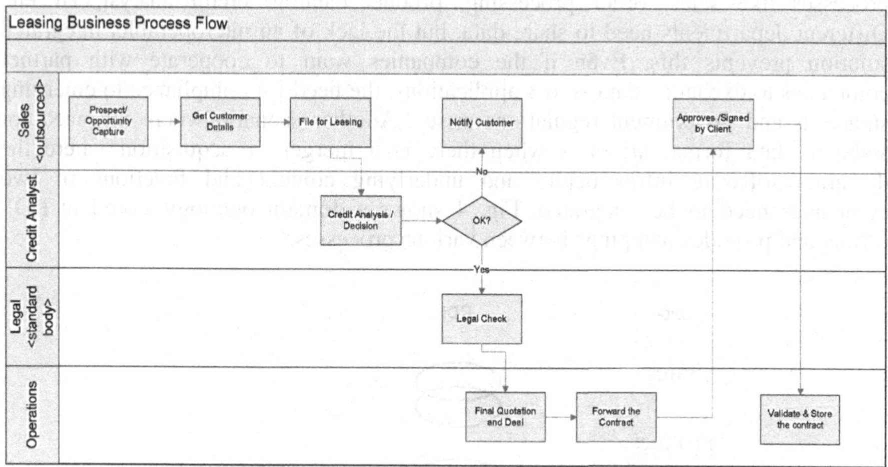

Fig. 3. Part of flow diagram of Leasing Business

5.2 AS-IS → TO-BE

The purpose of this exercise is to transform the manual operated leasing business with discrete applications carried out in discrete departments to automated business process with optimal manual intervention maintaining business agility. Up to date, million dollars are spent to develop enterprise architectures as a basis for IT modernization have largely resulted in manual compliance exercises, producing reference documentation, disconnected from operations and management systems, and delivering no capability to business users (which is the AS-IS scenario). The goal is to provide a semantic based integration platform which avoids manual indulgence to an extent and provides a flexible and agile business process (which is termed as the TO-BE scenario).

5.3 Information Perspective

In this section, we present a case study on leasing business to provide a deeper insight for designing of ontologies and conceptual modeling. It also aims at providing solution strategies for global enterprise system. Information integration provides benefits and challenges for different domain and application areas. In order to have synchronization in data representation in various vendor system or for any future acquired business, data convergence and knowledge management is a challenge that needs to be tackled. This will give way to many data format or data nomenclature differentiation that occur due to various administrative / ownership domains involved. Few key data convergence strategies and its significance are mentioned in the following sub sections. Each key area have enhanced the information definition and helped the leasing system.

Enterprise data integration: RDF

Enterprises comprises of many processes for e.g. Leasing business consists of many processes like sales, order processing, product catalog, credit analyst, Hr etc. Different departments need to share data, but the lack of an interoperable, integrated solution prevents this. Even if the companies want to cooperate with partner companies to exchange data across applications, the need for compliance to emerging standards and government regulations arises. Another scenario where the need for standard data format arises is when there is a merger or acquisition where the disparate software infrastructure and underlying content and functions of two companies need to be integrated. Fig. 4 shows a domain ontology stored in RDF format and provides mappings between various processes.

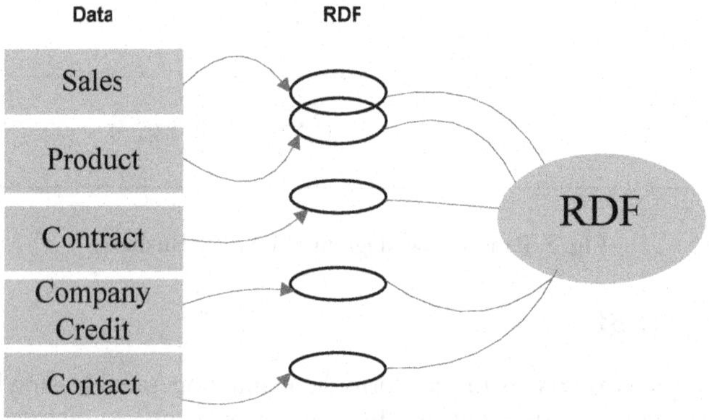

Fig. 4. Data integration within a Leasing Business enterprise application environment

Data Aggregation

An aggregator is an entity that collects and analyzes information from different data sources. Aggregation defines a new landscape in information retrieval for goods and services on the Internet. Aggregators provide access to comparisons of information and pricing that have not been possible in the past. In addition, after-aggregation information provides tremendous market intelligence whose value has yet to be realized.

Different data providers use different ways to structure their data, they use different identifiers to reference the same entities, there is acronym collision between the data sets. Even data is present in different formats namely file formats, XML schemas and relational models. RDF comes out as a better solution to overcome these problems. Fig 5 shows an example where prospect id and prospect code are alias names and refer to the same thing. RDF data format makes it easier to store the alias names and retrieves the data from both the processes if the query is "Get all details of prospect with prospect id: 10".

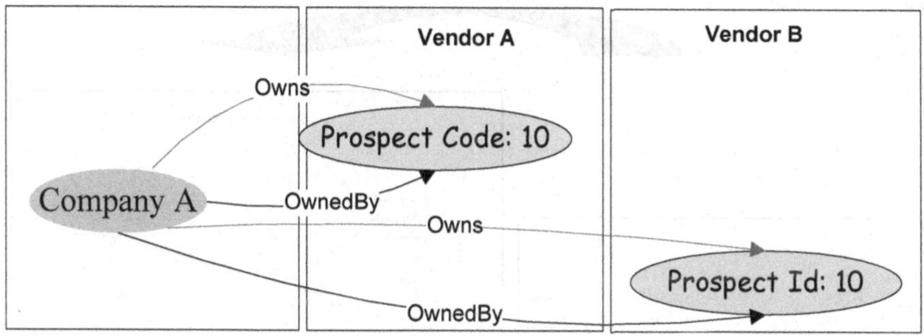

Fig. 5. Prospect Id alias Prospect Code

Content Aggregation

Content aggregation is done thorough Web 0ntology Language (OWL). Owl is for processing and interpreting the content on the Web.

Enterprise Search

The increase of both published and internal information presents a challenge in enterprises. Traditional search-based methods are unable to find relevant information in the required time scales.

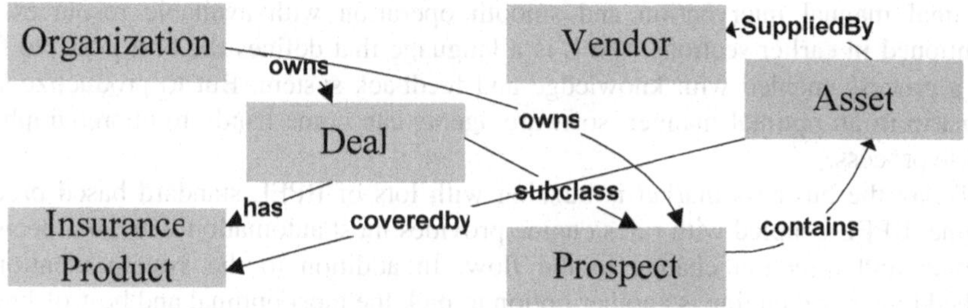

Fig. 6. Graph representation of RDF

As every relation in RDF is binary search becomes easier. Data is RDF is stored as directed graphs.

Managing Grid Resources

RDF refers to Resources, identified by URLs. This means that information about a single resource can come from many sources. Hence, having distributed data is easier in RDF format.

Mapping of ER diagram to RD

Most of the enterprises store data in relational model databases. It is not possible to model the data in RDF format from scratch, hence need for conversion of relational model databases into RDF formats arises. Fig. 9 shows one such conversion taking a part of ER diagram from leasing business using the method proposed in paper [13].

v v

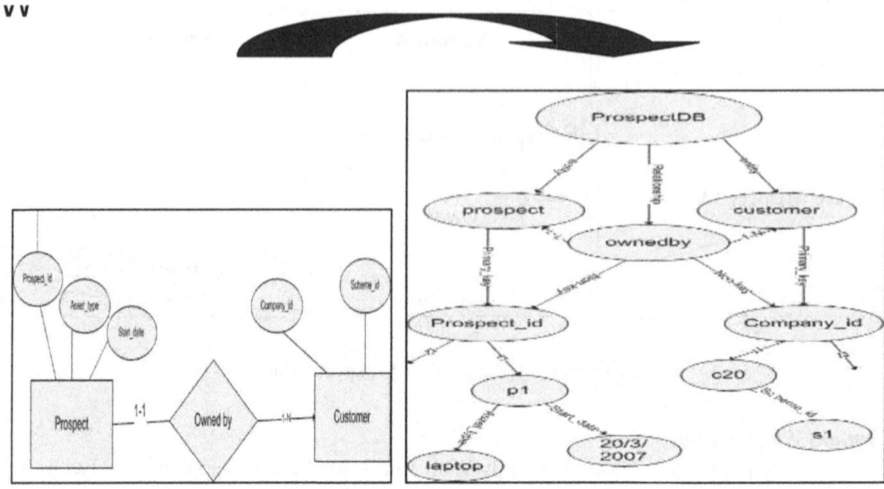

Fig. 9. An RDF equivalent of an ER diagram

5.4 Process Perspective

Once data or information has been streamlined to be understood by machine and across systems, now comes the part of automating the process to execute without any minimal manual intervention and smooth operation with available resources. As mentioned in earlier sections, OWL is a language that defines the best possible flow for a process enabled with knowledge and feedback system. But to productize such scenario in an optimal manner, software agents can come handy to choreograph the whole process.

Today the business market is buzzing with lots of BPEL standard based process engine. BPEL coupled with rules engine provides most automation with auto decision making and direction change in the flow. In addition to the system mentioned, embedding a grid engine is another option to pick the most optimal and best-of-breeds service.

Most of the other integration platform supports Service Component Architecture, which by and large, emulates the choreography strategy of process flow. This solution does not depend on one centralized component or a conductor to decide the route of a process but mediates through the services by intelligence and knowledge derived or calculated during the course of a process execution.

5.5 Positive Thought

The semantic EI approach includes semantic auto-discovery and mapping of legacy IT artifacts and documentation. This gives visibility and eliminates cost of as-is modeling, compliance auditing, and maintenance projects. Semantic discovery applied to IT artifacts gives the capability to scan source libraries, data schemas, and documentation, comments, etc. in order to identify unique artifacts, link and map dependencies, and do latent semantic indexing of the "as-is" world. The result is a repository of metadata (RDF/OWL), a very flat ontology that enables semantic (concept) search using business terms, without having to know the (often cryptic) as-built naming established by programmers. This could be thought of as a sort of "Google for IT" process that works bottom up, and also allows mapping linkages to enterprise architectures, or other governing models.

6 Assisting Technologies

6.1 Data Level

We have used RDF for data modeling and OWL for creation of ontologies. SPARQL is used as query language. Many publicly available editors are present for ontology creation and data modeling like

- **Protégé:** free open source editor and knowledge base framework.
- **Webnoto:** a tool providing Web-based visualization, browsing and editing support for developing and maintaining ontologies and knowledge models specified in OCML (an operational knowledge modeling language).
- **OilEd:** an ontology editor allowing the user to build ontologies using DAML+OIL. For further details and information about DAML+OIL.

We have used protégé to implement our case study.

6.2 Service Level Languages

We have used OWL-S to implement service level ontologies. We have used OWL-S plugin in protégé editor to model the ontologies. BPEL4WS has been used for service orchestration. Structurally, a BPEL4WS file describes a workflow by stating whom the participants are, what services they must implement in order to belong to the workflow, and what are the various orders in which the events must occur. The BPEL4WS process model is built on top of the WSDL 1.1 service model and assumes all primitive actions are described as WSDL port Types. That is, a BPEL4WS description describes the orchestration of a set of messages all of which are described by their WSDL definitions.

7 Future Work

We plan to use agent-based workflow management for service orchestration. The emergence of Web services and semantic Web facilitate the modeling of agent based system. In effect agent-based technologies provide the mechanism for components to seek work, enter into cooperative agreements and thus otherwise address the requirements of dynamic, heterogeneous environments.

8 Conclusions: Removal of Human Agents

The vision of Semantic Web has been to enable computer software to locate for us, relevant resources on the Web and also extract, integrate and index the information contained in the resources. Basically, make computers work on our behalf that is removing the human agents. In this paper, we have partially shown how information integration can be done in an enterprise using Semantic Web Services. We have used publicly available protégé tool to model the ontologies and store data in RDF Schema and OWL format. OWL-S is used for service aggregation and SPARQL is used for querying the data. We would like to extend our work by using agents for service aggregation and negotiation.

References

[1] Sheth, A., Larson, J.: Federated database systems for managing distributed, heterogeneous and autonomous databases. ACM Computing Surveys 22(3), 183–236 (1990)

[2] Jakobovits, R.: Integrating Autonomous Heterogeneous Information Sources (1997)

[3] Raman, V., Narang, I., Crone, C., Haas, L., Malaika, S., Mukai, T., Wolfson, D., Baru, C.: Data Access and Management Services on Grid (2002)

[4] Franconi, E.: Introduction to Data Warehousing

[5] Newcomer, E., Lomow, G.: Understanding SOA with Web Services, Addison Wesley, Reading (2004)

[6] Papazoglou, M.P.: Service-oriented computing: concepts, characteristics and directions. In: Proceedings of the Fourth International Conference on Web Information Systems Engineering, pp. 3–12 (December 2003)

[7] Birman, K.: Can Web Services Scale Up? IEEE computer (October 2005)

[8] Wang, H., Huang, J.Z., Qu, Y., Xie, J.: Web Services: problem and future directions. Journal of Web Semantics 1(3), 309–320 (2004)

[9] Uschold, M., Gruninger, M.: Ontologies: Principles, methods and applications. Knowledge Engineering Review 11(2), 93–115 (1996)

[10] Stuckenschmidt, H., van Harmelen, F.: Information Sharing on the Semantic Web. In: Advanced Information and Knowledge Processing, Springer, Heidelberg (2005)

[11] Laliwala, Z., Sorathia, V., Chaudhary, S.: Semantic and Rule Based Event-driven Services-Oriented Agricultural Recommendation System. In: ICDCSW'06. Proceedings of the 26th IEEE International Conference on Distributed Computing Systems Workshops, IEEE Computer Society Press, Los Alamitos (2006)

[12] Kabbaj, M.Y.: Strategy and Policy Prospects for Semantic Web Services Adoption in US online travel industry. MS thesis Submitted to Masters of Science in technology and policy at MIT

[13] Krishna, M.: Retaining Semantics in Relational Databases by Mapping them to RDF. In: IEEE/WIC/ACM (2006)

[14] Davis, M.: Semantic Wave: Executive guide to billion dollors

Policy Based Messaging Framework

Martin Eggenberger[1,2], Nupur Prakash[2], Koji Matsumoto[2], and Darrell Thurmond[3]

[1] SpinergyGroup, Piedmont, CA, USA
[2] Delta Dental of California, San Francisco, CA, USA
[3] KoolKode Technologies, LLC, Santa Monica, CA, USA

martin@spinergygroup.com, nprakash@delta.org, kmatsumoto@delta.org, koolkode@architect-alchemist.com

Abstract. Due to integration complexities to legacy as well as new systems, a Common Messaging Framework has been developed that is based on policies to control the behavior of the various enterprise services. These policies include both internal and external Quality of Service Policies as well as constraint based business process policies. This paper proposes and identifies a policy based messaging framework for both intranet and extranet services, upon which individual policies can be injected during runtime for individual messages, domains and or processes. Further more these policies can be customized on a per actor basis and dynamically changed during runtime by a console user without having to stop the process.

Keywords: Service Oriented Architecture, QoS, Policy, Dependency Injection, Adaptive Services, Ontologies, Queuing.

1 Introduction

Although there has been considerable attention been devoted in both industry and academia to the design and implementation of new services, little headway has been made to enable legacy systems to truly take advantage of a Service Oriented Architecture. Specifically, non–functional requirements within the Quality of Service (QoS) arena need to be further researched. In essence we found three problems associated with legacy integration using SOA.

First off, most legacy integrations are built using Point to Point integration solutions. Most large scale organizations use batch processes and batch transfers to exchange data between various point solutions and the primary communication channel is file based. Since the individual records in these files do not contain QoS policies and the rewriting of the code is not feasible, no policy enforcement is feasible.

Secondly, the error handling of legacy applications and processes are using different solutions such as log files, databases and simple process return codes. Since these applications were built over the last 20 years, we are faced with various problems in the application logging/monitoring and auditing policies. Specifically, the auditing policies have changed over the years; and therefore, we

B. Krämer, K.-J. Lin, and P. Narasimhan (Eds.): ICSOC 2007, LNCS 4749, pp. 497–505, 2007.

require an adaptive policy system to adjust to the changing regulatory requirements.

And lastly, the process orchestration used is mostly based on scheduling technology [1,2]; and therefore, only temporal properties are used for process orchestration. The nature of this orchestration limits the introduction of QoS policies, hence a new event driven processing mechanism was explored that enable policies for legacy and new systems.

To address these problems, we have developed a policy based messaging framework that support QoS policies. Our approach is based on a comprehensive messaging model for description, discovery, policy injection and policy enactment that are suited for a Service Oriented Architecture [3]. The messaging model defines a semantic model of the messages' purpose as well as the policy associated within the semantic model. To that end, a message consists of a set of processing instructions related to the domain and process it is used in, as well as a set of policies that are related to the domain, the process or the message itself. Further more we described the relationship between the caller's context (e.g. security context) and the associated policies. For example, a system user may define an Auditing Policy based on a specific computing domain such as Claim Processing. In the above example, the system user requesting such a service would specify what elements within the message have to be auditable.

Given such a description framework, we also required a message discovery framework [4,5] that allows us to apply and inject domain and process information into the individual message. To that end, we developed and implemented a domain and process ontology, that is used as the basis for domain and process discovery purposes. Having obtained the messages' domain and process, the policy set can be injected given the callers credentials.

Since all user and system credentials are stored in an enterprise directory, the individual policies can also be stored in the same directory as part of the user profile. Therefore, if a user authenticates him/herself we can cache the policy set associated with the user and apply case - based reasoning for injecting policies based on the message, process or domain. In general this injection occurs using a set of policy rules (e.g. business rules) that specify the injection behavior of the policies.

Once, all policies have been injected we need to worry about the enactment [5] of the specified policies as well as the monitoring of these policies.

2 Messaging Framework

The messaging framework is a conceptual model that describes messages within the enterprise. It not only allows us to model message payloads, but also message related processing information such as domain, process and policy information. This relationship between the individual messages' domain and process has an advantage over other frameworks [6,7,8] insofar that it allows policy granularity not only on the message, but also on the domain and process level. For example, when dealing with healthcare information during Claims Processing, all data access has to be auditable; and therefore an Audit Policy on the domain will be sufficient to control the auditing behavior. To that end any message received during processing that is correlated to the Claims domain will have the policy propagated to each message. The relationship between a message, process, domain and policy is shown in Fig.1. A message must belong to a domain and a process at all times. Further more a process must belong to at least one domain and vice versa. All three primary objects may depend on one or more policies that can be message, domain or process centric.

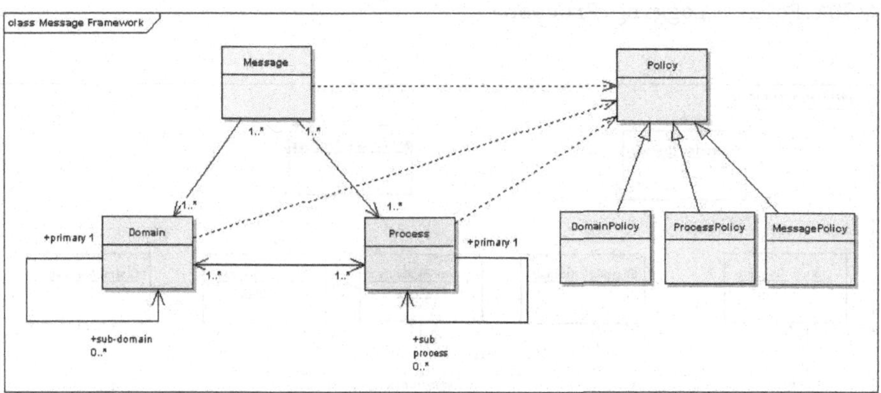

Fig. 1. Simplified Message Framework Model

2.1 Policy Definition Model

The policy definition model can be defined as a set of individual policies that define non-functional processing aspects related to the message itself. Before delving further into the definition model it is necessary to clearly define the difference between a policy and a rule. From our perspective a policy is an atomic enforceable constraint on a system [9] whereas a rule is a conceptualization of a business need. This distinction is necessary to both understand and use this framework. To that end, rules [10,11] maybe used to implement and enforce policies similar to assertions being used in application programming. Fig. 2 shows a simplified Domain and Process Ontology and the relationship between the three different kinds of policies. The domain may subscribe to a domain policy and subsequently all messages related to that domain will use policy propagation from the domain. Similarly, a process may subscribe to a specific process policy, and finally a message itself can subscribe to specific message policy. Below are two examples of defining policies; the first one defines an Auditing policy on the claims domain that specifies to audit every interaction, the second one defines a logging policy on the Adjudicate Claim Process that specifies that a log must be written on every message participating in the process.

```
<SOA.Policy.Audit.Domain Audit.Event="All">
     <SOA.Common.Domain
          Common.Domain.ID="1"
          Common.Domain.Type="Claim"/>
</SOA.Policy.Audit.Domain>
<SOA.Policy.Logging.Process Logging.Level="Debug">
     <SOA.Common.Process
          Common.Process.ID="1"
          Common.Process.Type="AdjudicateClaim"/>
</SOA.Policy.Logging.Process>
```

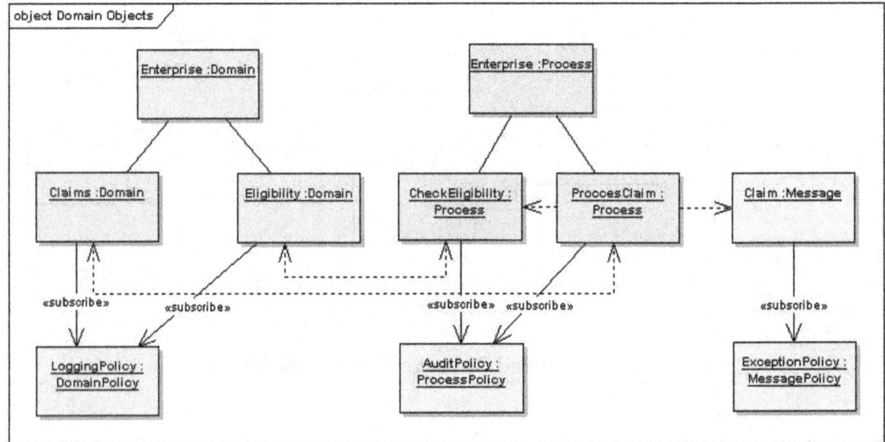

Fig. 2. Domain, Process Ontology with Policy Relationships

2.2 Policy Injection Model

Having defined the overall message model and their relationship with individual policies we now need understand how policies are injected. To that end we developed several policy injection scenarios: Static Injection and Dynamic Injection. Static Injection allows the provider of the message to programmatically specify the policies on the message itself. This approach requires a set of services to access the policy store for domain, process and policies. Dynamic injection on the other hand is based on the domain and process ontology that allows case-based reasoning on the message content and its relationship with the domain or process.

2.3 Policy Processing Model

The policy processing model is based on the translation of the policy definition language into a policy execution language as well as the execution of each policy. The policy execution language essentially invokes a service either synchronously or asynchronously to validate or enrich the message itself. For example, a logging policy may specify that a message is logged whenever it is being passed between business processes; and therefore, it will be executed asynchronously. A data field encryption policy on the other hand, will enrich the message by encrypting a data filed upon sending and decrypting upon receiving.

3 Message Model Formalization

In order to define and process policies we require a more formalized approach. In this section, we provide a brief introduction to the formalisms used in this research. This framework consists of a mathematical description to specify policies, domains, processes and messages. Further more we describe the mathematical relationship between the individual sets and provide a mathematical induction proof to validate the model.

Definition 1. *(Execution Definition). A message is used within a service S to perform an atomic operation. To that end we define a function f:M'M that takes as input an element of the Message Set M and returns a different element of the Message Set M.*

Definition 2. *(Message Definition). A single message is defined as a four- tuple that contains a payload subset P', a domain subset D', a process subset X' and a constraint subset C'. Therefore a single message is defined as follows.*

$$m_i = \{P', D', X', C'\} \quad i > 0; i \in N' \subset N \tag{1}$$

Given this definition we can define the space of all messages M that are permutations of all individual instances of the above definition. Since the number of permutations does not span a proper vector space we will prove that there exists a subset M' M that represent a valid vector space.

Definition 3. *(Payload Definition).The payload is defined as the data element to be processed within the message. We define the payload as follows:*

$$P' \subseteq P \cup \emptyset \tag{2}$$

Definition 4. *(Domain Definition). The domain is defined as the processing domain the payload is associated. We define the domain as follows:*

$$D' \subseteq D \cup \emptyset \tag{3}$$

Definition 5. *(Process Definition). The process is defined as the process (activity) the payload is associated. We define the process as follows:*

$$X' \subseteq X \cup \emptyset \tag{4}$$

Definition 6. *(Policy Definition). The policy is defined as the policy (constraint) associated with the payload.*

$$C' \subseteq C \cup \emptyset \tag{5}$$

Proposition 1. *(Policy Injection Rule). All policies are derived/defined from a domain, process, or the payload itself; and therefore we can define a function G, that maps a message M to a policy C.*

$$G : M \to C \tag{6}$$

We need to remember that the domain, process and payload are part of each message; and therefore, for each domain d_i there exists at least one constraint c_i ($\forall d_i \in D \to \{ \exists c_i \subseteq C' \}$). Similarly for each process x_i there exist a constraint (policy) c_i ($\forall x_i \in X \to \{\exists c_i \subseteq C'\}$). And finally for all messages m_i there exist a constraint (policy) c_i ($\forall m_i \in M \to \{\exists c_i \subseteq C'\}$).

Proposition 2. *(Policy Execution Rule). Since all policies are based on a message, we can define a function that H that maps the policy C back to a Message M. This is essentially an inverse function of G.*

$$H : C \to M \tag{7}$$

Theorem 1. *(Completeness of Execution). Let m_i be a message hat defines policies from n=0 .. m, we can proof by induction that the reverse function will exist on the subset M' of all messages.*
If no policies have been defined within a message m_i (n=0), the message will remain unchanged after injecting and executing the policy.

$$m_i = H(G(m_i)) \tag{8}$$

If a single policy n=1 is injected into the message m_i, the outcome of injection and executing the rule results in a message m_j that is part of the message set M' that will have no policies defined (n=0).

$$m_j = H(G(m_i)) \tag{9}$$

Since we defined the policy to be executable and computable on the message, we have proven by induction that the reverse function exists for all messages that have a computable policy set.

4 Architecture

The overall architecture we have chosen is based on highly scalable enterprise service bus (ESB) that acts as the intermediary for messaging [12,13]. The service bus provides asynchronous processing queues for primary business processes and domain activities that are implemented using BPEL [10]. In addition to these orchestrated services a set of utility services for data retrieval and cross-cutting concerns are registered on the bus. Using an enrichment pattern on the message bus, allows the individual messages to be extended and the policy and domain information to be added, and subsequently transformed into BPEL for the policies to be executed. Fig. 3 depicts the conceptual architecture of the solution.

The core of the system is the Message Bus and the Policy control framework responsible for policy injection, policy definition and policy execution. The Policy Control framework uses a policy store to retrieve policies given the context of the message (domain and process). Additionally, the diagram also shows the primary business process, Claim Processing, and the individual domain activities, Data Receiving, Data Pre – Processing, Data Validation and Data Adjudication.

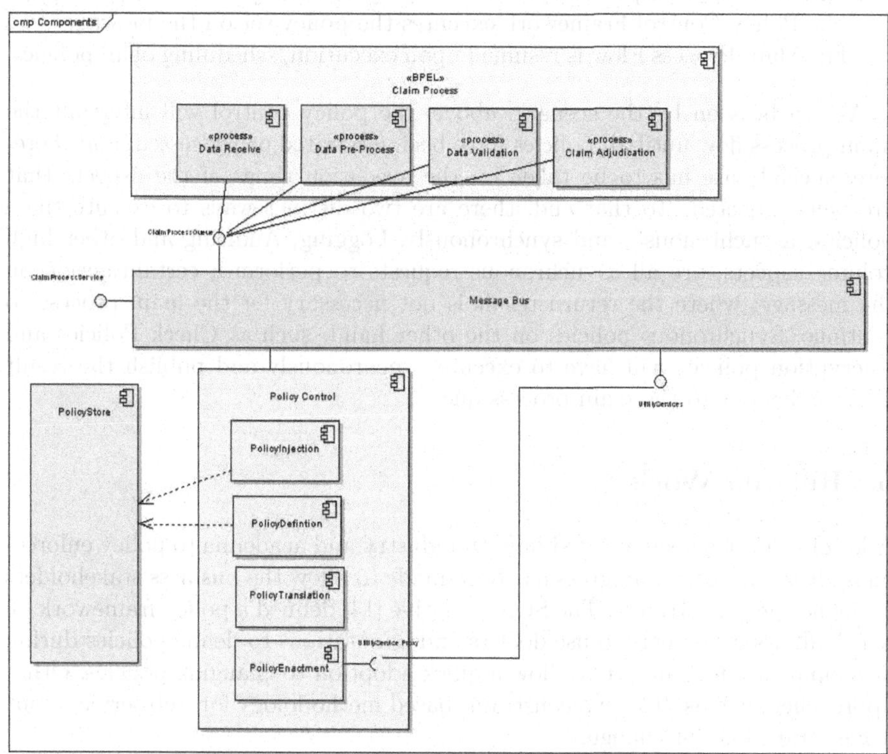

Fig. 3. Conceptual Architecture used by the messaging framework

Since each individual activity is a collaboration of data services that are based on our message model we can use a pipeline execution model to inject, transform and execute the policies using an interrupt pattern on the activity process flow.

4.1 Message Processing

Given that we use an enterprise service bus, the policy control framework will inspect the message while executing the business process orchestration. To that end the policy control framework will subscribe to the policy service queue that is invoked by the BPEL process. At that point the message is inspected, the domain, process and policy information injected. Once the message is complete the policies will be transformed into executable code and subsequently called based on the context. Once the policy enactment stage is complete, control is returned to the calling context. In other words, the pipeline execution model is guided by the policy control model. The typical flow of a message, once it is put onto a process or domain queue involves the following steps:

- The Message is published onto the primary/main flow queue.
- The Message is inspected synchronously by the policy control framework.
- The Policy Control Framework executes the policy set on the message.
- The Main Process Flow is resumed upon execution/scheduling of all policies.

As can be seen by the scenario above, the policy control will interrupt the main process flow until all policies have been evaluated or processed; and therefore, special care has to be taken on the execution times of the aspects that are being injected. To that end, there are two distinct ways to execute these policies: asynchronously and synchronously. Logging, Auditing and other high volume aspects, are all asynchronous requests to perform a certain action on the message, where the return result is not necessary for the main process to continue. Synchronous policies on the other hand, such as Check Policies and Encryption policies will have to execute synchronously and publish the result message back onto the main process queue.

5 Related Work

A lot of work has been devoted in both industry and academia to policy enforcement, little industrial progress has been made to allow the business stakeholders to define such constraints. The SCA initiative [14] defined a policy framework [8] which allows developers to use doclets and annotations to define policies during development which does not allow a quick adoption to changing policies. Other approaches such as [9], use a constraint based methodology for web services, but leave little room for change.

6 Conclusion and Future Work

Policy definition and policy enactment is an important issue in any successful implementation of a Service Oriented Architecture. In this paper we described an approach that allows various stakeholders in the ecosystem to define policies that will be executed during the execution of a business process or activity. Further more, we showed that policies can be defined coarse grained for optimal usability. Because our approach is unique insofar as the definition and execution of policies is concerned we provide adaptability to changing requirements and let the business and operational stakeholders constrain the business processes. In doing so we reduce the total cost of ownership as no further development effort is necessary, unless new processes have to be built. Our model could easily be extended to include the governance of any processes as it represents a way to constrain processes with policies, although our focus was based on an adaptable messaging model.

This work is at an early stage, and much more has to be done. The policy definition language, as well as the policy translation and execution language must be refined and evaluated. The performance of the policy control framework has to be considered and tuned as there are many times the injection and enactment algorithm has to be executed.

References

1. Brucker, P.: Scheduling algorithms. Springer, Berlin (2001)
2. Zhao, J.L., Stohr, E.A.: Temporal workflow management in a claim handling system. In: ACM SIGSOFT Software Engineering Notes, Proceedings of the international joint conference on Work activities coordination and collaboration WACC '99 (March 1999)
3. Fremantle, P., Weerawarana, S., Khalaf, R.: Enterprise Services, Examining the emerging field of Web Services and how it is integrated into existing enterprise infrastructures. Communication of the ACM 45(2) (October 2002)
4. Hoschek, W.: The Web Service Discovery Architecture. In: Proceedings of the 2002 ACM/IEEE conference on Supercomputing, Baltimore, Maryland, November 16, 2002, pp. 1–15 (2002)
5. Kozlenkov, A., Fasoulas, V., Sanchez, F., Spanoudakis, G., Zisman, A.: Service discovery and binding: A framework for architecture-driven service discovery. In: SOSE '06. Proceedings of the 2006 international workshop on Service-oriented software engineering
6. Anderson, A.: An Introduction to the Web Services Policy Language. In: POLICY'04. Fifth IEEE International Workshop on Policies for Distributed Systems and Networks, IEEE Computer Society Press, Los Alamitos (2004)
7. Web Services Policy Framework (ws-policy). Technical Report, IBM, BEA Systems, Microsoft, SAP AG, Sonic Software, VeriSign (March 2006)
8. Beisiegel, M., Kavantzas, N., Malhorta, A., Pavlik, G., Sharp, C.: SCA Policy Association Framework. In: Dan, A., Lamersdorf, W. (eds.) ICSOC 2006. LNCS, vol. 4294, pp. 613–623. Springer, Heidelberg (2006)
9. Aggarwl, R., Verma, K., Miller, J., Milnorm, W.: Constraint driven web service composition in METEOR-S. In: SCC'04. IEEE Conference on Service Computing, Shangahi China, pp. 23–30. IEEE Computer Society Press, Los Alamitos (2004)
10. Andrews, T., Cubera, F., Dholakia, H., Goland, Y., Klein, J., Leymann, F., Liu, K., Roller, D., Smith, D., Thatte, S., Trickovic, I., Weerawarana, S.: Business process execution language for web services version 1.1. Technical report, OASIS, `http://download.boulder.ibm.com/ibmdl/pub/software/dw/specs/ws-bpel/ws-bpel.pdf`
11. ILog JRules, `http://www.ilog.com/products/jrules`
12. Fowler, M.: Patterns of Enterprise Application Architecture. Addison-Wesley Professional, Reading (2002)
13. Hohpe, G., Woolf, B.: Enterprise Integration Patterns: Designing, Building, and Deploying Messaging Solutions. Addison-Wesley Professional, Reading (2003)
14. Service Component Architecture (SCA) Specifications, `http://www.osoa.org/display/Main/Service+Component+Architecture+Specifications`

Contextualized B2B Registries

U. Radetzki, M.J. Boniface, and M. Surridge

IT Innovation Centre
2 Venture Road
Chilworth
Southampton, SO16 7NP, UK
{ur,mjb,ms}@it-innovation.soton.ac.uk

Abstract. Service discovery is a fundamental concept underpinning the move towards dynamic service-oriented business partnerships. The business process for integrating service discovery and underlying registry technologies into business relationships, procurement and project management functions has not been examined and hence existing Web Service registries lack capabilities required by business today. In this paper we present a novel contextualized B2B registry that supports dynamic registration and discovery of resources within management contexts to ensure that the search space is constrained to the scope of authorized and legitimate resources only. We describe how the registry has been deployed in three case studies from important economic sectors (aerospace, automotive, pharmaceutical) showing how contextualized discovery can support distributed product development processes.

Keywords: Registry, discovery, B2B, SOA, SLA.

1 Introduction

Service discovery is a fundamental concept underpinning the move towards dynamic service-oriented business partnerships. Existing Web Service registries lack the possibility to register and discover resources in the context of dynamic business relationships. Business to Business (B2B) collaboration demands not only discovery of application resources based on available metadata, but also discovery of these resources in the context of agreed contracts, like Service Level Agreements (SLAs).

In this paper we present a novel contextualized B2B registry that supports users in querying resources based on management contexts like SLAs or trade accounts. The registry enables clients to ask queries like "Find SLAs providing MSC.NASTRAN applications where the CPU seconds of SLA is greater than 1000 and the Usage of SLA with respect to the used disk space is lower than 500MB". The registry is able to cope with any business context, resource and metadata as far as they can be represented in XML and identified by a WS-Addressing Endpoint Reference (EPR) [15]. It supports the dynamical adding of new business contexts and new relationships between these contexts. This information is defined in the registry domain model (RDM) of the contextualized B2B registry. The registry is provided as part of an overall service-oriented infrastructure (SOI) and has been deployed in case studies within key industrial sectors such as aerospace, automotive and pharmaceutical.

B. Krämer, K.-J. Lin, and P. Narasimhan (Eds.): ICSOC 2007, LNCS 4749, pp. 506–517, 2007.

2 Contextualized B2B Registries

An analysis of the business model for registration and discovery of software services unveils that the discovery process has different phases and actors that participate in establishing trusted business relationships, providing SLA offerings and procuring SLAs as well as demanding concrete resources. We have identified four different types of registries supporting each phase providing capabilities to constrain the search space based on the actor's context and business context within the discovery process.

2.1 Registries in B2B Collaborations

Service registration and discovery is an essential capability of service-oriented architectures (SOA). Service discovery ensures loose coupling between customers and service providers by allowing many service providers to publish service descriptions in a registry independently of customers, yet allowing the customers to connect directly to their selected service at the point of use. Registries can contain multiple services ensuring scalability and resilience is provided through redundancy of service provision to the customer. The principles of service discovery can be described in three stages 1) service providers publishing service descriptions 2) customers discovery available services based on some criteria 3) customers binding to discovered services at the point of use.

There are many service discovery initiatives ranging from high-level business registries [14, 3] through to low-level soft state registries [18] for dynamic resource information. UDDI, although part of the WS-I Basic Profile [17], has never been an appropriate registry for Web Service metadata due to its awkward TModel information structure. ebXML provides a better information model, however, the ebXML activity is not widely supported by all major middleware vendors. WSRF-SG supports the aggregation of arbitrary XML metadata but the relationship between XML documents is not supported and security is not considered. Recent initiatives [16] are looking more promising and the initial scope of WS-ResourceCatalog addresses taxonomies of resources but the specifications are evolving and no compliant registry service exists today. Other approaches combine matchmaking and information retrieval (IR) techniques. Service information based on WSDL is analyzed and service profiles are extracted which are matched against user requirements [12]. These profiles can contain, beside syntactic information, context information about location of services etc. allowing to retrieve services based on user contexts, like user location [8]. Recent research highlighted also that context information of services can change over time [2]. The context models, however, of these approaches are static and the IR approaches do not allow to search for business contexts, like SLAs, but only for ranked list of services. Nevertheless adding a fuzzy approach into contextualized discovery is quite promising.

The challenge for current registry developments is to understand the overall business model for registration and discovery in a market-based SOI. Many SOI users today imagine that an engineer, working for an aerospace company for instance, can search a registry to find and use services based their requirements. For example, find service provider that can provision an Aero-Acoustics service based on a 10 node cluster running against dataset A, B and C. However, the decision to trust and potentially pay for a service is not typically the responsibility of the engineer but rather a project or senior manager within their organization. The engineer may be able to find a service, but they may not be authorized to use it within their design activity because the service provider may not be trusted or maybe there is insufficient project budget available. Therefore, for the SOI to support dynamic service composition, discovery needs to include the actor's context and the business context to constrain the scope of the search space to authorized and legitimized services only.

Most customers and service providers assume that a SOI provides a central registry to support service discovery, however, the business model for operating such a registry has yet to be proved viable. On the web today, discovery businesses such as Google and Yahoo operate successfully providing discovery services to customers with a variety of business models such as advertising (Click-through Text-Ads, Banner Ads) and brokering (market-makers bringing buyers and sellers together and facilitate transactions). Therefore, for the SOI to facilitate market-based service provision business models need to be developed for central registry operators.

Market-based SOI extends the registration and discovery process to include interactions with key actors and incorporates business models for participating organizations. Fig. 1 illustrates actors and business contexts in the life cycle of B2B collaborations. This life cycle starts with the advertisement of business services by marketing managers. The business service presents information about the business area, company details, contact persons etc in its corresponding metadata, i.e. business metadata, service provider details, relationship details etc. This information is used as a starting point to establish trust between service providers (SPs) and service

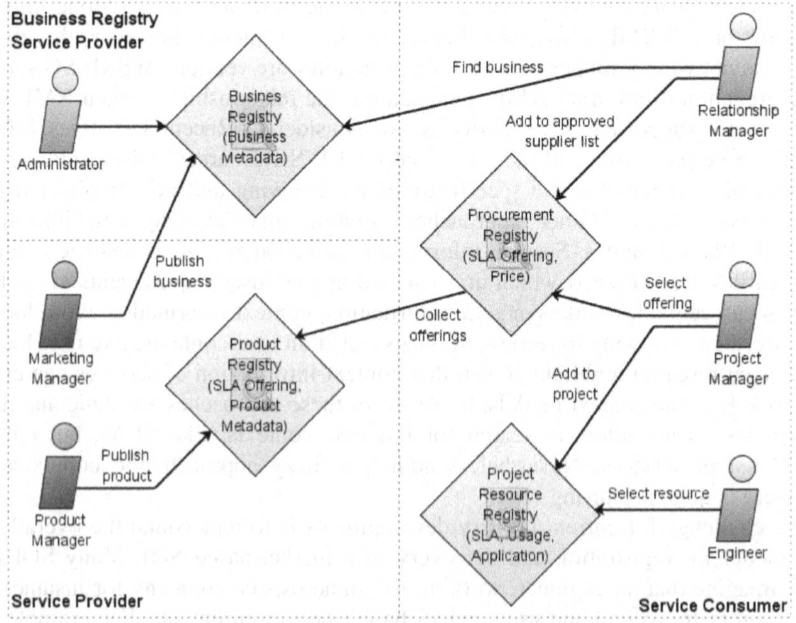

Fig. 1. Registration and discovery in B2B collaborations

consumers (customers). A business registry provided by a third party business registry service provider acts like an open market place similar to Yellow Pages.

Customer procurement experts, e.g. relationship managers, discover SPs based on business advertisements. They decide which SP to trust and manage these relationships in approved supplier lists (e.g. ISO9000 accredited businesses) stored in a procurement registry. After establishing trust, e.g. based on trade accounts and granted credit limits, the procurement registry collects SLA offerings from approved SPs' product registries, which are maintained by SPs product managers. It can also collect resource metadata used within the SLA offering. We assume that contracts between business partners are based on bi-lateral SLAs agreed between the customer and SP.

The procurement registry is used by project managers to identify resources and purchases resources through SLAs within the context of an organizations approved supplier list. Resources can be entire resource bundles containing other resources or they can be specific resources, like applications or databases (there might be other resources like laboratory equipment). Every resource is specified by resource metadata, containing details of the resource, like EPR, names, arguments, semantics etc. Project resources are registered by a project management within the project resource registry. Finally project users, like engineers, can discover and use resources within the context of a specific project, to which they have access to. This registry can also pull other information, like usage report spend on specific SLAs that can be augmented with other metadata stored in the project resource registry.

This life cycle demonstrates that registries in B2B collaborations require storing resources and relating them to different contexts as well as they have to support different user roles. In the following we will focus on these contextual aspects of B2B registries.

2.2 Registry Domain Model

We assume that contextualized B2B registries provide a registry domain model (RDM) that defines the different business contexts used within the registry, like

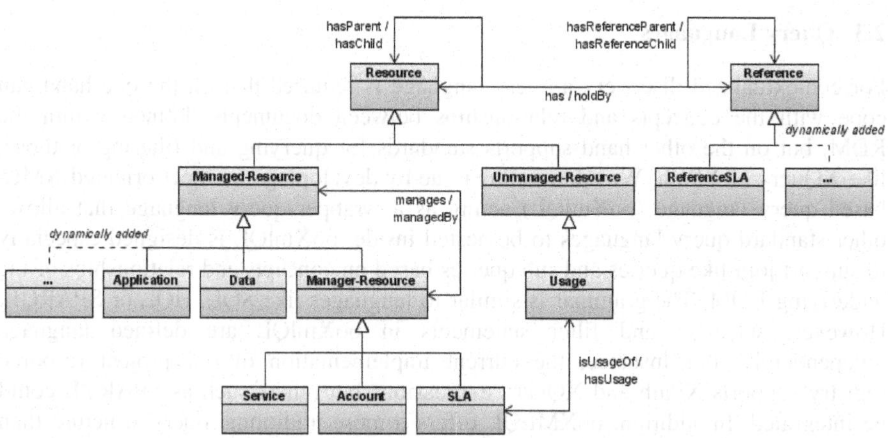

Fig. 2. Example RDM for a project resource registry

SLAs, projects, trade accounts etc. Business contexts are defined in terms of business concepts and relationships between these concepts. Objects (in general XML documents) are registered and can be retrieved with respect to these concepts and relationships. Relationships define dependencies between concepts that can be used for specifying 'join'-like queries. They allow users to navigate through the RDM in an object-oriented way. A special 'is-a' relationship is introduced for specifying hierarchies of concepts. Sub concepts inherit relationships from their super concepts. However, there is no assumption about the XML documents registered under a specific concept. Therefore schemas of objects of sub concepts belonging to the same super concept could be different. Even though this is possible, the situation should be avoided, or appropriate schema matching approaches have to be applied, but this topic is beyond the scope of this paper.

Fig. 2 depicts an example RDM we are using for a project resource registry (see Section 3.2). There are two top level concepts: 'Resource' and 'Reference'. Under the concept 'Reference' EPRs of resources are registered. Depending on the type of EPR new concepts as sub types of 'Reference' are dynamically added to the RDM, for instance a concept 'ReferenceSLA' for EPRs belonging to the SLA resources.

The concept 'Resource' is used to register data and metadata of resources, like WSDL documents, application metadata, SLAs, trade accounts etc. We divide resources into managed resources like applications or services and unmanaged resources like usage reports. Some resources like SLAs or trade accounts are used to manage other resources, like job or data services. These resources are specified by the concept 'Manager-Resource'. Relationships are represented in Fig. 2 as arrows between concepts. For instance the bidirectional relationship 'isUsageOf / hasUsage' combines usages reports with SLAs they belong to.

We suggest using the Web Ontology Language (OWL) [11] as a language for modeling of RDMs. However, OWL Lite already provides the mechanisms we require for such specifications. Concepts are specified using 'owl:Class', sub concepts are specified using 'rdfs:subClassOf' etc.; relationships are defined by 'owl:ObjectProperty', bidirectional relationships through 'owl:inverseOf' etc.

2.3 Query Languages

For contextualized discovery a query language is required that on the one hand can cope with the concepts and relationships between documents defined within the RDM, but on the other hand supports standards for querying and filtering of those, like XQuery or XPath. We address this issue by developing an object-oriented XML-based query language (ooXmlQL) acting as a wrapper query language that allows other standard query languages to be nested inside. ooXmlQL is designed especially to support join-like queries and sub queries based on concepts and relationships of the underlying RDM. The grammar is similar to languages like SQL, HQL or SPARQL. However, selection and filter statements in ooXmlQL are defined language independently. For instance, the current implementation of our project resource registry supports XPath and XQuery expressions but others such as SPARQL could be integrated. In addition, ooXMLQL offers a more traditional query structure than the programmatic style provided by XQuery.

```
SELECT $epr
FROM Application AS $app
JOIN ON hasParent OF Service AS $jobService
JOIN ON has OF Reference AS $epr
WHERE fn:contains($app//name, 'BLAST')
RESTRICT $jobService
IN (
  RETURN manages
  FROM Manager-Resource AS $manager
  WHERE $manager//type = 'SLAService'
)
```

Fig. 3. Query primitives of ooXmlQL

The example of Fig. 3 illustrates a query in ooXmlQL. This query expresses "Find EPRs ($epr) of job services that both support 'BLAST' applications and are managed by manager resources having the type SLAService". The keywords of ooXmlQL are represented in bold, upper case letters, like SELECT, FROM, JOIN etc.

Variables within ooXmlQL are sound, if they follow the XQuery specification, e.g. they have to have a leading '$'. From- and join-parts (FROM, JOIN) are expressed using concepts of the RDM. Joins are created using relationships defined within the RDM. A join expression is valid, if the relationship used (ON) is defined between the concept of the previous join- or from-part and the concept within the join (OF). For instance, the relationship hasParent(Application, Service) has to be defined within the RDM, in order to have a valid join 'JOIN ON hasParent OF Service AS $jobService'. This join is valid, because the concepts Service and Application are sub concepts of the concept Resource and hasParent is defined as hasParent(Resource, Resource).

```
DECLARE NAMESPACE addressing: http://www.w3.org/2005/08/addressing
...
DECLARE VARIABLE $max: fn:max( $usage//metric[@type="disc space"]//rate )
...
WHERE $usage//metric[@description="disc space"]//rate = $max
```

Fig. 4. Declaration of variables and namespaces in ooXmlQL

A similar validation strategy is applied on restrictions (RESTRICT). Restrictions specify sub queries on objects of one concept defined by a variable. A restriction on a variable is valid, if the relationship defined in the sub query (RETURN) is defined between the concept used in the from-part of the sub query and the concept the variable belongs to. For instance, the restriction on job services ($jobService) uses the relationship manages. $jobServices defines objects of the concept Service through 'JOIN ON hasParent OF Service AS $jobService'. Therefore, this restriction is valid, if manages(Manager-Resource, Service) is defined within the RDM, which is the case, because Service is a sub concept of Managed-Resource. Selection (SELECT) and filtering (WHERE) of XML resources is based on standard XQuery/XPath expressions following their specifications as shown in Fig. 3.

Further features of ooXmlQL contain the definition of namespaces and variables. Fig. 4 shows a corresponding example. Variable declarations, for instance, allow defining aggregate functions that can be used later on within filtering statements.

3 Inter-enterprise Service-Oriented Infrastructure

The design and development of the registry service has been driven by case studies from three important industrial sectors aerospace, automotive and pharmaceutical, as part of the EU IST SIMDAT Project [13]. Each of these sectors is exploring how dynamic SOIs can be used to integrate software services and expertise provided by external suppliers into product design processes. Typical processes in each of these sectors are represented by complex scientific workflows developed in a variety of sector specific problem solving environments such as [6, 7, 10].

The aerospace case study simulates the multi-disciplinary collaborative design of a low-noise, high-lift aircraft landing system. The prime contractor dynamically builds a distributed design team from service providers offering specialized engineering services such as optimization (University of Southampton), aerodynamics (BAE SYSTEMS), aero-acoustics (EADS) and structures (MSC) that are incorporated into an overall parameterized design optimization workflow. The automotive case study demonstrates how a car manufacturer (Renault) can collaborate with design suppliers (IDEStyle) for the purpose of designing a car that conforms to safety regulations. A trusted-third party service provider hosts an integrated simulation infrastructure that allows the participants to manage and orchestrate the design process whilst protecting the intellectual property rights associated with each component. The pharmaceutical case study focuses on the use of bioinformatics during the target identification phase of the drug discovery pipeline. Workflows developed by scientists at GlaxoSmith-Kline can now access both internal resources and augment these with high-value services procured from biotechnology service providers. For example, Inpharmatica/Galapagos has offered their Bioclips product [1] to provide detailed annotation of protein data supporting similarity searching based on structure, ligand binding sites and annotations.

The case studies show how inter-enterprise capabilities can be procured from service providers and integrated into design processes through SOIs. Contextualized discovery and selection is an essential part of this process from relationship management through to service procurement and use. For example, within the aerospace case study the prime contractor builds a distributed design team by selecting service providers from their approved suppliers list and procuring service through the negotiation of SLAs. The resulting SLAs are added to a project resource registry that is available to engineers who are developing and executing the design optimization workflows.

3.1 GRIA

The registry service forms part of the client management package distributed with the GRIA middleware [5]. GRIA is a SOI designed to support B2B collaborations through service provision across organizational boundaries in a secure, interoperable and flexible manner.

GRIA supports business relationship management through conventional business procurement models. When a consumer wants to buy services from a provider, they first have to open a trade account with the service provider. This trade account represents a trust relationship between a customer and service provider, based on the customer's willingness to pay for services provided. The two sides can constrain the level of trust by specifying a credit limit for each trade account, which represents the maximum amount of service the provider is willing to deliver before being paid, or the maximum amount of service the consumer is willing to pay for, whichever is the smaller.

GRIA allows service providers and customers to trade resources (applications, data, processing, and storage) under the terms of bilateral SLAs. An SLA describes quality of service (QoS) and other commitments by a service provider in exchange for financial commitments by a customer against an agreed schedule of prices and payments. GRIA allows service providers to advertise SLA offerings that are proposed by customers during SLA negotiation. Service providers deploy application services appropriate to their business operation. These services generate usage reports using their own QoS criteria which may be qualitative (e.g. error conditions) or quantitative (e.g. processing time, data transferred). GRIA uses these reports to monitor customer usage and the level of commitments from existing agreements compared with available capacity.

3.2 GRIA's Project Resource Registry

The contextualized project resource registry (PRR) allows project managers to register different kinds of services and business data required in their project. Project members, if they have the appropriate access rights, can use this information later on for discovering required services in the context of business constraints, like CPU

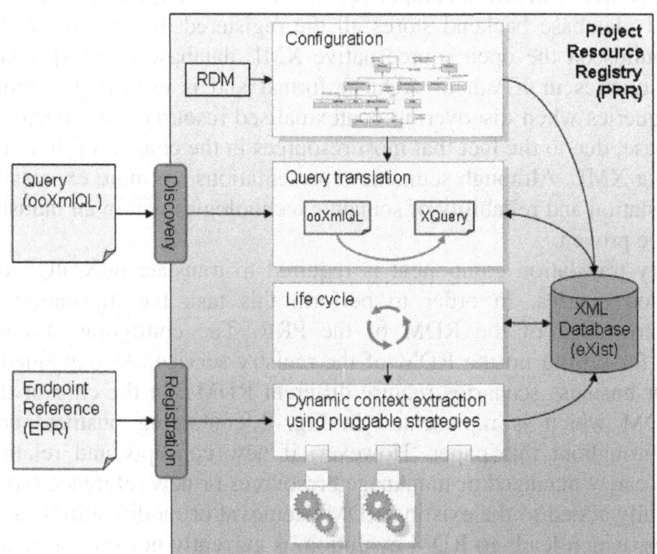

Fig. 5. Project Resource Registry Architecture

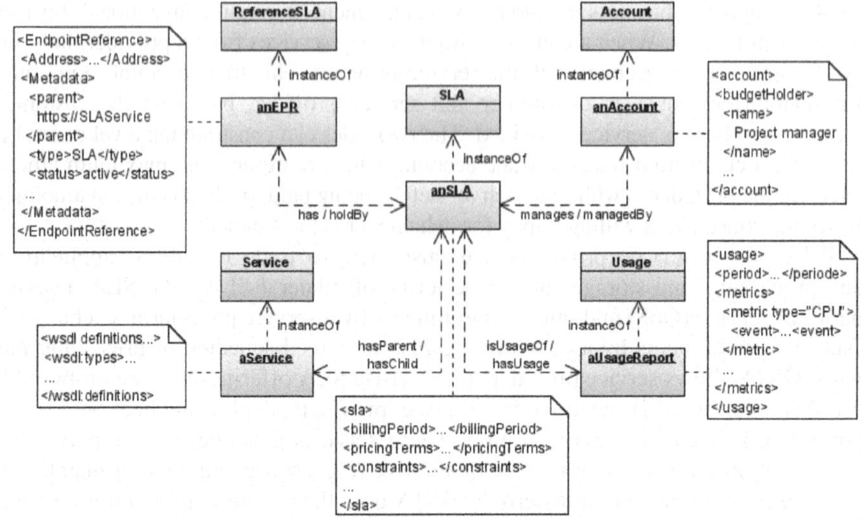

Fig. 6. Registry snapshot after SLA registration

provided by an SLA, usage reports of services, etc. Furthermore, project managers can use the registered information to keep track of signed SLAs, established trust relationships based on approved trade accounts, services provisioned by signed SLAs, etc. Thus, the PRR can act as a basis for business analysis and future business strategies and decisions.

Fig. 5 depicts the software architecture of the PRR which consists out of five major building blocks: configuration component, query translation component, life cycle component, context extraction component and XML database backend.

The XML database backend stores all the registered information as XML document and builds on the open source native XML database eXist[4]. eXist supports performing queries in XPath or XQuery format and is used as the foundation for ooXmlQL queries when discovering contextualised resources. We decided to use an XML database, due to the fact that most resources in the context of SOI are described already using XML. Although semantic representations are more expressive, the cost of data translation and reliability of semantic technologies within an industrial context remains to be proven.

The query translation component is required to translate ooXmlQL queries into XQuery-based queries. In order to perform this task the translation component demands knowledge of the RDM of the PRR. The configuration component is responsible for setting up the RDM of the registry service. As explained in Section 2.1 different business scenarios require different RDMs. In the case of the PRR we use the RDM which is represented in Fig. 2 containing business concepts we described throughout this paper. However, if new concepts and relationships are required, like new managed or unmanaged resources or new reference types, they can be dynamically added to the existing RDM. Removal or modifications of concepts or relationships, which leads to RDM evolution, is currently not supported and topic of future work.

The life cycle component periodically makes updates and pulls data from registered entities. Especially usage record spend on SLAs and information about trade accounts are important to be updated and pulled in order to allow project managers to carry out business analysis and project members to select services which are appropriate for their current task. Further, the status of a resource could change over time as well, for instance if a trade account is closed or a service becomes unavailable. Different policies could be applied to handle these status changes as well as the status information could be used in queries, for instance to select only trade account which are currently open.

The context information of a resource and the relationship to other resources entirely depends on the type of resource a user registered. Therefore, we applied the concept of dynamical selection of pluggable context extraction strategies. The context extraction component is fulfilling the task of selecting an appropriate strategy for a given resource. If a new resource type emerges, a new strategy can easily be discovered and plugged in. However, if no specialized strategy can be found, a default strategy will be automatically applied, which for instance stores the endpoint reference (EPR) of the resource. In future, we also plan to define default strategies for accessing and storing metadata based on standards like MEX[9] or WS-RT[19].

3.3 Registration and Discovery: A Business Use Case

In the following use case scenario we assume a project manager who registers an SLA signed with a trusted SP and afterwards discovers SLAs in a specific business context. The registration process starts with the EPR of the SLA which will be registered using the registration interface of the PRR. In a first step, based on the EPR an appropriate SLA context extraction strategy is selected. This strategy stores the EPR and the actual SLA under the corresponding business concepts as well as it establishes a relationship between these two objects (has/holdBy). Subsequent additional relationships between objects of trade accounts (manages/managedBy), parent services (hasParent/hasChild), and usage reports (isUsageOf/hasUsage) are inserted. The final snapshot of the registered objects and relationships is presented in Fig. 6.

Depending on the kind of policy applied to the PRR it is also possible that a context extraction strategy automatically registers missing objects, if a relationship exists but the target object is missing. For instance, assume the object aService of Fig. 6 is missing, but the relationship hasParent is identified by the SLA context extraction strategy, then the corresponding service could be contacted and the required information requested and inserted into the registry. To be able to register the information about the service another context extraction strategy will be selected. This kind of registration process cascades until all the required objects are registered by the different strategies and the relationships are inserted.

Knowing the RDM the project manager can start formulating queries fulfilling business requirements. One standard request is finding SLAs fulfilling different constraints. For instance the project manager might want to know, which SLAs provide the specific application MSC.NASTRAN but the disc space spend on the SLAs in their usage reports is not higher than 0.0. This might lead to SLAs which are not used in the project at all and trigger an analysis of the circumstances why this kind of SLAs is not used. The corresponding query of this request is illustrated in Fig. 7.

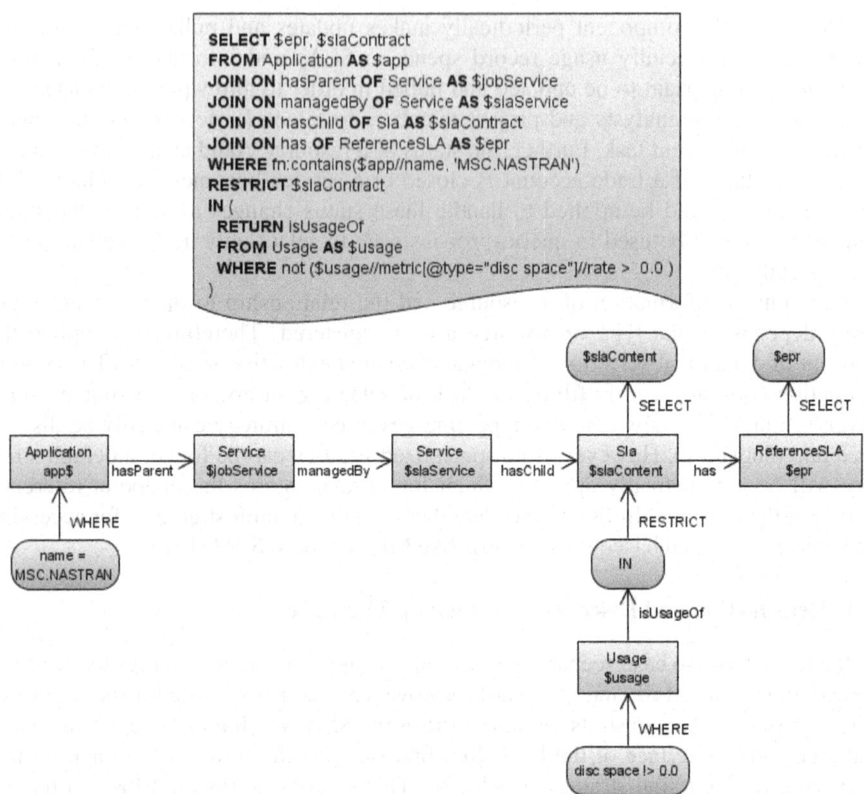

Fig. 7. Example query finding SLAs with specific business constraints

Fig. 7 shows also how joins are used to navigate through the RDM and sub queries are used to restrict these elements. The query starts with application metadata (concept Application) and navigates through different relationships until it reaches the EPR of an SLA (concept ReferenceSLA). The SLA as well as the EPR is returned using SELECT. SLAs and applications are further constraint. The difference between these two is that one use sub queries (RESTRICT) whereas the other use WHERE. WHERE clauses are directly applied to documents which are represented by the corresponding variable. Sub queries restrict documents belonging to a specific variable by restricting other documents that are related to this variable.

4 Conclusion

In this paper we presented a novel contextualized B2B registry that supports dynamic registration and discovery of resources within management context to ensure that the search space is constrained to the scope of authorized and legitimate resources only. This kind of business-related contextualized discovery is a fundamental requirement to move towards dynamic service-oriented business partnerships. The main contribution of our registry is twofold: an OWL-based Registry Domain Model (RDM) supporting the specification of business concepts and relationships and a query language enabling contextualized query resources based on the RDM. We described how the registry has been deployed in three case studies from important economic sectors (aerospace, automotive, pharmaceutical) showing how contextualized discovery can support distributed product development processes.

Acknowledgements

The SIMDAT project has received research funding from the EC's Sixth Framework Programs (project EU IST-2002-511438 STP under the Information Society Technologies Programs).

References

[1] BioClip<Superscript>TM_</Superscript> an Annotation Express<Superscript>TM </Superscript> Module, Inpharmatica (Galapagos), http://www.inpharmatica.co.uk/ BioClip/bioclip.htm

[2] Cuddy, S., Katchabaw, M., Lutfiyya, H.: Context-Aware Service Selection Based on Dynamic and Static Service Attributes. In: IEEE Int. Conf. on WiMob, vol. 4, pp. 13–20. IEEE Computer Society Press, Los Alamitos (2005)

[3] Electronic Business using eXtensible Markup Language (ebXML), http://www.ebxml.org/

[4] eXist - Open Source Native XML Database, http://exist.sourceforge.net/

[5] GRIA - A Grid For Today, IT Innovation Centre, http://www.gria.org/

[6] InforSense KDE (Knowledge Discovery Environment), InforSense Ltd., http:// www.inforsense.com/

[7] iSIGHT-FD, Engineous software, http://www.engineous.com/

[8] Kuck, J., Reichartz, F.: A collaborative and feature based approach to Context-Sensitive Service Discovery. In: 16th Int. WWW Conf., 5th WWW Workshop on Emerging Applications for Wireless and Mobile Access, Banff, Alberta, Canada (2007)

[9] Web Services Metadata Exchange (WS-MetadataExchange) - Version 1.1 (August 2006), http://specs.xmlsoap.org/ws/2004/09/mex/

[10] Model Center, Phoenix Integration, http://www.phoenix-int.com/

[11] OWL Web Ontology Language, W3C Recommendation (Febuary 10, 2004), http://www.w3.org/TR/owl-features/

[12] Radetzki, U., Leser, U., Schulze-Rauschenbach, S.C., Zimmermann, J., Lüssem, J., Bode, T., Cremers, A.B.: Adapters, shims, and glue - service interoperability for in silico experiments. Bioinformatics 22(9), 1137–1143(7) (2006)

[13] SIMDAT - Grids for Industrial Product Development, www.simdat.eu

[14] Universal Description: Discovery, and Integration (UDDI), http://www.uddi.org

[15] Web Services Addressing (WS-Addressing): W3C Member Submission (August 10, 2004), http://www.w3.org/Submission/ws-addressing/

[16] Toward converging Web service standards for resources, events, and management, Version 1.0, http://devresource.hp.com/drc/specifications/wsm/index.jsp

[17] WS-I Basic Profile Version 1.0 (April 2004), http://www.ws-i.org/Profiles/BasicProfile-1.0.html

[18] Web Service Group 1.2 (WS-ServiceGroup) (June 2004), http://docs.oasis-open.org/ wsrf/2004/06/ wsrf-WS-ServiceGroup-1.2-draft-02.pdf

[19] Web Service Resource Transfer (WS-ResourceTransfer) (August 2006), http:// schemas.xmlsoap.org/ws/2006/08/resourcetransfer/

Bridging Architectural Boundaries Design and Implementation of a Semantic BPM and SOA Governance Tool

Christoph F. Strnadl

Software AG (Austria), Guglgasse 7–9, A-1030 Wien, Austria
christoph.strnadl@softwareag.com

Abstract. In order to increase IT and business agility or to improve IT systems and business processes integration many organizations are currently implementing business process management systems (BPMS) or adopting a service-oriented architecture (SOA) paradigm. However, in doing so, IT complexity will admittedly increase and IT managers then are in need of effective governance techniques covering both strategic initiatives, BPM and SOA. This contribution re-examines the problem domain in the novel *Enhanced Process-Driven Architecture* (ePDA) model in order to systematically derive the requirements for combined BPM and SOA governance. We then formulate a semantic meta model capable of capturing necessary artifacts and describe its technical implementation in Software AG's and Fujitsu's joint CentraSite governance registry/repository. As "lessons learned" from several projects we systematically derive governance benefits using the Analytic Hierarchy Process (AHP) and highlight measures on software deployment issues.

Keywords: SOA Governance, BPM Governance, Business Process Management, IT Governance, Analytic Hierarchy Process (AHP).

1 Introduction

Currently many IT organizations of large enterprises face mounting pressure towards increasing IT and business agility and/or improving the integration of IT systems with business processes. This has already enticed several IT departments to either implement business process management systems (BPMS) or to adopt a service-oriented architecture (SOA) paradigm. While each of these strategies is certainly viable in itself, IT leaders now discover that, when implementing these initiatives, IT complexity has increased noticeably. This situation is exacerbated by the fact that quite a few IT executives lack effective management and governance processes and tools for dealing with that growing amount of complexity.

This has prompted some IT departments to implement first generation (IT) governance tools which either are rather IT system focused (the corresponding attitude often called "Business Systems Management," BSM), or to remain with classic "SOA registries". In both cases IT management now recognizes the limitations

B. Krämer, K.-J. Lin, and P. Narasimhan (Eds.): ICSOC 2007, LNCS 4749, pp. 518–529, 2007.

of these isolated approaches due to their lack of integration with each other: SOA registries being agnostic about business process management (systems), and BSM being ignorant about SOA and BPMS systems. This situation is aggravated by current best practices acknowledging the need for a converging BPM *and* SOA ecosystem as opposed to disentangled and separated implementation strategies, *viz.* a BPMS project *alone* or a SOA strategy *alone*.

This paper addresses this disparate state of affairs and proposes methods and an actual implementation architecture capable of bridging the currently isolated architectural boundaries between BPM and SOA regarding their holistic governance.

The organization of the paper is as follows: In Section 2 we first re-examine the problem domain and the mission of combined SOA/BPM governance. Section 3 introduces a semantical model and the technical implementation chosen by Software AG and Fujitsu to fulfill the requirements posited in Section 2. We highlight our experiences from implementing or testing this solution in several large organizations in Section 4 including a systematic benefits analysis based on the Analytic Hierarchy Process (AHP) and a demonstration how software deployment and lifecycle issues may (and must) be addressed as well by a holistic governance solution.

2 Governance Requirements

2.1 Governance Definition

While we acknowledge that no universal and concordant definition of (SOA/BPM) governance currently exists we have found the following pragmatic definition to provide a good basis for further "customizing" an organization's governance framework [1]–[3]:

> ***SOA/BPM Governance*** *specifies the decision rights and accountability framework to encourage desirable behavior in the context of SOA and BPM. This consists of leadership, organizational structure and processes to direct and control the enterprise in order to sustain and extend the organization's strategies and objectives by utilizing SOA and BPM methodologies and tools.*

In a nutshell, SOA/BPM governance answers the following three questions:

1. **Who** decides and enforces
2. **which** SOA or BPM relevant **questions**
3. according to **which** decision making and enforcement **processes**?

We also urge the reader to take notice how this definition elegantly introduces both *design-time* (*arg.* notions linked to decision making) and *run-time* (*arg.* concepts linked to enforcement) related aspects of governance.

2.2 Enhanced Process-Driven Architecture (ePDA)

In order to capture all relevant (but not more) architectural layers and tiers we extend the original *Process-Driven Architecture* (PDA) model [4] into the *Enhanced Process-Driven Architecture* (ePDA). While the original PDA stays at a somewhat superficial level sufficient to address the issues of bridging the business / IT divide on a business executive level, we clearly admit the necessity of an additional level of detail in order to effectively address IT governance issues.

Experiences from our projects strongly suggest that the resulting (limited) complexity of the ePDA suffices to conduct even technical discussions (cf. Fig. 1).

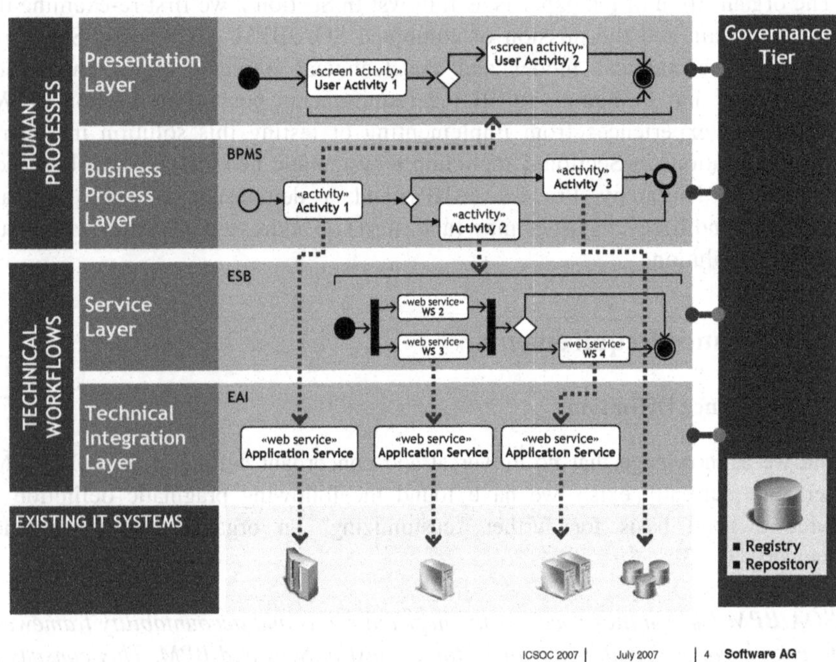

Fig. 1. Enhanced Process-Driven Architecture (ePDA) Model

On top of the existing IT systems and infrastructure layer the ePDA recognizes four conceptually independent layers emphasizing different elements of a full-fledged SOA including explicit business process management using business process management systems (BPMS) and workflow management systems (WfMS) [5]–[7].

We would like to highlight the fact that the horizontal and conceptually independent layers are explicitly linked by a vertical *Governance Tier*.

This architectural diagram already captures and depicts **two fundamental questions** of SOA/BPM governance:

1. Which artifacts **exist** on a given layer, both at design-time and at run-time?
2. How are different artifacts **linked** to each other — not only *within* a single layer but also to artifacts of a different layer?

We take particular notice of issue (2) which is brought about by the necessary orchestration (or, *vice versa*, decomposition) of functionality embodied in one layer by artifacts from another (higher/lower) layer: Business processes utilize different screen templates and forms and, simultaneously, consist of a suitably structured set of activities which, in turn may be composed by appropriately "orchestrated" or "choreographed" (Web) services wrapped around modules of existing applications. We also observe that the notion of "linkage" of services also explicitly encompasses run-time interactions and dependencies, situations of service availability (or, rather, unavailability) and service level agreements (SLA) and SLA management

Contrary to question (1), which may be addressed within a simple *registry* approach (*viz.* by employing a directory), issue (2) requires a different — and as we demonstrate, a semantic — *Ansatz*.

2.3 Domain Meta-model

Based on the ePDA and the observations in Subsection 2.2 above we have extended the model introduced by [8] to develop the following Domain Meta-Model (cf. Fig. 2, abridged).

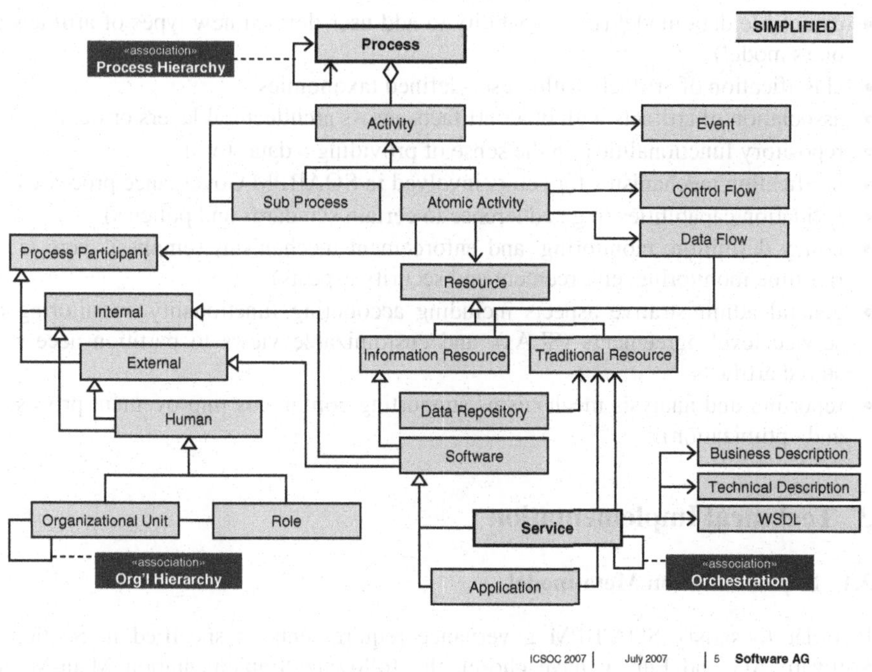

Fig. 2. Domain Meta-Model

This model not only captures relevant entities or concepts *within* a particular layer of the ePDA but also explicitly incorporates associations *between* artifacts irrespective of their layer. We also like to point out how named associations are used to specify a hierarchy or taxonomy within artifacts of the same "type" (e.g., the *«association»* "Process Hierarchy" classifying artifacts of "type" Process).

2.4 SOA and BPM Specific Governance Requirements

Based on the definitions and ePDA architecture given above our SOA/BPM implementation pilots and projects suggest the following system-level and organizational requirements for a holistic SOA and BPM governance. In all circumstances these requirements would apply to design time and, *mutatis mutandis,* run-time environments equally.

- identification and description of artifacts (e.g., services, business processes, activities, resources, roles, etc.) in the sense of a registry
- search & locating capabilities (during run-time this also involves the detection of rogue, i.e., unregistered, services)
- service discovery, binding, and (service) endpoint management
- SOA service and process lifecycle management support
- means for dynamically invoking services
- extensible data model (i.e., capability to add user-defined new types of artifacts to one's model)
- classification of artifacts within user-defined taxonomies
- association of artifacts with other artifacts across architectural layers or tiers
- repository functionalities (in the sense of providing a data store)
- notification mechanisms for actors involved in SOABPM Governance processes
- validation capabilities (e.g., adherence to certain standards and policies)
- policy definition, monitoring, and enforcement mechanisms (emphasis here is on run-time monitoring, enforcement and security aspects)
- general administrative aspects including accounting functionality, monitoring of service level agreements (SLAs), and customizable views to partition access to stored artifacts
- reporting and analysis mechanisms supporting continuous improvement processes and optimization)

3 Technical Implementation

3.1 Implementation Meta-model

In order to satisfy SOA/BPM governance requirements as specified in Section 2 Software AG and Fujitsu have chosen the following Implementation Meta-Model when developing the CentraSite™ SOA/BPM Governance solution (cf. Fig 3. below). The meta-model is based on the JAXR standard (Java API for XML Registries [9], [10]).

While it is evident that the domain meta-model (cf. Fig. 2) is ill-suited to be natively implemented in a strict relational (database) model requiring tedious normalization steps the power of an entity-relationship model (ER) should, in principle, suffice. There are two reasons, though, which have prompted us to go beyond traditional ER models towards higher level semantics:

- language and technology proximity of the meta-model to the field of semantics;
- preparation for the Semantic Web or Semantic Web Services

When comparing the conceptual power of our implementation meta-model with other initiatives in the "Semantic Web" or "Semantic Web Services" (SWS) areas we clearly observe that our model is neither as rich as pure RDF or OWL [11] nor does it fully address requirements or capabilities of SWS like WSMO (Web Services Modeling Ontology [12]) or SWSL (Semantic Web Services Language, [13]–[15]). On the "ontology spectrum" [16], though, the expressive power of CentraSite's information model clearly exceeds any pure thesaurus or taxonomy and nearly reaches the level of a "Conceptual Model".

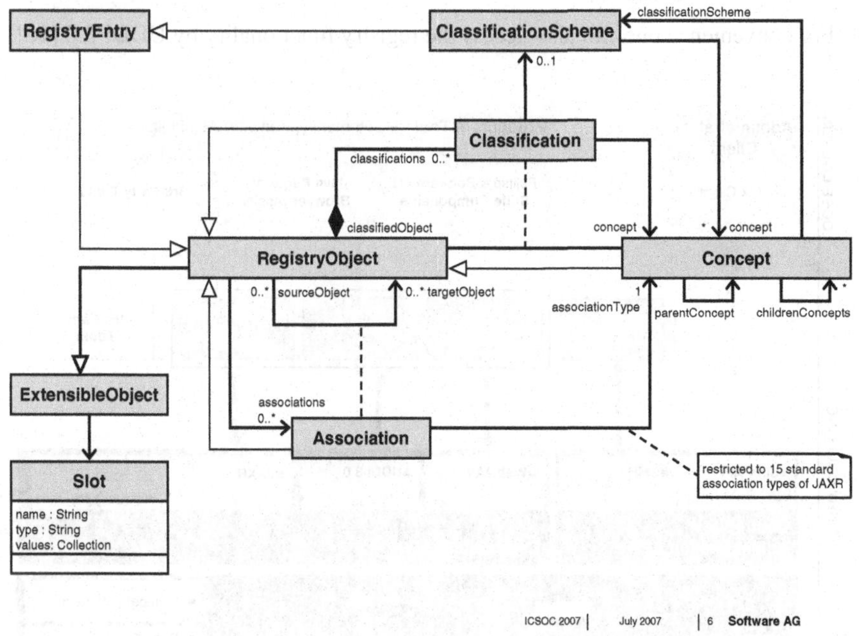

Fig. 3. CentraSite's information model

Identity of different artifacts is maintained through a unique UUID for every `RegistryObject` (implemented as JAXR `Key` interface; not shown in Fig. 3). This allows correlation of CentraSite objects to other management level systems that have their own identity schemes for the "same" entity.

We also note that the CentraSite's current information model does not (yet) include *ad hoc* classification schemes such as tagging or social bookmarking (`http://del.icio.us` style).

3.2 Implementation Architecture

The actual implementation architecture of CentraSite is illustrated in Fig. 4 below.

Software AG's native XML database TAMINO serves as the underlying data store providing security, versioning, and the basic metadata manager. From point of view of any user of CentraSite, though, TAMINO is completely transparent and hidden by the generic CentraSite API for SOA/BPM Governance activities, and a set of administrative APIs either utilizing Software AG's proven SMH (System Management Hub) technology or the Java Management Extension (JMX).

The CentraSite APIs are principally based on open international standards, namely

- **Registry functionality:** JAXR (Java API for XML Registries, [9], [10])
- **Repository functionality:** WebDAV (Web Distributed Authoring and Versioning, [17])

For convenience one can also access the registry functionality by UDDI 3.0 [18].

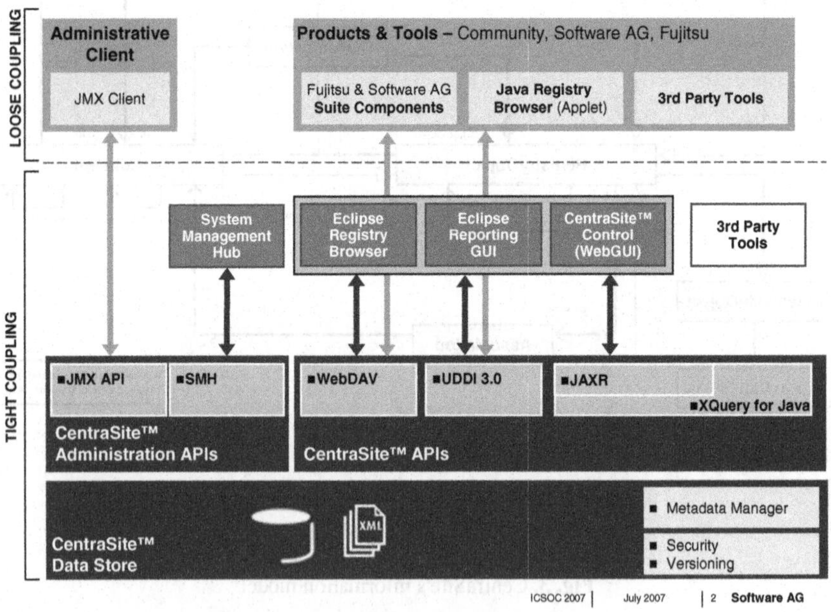

Fig. 4. CentraSite implementation architecture

Initially, our implementation has been biased somewhat towards *design time* governance functionality at the expense of *run time* governance. With the successful completion of Software AG's acquisition of webMethods Inc. (USA) per July 2007 we are currently working on extending CentraSite with run time governance functionality based on webMethods' Infravio product, notably in the areas of policy management and enforcement.

4 Experiences

In this Section we want to highlight experiences and "lessons learned" from several large-scale implementations, pilot projects, or proof-of-concept situations with CentraSite. In order to preserve anonymity of our CentraSite customers individual "lessons learned" are not attributed to a particular client and have been disguised.

4.1 Governance Benefits Analysis

When attempting to measure the benefit of (good) governance or management practices and processes, many if not all traditional, mostly accounting oriented methods such as ROI (return on investment) or DCF (discounted cash flow) analysis miserably fail.

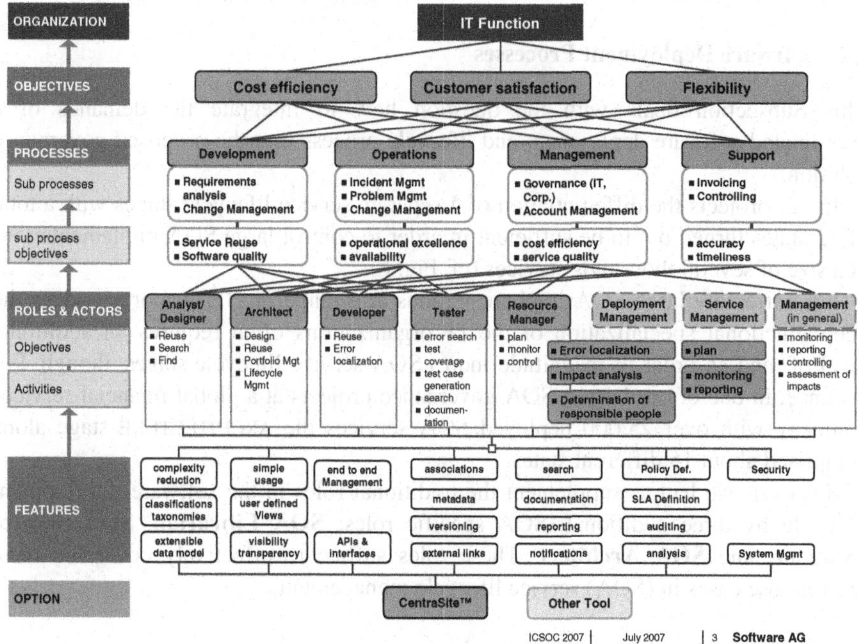

Fig. 5. AHP benefits hierarchy of a SOA/BPM Governance tool

Obviously, this is due to the fact that governance *in itself* does not create business value *on its own* (that is achieved through value-adding business processes), but only *indirectly* contributes to organizational efficiency and effectiveness.

In our projects we have been very successful in applying the Analytic Hierarchy Process (AHP) [20], [21] in order to capture qualitatively and quantitatively the indirect manner in which governance operates.

Within the AHP we use the so-called *Forward Planning* in the following 4-level hierarchy as shown in Fig. 5:

- **Features** — focusing on the particular features or properties of a SOA/BPM governance tool;
- **Roles & Actors** including their objectives and activities;
- **Processes of the IT organization** including suitable sub processes and process objectives. Note that the five horizontal separately displayed processes ("Error Localization", "Impact Analysis" through "Monitoring & Reporting") apply to all actors equally);
- **objectives of the corporate IT function**

As usual within the AHP a pair-wise comparison process of lower level elements with respect to their influence on upper level "criteria" lets one determine a ranking of positive contributions of SOA/BPM Governance (not shown in Fig. 4). In addition, the very same AHP hierarchy could be used to compare and select different SOA/BPM Governance tools on the OPTIONS Layer (the "Other Tool" in Fig. 5).

4.2 Software Deployment Processes

This Subsection deals with the question how to integrate the demands of a coordinated software deployment and lifecycle process into the proposed governance solution.

In our projects the differentiation of 4 separate service lifecycle stages with a total of 12 states turned out to be sufficient in order to control large SOA implementations at a size of several thousands services (cf. Fig. 6).

For extremely large SOA implementations at a range of 10^4 or more services the deep functional specialization of the IT organizations often requires an additional level of (and an order of magnitude more) SOA service lifecycle stages, though. For instance, in one of our largest SOA governance projects at a global financial services company with over 25,000 deployed SOA services the ARCHITECTURE stage alone comprised about 15 different states.

However, we had to supplement the traditional roles in the software development lifecycle by three additional, SOA specific roles: **SOA Librarian**, **SOA Service Designer**, and **SOA Architect**. These roles suffice to effectively cover the most relevant use cases in (SOA) service lifecycle management:

- match business requirements
- design new service
- develop (new) service
- deploy (new) service
- test system
- set service productive
- apply temporary production change
- conduct run-time analysis
- conduct impact analysis
- undeploy service
- retire service

In that connection we also have found the role of an **SOA Architect** to be much stronger (i.e., endowed with more *formal* decision authority) than that of a traditional Software or IT Systems Architect.

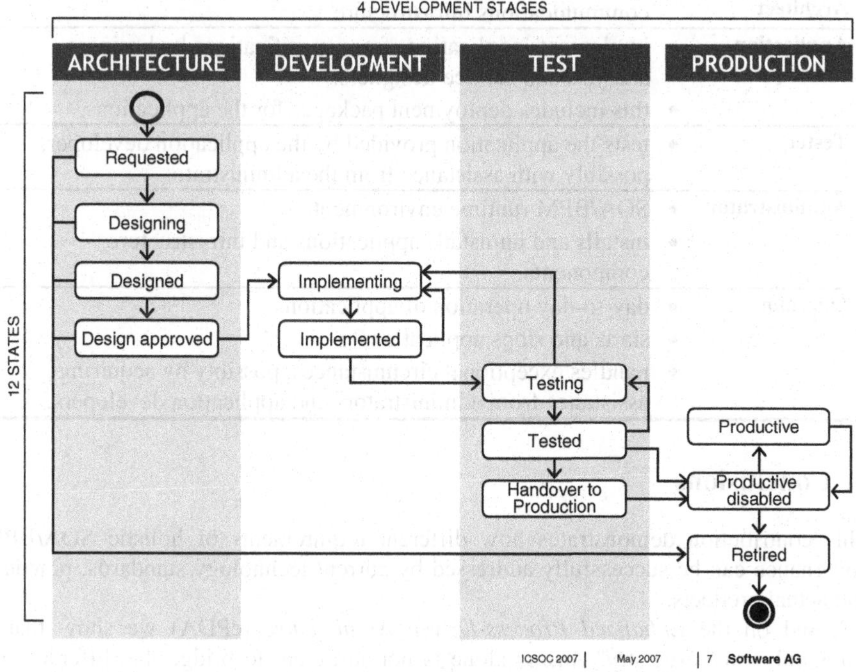

Fig. 6. Service lifecycle states and stages

The full set of lifecycle specific roles is depicted in Table 1 below.

Table 1. SOA Roles

Role	Responsibilities
SOA Librarian	• service registry and consistency • establishes rules and guidelines for services • approves additions and changes to service registry content
Business Analyst	• owns business requirements • represents potential service consumers • ensures business requirements are met
SOA Service Designer	• creates technical service design from business requirements for the application developer to implement

Table 1. *(continued)*

SOA Architect	• *logical and physical architecture of the SOA/BPM landscape* • *approves application architectures*
Infrastructure Architect	• planning and organizing the network, server, and communications infrastructure
Application Developer	• implements applications from specifications by business analysts and service designers. • this includes deployment packages for the applications.
Tester	• tests the application provided by the application developer, possibly with assistance from the administrator
Administrator	• SOA/BPM runtime environment • installs and uninstalls applications and infrastructure components
Operator	• day-to-day operation of applications • starts and stops applications • handles exceptional circumstances, possibly by acquiring assistance from administrators and application developers.

5 Conclusions

This contribution demonstrates how different requirements of holistic SOA/BPM governance can be successfully addressed by current technology standards, practices and actual products.

Based on the *Enhanced Process-Driven Architecture* (ePDA) we show that a commonly tried "registry" *Ansatz* alone is not sufficient to bridge the different and necessary layers of the architecture but needs to be complemented by suitable semantic methods at a sophistication level of a "Conceptual Model".

Building on Software AG's and Fujitsu's implementation of the corresponding information model in their CentraSite™ SOA/BPM Governance tool we highlight experiences and lessons learned when implementing SOA/BPM governance in large and complex organizations. Specifically, we derive a fairly generic SOA/BPM benefits hierarchy using the Analytic Hierarchy Process (AHP), and define a suitable Service Lifecycle Model comprising four stages and 12 states.

Finally, and concluding from our implementation projects, we want to stress the fact that SOA/BPM Governance is definitely more an organizational challenge than a technical one — as long as organizations use sufficiently advanced information technology, such as CentraSite.

Acknowledgments. The author wants to acknowledge the stimulating and intriguing discussions within Software AG's (global) SOA Infrastructure & Governance Group headed by Javier Camara Melgosa.

Special thanks (again) go to Javier Camara (Software AG Spain) for meticulously and thoroughly reading and commenting an earlier version of this paper (key word: *run-time governance*) and Christian Schultes (Software AG Austria) for providing *en passent* valuable information about international real-life SOA Governance projects.

We also appreciate the comments of the anonymous reviewers which helped in sharpening certain aspects of this paper.

References

1. Weill, P., Broadbent, M.: IT Governance. How Top Performers Manage IT Decision Rights for Superior Results, pp. 30–34. Harvard Business School Press, Boston, MA (2004)
2. IT Governance Institute (ITGI), CobIT Executive Summary Version 3, p. 3 (July 2000)
3. IT Governance Institute (ITGI), CobIT Version 4. Rolling Meadows, IL: IT Governance Institute, p. 5
4. Strnadl, C.F.: Aligning Business and IT. The Process-Driven Architecture Model. Inf. Syst. Manage 23(4), 235–241 (Fall 2006)
5. Smith, H., Fingar, P.: Business Process Management. In: The Third Wave, Meghan-Kiffer Press, Tampa, FL (2003)
6. Weske, M., van der Aalst, W.M.P., Verbeek, H.M.W.: Advances in business process management. Data & Knowledge Eng. 50, 1–8 (2004)
7. van der Aalst, W., van Hee, K.: Workflow Management. In: Models, Methods, and Systems, ch. 5, MIT Press, London, UK (2004)
8. List, B., Korherr, B.: An Evaluation of Conceptual Business Process Modeling Languages. In: Proc. 21st Annual ACM Symposium on Applied Computing, Dijon, France, 23-27 April, 2006, pp. 1532–1539. ACM Press, New York (2006)
9. Najmi (ed.): Java<Superscript>TM</Superscript> API for XML Registries (JAXR) Specification 1.0. SUN JSR-093 (April 10, 2002)
10. Perrone, P.J., Chaganti, V.S.R.R., Schwenk, T.: J2EE Developer's Handbook, ch. 13. Sams Publishing Developer's Library, Indianapolis, IN (2003)
11. Decker, S., Melnik, S., van Harmelen, F., Fensel, D., Klein, M., Boekstra, J., Erdmann, M., Horrocks, I.: The Semantic Web: The Role of XML and RDF. IEEE Internet Comp. 4(5), 63–73 (2000)
12. See directly: www.wsmo.org
13. Burstein, M., Bussler, C., Zaremba, M., Finin, T., Huhns, M.N., Paolucci, M., Sheth, A.P., Williams, S.: A Semantic Web Services Architecture. IEEE Internet Comp. 9(5), 72–81 (2005)
14. Hepp, M.: Semantic Web and Semantic Web Services. Father and Son or Indivisible Twins? IEEE Internet Comp. 10(2), 85–88 (2006)
15. Zhou, C., Chia, L-T., Lee, B-S.: Semantics in Service Discovery and QoS Measurement. IT Professional 7(2), 29–34 (2005)
16. Daconta, M.C., Obrst, L.J., Smith, K.T.: The Semantic Web. A Guide to the Future of XML, Web Services, and Knowledge Management. Indianapolis, IN: Wiley, p. 157 (2003)
17. See directly, www.webdav.org
18. Clement, L., Hately, A., von Riegen, C., Rogers, T. (eds.): UDDI Version 3.0.2. UDDI Spec Technical Committee Draft Dated 20041019. OASIS, http://uddi.org/pubs/uddi_v3.htm
19. Shapiro, R. (ed.): XML Process Definition Language Version 2. Lighthouse Point, FL: Workflow Management Coalition, Doc. Nr. WFMC-TC-1025 (version 2) (October 3, 2005)
20. Saaty, T.: The Analytic Hierarchy Process. Planning, Priority Setting, Resource Allocation, McGraw-Hill, New York, NY (1980)
21. Saaty, T.: Decision Making for Leaders.The Analytic Hierarchy Process for Decisions in a Complex World, 3rd edn. 2001, Lifetime Learning Publications, Belmont, CA (1982)

SOA and Large Scale and Complex Enterprise Transformation

Mansour Kavianpour

Executive Architect, Unisys Corp USA
Mansour.Kavianpour@Unisys.com

Abstract. Service-oriented architecture (SOA) is an architectural approach to development that turns traditional techniques upside down. SOA encourages organizations to think in terms of actual business services and the associated data, rather than low level technology details. Instead of developing applications from the ground up, SOA frees organizations to start with high level business definitions for data, interfaces, documents, and processes. SOA then maps these high level service definitions onto new or existing infrastructure, regardless of the details, location, or programming language in which the systems were written[1],[2].

In this paper we share our practical experience regarding application of SOA to a very large and complex enterprise transformation. By transformation we mean modernization of legacy applications, operating systems, server components, development of new applications, and business process automation with incremental deployment option using either a traditional distributed heterogeneous environment or a set of Virtual machines deployed on a set of utility computing platforms (on-demand computing).

Transforming a large and complex enterprise requires digital visibility into the holistic view of the enterprise. This holistic view is captured as a set of interrelated models. Models are digital representations of the enterprise business architecture, the associated technology architecture, and their semantic dependencies. Models are stored in a living and manageable repository with impact analysis capability to accommodate for SOA modernization to be driven by the business needs.

We describe our 3D Visible Enterprise (3D-VE)[3] modeling methodology as the analysis phase of our SOA approach. We then describe how such analysis guided us through modernization styles, where each style prescribes the transformation of a legacy entity into its modernized form while following our SOA governance. In this approach the modernization requirements are mapped into the appropriate transformation styles and finally to technical implementation. The mapping follows our SOA governance, a set of guidelines

[1] Principles of SOA Design, A whitepaper from Cape Clear Software Inc.

[2] Best Practices for SOA with Cape Clear ESB.

[3] 3D VE (3 Dimensional Visible Enterprise) is the Unisys modeling approach to creating a more visible enterprise. It's a proven business and systems modeling framework and methodology that integrates business vision with IT execution to create organizational visibility (www.unisys.com).

B. Krämer, K.-J. Lin, and P. Narasimhan (Eds.): ICSOC 2007, LNCS 4749, pp. 530–545, 2007.

regarding transformation style selection, and the SOA design & run time governance.

Relevant SOA standards and products supporting modernization implementation are used to carry the implementation. In particular, some aspect of modernization approach and Unisys SOA governance are described as well.

In this paper we tried to describe three important areas of our overall SOA solution methodology, namely the 3D VE modeling, the Architecture Driven Modernization and applied SOA governance to the ADM style. Our plan is to publish subsequent papers each describing the details of our SOA solution methodology, specifically the modeling phase, the tools and methods used to implement the applied ADM styles, criteria selecting ADM style, the SOA governance and the associated SOA standards and products.

The paper concludes with lessons learned through such a complex transformation, especially the importance of the front-end business process analysis leading us to identify the components or a subset of the enterprise computing environment for systematic and incremental SOA transformation. Finally we discuss some of the pros and cons of the transformation applying SOA.

1 Introduction

To protect our contractual obligation we would like to avoid to reveal the name of our client organization instead we use the term “the enterprise”. The enterprise subject to the transformation is a multi billion dollar global pharmaceutical company with distributed IT infrastructures supporting its daily businesses. A modest inventory of such a complex environment includes more than 600 applications, over 3000 window stations, 3000 UNIX stations, 10s of VAX machines, mainframe computers and numerous data sources, middlewares, massive storage and network installations, proprietary securities, with software-enforced US government policies, and regulations with complex existing firewalls, numerous business and employee portals, web and complex financial applications.

The transformation asks for replacement of old computers, consolidation of applications, data sources, and middleware into a secure SOA environment. The transformation further asks for enterprise architecture with a deployment option on an on-demand computing platform using virtualization technology. The overall transformation will take 5 years with multiple phases.

Transformation can not be performed in isolation. For such a large and complex enterprise the transformation requires digital visibility into the holistic view of the enterprise. This holistic view a) allows systematic identification of hosted applications, and b) facilitates for business impact and risk analysis of the hosted applications running on the retired VAX machine. Similarly other platforms like MVS, HP-3000, AS400 and the like will eventually require to be modernized and therefore their business impact must be known before any modernization activities. Similar to a large scale, distributed software development where the design phase plays the critical role in success of the project, capturing holistic views of the existing enterprise for analysis is the key to the successful transformation. It is this level of visibility that allows for systematic impact analysis, modernization and consolidation planning, the associated risk assessment and mitigation and project planning. Section Unisys 3D VE Methodology briefly introduces the Unisys 3D VE transformation methodology. This section sets the stage for our next step in our road map, the actual modernization.

Once the elements of the enterprise are selected for the modernization, the modernization itself requires a proven method. Unisys adopted Architecture Driven Modernization (ADM) which is an IT Modernization discipline using a model-driven approach. Unisys ADM is based on the Object Management Group (OMG) Model Driven Architecture (MDA)[4]. We apply this method to each step of transformation to implement the required modernization. Section Architecture Driven Modernization briefly describes our ADM transformation approach.

Our target enterprise architecture must address some challenging requirements. For example the client wanted an agile architecture to allow non intrusive application replacement, integration, data migration, application modernization, server modernization, and middleware and database consolidation. We adopt SOA with supporting governance. Without architecture governance ad-hoc transformation will soon create a costly IT chaos. Section SOA Architecture and Governance briefly describes the SOA governance we applied to each transformation styles.

The final SOA environment accommodates for two radically different deployment architectures, namely a traditional distributed network computing, or an on-demand Real Time Infrastructure (RTI) computing platform. The Unisys RTI approach is not discussed in this paper. We believe, due to its complex nature, a separate paper should be allocated to this topic. It is worth to mention that our RTI approach takes the on-demand computing to a new level where the demand for resources are detected at runtime and dynamically allocated.

Section Conclusion highlights the lesson we learned during the design and the description of the road map of the transformation. Some specific application of SOA technology that helped us during the transformation design is highlighted as well.

2 Unisys 3D VE Methodology

Transforming large and complex environments require modeling and blueprinting of enterprise subject to transformation in form of digital models that provide risk free, predictable, repeatable and cost effective transformation.

The 3D Visible Enterprise (3D-VE) is the Unisys modeling approach. 3D-VE makes visible the relationships between the business and the technology that supports it. It reveals the connections business strategy, business process, infrastructure and traceability. It shows how infrastructure applications, hardware and management processes work together. And it anticipates the results through impact analysis and "what-if" simulation of proposed changes.

---

[4] Model Driven Architecture (MDA) is a framework based on the Unified Modeling Language (UML) and other industry standards for visualizing, storing, and exchanging software designs and models. MDA promotes the creation of machine-readable, highly abstract models that are developed independently of the implementation technology and stored in standardized repositories.

Our methodology takes a holistic view across all dimensions of an enterprise. This holistic view includes modeling of Enterprise's *Business Architecture* and *Technology Architecture*. Modeling the business architecture includes modeling the Enterprise's Business Strategy and Business Process while modeling the technology architecture includes modeling of the Enterprise Applications and Infrastructure components.

Blueprinting provides a unique, four layered structure that reveals the complex relationships between business strategies, business processes, applications, and the IT infrastructure. By making these relationships visible, a high degree of traceability is achieved — making response to change a reality. This approach enables capture of Enterprise's' organization knowledge and end-to-end dependencies in a number of artifacts which continuously maintained in a Repository.

The processes involved in building the relevant Blueprints (aka knowledge repository) take two paths. The first path captures the Enterprise's business models in a number of logically related layers using existing documentations and SMEs. These layers, as defined below, are abstracting the Enterprise overall operations. Artifact models specific to each layer will be developed using Unisys 3D Blueprinting tools. A quick summary of sample Blueprints are given below. These models are all developed using ProVision[5].

- **Business Visions and Operations Models** -- Layer1 artifacts: At this level we capture the Enterprise's organizations, goals and business opportunity models. The data is gathered using organization charts, company goals and interview with management.
- **Business Process Models** – Layer2 artifacts: At this level we capture the business processes fulfilling organizations', goals' and opportunities' captured in Layer1. These models are captured as Business Swim Lanes and the Business Interaction Model. The data regarding business processes are gathered via interview with business people and subject mater expert.
- **Functional and Application Models** – Layer3 artifacts: At this level we capture Business Use Case Model, Cost Model, and Deployment Model related to business processes capture in Layer2. In most cases we discovered that business use cases for identified processes must be developed from scratch. Similarly we have to develop the cost model and deployment model. The data for creating these models usually do not exits and has to be developed.
- **Infrastructure Models** – Layer4 artifacts: At this level we capture Infrastructure Service Architecture Model, Infrastructure Service Usage Specification model supporting IT components captured in Layer3. These models capture application and node topology (the actual IT components topology). The data required to develop this model is gathered using our network agent toolset. Metadata about applications, their locations, IP address of servers, etc. are all gathered and used as input to develop the infrastructure models.

These models once are captured are the foundation for delivering an intelligent infrastructure vision. They are used to abstract and represent data and metadata

[5] We have customized Proforma Provision modeling tool with Unisys Meta schema to allow the development of 3D VE models.

describing the various IT components, their dependencies and relationships needed for transformation as well as a knowledgebase to realize a real-time infrastructure. The models are kept and managed in a repository. A graphical representation of the 3D VE is illustrated in the following diagram, the layer and the dependencies are high lighted.

Business and IT Alignment

Business operations are formally modelled in order to share and scale best practices

- **Traceability is the backbone for maintaining and managing the alignment between business and IT.**

Strategic Goal Model, Measurement Model

Process & Organization Models

Information & Component Models

Infrastructure & Topology Models

If you can't model it you can't fully understand or predict behavior

Models were used for impact analyses. For example, the organization artifact model (organization model captured at layer1) is traced to one or more associated business processes (business process swimlane captured in layer2). The dependency implies that the Enterprise organization uses certain business processes. Similarly, each business process will be traced to its business use cases (business use case model captured in layre3), and finally each business use case artifact will be traced to application and computing node (Infrastructure Service Architecture Model captured in layer4).

We needed this level of visibility in order to decide on partitioning and isolating the legacy entities to be transformed into the new SOA environment. This living and maintainable repository of models and multi dimension traceability provided a complete enterprise view to the subject Enterprise business operation.

We used the business process workflow analysis (a top down analysis) to improve the existing business processes, identify processes creating backlogs, identify unwanted processes, etc. These activities are ProVision specific and are not discussed here. Once improvement identified, we used the Impact Analysis tool to identify risks, formulate risk mitigation, estimate cost before starting the modernization project. We used Impact Analysis for removing server, or application(s) to assess and measure the impact on the Enterprise's business operation (a bottom up analysis).

In summary, the repository of models helped us with modernization implementation planning, prioritizing and planning for retirement of the existing components, consolidation, and preparation of knowledge extraction, and application of our Architecture Driven Modernization (ADM) aka Enterprise Modernization methodology.

The captured as-is models are enhanced with more related data during modernization analysis phase. We applied our ADM methodology to actually make the implementation decision which transforms a legacy entity into the desired target SOA component following our SOA governance.

In summery the repository of models, among others, provided numerous advantages. For example:

- Better strategic decision making for new modernization projects such as a legacy application replacement, server, database, and middleware consolidation.
- Helping with phasing and incremental transformation planning.
- Allowed the organization to identify, across the whole portfolio; exactly what processes, business rules, and application code are impacted by a change (market, legislative or otherwise). A process we used to identify and select applications subject to modernization, the respective project plan, risk and risk mitigation plan associated with the modernization.
- The repository became a key business asset, maintained and upgraded just as key operational and decision support systems are.
- It used as the source for Business Process Improvement and automation.
- It enabled for systematic identification of data sources, applications, external systems used internally or externally collectively called "touch points" to help with integration architecture, estimating and managing integration cost, risks and overall project management.
- Used as a secure repository for generating reports for government regulatory such as Sarbanes-Oxley.
- Used as a decision making for the overall consolidation.

Next section takes us into the ADM method and describes how we applied ADM to each entity subject to modernization.

3 Architecture Driven Modernization

Management of enterprise critical business knowledge starts with capture of the business architecture/organization knowledge in form of several models – both the current architecture and the new one as it is created. Business models in support of the model driven approach are the best way to do this. As modernization process starts and a particular process and its corresponding application(s) are selected, the impact to the existing business model and propagation of such change must be analyzed. Model-driven approach supports automated forward engineering of the business rules into services that can ultimately be hosted and executed in a .NET framework, a J2EE app server, a Web server, an ORB server, a JVM, or any proprietary runtime environments.

Unisys IT Modernization Framework is based on the Object Management Group (OMG) MDA standard. It is a framework that helps to define and analyze major enterprise transformation styles. Each transformation style requires Knowledge Mining and Abstraction (KMA). We used the ADM (1 + 5)[6] mutually complimentary transformation styles to address the enterprise modernization requirements. In this approach the modernization requirements are mapped to the appropriate ADM transformation styles and finally to technical implementation. Relevant standards and products addressing modernization requirements are used but not discussed here. The Technical Implementation is actually the fruit of the ADM analysis which helped us to formulate standard SOA solutions based on available widely used vendor products.

Unisys IT Modernization Framework

Enterprise IT Modernization includes understanding, monitoring, maintaining, upgrading and replacement of the existing Enterprise applications. It relies on mining knowledge from existing applications and its abstraction to the level required for the specific modernization project. All IT Modernization styles utilize the outcome of the KMA effort in one way or another. The IT Modernization Framework is organized along two dimensions:

1- Scenario – a scenario is a distinct type of IT Modernization effort. The major IT transformation styles, also known as 1 + 5 ADM building blocks are:
   - One
     - Discovery
   - Five
     - Refactoring/Consolidation
     - Translation/Porting
     - Wrapping
     - Replacement – Redesign/COTS
     - Orchestration

2- Purview – a purview is a collection of artifacts at a given level of abstraction. All ADM building blocks involve effort in Knowledge Mining and Abstraction (KMA).

   The outcome of the KMA building block is a set of artifacts in the form of a model or a less formal description of the existing application at required level of abstraction. These artifacts are used as an input for each of other 5 ADM building blocks. These models also provide a single point of maintenance, a place that captures the business rules in business-like structured English and business processes in easily readable formats.

The following diagram gives an abstract view of the Unisys ADM Framework.

---

[6] They are (Discover) + (Refactor, Translate, Wrap, Replace and Orchestrate).

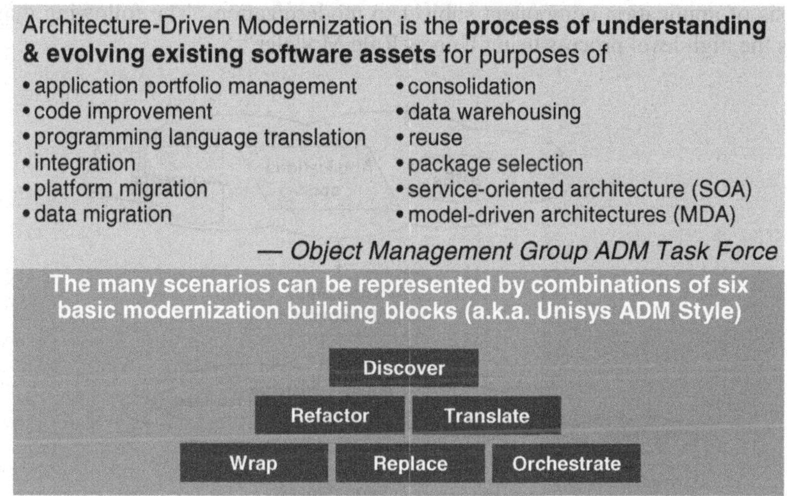

ADM Definition
Architecture-Driven Modernization is the process of understanding & evolving existing software assets for purposes of
• application portfolio management
• code improvement
• programming language translation
• integration
• platform migration
• data migration
• consolidation
• data warehousing
• reuse
• package selection
• service-oriented architecture (SOA)
• model-driven architectures (MDA)
— Object Management Group ADM Task Force
The many scenarios can be represented by combinations of six basic modernization building blocks (a.k.a. Unisys ADM Style)
Discover
Refactor
Translate
Wrap
Replace
Orchestrate

The ADM building blocks are orthogonal in the sense that they require different models produced as a result of the KMA effort and are complimentary. For example, knowledge discovery process may apply to business applications running on the VAX Open VMS, while Orchestration applies to ready-to-go application services. These building blocks serve as implementation selection category for our Enterprise modernization.

The ADM building blocks allow composing styles with the following common characteristics - at the beginning of scenario execution, the existing Enterprise's applications are analyzed and at the end – a target application is created. The target application replaces the existing application and satisfies the same (or enhanced/ modified) requirements as the existing application.

Styles or their combinations may apply to any modernization. For example, a typical modernization may require *Discovery* of existing environment and applications, *Refactoring/Consolidation* of existing applications (packaged app or custom app), *Translation/Porting* of an old system, *Wrapping* of legacy systems, *Replacement/ Redesign* of legacy components with some COTS, exposing existing and new applications as services and *Orchestration* of these services, or combination of the above. Our SOA governance has been used as an enforceable set of guidelines for development of the target application in each scenario.

The detail of "how" each ADM style are implemented will be published in future and do to space limitation are not discussed in this paper. Instead the high level descriptions of each transformation style are introduced below. Due to diversity of different Enterprise Modernization requirements, Unisys has established partnerships with a large number of translation and migration tool vendors. We purposely avoid naming any vendor in this paper.

Discovery – Remember the 3D VE analysis helped us to pinpoint the application components of the old architecture subject to modernization. This process as described above is driven by the business needs. The Discovery phase is about analysis of application component subject to modernization. The following diagram shows the high level process using Unisys Rule Modeler[7].

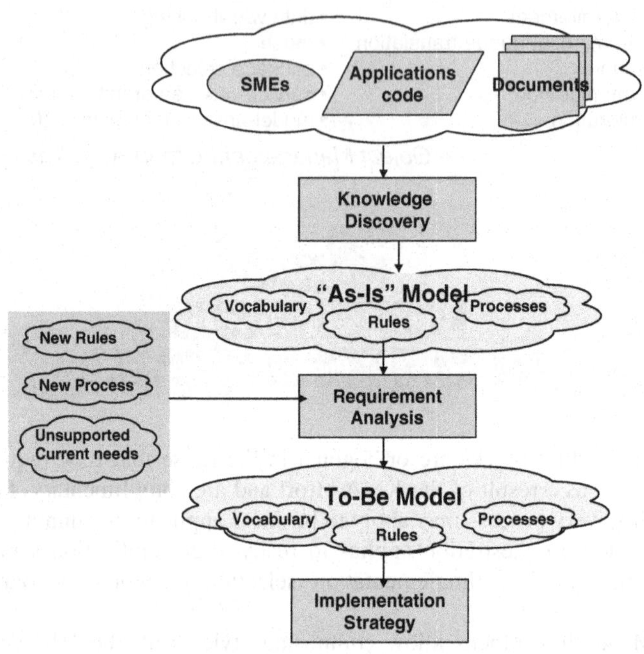

The "As-Is" Model will be extracted from the legacy application. The source for knowledge discovery is the existing application source code, existing documentation as well as SME (if is available). The main information captured at this level is the existing business processes, the existing business rules and the existing business vocabulary. A business process may include one or more automated and manual activities to perform a business function (e.g., fulfill an Order). A business rule specifies conditions/terms which must be satisfied (e.g., government legislation, etc). A vocabulary represents a business term such as "employee", "address", "salary", etc. This data elements form the As-Is model.

In next step, the As-Is Model will be augmented with new requirements to produce the To-Be Model. This activity usually includes client requirements analysis, addition of new rules, new business processes and the associated vocabularies. Models are kept and managed in a technology independent abstract representation (not shown in the diagram). Solution Modeler captures these in an Abstract Syntax Tree Metamodel (ASTM – defined by OMG). The abstract representation is used by proper tools

[7] Unisys Rules modeler is an integrated part of Unisys Solution modeler capable of extracting business rules, business terms and business vocabulary from the legacy application components.

(not discussed here) for generation of application component (modernized app) as well as generation of test scripts. For example, the discovered business Vocabulary is used to automatically generate the required database schema. The business rules and processes are used to generate the application code. This step requires Unisys Rules/Solution Modeler and Unisys consultant to perform the Discovery task. Rules Modeler and details of transformation are not discussed due to space limitation in this paper. In average we experienced 80% of the process above driven by the tool (automated) while 20% required manual activities.

Refactoring/Consolidation -- This style includes all types of existing application improvements such as rewriting data definitions, removing data redundancies, data consolidation and migration to relational databases, code streamlining, removing code redundancies, performance improvements, etc. Refactoring does not include improvements which significantly enhance or modify the set of requirements. Modern translation technique, including OMG-like Knowledge Mining and Abstraction techniques are used to semi-automate the Refactoring process. For example, a code fragment representing a sub-tree structure of an Abstract Syntax Tree (AST) generated during discovery can be map to re-factored code and new re-factored code can be generated using the same AST. There are few vendor tools that allow re-factoring and re-architecting to be exercised at AST level before generating the target code. Some advanced tools provide rule based AST generation. The rules include code patterns that need to be defined manually. We found AST to AST re-factoring much efficient than code level re-factoring. Code level re-factoring complicates the version management and maintenance.

Enforced SOA Governance -- The final re-factored application architecture follows Unisys SOA Design Time Application Governance.

Translation/Port -- This building block involves automated or semi-automated porting of the existing system, packaged or custom applications to the new platform or its translation to a modern (usually object-oriented) language. In most legacy modernization vendor products and tools are used to perform automatic translation. Unisys has specified a number of translation tools. Based on application implementation language and operating systems, specific tools will be used for translation. This scenario well suited for applications where direct translation results in better ROI. This scenario applied to all applications running on the VAX VMS platforms. Almost all translated apps needed re-factoring. There are few vendor tools that includes modern compiler technique in generation of language parser, rule based AST generation, and complete separation of data migration from code migration. We found rule based AST translation much more efficient than direct code translation. In direct code translation data and code migration can not be separated due to one-on-one dependency of code to data at transformation time.

Enforced SOA Governance -- The final Translated application architecture follows Unisys SOA Design Time Application Governance.

Wrapping -- This building block breaks the existing monolithic application into multiple parts, each represented as service using SOA techniques (mostly exposing the parts as Web Services). This style is an essential part of one of the most occurring styles used in most modernization and is used for those applications where the Enterprise has made significant investment. SOA tool vendors almost all provide support for wrapping of applications written in .NET and J2EE. The real challenge is legacy languages. Very few SOA vendors provide IDE environment for wrapping legacy components written in languages like COBOL, C, C++ and others. Selection of right SOA tools plays important role in success of transformation. Wrapping techniques exist for exposing CORBA, COBOL, .NET, J2EE, Java, and C++ components as Web Services.

Enforced SOA Governance -- The final application architecture follows Unisys SOA Design Time Application Governance.

Replacement – Redesign/COTS -- This style includes a comprehensive transformation using Unisys Solution Modeler application generation. Note that To-Be Model is a technology-independent model. For this style of transformation we will perform feature gap analysis verses packaged or COTS products. If match found we will use the COTS app, if match not found and cost analysis (not discussed here) suggest to develop a new application, we then use our solution modeler application generation. Applications can be generated for either .NET or J2EE platform. The gap analysis is a great exercise (we used Rational RequisitePro for gap analysis) for specifying configuration parameters if COTS component if we decide to use COTS. We found rule based AST translation approach is the best fit when COTS component replacing a large portion of the existing legacy applications. The interface to the COTS component is modeled in the translation rules, providing semantically correct AST generation as well as final target language code generation.

Enforced SOA Governance -- The final application architecture must follow Unisys SOA Design Time Application Governance. The COTS selection follows Unisys SOA COTS selection guidelines.

Orchestration – Applying any style of transformation discussed above finally produces a modernized component adhering to Web Services standard architecture, i.e., Service components with WSDL as its interface. This orchestration assumes that the To-Be Model has already been developed. Part of the To-Be Model includes the To-Be processes. Solution Molder is used to generate the corresponding orchestration in BPEL (Business Process Execution Language) standards. BPEL script is loaded into a COTS orchestration engine. The BPEL engine finally executes the orchestration, according to the business processes defined in the to-be Model, while invoking the modernized components using their corresponding WSDL interface.

The orchestration may include other components such as security interceptors, transformation components, auditing and more. This style is an essential part of the modernization with requirement for business process automation. It is applied once and maintained after.

Enforced SOA Governance -- Orchestration is a native architectural aspect of Unisys SOA Governance which follows the industry standard, i.e., Web Services and other related open standards. BPEL applies to those application components that have already confirmed to SOA Governance, i.e., they are transformed into first class Web Service.

As we have stated in the introduction to this paper, the detail of transformation, the technique and tooling, and the translation processes deserve a complete separate paper. We plan to publish subsequent papers regarding the overall transformation and SOA techniques used in this project.

We now very briefly describes our SOA Governance, a set of guidelines helped us during transformation, i.e., design and implementation of services, service policy and runtime governance. This is indeed an introduction only. We plan to publish a separate paper discussing for example how we deploy the Enterprise Service Bus to manage runtime policy and governance.

At the time of writing this paper we have completed a successful pilot project to demonstrate our overall Enterprise Modernization methodology, tools and technique. Large scale modernization planned to follow.

4 SOA Architecture and Governance

The Enterprise Modernization style briefly described in the Unisys MDA section form the mechanisms for our transformation. These mechanisms followed the Unisys SOA Governance. Our governance includes SOA reference models, the corresponding SOA reference architectures and our SOA maturity model (none discussed in this paper).

The scenario driven (ADM) uses this governance guidelines during implementation. The following diagram summarizes our Governance.

SOA Lifecycle

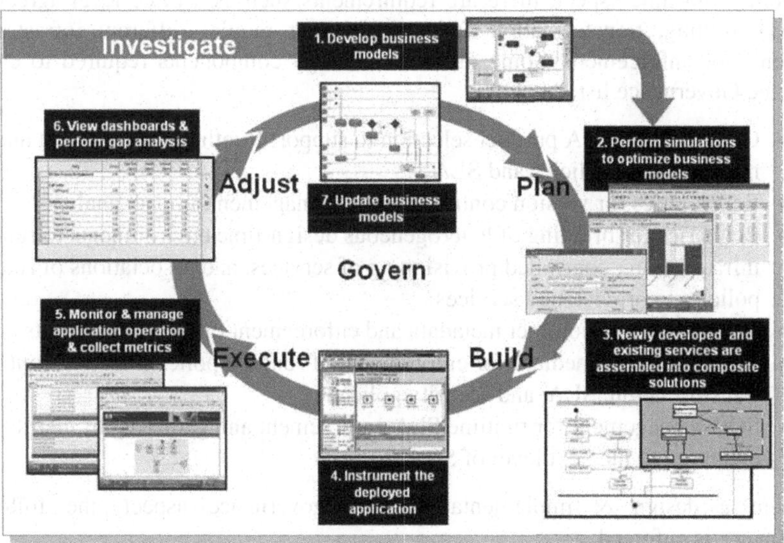

Our SOA Governance is an agile and efficient decision and accountability framework that provides the capability to organize, understand, and manage SOA information to govern the planning, building and managing of a SOA system. In support of this goal, our SOA governance works to enable the success of the following key assets in delivering SOA:

- Prioritized enterprise and business unit service roadmaps
- Service lifecycle (specification, design, development, deployment, operation)
- Best practices, standards selection, and enforcement
- Funding models, financial metrics
- Reference architecture
- Change management to control services and registry sprawl

The governance also enables and tracks the following cultural and team transformation activities:

- Education and skills development for both business and technology groups
- Organization structure alignment for SOA, including clear roles and responsibilities for stakeholders
- Removal of organizational issues around joint ownership of processes and assets, clarified communication channels, and processes
- Enablement of successful cross-functional collaboration throughout the service lifecycle
- Individual incentive and measurement changes for SOA

It's important to establish both the organizational aspects of SOA governance, such as those outlined above, concurrent with technology enablers to enforce governance at both design and runtime. The technology aspect of the governance includes Design time and Runtime governance.

From a run-time aspect, there are requirements such as service level agreements (SLAs), routing, transformation and security that require different infrastructure elements for enforcement. Some of the technology components required to enforce Runtime Governance listed below:

- Guideline for SOA product selection to support Runtime management and monitoring of policies and SLA's.
- Repositories for version control, change management, impact analysis
- Registries for bridging of heterogeneous design-time environments to runtime infrastructure, controlled provisioning of services, and associations of runtime policies to provisioned services
- Management of contract metadata and enforcement of service contracts
- Messaging intermediary for enforcement of runtime policies such as routing, transformation, SLA, and security policies
- SOA management for runtime SLA enforcement and gathering of metrics for evolution to the next level of SOA maturity

From a design & implementation time governance aspect, the following governance is enforced:

- **Design Governance**
  - 3D VE guidelines for capturing business and technology architectures of as-is models. Impact analysis to guide through selection of the existing IT elements for modernization.
  - ADM guidelines for Knowledge Mining and Abstraction (KMA) of the identified IT elements.
  - ADM guidelines for discovery and scenario selections and analysis of the identified IT elements.
  - Standard Tools to support lifecycle processes -- capture of as-is models, and capture of to-be models.
  - Business service governance
- **Implementation Governance**
  - Guideline for use of SOA IDE (pluggable to Eclipse)
  - Guidelines for service granularity
  - Design Guideline for exposing legacy components, legacy data, legacy applications
  - Guideline for building services and orchestrations
  - Guideline for Service Registry
  - Guideline for Test the services and orchestrations
  - Guideline for deploying services and orchestrations
  - Standard Repositories of service assets and all the associated documentations that goes along with it
  - Guideline for Quality assurance
  - Guideline for Discovery mechanism for service consumers and orchestrations

And finally from the Management aspect the following governance is enforced:

- A distributed secure SOA console providing features such as:
  - Policy Management
  - Service security management
  - Service Registry
  - Service configuration and customization
  - Protocol management
  - Service Quality Assurance and Validation

Additional technologies were also utilized to facilitate non-policy facets around SOA governance. Some of the technologies considered are:

- Portals for centralized dissemination of SOA information and access control of SOA assets such as reference architecture documentation
- Dashboards for graphical representation of SOA metrics
- Business intelligence to enable SOA metrics trend analysis and scenario forecasting
- Workflow to automate SOA governance processes and enable quality and control gateways
- Service and project portfolio management to enable a holistic and more informed decision process around service candidate selection, service versioning, service retirement, and SOA investment decisions.

We found the governance a necessary element for the successful and consistent transformation into the SOA. Adhering to the underlying principle of SOA, SOA governance spans both organizational and technical boundaries. It is the critical element to enabling an organization to successfully manage and control the cross-divisional, distributed nature of SOA. Successful SOA governance ensures that an organization is prepared to respond to changing market requirements in a more agile manner. This is dependent upon the establishment and enforcement of SOA organization and governance practices via all elements outlined above—structure, process, and technology.

5 Conclusion

Having access to holistic view of the enterprise provided us with systematic but business driven transformation selection. Gathering holistic views of the enterprise as a set of interrelated models helped us with modernization implementation planning, prioritizing and planning for retirement of the existing components, consolidation, and preparation of knowledge extraction, and application of ADM. Prioritizing implicitly help with incremental modernization. Legacy components are modernized in a logical order as defined in the captured 3D VE models.

We believe ad-hoc selection of old application components without knowing the business impacts will cause the SOA modernization to fail. ROI is a vital part of large scale modernization and having a systematic methodology to help with selecting, prioritizing and planning of the old IT touch points for modernization significantly reduces the risks while guarantee the SOA project to succeed.

In a large and complex environment without a transformation framework like MDA, the modernization will become almost impossible. We believe ad-hoc selection of old application components, with ad-hoc SOA implementation strategy for the required transformation will hardly succeed. MDA styles guided with supporting SOA governance are the key to success of large scale SOA transformation. The governance specific to each styles removes any ambiguities regarding implementation approach.

SOA governance spans both organizational and technical boundaries. It is the critical element to enabling an organization to successfully manage and control the cross-divisional, distributed nature of SOA. Successful SOA governance ensures that an organization is prepared to respond to changing market requirements in a more agile manner. This is dependent upon the establishment and enforcement of SOA organization and governance practices via all elements outlined above—structure, process, and technology.

SOA like any other technological innovation requires proper skills. SOA implicitly must meet a set of challenging requirements, and that is the integration and interoperation of disparate applications, systems, databases, middlewares, and more. This vast area of integration technology opens numerous opportunities for SOA vendors to inject their own proprietary, none-interoperable features. Uneducated selection of SOA vendor products could quickly produce yet another proprietary (legacy) environment! Likely numerous Web Services standards have been produced by standard bodies and implemented by a number of SOA vendors. To move into real

SOA environment, we strongly recommend the use of SOA products that adhere to the open standards. For example an Enterprise Service Bus without using XML standards, the de-facto messaging, routing, transformation, and security mechanisms and more, will fall into EAI category, where each EAI hub used to introduce their own proprietary messaging scarifying interoperability and therefore orchestration. Service granularity, design time decisions, runtime policies must some how be defined before any service being designed and implemented. This is where SOA Governance plays a key role in success of solid design, test, deployment and maintenance of a large SOA environment.

Run-Time Adaptation of Non-functional Properties of Composite Web Services Using Aspect-Oriented Programming

N.C. Narendra[1], Karthikeyan Ponnalagu[1], Jayatheerthan Krishnamurthy[2], and R. Ramkumar[2]

[1] IBM India Research Lab, Bangalore, India
{narendra, karthik.ponnalagu}@in.ibm.com
[2] IBM India Software Lab, Bangalore, India
{jayatheerthan, ramkumar_rj}@in.ibm.com

Abstract. Existing web service composition and adaptation mechanisms are limited only to the scope of web service choreography in terms of web service selection/invocation vis-à-vis pre-specified Service Level Agreement constraints. Such a scope hardly leaves ground for a participating service in a choreographed flow to re-adjust itself in terms of changed non functional expectations and most often these services are discarded and new services discovered to get inducted into the flow. In this paper, we extend this idea by focusing on run-time adaptation of non-functional features of a composite Web service by modifying the non-functional features of its component Web services. We use aspect-oriented programming (AOP) technology for specifying and relating non-functional properties of the Web services as aspects at both levels of component and composite. This is done via a specification language for representing non-functional properties, and a formally specifiable relation function between the aspects of the component Web services and those of the composite Web service. From the end users' viewpoint, such up-front aspect-oriented modeling of non-functional properties enables on-demand composite Web service adaptation with minimal disruption in quality of service. We demonstrate the applicability and merits of our approach via an implementation of a simple yet real-life example.

1 Introduction and Motivation

Web services have emerged as a major technology for deploying automated interactions between heterogeneous systems. They possess certain key properties [8, 12], viz., independent from specific platforms and computing paradigms, developed primarily for inter-organizational situations, and composable into composite Web services. Web service composition primarily concerns requests of users that cannot be satisfied by any atomically available Web service, but satisfied by a composite service obtained by combining a set of available Web services [13]. The dynamic nature of the business world highlights the continuous pressure to reduce expenses, to increase revenues, to generate profits, and to remain competitive. This requires Web services to be highly reactive and adaptive to business centric changes. In particular, composite Web services should be equipped with mechanisms to ensure that their constituent component Web services are able to adapt to meet changing requirements.

B. Krämer, K.-J. Lin, and P. Narasimhan (Eds.): ICSOC 2007, LNCS 4749, pp. 546–557, 2007.

In this paper[1], we consider the important research issue of engineering adaptations on component Web services based on changed non-functional requirements imposed on the composite Web service, such as improved security, better scalability, etc. In particular, we focus on how non-functional requirements changes in the composite Web service can be met via appropriate pre declared modifications to the component Web services code, without affecting their core functionality. Our approach uses distributed aspect-oriented programming (AOP) technology [1, 4, 5] to dictate these modifications in component Web services in a non-intrusive manner. In addition, from the viewpoint of the users of the composite Web service, such an approach enables on-demand adaptation with minimal disruption. To the best of our knowledge, this is the first non-intrusive distributed AOP mechanism, especially applied to Web services. Hence our main contributions are the following: a distributed system architecture for non-functional adaptation of Web services via AOP (implemented on top of PROSE [2,3], a well-known AOP implementation environment[2]), a specification language for specifying non-functional properties of Web services, a formally specifiable relation function between the non-functional properties of the component and composite Web services, and a non-intrusive concern extraction and manipulation implementation for component Web services based on the relation function.

Our paper is organized as follows. We review related work in section 2. Section 3 introduces our approach and conceptual architecture. We then describe our running example in Section 4, and then use it to explain our approach in detail. In Section 5, we describe our specification language for describing non-functional properties of component and composite Web services. In Section 6, we discuss how multiple aspects can be weaved together, via a discussion of their inter-relationships. The detailed implementation of our running example is presented in Section 7. Finally, Section 8 concludes the paper with suggestions for future work.

2 Related Work

Aspect-oriented programming (AOP) [1,4,5] is an extension of other software development paradigms; it allows capturing and modularizing concerns called aspects that crosscut a software system. AOP makes very powerful program transformations possible, through a composition process where aspect *advices* are *woven* into the core program at locations called *pointcuts*. Members and methods can also be inserted in classes through an aspect construct called introduction. Aspects have the ability to introduce functionality in a core program in a non-invasive way, making it possible to alter the behavior of a system a posteriori. This aspect weaving can be done at any time – compile time, load time or run time.

Regarding Web services, existing web service composition and adaptation mechanisms are limited only to the process of web service choreography in terms of web service selection/invocation vis-à-vis pre-specified (Service Level Agreement) SLA constraints. Such a technique has many deficiencies, such as inability to manage ad-

[1] This is an expanded version of a paper that will appear in WS-Testing Workshop (co-located with SCC 2007).

[2] We have used version 1.3.0 of PROSE.

aptation, code duplication, inability to invoke an alternate Web service in case of failure, etc. To that end, several researchers are investigating AOP for improving the manageability of Web service compositions. For example, Cibrán and Verheecke propose a method for modularizing Web services management with AOP [11].

Charfi et. al. have approached this problem from a different direction [10]. They have proposed an extension to the BPEL language, which they called aspect-oriented BPEL (AO4BPEL). Their language brings in modular and dynamic adaptability to BPEL, since mid-flight adaptations can be implemented via advices in AO4BPEL. Ortiz et al. develop an aspect-oriented solution for Web services composition (of type orchestration) and for interaction patterns [6]. Orchestration is, here, defined as the process by which the Web services interactions are monitored and managed. The authors' work is motivated by the lack of standards associated with composition. More particularly, Ortiz et al. raised multiple questions related to the possibility of reusing interaction patterns previously implemented, and the efforts to put in for modularizing these patterns rather than scattering the code.

One recent approach towards service adaptation via AOP methods is described in [15]. In that paper, however, the authors have primarily focused on a template-based approach that enables the selection of the appropriate advice to be weaved into the Web service code based on mismatches with other participating Web services in the composite Web service. The focus in our paper, on the other hand, is on joint modeling and sharing of non-functional properties expressed as cross-cutting concerns via aspects. Hence we view the ideas in [15] as being complementary to our work. Similar to [15], our earlier work [14] proposes a method for decoupling security concerns in Web services via aspects, by expressing these concerns as contextual information separate from the core Web services functionality. This too, is complementary to the work reported in this paper.

One of the most well-known AOP implementations available today, is PROSE [2,3]. PROSE works by implementing methods – known as "hooks" – that intercept method calls in the Java Virtual Machine (JVM) at the point where the aspects are to be executed. Hence PROSE uses a modified version of the Java just-in-time compiler to insert code that checks for the presence of aspect advice at every possible join point, so as to implement system behavior modification at runtime. However, PROSE is not a distributed implementation, and works only to alter the behavior of a single component. Our system, therefore, seeks to extend PROSE for the distributed environment of web service composition and execution. Our system is also different from other distributed AOP systems [9], since it does not directly manipulate the source code of the individual component Web services; instead, it works by specifying advices to the individual component Web services so that they can change their functionality themselves.

Our solution approach uses WS-Policy and WSLA for implementing the negotiation of service requirements and capabilities between the service provider and the consumer, rather than using an enterprise service bus (ESB)-based approach. An ESB solution by itself does not provide native support for implementing negotiation of service requirements, but instead works in conjunction with WS-Policy and WSLA to implement the negotiation between the participating web services.

3 Solution Architecture and Approach

The composite web service model is extended to contain the list of its cross-cutting concerns that have a bi-directional mapping to those of the participating individual component web services. Each of these concerns, in turn, will have a mapping to the SLA constraints representing the different non-functional requirements. Hence there are two mappings to be established and maintained (These mappings need to be established between the composite and component Web services by prior agreement during the build time phase of the composite web service):

- The mapping between the non-functional requirements and the different cross cutting aspects of the composite web service
- The mapping (also known as relation function) between each aspect of the composite web service and the individual aspects of the component web services

The overall solution architecture is depicted in Figure 1.

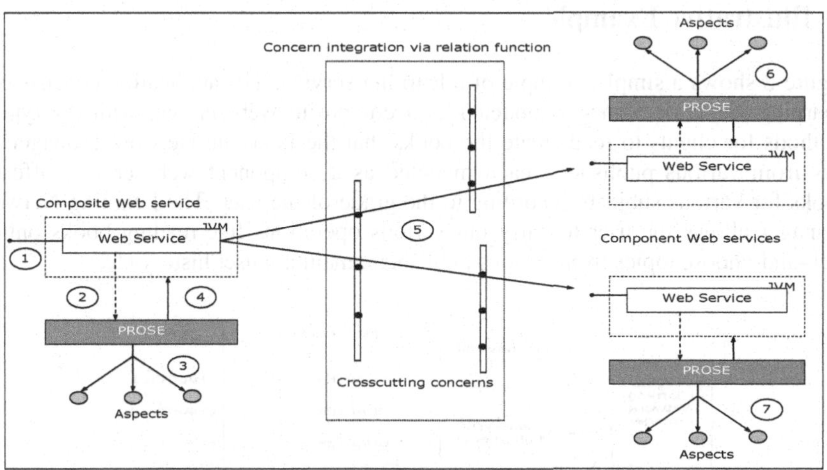

Fig. 1. Solution Architecture & Approach

Briefly, our system works as follows: at run time, in response to a change in a non-functional requirement imposed on the composite Web service by its user (1), the composite web service determines the appropriate aspect changes needed (2) to meet the change. The composite Web service makes this determination using the relation function (depicted via the "concern integration" rectangle in Figure 1) which it maintains. The composite Web service will therefore invoke the relation function (3, 4) to determine those aspects of the individual web services that need to be modified. It will then send messages (5) to the component web services, asking them to "re-weave" their functionalities in order to meet the changed requirements (6, 7). In case a component web service is not able to do so, it will send a reply to the message, upon which the composite web service will need to implement the appropriate exception handling mechanisms, for responding back to the initial user request.

We model the composite web service comprising aspects A_1 through A_n. Each component Web service W_i also possesses aspects a_{i1} through a_{in}. Each aspect A_i in the composite web service is related to the aspects a_{ij}, via the relation function:

$$A_i = f_i(a_{ij}, 1 <= i <= m, 1 <= j <= n)$$

Of course, not all aspects a_{ij} will be affected by A_i, hence the relation function for each A_i would be different. Indeed, at its most elementary level, the relation function f_i is merely a mapping between A_i and the individual a_{ij} aspects, where each mapping could be suitably annotated with machine-readable information encoded in an XML formatted file.

It is to be stressed that our solution approach is *not* dependent on the choice of PROSE as an implementation mechanism. Different component Web services can have their own aspect-oriented implementation mechanisms (of which several exist in the literature[3]), as long as they can interoperate on sending/receiving advices for non-functional adaptation.

4 Illustrative Example

Figure 2 shows a simple example of a learning service. The application consists of a Learning Network Manager modeled as a composite web service, with the typical methods for clients to read/create the books that the Learning Network Manager offers from various publishers (each modeled as a component web service) offering books for various subjects according to the grade of the user. The Learning Network Manager allows the user to carry out various operations like reading books online, pick-and-choose topics from various publishers, maintain user history etc.

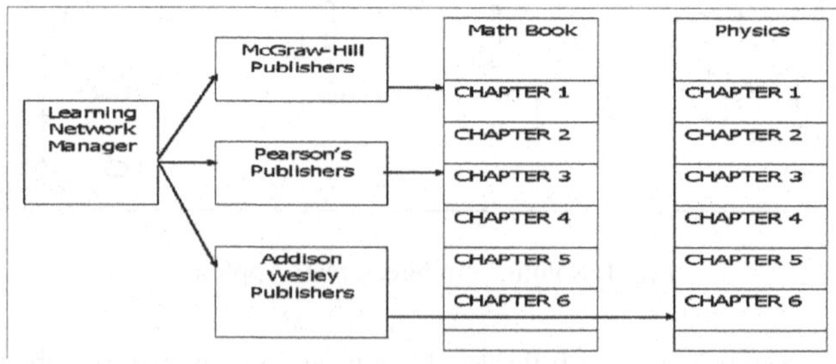

Fig. 2. Learning Network Manager and Associated Component Web Services

In this distributed environment, the Publishers and Learning Network Manager are required to customize their code to accommodate various kinds of customers with dynamic requirements. We have identified some of the important cross-cutting concerns. For example, the Publisher and Learning Network Manager need to accommodate the *timing* property in order to calculate the time taken by the customer to access the Web services. This function is important for tracking the performance of the system, especially under heavy load conditions. The second important concern is

[3] http://en.wikipedia.org/wiki/Aspect-oriented_programming#Implementations

scalability - in order for the Learning Network Manager to support a larger user base, it may expect the publishers also to support the same. Also, maintaining the *history* of each user, for future reference, is another important cross-cutting concern, which needs to be maintained by each publisher. Finally, *security* is needed for ensuring access to only authorized users.

The above cross-cutting concerns can also be used to identify their respective pointcuts, viz., Timing, System Tuning (for scalability), User History and Security.

5 Specification Language for Non-functional Properties

In order for a composite web service to locate a component web service at runtime, based on its '*capabilities*' to adapt to a changing non-functional requirement, the component web service must declare its capabilities in a program readable format, which could be interpreted by the composite web service to make a decision at run-time whether or not to invoke a particular component web service. Hence in this section, we discuss a specification language for representing non-functional properties that is built on existing standards such as WS-Policy[4] and WSLA[5]. While we use the WS-Policy framework to represent the capabilities and requirements of a Web service, WSLA is used to publish the QoS and related parameters that a web service can offer to its clients.

5.1 WS-Policy Based Specification of Non-functional Properties

WS-Policy provides a general purpose XML model to define capabilities and requirements of a Web Service. A policy is a collection of policy alternatives, which are in turn a collection of policy assertions. A policy assertion represents an individual requirement, capability or other property of behaviour. In our model, we extend the WS-Policy grammar by adding the `policy-assertion` and `NonFunctional-Property` tag elements as illustrated below.

```
<wsp:Policy
     xmlns:wsp="http://schemas.xmlsoap.org/ws/2004/09/policy"
     xmlns:nfp="http://www.ibm.com/schemas/nfp">
 <wsp:All>  <!-- policy alternative -->
  <nfp:policy-assertion name="…" type="…" category="…">
   <nfp:NonFunctionalProperty name="…">
    <nfp:Attribute name="…" value="…"/>
     <nfp:Parameter name="" value="" mandatory="(true | false)"/>
     <nfp:custom-tags/>
   </nfp:NonFunctionalProperty>
  </nfp:policy-assertion>
 </wsp:All>
</ws:Policy>
```

Each `policy-assertion` has the following attributes:

---

[4] http://www.w3.org/Submission/WS-Policy/

[5] http://www.research.ibm.com/wsla/WSLASpecV1-20030128.pdf/

- `name:` A qualified name for the policy assertion that could be referred to by another element in the policy document.
- `type:` Type specifies whether this policy assertion represents the 'requirement' or the 'capability' of the web services defining the policy.
- `category:` Domain specific category name of the assertion. Example: *Security*, *Performance* etc.

While the <Attribute> tag would be used to provide more description about the <NonFunctionalProperty>, the <Parameter> tag accepts input parameters to be passed to the target application (component service or an aspect implementation). For example, the non-functional property 'ResponseTime' may have an *attribute* called 'units' that may specify the unit of time that would be used to track the response time (like seconds, milliseconds etc), while at the same time, may accept a *parameter* called 'round-off-digits=nnn' with which a composite service may inform to the component service as to how many digits should the Response time output be rounded off to. The <custom-tags/> in the policy specification above provides flexibility for the participating web service to specify any domain specific custom tags that would be required to define the non-functional properties in a more detailed manner. However, please note that the XML schema definition and the interpretation of the <custom-tags/> is to be exchanged between the participating web services a priori.

Given below is an example of how the above mentioned model would be instantiated. The example below depicts a component web service that declares its *capability* of supporting 'Authentication' as a non-functional property. Please note that the policy-assertion type is 'capability' since the component web service exposes its ability to support 'authentication' as one of its non-functional properties.

```
<wsp:Policy
   xmlns:wsp="http://schemas.xmlsoap.org/ws/2004/09/policy"
   xmlns:nfp="http://www.ibm.com/schemas/nfp">
 <wsp:All>  <!-- policy alternative -->
  <nfp:policy-assertion name="SecurityAuthSpec"
                   type="capability" category="Security">
    <nfp:NonFunctionalProperty name="authentication">
       <nfp:Parameter name="username" mandatory="true"/>
       <nfp:Parameter name="password" mandatory="true"/>
    </nfp:NonFunctionalProperty>
  </nfp:policy-assertion>
 </wsp:All>
</ws:Policy>
```

Please note that our specification language differs from WS-CoL [18] in that WS-CoL extends WS-Policy to define 'constraints' to be imposed during the execution of web services as well as to retrieve external data required to evaluate a constraint expression whereas our extension of WS-Policy provides a facility to specify the 'capabilities' and 'requirements' of a service. Our specification is domain independent due to the support of a generic <NonFunctionalProperty> tag as well as the <custom-tags/> place holder to support domain specific extensions and representations of non-functional properties.

5.2 Service Level Agreement

A service level is used to define the expected performance behavior of a deployed Web service, where the performance metrics are, for example, average response time, supported throughput, service availability, etc. During deployment of a Web service, the resources of an underlying Web service container can be reconfigured to provide a certain service level. Even the same Web service can be offered at different service levels to different clients by dynamically allocating resources for execution of individual Web service requests. Hence, to receive assurances on the service level, a client creates a priori a service level agreement (SLA) associated with this Web service with the service provider.

In our running example, a Publisher's web service would have an SLA defined for 'ResponseTime' using WSLA, representing the Timing pointcut introduced in Section 4. Given below is a sample SLA document defining an SLAParameter called 'ResponseTime' and the metric used to measure it.

```
<OperationGroup name="ReadOperations">
   <Operation name="WSDLSOAPGetChapter">
      <SLAParameter name="ResponseTime" type="float"
                    unit="seconds">
          <Metric>AverageResponseTime</Metric>
      </SLAParameter>
   </Operation>
</OperationGroup>
```

An SLAObligation for the above mentioned example may be defined as below:

```
<ServiceLevelObjective name="SLO_for_ResponseTime">
  <Obliged>McGrawHillPublisher</Obliged>
  <Expression>
    <Predicate xsi:type="Less">
       <SLAParameter>ResponseTime</SLAParameter>
       <Value>2</Value> <!-- 2 seconds -->
    </Predicate>
  </Expression>
</ServiceLevelObjective>
```

6 Aspects and Their Relationships

We relate each of the above identified point-cuts to an aspect. An aspect of a component web service is affected by zero or more aspects of the composite web service. Aspect interactions can be complex, subtle and very difficult to identify. Please note that finding such interactions is outside the scope of our research. In our work we assume a fixed ontology of aspects, with all interactions explicitly identified ahead of time. We provide an XML file representation for specifying the aspect interaction and conflicts. Our model is extensible and hence we can contain any level of complex relationships here. Our model of aspect interactions is leveraged from [7]), and features the following: *Orthogonal* – if the combined contribution of both aspects is equal to the sum of their individual contributions (e.g., user-history aspect of component & composite Web services); *Complementary* – if their combined contribution is greater than the sum of their individual contributions (e.g., authentication and timing aspect), *Depends* – if they can only be deployed along with each other (e.g., timing aspect of composite Web service and timing aspects of component Web service); *Conflict* – if their combination has a negative effect on the behavior of the composite Web service (e.g., timing and user-history aspect may conflict, especially if the policy of charging the customer is based on the content accessed); *Prevents* – if the application of one aspect prevents the application of the other (e.g., if one aspect measures the response time with respect to a threshold, which would deactivate other aspects such as caching, security and logging); *Equivalent* – if their individual effects are the same (e.g., different logging types such as CBELogging, JTraceLogging, etc.)

7 Implementation Details

Our learning network manager is modeled as a composite web service, with operations such as authenticateUser, showBooks, showSubjects, showTopics, showContents and createBook exposed for clients to read/create the books that the Learning Network Manager offers from various publishers (see Figure 3). Each publisher is modeled as a component web service offering books for various subjects through their exposed operations. (We have not displayed the details of the WSDL-based interfaces of the Web services in this Section, since we have chosen to focus on the non-functional property modeling aspects.)

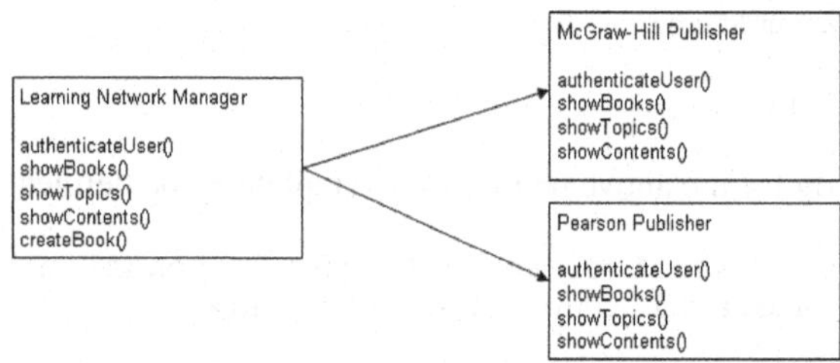

Fig. 3. Service Operations

The timing aspect relationship between the Learning Network Manager and any of the publishers is depicted in Figure 4.

```
<ar:aspect-relation xmlns:ar="http://www.ibm.com/aspectrelationship">
    <ar:source-aspect id="a1" component="ws1">
        <ar:aspect class="class1">
            <pointcut name="methodAround" expression="execution(* class1.methodAround(..))"/>
            <advice name="advice1" type="around" bind-to="methodAround"/>
            <parameters>
                <parameter name="p1" value="v1"/>
                <parameter name="p2" value="v2"/>
            </parameters>
        </ar:aspect>

        <ar:relation type="depends">
            <ar:target-aspect id="a2" component="ws2"/>
                <ar:aspect class="class2">
                <pointcut name="methodAround" expression="execution(* class2.methodAround(..))"/>
                <advice name="advice1" type="around" bind-to="methodAround"/>
                <parameters>
                    <parameter name="p1" value="v1"/>
                    <parameter name="p2" value="v2"/>
                </parameters>
                </ar:aspect>
            </ar:target-aspect>
        </ar:relation>
    </ar:source-aspect>
</ar:aspect-relation>
```

Fig. 4. Timing aspect relationship between component and composite services

Given below is the Timing Aspect implementation for McGrawPublisher service in PROSE.

```
public aspect TimingAspect
{
    private long McGrawPublisher.timeBeforeMethod = 0;
    private long McGrawPublisher.timeAfterMethod = 0;
    private long McGrawPublisher.timeBetweenMethods = 0;

    pointcut setter(McGrawPublisher m): call(void McGrawPublisher.show*(*)) && target(m);

    void around(McGrawPublisher m): setter(m) {
        timeBeforeMethod = System.currentTimeMillis();
        proceed(m);
        timeAfterMethod = System.currentTimeMillis();
        timeBetweenMethods = timeAfterMethod - timeBeforeMethod;
    }

    private long PearsonPublisher.timeBeforeMethod = 0;
    private long PearsonPublisher.timeAfterMethod = 0;
    private long PearsonPublisher.timeBetweenMethods = 0;

    pointcut setter(PearsonPublisher p): call(void PearsonPublisher.show*(*)) && target(p);

    void around(PearsonPublisher p): setter(p) {
        timeBeforeMethod = System.currentTimeMillis();
        proceed(p);
        timeAfterMethod = System.currentTimeMillis();
        timeBetweenMethods = timeAfterMethod - timeBeforeMethod;
    }
}
```

Figure 5 depicts a snapshot of WS-Policy declared by `LearningNetworkManager` Web Service stating that it *'expects'* the component services (Mc-GrawHill and Pearson publishers) to support the tracking of *'Response Time'* of `ShowBooks()` service. The component service would also weave an aspect code dynamically into its AOP runtime system to handle the change in non-functional requirement.

```
<wsp:Policy xmlns:wsp="http://schemas.xmlsoap.org/ws/2004/09/policy"
            xmlns:nfp="http://www.ibm.com/schemas/nfp">

  <wsp:All>  <!-- policy alternative -->
    <nfp:policy-assertion name="ResponseTimeTracker" type="requirement" category="Timing">
      <nfp:NonFunctionalProperty name="ResponseTime">
        <nfp:Attribute name="units" value="seconds"/>
        <nfp:Parameter name="round-off-digits" value="3"/>
      </nfp:NonFunctionalProperty>
    </nfp:policy-assertion>
  </wsp:All>
</ws:Policy>
```

Fig. 5. WS-Policy defining composite service's Non Functional Property requirement

In response to the above mentioned requirement, the component service (eg., Mc-GrawHill publisher), would generate an SLA and publish it to the requesting service. Section 5.2 above shows a snapshot of the SLA published by the component service.

Given in Figure 6 below is a self-explanatory sequence of screen shots that explain the flow of the implementation. The Figure shows the ShowBooks() service of the McGrawHill and Pearson publisher services, *before* and *after* the invocation of the Timing aspect.

(**a**) Invocation of ShowBooks() operation

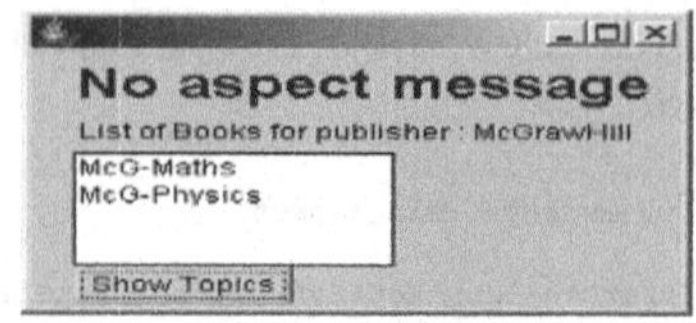

(**b**) ShowBooks() returns no aspect message

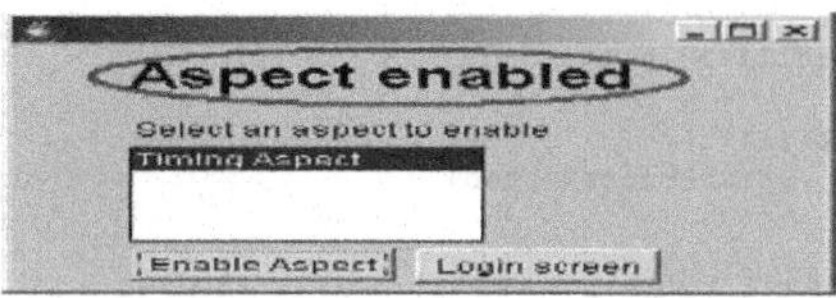

(**c**) Enabling of Timing Aspect

(**d**) Invoking ShowBooks() after enabling aspect

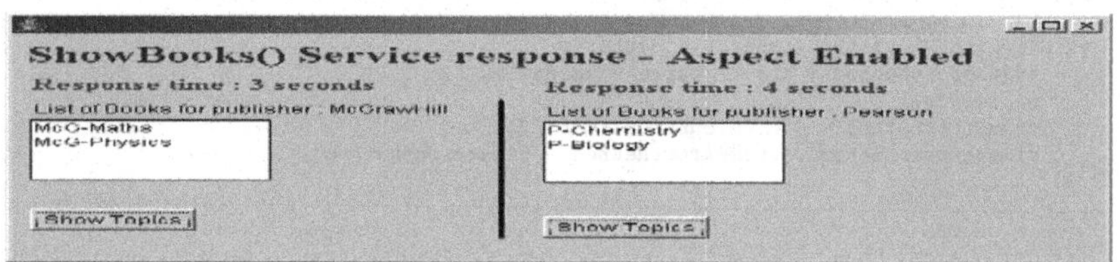

(**e**) Due to dynamic weaving of aspects, component service responds back to composite service with Response time details

Fig. 6. Screenshots of Implementation

8 Future Work

Future work will involve integrating our work with self-healing Web services environments as modeled in [16]. Additionally, we will also evaluate the recent work of a joinpoint inference technique based on behavioral specifications of state machine specifications [17], and investigate how it can be used to provide a formal specification of aspect interactions between the composite and component Web services.

Acknowledgement. The authors wish to thank Sumanth Vepa, Zakaria Maamar, Dipayan Gangopadhyay and the anonymous ICSOC reviewers for their feedback.

References

[1] Kiczales, G., Lamping, J., Mendhekar, A., Maeda, C., Lopes, C., Loingtier, J., Irwin, J.: Aspect Oriented Programming. In: Aksit, M., Matsuoka, S. (eds.) ECOOP 1997. LNCS, vol. 1241, pp. 220–242. Springer, Heidelberg (1997)

[2] Popovici, A., Gross, T., Alonso, G.: Dynamic Weaving for Aspect Oriented Programming. In: Proceedings of 1st International Conference on Aspect-Oriented Software Development, Enschede, The Netherlands (2002)

[3] Nicoara, A., Alonso, G.: Dynamic AOP with PROSE. Department of Computer Science, Swiss Federal Institute of Technology Zurich (ETH Zurich), CH-8092 Zurich, Switzerland, accessible from http://prose.ethz.ch/

[4] Popovici, A., Alonso, G., Gross, T.: Just in Time Aspects: Efficient Dynamic Weaving for Java. In: Proceedings of 2nd International Conference on Aspect-Oriented Software Development, Boston, USA (2003)

[5] Kiczales, G., Hilsdale, E., Hugunin, J., Kersten, M., Palm, J., Griswold, W.G.: An Overview of AspectJ. In: Knudsen, J.L. (ed.) ECOOP 2001. LNCS, vol. 2072, pp. 18–22. Springer, Heidelberg (2001)

[6] Ortiz, G., Hernandez, J., Clemente, P.J.: Decoupling Non-Functional Properties in Web-Services: As Aspect-Oriented Approach. In: ICSOC'2004. Proceedings of The 2nd International Conference on Service Oriented Computing, New-York, USA (2004)

[7] Wohladter, E., Tai, S., Thomas, A., Rouvellou, I., Devanbu, P.: GlueQoS: Middleware to Sweeten Quality-of-Service Policy Interactions. In: ICSE. Proceedings of International Conference on Software Engineering, Edinburgh, UK (2004)

[8] Ma, K.J.: Web Services: What's Real and What's Not. IEEE IT Professional 7(2) (2005)

[9] Nishizawa, M., Chiba, S., Tatsubori, M.: Remote Pointcut – A Language Construct for Distributed AOP. In: AOSD'04. Proceedings of International Conference on Aspect-Oriented Software Development, Lancaster, UK, March 22-26, pp. 7–15. ACM Press, New York (2004)

[10] Charfi, A., Schmeling, B., Heizenreder, A., Mezini, M.: Reliable, Secure and Transacted Web Service Compositions with AO4BPEL. In: ICSOC'2004. Proceedings of The 2nd International Conference on Service Oriented Computing, New-York, USA (2004)

[11] Cibrán, M.A., Verheecke, B.: Modularizing Web Services Management with AOP. In: Cardelli, L. (ed.) ECOOP 2003. LNCS, vol. 2743, Springer, Heidelberg (2003)

[12] Benatallah, B., Sheng, Q.Z., Ngu, A.H.H., Dumas, M.: Declarative Composition and Peer-to-Peer Provisioning of Dynamic Web Services. In: ICDE. Proceedings of International Conference on Data Engineering (2002), also available from http://csdl.computer.org/comp/proceedings/icde/2002/1531/00/15310297abs.htm

[13] Berardi, D., Calvanese, D., De Giacomo, G., Lenzerini, M., Mecella, M.: A Foundational Vision for E-Services. In: Eder, J., Missikoff, M. (eds.) CAiSE 2003. LNCS, vol. 2681, Springer, Heidelberg (2003)

[14] Kouadri Mostefaoui, G., Maamar, Z., Narendra, N.C., Sattanathan, S.: Decoupliing Security Concerns in Web Services Using Aspects. In: ITNG 2006. Proceedings of Information Technology – New Generations, IEEE Computer Society Press, Los Alamitos (2006)

[15] Kongdenfha, W., Saint-Paul, R., Benatallah, B., Casati, F.: An Aspect-Oriented Framework for Service Adaptation. In: Dan, A., Lamersdorf, W. (eds.) ICSOC 2006. LNCS, vol. 4294, Springer, Heidelberg (2006)

[16] Kouadri Mostefaoui, G., Maamar, Z., Narendra, N.C., Thiran, Ph.: On Modeling and Developing Self-Healing Web Services Using Aspects. In: COMSWARE 2007. Proceedings of 2nd International Conference on Communication Software and Middleware, IEEE Communications Society, Los Alamitos (2007)

[17] Cottenier, T., van den Berg, A., Elrad, T.: Joinpoint Inference from Behavioral Specification to Implementation. In: ECOOP. Proceedings of European Conference on Object-Oriented Programming (2007) (to appear)

[18] Baresi, L., Guinea, S., Plebani, P.: WS-Policy for Service Monitoring. In: Proceedings of TES 2005 (September 2005)

Software as a Service: An Integration Perspective

Wei Sun[1], Kuo Zhang[1], Shyh-Kwei Chen[2], Xin Zhang[1], and Haiqi Liang[1]

[1] IBM China Research Lab
[2] IBM T.J Watson Research Lab
{weisun, zhangkuo, zxin, lianghq}@cn.ibm.com, {skchen}@us.ibm.com

Abstract. Software as a Service (SaaS) is gaining momentum in recent years with more and more successful adoptions. Though SaaS is delivered over Internet and charged on per-use basis, it is software application in essence. SaaS contains business data and logics which are usually required to integrate with other applications deployed by a SaaS subscriber. This makes Integration become one of the common requirements in most SaaS adoptions. In this paper, we analyze the key functional and non-functional SaaS integration requirements from an industry practitioner point of view; and summarize the SaaS integration patterns and existing offerings; then point out the gaps from both technology and tooling perspectives; finally we introduce a SaaS integration framework to address those gaps. Considering there is no much academic work on SaaS service modeling, we come up with a SaaS service description framework as an extension of Web Service description, so as to model SaaS unique features in a unified way. With the supported tooling and runtime platform, the framework can facilitate the SaaS integration lifecycle in a model-driven approach.

1 Introduction

Software as a Service (SaaS) is a software delivery model, which provides customers access to business functionality remotely (usually over the internet) as a service [1, 2]. The customer does not specially purchase a software license. The cost of the infrastructure, the right to use the software, and all hosting, maintenance and support services are all bundled into a single monthly or per-use charging. As SaaS brings lower Total Cost of Ownership (TCO) and better Return On Investment (ROI), SaaS services achieve a prosperous development and cover most of the well-known application areas, e.g. Customer Relationship Management(CRM) service from Salesforce.com, Human Resource Management(HRM) service from Employease.com [3, 4].

The functionalities of services delivered through SaaS may vary. Complete or full-blown solutions can be costy and hard to configure. Simple services normally provide specific functionalities, but a need exists to integrate several services together to achieve a desired business operation [7]. There are no standards or guidelines for clients to make technical decision. It becomes a critical problem when disparate services come from different software providers, through different service protocols and with various functionalities. The integration requirement of SaaS customers has been studied by different SaaS market research efforts. According to the survey of 639 companies by AMR research, more than 70% companies expect that the SaaS solution can be integrated with their on-Premises legacy applications or other SaaS solutions

B. Krämer, K.-J. Lin, and P. Narasimhan (Eds.): ICSOC 2007, LNCS 4749, pp. 558–569, 2007.

they subscribed/plan to subscribe [8]. IDC conducted a SaaS solution adoption trend study in 2004 and found that more than 50% of the survey respondents selected "Better integration with in-house applications" as one of the top 3 drivers, making SaaS solution more attractive [9].

There are many industry players and offerings addressing the SaaS integration issues. AppExchange from Salesforce.com provides a hosting platform and web based programming tools for third party vendors to develop/integrate add-on SaaS services on top of its CRM service [4]. Jamcracker enables a hosted SaaS integration hub [10]. IBM SaaS showcase provides a portal of different SaaS services which can be subscribed and integrated [11]. OpenKapow focuses on wrapping SaaS services' capability with Web user interface into a standardized component called "Robot", and leverages Mashup technologies to facilitate the composition of "Robot" come from different SaaS services and Web Services [29]. However, there are few academic works in this area. Seltsikas explored the integration challenges for application service providers from business model point of view [12]. Elfatatry studied SaaS from contract negotiation point of view [13]. Turne summarized SaaS related Web Services technologies [14]. Ottinger from Mule open source group [30] analyzed some SaaS integration requirements, which highlighted several SaaS integration unique issues around corporate firewall, network latency of the integration. However there is not a relatively complete and deep analysis about the SaaS integration requirements as well as the demand for any new technologies in a holistic view.

In this paper, we analyze and identify the SaaS integration requirements and technology gaps, and then propose reference architecture of the SaaS integration framework, which includes a SaaS Description Language (SaaS-DL) to support model driven integration approach, tooling and runtime components as well as different configurations. SaaS can cover very broad areas of Web Services, in this paper, SaaS specially focuses on those business applications (e.g. CRM [4, 16]) delivered in Web Services model. The rest of the paper is organized as follows. Firstly, we will analyze the SaaS integration requirements, common patterns as well as challenges in section 2; based on these analysis, a SaaS-DL and integration framework reference architecture will be introduced in Section 3; then in section 4 prototype implementation of the framework is presented; a case study is introduced in Section 5 to illustrate how the integration framework works; finally, conclusions and future work will be summarized in section 6.

2 SaaS Integration Requirements and Patterns

Most SaaS service subscribers, especially those medium to large companies, have certain applications already deployed on their premises. This makes the application environments of those companies become a hybrid model illustrated in the figure 1. SaaS service is usually a web application which can be accessed by different customers through Internet. Just like normal web based business application, SaaS application is composed by three major layers: user interface, business logic, and data. On the other hand, the SaaS application is special. It usually involves the metering and billing for the usage of the service consumer. Its Quality of Service (QoS) should achieve Service Level Agreement (SLA) between the service provider and consumer according to the service contract. In this section, we will explore the SaaS integration requirements from both functional and non-functional perspectives.

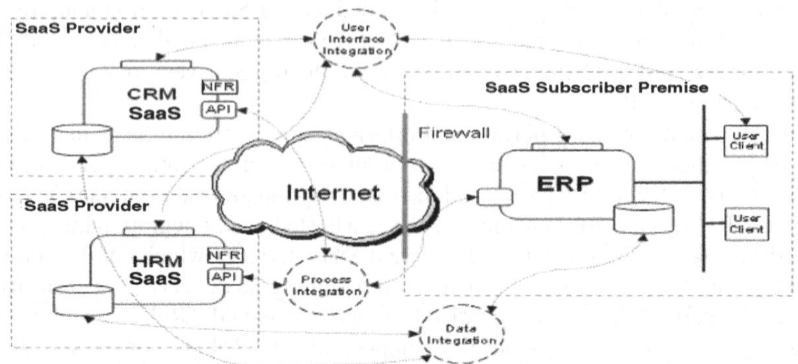

Fig. 1. SaaS Consumption Environment and Integration Requirements

2.1 SaaS Integration Functional Requirements and Patterns

SaaS subscriber leverages SaaS services to support certain business functions, e.g. CRM, HRM. However any business function cannot be isolated from others in most cases. For example, the sales person's commission calculation in HRM should be supported by the sales' performance data managed in CRM. Therefore the different applications/services a company deployed/subscribed should be integrated together. The integration will happen in all the three layers of the SaaS application.

a) User Interface(UI) Integration

Every application has its own user interface and related access control. So the SaaS subscribers should switch among different user interfaces with different user identity and password information required by SaaS services and on-premise applications. As illustrated in figure 2, pattern U-I, Single Sign On (SSO), is a very common UI integration requirement. SSO can enable users log on once and then access all the authorized user interfaces from different applications/SaaS services. Pattern U-II, Mash-up [7, 15], can enable users to access one application/SaaS service's data through another SaaS service/application's user interface.

b) Process Integration

A business process supported by a SaaS service usually can trigger business process supported by another SaaS service or on-premise application. For example, an order process from CRM service should trigger an order fulfillment process managed by ERP application. Therefore process integration can automate the end to end business process transaction span across multiple SaaS services and on-premise applications. There are four key process integration patterns that are usually required. Pattern P-I and P-III can support invoking another process or receiving an invocation through Web Services technology. P-II can support scheduled process invocation in pulling mode. Pattern P-IV can support complex process integration scenario using workflow, in which different people and applications will be involved to link different processes.

c) Data Integration

There are two types of data in a SaaS service: master data and transactional data. As illustrated in Pattern D-I and D-II, these data should be synchronized or migrated from

SaaS services to on-premise applications or vice versa. One type of data in a company's application environment should have only one master data source. The master data source should populate or synchronize the data to other applications/SaaS services timely that need to store that data locally. For example, if a company subscribed a CRM SaaS service, the customer information related data should be a type of master data maintained by CRM SaaS service, though ERP application need to store customer information as well to support fulfillment processes (scheduling, shipping, billing, etc), these data should be always synchronized from CRM service.

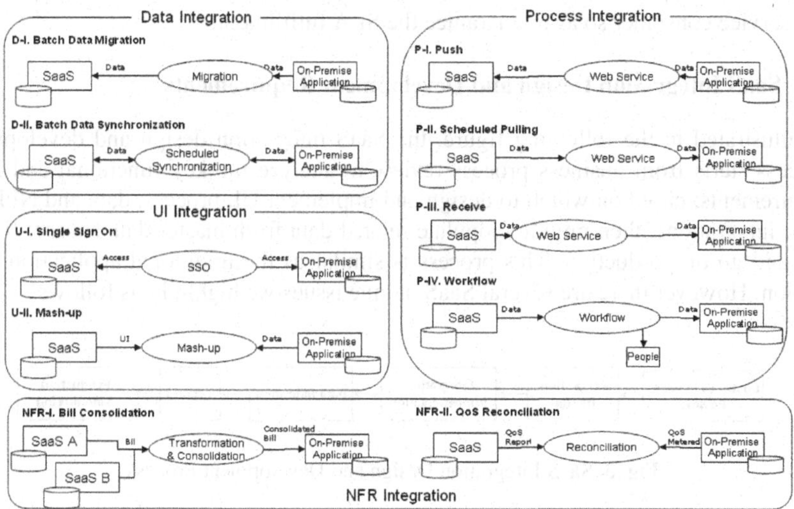

Fig. 2. SaaS Integration Common Patterns

2.2 SaaS Integration Non-Functional Requirements(NFR) and Patterns

SaaS services can be treated as Web Services from both macro level (services delivered over web) and micro level (leverage web services technologies to support integration). Most the NFR requirements brought by Web Services exist in SaaS domain as well, e.g. Security and Privacy. Here we point out the following three important requirements in the integration point of view.

a) Security and privacy

In most cases, all the SaaS subscribers' business data are centrally stored and managed by SaaS provider in a remote side over Internet. In the integration scenario, business data of every SaaS subscribers flow back and forth among the SaaS service and their on-premise applications over Internet. The integration technology should guarantee the subscriber's data should not be hacked and accessed by any third party.

b) Bill reporting and management

SaaS services are charged by usage. A bill is usually issued to the SaaS subscriber in certain timeframe by SaaS provider. As different SaaS providers issue different bills in terms of format and delivery method, the ideal integration scenario related with bill is illustrated in pattern NFR-I: different bills from different SaaS providers use same format or can be transformed into same format, then could be centrally managed and fed into subscriber's finance and accounting application.

c) QoS reporting and reconciliation with SLA
SLA is usually included in a SaaS service contract between SaaS provider and SaaS subscriber. SLA often states the QoS related performance indicators, e.g. availability, response time. Most SaaS providers do provide QoS reports, however the reports are generated from service provider point of view only. As shown in pattern NFR-II, if the QoS of the SaaS services can be metered by the SaaS subscriber and generate report from consumer point view, then the QoS can be reconciled between service provider and service consumer so as to guarantee the SLA fulfillment.

2.3 SaaS Integration Design and Development Requirements

As illustrated in the following figure, the SaaS integration design and development process starts from business process review to analyze the key functional and NFR requirements; based on which to design and implement UI, process, data and NFR related integrations; then migrate/populate related data from master data source; finally test and go on production. This process is similar as the traditional application integration. However there are several SaaS unique issues we highlight as follows.

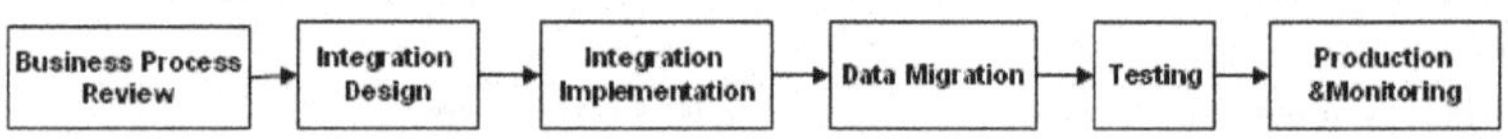

Fig. 3. SaaS Integration Design and Development Process

a) SaaS related policies' visibility
SaaS services have many policies which should be considered and utilized during the integration design and development process, e.g. configuration and customization policies. SaaS service usually serves many customers in multi-tenancy mode. Most customers usually have personalized requirements on the SaaS service. However the business model of SaaS is fundamentally about economic scale, which can only allow service configuration and customization within certain scope supported by self-service mode. Therefore the integration specialist should be instructed for the service configuration and customization policies during the integration design and development lifecycle. However, there is no related industry standard to support the definition of service's configuration and customization policies. Furthermore, to support those SaaS NFR integration requirements, the NFR policies of SaaS should be visible in the integration design and development environment.

b) Accommodation of different SaaS services in a unified environment
Currently different SaaS vendors have different toolkits to support integration, and System Integrators (SI) use different tools as well [4, 17]. However, a unified tooling environment can standardize the SaaS integration approach, so as to improve integration productivity, efficiency and accelerate the SaaS adoption accordingly. Since most SaaS services adopt Web Services technologies, it provides a very good foundation to accommodate different SaaS services in a unified tooling environment.

For most SaaS subscribers, functional integration requirements always have higher priority, NFR integration requirements can be value add features. In the following sections, a SaaS integration framework will be presented. This framework aims to streamline the SaaS integration design and development process for SI, supports the functional and NFR integration requirements accordingly.

3 SaaS Integration Framework

To address those SaaS integration requirements, in this section we introduce a SaaS integration framework reference architecture based on model driven integration approach [18], including SaaS-DL, tooling and runtime components.

3.1 SaaS-DL

SaaS can be treated as a kind of complex Web Services. Though Web Services Description Language (WSDL) can be used to describe interface related information, other information of SaaS services should be captured to support model driven SaaS integration. *WS-Policy [19] represents a set of specifications that describe the capabilities and constraints of the security (and other business) policies on intermediaries and end points, and how to associate policies with services and end points.* However, it does not address customization policy and some specific NFR policies clearly, which is strongly required in integration perspective. *In this section, we* will introduce the design of SaaS-DL that is an extension to WSDL standards. The overall structure of SaaS-DL is depicted in figure 4. It leverages the WS-Policyattachment specification to bind itself to WSDL and XSD schemas; WSDL is also referenced in SaaS-DL, which describes the integration programming interfaces of the SaaS service. Three additional aspects are included. They are Customization Policy, Billing Policy, and Data Object Relationship Model.

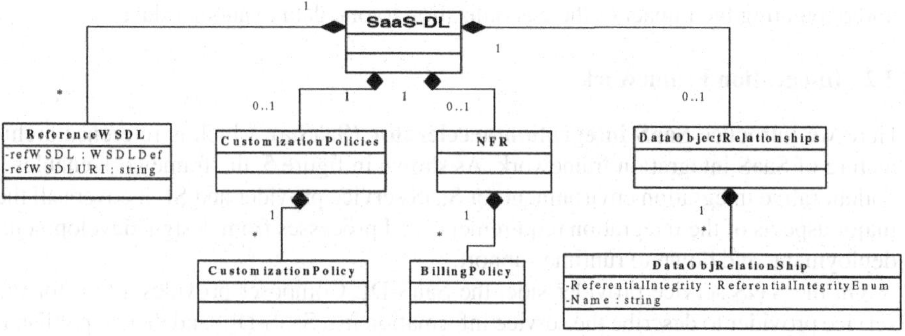

Fig. 4. Structure of SaaS-DL

Customization Policy

As analyzed in Section 2, SaaS services usually need to be customized to satisfy specific subscriber's requirements. Current Research topics on web services customization usually focus on semantic discovery or virtual wrappers [20, 21]; we propose a novel approach by defining customization policy in SaaS-DL, and consuming it through SaaS integration lifecycle. Customization policy can be defined by SaaS provider, which annotates the SaaS service's customization capability to its subscribers; customization policy, customization process and related enablement technologies can streamline a standardized approach for the collaboration between providers and subscribers for the entire service customization lifecycle, the detailed design is discussed in paper [22].

Billing Policy

Billing is one of the most important NFR technologies required by SaaS. Many research works have been done on metering and accounting for Web Services [23, 24]. However, Web Services accounting is only one factor of SaaS billing concerns. Other factors should be considered, such as storage usage, and the membership types of SaaS subscribers. How to reasonably reflect the composite values, and consolidate different bills from different providers with different formats and styles, are important concerns. Therefore, a structuralized hierarchical model is proposed to organize the bill items and their relationships in a billing policy. Bill item is an atomic unit to describe the rule of billing, while the relationships in billing policy provide the power to specify how to compose a complex bill by combining atomic items recursively. The billing policy can be used to guide the metering of service usage so as to generate bill. Based on the policy, bill report structure can be standardized, so the bill reports from different SaaS providers can be easily consolidated into one bill for the SaaS subscriber.

Data Relationship Model

A SaaS service generally depicts a relatively complex service that involves many business objects (or data types) and their operations. As data relationship is not covered in WSDL, incorrect data manipulation can easily happen, for example, deleting one data object will bring major influence to another data. We propose to depict the data relationships of SaaS data in the SaaS-DL. This data relationship model in SaaS-DL is very much like that Entity Relationship(ER) diagram[25], where a data relationship is a triple of three elements: source object, target object, and its cardinality. Representing data relationships in SaaS-DL will also help SaaS customization process by analyzing and populating the impact of the customization to one data to another data.

3.2 Integration Framework

Here we introduce **SaaS integration accelerator** (SaaSia), which is reference architecture of SaaS integration framework. As shown in figure 5, the framework enables a collaborative integration environment for SaaS service provider and SI. It covers all the major aspects of the integration requirements and processes from design, development, deployment, and down to runtime support.

On the SaaS service provider side, the SaaS-DL Composer provides a tool for the service provider to describe the service information in a SaaS-DL, and then to publish it into the service registry to share with service subscribers. The Customization Engine provides a standardized interface to fulfill the customization requests. Through validating, analyzing, and decomposition, the Customization Engine weaves these requests into existing SaaS services, updates its implementation/configuration, and dynamically loads the upgraded service for the requestor. The NFR Reporting Service offers web services interfaces for subscribers to access NFR reports, e.g. bill, QoS report.

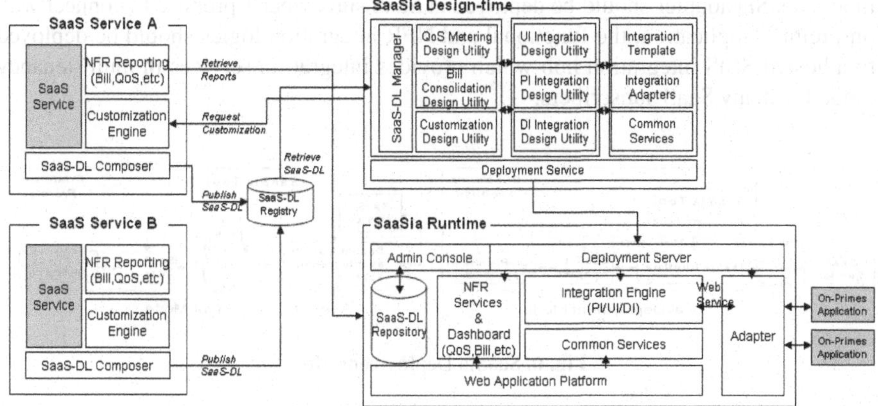

Fig. 5. SaaSia Framework Reference Architecture

On the SaaS service subscriber side, SI can use the design-time integration tool to design/develop the SaaS integration artifacts and deploy them into runtime environment, then automates the execution of integration logics on the runtime platform to meet its customer's needs. The SaaS-DL Manager component retrieves SaaS-DL from service registry and manages it in local repository. Customization Design Utility provides the customization controller for SI to handle the customization requirements in the whole integration lifecycle. The requirements are controlled within the scope defined by customization policy in SaaS-DL. The utility generates customization requests and send to SaaS service' Customization Engine to fulfill. The Bill Consolidation Design Utility can be used to design how the bills are retrieved from SaaS providers and then consolidated as one bill. QoS Metering Design Utility is used to define how the SaaS service's usage is metered so as to generate QoS report locally. Beside the core components introduced above, SaaSia design-time leverages common PI/UI/DI Design Utilities(e.g. BPEL[26]). The Deployment Service packages all the integration artifacts and deploys the package to runtime environment.

SaaSia runtime provides fundamental services and integration capabilities from different perspectives. The SaaS Repository manages the SaaS-DL and provides interface for runtime usage. NFR Services include two key services: QoS Metering service meters the SaaS services' utilization(transaction numbers, response time, exception rate, etc); the Bill Retrieval and Consolidation service fetches the bill reports from SaaS provider, transform and consolidate multiple bills into one integrated bill. The NFR Dashboard component provides a visualized presentation about the bill and service utilization information. The Adaptor is a runtime framework to enable the integration with on-premise application using required network protocol and programming interfaces.

The SaaSia runtime architecture can be implemented in two different deployment modes illustrated in figure 6. If the SaaS subscribers have strong integration requirements about security and privacy, they should select the local deployment mode which provides dedicated SaaSia runtime; If the SaaS subscribers prefer to get the integration capability as hosted services, they should use the remote deployment mode. In this mode, SaaSia adapter should be deployed at SaaS subscriber's premise to connect with on-premise application, the functional and NFR integration logics should be deployed to a hosted SaaS integration hub which provides integration services in multi-tenancy mode for many SaaS subscribers.

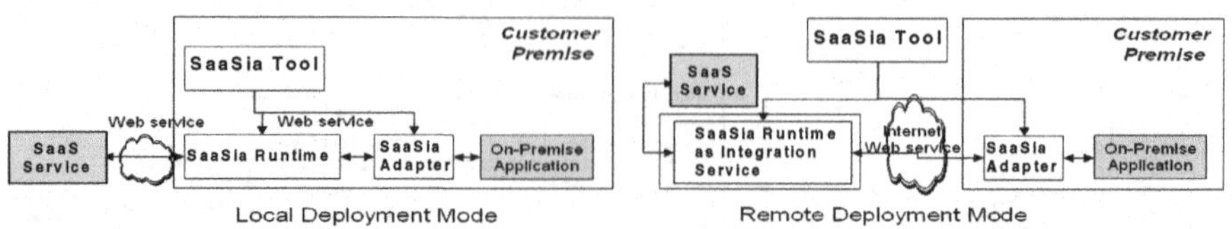

Fig. 6. SaaSia Deployment Mode

3.3 SaaSia Prototype

According to the reference architecture, a SaaSia prototype is built. The tooling prototype embraces the lightweight and open Eclipse platform. It also benefits from the full functionalities brought by the Eclipse projects, e.g., web tool by Eclipse WTP, data transformation by Eclipse DTP, dashboard by Eclipse BIRT, and BPEL programming by Eclipse BPEL [27]. There are also pre-built assets to accelerate the integration design/development, including Common Services (e.g., scheduling, logging), Integration Adapters(e.g. Adapter for SAP, Quickbooks) and Integration Templates(e.g. CRM opportunity to ERP order fulfillment). As illustrated in figure 7, SaaS-DL Manager, SaaS Customization, NFR Dashboard Design Utilities and Deployment Utility can integrate with these Eclipse components as a SaaS integration design and development toolkit.

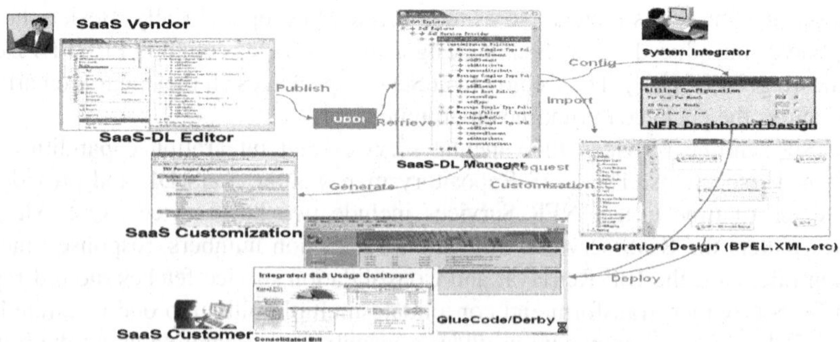

Fig. 7. SaaSia Design-Time Prototype

The SaaSia Runtime prototype adopts the local deployment mode. It focuses on lightweight integration capability at SaaS subscriber premise environment. SaaS runtime is an integrated platform built by leveraging open source and existed components as much as possible. As shown in figure 8, SaaS runtime provides three key modules: administration console, integration platform, and SaaS utilization dashboard. The integration module provides integration related capabilities such as BPEL engine, ETL engine, and legacy application integration through JCA adaptor. SaaS NFR dashboard demonstrates the result of SaaS usage metering and bill consolidation. Administration components offer the SSO and SaaS-DL management services.

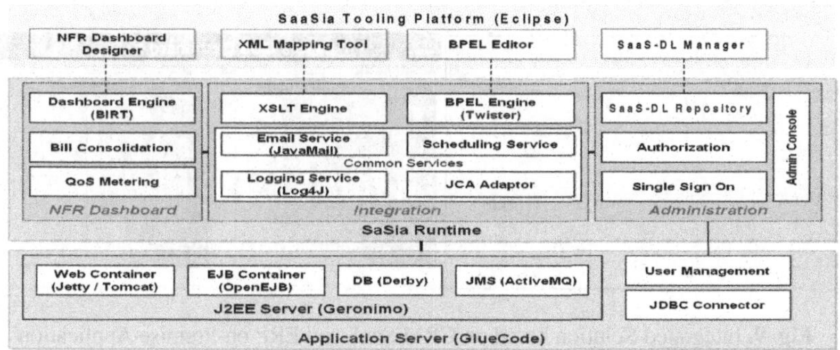

Fig. 8. SaaSia Prototype Architecture

4 Case Study

In this section, a case about integrating CRM SaaS service and ERP on-premise application is studied. The customer company has hundreds of employees and 4 offices in different cities in China. An ERP application has been deployed for several years to support manufacturing related business. Recently the company subscribed a SaaS CRM service to better support their customer related business. Though they started to use the

Table 1. Business Requirements and corresponding pattern and actions

Business Requirements	Pattern	Integration Actions
"Product" information synchronization from ERP to CRM service; "Account" information synchronization from CRM service to ERP	D-II	Customize the "Product" & "Account" data structure on CRM service to map with ERP; Leverage Scheduling service and CRM service & ERP application api to synchronize data
Pass new "Order" information from CRM service to ERP	P-III	Customize the "Product" & "Account" data structure on CRM service to map with ERP; Leverage Scheduling service and CRM service & ERP application api to synchronize data
Pass new "Shipping Notice" and "Invoice" information from ERP to CRM service and update original "Order"'s status	P-I	Create new data structure "Shipping Notice" and "Invoice" and build relationship with "Order" using Order_ID; Develop new web service to feed the data into CRM services
Sales Person creates a new "Product" request according to customer's special requirements, the request will be sent to Product Manager to approve, and then feed into ERP system to guide fulfillment.	P-IV	Create a workflow and link the workflow with CRM service/ERP application api
Have an integrated user interface to access both CRM service & ERP application	U-I	Create a new web page to accommodate the ERP & CRM service with UI supported by SSO.
Collect the usage statistical information of the CRM service	NFR-II	Configure NFR dashboard based on web service metering capability

SaaS service as a standalone application, they eventually found that it had to be integrated with their on-premise ERP application. The detailed requirements, patterns applied and developed integration actions are listed in the following table1.

As illustrated in figure 9, the requirements listed above have been fulfilled by SaaSia prototype technologies. There are two important lessons gained through our practice:

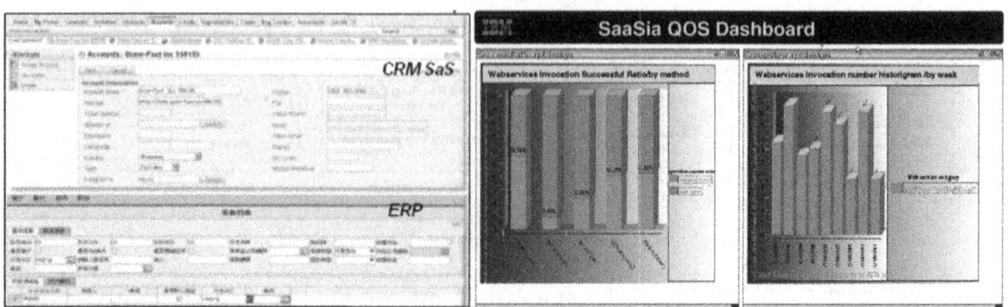

Fig. 9. Integrated Solution based on CRM SaaS and ERP on-Premise Application

a) Most SaaS services don't provide programmatic interfaces for customer to retrieve QoS and Billing reports. Different SaaS services use their own tools to describe customization capability and perform customization actions. So SaaS related standards should include these perspectives to benefit the SaaS growth.

b) As currently most SaaS services' subscribers are SMBs [6]. They strongly -expect integration to be done with very small footprint in agile way. The current SaaSia prototype is standard based, e.g. Eclipse, BPEL. But to gain SMB adoption we need to explore more lightweight approach including browser based integration tool and programming model based on Web 2.0 technologies [12, 28].

5 Conclusions and Future Work

In this paper, we analyzed the key requirements for SaaS integration and presented several integration patterns. A SaaS integration framework, SaaSia, is proposed to address those requirements. Also a prototype and corresponding case study is introduced. We learned two valuable lessons. Firstly, most SaaS integration functional requirements can be fulfilled by existing SOA integration technologies [5]; Secondly SaaS involves some NFR requirements which should be addressed by extending exiting integration technologies. We plan to pursue future work in two directions. As there lacks of industry standards to streamline SaaS integration, we will conduct more research around the concept of SaaS-DL [22] in Enterprise Application Integration, leverage and Enhance BPEL or ESB; we will also dive into the latest Web2.0 technology [12, 28], e.g. apply SaaS-DL in Mash-up description languages, to explore a more lightweight and generic SaaS integration platform for SMB.

References

[1] Knorr, E.: Software as a Service: The Next Big Thing, http://www.infoworld.com/article/06/03/20/76103_12FEsaas_1.html

[2] Summit Strategy Report: The Future of Software as Service-And the Partners ISVs will Need to Get There (2004)
[3] Web Site, http://www.employease.com
[4] Web Site: Salesforce.com AppExchange, [Online]: http://www.salesforce.com
[5] Newcomer, E., Lomow, G.: Understanding SOA with Web Services. Addison-Wesley, Reading (2004)
[6] Baumol, W.: Small Firms: Why Market-Driven Innovation Can't Get Along Without Them., The Small Business Economy: A Report to the President, Ch. 8, pp. 183–206 (2005)
[7] Web Site: Mashups and the Web as Platform, http://www.programmableweb.com/
[8] AMR Research Report: Software as a Service: Managing Buyer Expectations as We Pass the Tipping Point from Novelty to Necessity (2005)
[9] IDC report: Software as a Service in the Mid-market: Adoption Trends and Customer Preferences (2004)
[10] Web Site, [Online]: http://www.jamcracker.com
[11] Web Site, SaaS Showcase, [Online]: http://www-19.lotus.com/wps/portal/showcase/SaaS
[12] Seltsikas, P., Currie, W.L.: Evaluating The Application Service Provider (ASP) Business Model: The Challenge of Integration. In: Proceedings of the 35th Hawaii International Conference on System Sciences (2002)
[13] Elfatatry, A.: Software As A Service: A Negotiation Perspective. In: COMPSAC'02. Proceedings of the 26th Annual International Computer Software and Applications Conference (2002)
[14] Turne, M.: turning Software into a Service, Computer (October 2003)
[15] O'Reilly: What is Web 2.0, Design Patterns and Business Models for the Next Generation of Software (2005)
[16] Web Site: NetSuite Small Business, [Online]: http://www.netsuite.com/
[17] Web Site, [Online] available: http://www.aboveall.com
[18] OMG: An Architecture for Modeling, http://www.omg.org/mda
[19] W3C WS-Policy standard: http://schemas.xmlsoap.org/ws/2004/09/policy/
[20] Mandell, D., McIlrait, S.: Automating Web Service Discovery, Customization, and Semantic Translation with a Semantic Discovery Service. The Twelfth International World Wide Web (2003) (reference 26)
[21] Rykowski, J.: Virtual Web Services - Application of Software Agents to Personalization of Web Services. In: 6th International Conference on Electronic Commerce ICEC 2004: Engineering the New Landscape, pp. 419–428. ACM Publishers, New York (2004)
[22] Zhang, K., Sun, W., Zhang, X., Liang, Hq., Huang, Y., Liu, X.: A Policy-Driven Approach for SaaS Customization. In: The 9th IEEE Conference on E-Commerce Technology, IEEE Computer Society Press, Los Alamitos (2007)
[23] Aboda, B., Arkko, J., Harrington, D.: Introduction to Accounting Management, RFC2975 (October 2000)
[24] Agarwal, V., Karnik, N., Kumar, A.: Metering and Accounting for Composite e-Services. In: CEC'03. Proceedings of the IEEE International Conference on E-Commerce, IEEE Computer Society Press, Los Alamitos (2003)
[25] Web Site, [Online] available, http://www.umsl.edu/~sauter/analysis/er/er_intro.html
[26] IBM: BEA Systems, Microsoft, SAP AG, Siebel Systems, Business Process Execution Language for Web Services version 1.1
[27] Web Site, [Online] available, http://www.eclipse.org
[28] Gross, C.: Ajax Patterns and Best Practices, Apress (2006)
[29] Web Site, OpenKapow, http://openkapow.com/
[30] Ottinger, J.: Software as a Service Integration via Mule, http://www.theserverside.com/news/thread.tss?thread_id=44456

Building Data-Intensive Grid Applications with Globus Toolkit – An Evaluation Based on Web Crawling

Andreas Walter[1], Klemens Böhm[2], and Stephan Schosser[2]

[1] IPE, FZI Forschungszentrum Informatik, Haid-und-Neu-Straße 10-14, 76131 Karlsruhe
awalter@fzi.de

[2] IPD, Universität Karlsruhe, Am Fasanengarten 5, 76131 Karlsruhe
{boehm, schosser}@ipd.uka.de

Abstract. Nowadays, there is a trend to create resource-consuming applications without building heavy computer centers, but to use resources on computer systems distributed over the internet. Grid middleware is a framework to access these resources. The concern of this paper is the evaluation of a specific grid middleware, namely Globus Toolkit, for data-intensive applications. As a test case, we have designed and implemented a service-based distributed web crawler on top of this middleware: A web crawler is a complex application consisting of many nodes. It imposes significantly higher demands on grid middleware regarding administrative flexibility compared to grid applications that allocate computing power of grid nodes. We have observed that some components of Globus Toolkit are flexible enough to provide the control functionality necessary for a web crawler, while others are not. For these other components, we propose possible extensions. Since we expect the combination of those characteristics to occur with many other grid applications as well, our study is of broader interest, beyond web crawling.

Keywords: Globus Toolkit, Grid-Services, Complex Grid Applications, Usability of grid-services, requirements for data intensive grid applications.

1 Introduction

Grid middleware facilitates the creation of a "grid" to develop and run distributed applications (aka. grid applications). It contains components for the coordination, allocation and management of resources in a grid. Different grid-middleware solutions exist, which help to implement such applications. In this paper we focus on Globus Toolkit (GT4) [10], the de-facto standard for grid middleware. GT4 – in contrast to other grid middleware – uses a service-oriented approach to manage resources: It uses a kind of web service, the *grid service*. Grid services serve two purposes: First, they provide high-level functionality that is needed frequently (e.g., user management). Second, they make operating-system-specific functionality such as security features transparent. The concern of this paper is to evaluate GT4, in combination with grid services, as a platform for data-intensive applications.

B. Krämer, K.-J. Lin, and P. Narasimhan (Eds.): ICSOC 2007, LNCS 4749, pp. 570–581, 2007.

Grid applications typically make excessive use of resources on computer systems connected to the internet, in contrast to arbitrary distributed systems which may also run in a local network. Existing evaluations focus on grid applications which perform complex computations or transfer large data sets [8]. In this paper we choose a different focus: To evaluate that middleware, we have developed a highly distributed web crawler. One reason why we have used web crawling as an application is its relatively high complexity. A crawler loads web pages from the internet. It has a high consumption of bandwidth and memory. In addition, it requires a control system that can handle a list of addresses of web pages. A crawler will request such addresses (aka. jobs) and then load the web pages. It should not process a job more than once. This calls for bookkeeping by the control system. In our case, we have designed a control system that can fulfill these requirements. In addition, this control system is distributed to guarantee high availability and scalability. Its nodes must communicate extensively. All this leads to strong requirements on resources and coordination. Using our web crawler for illustration, we also describe our experiences in designing and implementing a complex application in GT4 and missing features that can help in creating such an application flexibly. Many grid applications in real world setups run on systems that share their resources among several applications running in parallel. Therefore, our evaluation puts a focus on usability, performance and stability of GT4, by running our service-based web crawler in shared environments.

Paper outline: Chapter 2 gives an overview of GT4 and its concepts for integrating services. In Chapter 3, we describe related work and extensions of GT4 that can help in building grid-based applications. Chapter 4 introduces our crawler architecture. In Chapter 5 we use this architecture to develop a web crawler based on GT4. We then report on our experiences in Chapter 6. Chapter 7 concludes.

2 Services in Globus Toolkit

Grids allow the creation of distributed applications with high resource requirements. Grid participants share resources, e.g., CPU or memory on their computers, which communicate via the internet [7]. Grid middleware simplifies application development. It consists of tools frequently needed in a grid scenario. The objective of GT4 is to let individuals share computing power, databases and other tools securely online, without sacrificing local autonomy. As grid nodes are connected over the internet, the requirements exceed those on a local network. The requirements and the design of the components go back to Foster et al [6, 7]. The requirements are safety, fairness, control, flexibility and a common runtime. [16] discusses these requirements in detail. Besides these requirements concerning the functionality offered, grid middleware has to integrate heterogeneous resources. This heterogeneity should be transparent to the users and their applications. To accomplish this, GT4 uses a service-based approach based on XML. Services in GT4 are called *grid services*.

Grid services are similar to web services. *Service containers* solve the problem of heterogeneity: All grid services are executed within the service container, which is adaptable to different operating systems. For the integration of resources, there are standardized mechanisms to describe services and exchange objects between them [4, 12]. Grid services communicate using standard WWW protocols, e.g., http and https.

Besides the security infrastructure, grid services are the most important concept in GT4 [9]. All of its components are implemented as grid services. We will use grid services as well to realize our distributed web crawler.

3 Related Work

Current grid applications focus on the allocation of computing power and the transfer of large data sets. A grid-based crawler needs components that address the requirements of data-intensive applications with a large control overhead. The standard service for the allocation and management of resources in GT4 is not flexible. It cannot handle clusters of computers and does not allow for the definition of complex rules for resource allocation [9]. A distributed web crawler mainly consumes the resources bandwidth and memory. There are several GT4 extensions for the management and allocation of CPU time. *Condor* [5] for instance allocates jobs in clusters of computers. *Sun Grid Engine* [14] extends the resource management with accounting functionality, to limit CPU consumption. Both extensions are not suitable to manage bandwidth usage.

Web crawlers require a resource-management system that can either define the maximal bandwidth that a user is willing to share or the maximal amount of data that may be transferred over his internet connection. The resource allocation and management in the 'Distributed Aircraft Maintenance Environment' *(DAME)* [1] controls the analyses of errors in airplanes. This is a complex task with high safety requirements. They extend GT4 with a resource management and an allocation service that allows the definition of service-level agreements. One can reuse their extended control service for tasks with high safety requirements, but not for bandwidth-intensive tasks such as ours. The middleware OGSA *DAI* (Data access and integration) [15] aims to integrate heterogeneous database systems in a grid. *DRS* (Data Replication Service) [10] can help in replicating data. For the evaluation of our web crawler, we will integrate the repositories needed with a service of our own. The reason is that it has to fulfill additional tasks, such as the filtering of web pages already processed. So we cannot use OGSA-DAI. Further, we leave aside replication in our study, i.e., we did not use DRS either.

Other grid middleware like *BOINC* [3] and *UNICORE* [19] is based on a framework to create grid applications. They do not contain any features that address the heterogeneity problem. This is in contrast to GT4, which uses grid services to this end. We have deemed GT4 the most promising platform for a crawler application because of its service concept and its advantages for heterogeneous environments.

4 Structure of a Highly Distributed Web Crawler

A web crawler has very high demands regarding resources (bandwidth and CPU) and coordination: The web consists of billions of web pages. Most of them change frequently. Thus, a good web crawler must analyze pages fast and revisit them in time intervals of a few days. Large computer centers can do this fast [3]. But grid-based web crawlers might accomplish this as well. We expect that the more nodes there are, the more web pages can be processed per time unit. We will present a service-based crawler architecture which benefits from the advantages of GT4 (we hypothesize).

Web crawlers contact web servers, download web pages, and send the results to repositories. A crawler needs components to load pages, extract links, and store pages. In addition, a control system is required. It assigns the next URLs to process to the crawler. [13] proposes a reference architecture for a distributed web crawler. Its control overhead increases with the number of crawlers and repositories and becomes a bottleneck. Hence, the control system should be distributed as well, and [13] suggests an extension of the reference architecture for a high degree of distribution. The crawlers and the repositories are assigned evenly to the distributed components of the control system. If one of these components breaks down, other components can take over its crawlers and repositories. With our distributed web crawler, we will follow this suggestion. To ensure that each node of the distributed control system handles roughly the same number of crawlers and repositories, a component management is needed, as a further extension of the distributed control system.

The bandwidth of most internet connections is not as high as in a local environment. The transfer of data takes more time and is more expensive [11]. Thus, the repositories themselves should analyze the data, instead of sending it to a control system. In contrast to the reference architecture, our distributed control system performs coordination tasks instead of filtering links to web pages. Each repository is responsible for a number of web sites. The repositories have to communicate with each other to locate the node responsible for a web site. We do not describe the communication of the nodes and the allocation of web sites to them in detail. This is because the issue is orthogonal to the concern of this paper. We refer the interested reader to [16]. We only mention that the allocation principle is based on characteristics of the link structure in web sites: More than 75 percent of the links are intra links [2]. They do not require any additional communication between the repositories. The crawlers load web pages and extract new links from them before sending both to the repositories. In a local network environment, there is a direct view and control over the components. In contrast, components in a highly distributed grid environment are not as easy to control. Unauthorized access to the highly distributed web crawler has to be avoided. The owners of each node must be able to specify the bandwidth and the memory they are willing to provide. Thus, we have two aspects of control. One is the allocation of resources by the owners. The other one is the control over all shared resources in the context of our web crawler. The control system of the reference architecture described before only deals with the second aspect. We therefore extend the reference architecture to fulfil grid-specific requirements, as described next.

5 Mapping the Web Crawler to Globus Toolkit

Using GT4, all components have to be implemented as grid services. Our first approach for the design of the data-intensive crawler application was to use standard services provided by GT4 – these are a directory service, resource management, control services and a monitoring service. Standard services address requirements of many grid applications and reduce design and implementation time. While this is promising in our context as well, it has turned out to be insufficient: Most of the standard services for control and coordination tasks focus on applications with a high demand on computing power. When we designed the grid-based web crawler, it turned out that the standard services lack functionality for the coordination of such an application. In particular, the assignment of jobs to nodes must be more flexible than with current GT4 control services. Hence, we implemented missing functionality with own grid services. Figure 1 gives an overview of our architecture. To control the crawler components, the standard service 'resource management and allocation' provided by GT4 becomes part of the architecture. To observe the current usage of the resources in the grid, the monitoring service is included, too, as is the directory service in GT4. It promises scalability, since new components can be added dynamically.

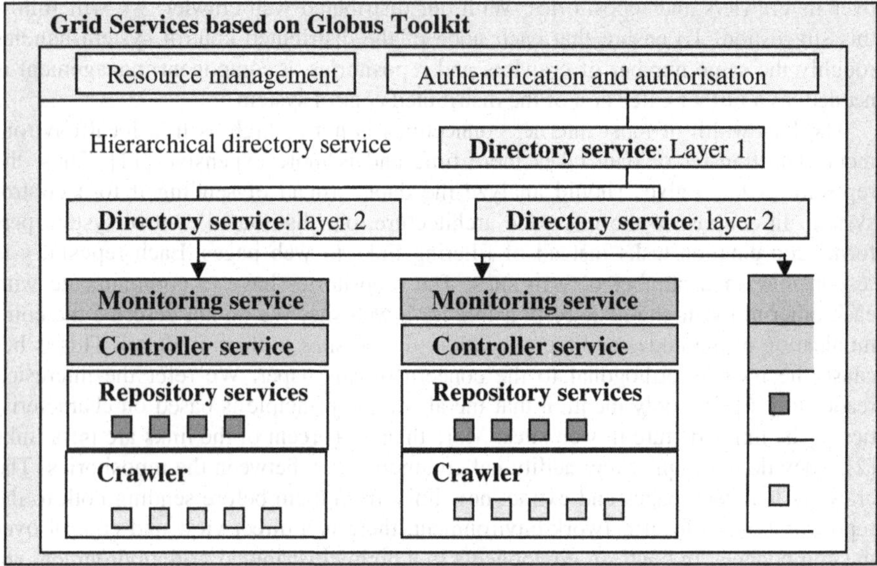

Fig. 1. Overview of our grid-based crawler architecture

Directory Service

The directory service in GT4 allows discovering available services. New services can be added dynamically. Grid applications must know the addresses of the nodes running the directory services. GT4 requires specifying these addresses in configuration files on each node that wants to publish grid services. The GT4 directory service has three drawbacks when applied to a distributed web crawler.

First, the number of entries in the directory service is large if there are many services in the grid. This calls for a distributed service. To add a new directory service, the configuration files of GT4 would have to be updated. Hence, it is not possible to add a new node for the distributed directory service dynamically. The second problem is that we need to find an efficient way to partition the distributed directory service evenly. Each directory service should be responsible for some of the services in the grid. Third, the directory service in GT4 always returns the complete list of services requested. The requestor then chooses one service from the list. This does not exactly help to achieve a balanced load of the grid nodes. To eliminate these problems, we have designed a directory service of our own. It has a hierarchical structure. If the number of entries in a node is too large, it is split into a new layer of the hierarchy. If a node breaks down, nodes in the same hierarchy level or in a higher one take over its services. Instead of returning a list of services of a type requested, the directory service already performs load balancing among crawlers and repository services and returns only the service to be used by the requestor.

Monitoring Service

The monitoring service controls the services by querying their states periodically. The queried values can then either be displayed to users of the grid, or extensions can process them further. Such extensions can trigger error handling or notify users in cases of errors. In GT4 there is no standalone service for monitoring. The functionality for the directory and monitoring are part of one service named 'Monitoring and Discovery Service'. Because our directory service is proprietary, we cannot use the standard monitoring service either. We had to develop a monitoring service that is distributed as well. Its basic tasks are to query the states from the repository services, e.g., memory available. The control services and the participants of the grid can then query the monitoring services for these values.

Repository Service

GT4 contains standard services for reliable file transfer, but no repository service. Hence, we had to build such a service that can be configured to store web pages. In addition, it needs to filter web pages, as described before. Each node of our distributed repository service is connected to a relational database. For fast communication, the database system lies in the local network where the service is installed. The tasks of the repository services are to store the web pages and the links. Each repository service is responsible for a number of web sites. For each web site, it knows the web pages already processed and the ones waiting to be crawled.

Resource Management and Control Service

To meet the requirements fairness and control, GT4 contains an independent service for resource allocation and management. When a user offers resources, he can define rules how these may be used. The standard service in GT4 allows limiting the CPU usage allowed. More complex rules about CPU usage, e.g., user groups and budgets allowed, are definable with extensions like Sun Grid Engine. The resource-allocation component then controls the resource usage. It can choose resources in the grid and allocate the requests evenly. It can also choose alternative resources in case of execution errors.

Our web crawler requires the resources bandwidth, CPU time, and memory. The resource allocation must be able to distribute the requests to nodes with sufficient resources of all three kinds. With the standard service in GT4 and with extensions like Condor, only the even allocation of CPU time is possible. As the standard resource allocation and management service is not applicable to our scenario, we have developed a 'control service' which integrates the functionality of both of them. It handles the requirements of the control system of a web crawler. Each node of this service knows some repository services as allocated through the directory service responsible. For quick responses to requests from crawlers for new addresses of web pages, each control service maintains a stack. When it is empty, the control service queries the repository services for new addresses to process.

6 Experiences with Globus Toolkit

Running a crawler application on a grid middleware requires a stable service infrastructure for the grid services implemented. For the success of GT4 in practice, three requirements are essential. First, the benefits of grid services, especially the integrated security infrastructure and resource management, must go beyond the ones of plain web services. Second, GT4 as a service infrastructure (i.e., the platform where the services run) must be comparative to other infrastructures, e.g., Apache Tomcat [17], both with regard to resource consumption and ease of installation. Third, GT4 must be stable when running grid services. (For us, data intensive applications are in the center of interest.)

In real-world setups, a grid application can run on many nodes – each one sharing many applications, e.g., file sharing, communication and office applications. In such environments, it is not possible to use the entire CPU and memory of the nodes. Therefore, our evaluation does not focus on comparing our grid-based crawler with crawler benchmarks [15] using high end systems. Rather, we are interested in the benefits of grid services and the minimal requirements for running them on shared systems.

Our evaluation focuses on three aspects: the runtime of grid services compared to web services, the performance of GT4 when running web-crawler-specific services that generate and transfer a lot of data, and the stability of GT4. Note that a single grid node is sufficient to evaluate these characteristics of GT4. For our experiments, we used a simple standard PC, a Pentium Centrino with 1.600 MHz CPU and 512 MB RAM.

Installation

Version 4 of Globus Toolkit requires a UNIX-based operation system for installation. Hence, it cannot be installed on Windows systems without emulation of UNIX specific functions. This is not exactly in line with the requirement that a grid should support as many environments as possible. Installation of Globus Toolkit is more complex than the installation of the web-service environment Apache Tomcat: First, for the installation, the toolkit requires the configuration of the desired location. Afterwards, GT4 runs without security options. Second, to enable authentification and authorization, SSL certificates need to be created. Third, description files, containing the name of the grid and information about the security policies, need to be created. These files are required on each node participating in the grid. Finally, the standard services need to be configured, e.g., one needs to specify the address of a directory service for publishing grid services. When following these steps, we observed several problems: Using all standard services proposed, Globus Toolkit throws a lot of errors on start up. The reason is that the services are not configured correctly. Further, errors concerning security arise, even when the platform is started following the second step, i.e., security is deactivated. We also had problems of different behavior of the middleware on different systems. We encountered different, uncommented errors on different UNIX distributions. The complete installation requires a lot editing of configuration files with the correct parameters. We hope for an installation dialogue which handles the desired features to allow for a faster installation of Globus Toolkit, so that installing GT4 can be as easy as installing web-services containers.

Runtimes of Grid Services

We were interested in the runtimes of grid services compared to web services, to assess the current grid infrastructure. Therefore we compared the runtimes of grid services with Globus Toolkit 4.0.1 to simple web services with Tomcat 5.5. In each run, the control service counts the time passed between the first request of a web page and the end of the process. Each test ends when 5,000 jobs were processed. A job in our context is defined as a set of two addresses. The first one is the web page that will be loaded, and the second one is the address of the repository that will store the results. Each service container can be started using an unsecured or a secured connection. The secured connections of both web services and grid services use SSL certificates to identify the server and client side on the standard port 443 for secured connections. We expect runtimes of services to be different with and without such data encodings. Hence, the comparison of runtimes consists of four different setups: each combination of 'web service' or 'grid service' on the one hand and of 'secured' and 'unsecured' on the other hand. Normally, the service container for grid services is started using a secure connection. Only then authorization and authentification are possible. We expect that this type of connection is slightly slower than the one for web services, because of more components in GT4. Table 1 shows the results. Web services with an unsecured connection are the fastest. The unsecured connection with GT4 is only slightly slower than the unsecured connection of web services running in Tomcat. The secure connection with web services took about 20 percent longer than the unsecured one. The secure connection for GT4 takes more time than the secure connection for web services. The general (albeit expected) conclusion is that there is a difference in the runtimes of grid services and web services. In more detail, we think that the (not so much) slower performance of a grid service is acceptable. The reason is that, unlike web services, grid services are integrated in a grid infrastructure featuring security, resource allocation and resource management and allowing a fast implementation of all requirements that are requested to a grid based application.

Table 1. Runtimes of grid services compared to web services

Tomcat/Unsecured	**Tomcat**/Secure	**GT4**/Unsecured	**GT4**/Secure
2.130 sec	2.610 sec	2.390 sec	3.130 sec

Running Globus Toolkit

After the comparison of web services and grid services, we now focus on features of GT4. With the following experiment, we measure the time overhead that is required to exchange data. We modified our test setup with different numbers of jobs requested by the crawler from the control service in parallel. Even though crawler and control service run on the same node in our experiment, this is intended: Data is exchanged using the communication channels of GT4. In contrast to an evaluation using multiple nodes, latency based on other network components will not affect the outcome of the experiment. The crawler sends the parameter "number of jobs" to the control service. It returns this number of web pages to the crawler. The control service measures the

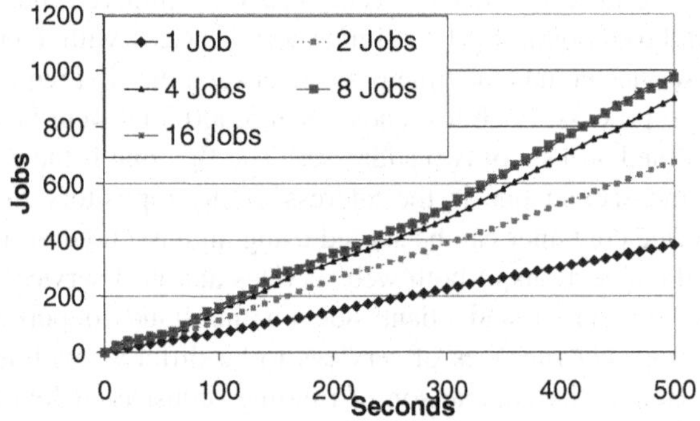

Fig. 2. Overhead on requesting jobs

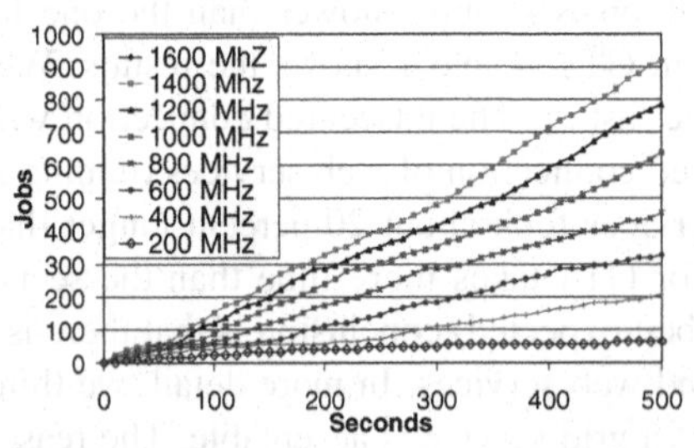

Fig. 3. Number of jobs with limited CPU

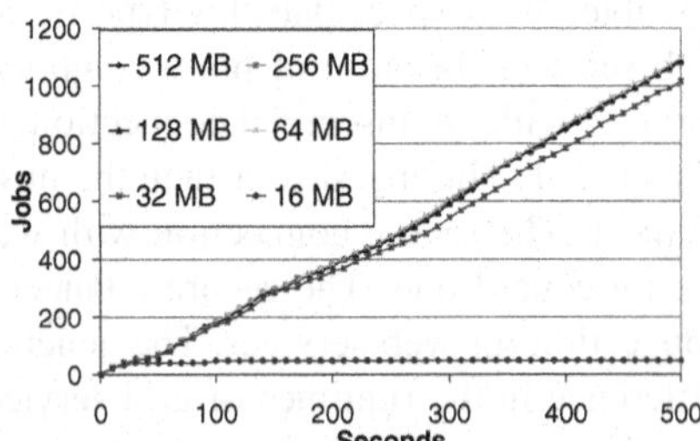

Fig. 4. Number of jobs with limited RAM

time that the crawler needs to process one thousand web pages for different numbers of jobs requested. It may be obvious that the request of every single job generates the highest overhead of data transfer for requests. Too many jobs per request in turn would give way to inflexibility and redundancy. We are now interested in the number of jobs that should be requested in parallel to achieve optimal run times. At the same time we try to keep the data overhead for requesting new jobs very low. Figure 2 shows the results. While the run times of 16 requested jobs and 8 parallel requested jobs are nearly equal, 4 parallel jobs take some more time to exchange the data needed. Hence, to arrive at acceptable runtimes of the web crawler, at least 4 jobs in parallel should be requested. As a general conclusion, a lower number of requests with more content can be performed faster than a high number of requests with less content. For data intensive applications, this means the following: one should keep the number of calls to coordination nodes as low as possible and request a large number of new jobs with every call.

Stability

A data-intensive grid application requires a stable grid middleware. To test the stability of GT4 with limited resources, we reduced the system resources of our computer system step by step. We want to verify that GT4 also runs stable in environments shared by a lot of applications – that is often the case in real-world setups. A reason for instable behavior of GT4 could be that it requires a minimum amount of CPU. To verify this, we started GT4 (and four parallel crawlers as clients on a different system) with 100% of CPU Power (1600 MHz). Then we reduced the CPU power step by step in intervals of ten percent down to ten percent of CPU power remaining. The services were still running, albeit slowly, and we noticed no error (Figure 3). Thus, GT4 is able to run on machines where little CPU time is allocated. Our next test focused on the RAM required for our setup. We expected that the platform will stop with an error when the available RAM is not sufficient for running the platform correctly. Therefore, we reduced the RAM that the container may use – starting with 512 MB down to 16 MB. GT4 and the grid services also started with 16 MB RAM (Figure 4). With only 16 MB of RAM, the services stopped working after about one minute with the error 'Out of memory'. The platform itself was still running and available. Hence, insufficient memory lets grid services crash, while the platform itself is still running. For a highly distributed grid application with many nodes, this is a problem. Nodes different from the one where GT4 is running cannot detect such an error caused by RAM limitations. Thus, we would like to see a suitable error handling inside of GT4, e.g., automatic generation of an email to a system administrator. Currently, there is no such error handling by GT4. Our test with 16 MB showed the behavior when a grid service has problems with RAM limitations. The same reaction would occur when a RAM-consuming service reaches its limit. This is a weakness since errors based on a lack of memory cannot be detected outside of the platform. The experiments concerning RAM and CPU requirements lead to the following conclusion: There is an insufficient error handling in GT4 when a grid service has insufficient memory. A solution to this problem is urgent. This is because those errors cannot be detected outside of GT4.

7 Conclusions

During the last years, different implementations of grid middleware have emerged. A prominent one is Globus Toolkit. In this paper we evaluated its Version 4 using an implementation of a distributed web crawler. In contrast to other grid applications, a web crawler has significantly higher demands concerning administrative flexibility and is therefore a realistic test case.

Grid services allow to reuse standard services for resource management, monitoring, directory of given nodes and control services to develop grid applications, to reduce implementation and testing time. The grid services in GT4 are designed to fulfill Foster's grid requirements [9]. The focus of current grid applications is the allocation of distributed CPU power. The resource-management service of GT4 does not allow for the management and allocation of other resources, e.g., bandwidth. Ideally, however, it should even allow for an integrated perspective on different resources. To investigate the issue, we have proposed a highly distributed web-crawler architecture based on grid services and extensions of the standard services, in order to fulfil the requirements of data-intensive applications with a large control overhead.

We have shown that data intensive, complex applications can be developed using GT4 and have advantages over standard web services that run in simple service environments, e.g. regarding security issues. Our setting however required a reimplementation of most of the standard services of GT4. We expect such extensions to be part of newer versions of Globus Toolkit. Its standard services should be more flexible concerning the integration of many different resources and complex control requirements. As soon as this is the case, the framework should be reevaluated.

References

1. Austin, J.: DAME - Distributed Aircraft Maintenance Environment: (last visited 2006-07-24) (2004) http://www.cs.york.ac.uk/dame/
2. Bharat, K., et al.: Who links to whom: Mining linkage between web sites. In: ICDM '01. Proceedings of the IEEE, International Conference on Data Mining, San Jose, USA, IEEE Computer Society Press, Los Alamitos (2001)
3. BOINC, http://boinc.berkeley.edu
4. Brin, S., Page, L.: The anatomy of a large-scale hyper textual Web search engine. In: Computer Networks and ISDN Systems, vol. 30 (1998)
5. Chinnici, R., et al.: Web Services Description Language (WSDL) Version 2.0, W3C Whitepaper last visited (2006-07-24) (March 2006), http://www.w3.org/TR/2006/CR-wsdl20-20060327/
6. Condor – High Throughput Computing, http://www.cs.wisc.edu/condor
7. Foster, I., Kesselman, C.: The Anatomy of the Grid. In: Sakellariou, R., Keane, J.A., Gurd, J.R., Freeman, L. (eds.) Euro-Par 2001. LNCS, vol. 2150, Springer, Heidelberg (2001)
8. Foster, I., Kesselman, C., Nick, J., Tuecke, S.: The Physiology of the Grid, Global Grid Forum (June 2002)
9. Foster, I., Kesselman, C.: The Grid. Blueprint for a New Computing Infrastructure, 2nd edn. Morgan Kaufmann Publishers, San Francisco (2003)
10. Foster, I.: Globus Toolkit Version 4: Software for Service-Oriented Systems. In: Jin, H., Reed, D., Jiang, W. (eds.) NPC 2005. LNCS, vol. 3779, Springer, Heidelberg (2005)
11. Globus Toolkit, http://www.globus.org
12. Gray, J., Szalay, A.: The World Wide Telescope. Science Bd. 293 (2002)
13. Gudgin, et al.: Web Services Addressing 1.0 – SOAP Binding, W3C Whitepaper, (March 2006)
14. Planet Lab, http://www.planet-lab.org

15. Shkapenyuk, V., Suel, T.: Design and implementation of a high-performance distributed Web crawler. In: Proceedings of the 18th International Conference on Data Engineering, San Jose, pp. 357–368 (2002)
16. Sun N1 Grid Engine, http://www.sun.com/software/gridware/
17. Tomcat 5.5, tomcat.apache.org
18. The OGSA-DAI Project, http://www.ogsadai.org.uk
19. UNICORE, http://www.unicore.com
20. Walter, A., Schosser, S., Böhm, K: Überlegungen zur Entwicklung komplexer Grid-Anwendungen mit Globus Toolkit. In: Proceedings of the GI Fachtagung für Datenbanksysteme, Technologie und Web (BTW), Aachen, Germany (2007)

QoS-Aware Web Service Compositions Using Non-intrusive Policy Attachment to BPEL

Anis Charfi[1], Rania Khalaf[2], and Nirmal Mukhi[2]

[1] SAP Research CEC Darmstadt
Darmstadt, Germany
[2] IBM TJ Watson Research Center
Hawthorne, New York, USA

Abstract. Supporting Quality of Service properties in BPEL processes is essential to enable Web Service based production workflows. In fact, when implementing a Web Service composition with a BPEL process, appropriate means are needed to express and enforce various QoS properties such as security, reliable messaging, and transactions.

In this paper, we present a generic and non-proprietary approach to express QoS properties in BPEL processes using policies. This approach uses XPath, WS-Policy, and the external policy attachment mechanism of WS-PolicyAttachment to enable a separate and non-intrusive specification of both the messaging-level and process-level QoS requirements in BPEL processes. We also present a prototype implementation on top of the Colombo BPEL engine, which supports the enforcement of policies that are attached to BPEL activities.

1 Introduction

Several Quality of Service requirements arise when defining a Web Service composition in BPEL such as security, reliable messaging, and transactions. In [5], these requirements were presented and classified into *messaging-level* and *process-level* requirements. For instance, message encryption is a QoS property that may be required for an interaction with a partner via an *invoke* activity. Message delivery with exactly-once semantics is another example of messaging-level requirements. Moreover, a set of activities that are nested in a *sequence* activity may require transactional execution either as an atomic transaction or as a business activity [18]. Supporting all these requirements is essential to enable Web Service based *production workflows* [14].

With respect to the expression of QoS requirements, the BPEL specification leaves out QoS issues for several good reasons such as keeping language simplicity, separation of concerns, and interoperability. Moreover, it is widely assumed that QoS concerns are deployment issues that the BPEL engine should deal somehow with. However, most state of the art BPEL engines lack appropriate means for the expression and the enforcement of many important QoS properties. A few engines support the expression of certain requirements either at the partner link level as in [7] and [17] or by introducing specific language extensions

B. Krämer, K.-J. Lin, and P. Narasimhan (Eds.): ICSOC 2007, LNCS 4749, pp. 582–593, 2007.

as in [12]. Both approaches suffer from problems. In the first one, granularity is an issue as it is not possible to define different QoS properties for different interactions with the same partner. In the second approach, concern-specific language extensions are needed for each concern, which increases the complexity of the BPEL language and breaks its portability.

With respect to the enforcement of QoS requirements, current BPEL engines rely on implementations of WS-* specifications such as WS-Security and WS-ReliableMessaging, which are provided through some message handlers or through an Enterprise Service Bus. That is, the enforcement of the QoS requirements is done outside and independently of the BPEL interpreter. Consequently, process-level requirements such as the transactional execution of a *sequence activity* cannot be supported because they require knowledge about the process structure, BPEL semantics, and the process execution state. Moreover, such an approach does not allow to distinguish different messaging activities that call the same operation on the same partner.

Some work has been done by the authors on the expression of QoS requirements in BPEL. In [18], policies were used to specify the transactional behavior of BPEL processes by attaching policies to scopes. The policy attachments are inlined within the BPEL file, i.e., the specification of QoS requirements is not separated from the specification of the process business logic. In [5], a proprietary deployment descriptor was introduced to express QoS properties of BPEL activities such as security and reliable messaging separately from the BPEL process. However, matching the requirements expressed in that descriptor with the real policies of the live partner Web Services (generally published using WS-Policy) is quite difficult.

To support a generic, fine-grained, non-intrusive, and non-proprietary expression of QoS properties in BPEL, we introduce a novel approach that leverages our previous works. This approach is based on XPath, WS-Policy, and WS-PolicyAttachment [4]. It introduces external policy attachment files that use XPath based selectors to refer to the activities to which a certain policy must be attached. Our approach is generic as it works for various QoS concerns (e.g., security, reliable messaging, transactions) by using the respective policy assertion languages. Moreover, it uses the widely accepted WS-Policy specification rather than introducing proprietary and engine-specific deployment descriptors.

In addition, we will show how our approach was implemented by extending the Colombo [9] BPEL engine. To enforce the requirements of the process activities, that engine was modified in an event-driven manner so that the policy handling component is notified about different events in the execution of process activities. Such a design can be easily incorporated in other BPEL engines that would adopt our approach.

The remainder of this paper is organized as follows: Section 2 gives some background knowledge and motivates the need for policy attachment to BPEL. Section 3 presents the proposed policy attachment syntax and Section 4 describes our prototype implementation within the Colombo framework. Section 5 reports on related work and Section 6 concludes the paper.

2 Motivation

This section provides some background knowledge. Then, it motivates the need for the external attachment of policies to BPEL.

2.1 Background

BPEL [10] is a workflow-based Web Service composition language, i.e., a workflow process specifies the Web Services that participate in the composition, the ordering of their interactions, and the flow of data between them. The main building blocks of BPEL processes are called activities, which can be *primitive* such as *invoke* or *structured* such as *sequence.*

WS-Policy [13] is a specification that provides a generic model and an XML-based syntax for Web Services to publish their policies, i.e., their requirements, capabilities, and preferences. A policy is a collection of policy assertions that can be combined using several operators. There are many domain-specific assertion languages for different purposes such as WS-SecurityPolicy [3], which defines typical security assertions such as message confidentiality and message integrity. Listing 1 shows an example policy that defines a security assertion requiring message encryption using the triple DES algorithm and a reliable messaging assertion requiring ordered message delivery with the at-most-once semantics.

```
<wsp:Policy xmlns:wsp="http://schemas.xmlsoap.org/ws/2002/12/policy/"
    xmlns="http://schemas.xmlsoap.org/ws/2002/12/policy/"
    Name="RMConfidentialityPolicy"
    TargetNamespace="http://www.research.ibm.com/colombo/">

 <wsp:All xmlns:wsrm="http://schemas.xmlsoap.org/ws/2004/03/rm/"
                  xmlns:wsse="http://schemas.xmlsoap.org/ws/2002/04/secext/">
  <wsse:Confidentiality wsp:Usage="Required">
    <wsse:Algorithm Type="wsse:AlgEncryption"
     URI="http://www.w3.org/2001/04/xmlenc#tripledes-cbc"/>
  </wsse:Confidentiality>
  <wsrm:IsReliable assurance="wsrm:AtMostOnce" inOrder="true"
                  wsp:usage="Required"/>
 </wsp:All>
</wsp:Policy>
```

Listing 1. An example of WS-Policy

Web Service Policies are typically attached to elements of WSDL bindings e.g., to an interface as a whole or to a particular binding operation. Attachments to other WSDL structures such as interface or message definitions, though not typical, are also possible. WS-PolicyAttachement [4] defines a general-purpose mechanism for associating policy expressions with subjects such as WSDL documents, UDDI entries, or any other resources. It provides two association approaches: *internal attachment* where the policy is defined as part of the definition of the subject and *external attachment* where the policy is defined independently of the subject and associated to it through an external binding.

2.2 Quality of Service Requirements in BPEL

In [5], QoS requirements in BPEL are classified into *messaging-level* requirements, which are associated with messaging activities and *process-level* requirements, which are associated with higher-level language constructs such as the composite activities *sequence* and *scope*. In the following, we illustrate QoS requirements in BPEL processes using the loan approval process that is presented in the BPEL 1.1 specification [10]. Then, we motivate the need for a new approach to expressing QoS requirements in Web Service compositions.

The loan approval process composes two partner Web Services: a *risk assessor*, which decides on the risk level of the loan application and a *loan approver*, which approves or rejects the loan request in risky cases. If the requested loan amount is small (below a certain value) then the loan is approved directly without invoking the loan approver. Interactions of the loan approval process with the risk assessor and the loan approver via messaging activities go through the Internet, which poses several risks w.r.t security and reliable messaging.

For example, a malicious third-party could see the exchanged messages and even modify them or claim to be the loan approver Web Service and resend client messages to the BPEL process (replay attacks), etc. In addition, the messages exchanged during the execution of the BPEL process could be lost, delivered several times, or in the wrong order.

As an example of a process-level requirement, consider a *sequence* activity that constrains the order in which three invocations of partner Web Services are performed. If these invocations represent an atomic unit of work, it may be necessary to execute the *sequence* using a distributed atomic transaction [18].

Moreover, if these invocations are asynchronous one-way interactions, it may be necessary to guarantee that the corresponding messages are received by the partners without any reordering. This requirement of ordered multi-party message delivery [5] is not guaranteed even if the invocations are performed in order.

2.3 Why Should Policies Be Used to Define QoS Properties?

In a previous work, we introduced an XML-based deployment descriptor to define QoS properties in BPEL processes as part of the process container framework [5], in which an aspect-based process container is generated automatically from the deployment descriptor to enforce QoS requirements.

A major advantage of that deployment descriptor over the usage of policies is that it provides means to define the necessary parameters to enforce a certain requirement. Policies are too declarative (focus on what) and they do not provide any means to pass parameters. That is another way to pass parameters should be found. On the other hand, the requirements specified in the deployment descriptor may conflict with the real policies of the partner Web Services, which can be defined using WS-Policy and policy attachment to WSDL. For instance, the deployment descriptor may specify that authentication with username tokens is required for certain messaging activities that interact with a certain partner Web Service whilst the published policy of that Web Service states that only binary tokens are supported. This example shows that using policies to define the QoS properties of the BPEL process would allow a combined policy to be calculated out of the required policies (defined at the composition side) at the real partner policy (defined at the partner service side). Moreover, conflicts between the QoS requirements of the process and the policy of the partners will be detected easily.

2.4 Why Is Policy Attachment to WSDL Not Sufficient?

Colombo is a light-weight platform for service-oriented applications. Several messaging-level requirements are supported by attaching policies to the WSDL of the composition or its partner Web Services (i.e., the association of policies to elements of the WSDL document such as operations, messages, and port types). However, this approach does not allow two different messaging activities with the same attributes to have different policies. For example, consider a process with two *receive* activities that run sequentially. Clients of this Web Service should call a certain operation twice and then cause some business logic to be executed. Policy attachment to WSDL does not allow to differentiate the two *receive* to express, e.g., that the first *receive* requires authentication and the second requires encryption because they match one same WSDL operation. A finer attachment granularity in the case of BPEL processes is needed.

Moreover, process-level requirements cannot be supported with policy attachment to WSDL because these requirements arise from higher-level language constructs such as composite activities and variables.

Composite activities in BPEL such as *sequence* and *scope* can be used to group a set of interactions. WSDL merely defines the service interface, making it impossible to specify a QoS requirement that spans multiple interactions. For example, one cannot use policy attachment to WSDL to express that three invocations of partner Web Services have a shared coordination context. WSDL does not provide means to specify the transaction boundaries across different operations. Moreover, the two operations that are called by the BPEL process may be defined in different WSDL files.

2.5 Why Should Policies Be Separated from Process Definitions?

The idea of using policies with BPEL was first presented in [18], where policies are used to specify transactional behavior for BPEL processes. In that work, transaction policies are attached to scopes and policy attachments are inlined within the BPEL file, which is quite intrusive. To enforce these policies, an implementation of WS-AtomicTransaction and WS-BusinessActivity is used.

As QoS policies address concerns often orthogonal to the business logic of a BPEL process such as security and reliable messaging, we advocate an even more loosely coupled approach to specifying them: the business logic of the process and the technical details about QoS policies should be defined in separate files, which would bring several benefits:

- It supports the principle of Separation of Concerns as the specification of the process business logic is separated from the specification of technical QoS

properties. Thus, the policies and the BPEL file can be modified independently of each other and the policies can be even modified at runtime.
- It reduces the complexity of the resulting process definition and makes it easier to understand, to maintain, and to evolve.
- It increases reuse as the process can be deployed with various QoS settings in different environments. Rather than several versions of the process, one would have one process (bpel file) and different policy configuration files.
- More flexible attachments schemes can be enabled: one could select a set of activities first (e.g., all *invoke* activities on a partner foo) and then attach a policy to the whole selection (quantification). One could also attach a policy to specific process instances. Without this separation, one would have to find all the *invoke* activities and then attach the policies to them manually.

3 Policy Attachment to BPEL

In this section, we present our assumptions and the proposed syntax for policy attachment to BPEL. Then, we illustrate our approach using an example.

3.1 Assumptions About the BPEL Design and Runtime System

At development time, we assume that the developer is working with a set of Web service definitions (described using WSDL) that are being composed using BPEL. Note at this time that the composition is *abstract*, i.e. no live services need to exist in order for the composition to be created. Once the BPEL definition of the composition is complete, the developer can begin to meet non-functional requirements by adding policies. Policies may be specified by annotating WSDL definitions, which is the standard practice. However, our system additionally allows those non-functional requirements associated with the composition itself to be specified along with the BPEL definition.

At deployment time, the set of WSDL definitions, BPEL definition and policies is mapped into a *live* service composition, with an endpoint for accessing the BPEL process and live partner Web services. During deployment, actual service endpoints are chosen for the Web Services being composed. The policies specified at development time may not match with those required by the selected services. In that case, deployment fails. Our system does not perform matchmaking of any kind; it only computes required policies for the services that are expected to be met by the chosen endpoints.

At runtime, message exchanges and process state may trigger policy handling, i.e. some action by the system middleware to support a QoS requirement such as atomicity or reliable messaging. Here again our system differs from traditional approaches where message exchanges are the only trigger to such actions.

3.2 Syntax of Policy Attachment to BPEL

In WS-PolicyAttachement [4], a syntax is presented for *external* policy attachment to arbitrary resources. We use that syntax to associate externally defined policies to BPEL activities and to partner links. In the last case, the semantics is that the policy applies to all interactions of the process with the partner [18].

We introduce policy attachment files (*.pat files* for short), which are XML files that contain an *appliesTo* element with a nested *selector* element. The content of the latter is an XPath expression for selecting a set of activities. In addition, the *.pat* file contains either a policy or a policy reference.

Inspired by the *quantification* concept [11] that is introduced by Aspect-Oriented Programming, the usage of XPath expressions in the activity selectors enables a flexible and advanced attachment mechanism. In fact, a set of activities that may be defined in different processes can be selected based on certain attribute values (e.g., all interactions with a certain partner or all calls to operations of a given port type) and the policy will be attached to the whole set in one go.

If some policy should be applied only to the request message or response messages of an *invoke* activity then the *inputVariable* attribute (respectively the *outputVariable* attribute) should be used in the XPath expression.

```
<wsp:PolicyAttachment
    xmlns:wsp="http://schemas.xmlsoap.org/ws/2002/12/policy/"
    xmlns:bpat="http://www.research.ibm.com/bpel-attachment/"
    xmlns:bpel="http://schemas.xmlsoap.org/ws/2003/03/business-process/">
 <wsp:AppliesTo>
   <bpat:selector>
   //bpel:process[@name="loanapproval"]//bpel:reply[@operation="approve"]
  </bpat:selector>
 </wsp:AppliesTo>
 <wsp:PolicyReference
 URI="http://www.research.ibm.com/colombo/RMConfidentialityPolicy"/>
</wsp:PolicyAttachment>
```

Listing 2. Syntax of policy attachment to BPEL

Listing 2 shows an example *.pat* file that associates a confidentiality policy to the *reply* activity contained in the BPEL process *loan approval* by using a policy reference. This *.pat* file contains a reference to the policy that was shown in Listing 1.

3.3 Policy Enforcement

In the following, we explain in a generic way how policies attached to BPEL activities are enforced. To support QoS policies defined in this manner, the system needs to first read and load the policy attachment files and the attached policies. The system may choose to load the *.pat* file, interpret the context and configure the middleware at deployment time (i.e. when the BPEL process is deployed to the system with associated policy attachment files), or even at runtime by checking dynamically for new policy attachments.

Then, the system needs to identify the processes to which the policy is attached and establish a mapping between the activities selected by the *AppliesTo* element and the respective policies. For example, for the policy attachment file shown in Listing 2, the system will locate all instances of the business process named *loanapproval* and load the policy referenced by the *policyReference* element in the *.pat* file (shown in Listing 1). Next the system establishes a mapping between the selected *reply* activity and that policy.

Consider a BPEL system with a policy handler mechanism for Web services, which supports policy attachment to WSDL. If one aims to add support for policies attached to BPEL constructs in such as system, then the BPEL engine and the policy handlers need to interact to exchange state information relevant to the BPEL activities being executed. For example, if a process has some transaction policy attachments to a *sequence* activity then the transaction policy handlers need to be notified about relevant events in the execution of that activity such as start, completion, and the execution of nested messaging activities.

Figure 1 shows how various reliable messaging and security policies are attached to the activities of the loan approval process. In this figure, three different policies are used for interacting with each partner of the process (via the activities *receive*, *reply*, and *invoke*.

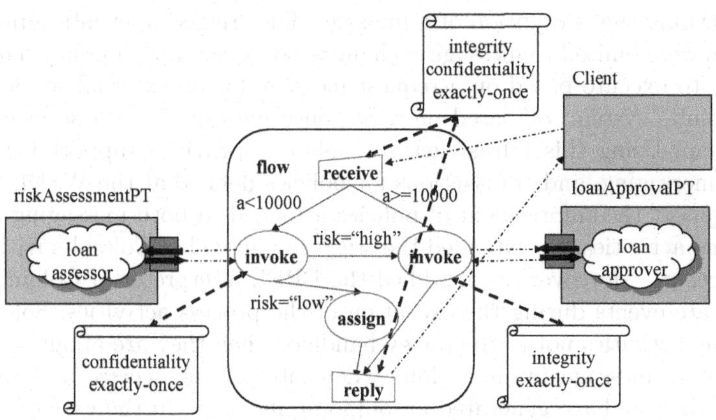

Fig. 1. A secure and reliable loan approval process

4 Implementation

Colombo [9] is a light-weight platform for developing, deploying, and executing service-oriented applications. It offers native and optimized runtime support for the service-oriented computing model, as opposed to approaches layering service-oriented applications on a legacy runtime.

Colombo provides a multi-language service programming model supporting Java and BPEL. The deployment and discovery models of Colombo are based on declarative service descriptions in WSDL and WS-Policy. The unit of development and deployment is called *servicelet*. The Colombo platform consists basically of a *SOAP message processing engine*: messages flow into the system via channels and are examined and dispatched to the intended recipient according to a set of predefined rules to the respective servicelet manager (one for

BPEL and one for Java). The latter provides the connective layer between the servicelet implementation and the system's infrastructure. Colombo also comes with a set of middleware services such as security, transaction, persistence, etc. In addition, there is a policy framework responsible for collecting, interpreting, and enforcing policies.

The deployment of BPEL servicelets in Colombo looks for *.car* files that contain the servicelet definition files and the WSDLs of the partner Web Services. If some policies are attached, e.g., to some operations in the WSDL of the partner Web Services, these policies are parsed and a mapping is established between the SOAP message corresponding to these operations and the respective policies. To support policy attachment to BPEL, the deployment process also looks for *.pat* files in the *car* file. Once those files are found, the BPEL activities that are matched by the XPath selectors are computed, the attached policies are parsed, and a mapping is established between the activities and the respective policies.

Colombo's policy enforcement model is based on a set of triggering events that result in policy handlers being executed. A policy handler is responsible for the enforcement of a specific policy, for example supporting confidentiality by performing the encryption of a message. The triggering events supported by Colombo were limited to message exchanges, so for example a policy handler can be made to execute based on a request message for an external service leaving the Colombo system, or based on a response message from a service entering the system. Using this infrastructure, Colombo provides support for security, reliable messaging, and transactions for policies defined at the WSDL level.

To support the enforcement of policies attached to both messaging and non-messaging activities, we extended the triggering model of Colombo with *activity trigger events*. Moreover, we modified the BPEL interpreter of Colombo to fire appropriate events during the execution of the process activities. For instance, messaging activities notify the policy handlers when they are about to consume an incoming message (as it is done when interpreting *receive* and *invoke* activities), or they have generated an outgoing message (in the case of *reply* and *invoke*). Structured activities such as *scopes* notify the policy handlers when they are entered, exited, and when the lifecycle of their child activities changes. When the policy handlers receive such events, they check the list of activity-to-policy mappings that was established at deployment time. If the source activity of the events is found in one of those mappings, the respective policy is enforced by the appropriate policy handler.

The version of Colombo modified in this manner is now able to support activity triggers in addition to message triggers. Moreover, policies are applied on SOAP messages (e.g., encryption), on activities (e.g., creation of a sequence when a scope with reliable messaging policy is entered), or on a combination of both (e.g., creation of a transaction context at the beginning of a scope).

If a certain policy *p1* is defined for a messaging activity via policy attachment to BPEL and a policy *p2* is defined via policy attachment to WSDL, both policies are combined into an effective required policy that is calculated as described in [15]. When the partners are matched with real Web Services, the effective required policy should be matched with the policy of the real Web Service.

5 Related Work

In [6], Charfi and Mezini presented AO4BPEL, which extends BPEL with aspect-oriented concepts. Unlike other aspect-oriented extensions to BPEL, which allow only the modularization of process-level concerns such as [8] and [2], AO4BPEL aspects support also middleware-related QoS concerns [5] because AO4BPEL provides suitable language concepts for that such as *internal join points*, *cross-layer pointcuts*, and appropriate context collection constructs that the advice can use to access the SOAP messaging layer.

Based on AO4BPEL, Charfi et al. presented a process container framework that also addresses QoS requirements in BPEL processes in [5]. Unlike the current proposal, the process container framework introduces a declarative XML-based *deployment descriptor* to express QoS requirements. To enforce QoS requirements, a set of AO4BPEL container aspects is generated automatically from the deployment descriptor using XSLT. These aspects intercept the execution of the process activities and call dedicated *middleware Web Services* to enforce the requirements. The current paper uses WS-Policy to define QoS requirements, which allows an easier matching of the QoS requirements of the BPEL process with the real policies of partner Web Services. Another important difference is that the logic for enforcing requirements is part of the policy handler in Colombo (i.e., how policies are enforced is hidden) whilst that logic is part of the container aspects in AO4BPEL (i.e., it is visible to the user).

The work presented in this paper is also aspect-oriented to some extent. The XPath expressions used in the policy attachment file are similar to the pointcut concept in AO4BPEL. The attached policy is similar to the advice but it is more declarative as it specifies what should be done but not how it should be done. Note however, that policies and aspects can complement each other as it is possible for example to use AO4BPEL aspects to enforce certain policies.

The idea of using aspects to enforce policies is also mentioned in [16]. In that work, Ortiz and Leymann use WS-Policy [13] to describe the requirements of Web Services and propose generating AspectJ aspects to enforce the policies. The use of aspects in that proposal allows for a more modular and reusable implementation of the Java based Web Service. However, no implementation is provided on how aspects can be generated. Moreover, Web Service compositions that are implemented in BPEL are not supported as the approach is specific to Java-based Web Services.

In [12], the authors defined transactions support to BPEL in a way that is extremely tightly coupled with the process definition: They directly extended the BPEL language by new constructs and proposed adding the extensions to the specification. This approach breaks the portability of BPEL and makes it very complex. Moreover, with such an approach, one would have a specific language extension for transactions, for security, for reliable messaging, and so on. We choose to attach policies in a non-intrusive manner that distinguishes our work from this and other works.

The idea of using policies with BPEL was first presented in [18], where policies are used for specifying transactional behavior for BPEL processes by attaching them to scopes and partner links. That work focuses on the issues of supporting specifically transactions in BPEL (policy syntax, programming model, middleware implications). That is, how one can combine coordination (WS-Coordination) and composition (BPEL). It does not delve into policy attachment mechanisms and granularities for general non-coordination related QoS. As a result, that work itself is not concerned with *how* one attaches these policies. In the current paper, our focus is on the issues of a generic, flexible, external attachment mechanism of policies to BPEL processes and constructs, e.g., to an *invoke*, a *sequence*, etc. We enable one to use quantification for policy attachment and our approach can be used for all BPEL constructs.

The design of Colombo's policy framework is described in [9] and [15]. One of the design goals is to support policy attachment and enforcement independently of the service implementation. This goal is consistent with the Web Services middleware layer being viewed as a veneer to facilitate interaction with the business logic as a service. However, as we have seen, this goal causes problems when the business logic and QoS properties are related to each other so that it is impossible to specify QoS as a wrapper to a black box implementation.

6 Conclusion

In this paper, we used policies to specify the QoS properties of BPEL processes. We introduced a syntax for attaching policies to BPEL activities using WS-PolicyAttachment and XPath activity selectors. We also explained how policies that are attached in that way can be enforced by the BPEL runtime. Moreover, we presented a prototype implementation based on the Colombo framework.

As future research, one could extend the *AppliesTo* element for policy attachment with an endpoint reference (EPR) [1]. This would allow the attachment of a policy to a specific process instance. In the current implementation, the policy is attached to the selected activities in all instances of the process. Second, one could develop a command line tool for the dynamic modification of policies. This tool will take a *.pat* file as parameter and support attaching policies to running BPEL processes.

Acknowledgments

The authors acknowledge Francisco Curbera for the inception of this project, and the discussions and ideas during its creation. Moreover, the first author thanks Mira Mezini for enabling this collaboration.

References

1. Box, D., Curbera, F. (eds.): Web Services Addressing (WS-Addressing) (August 2004)
2. Braem, M., Verlaenen, K., Joncheere, N., Vanderperren, W., Van Der Straeten, R., Truyen, E., Joosen, W., Jonckers, V.: Isolating process-level concerns using padus. In: Dustdar, S., Fiadeiro, J.L., Sheth, A. (eds.) BPM 2006. LNCS, vol. 4102, Springer, Heidelberg (2006)
3. Kaler, C., Nadalin, A. (eds.): Web Services Security Policy Language (WS-SecurityPolicy) Version 1.1 (July 2005)
4. Sharp, C. (ed.): Web Services Policy Attachment (WS-PolicyAttachment) (September 2004)
5. Charfi, A.: Aspect-Oriented Workflow Languages: AO4BPEL and Applications. PhD thesis, Darmstadt University of Technology, Darmstadt, Germany (2007)
6. Charfi, A., Mezini, M.: Ao4bpel: An aspect-oriented extension to bpel. World Wide Web Journal: Recent Advances in Web Services (March 2007)
7. Cape Clear. Cape clear orchestrator 6.5
8. Courbis, C., Finkelstein, A.: Towards aspect weaving applications. In: Proceedings of ICSE, pp. 69–77 (May 2005)
9. Curbera, F., Duftler, M.J., Khalaf, R., Nagy, W.A., Mukhi, N., Weerawarana, S.: Colombo: Lightweight middleware for service-oriented computing. IBM Systems Journal 44(4), 799–820 (2005)
10. Curbera, F., Goland, Y., Klein, J., et al.: Business Process Execution Language for Web Services (BPEL4WS) Version 1.1 (May 2003)
11. Filman, R., Friedman, D.: Aspect-oriented programming is quantification and obliviousness. In: Workshop on Advanced Separation of Concerns in conjunction with OOPSLA 2000 (October 2000)
12. Flechter, T., Furniss, P., Green, A., Haugen, R.: BPEL and Business Transaction Management, Choreology submission to OASIS (2003)
13. Schlimmer, J. (ed.): Web Services Policy Framework (September 2004)
14. Leymann, F., Roller, D.: Production Workflows. Prentice-Hall, Englewood Cliffs (2000)
15. Mukhi, N.K., Plebani, P.: Supporting policy-driven behaviors in web services: experiences and issues. In: Proc. of ICSOC, pp. 322–328. ACM Press, New York (2004)
16. Ortiz, G., Leymann, F.: Combining ws-policy and aspect-oriented programming. In: Proceedings of AICT-ICIW '06, Washington, DC, USA, p. 143. IEEE Computer Society Press, Los Alamitos (2006)
17. OpenLink Software. Virtuoso universal server 4.5
18. Tai, S., Khalaf, R., Mikalsen, T.: Composition of coordinated web services. In: Jacobsen, H.-A. (ed.) Middleware 2004. LNCS, vol. 3231, pp. 294–310. Springer, Heidelberg (2004)

Execution Optimization for Composite Services Through Multiple Engines*

Wubin Li[1], Zhuofeng Zhao[1], Jun Fang[1], and Kun Chen[2]

[1] Research Centre for Grid and Service Computing
Institute of Computing Technology, Chinese Academy of Sciences
P.O.Box 2704, 100080, Beijing, China
[2] Department of Computer Science and Technology
Shandong University of Science and Technology, Qingdao 266510, China
{liwubin, zhaozf, fangjun, chenkun}@software.ict.ac.cn
http://sigsit.ict.ac.cn/

Abstract. Web services are rapidly emerging as a popular standard for sharing data and functionality among heterogeneous systems. We propose a general purpose Web Service Management System (*WSMSME*) that enables executing composite services through multiple engines. This paper tackles a first basic *WSMSME* problem: execution optimization for composite services through multiple engines. Our main result comprises two dynamic programming algorithms. One helps minimizes the number of engines required to complete a composite service when computational capability of each engine is relatively changeless; the other optimally minimizes the heaviest load of engines by segmenting a pipelined execution plan into sub-sequences before they are dispatched and executed; Both of the two can obtain optimal solutions in polynomial time. Experiments with an initial prototype indicate that our algorithms can lead to significant performance improvement over more straightforward techniques.

Keywords: Web Services, Execution Optimization, Multiple Engines, Dynamic Programming.

1 Introduction

Web services [1] are becoming a standard method of sharing data and functionality among loosely-couple, heterogeneous systems. Many organizations and enterprises are considering exposing their existing data and business logic as Web services (to both internal and external audiences). On the other hand, the composition of Web services to handle complex transactions such as finance, billing, and traffic information services is gaining considerable momentum as a way to enable business-to-business (B2B) collaborations. There has been a considerable amount of recent work [2, 3] on the challenges associated with discovering

* This work is supported in part by the National Science Foundation of China (Grant No. 90412010), the National Basic Research Program of China (973 Program) (Grant No. 2007CB310805), and the China R&D Infrastructure and Facility Development Project (Grant No. 2005DKA64201).

B. Krämer, K.-J. Lin, and P. Narasimhan (Eds.): ICSOC 2007, LNCS 4749, pp. 594–605, 2007.

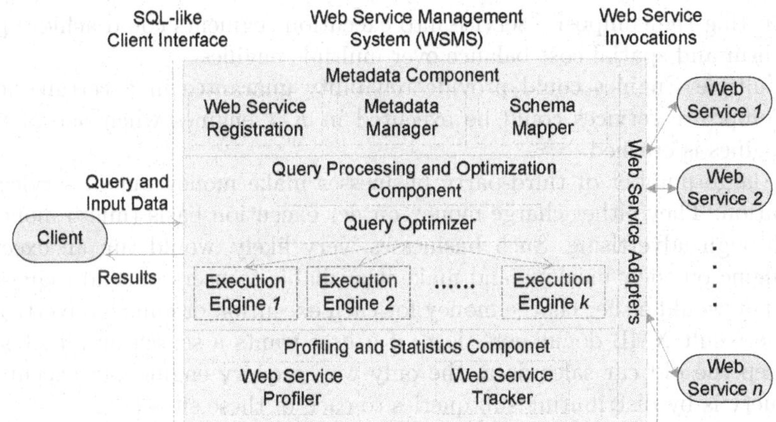

Fig. 1. A Web Service Management System with Multiple Engines (*WSMSME*)

and composing web services to solve a given problem. We are interested in the more basic challenge of providing scheduler-like capabilities when scheduled jobs are composite services. To this end we propose the development of a Web Service Management System with Multiple Engines *WSMSME*: a general-purpose system that enables clients to execute composite services simultaneously in a transparent and integrated fashion.

Overall, we expect a *WSMSME* to consist of three major components; see Figure 1. The *Metadata* component deals with metadata management, registration of new web services, and mapping their schemas to an integrated view provided to the client. Given an integrated view of the schema, a client can request the *WSMSME* through a client interface. The *Execution Processing and Optimization* component handles optimization and execution of such declarative request, i.e., it chooses and executes a plan whose operators invoke the relevant composite service which comprise several web services. The *Profiling and Statistics* component profiles web services for their response time characteristics, spatial cost; and maintains relevant statistics over the web service data, to the extent possible. This component is used primarily by the execution optimizer for making its optimization decisions.

What make *WSMSME* different from other congeners [13] are the number of execution engines and the locations of them. We argue that, multiple execution engines and distribution could be exploited to achieve parallelism in execution and reduce the response time to the user. One can expect a reasonable speedup and cost-like load balancing because of the following reasons:

- A single Engine might be incapable to finish the whole process especially when computational capability and resources are insufficient in a separate machine.
- Architecture with multiple engines distributed in different systems is usually a preferable solution. Distributing the query makes more computational power available for the execution of the composite service.

- Cutting the composite service into execution segments could achieve parallelism and spatial cost balance over multiple engines.
- Multiple Engines could provide reliability guarantee in a certain degree. Composite services could be executed in *K-1* engines when one of the *K* engines is crashed.
- A large number of third-party businesses make money out of service execution. They either charge money on per execution basis (micro money) or through advertising. Such businesses, very likely, would run an execution engine on their machine and make it available to users to send requests to. They would either charge money for each execution or embed advertising in the result XML documents. E.g., if a user wants a search on all sites that keep the old car sales data, the only way a query engine can execute this query is by distributing sub queries to each of these sites [13].

Moreover, our *WSMSME* architecture is similar to mediators in distributed data integration system [16, 17, 18, 19, 20];

2 Related Work

2.1 Parallel and Distributed Execution Processing

In our setting of execution processing over web services, only data shipping is allowed, i.e., dispatching data to web services that process it according to their preset functionality. In traditional distributed or parallel execution processing, each of which has been addressed extensively in previous work [4,5,6], in addition to data shipping, code shipping also is allowed, i.e., deciding which machines are to execute which code over which data. Due to lack of code shipping, techniques for parallel and distributed execution optimization, e.g., fragment-replicate joins [6], are inapplicable in our scenario. Moreover, most parallel or distributed execution optimization techniques are limited to a heuristic exploration of the search space whereas we provide provably optimal plans for our problem setting.

2.2 Web Service Composition and Choreography

A considerable body of recent work addresses the problem of composition (or orchestration) of multiple web services to carry out a particular task, e.g. [7, 8]. In general, that work is targeted more toward workflow-oriented applications (e.g., the processing steps involved in fulfilling a purchase order), rather than applications coordinating execution optimization through multiple engines, as addressed in this paper. Although these approaches have recognized the benefits of pipelined processing, they have not, as far as we are aware, included formal cost models or techniques that result in provably optimal pipelined execution strategies.

Languages such as *BPEL4WS* [9] are emerging for specifying web service composition in workflow-oriented scenarios. While we have not yet specifically applied our work to these languages, we note that *BPEL4WS*, for example, has constructs that can specify which web services must be executed in a sequence and which can be executed in parallel. But there is no consideration about running environments, nor optimal execution plans - no specification relative about how to complete the executions through multiple engines. We are hopeful that the optimization techniques developed here will extend to web-service workflow scenarios as they become more standardized, and doing so is an important direction for future work.

3 Preliminaries

Consider a *WSMSME* as shown in *Figure 1* that provides an integrated interface to invoke a composite service which involves n web services $WS_1,...WS_n$. We assume that each web service possesses a property (referred to as C) which represents how much cost that is required to finish executing it. C might include time, memory sizes, money, etc. consequently, we write WS_i (C_i) to denote that, treating WS_i as a program whose running cost is C_i. An important direction of future work is to provide more sophisticated mechanisms to describe those requirements, because every-way, the notion of a single cost factor C is overly a little bit simplistic.

3.1 Composite Pattern Considered

The composite patterns of service we consider for optimization are sequential services over one or more web services $WS_1,...WS_n$. We assume that the correspondence among various inputs of services is tracked by the Metadata component of the *WSMSME* (*Figure 1*).

DEFINETION 3.1 (SEQUENTIAL SERVICES).

Input
$I \rightarrow (WS_1) \rightarrow (WS_2) \rightarrow \cdots\cdots\cdots \rightarrow (WS_n) \rightarrow$ *Results*

Where inputs of WS_{i+1} come from the outputs of WS_i ,where $i \in [1,2...n\text{-}1]$.

We assume in *Definition 3.1* that all web services run in order: In a given process, WS_{i+1} can not be executed before WS_i has been executed. We also assume that inputs of each web service can be delivered accurately without any other consideration about how it can be.

EXAMPLE 3.1. *Suppose a credit card company wishes to send out mailings for its new credit card offer. The company continuously obtains lists of potential recipients from which it wants to select only those who have a good payment history on a prior credit card, and who have a credit rating above some threshold. For processing this query, the company has the following three web services at its disposal.*

WS_1 : name (n) $\rightarrow$ credit rating (cr)
WS_2 : name (n) $\rightarrow$ credit card numbers (ccn)
WS_3 : card number (ccn) $\rightarrow$ payment history (ph)
With a WSMSME, one possible way of executing the query is as follows: The Company's initial list of names (we assume names are unique) is first processed by WS_1 to determine the corresponding credit ratings, and those below threshold are filtered out (either by WS_1 itself or by the WSMSME). The remaining names are then processed by WS_2 to get the corresponding credit card numbers. Each card number is then processed by WS_3, and if the card is found to have a good payment history, then the name is output in the result of the query, as below.

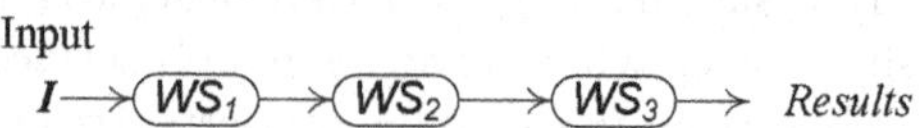

Fig. 2. Plan for Example 3.1

Other patterns mentioned in previous works [12] are left out of in this paper, and would be kept for the future work.

3.2 Problem Definition

There are two basic scenarios involved in this paper, and we try to solve problems related with those scenarios. Such problems are all about execution optimization through multiple execution engines in *WSMSME*.

3.2.1 Scenario A: Minimize the Number of Execution Engines

In this scenario, we suppose that there are K execution engines available in *WSMSME*, and client requests arrive in chunks. Web service WS_i of a composite service requires *C_i-weighed* resources so that it can be executed correctly. In order to keep the number of available execution engines as great as possible, we try to minimize the number of execution engines required when a request of a composite service arrives, then allocate the chosen engines to the composite service being invoked. Suppose there are 8 execution engines available when a request of composite service *CS* comes, we can allocate 5 engines to complete this request; but if 2 is ok, then we choose 2 and thereby 6 is left before others become available again. Currently, we also simply assume that the computational capability of each engine is equivalent relatively, and we write a value L to denote this.

EXAMPLE 3.2.1. *Consider the plan in Figure 2. Let the requirement of the web services and L to be as follows:*

i	*1*	*2*	*3*
Requirement of WS_i (C_i)	*4*	*2*	*3*
Value of L	*6*		

Then if we dispatch each service to a different execution engine (it is possible because L is greater than C_i), 3 execution engines are needed. Obviously, it is not the optimal solution. At least, we have two more plans for this problem: (a) allocate an execution engine to run WS_1 and WS_2, and another for WS_3; (b) allocate an execution engine to run WS_1 and another for WS_2 and WS_3.

Now we can not tell which is better, because plan a and b both need 2 execution engines. To evaluate how a plan is different from another that needs the same number of execution engines, we introduce a dissatisfaction index function(referred to as *DI*) to calculate how bad the plan is. Suppose two different plans both need M engines (referred to as EE_1, EE_2,...EE_M), then:

$$Dissatisfaction\ Index = \sqrt{\frac{\sum_{i=1}^{M}(L - \sum_{EE_i\ is\ allocated\ to\ WS_k} C_k)^2}{M}}$$

In this scenario, we treat C_i as a random variable, whose dissatisfaction is the standard deviation. The standard deviation is the root mean square (RMS) deviation of values from their arithmetic mean, and it is most common measure of statistical dispersion, measuring how widely spread the values in the data set $\{C_1, C_2, ...\}$ are. The less that standard deviation is, the better the solution is. Concretely, if dissatisfaction index is large, that means many C_i are far from the mean, and correspondingly,vast sum of resources of engines are wasted.

We can now calculate which is better in Example 3.2.1, because $DI(a) = \sqrt{\frac{(6-4-2)^2+(6-3)^2}{2}} = \frac{3\sqrt{2}}{2}, DI(b) = \sqrt{\frac{(6-4)^2+(6-2-3)^2}{2}} = \frac{\sqrt{10}}{2}$.

Apparently, *Dissatisfaction Index(a)>Dissatisfaction Index(b)* which tells that plan *b* is more optimal than plan *b*, then we choose the preferable one.

3.2.2 Scenario B: Load Balancing Through Multiple Engines

In this scenario, which is independent with scenario A, we try to dispatch K web services (which comprise a composite service) to M available engines and obtain load balancing over those M engines.

EXAMPLE 3.2.2. *Consider the plan in Figure 2. Let the requirement of the web services and L to be as follows:*

i	*1*	*2*	*3*
Requirement of WS_i (C_i)	*4*	*2*	*3*
Value of L	*7*		
Number of Engines Allocated	*2*		

And now we have two plans for this problem: (a) allocate an execution engine M_1 to run WS_1 and WS_2, and another M_2 for WS_3; (b) allocate an execution engine M_1 to run WS_1 and another M_2 for WS_2 and WS_3. In this scenario, we can easily tell that plan (a) is better, because the maximum load among M_1 and M_2 is 6 (the sum of C_1 and C_2), which is less than that of plan (b). In other *words, we redefine the dissatisfaction index function(calculate the maximum load of engines) in this scenario to be as follows:*

$$Dissatisfaction\ Index = \max_{M}\left\{\textstyle\sum_{EE_i \text{ is allocated to } WS_k} C_k \middle| i \in [1, 2...M]\right\}$$

For EXAMPLE 3.2.2, we get

$$DI(a) = \max\{(2+4), 3\} = 6, DI(b) = \max\{2, (4+3)\} = 7$$

Which shows that plan (a) is preferable.

4 Algorithms for Execution Plans in the Two Scenarios

4.1 Optimal Execution Plans for Scenario A

To solve the problem described in scenario A, we use the optimal substructure to show that we can construct an optimal solution from optimal solutions to subproblems. Firstly, we make two denotations as follows:

- □ $F(k)$:The minimum number of execution engines to complete the first k web services in a composite service.
- □ $D(k)$:The value of dissatisfaction index when the first k web services are optimally scheduled.

Thus, the minimum number of execution engines to complete the first *k+1* web services $F(k+1)$ is either of

1. $F(k)+1$, that is to say, allocate a new engine to the web services WS_{k+1}.
2. $F(j)+1$,when allocating services WS_{j+1}, WS_{j+2},...WS_{k+1} the same engine.

Using this we get:

$$F(k+1) = Min\{F(k)+1, F(j)+1 \big| j < k+1 \& \textstyle\sum_{i=j+1}^{k+1} C_i \leq L\}$$

Moreover, we can update $D(k)$ when computing $F(k)$.

Algorithm Dynamic Programming A

$F(1) \leftarrow 1, D(1) \leftarrow \sqrt{(L-C_1)^2}, k \leftarrow 1, T \leftarrow number\ of\ webservices$
$While(k+1<T)$
    $F(k+1) \leftarrow \infty, D(k+1) \leftarrow \infty$
    $While(j<k+1 \& \sum_{i=j+1}^{k+1} C_i \leq L)$
        $if(F(k+1)>F(j)+1)$
            $F(k+1) \leftarrow F(j)+1$
            Re−calculate D(k+1) using Dissatisfaction Index Function.
        $elseif(F(k+1)=F(j)+1)$
            Re−calculate D(k+1) using Dissatisfaction Index Function.
$Return F(T), D(T)$.

4.2 Optimal Execution Plans for Scenario B

Conditions involved in scenario B are different from that of scenario A, but the solution is similar. And we still using dynamic programming algorithms to solve that problem. We write $F(i,j)$ to denote the maximum load among j engines when executing i web services through those j engines. Thus, considering the definition of F, we get

$$F(i,j) = Min\left\{ Max\left\{ F(i-1,t-1), \sum_{k=t}^{i} C_k \right\} \middle| t \geq i \right\}.$$

Using the equation above, we get algorithm as follows:

Algorithm Dynamic Programming B

$k \leftarrow number\ of\ available\ execution\ engines, n \leftarrow number\ of\ web\ services$
$for(i = 1; i \leq n; i++)$
$\quad F(1,i) = SUM(C_1, C_2...C_i)$
$for(i = 2; i \leq k; i++)$
$\quad for(j = i; j<n; j++)$
$\quad\quad for(t = j; t \geq i; t--)$
$\quad\quad\quad tem = Max\{F(i,t-1), \sum_{k=t}^{i} C_k\}$
$\quad\quad\quad if(tem<F(i,j))$
$\quad\quad\quad\quad F(i,j) \leftarrow tem$
$ReturnF(k,n)$.

4.3 Analysis of Algorithms

See the algorithms above, algorithm A computes an optimal plan in $O(n^2)$ time where n is the number of web services involved in the composite service which is invoked; algorithm B computes an optimal plan in $O(kn^2)$ time where n is the number of web services and k is the number of engines.

5 Implementation and Experiments

We implemented an initial prototype *WSMSME*, described in*Section 5.1*. Here we report on a few experiments with it. Not surprisingly, in our experiments, plan execution performance of composite service reflects our theoretical results (thereby validating our cost model). Using minimum number of execution engines on demand and maximum load among execution engines as metrics, we compared the execution plan produced by our optimization algorithm (referred to as Optimizer) against the plans produced by the following simpler algorithms:

1. *Greedy*: This algorithm attempts to exploit the minimum possible number of execution engines by dispatching services to execution engine whenever possible. For example, if a subsequent service WS_i is supposed to require 40M memories, and the available computational capability of execution engine

EE_k is 46M (which is greater than 40M), then WS_i would be dispatched to execution engine EE_k, and that would decrease the available computational capability of EE_k to be 6M. Thereby, if the following service WS_{i+1} requires more than 6M to complete, an additional execution engine is needed. Greedy is used to finish a comparison with our algorithm in the first scenario (scenario A) that mentioned before.

2. *Random*: Segmenting a composite service into K sub-sequences can be obtained randomly. Random is used to finish a comparison with our algorithm in the second scenario (scenario B) that mentioned.

We first describe our *WSMSME* prototype and the experimental setup in *Section 5.1.* We then describe our experiments for scenarios mentioned before.

5.1 Prototype and Experimental Setup

The experimental setup consists of two parts: the client side, consisting of our *WSMSME* prototype, and the server side, consisting of web services set up by us.

Our *WSMSME* prototype is a multithreaded system written in Java [14]. It implements the two core dynamic programming algorithms we proposed in this paper. For communicating with web services using SOAP, our prototype uses Codehaus XFire [11] tools. Given a description of a web service in the Web Service Definition Language [15], Xfire generates a class such that the web service can be invoked simply by calling a method of the generated class. The input and out types of the web service are also encapsulated in generated classes. The function of executing a web service is realized inside Execution Engines. Execution engine here is a little bit "virtual" within our prototype, and it is implemented to be a common multi-threaded object (*ExecutionEngine*) which possesses of one special property (*ComputationalCapability*) that specifies its computational capability, which means we can create and delete an engine that has specific computational capability on demand.

We use Apache Tomcat [10] as the application server and Codehaus XFire [11] tools for web service deployment. Each of our experimental web services WS_i runs on a different machine, and has a table T_i (int a, int b, primary key a) associated with it. Given a value for attribute a, WS_i retrieves the corresponding value for attribute b from T_i (by issuing a SQL query) and returns it. The tables T_i are stored using the lightweight MySQL DBMS. Since attribute a is the primary key, MySQL automatically builds an index on a.

For our experiments, we needed web services with different costs and requirements. To obtain different costs, we introduce a delay between when a web service obtains the answer from its database and when it returns the answer to the caller of the web service. The web service cost is varied by varying this delay. The *WSMSME* is run on a different machine from the ones on which the web services were running. Each composite service is compromised by a series of web services sequentially (other types of composite patterns are left out of our discussion currently).

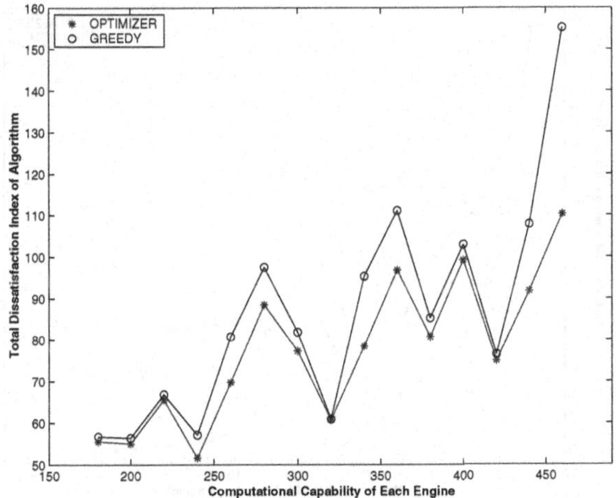

Fig. 3. Comparison of Total Dissatisfaction Index in Scenario A

5.2 Scenario A: Minimize the Number of Engines

In this experiment, given a composite service comprised by a sequence of web services with certain costs, we try to minimize the number of engines required to complete a composite service when computational capability of each engine is relatively changeless and equivalent. Furthermore, if there are multiple schedules with the minimum number of engines, we also minimize the Total *Dissatisfaction Index*. We developed 19 web services, and make them a composite service. Costs of the web service ranges from 50 to 180. When running this composite service, we dynamically increased the computational capability of engine from 170 to 460. Surprisingly, we found that the minimum possible number of engines required is nearly the same when using *OPTIMIZER* and *GREEDY*, while the *Total Dissatisfaction Index* is completely different as *Figure 3* shows.

Figure 3 shows that, the advantage of *OPTIMIZER* mounts up as the computational capability of each engine (referred to as *cmp*) increases. Only when the *cmp* is small do the *GREEDY* obtain the similar schedule plan as *OPTIMIZER*.

5.3 Scenario B: Minimize the Heaviest Load of Engines

In this experiment (independent with the last one), we try to minimize the heaviest load of engines by segmenting a pipelined execution plan into subsequences before they are dispatched and executed. Namely, it is an experiment about load balancing among multiple engines. We use the services we've mentioned in Section 5.2, and increased the number of execution engines from 1 to 15.

See the performances produced . Not surprisingly, the maximum load among execution engines descends as the number of engines increase, no matter which algorithms were applied. Nevertheless, results obtained from *OPTIMIZER* were always more excellent than that from *RANDOM*.

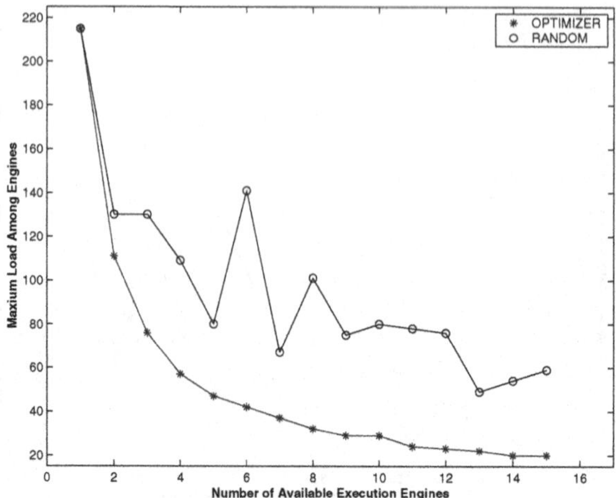

Fig. 4. Maximum Load among Engines in Scenario B

6 Conclusions and Future Works

Web services have received significant attention and there is a great deal of industry excitement around the opportunities afforded by them. While most of this attention has focused on middle-tier Web services, an increasing interest in composite service has recently emerged as organizations encapsulate their existing legacy services to be web services. In this paper, we focus on execution optimization issues that arise in a *WSMSME*. Towards two basis scenarios, we've devised new algorithms to: (a) help minimize the number of engines required to execute a composite service when computational capability of each engine is relatively changeless and (b) optimally minimizes the heaviest load of engines (namely load balancing) by segmenting a pipelined execution plan into subsequences before they are dispatched and executed. While the algorithms in this paper form the basis of a *WSMSME* execution optimizer, we believe they only scratch the surface of what promises to be an exciting new research area. There are several interesting directions for future work:

- An important next step is to extend our algorithms to support composite services which are comprised in more complicated patterns such as those mentioned in [12].
- We have not considered web services with monetary costs or other special types of costs. In those scenarios, we may wish to use optimization algorithms that minimize the running of a composite service to a certain budget limit. Moreover, it is also interesting to achieve load balancing when costs of web services are monetary or else.
- Our algorithms currently do not take much consideration about the metric of each execution engine's computational capability. We just simply expect

that it is equivalent the same. However, as the case stands, computational capability of executions might obviously vary.

- More work on service composite languages such as *BPEL4WS* is needed; Extension of our algorithms to such specifications is an interesting direction of future work.

References

1. Web services (2002), `http://www.w3.org/2002/ws`
2. Florescu, D., Grunhagen, A., Kossmann, D.: XL: A platform for web services. In: CIDR. Proc. First Biennial Conf. on Innovative Data Systems Research (2003)
3. Ouzzani, M., Bouguettaya, A.: Efficient access to web services. IEEE Internet Computing 8(2), 34–44 (2004)
4. DeWitt, D., et al.: The Gamma Database Machine Project. IEEE Trans. on Knowledge and Data Engineering 2(1), 44–62 (1990)
5. Hong, W., Stonebraker, M.: Optimization of parallel query execution plans in XPRS. In: Proceedings of the First Intl.Conf. on Parallel and Distributed Information Systems, pp. 218–225 (1991)
6. Ozsu, M., Valduriez, P.: Principles of distributed database systems. Prentice-Hall, Inc, Englewood Cliffs (1991)
7. Florescu, D., Grunhagen, A., Kossmann, D.: XL: A platform for web services. In: CIDR. Proc. First Biennial Conf. on Innovative Data Systems Research (2003)
8. Ouzzani, M., Bouguettaya, A.: Efficient access to web services. IEEE Internet Computing 8(2), 34–44 (2004)
9. BPEL4WS: Business Process Execution Language for Web Services, `ftp://www6.software.ibm.com/software/developer/library/wsbpel.pdf`
10. Apache Tomcat, `http://tomcat.apache.org/`
11. Codehaus XFire, `http://xfire.codehaus.org/`
12. Russell, N., ter Hofstede, A.H.M.: WORKFLOW CONTROL-FLOW PATTERNS-A Revised View, `http://workflowpatterns.com/documentation/documents/BPM-06-22.pdf`
13. Srivastava, U., Munagala, K., Widom, J., Motwani, R.: Query optimization over web services. In: Proceedings of the 32nd international conference on Very large data bases, vol. 32, pp. 355–366 (2006)
14. Java API, `http://java.sun.com/j2se/1.5.0/docs/api/`
15. Web Services Description Language, `http://www.w3.org/TR/wsdl`
16. Casati, F., Dayal, U. (eds.): Special Issue on Web Services, IEEE Data Eng. Bull., vol. 25(4) (2002)
17. Garcia-Molina, H., et al.: The TSIMMIS approach to mediation: Data models and languages. Journal of Intelligent Information Systems 8(2), 117–132 (1997)
18. Miller, R. (ed.): Special Issue on Integration Management, IEEE Data Eng. Bull., vol. 25(3) (2002)
19. Roth, M., Schwarz, P.: Don't Scrap It, Wrap It! A Wrapper Architecture for Legacy Data Sources. In: Proc. of the 1997 Intl. Conf. on Very Large Data Bases, pp. 266–275 (1997)
20. Viglas, S., Naughton, J.F., Burger, J.: Maximizing the output rate of multi-join queries over streaming information sources. In: Proc. of the 2003 Intl. Conf. on Very Large Data Bases, pp. 285–296 (2003)

Service Design Process for Reusable Services: Financial Services Case Study

Abdelkarim Erradi[1,3], Naveen Kulkarni[2], and Piyush Maheshwari[3]

[1] School of Computer Sc. and Eng. University of New South Wales, Sydney, Australia
[2]SetLabs Infosys Technologies Ltd, Bangalore, India
[3]IBM India Research Lab (IRL), New Delhi, India
aerradi@cse.unsw.edu.au, Naveen_Kulkarni@infosys.com, pimahesh@in.ibm.com

Abstract. Service-oriented Architecture (SOA) is an approach for building distributed systems that deliver application functionality as a set of business-aligned services with well-defined and discoverable contracts. This paper presents typical a service design process along with a set of service design principles and guidelines for systematically identifying services, designing them and deciding the service granularity and layering. The advocated principles stem from our experiences in designing services for a realistic Securities Trading application. Best practices and lessons learned during this exercise are also discussed.

1 Introduction

Service Oriented Architecture (SOA) is a promising architectural approach to integrate heterogeneous and autonomous software systems. It promises effective business-IT alignment, improved business agility and reduced integration costs through increased interoperability and reuse of shared business services. SOA decomposes a system in terms of loosely coupled and replaceable services that interact via the exchange of messages conforming to well defined contracts [5]. SOA principles place a strong emphasis on decoupling the service consumers from the service providers via: (1) strict separation of service interface description, implementation and binding, thus allowing service changes to occur without impact on service users (2) declarative constraints and policies to govern the service behavior and the interactions between collaborating services (3) message-centric and standards-based interactions between participating services, thus allowing easier interoperability between systems inside and across enterprise boundaries. The perceived value of SOA is that it provides a flexible model that allows new applications/services to be created through the assembly of existing internal/third party services. Additionally, some of the new business requirements can be realized by re-composition of component services rather than by changing the services implementation. Therefore, SOA can help reduce the integration costs via eliminating the redundancy of overlapping and duplicate functionality as well as the consolidation and reuse of services across processes, lines of business, or the enterprise.

B. Krämer, K.-J. Lin, and P. Narasimhan (Eds.): ICSOC 2007, LNCS 4749, pp. 606–617, 2007.

Technology and standards are important in building service-oriented distributed applications but they are not sufficient on their own. Moving to service-orientation is a non trivial one and requires far more than simply wrapping software entities with Web services interfaces. An effective approach for modeling and designing services is crucial for achieving the full benefits of SOA. In this paper, we present the set of design principles and processes for identifying, designing and layering services in a repeatable and non-arbitrary fashion. These have been derived from an elaborate SOA example involving the modeling of financial services for Securities Trading domain. The rationale behind design decisions is captured and the lessons learned are reported.

The rest of the paper is organized as follows. In Section 2 we provide an overview of the securities domain focusing on the pain points inherent in this area. Subsequently, in Section 3 we briefly discuss our suggested service-based decomposition framework. Section 4 details the suggested service design for our case study. Section 5 presents the lessons learned and the key service design considerations. The last section concludes the paper and provides some directions for future work.

2 Background and Problem Area

Despite the wide range of advocated advantages associated with the introduction of SOA, comprehensive SOA implementation case studies continue to be scarce in the literature. This paper aims to present a practical service design process along with key design principles derived from a Stock Trading service enablement case study.

For our case study, the key issues that SOA adoption aims to address are: (i) Heterogeneous IT portfolio with proprietary and brittle point to point connections that impact flexibility, (ii) Redundant and overlapping functionality leading to cost overheads and increased time to market. A specific example may be the use of individual pricing engines along with individual market data servers for multiple trading instruments, (iii) Inflexible and costly legacy applications portfolio.

The main business drivers for adopting service-orientation for our case-study are: (i) accelerate the securities trade processing towards Straight Through Processing (STP) allowing the final settlement to happen on the day of transaction, (ii) Make the securities trading accessible from various channels such the Web and mobile devices.

Many researches from academia and industry are suggesting various approaches to guide the service modeling and design. One of the outstanding efforts is this space is IBM's Service-Oriented Modeling and Architecture (SOMA) [1]. SOMA is a methodology for the identification, modeling and design of services that leverages existing systems. It consists of three steps: identification, specification and realization of services. However, SOMA lacks openly available detailed description of the methodology, which makes it difficult to further analyze its capabilities.

3 Service Oriented Decomposition Process

Service-based decomposition is an iterative process for arriving at an optimal partitioning of business capabilities into services. The first step is to first establish clear and well-defined boundaries between collaborating systems, followed by reduction of interdependencies and limiting of interactions to well-defined points. The key tasks in the service oriented decomposition process include identification of services along with deciding service granularity and appropriate layering of services.

3.1 Service Identification

As shown in Figure 1, for service identification we advocate a hybrid approach combining top-down domain decomposition along with bottom-up application portfolio analysis. This yields a list of candidate services that further need to be rationalized and consolidated. The top-down analysis of a business may be decomposed into products, channels, business processes, business activities and use cases. The business activities are often good candidates for business services. For example, the activity of obtaining a price for a specific security during an equity trading business process may be a logical candidate service. On the other hand, a broker could offer equity trading as a product which requires instantiating order placement and settlement processes, whose activities could be realized by services harvested from functionalities embedded in existing applications. The harvesting can be facilitated by reverse-engineering techniques and tools to extract data and control flow graphs that provide different views of abstraction of operational systems.

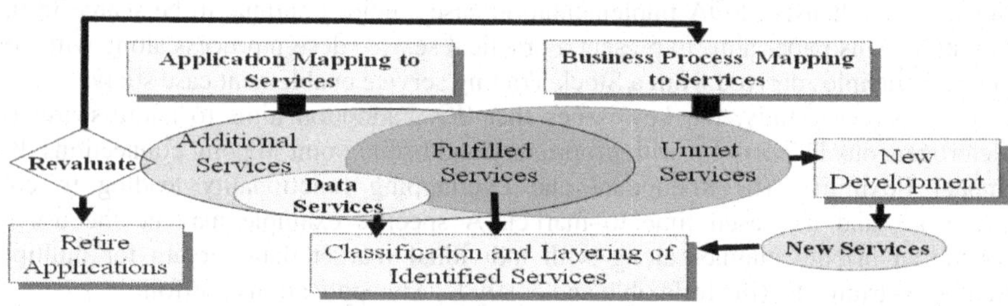

Fig. 1. Service identification framework

Our proposed service identification framework is initiated by a top-down capture and comprehension of key business processes as well as the mapping of the business processes to the existing application portfolio. This is followed by defining the To-be business process models (BPM) so that business services can be properly identified. BPM consists of the decomposition of the business domain into functional areas and business use cases. The level of functional decomposition of business processes depends on the level of complexity, for example a business process could be decomposed into business sub-processes, which in turn are decomposed into high-level business use cases comprised of a set of activities. For instance, the registration of a new customer is a business use case in a Trade Order process. The coarse grained business services are then defined on the basis of logical business activities. It needs to be noted that the services identified here may be applicable across use cases and business processes. Once the To-be BPMs are captured, a Process-to-Application Mapping (PAM) is required to examine existing software assets in order to discover candidate application functionality (e.g., APIs, sub-systems and modules from legacy, custom and packaged applications) for realizing identified business services. The mapping is performed between the business activities and the operational applications. This provides the basis for identifying applications that support a particular business process. Also the PAM helps to highlight possible redundancies and overlaps in the application portfolio, and to identify applications that offer potential shared services across channels and LOBs. In addition gaps and services that need new development can be uncovered. The important aspect of this exercise is that we end up with a conceptual map of the business services and maintain the association with the systems that may fulfill those services based on the existing IT portfolio. This is an important artifact that is essential towards matching the required services with existing services and to plan for new services that need to be built or acquired.

Apart from top down modeling, our framework also identifies functionality existing in the current enterprise IT portfolio. This can be accomplished by a combination of tools as well as interviews with application stakeholders. The outputs of this activity are typically fine-grained functional modules such as: updating customer's personal information, updating a customer's financial information, updating accounting entries for a cash payment transaction, etc. Collating all these functional activities will provide a comprehensive list of all the fine-grained activities performed by the application portfolio. This list of functionalities must be consolidated in a meaningful way to come up with reasonably coarse level activities that may be used to align with the services identified from the top down business process modeling effort.

The service identification also covers identifying reusable infrastructure services, currently supporting non-service oriented applications, which may be leveraged to support business services. For example security services providing authentication, authorization and secure communication, message delivery services to send messages and alerts to a variety of devices, such as email, SMS and fax. Another example might be provisioning services that manage subscriptions, SLAs, provisioning contracts, monitoring, metering and billing.

Figure 2 shows the meta-model we defined to guide service based decomposition activities. First the identification of candidate services starts with the services representing communication points between the parties involved. This is followed by capturing and describing the externally observable behavior of the identified services. In the current case study, the meta-model shown in Figure 2, provided the framework to identify the different types of services and their granularity.

An illustration of service-based decomposition of the Securities Trading application is depicted in Figure 3. During the service identification the primary view point should be towards achieving a common business goal through a single service. The business processes usually are modeled to achieve a single goal and hence would provide a natural boundary. For example a Trade Settlement service would aggregate various correlated activities like allocation matching, trade billing (commission, tax, fees etc) to achieve the goal of trade settlement.

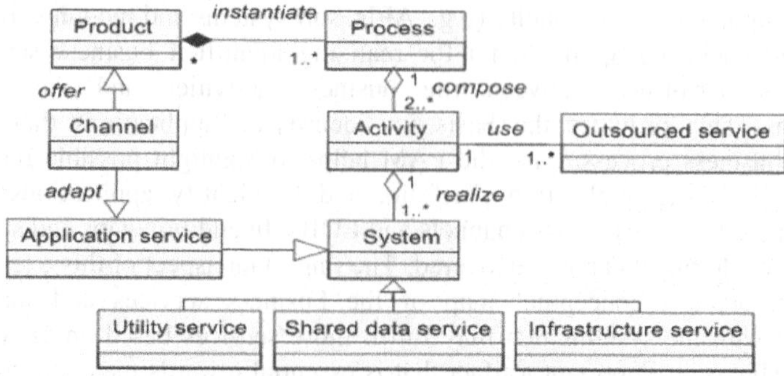

Fig. 2. Service conceptualization Meta-model

The identified services can be classified and grouped in a variety of ways. The services can be classified according to their scope into cross-business services, cross Line of Business (LOBs)/channels services, and LOB/channel specific services. The classification can also be based on their degree of reuse such as core enterprise services used by all (like a Customer Information Service), common services, or services unique to a specific application. The service classification activity is crucial to guide the non-functional aspects of services design, for example core and common services need to be designed and deployed with more emphasis on scalability and high availability.

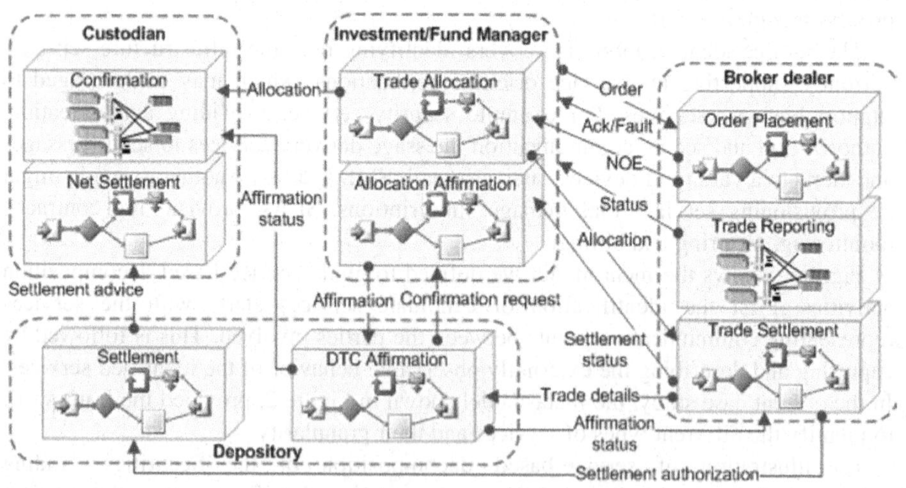

Fig. 3. High-level view of key Securities Trading services and their choreography

3.2 Service Granularity

The service granularity is considered a key design decision for service enablement. Services may be offered at different layers with different granularity. Service granularity refers to the service size and the scope of functionality a service exposes.

The service granularity can be quantified as a combination of the number of components/services composed through a given operation on a service interface as well as the number of resources' state changes like the number of database tables updated. The service should have the right granularity to accomplish a business unit of work in a single interaction. If the service is too coarse-grain, the size of exchanged messages grows and sometimes might carry more data than needed. Also it yields more complex interfaces and represents more possibilities to be affected by change. On the other hand if the service is too fine grained multiple round trips to the service may be required to get all the required data/functionality.

Hence a balance is struck, depending upon the level of abstraction, likelihood of change, complexity of the service, and the desired level of cohesion and coupling. A tradeoff needs to be made while taking into account non-functional requirements particularly performance.

Deciding the appropriate service granularity remains a challenge, but generally speaking services exposed to other systems should provide operations that correspond to business functions and they should be sufficiently generic to allow their reuse in different processes and/or by different users. Fine-grained component services may be used within a business service, but should not be exposed to other systems.

We have employed a business driven approach guided by the meta-model presented earlier to arrive to pragmatic granularity. The identified services, such as Trade Order Service and Trade Settlement Service, are business meaningful services that offer a single operation to fulfill a complete business task. Notice that we refer to the services as nouns, not verbs. In the contrary, focusing on the actions (verbs) rather than the service (nouns), such as Add Trade Order, often yields fine grained services.

There is no theory-founded method for deciding the correct level of granularity. The following guidelines can help in defining an acceptable level of granularity:

- **Reusability:** the optimal service design with respect to reusability is to provide a generalized set of services, compared to the development of a specific service for a specific consumer application. This enables the users to assemble a wide array of business applications using these services. Increased reusability stems mainly from accurate, complete and generalized service contract design capturing all possible message variants. This allows covering a larger number of usage scenarios through altering the service behavior simply by supplying varying message instances conforming to a subset of a super-schema defined by the service contract. For example designing an Insurance Quote Service based on a comprehensive schema definition like ACORD [2] allows the service to serve Quotes for individual as well as corporate users regarding various life insurance products and their variants. In the current case study, the process services such as Order Placement Service or Trade Settlement Service were envisioned to be reused across various products.

- **Business-alignment:** exposed business services need to add tangible business value and support a business use case. A service could be designed to represent a single important business concept, like a customer information service, thus forming clear traceability to the business model.

- **Design for assembly:** it is important that a service interface is defined in a way that its encapsulated functionality can be used and composed in different contexts with minimal effort so as to increase the service reuse potential. Simply exposing services directly off existing systems often yields non-optimal services that require considerable effort by the consumer to aggregate and refine them into useful services. Also the service interface should not be unnecessarily complicated so that it can be used and assembled with little complexity.

- **Reduce ripple-effects of applications changes:** services need to be self-contained and encapsulated in a way so that changes behind the interface can be done with no or minimal disruption to the service consumers. This increased isolation helps reduce change propagation and contain regression testing efforts and in turn reduces maintenance and evolution costs. In addition existing services may be swapped by new service implementations from potentially different providers without disturbing the service users.

- **Performance and size:** Services are often accessed remotely and might incur significant overhead to making a round trip. Hence the service design should expose coarse-grained operations covering a greater range of related functionality within a single service invocation in order to reduce the number of Service requests necessary to accomplish a task. In other words, a service should expose a significant business process capability, as opposed to low-level business functions. For example, the Trade Order Service should offer one operation (e.g., Place Order) to accept a Trade Order in one call instead of offering multiple operations consisting of "Create Trade Order Header" followed by a call to "Add Line Item" for each line item. However, coarse-grained operations might yield large size messages. Hence the size of messages should be constrained to what the service can process efficiently. So, the optimal size of exchange messages could guide the required adjustments to the service granularity.

4 Service Design

This Section briefly presents key service design principles. Then it discusses the main service design decisions for our Securities Trading case study and their rationale.

4.1 Service Design Principles

The service design should take into account the basic principle of high cohesion and low coupling among services [4] in order to minimize interdependencies and the impact of change while facilitating reuse. This ensures that the resulting services are self-contained, replaceable and reusable. **Service Cohesion** refers to the strength of functional/semantic relatedness of activities carried out by a service to realize a business transaction [4]. High cohesion ensures that a service represents a single abstraction and exposed interface elements are closely related to one another. **Service Coupling** refers to the extent to which a service is inter-related with other services, in other words it measures the degree of isolation of one service from changes that happen to another [3]. Low coupling can be achieved by reducing the number of connections between services, eliminating unnecessary relationships between them, and by reducing the dependencies between services to few, well-known dependencies [4]. Additionally, the service interfaces should be defined to be as independent as possible from the service implementation. This allows services to be independently deployed, and allows the assembly of applications that make no assumptions about service implementation beyond the characteristics published in the service contract. This way the service implementation can change without affecting service users so long as the service interface is unchanged.

Another key service design principle is that of stateless service design, services should not require context or state information of other services, nor should maintain state from one request to another. This implies that the exchanged messages should be self-contained with sufficient correlation information and metadata (such as links to persisted data) to allow the destination service to establish the message context [5]. On the contrary, a stateful interface tend to increase coupling between the service consumer and provider by associating a consumer with a particular provider instance.

Additionally, the service interface should be expressed in terms of meaningful business operations rather than generic or fine-grained primitive methods such as CRUD (Create, Read, Update and Delete) interfaces. The operations should correspond to specific business scenarios such as placing an order. Additionally the message contracts associated with the service operations should be coarse-grained encapsulation of business domain entities.

Sound interface design has to anticipate and meet the current and future needs of varied clients using the service in different contexts and different functional and QoS expectations. The service interface should capture and describe externally observable service behavior hiding the implementation details. This ensures that changes to the implementation are localized and do not necessitate changes in the service consumer.

The Service design should also accommodate multiple invocation patterns to be able to meet the requirement of various service consumers. A service consumer should be able to invoke the offered services using a variety of different invocation patterns such as synchronous invocation using SOAP over HTTP or asynchronous invocation using SOAP over JMS.

Optimal service granularity is crucial in ensuring maximum reuse in SOA. If the service is too coarse-grained, the size of the exchanged messages grows and sometimes might carry more data than needed. On the other hand if the service is too fine grained, multiple round trips to the service may be required to get the full functionality. Usually a balance is established, depending upon the level of abstraction, likelihood of change, complexity of the service, and the desired level of cohesion and coupling. A tradeoff needs to be made while taking into account non-functional requirements particularly performance. During service design, reusability can be maximized by using generalized service schema design, where the variations of the service behavior can be captured simply by supplying varying message instances conforming to a subset of a super-schema defined by the service schema.

4.2 Service Design Tasks

SOA is more about assembly of an integrated whole from independent parts. Hence, sound interface design is the essence of the integration design and it is a key tenet for reusable services. The challenge is that the service interface design has to anticipate and meet the current and future needs of varied clients using the service in different context and with different functional and QoS expectations. The service interface should capture and describe externally observable service behavior without leaking the details of the underlying implementation nor the service inner working and internal object model. Following this principle ensures that changes to the implementation are localized and minimize required interface changes.

Designing service-oriented applications involves a variety of tasks that may be enumerated as below, the aim to produce the design artifacts shown in Figure 4:

- Specifying the information model of the service as well as the structure and the data types of exchanged messages using a schema definition language such as XML Schema. The outcome of this task is to produce the Service Contract along with the associated Operations Contract, Messages Contract, Data and Faults Contract.
- Defining the behavioral model of the service comprising the service operations as well as the incoming and outgoing messages that are consumed or produced by the service. The service interface should also specify the supported Message Exchange Patterns (MEPs), such as one-way/notification and request-response pattern.
- Modeling of supported conversations and the temporal aspects of interacting with service, such as defining the order in which messages can be sent and received. For example, in the Order Placement Service, the actions available to a service consumer include presenting credentials, then placing an order.
- Specifying the service policy to advertise supported protocols, the constraints on the content of exchanged messages and QoS features, such as security, availability, response time, and manageability assertions. The key service attributes that need special attention are the transactional aspects of the service and whether the service is idempotent. These QoS requirements also dictate the Service Bindings and the Service Hosting options.

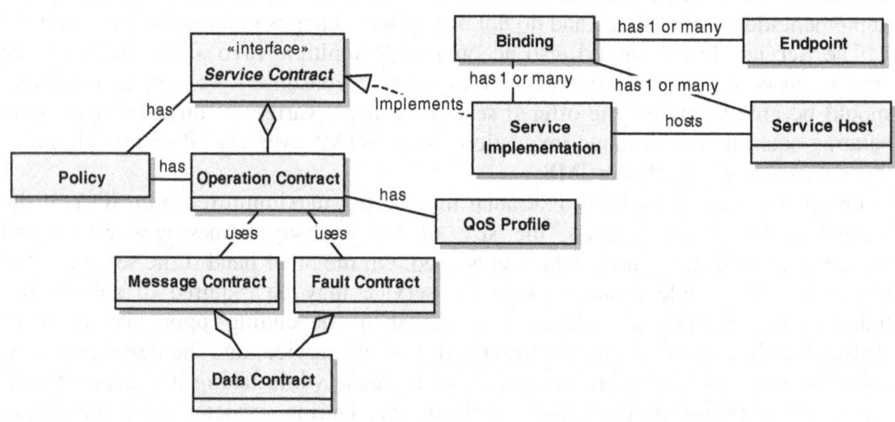

Fig. 4. Service Design Artifacts

4.3 Services for the Securities Case Study

The identified services are layered according to their granularity into four functional layers. Each layer has a set of roles and provides services to the layers above it. The top layer describes business processes made up of a sequence of business activities. The second layer defines business services that automate specific business process activities. The third level defines software components that allow the business services to leverage enterprise-level shared resources. The operational resources layer comprises applications, packages and databases that implement the services. For example, the Order Placement Service is implemented through wrapping relevant functionalities from the existing Order Management System (OMS) while the Allocation Matching Service is provided by the Trade Processing System (TPS).

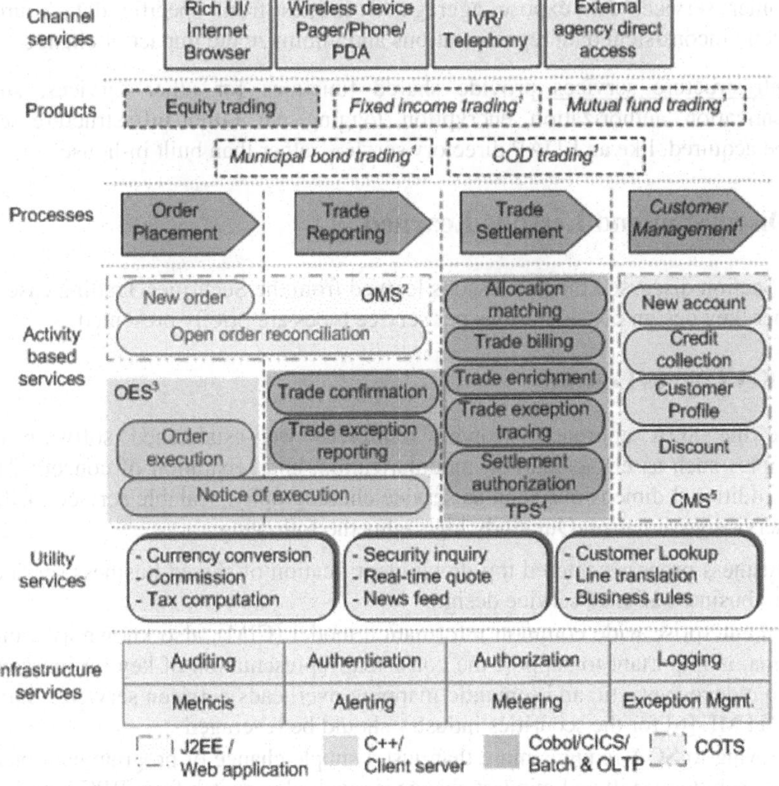

Fig. 5. Equity trading key services from the Broker viewpoint

Our design considers four types of services:

- Process services represent workflows that the Broker uses to deliver products offerings, like Equity Trading, through various channels like the Web, telephony or direct access. Process services, like Order Placement, expose access points that allow business partners to participate in the process. Process services also automate the information flow across disparate systems and eliminate duplicate data entry, manual data transfer and redundant data collection.

- Application services represent business activities that are useful across business units. For example, services like the Securities Pricing service is required across multiple business lines such as equity trading, fixed income trading, asset management, mutual fund trading etc. Application services provide shared and consolidated functional services to reduce/eliminate redundant/overlapping implementations.

- Shared data services map multiple schemas from different data sources to a single schema which is presented to collaborating applications. They provide the ability to unify and hide differences in the way key business entities are represented within the organization or between different business partners. Shared data services, like a

Customer service, can expose aggregated entities from specific data sources to reconcile inconsistent data representations and minimize the impact of change.

- Infrastructure services provide shared functions for other services, such as authentication, authorization, encryption, logging, etc. Often infrastructure services can be acquired, like an LDAP directory service, rather than built in-house.

5 Discussion and Lessons Learned

This Section discussed the key lessons learned from the Securities Trading case study. Further, key design considerations per service types are briefly presented.

5.1 Key Lessons Learned

While the SOA approach strongly reinforces well-established software design principles such as encapsulation, modularization, and separation of concerns, it also adds additional dimensions such as service choreography, scalable service mediation, and service governance. Our study highlights the following:

- Business process centered top-down identification of shared business services can lead to business aligned service design.
- An enterprise wide common information model (CIM), also known as Canonical Schema, is important to support the consistent representation of key business entities and to reduce syntactic and semantic mapping overheads between services. Standards like STPML [6] for the securities industry should be leveraged.
- Moving to SOA requires more than just a simple change of programming practices, rather a paradigm shift and mindset change is required to switch from RPC-based/object-based architecture to a loosely-coupled, message-focused and service-oriented architecture. A true SOA is realized when applications are built as self-contained, autonomous business services that interact by exchanging messages that adhere to specified contracts
- When service-enabling Mainframe CICS applications, it would be wise to expose one service per screen flow, and avoid translating all transactions to services. This involves identifying the required screens navigation to achieve key capabilities of the application, like CustomerCreation for instance, and then exposing the entire screen flow as a service.
- To ease service discovery and reuse, there is a need for clear service naming guidelines and a services metadata management repository to support governance and easy identification of services based on business function.

5.2 Design Considerations Per Service Type

For process services design the focus should be on the ease of modification and customization as these services are subject to higher change frequency. Hence, they should declaratively capture only the routing logic to manage the data and control flow between activity services. Further, complex business rules should be abstracted and externalized from processes so that they can be managed by a dedicated rules engine. Further, robust exception handling/compensation design is required.

Application services can have a verb-focused design by exposing key verbs as service methods, which unfortunately require RPC like behavior and sometimes might reveal the internal state of the service. We advocate a message-centric design to allow message content-driven service behavior and generalized service interface that can be used and composed in various applications. Command design pattern is used where the service performs dynamic content-based routing to direct the received messages to the appropriate implementation. This practice is acceptable when the resulting service contract is coherent and deals with closely-related business concepts. For example a generic Securities Price Lookup service could be provided to retrieve the price from various stock exchanges using content-based routing. Services need to be idempotent so that requests arriving multiple times are only processed once.

Shared data services uses noun-based design and usually expose CRUD interfaces representing simple atomic operations on an entity.

Infrastructure services are usually acquired and act on messages depending on the message context like the channel through which the message has arrived.

6 Conclusion and Future Work

Service-orientation is gaining momentum as a promising approach to deliver increased reusability, flexibility and responsiveness to change. However, the practical design of services requires sound engineering principles. The main contribution of this paper is a service-enablement case study in the securities trading domain to illustrate the issues and the challenges related to service design. The paper also emphasized the importance of service design in a Service-Oriented Architecture as well as the importance of focusing on the services' business value to guide the service requirement gathering, service identification and service design. Furthermore, we discussed the lessons learned with respect to the service design best practices and guidelines. Future work will focus on empirical studies of how the level of service granularity affects cohesion and coupling. We are also looking at developing an integrated toolset and a Domain Specific Language (DSL) supporting our service design methodology.

References

[1] Arsanjani, A.: Service-oriented modeling and architecture (SOMA) (2004), http://www-128.ibm.com/developerworks/webservices/library/ws-soa-design1/

[2] Association for Cooperative Operations Research and Development (ACORD) (2007), http://www.acord.org

[3] Briand, L.C., Daly, J.W., Wüst, J.: A Unified Framework for Coupling Measurement in Object-Oriented Systems. IEEE Transactions on Software Engineering 25(1), 91–121 (1999)

[4] Papazoglou, M.P., van den Heuvel, W.J.: Service-Oriented Design and Development Methodology. Int'l Journal of Web Engin. and Technology (IJWET) (2006) (to appear)

[5] Parastatidis, S., Webber, J.: Realising Service Oriented Architectures Using Web Services. In: Service Oriented Computing, MIT Press, Cambridge (2005)

[6] Straight Through Processing Markup Language (STPML) (2007), http://www.stpml.org

UMM Add-In: A UML Extension for UN/CEFACT's Modeling Methodology

B. Hofreiter[1], C. Huemer[2], P. Liegl[3], R. Schuster[3], and M. Zapletal[4]

[1] University of Technology Sydney
birgith@it.uts.edu.au
[2] Vienna University of Technology
huemer@big.tuwien.ac.at
[3] Research Studios Austria
{pliegl, rschuster}@researchstudio.at
[4] Vienna University of Technology
marco@ec.tuwien.ac.at

1 Introduction

The tighter coupling of enterprises in regard to information system technology has also changed the way business processes are modeled. Modeling inter-organizational business processes is necessary in order to gain a profound and unique representation of the processes involved. However this requires a new methodology especially designed for modeling inter-organizational business processes. The United Nation's Center for Trade Facilitation and Electronic Business (UN/CEFACT) took up the challenge and started to develop such a methodology. The research efforts became known as UN/CEFACT's modeling methodology (UMM) [1]. UMM enables the business modeler to capture the business knowledge independent of the underlying implementation technology such as ebXML or Web Services.

Due to the popularity of the Unified Modeling Language (UML) the UMM is built on top of it. UMM is defined as a UML profile - i.e. a set of *stereotypes*, *tagged values* and *constraints* - in order to customize the UML meta model for the specific purpose of modeling the collaborative space in B2B.

Although the standard is well developed and documented, its complexity and mightiness make it difficult for the novice user to perceive from scratch. Therefore a tool, supporting the modeler in creating a valid UMM model would help those inexperienced with UMM. We have developed such a plug-in for the UML modeling tool Enterprise Architect [1] called *UMM Add-In* [2]. We highlight the main features of the Add-In and show how the tool facilitates the use of the methodology.

2 The UMM Add-In

The UMM Add-In consists of several distinctive features helping the modeler on his way towards a valid UMM model.

[1] http://www.sparxsystems.com.au
[2] http://ummaddin.researchstudio.at

B. Krämer, K.-J. Lin, and P. Narasimhan (Eds.): ICSOC 2007, LNCS 4749, pp. 618–619, 2007.

UMM specific toolbar. In order to create a UMM model it is convenient to drag and drop UMM stereotypes from a toolbar onto the modeling canvas. Thus, the stereotypes as defined in the UML profile for UMM are integrated into Enterprise Architect and provided in a toolbar.

UMM Requirements Engineering support. While elaborating a UMM model the business knowledge is collected during interviews between business domain experts and business analysts. The information gathered is captured in so called UMM worksheets. Traditionally worksheets were completed using a word processor and stored separately to the model. With the introduction of the UMM worksheet editor in the UMM Add-In the modeler can store model and worksheet information together which guarantees consistency and accuracy.

Semi automatic generation of UMM artifacts. Most activities while creating a UMM model are reoccurring and follow similar patterns. One of the major goals of the UMM Add-In is to relieve the modeler from repeating activities and provide support for the semi automatic generation of modeling artifacts. E.g. the creation of the initial structure of a UMM model is performed automatically by the UMM Add-In.

Validation of the UMM model. Any UMM model is valid if it follows the constraints specified in the UMM specification. During the modeling process artifacts are created in an iterative manner and often errors occur. The UMM Add-In provides a UMM validator checking the constraints specified in the specification against any given UMM model. In case of factual errors in the model the user is provided with detailed error messages helping to correct the model.

Transformation to choreography languages. Once a valid UMM model is created, it is envisioned to transform the business logic defined into IT-platform specifics. Currently the UMM Add-In supports the mapping of the process definitions to process specification languages as used in services oriented architectures namely ebXML's Business Process Specification Schema (BPSS) and Business Process Execution Language (BPEL).

Modeling business documents using UN/CEFACT's Core Components. Apart from the business process specific extensions, the UMM Add-In also offers features to model the business documents exchanged in a business process. For business document modeling the current implementation supports the use of the UML profile for UN/CEFACT's core components (UPCC). The data model created can then be used to automatically generate XML schema representations.

References

1. UN/CEFACT: UN/CEFACT's Modeling Methodology (UMM), UMM Meta Model - Foundation Module. Technical Specification V1.0 (September 2006), `http://www.unece.org/cefact/umm/UMMFoundationModule.pdf`

CP4TWS - A Prototype Demonstrating Context and Policies for Transactional Web Services

Sattanathan Subramanian[1], Zakaria Maamar[2], Nanjangud C. Narendra[3], Djamal Benslimane[4], and Philippe Thiran[1]

[1]IMRU-FUNDP, University of Namur, Namur, Belgium
[2]CIT, Zayed University, Dubai, United Arab Emirates
[3]IBM India Research Lab, Bangalore, India
[4]LIRIS, Claude Bernard Lyon 1 University, Lyon, France

Transaction management has become important in Web services composition [1]. The goal is to guarantee the consistency of the business processes to implement as Web services. This demo paper presents CP4TWS prototype that validates our approach for context-driven transactional Web services using policies [2]. In this approach, context tracks Web services, policies specify Web services' transactional behaviors, and backward/forward adaptation strategies support Web services' exception handling.

Fig. 1 (a) presents the running scenario, which is a composite Web service providing transportation plans to tourists. Initially, a tourist invokes *Itinerary WS* that proposes routes, e.g., hotel to museum. *Itinerary WS* consults *Weather WS* and requests *Location WS* for details on the origin and destination places. In case of bad weather, a taxi booking is made for the tourist using *Taxi WS*. Otherwise, the tourist uses public transport. Hotel and museum locations are submitted to *Bus Schedule WS*, which returns the bus numbers to ride. Traffic jams make *Bus Schedule WS* interact with *Traffic WS* regarding the status of the traffic network. This status is fed into *Bus Schedule WS* for adjustment needs. Each Web service in this running scenario has a dedicated state chart diagram that reflects its transactional property (e.g., pivot, retriable, compensatable). The diagram of a pivot Web service is given in Fig. 1 (b).

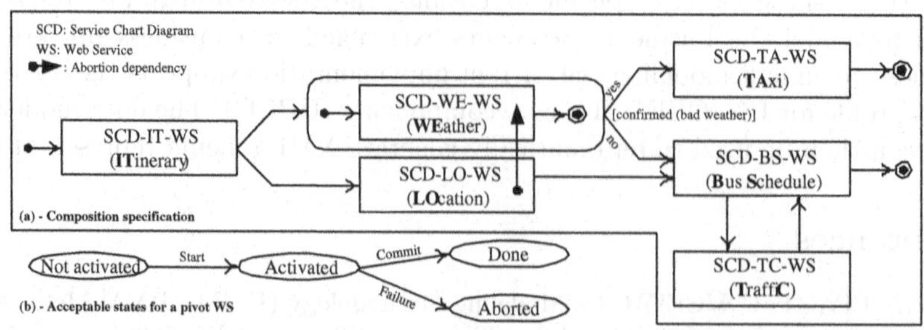

Fig. 1. Scenario specification/Acceptable states for a pivot Web service

B. Krämer, K.-J. Lin, and P. Narasimhan (Eds.): ICSOC 2007, LNCS 4749, pp. 620–622, 2007.

(a)

RetriableActivated Policy Parameters	Values
TransactionalProperty	Retriable
CurrentState	Suspended
PreviousState	Activated
TranstitionOut	Retry
NextEffectiveState	Activated

(b)

RetriableDone Policy Parameters	Values
TransactionalProperty	Retriable
CurrentState	Activated
PreviousState	Notactivated
TranstitionOut	Commit
NextEffectiveState	Done

Fig. 2. Some of Location WS's policies

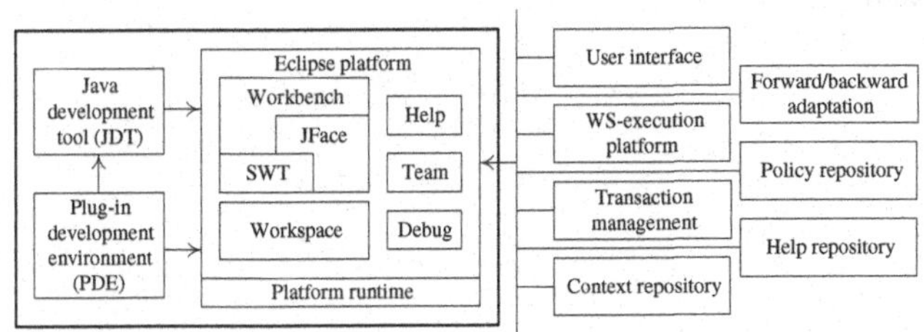

Fig. 3. Architecture of $\mathcal{CP}4\mathcal{TWS}$

In this paper we only report on the forward adaptation strategy. To this end, we consider the failure of *Location WS*. Fig 2 shows the policies of this Web service. For example, *WS-Retriable.Policy*$_{activated}$ corresponds to the policy that would allow the retriable *Location WS* to bind a new state upon context assessment and validation.

When *Location WS* fails, the set of the post-affected Web services consists of {*Bus Schedule WS*, *Traffic WS*, *Taxi WS*, *Weather WS*}. If *Location WS* is retried successfully, the execution will then proceed normally. If not, *Location WS* will need to be aborted. While *Location WS* is being retried, *Weather WS* is kept suspended, until *Location WS* either succeeds or fails. In case *Location WS* fails, *Weather WS* will be aborted as per the abortion dependency between these two Web services (Fig. 1 (a)). This leads to a redesign of the composition specification starting from *Itinerary WS*.

Fig. 3 shows the architecture of $\mathcal{CP}4\mathcal{TWS}$. The following tools were used: *Eclipse 3.2*, *JDK1.4.2*, *W3C DOM* to process XML information, *XACML* to represent policies, and *SWT* for GUI needs. The development of $\mathcal{CP}4\mathcal{TWS}$ has called for seven plug-ins. WS-execution platform plug-in extends the workspace in terms of project nature (i.e., contextual Web services) and builder (i.e., context assessment, validation, and reasoning). Forward/backward adaptation plug-in implements the adaptation strategies for Web service composition. Transaction management plug-in executes different policies of transactional properties of Web services by monitoring the different contexts. Context/policy repository plug-ins store and retrieve details on contexts/policies. Finally, help repository plug-in provides the necessary documentation for using $\mathcal{CP}4\mathcal{TWS}$.

References

1. Bhiri, S., Perrin, O., Godart, C.: Ensuring Required Failure Atomicity of Composite Web Services. In: WWW'2005. Proceedings of The Fourteenth International World Wide Web Conference, Chiba, Japan (2005)
2. Maamar, Z., Narendra, N.C., Benslimane, D., Subramanian, S.: Policies for Context-driven Transactional Web Services. In: CAiSE'2007. Proceedings of The 19th International Conference on Advanced information System Engineering, Trondheim, Norway (2007)

WSQoSX – A QoS Architecture for Web Service Workflows

Rainer Berbner, Michael Spahn, Nicolas Repp, Oliver Heckmann, and Ralf Steinmetz

Dept. of Computer Science, Darmstadt University of Technology, Germany
{berbner,spahn,repp,heckmann,steinmetz}@kom.tu-darmstadt.de

Web Services as a technology to enable distributed business processes gain in importance, especially in the area of Enterprise Application Integration (EAI) and Business Process Outsourcing (BPO). However, the support of Quality of Service (QoS) is crucial in this context. Without any guarantee regarding QoS, no enterprise is willing to rely on external Web Services within critical business processes. Thus, we designed and implemented the *Web Service Quality of Service Architectural Extension (WSQoSX)* as an integrated Web Service system with comprehensive QoS support [2, 4]. WSQoSX supports the assessment of Web Services to assure that only Web Services will be used in critical business processes that satisfy the requirements defined by the user. The selection and execution of a certain Web Service depends on its QoS-properties described by a Service Level Agreements (SLAs) document. The compliance with given SLAs is monitored by WSQoSX as well. In case of a Web Service not being able to fulfil the requirements, it can be replaced during runtime by selecting an alternative Web Service out of a pool of similar Web Services. Additionally, providers can register their Web Service offerings using the same Web-based interface, making WSQoSX a marketplace for Web Services.

If a workflow managed by WSQoSX is started, the workflow engine does not invoke a Web Service directly. Web Service invocation is managed by a Proxy Component instead. This Proxy Component can determine which category (e.g. shipping) has been triggered for invocation and hands this information over to the Selection Component. The Rating Component calculates a score for each Web Service according to specific user preferences. Based on these calculations the Selection Component chooses and invokes the best suitable Web Service. The Accounting Component tracks detailed information about which Web Services have been invoked and their runtime behaviour. This data is used by the QoS Monitoring Component to detect SLA violations during the execution of Web Services [1]. The management components (Figure 1) of WSQoSX described above are implemented in Java.

The QoS-aware selection of Web Services is based on a QoS-model on which selection algorithms are applied [1]. The algorithms used mainly emanated from the operations research discipline, adapted to the special needs of Web Service selection. For this, a utility function maximizing the overall QoS subject to particular QoS constraints is introduced. This leads to an optimization problem that is NP-hard. Thus, we propose a heuristic based approach to solve the QoS-aware Web Service composition problem. For this, we design a heuristic H1_RELAX_IP that uses a backtracking algorithm on the results computed by a relaxed integer program. The evaluation of H1_RELAX_IP reveals that this heuristic is extremely fast and leads to

B. Krämer, K.-J. Lin, and P. Narasimhan (Eds.): ICSOC 2007, LNCS 4749, pp. 623–624, 2007.

results that are very close to the optimal solution. H1_IP_RELAX outperforms the linear integer programming based solution of a solver with regard to the computation time, especially with increasing number of candidate Web Services and process tasks.

Due to the volatile nature of the Web Service environment the actual runtime behaviour of Web Services may deviate from the one estimated in the planning phase. Thus, we introduce a heuristic based replanning mechanism for adapting a workflow to the real behaviour ensuring that its execution remains feasible, valid and optimal subject to the preferences and constraints defined by the user [3].

Using WSQoSX enterprises are enabled to build flexible and agile business processes, generating the foundation for future cost savings.

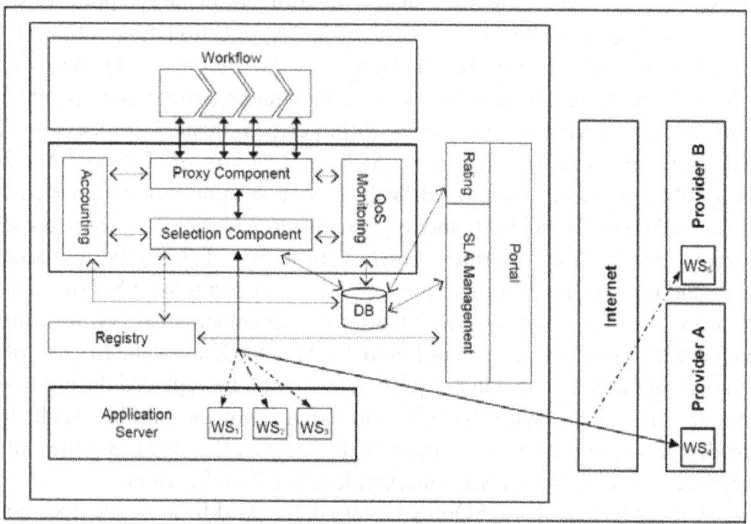

Fig. 1. WSQoSX – Architectural blueprint

References

1. Berbner, R., Spahn, M., Repp, N., Heckmann, O., Steinmetz, R.: Heuristics for QoS-aware Web Service Composition. In: ICWS 2006. Proc. 4th IEEE International Conference Web Services, Chicago, IL, USA, pp. 72–82. IEEE Computer Society Press, Los Alamitos (2006)
2. Berbner, R., Grollius, T., Repp, N., Heckmann, O., Ortner, E., Steinmetz, R.: An approach for the Management of Service-oriented Architecture (SoA) based Application Systems. In: EMISA 2005. Proc. Enterprise Modelling and Information Systems Architectures, Klagenfurt, Austria, pp. 208–221 (2005)
3. Berbner, R., Spahn, M., Repp, N., Heckmann, O., Steinmetz, R.: An Approach for Replanning of Web Service Workflows. In: AMCIS 2006. 12th Americas Conference on Information Systems, Acapulco, Mexico (2006)
4. Berbner, R., Heckmann, O., Steinmetz, R.: An Architecture for a QoS driven composition of Web Service based Workflows. In: NAEC 2005. Networking and Electronic Commerce Research Conference, Riva Del Garda, Italy (2005)

ReoService: Coordination Modeling Tool

Christian Koehler*, Alexander Lazovik**, and Farhad Arbab

CWI, Amsterdam, Netherlands
{koehler,a.lazovik,farhad.arbab}@cwi.nl

Coordination in SOA addresses dynamic topologies of interactions among services. Most efforts up to now have been focused on statically defined composition of services, e.g., using BPEL. To the best of our knowledge, there are no serious means to address the issues of dynamic coordination to accommodate continuously changing requirements. While BPEL is a powerful standard for service composition, it lacks support for typical coordination constraints, like synchronisation, mutual exclusion, and context-dependency.

In this paper we present ReoService, which is a modeling tool for coordinating business processes. ReoService is based on Reo [2] – a general framework for coordinating components in distributed systems. Reo is a channel-based exogenous coordination language wherein complex coordinators, called connectors, are compositionally built out of simpler ones. The simplest connectors are a set of user-defined communication channels with well-defined behavior. The emphasis in this model is on connectors, not on the services to connect. In this sense, ReoService acts as a "glue" language that interconnects and coordinates services in a distributed business process.

The Reo coordination tool is developed to aid the process designers who are interested in complex coordination scenarios. The ReoService and its underlying Reo framework are implemented in Java as a set of plug-ins [1] on top of the Eclipse platform (www.eclipse.org). Currently the framework consists of the following parts: (i) graphical editors, supporting the most common service and communication channel types; (ii) a simulation plug-in, that generates flash animated simulations on the fly; (iii) BPEL converter, that allows conversion of Reo connectors to BPEL and vice versa; (iv) Java code generation plug-in, as an alternative to BPEL, represents service coordination model as a set of Java classes; (v) validation plug-in, that performs model checking over coordinations represented as constraint automata.

We now describe the Reo framework architecture that is shown in Figure 1. The central part of the framework is a visual editor for Reo connectors. It represents the actual coordination model with services and communication channels. The developed tool also allows us to represent Reo in terms of constraint automata [4]–an alternative behavioral model. This is useful if additional validation based on model checking techniques [6] is required. Q-Automata [5] is used if

* The work in this paper is supported in part by a grant from the GLANCE funding program of the Dutch National Organization for Scientific Research (NWO), through projectWoMaLaPaDiA (600.643.000.06N09).

** This work was carried out during the tenure of an ERCIM "Alain Bensoussan" Fellowship Programme.

B. Krämer, K.-J. Lin, and P. Narasimhan (Eds.): ICSOC 2007, LNCS 4749, pp. 625–626, 2007.

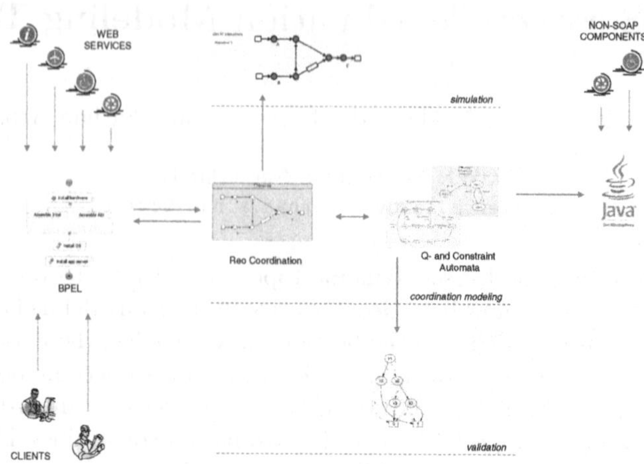

Fig. 1. Reo coordination framework for services

QoS aspects of communication channels are important. Along with editing, the Reo editor maintains simultaneous conversion to BPEL. To test the coordination model, one may run an animated simulation using the animation plug-in. In some situations it is desirable to use a coordination model in a non-web service scenario: in this case, generation of Java code is used. In the generated code non-SOAP components are represented by wrappers over Java threads.

However, our tools currently lack adequate support for certain concerns that are specifically important for services, e.g., preferences, extended service descriptions, and temporal constraints. While some of these concerns, e.g., temporal constraints, are naturally supported by our coordination language [3], others as extended service descriptions and preferences to provide users with better control over instantiated process execution require extensions that go beyond the scope of a general purpose coordination language. Improving our tools to support temporal aspects of Reo circuits is in our agenda. We also plan to address extended service descriptions and investigate preferences in our future work.

References

1. Eclipse coordination tools, `http://homepages.cwi.nl/~koehler/ect`
2. Arbab, F.: Reo: a channel-based coordination model for component composition. Math. Structures in CS 14(3), 329–366 (2004)
3. Arbab, F., Baier, C., de Boer, F., Rutten, J.: Models and temporal logics for timed component connectors (2004)
4. Baier, C., Sirjani, M., Arbab, F., Rutten, J.: Modeling component connectors in reo by constraint automata. Sci. Comput. Program. 61(2), 75–113 (2006)
5. Chothia, T., Kleijn, J.: Q-automata: Modelling the resource usage of concurrent components. In: FOCLASA 2006 (2006)
6. Klueppelholz, S., Baier, C.: Symbolic model checking for channel-based component connectors. In: FOCLASA'06 (2006)

Author Index

Lecture Notes in Computer Science

Sublibrary 2: Programming and Software Engineering

For information about Vols. 1–4038
please contact your bookseller or Springer

Vol. 4749: B.J. Krämer, K.-J. Lin, P. Narasimhan (Eds.), Service-Oriented Computing – ICSOC 2007. XIX, 629 pages. 2007.

Vol. 4670: V. Dahl, I. Niemelä (Eds.), Logic Programming. XII, 470 pages. 2007.

Vol. 4634: H.R. Nielson, G. Filé (Eds.), Static Analysis. XI, 469 pages. 2007.

Vol. 4615: R. de Lemos, C. Gacek, A. Romanovsky (Eds.), Architecting Dependable Systems IV. XIV, 435 pages. 2007.

Vol. 4610: B. Xiao, L.T. Yang, J. Ma, C. Muller-Schloer, Y. Hua (Eds.), Autonomic and Trusted Computing. XVIII, 571 pages. 2007.

Vol. 4609: E. Ernst (Ed.), ECOOP 2007 – Object-Oriented Programming. XIII, 625 pages. 2007.

Vol. 4608: H.W. Schmidt, I. Crnkovic, G.T. Heineman, J.A. Stafford (Eds.), Component-Based Software Engineering. XII, 283 pages. 2007.

Vol. 4591: J. Davies, J. Gibbons (Eds.), Integrated Formal Methods. IX, 660 pages. 2007.

Vol. 4589: J. Münch, P. Abrahamsson (Eds.), Product-Focused Software Process Improvement. XII, 414 pages. 2007.

Vol. 4574: J. Derrick, J. Vain (Eds.), Formal Techniques for Networked and Distributed Systems – FORTE 2007. XI, 375 pages. 2007.

Vol. 4556: C. Stephanidis (Ed.), Universal Access in Human-Computer Interaction, Part III. XXII, 1020 pages. 2007.

Vol. 4555: C. Stephanidis (Ed.), Universal Access in Human-Computer Interaction, Part II. XXII, 1066 pages. 2007.

Vol. 4554: C. Stephanidis (Ed.), Universal Acess in Human Computer Interaction, Part I. XXII, 1054 pages. 2007.

Vol. 4553: J.A. Jacko (Ed.), Human-Computer Interaction, Part IV. XXIV, 1225 pages. 2007.

Vol. 4552: J.A. Jacko (Ed.), Human-Computer Interaction, Part III. XXI, 1038 pages. 2007.

Vol. 4551: J.A. Jacko (Ed.), Human-Computer Interaction, Part II. XXIII, 1253 pages. 2007.

Vol. 4550: J.A. Jacko (Ed.), Human-Computer Interaction, Part I. XXIII, 1240 pages. 2007.

Vol. 4542: P. Sawyer, B. Paech, P. Heymans (Eds.), Requirements Engineering: Foundation for Software Quality. IX, 384 pages. 2007.

Vol. 4536: G. Concas, E. Damiani, M. Scotto, G. Succi (Eds.), Agile Processes in Software Engineering and Extreme Programming. XV, 276 pages. 2007.

Vol. 4530: D.H. Akehurst, R. Vogel, R.F. Paige (Eds.), Model Driven Architecture - Foundations and Applications. X, 219 pages. 2007.

Vol. 4523: Y.-H. Lee, H.-N. Kim, J. Kim, Y.W. Park, L.T. Yang, S.W. Kim (Eds.), Embedded Software and Systems. XIX, 829 pages. 2007.

Vol. 4498: N. Abdennahder, F. Kordon (Eds.), Reliable Software Technologies - Ada-Europe 2007. XII, 247 pages. 2007.

Vol. 4486: M. Bernardo, J. Hillston (Eds.), Formal Methods for Performance Evaluation. VII, 469 pages. 2007.

Vol. 4470: Q. Wang, D. Pfahl, D.M. Raffo (Eds.), Software Process Dynamics and Agility. XI, 346 pages. 2007.

Vol. 4468: M.M. Bonsangue, E.B. Johnsen (Eds.), Formal Methods for Open Object-Based Distributed Systems. X, 317 pages. 2007.

Vol. 4467: A.L. Murphy, J. Vitek (Eds.), Coordination Models and Languages. X, 325 pages. 2007.

Vol. 4454: Y. Gurevich, B. Meyer (Eds.), Tests and Proofs. IX, 217 pages. 2007.

Vol. 4444: T. Reps, M. Sagiv, J. Bauer (Eds.), Program Analysis and Compilation, Theory and Practice. X, 361 pages. 2007.

Vol. 4440: B. Liblit, Cooperative Bug Isolation. XV, 101 pages. 2007.

Vol. 4408: R. Choren, A. Garcia, H. Giese, H.-f. Leung, C. Lucena, A. Romanovsky (Eds.), Software Engineering for Multi-Agent Systems V. XII, 233 pages. 2007.

Vol. 4406: W. De Meuter (Ed.), Advances in Smalltalk. VII, 157 pages. 2007.

Vol. 4405: L. Padgham, F. Zambonelli (Eds.), Agent-Oriented Software Engineering VII. XII, 225 pages. 2007.

Vol. 4401: N. Guelfi, D. Buchs (Eds.), Rapid Integration of Software Engineering Techniques. IX, 177 pages. 2007.

Vol. 4385: K. Coninx, K. Luyten, K.A. Schneider (Eds.), Task Models and Diagrams for Users Interface Design. XI, 355 pages. 2007.

Vol. 4383: E. Bin, A. Ziv, S. Ur (Eds.), Hardware and Software, Verification and Testing. XII, 235 pages. 2007.

Vol. 4379: M. Südholt, C. Consel (Eds.), Object-Oriented Technology. VIII, 157 pages. 2007.

Vol. 4364: T. Kühne (Ed.), Models in Software Engineering. XI, 332 pages. 2007.

Vol. 4355: J. Julliand, O. Kouchnarenko (Eds.), B 2007: Formal Specification and Development in B. XIII, 293 pages. 2006.

Vol. 4354: M. Hanus (Ed.), Practical Aspects of Declarative Languages. X, 335 pages. 2006.

Vol. 4350: M. Clavel, F. Durán, S. Eker, P. Lincoln, N. Martí-Oliet, J. Meseguer, C. Talcott, All About Maude - A High-Performance Logical Framework. XXII, 797 pages. 2007.

Vol. 4348: S.T. Taft, R.A. Duff, R.L. Brukardt, E. Ploedereder, P. Leroy, Ada 2005 Reference Manual. XXII, 765 pages. 2006.

Vol. 4346: L. Brim, B. Haverkort, M. Leucker, J. van de Pol (Eds.), Formal Methods: Applications and Technology. X, 363 pages. 2007.

Vol. 4344: V. Gruhn, F. Oquendo (Eds.), Software Architecture. X, 245 pages. 2006.

Vol. 4340: R. Prodan, T. Fahringer, Grid Computing. XXIII, 317 pages. 2007.

Vol. 4336: V.R. Basili, D. Rombach, K. Schneider, B. Kitchenham, D. Pfahl, R.W. Selby (Eds.), Empirical Software Engineering Issues. XVII, 193 pages. 2007.

Vol. 4326: S. Göbel, R. Malkewitz, I. Iurgel (Eds.), Technologies for Interactive Digital Storytelling and Entertainment. X, 384 pages. 2006.

Vol. 4323: G. Doherty, A. Blandford (Eds.), Interactive Systems. XI, 269 pages. 2007.

Vol. 4322: F. Kordon, J. Sztipanovits (Eds.), Reliable Systems on Unreliable Networked Platforms. XIV, 317 pages. 2007.

Vol. 4309: P. Inverardi, M. Jazayeri (Eds.), Software Engineering Education in the Modern Age. VIII, 207 pages. 2006.

Vol. 4294: A. Dan, W. Lamersdorf (Eds.), Service-Oriented Computing – ICSOC 2006. XIX, 653 pages. 2006.

Vol. 4290: M. van Steen, M. Henning (Eds.), Middleware 2006. XIII, 425 pages. 2006.

Vol. 4279: N. Kobayashi (Ed.), Programming Languages and Systems. XI, 423 pages. 2006.

Vol. 4262: K. Havelund, M. Núñez, G. Roşu, B. Wolff (Eds.), Formal Approaches to Software Testing and Runtime Verification. VIII, 255 pages. 2006.

Vol. 4260: Z. Liu, J. He (Eds.), Formal Methods and Software Engineering. XII, 778 pages. 2006.

Vol. 4257: I. Richardson, P. Runeson, R. Messnarz (Eds.), Software Process Improvement. XI, 219 pages. 2006.

Vol. 4242: A. Rashid, M. Aksit (Eds.), Transactions on Aspect-Oriented Software Development II. IX, 289 pages. 2006.

Vol. 4229: E. Najm, J.F. Pradat-Peyre, V.V. Donzeau-Gouge (Eds.), Formal Techniques for Networked and Distributed Systems - FORTE 2006. X, 486 pages. 2006.

Vol. 4227: W. Nejdl, K. Tochtermann (Eds.), Innovative Approaches for Learning and Knowledge Sharing. XVII, 721 pages. 2006.

Vol. 4218: S. Graf, W. Zhang (Eds.), Automated Technology for Verification and Analysis. XIV, 540 pages. 2006.

Vol. 4214: C. Hofmeister, I. Crnkovic, R. Reussner (Eds.), Quality of Software Architectures. X, 215 pages. 2006.

Vol. 4204: F. Benhamou (Ed.), Principles and Practice of Constraint Programming - CP 2006. XVIII, 774 pages. 2006.

Vol. 4199: O. Nierstrasz, J. Whittle, D. Harel, G. Reggio (Eds.), Model Driven Engineering Languages and Systems. XVI, 798 pages. 2006.

Vol. 4192: B. Mohr, J.L. Träff, J. Worringen, J. Dongarra (Eds.), Recent Advances in Parallel Virtual Machine and Message Passing Interface. XVI, 414 pages. 2006.

Vol. 4184: M. Bravetti, M. Núñez, G. Zavattaro (Eds.), Web Services and Formal Methods. X, 289 pages. 2006.

Vol. 4166: J. Górski (Ed.), Computer Safety, Reliability, and Security. XIV, 440 pages. 2006.

Vol. 4158: L.T. Yang, H. Jin, J. Ma, T. Ungerer (Eds.), Autonomic and Trusted Computing. XIV, 613 pages. 2006.

Vol. 4157: M. Butler, C. Jones, A. Romanovsky, E. Troubitsyna (Eds.), Rigorous Development of Complex Fault-Tolerant Systems. X, 403 pages. 2006.

Vol. 4143: R. Lämmel, J. Saraiva, J. Visser (Eds.), Generative and Transformational Techniques in Software Engineering. X, 471 pages. 2006.

Vol. 4134: K. Yi (Ed.), Static Analysis. XIII, 443 pages. 2006.

Vol. 4119: C. Dony, J.L. Knudsen, A. Romanovsky, A. Tripathi (Eds.), Advanced Topics in Exception Handling Techniques. X, 302 pages. 2006.

Vol. 4111: F.S. de Boer, M.M. Bonsangue, S. Graf, W.-P. de Roever (Eds.), Formal Methods for Components and Objects. VIII, 447 pages. 2006.

Vol. 4089: W. Löwe, M. Südholt (Eds.), Software Composition. X, 339 pages. 2006.

Vol. 4085: J. Misra, T. Nipkow, E. Sekerinski (Eds.), FM 2006: Formal Methods. XV, 620 pages. 2006.

Vol. 4079: S. Etalle, M. Truszczyński (Eds.), Logic Programming. XIV, 474 pages. 2006.

Vol. 4067: D. Thomas (Ed.), ECOOP 2006 – Object-Oriented Programming. XIV, 527 pages. 2006.

Vol. 4066: A. Rensink, J. Warmer (Eds.), Model Driven Architecture – Foundations and Applications. XII, 392 pages. 2006.

Vol. 4063: I. Gorton, G.T. Heineman, I. Crnkovic, H.W. Schmidt, J.A. Stafford, C.A. Szyperski, K. Wallnau (Eds.), Component-Based Software Engineering. XI, 394 pages. 2006.

Vol. 4054: A. Horváth, M. Telek (Eds.), Formal Methods and Stochastic Models for Performance Evaluation. VIII, 239 pages. 2006.

Vol. 4053: M. Ikeda, K.D. Ashley, T.-W. Chan (Eds.), Intelligent Tutoring Systems. XXVI, 821 pages. 2006.

Vol. 4044: P. Abrahamsson, M. Marchesi, G. Succi (Eds.), Extreme Programming and Agile Processes in Software Engineering. XII, 230 pages. 2006.

Vol. 4039: M. Morisio (Ed.), Reuse of Off-the-Shelf Components. XIII, 444 pages. 2006.